THE NEW ANNALS OF THE CIVIL WAR

Edited by Peter Cozzens and Robert I. Girardi

STACKPOLE
BOOKS

Published by
STACKPOLE BOOKS
5067 Ritter Road
Mechanicsburg, PA 17055
www.stackpolebooks.com

Printed in the United States of America

10 9 8 7 6 5 4 3 2 1

FIRST EDITION

Library of Congress Cataloging-in-Publication Data

The new annals of the Civil War / edited by Peter Cozzens and Robert I. Girardi.— 1st ed.
p. cm.
Includes index.
ISBN 0-8117-0058-5
1. United States—History—Civil War, 1861–1865—Personal narratives.
2. United States—History—Civil War, 1861–1865—Campaigns. I. Cozzens, Peter, 1957– II. Girardi, Robert I.
E464 .N48 2004
973.7—dc22

2003019881

For my son, Eric,
from your devoted father,
Robert I. Girardi
and
For you, Izzy,
from your loving father,
Peter Cozzens

CONTENTS

PART FIVE: The War in 1865

LIST OF ILLUSTRATIONS AND MAPS

ILLUSTRATIONS

MAPS

INTRODUCTION

Alexander Kelly McClure never fired a shot in anger during the Civil War, but he was devoted to the Union cause nonetheless. Born on a farm in Perry County, Pennsylvania, on January 9, 1828, McClure early became a staunch adherent to Whig political principles and active in the public life of his state. At age twenty-one he was commissioned a colonel in the Pennsylvania militia, and in 1850 he was appointed deputy United States marshal for Juniata County. McClure was admitted to the bar in 1856 but gave most of his attention to the Franklin *Repository*, a Chambersburg newspaper of which he was part owner.

Like most northern Whigs, McClure transferred his allegiance to the fledgling Republican Party, and he was a member of the party's first state convention in 1855. As a delegate to the Republican National Convention in 1860, McClure was instrumental in switching the Pennsylvania vote to Abraham Lincoln after it became apparent that favorite son Simon Cameron had no chance. During the Civil War McClure served in the state senate. As chairman of the committee on military affairs, he aggressively supported both state and Federal efforts to restore the Union. At the request of President Lincoln, McClure accepted a commission as assistant adjutant general of the army and placed seventeen regiments in the field.

After the war McClure devoted himself to his law practice and to civic affairs. He supported Grant in the 1868 election but broke with the state party machine in 1872 to become chairman of the Pennsylvania delegation to the Liberal Republican National Convention, which nominated Horace

Greeley for the presidency. McClure himself won election to the state senate on the Citizen's Party ticket. Two years later, running on an anticorruption platform, he was defeated as the Citizen's-Democratic candidate for mayor of Philadelphia.

To give greater voice to the independent political elements in the city, McClure and Frank McLaughlin established the Philadelphia *Weekly Times* in 1875. Two years into publication, McClure and McLaughlin decided to dedicate the better part of the paper's front page to specially commissioned, reminiscent articles on the Civil War, "with the view," said McClure, "of correcting many of the grave errors of the hastily compiled, heedlessly imperfect, and strongly partisan histories which appeared during and soon after the close of the war."

McClure's national reputation enabled him to assemble a distinguished group of contributors for the series, which was called "The Annals of the War." Former Union secretary of the navy Gideon Welles wrote the premiere article, entitled "The First Ironclad." It appeared in the March 3, 1877, number of the *Weekly Times*. Perhaps because he had broken with the Republican Party, McClure had little trouble enlisting ex-Confederates in the endeavor. Former Southern lieutenant general Richard Taylor contributed the second article, a story of the final days of the war west of the Mississippi, entitled "The Last Confederate Surrender." The series caught on, and the roll call of contributors during the first year included former Union generals William B. Franklin, James H. Wilson, and Andrew A. Humphreys, as well as Confederate notables James Longstreet, John Singleton Mosby, and Joseph E. Johnston.

McClure assembled 56 of the 175 articles that appeared in the *Weekly Times* between March 1877 and December 1878 and presented them to the public in book form in the spring of 1879 as *The Annals of the War, Written by Leading Participants North and South.*

The Annals of the War, McClure opined, "furnish the most valuable contributions to the future historian which have yet been given to the world. They are far from being perfect," he conceded, "but they have elicited the truth to a degree that no other means could have accomplished. That they are entirely free from prejudice or from the coloring that all must accept in describing momentous events with which they were interwoven by every inspiration of devotion and ambition is not to be pretended; but that they are written in integrity of purpose, and that they give the substance of the truth, can be justly claimed for them."

At the time he made them, McClure's lofty claims for *The Annals of the War* were largely justified. Most of the books to appear on the Civil War in the first two decades after the conflict were heavily biased, poorly researched, and weakly written narratives or general histories. Also, McClure's *Weekly Times* had been the first prominent newspaper or magazine to feature a significant number of quality articles on the war. The *Southern Historical Society Papers* began publication in 1876, but most of the early contributions to it were hopelessly prejudiced "Lost Cause" missives. Two other Southern publications, *The Land We Love* and *Our Living and Our Dead*, were even worse. The generally excellent *Confederate Veteran* would not begin publication until 1893. The *National Tribune*, which for four decades would offer its readers—most of them Union veterans—a steady stream of Northern reminiscences, did not run war-related articles on a regular basis until 1881. Popular periodicals such as *Scribner's, Harper's New Monthly Magazine*, and *The Atlantic Monthly* rarely carried war stories. And the *Century Magazine* did not enter the field with its acclaimed "Battles and Leaders" series until 1884.

Tens of thousands of books and articles on the Civil War have appeared in the 124 years since *The Annals of the War* was published, but the work has stood the test of time as well as McClure and his legion of contributors could have hoped. Writing in *Civil War Books: A Critical Bibliography*, the distinguished Civil War historian James I. Robertson, Jr., termed the articles collected in *The Annals of the War* "excellent commentaries on campaigns," of greater reliability than those found in *Battles and Leaders of the Civil War.* "Livelier and more provocative than [the *Battles and Leaders*] series," said Pulitizer Prizewinning historial James M. McPherson, "these articles address some of the numerous swirling controversies about the war." "*Annals* is absolutely essential," wrote T. Michael Parrish in the *Civil War News. The Annals of the War* "offers a rich lode of testimony from Union and Confederate witnesses. . . . No other single volume boasts a more impressive roster of contributors or presents greater breadth of coverage," averred Gary W. Gallagher.

We are confident that the plaudits accorded the original *Annals of the War* by these and other historians may be applied with equal if not greater force to *The New Annals of the Civil War.* Whereas McClure had only the initial two years' *Weekly Times* offering of 175 articles from which to draw monographs for his book, we have drawn on the best of the remaining 681 articles that appeared between January 4, 1879, and July 7, 1888, when the Philadelphia *Weekly Times* concluded the "Annals of the War" series with the article "The Blue and Gray, Clasping Hands Fraternally on the Field of Gettysburg."

Of especial benefit to the modern reader or researcher, the majority of the articles we have selected for the *The New Annals of the Civil War* are from Confederate contributors, a intentional effort on our part to help correct the glaring quantitative imbalance between Northern and Southern accounts of the war.

We present these articles to the reader largely as they appeared on the pages of the Philadelphia *Weekly Times*. Wishing to allow the authors of the articles gathered here to speak posthumously for themselves, we have not edited the pieces for accuracy in details, nor have we done much more than silently correct misspelled names, complete partial references to persons with bracketed insertions, break up paragraphs of unwieldy length, or correct egregious errors of punctuation and grammar.

Peter Cozzens
Panama City, Panama

Part One

The War in 1861

Ellsworth's Career

FRANK E. BROWNELL,
SERGEANT, 11TH NEW YORK VOLUNTEER INFANTRY

Philadelphia *Weekly Times* 5, no. 17, June 18, 1881

There is perhaps no more interesting and remarkable incident of the War of the Rebellion than that which resulted in the death of Col. Ephraim E. Ellsworth, in the city of Alexandria, Va. on May 24, 1861. The fact that his was the first Union blood shed on rebel soil alone gives it an historical interest. The fact that Ellsworth was a loved protégé and bosom friend of Abraham Lincoln and that both fell by assassination—the one the very first, the other the very last to bleed—makes one of those remarkable coincidences which border on the marvelous. There is evidence of the existence of a singular sameness in the lives of these two heroes of an unhappy era in American history, as well as in their untimely taking off. It was given to them the rare lot to subserve a greater purpose in the manner of their dying than in the acts of life. But the most minute acts and words of Mr. Lincoln have become as familiar as household words. It remains to clear away the rubbish of abuse and the cobwebs of misapprehension from his humbler prototype to show a character as clearly cameo cut and as interesting as the tragic event which abruptly closed his career and roused the men of the North. The event is far enough behind us to claim the attention of a new generation, and not too far to prevent a correct chronicle. It is wise to thus take the hour when living witnesses may give their testimony. It is only by a brief review of this short career that the true significance of the tragedy at Alexandria can be understood and appreciated. My own part in that tragedy as the instrument in the hands of Providence to visit sudden and condign punishment on the murder of Ellsworth makes it fitting that I should bear this testimony to the memory of a gallant soldier, a pure-hearted gentleman and an exalted patriot.

Ephraim E. Ellsworth was born April 11, 1837, at Saratoga, N.Y., and went to New York City in 1854. He remained there about a year and then went West, residing in several Western cities, but finally locating in Chicago.

At a very early age Ellsworth appears to have been stricken with the military fever. He joined a company in Chicago called the National Guard Cadets. Without any apparent definite purpose he took up the study of military tactics. He was made first sergeant of the Chicago company, but his rigid ideas of drill and military discipline made him unpopular and he was soon forced out of the organization. He went from Chicago to Elgin, Illinois, carrying his military spirit with him, and there organized a company. It was not long after that he extended a challenge to his former companions in Chicago to a competitive drill, in which his Elgin company so effectually put them to blush that they returned to Chicago humiliated and sore over defeat. Realizing their mistake in losing such a drillmaster the Chicago boys never rested from that time until they secured his return as captain of their organization. This was in the spring of 1859.

At this time Ellsworth told his mother that he was so engrossed with military matters and military ideas that he could fix his mind on nothing else, and henceforth he would make military matters the study and business of his life. His mother replied that it was very unfortunate that he was not born in Europe, where there was war nearly all the time, as there was no prospect of utilizing his talents in this country. With words that in the light of after events seem almost like prophecy he wrote that he could not but feel that this country would soon need his services and the services of a large and well-drilled army. He said the political struggle being waged between different sections could result in nothing but war. "Would to God," he exclaimed, "that I might believe otherwise."

Ellsworth was very poor at this time, having neglected all other business for the business that did not pay. His diary of that date tells the story:

> April 11, 1859
>
> Room No. 5, 79 Dearborn Street, Chicago
>
> Have decided to keep a diary. Shall wrote a sketch of my life to the present time and place it in front of this book. I do this because it seems very pleasant to be able to look back upon one's past life and note the gradual change of sentiment and views and because my life has been and bids fair to be such a curious jumble of strange incidents that should I ever become anybody or any-

> thing this will be useful as a means of showing how much suffering and temptation a man may undergo and still keep clear of despair and vice.

The last line of this day's entry is as follows: "One dozen pages Blackstone today. Sleep on office floor tonight." This office was where he copied law papers and thereby eked out a scanty living.

On Thursday, April 14, he wrote:

> Rose 6:30 A.M. According to promise went for Mrs. Smith and took her to [dinner] at Tremont House. She insisted on paying her fare in omnibus. She meant right and I could take no offense. I simply insisted on dropping the matter and paid it myself. (Charged it to my dinner.) "Very pressing invitation." Nay, command, to take dinner at Tremont with Mrs. S——. Refused. Gentlemen who like myself live on crackers and water seldom dine at hotels. (Reason very obvious to inquiring mind.)
>
> Received a letter from home. Mother well, but father sick with rheumatism. Will the time ever come when I can place my parents above the necessity of labor?

As the day's record winds up with the inevitable crackers and the office floor the prospect of helping his parents into comfortable circumstances must have been very dull indeed. The next day he wrote:

> I almost feel downhearted tonight. Copying consumes so much time that I cannot study to advantage, although I rise early and work late. I am unable to fix my mind on my studies, for I am forced continually to think there is so much copying which must be done or nothing to eat to-morrow. I can't starve. Oh! That the want of a few paltry dollars should retard my progress in this way!

It was on April 16, according to this diary, when he received a visit from the secretary of the Chicago Cadets with a letter notifying him of his selection as their captain. He was very much surprised that a company of young men which included many of the flower of the city should seek out a penniless youth to take command of them—more especially since he had been driven out from among them less than a year before. But he discusses their shocking want of discipline in a business like way and promises his decision on the following Tuesday. On that night he attended the meeting of the cadets, made a speech to them and accepted the proffered captaincy. His amusing self-congratulation appears pardonable under the circumstances:

> Had meeting and drill of cadets tonight. This is something of a triumph for me—a small one, it is true, but nevertheless pleasant. After having taken from them every particle of military prestige and reputation—met them on equal ground—now, they come supplicating to me, the person of all others in the world they have left no stone unturned to wrong, whose reputation they have tried by every means in their power to best—they come to me to command them. It makes me laugh. Time will tell. Five pages Blackstone tonight. Nothing to eat today and I'm tired and hungry tonight. Onward flow tonight!

It was on April 29 that he accepted the captaincy, which he coupled with these severe conditions: He wanted soldiers in every sense of the word and insisted they should be strictly moral, obedient and should allow themselves to be ruled with the iron hand of military discipline. If they would do this he would make them the best company in the United States; if they wouldn't he would have nothing to do with them. He was unanimously chosen. The next day he got some money and bought a lounge for three dollars and seventy-five cents, and congratulates himself on having a comfortable place to sleep. He had concealed his uncertain life from his parents:

> I was very lucky in getting my lounge just when I did for mother would be put off no longer and wanted to know in her letter today where I was boarding. So I can write back to her that I have a good lounge to sleep on. The eating part is getting along nicely. There is no use of making father and mother (God bless them!) miserable by the knowledge of my circumstances. I owe them more already than I can ever repay.

From this time the whole soul of young Ellsworth was swallowed up in his military company. He drew up a code of regulations, which were printed in all the Chicago papers and excited general comment. In this code expulsion was the penalty of entering any drinking saloon while wearing the uniform of the corps, attending public masked balls in uniform and the use of language unbecoming a gentleman while in the reading or drill room. To get rid of objectionable members he disbanded the "National Guard Cadets," and on the nucleus of the best formed the "U.S. Zouave Cadets."

By this rigid course he began to gather around him the aid and sympathy of the best citizens of Chicago. He still kept up his law studies, copied and lived on crackers and water. In military drill he was indefatigable. He pasted on his desk a schedule of time, which he lived up to regularly. It ran as follows:

> Mondays, Thursdays, and Saturdays—Rise at 5:00 A.M.; 5 to 10, study; 10 to 1, copying; 1 to 4, business; 4 to 7, study; 7 to 8, exercise; 8 to 10, study. On Tuesdays, and Wednesdays and Fridays—Rise at 6:00 A.M.; 6 to 10, study; 10 to 1, business; 1 to 7, study and copying; 7 to 11, drill.

Here was a rigid disciplinarian willing and able to apply rules to his own daily life that followed by any young man who possessed a fair amount of ability would command success in any walk of life. It appears that he carried his exercise to include the use of the sword. On May 14 he writes, "Have received a challenge to trial of skill with a very expert fencer in daily practice. As I have not practiced with a master for nearly eighteen months he will probably worst me. Nevertheless, I shall foil with him, as I must fence with some expert or lose my skill altogether. One and a half pound crackers and meat tonight."

About this date he appears to have become so thoroughly engrossed in his military ideas, exercise, drill and details that he dropped Blackstone and only kept up his copying to keep soul and body together. His diary falls off and but fitful entries appear at intervals. In one of these he relates an experience with a toothache. He was recommended to smoke by some of his "boys," as he familiarly calls them. After having gone to his lounge sick that night he says he made up his mind there was one thing worse than toothache. So he gave up smoking. His indefatigable energy and his success with the organization of which he was captain began to attract the attention of the authorities of the State of Illinois and of military men everywhere. His journal begins to fondle military names and his mind to embrace state plans and national ideas. He received proposals to drill the officers of the State militia of both brigade and regimental staff, and an invitation to visit West Point at the graduation exercises.

On July 4, 1859, his corps gave an exhibition drill in which other organizations competed. Their performance raised a perfect furor in Chicago, and the Ellsworth Corps rose at a bound to the topmost round of popularity. At 2:00 A.M. on the fifth he enters the following record in his diary: "Victory! And, I thank God, a triumph for me."

The personal pride and sensitiveness of young Ellsworth surpasses belief. While he was achieving all this success which was so dear to his heart, being flattered by army officers and high state officials, he was living on, or rather starving on, his crackers and dried beef and water. And when these flatterers accused him of overworking himself and breaking himself down with excitement he merely writes, in the loneliness of his office: "It is under-eating," and goes on in the same indomitable spirit as before.

One day he returned to his room thoroughly dispirited, and confessed in his tablets that he had just indulged in a hearty, womanish cry. This was because of a sense of despair at being unable to marry, or to promise to marry, a young lady with whom he had conceived a deep attachment. He says after his cry he prayed. That night he had a good supper and slept on a bed for the first time in a year. The next week he received an invitation to go to California to teach the Zouave drill to a crack San Francisco corps. His fame had spread rapidly. He was wanted at Rockford and at Springfield to teach local companies. He consulted Col. [Joseph H.] Eaton, who advised him to continue his connection with the cadets. Colonel Eaton introduced him to many people. Among others the adjutant general of Illinois pressed him to accept a position on his staff. Several other military honors were thrust upon him, but nothing to eat, except titles, and he says rank was even less substantial than crackers and water. Together with several officers he attempted to secure the passage of a law for the complete reorganization of the militia system of Illinois. This seems to have been a pet idea. After wasting a good deal of time on it, however, the thing failed, though the system proposed by Ellsworth was considered the most perfect. The bill passed one house and fell.

On February 2, 1860, Ellsworth submitted a plan of drill to the Zouave Cadets and a comprehensive plan for state skeleton regiments of trained officers. The latter was complete in every detail, from the sword drill of officers, with accompanying sketches, to the fastening of the soldiers' shoes. It included every particular of uniform, with sketches and price, movements (from the French drill) of the company and battalion, with illustrations, and finally a code of moral law and discipline that presupposed the perfect human machine. Shortly after this Ellsworth and his Zouaves began the famous tour of the United States. Perhaps nothing ever excited more attention and emulation than this remarkable trip. His company drilled in all the principal cities of the North during the summer of 1860 and stirred up a military fever wherever they went. Immense crowds greeted them everywhere.

The organization of military companies followed in their wake. The Wide Awakes of the presidential campaign took up the Ellsworth drill and all went to prepare the popular mind for the great struggle of the following year. Thousands of people will still remember the electric effect of the famous Ellsworth Zouaves, and thousands now past the prime of manhood will date their first hot throb of the military fever, the burning desire to be a soldier, from witnessing their wonderful maneuvers.

It was at the close of this tour, when he had just given a return drill at the wigwam in Chicago, that Ellsworth first met Abraham Lincoln. A friendship immediately sprung up between these two. Lincoln inquired about the young man's private life from his friends, and before they separated the then presidential candidate extended him an invitation to go to Springfield and complete his law studies in his office and under his immediate supervision. The young man was quick to accept. During the campaign which followed he took the stump in Illinois for Mr. Lincoln's election. When the president-elect started for Washington Ellsworth was one of the party. From this time forward Colonel Ellsworth becomes a national character.

There were loud threats of disunion throughout the country. United States senators from the South were openly declaring the doctrine of secession from their place in the Senate chamber. The warning had been sent from one end of the country to the other that Mr. Lincoln's assumption of the executive office would be the signal for secession. Threats of death if he made the attempt were freely bandied about in the streets of Baltimore. Lincoln was advised of this, and it was in one of his remarkable speeches at that time that he accepted the issue without faltering.

Mr. [William S.] Wood was the superintendent of the presidential escort, of which Ellsworth was an important member. I have before me a copy of Wood's instructions, which Ellsworth carried out that day. It is as follows:

> To the Committee of Arrangements for the Reception of the president-elect
>
> Gentlemen: Being charged with the responsibility of the safe conduct of the president-elect and his suite to their destination, I deem it my duty, for special reasons which you will readily comprehend, to offer the following suggestions: First—The president-elect will under no circumstances attempt to pass through any crowd until such arrangements are made as will meet the approval of Colonel Ellsworth, who is charged with the responsibility of all

> matter of this character, and to facilitate this you will confer a favor by placing Colonel Ellsworth in communication with the chief of your escort immediately upon the arrival of the trains, Second—Arrangement of Carriages—First Carriage—The president-elect, Colonel Lamon, or other members of his suite, one or two members of the escort or committee. Second Carriage—Colonel E. V. Sumner, U.S.A.; Major David Hunter, U.S.A.; Hon. N. B. Judd, of Illinois: Hon. David Davis, of Illinois. Third Carriage—Colonel E. E. Ellsworth, Captain Hazzard, John G. Nicolay, Esq., private secretary, member of the escort. Fourth Carriage—Robert T. Lincoln, John M. Hay, assistant secretary; two members of the escort. The other members of the suite may be arranged at your pleasure by your committee in the cars. Two carriages will be required to convey Mrs. Lincoln and family and her escort from the cars.

Here we have the young man who a few months earlier was sleeping on his office floor in Chicago and living from hand to mouth on bread and water now suddenly transformed into the confidential companion of the president of the United States and entrusted with the responsibility of his personal safety on a journey then considered perilous and full of terrible possibilities. That journey was the theme of the nation. Nor does it appear that Colonel Ellsworth underrated his responsibility. In a conversation with John Hay the latter suggested a doubt whether the people of the North would sustain the president in active measures of coercion. Ellsworth replied warmly that patriotism was not yet dead. "As for me," said he, "I would wish for no better death than to fall before Sumter next week!"

As yet no overt act had been committed and very few yet believed that rebellion would actually come. Ellsworth was not one of these. So certain was he of war that a short time before, when he urged his views upon Mr. Lincoln and declared that war was inevitable, he was merely smiled benignly upon as a father would smile upon his enthusiastic boy. Nevertheless he was tendered a lieutenancy in the regular dragoons, where, the president laughingly assured him, he might at least drill. This he declined, with the belief that he could be of more service shortly elsewhere. He was still at the White House every day or two waiting for the great event.

He had not long to wait. On April 12 the Rebel guns opened upon Sumter. The whole country was in an uproar within twenty-four hours. The next day Sumter capitulated and the nation throbbed in the first throes of revolution. Two days later the president issued his call for seventy-five thousand men.

Before that call had passed the wires of the telegraph offices Colonel Ellsworth was on his way to New York. There is a military precision about his every movement, which furnishes a key to the man's indomitable character. The next day he visited the New York Fire Department and consulted with the officers and decided to raise a regiment out of that brave material. The following day posters appeared as if by magic in every engine house in New York. This was on Saturday. On Monday the rolls were full. They were more than full, 2,300 names having been subscribed.

There was no time to lose and there were none lost. He had come to raise a regiment. Here were men enough for two. They were drawn up in open ranks and Ellsworth passed through and picked his men. I had just come down from Troy and joined out of my confidence in the commander and admiration of his character. The hat was hastily passed around in the Fire Department and money enough subscribed within twelve hours to purchase uniforms, arms and equipments. Oh, they were terribly in earnest! And such arms! There were at least ten different patterns and had to be thrown away as quick as we got to Washington.

The regiment left New York on April 29. There was an effort to prevent us from leaving, the alleged ground being that we were taking more men than the state law provided. But Ellsworth commanded his men to go on board the steamer *Baltic*, having received orders to that effect from [Brig. Gen. John E.] Wool, and they were not molested. We went to Annapolis by steamer, thence to Washington by rail. Before leaving we had been presented with a stand of colors from the New York Fire Department and a flag from Mrs. John Jacob Astor and one from Miss Laura Keene, the actress.

Colonel Ellsworth's Fire Zouaves attracted much attention on their arrival in Washington. They were the first volunteers on the ground. A good many militia organizations were already at the capital, but Ellsworth's command was the first volunteer regiment in the field which had had no previous organization.

The city began to bristle with bayonets, and the sound of drums and the tread of marching columns drew excited crowds into the streets. There were no quarters for the soldiery. Ellsworth's command was quartered in the House of Representatives. There were some pretty hard characters among his men, and it was not more than a day or two before some sets of lawlessness raised a storm of indignation in the city and created a prejudice against the whole regiment. Ellsworth privately ascertained the extent of the damages and paid the amount out of his personal picket. Nevertheless the feeling against the regiment was so strong that it was finally decided to move it out of the city. Before this was done, however, a big fire at Willard's Hotel on May 9 enabled the Zouaves to recover their prestige. They were at home at a fire and at this one their conduct was such as to excite admiration, for they unquestionably not only saved the hotel building but the remaining property on the square. The sum of $500 was raised and presented to the regiment for their benefit in recognition of their services.

On May 10, however, Ellsworth's command was moved into camp near the Insane Asylum and shortly afterward down to Giesboro Point below. There was much discontent among the members. They had been promised many things at New York and their muster was irregular, they having been sworn in "for the war." There was trouble about their arms. While this was going on Ellsworth greatly felt the need of trained officers and privately sent to Chicago for several of his old associates in the cadets. He was fortunate enough to secure several good officers. But the monotony of camp life was more than the New York firemen could bear. Acts of insubordination were of daily occurrence.

In a few days it was whispered about headquarters that a movement was to be made on Alexandria. Ellsworth went immediately to the president and said that he would regard it as a personal favor to move in the advance. He went further and declared that the morale of his command required some active duty. "They must be got into the field," said he, "and they must be got in first." The president replied that the first movement on Southern soil was one of great delicacy. Much depended thereon. He desired to avoid all violence. The people of Virginia were not in a mass disloyal and he wanted nothing to occur that might incense them against the government, but rather wished to so conduct the movement that it would win them over. At present the city of Alexandria was in possession of the insurgents; they must be driven out or taken without bloodshed, if possible.

This position of President Lincoln was fully understood and appreciated by Colonel Ellsworth. He promised to be responsible for his command if they were allowed the advance, otherwise not. Discipline was now at an end here. This conference was, of course, unknown to the command. On the night of May 23 they were ordered into line at 9:00 P.M. The call was greeted with a yell of enthusiasm which could not be suppressed. When the men were drawn up Colonel Ellsworth made a short address to them. He told them of the importance of discipline and said he had pledged his bones that they would act like men. He had told [Brig. Gen. Joseph K. F.] Mansfield that he would, for them, consider it an affront if they were not allowed to lead the army into the enemy's country. They were the first to answer the call, the first sworn in for the war. He had demanded it as their right. It had been granted. They would move across the Potomac in two hours. He then impressed upon them the importance of the utmost circumspection. "For the army which comes after will be judged by you. We are to kill nobody except of kindness. Not a shot is to be fired except by orders."

The colonel then retired to his tent and wrote the following touching letter to his mother and father:

> Washington, D.C., May 22, 1861
>
> My Dear Parents,
>
> The regiment is ordered to move across the river tonight. We have no means of knowing what reception we will meet with, although I am of the opinion that our entrance of the city of Alexandria will be hotly contested, as I am just informed that a large body of troops arrived there today. Should this happen, my dear parents, it may be my lot to be injured in some manner. Whatever may happen I shall have the consolation of knowing I was engaged in the performance of a sacred duty, and tonight, thinking of the possibility of tomorrow and the occurrences of the past, I am perfectly content to accept whatever my fortune may be, confident that He who noted the fall of a sparrow will have some purpose even in the fate of one like me.
>
> My darling and ever-loved parents, good bye! God bless, protect and care for you! Ellsworth.

At 2:00 A.M. on May 24 the boats containing the Ellsworth Fire Zouaves silently dropped down the river. When we arrived off Alexandria a small boat shot out from the shadow of the gunboat *Pawnee* and landed at the wharf simultaneously with us. This boat contained an officer bearing a white flag. A hurried consultation was held between that officer and Colonel Ellsworth. I have always understood that the colonel was informed that the town had either surrendered or had been placed under a flag of truce or that the people had been given time to leave the city. We were the only Union troops there at this time.

We landed at the foot of Cameron Street, a square above the present ferry wharves. When we had disembarked the regiment was formed on the wharf. Colonel Ellsworth, in company with the chaplain of the regiment, Mr. Dodge; the correspondent of the *New York Times*, Mr. Windsor, and Mr. E. H. House, correspondent of the New York *Tribune*, started up Cameron Street. It was understood they were going to the telegraph office.

As they passed the right of Company A an officer suggested that they had better take a guard with them. It was broad daylight—after 5:00 A.M., yet so far from the excitement such an occasion might be expected to create not a soul seemed to be stirring. There were two or three shots heard up town, as if pickets had given warning, but otherwise the city was dead and silent as the grave. Not even a face could be seen at a shutter. The silence was actually painful.

The hint of a guard was accepted and Ellsworth called for the first squad on the right of the first company, consisting of five men, to follow. I was one of that party. All immediately then went up Cameron Street two squares and turned to the left, down Royal Street to King. As we turned the corner at King and Royal we came in full view of the Marshall House, on which a Confederate flag was fluttering in the breeze. The Marshall House was a square further west, on the opposite side of King Street, up which we proceeded. It was an old-fashioned tavern, three stories of dingy brick, with two old-fashioned dormer windows bulging from its shingle roof. There was a wide double entrance on King Street and an ordinary door to the left of it, while half a dozen wooden steps took in all together. The wide doors of glass led to the office, the ordinary door to the foot of the stairway in the hall.

What seemed most remarkable to me was the entire absence of life. No one was on the street, no one was lounging about the hotel. It might have been a cemetery.

At the sight of the rebel flag Ellsworth halted us. Turning to the sergeant he said, "Marshall, go back and tell Captain Coyle, of Company A, to hurry up his company here as soon as possible."

We then passed up King Street on the opposite side until we crossed the next street. Colonel Ellsworth and the newspapermen were a little in advance. I naturally supposed he was going to leave Captain Coyle to take care of the flag when he came up with his company. If that was his intention he changed his mind, for he suddenly turned and went diagonally across the street toward Marshall House. Probably he remembered his promise to the president and feared that a sight of that flag on a whole company would so inflame the men that Captain Coyle would be unable to control them. At any rate he turned and went back to the house, entered and was followed into the office. There was but one person visible—the first man we had yet met—and he stood behind the counter in the office. Ellsworth asked him for the proprietor. He replied in a surly manner that he was not about.

We did not stay to bandy words with him, but the whole party went into the hall from the office and started up the stairway to the attic.

Nobody offered to stop us and there was nobody to be seen to do so. When we reached the attic Ellsworth mounted a step-ladder leading to the roof, where the flag halyards came through a scuttle, and pulled in the offending bunting and threw it down the ladder. We started downstairs—an old-fashioned wooden zigzag stair, broken with landings between each story. I was in the advance.

Up to this time everything had been so quiet, peaceful and dead that none of us dreamed of violence. As I made the turn of the landing in the middle of the flight leading to the third floor I saw a man standing on the floor below at the side of the stairs with the barrel of a double-barreled gun resting on the banisters. He was a brawny-looking fellow and was in his shirtsleeves. I saw as quick as a flash what that man and that gun meant. It was in his eye.

By the instinct of self-preservation rather than anything else I jumped to the foot of the stairs at a bound. As I alighted beside him I struck down his gun with my own. Both pieces struck the banister together. Both glanced downward until they slipped off the end of the banister, where the guns separated. By this time Ellsworth had appeared in sight at the landing I had just left.

Without a word, and before I could recover my equilibrium, the man [James T.] Jackson quickly raised his gun again and fired. The muzzle of his shotgun was not more than three or four feet distant.

Colonel Ellsworth, with the single exclamation, "My God!" pressed his hand on his breast and fell dead at the foot of the stairway. The heavy charge of buckshot had pierced him just above the heart.

In the meantime I had jumped back and just as Jackson raised his gun the second time I fired upon him. Without stopping to see the effect of my shot I sprang toward him and with a quick thrust of the bayonet forced him to the floor. It was all done so quickly I had no time to think.

As Jackson fell it was with one convulsive grip upon the trigger, and his other barrel was discharged so close to my head that it seemed to paralyze me. The charge went into the wall just above my head. As the body of the dead rebel slipped from my bayonet it rolled to the landing below. Jackson had never spoken a word from the first and died without a sign. The story that his body was mutilated after death is false.

By this time the entire party had reached the scene. Great excitement ensued. People came rushing from the rooms and the street. I reloaded my gun and the squad stood on the landing for a minute back to back, in anticipation of an attack. We compelled them to stand up in a row, where we could command the situation. Mr. House was the first to go out of the building for succor, which he did at the imminent risk of his life. In a few moments Col. [Orlando B.] Willcox, of Michigan, since a general, came upstairs, with Captain Coyle and the regimental surgeon. The body of our dead colonel was wrapped in a blanket and I accompanied it to the Navy Yard, where it was placed in the engine house, for the purpose of embalming. I went over to the quarters of the 71st New York and lay down to rest my aching head.

It was only a short time, however, when a message came that the president wished to see me at the engine house. I went. There was no one but the president, Captain [Gustavus V.] Fox, of the navy, and the undertaker. Mr. Lincoln was walking up and down the floor, very much agitated. He was wringing his hands and there was, I thought, the trace of tears upon his cheek. He did not appear to notice my entrance at first. Lifting the cloth from the face of the dead man, he exclaimed with a depth of pathos I shall never forget, "My boy, my boy! Was it necessary this sacrifice should be made!"

After awhile he made me relate the whole occurrence in detail. I had scarcely finished before Mrs. Lincoln came and I was again asked to repeat the story of the tragedy to her.

A correspondent who visited the Executive Mansion on the morning of May 24 gives the following account of how the news was first received by the president. He said:

> I called at the White House this morning with Senator [Henry] Wilson to see the president on a matter of pressing public business, and as we entered the library we marked the president standing before a window looking across the Potomac, running at the foot of the grounds of the Executive Mansion. He did not move until we approached very closely, when he turned around abruptly and advancing toward us extended his hand, saying, "Excuse me; I cannot talk." We supposed his voice had given way from some cause and we were about to inquire when, to our surprise, he burst into tears and concealed his face in his handkerchief. He walked up and down the room for some moments and we stepped aside in silence, not a little moved at such an unusual spectacle in such a man and in such a place. After composing himself somewhat the president took his seat and desired us to approach. He said: "I will make no apology, gentlemen, for my weakness, but I knew poor Ellsworth well and held him in very high regard. Just as you entered the room Captain Fox left me, after giving me the details of Ellsworth's

unfortunate death. The event was so unexpected and the recital so touching that it has quite unmanned me." The president here made a violent effort to restrain his emotions, and after a pause proceeded to give us the incidents of the tragedy. As he closed his relation he exclaimed: "Poor fellow! It was undoubtedly an act of rashness, but it only shows the heroic spirit that animates our soldiers from high to low in this righteous cause of ours. Yet who can restrain their grief to see them fall in such a way as this, not by the fortunes of war, but by the hand of an assault.

"There is one fact that has reached me which is of great consolation to my heart and quite a relief after this melancholy affair. I learn from several persons that when the Stars and Stripes were raised again in Alexandria many of the people actually wept for joy and manifested the liveliest gratification at seeing this familiar and loved emblem once more floating above them."

The following letter from Mr. Lincoln to the parents of Ellsworth has, I believe, never been in print:

> In the untimely loss of your noble son our affection here is scarcely less than your own. So much of promised usefulness to one's country and of bright hopes for one's self and friends have rarely been so suddenly darkened as in his fall. In size and years and in youthful appearance a boy, his power to command men was surprisingly great. This power, combined with a fine intellect and indomitable energy and a taste altogether military, constituted in him, as seemed to me, the best natural talent in that department I ever knew. And yet he was singularly modest and deferential in social intercourse. My acquaintance with him began less than two years ago, yet through the latter half of the intervening period it was as intimate as the disparity of our ages and my engrossing engagements would permit. To me he appeared to have no indulgences or pastimes, and I never heard him utter a profane or intemperate word. What was more conclusive of his good heart, he never forgot his parents. The honors he labored for so laudable, and in the sad end so gallantly gave his life, he meant for them no less than for himself. In the hope that it may be no intrusion on the sacredness of your sorrow I have ventured to address this tribute to the memory of my young friend and your brave and early-

fallen child. May God give you the consolation which is beyond all earthly power. Sincerely your friend in a common affliction.

A. Lincoln

The body of Ellsworth was taken to the White House at Mr. Lincoln's request, where funeral services were performed. It was then conveyed to New York and funeral services repeated over it at the Astor House. When it was taken away the entire New York Fire Department escorted it to the steamer by which it went to Albany. There it laid in state in the capitol. Thence it went to Troy, where another funeral was held, at which the whole city turned out. It was finally interred at Mechanicsburg, New York, at the home of his parents. The events of that trip could never be forgotten, as they can never be described. The entire country seemed up in arms. The excitement was intense. It was felt that a hero had fallen. If there had been any faltering in the North it had now ceased, and the resolve to crush the rebellion was sealed in Ellsworth's blood.

The time is recalled to me now as I look upon a badge he used to wear. It is simply "U.S." worked in gold upon a black cloth ground and surrounded by a wreath. It is hard and gory and black red with his blood. I took it from beneath him on the day he fell and it is very precious to me. On the same day he wore a small gold badge upon his breast. It was about the size of a twenty-cent piece. It was a badge of the Baltimore City Guard and it hung upon his vest. On one side was the letters "B.C.G.," surrounded by a blue garter with the motto, "Non solum nobis sed prope patris." That badge was shot into his breast, whence it was removed by the surgeon. "Not only for myself, but for my country."

The Battle of Belmont

Benjamin F. Sawyer,
Colonel, 24th Alabama Infantry, C.S.A.

Philadelphia *Weekly Times*, 8, no. 25, August 9, 1884

In the combats that followed in such rapid succession, electrifying the continent and astounding the world, the comparatively insignificant battle of Belmont was forgotten. In the roll of mightier events it is hardly to be counted in the lists of battles. It is only to those who were engaged, the beginners who were that day matriculated in war, that its scenes were made memorable as long as life shall last. Some ten thousand men were for the first time brought face to face with danger and with death; for the first time realized the horrible work to which they had dedicated their lives. It is not likely that one of those, so engaged, will ever forget the experience of that day.

In itself, so far as any material results were effected, the battle was almost a sham, a tactical exercise gotten up by the opposing generals to test the efficiency and pluck of their troops. Perhaps it was; it seems difficult now, as it did then, hard as one may try, to conceive any other reason why it should have been fought. There was no strategy displayed by either general; there was no chance for any. [Brig. Gen. Gideon J.] Pillow's outlying camps on the Missouri side of the river were too well protected by the over-ranging batteries of Columbus to permit their occupation, if once captured. This [Brig. Gen. Ulysses S.] Grant must have known, for he had come down under a flag of truce a few days before and taken in the possibilities of the situation. The position being untenable, why sacrifice the life of even one man to capture it? Surely it was not for the triumph of capturing a few straggling tents, the only possible damage that could be inflicted, that he came down in all the pomp and circumstance of war, with drums beating and banners flying, to hazard the die of battle. The game was hardly worth the candle.

But perhaps Grant thought better. He may have attached a more important value to canvas and straw than did the extravagant Confederates. Doubtless he did and as he stood on the deck of the saucy little tug (the *Grampus*) that brought him in the Confederate lines a few days before and by a coup d'oeil took in the tempting exposure of the outlying camps he may, in the inspiration of his genius, have evolved a brilliant strategic movement whereby the destruction of the tents might be compassed. At any rate he came in a martial array, with a fizz and a flourish, putting his brave troops in the heart of the battle, holding them there for awhile and then turning in utter abandonment of all order and discipline and scurrying back to his gunboats, leaving his dead to be buried and his wounded to be cared for by his enemy.

[Maj. Gen. Leonidas] Polk's Corps, constituting the then Army of the Mississippi, was occupying the strong position of Columbus, Kentucky. Its naturally strong points were further strengthened by a series of skillfully designed and well-constructed forts, connected by a triple line of earthworks. The beetling bluffs that overlooked the town below, the river and the plains of Belmont opposite, were crowned with heavy batteries, while a tier of casemated guns below raked every foot of water in sight and made its water approach impossible. The camp which so temptingly invited the assault of the enemy was occupied by General Pillow's Brigade, consisting of Col. James C. Tappan's 13th Arkansas Infantry Regiment, Col. Robert M. Russell's 12th Tennessee, Col. John V. Wright's 13th Tennessee, Col. Edward Pickett's 21st Tennessee and Col. Thomas J. Freeman's 22nd Infantry regiments, and part of Col. Samuel F. Marks' 11th Louisiana Infantry Regiment, with Lt. Col. Daniel Beltzhoover's Louisiana Battery of four guns. It was against this camp, protected by the formidable batteries of Columbus, that Grant, then a newly-fledged and curly brigadier, hurled his eager troops.

It was a sharp frosty morning in November (the sixth). We were still busied in strengthening our works and constructing quarters for the coming winter when he came. Our regiment (the Blythe Mississippi) had started out on fatigue duty, when we were met by our comrades of the 154th Senior Tennessee coming in at a double-quick and giving us the first intimation of the approaching danger. I happened to be in command of the fatigue party for that day and without waiting for orders I about-faced my command and started back to camp, also at a double-quick. We had proceeded but a short distance before we were met by a courier confirming the news and ordering me to hurry back to quarters and prepare for battle.

Arriving at camp a wild scene of excitement and confusion was presented. Officers flurried with the new and strange perturbation were hurrying to and fro, awkwardly dangling their swords between their legs; men hunting up mislaid accouterments and burnishing too-long neglected guns; ordnance officers confusedly distributing ammunition, issuing Enfield cartridges for muskets, ball and buckshot for rifles, for be it known at that early stage of the conflict our regiment, as were many others, was armed with an incongruous variety of guns, no two companies being armed alike—one company, A, having Sharp's rifles, another, Company G, being armed with double-barreled shotguns and still another, my own, Company I, having long-barreled rifles, caliber .32, while the others were armed with old picked up army muskets.

To supply the diverse needs of the regiment would have puzzled a general of ordnance himself in an hour of cool deliberation. No wonder then that poor Lieutenant Brownrigg, flushed with the surprise of his maiden fight, lost his head in frantic confusion and handed out the ammunition in reckless disregard of service. The company commanders, however, were not so flurried and by swapping around soon managed to supply their respective companies with suitable cartridges, and when the regiment was formed for hasty inspection each man was found amply served with ball and powder for the emergency. The morning's lesson was a valuable one, however, and care was taken, as soon thereafter as possible, to arm the regiment with guns of uniform caliber.

We had formed our lines and were resting on our arms, nervously awaiting developments, when the booming of Belthoover's guns and a desultory popping of musketry far across the river told that it was no false alarm we had to meet. Soon, the firing became more rapid and distinct as the battle drew nearer. We could tell by the shifting direction of the firing that Pillow was hotly engaged and getting pushed, yet still we remained idle, impatiently waiting orders to move forward to the fight. There is hardly any position more trying to one's nerves, and especially the nerves of a raw recruit, than to stand in sight and sound of a battle waiting one's turn to be put into it. We felt it keenly that morning and when the first enthusiasm of excitement began to wear off and the battle roared louder and nearer, we could feel our valor oozing out, as it were, at our fingers' ends; but still we had to stand and no orders came, but instead the rumor that the main Union army, under [Brig. Gen. Charles F.] Smith, was advancing from Paducah and the attack on Pillow was only a feint to divert Polk's attention to that point.

At length, however, toward noon, the pressure upon Pillow became too heavy to be longer withstood and a portion of [Brig. Gen. Benjamin F.] Cheatham's Brigade, consisting of the 154th Senior Tennessee, Col. Preston Smith, and the Blythe Mississippi, Col. A. K. Blythe, was ordered to his relief. At a double-quick we started and were marched to the river, reaching the overlooking bank in time to see Pillow's hard-fought troops broken in disorder, his battery captured and turned upon him and his camps in a blaze of destruction. It was not an encouraging sight to beginners, but we had little time to contemplate it, for, having caught our range, as in close column we crowded down to the landing, Belthoover's captured guns were turned upon us, chilling us to the marrow with a nameless dread. A more demoralizing position I do not remember in my four-years' experience of battle. I shudder even now to think of it.

Two transports, large side-wheel steamers, lay at the wharf ready for us. Aboard one of these, the *Prince*, we hurriedly embarked and in the face of the fire crossed over, four solid shots crashing through the boat during the transit, carrying away the cabin steps, but happily doing no other damage. Company G, Captain Faulkner, with my own Company I, was crowded upon the hurricane deck, which elevated position, while exposing us to an unpleasant share of the enemy's attention, gave us a comparative view of the field. It was a sad and discouraging sight we saw. Pillow's men, powder-begrimed and bleeding, were utterly demoralized, cowering under the river's sheltering bank like gangs of hogs that had been badgered by dogs in a cornfield, his tents all aflame and an exultant enemy defiantly daring us on. In an incredibly short time the landing was effected and we as quickly debarked; the band bravely trying to enthuse our flagging spirits by striking up Dixie. Forming in line of battle as we landed and hurriedly loading we were ready for action.

The gallant Cheatham was there ready to lead us. "Men, forward, and give them the devil!" was his curt command and forward we moved. Mounting the bank under which we had formed and by an oblique movement to avoid the impenetrable brush of fallen timber, we struck the exultant enemy on his right flank, delivering an unexpected fire. At this moment, as if just awakened from a paralysis of fright, the heavy batteries on the bluff of Columbus opened a well directed fire of shot and shell, dealing death and carrying consternation in the opposing ranks. It is surprising to see the magic transition from defeat to victory, from a deliberate courage to a demoralized cowardice. All men are subject to the weakness.

It is no derogation then to the bravery of the gallant Illinois troops, who had fought so hard all the morning and but an instant before stood filled with the proud sense of victory, that they should now stand for a moment

"The retreat became a run" (JOHNSON, *CAMPFIRE AND BATTLEFIELD*)

in seeming wonder at our sudden onslaught and then begin to give back—at first slowly and in order and then the retreat became a run and from a run it broke into a disorderly rout. Guns were thrown away, bayonets, cartridge boxes and even haversacks and all order was forgotten in the wild race for life. With little less demoralization we followed after, helter-skelter, over fields and through the woods, loading and firing as we ran, every now and then bringing down a poor fellow with a cruelty little less than murder. The whole affair was so different from our preconceived ideas of a battle that we could hardly realize its tragic actuality. The pursuit was as disorderly and inglorious as was the flight. Had we no officers and had each man been filled with liquor we could scarcely have made a wilder, more reckless, undisciplined mob than we were.

Had General Grant held one single company cool in hand he could have captured every man of the two regiments that followed him through that Missouri swamp to his gunboats, six miles away. But he had no such company; his entire army fled before that straggling rabble, not even stopping to throw out a skirmish line to protect the embarkation of his fugitive troops, but hurried aboard his transports pell-mell and the devil take the hindmost. So closely did we follow that the steamboat *City of Memphis* had to cut its lines and back out in the stream, leaving a number on the bank to surrender as prisoners. Forming as we came up, a vigorous fire was opened on the retreating transports, doing considerable execution. But they soon withdrew beyond our range and the gunboats *Essex* and *Lexington*, interposing between, in turn opened upon us. Fortunately for us the river was so low in its banks that the range had to be so elevated that the shells went shrieking high over our heads through the tree tops, bursting in the woods far in the rear. By lying on the ground we were perfectly safe, where we remained until, seeing the transports out of any further danger from us, the gunboats withdrew and left us free to return to our quarters.

The report of shells bursting in our rear for a time spread an uneasy fear in our inexperienced minds, we first thinking that the enemy had inveigled us into a trap and was now attacking us in the rear.

"By God, Captain, the devils are in our rear," said Colonel Blythe, turning to me.

"Well, Colonel, 'spose they am; hain't we'uns in thar rare too?" asked Private Monk, a tall, ungainly fellow, straightening himself up with the assuring suggestion.

It was nearly sundown when, the gunboats having entirely disappeared, we began our return down the river. Tired as the men were they could not refrain from loading themselves with trophies of the battle as we passed over the field on our way. My entire company gathered arms and accouterments enough to completely equip themselves and the heavy, unwieldy rifles were thrown away or sent home. By 10:00 P.M. we recrossed the river and wearily returned to our quarters too tired to eat the supper the day's exciting fast so urgently demanded. We had scarcely fallen into sleep before we were ordered to arouse and fall into line. Smith's long expected columns were approaching and would assault our works at daybreak. Such was the exciting rumor that alarmed the camp.

The remainder of the night was spent in watching and longing for the morning to come and yet half dreading the work it promised to bring. At last it came, but no enemy appeared. There was none nearer than Mayfield—the alarm being the work of a cavalry videttes scare. We were all willing enough to excuse him the falsity of his report. After breakfast I accompanied a detail to the battlefield for the purpose of removing the wounded and burying the dead. I was surprised to find so many wounded scattered in the woods and hidden under the brushwood, still uncared for. They had dragged themselves thither for safety and had there moaned the wretched night away. We had scarcely began our sad task, treating friend and foe alike, when a flag of truce came in from General Grant asking permission to look after his wounded and to bury his dead. The request was readily granted, and soon we were joined by an ambulance corps and fatigue party and together in friendly sympathy we finished the melancholy work.

Accompanying the Union detail was a number of officers of high rank, among others Col. John A. Logan, then colonel of an Illinois regiment. Quite a number of Confederate field officers were also present and it was pleasant to see the friendly relations quickly established between them. Colonel Logan was particularly jovial and pleasantly rallied his quondam friend, Col. John V. Wright, of the 13th Tennessee upon his unceremonious treatment of him the day before. They had been political friends and allies and members of Congress together the year before and had met yesterday on the field of battle for the first time since they had parted in Washington.

"I saw you yesterday, John," said Logan, "and hallowed for you to stop, but you didn't even say 'how do' to me."

"Yes, I heard you," replied Wright, "but I thought your greeting a little too warm for comfort, and besides, I had urgent business in the rear."

There was one wounded officer, Col. [Henry] Dougherty, commander of an Illinois brigade, whom I shall always remember. He was one of the handsomest men I ever saw—a perfect specimen of physical strength and manly beauty. He was wounded in the leg and had to have it cut off. He submitted to the painful operation without a murmur, winning by his patient, uncomplaining manner the friendly sympathy of all who saw him.

There is another sad episode of the after battle that I wish to record. It was the burial of a young surgeon. I cannot recall his name; I would give much to be able to do so. He also was from Illinois, but had left his home and his people to join his ill-fated life to our ill-fated cause. His young and lovely wife came with him. He had but the week before joined us, only the day before been assigned to duty. It was his first service and while recklessly exposing himself on the field was killed. We brought his body to Columbus and buried it with special honors. His wife was present and it was sad to witness the grief that almost crazed her as she realized the desolation of her bereavement—a widow and an alien from her home. Poor lady, eyes unused to weeping shed tears of pity for her that day. Our duty to the dead being finished the usual routine of camp life was resumed, not to be disturbed again until nearly four months later the triumphant salvos of artillery at Cairo, twelve miles distant, told us of the disaster of Fort Donelson and warned us of the wrath to come.

Regaining the Atlantic Coast

THOMAS HALL,
CHIEF SIGNAL OFFICER, STAFF OF ADMIRAL SAMUEL F. DU PONT

Philadelphia *Weekly Times* 3, no. 20, July 12, 1879

In November 1861 the illustrated papers of this country had a tremendous and unprecedented sale. *Harper's* and *Frank Leslie's Weeklies* presented full page pictures of the battle of Port Royal, in the middle distance of which the United States fleet of men-of-war were seen staffing a circle and firing red-hot and cold shot, shell and grape into the fortification indicated by a line of sand embankment in the background. It was the first important engagement of the war on the seacoast. Two months before [Maj. Gen. Benjamin F.] Butler and Cmdr. [Silas] Stringham, commanding respectively the forces of the army and navy represented at Hatteras Inlet, had broken the Confederate line of coast possession and effectually blocked the passage of blockade runners and privateers from out of these inland seas the Sounds of Albemarle and Pamlico. It was an important action, but the magnitude of the operations at Port Royal and the great results that accrued from holding it made the expedition and engagement inside of Hilton Head second to none in importance that transpired on the Atlantic Coast.

About a year ago the *Weekly Times* told the story of the sailing of the expedition from Fortress Monroe and the writer, himself a sailor, described with graphic power the scenes at sea when the elements tossed the ships and transports as playthings on their billows. Mr. [R. C.] Hance's narration ["The Expedition to Port Royal," Philadelphia *Weekly Times*, October 12, 1878], however, does not include these inside points of history which I, as chief signal officer of the fleet and attached to Commodore [Samuel F.] Du

Samuel F. Du Pont as an admiral
(*MAGAZINE OF AMERICAN HISTORY*)

Pont's flagship, was in possession of. Neither does his story embrace the history of the battle, which he witnessed from a transport outside of the harbor, and with a view of telling something that has never been told of this memorable action and of correcting a few errors in facts, I take up the thread of Mr. Hance's narrative.

Most of the fleet arrived from Fortress Monroe on Sunday, November 3, 1861, and came to anchor inside of the bar at Hilton's Head. The *Wabash* came in on Monday morning and the others, except the frigate *Sabine* came in during that day. The entire fleet had been dispersed by Sunday's storm. As soon as the *Sabine's* absence was discovered the commodore directed the steamer *Bienville* to proceed to the southward in search of her. During Tuesday the steamers *Mercury* and *Vixen*, under cover of several gunboats, advanced up the harbor to buoy out the channel and mark the lines of position and advance. This was accomplished successfully and proved one of the most admirable of the many well-laid plans that tended to our ultimate success. The points had been well-established, and the major part of the soundings obtained before the Confederate batteries opened fire, which they did upon the gunboats during the afternoon.

This fact was reported to the commodore, who asked: "Are they hitting anything?" "Nothing," was the reply. "Very good," said he; "signal them to stay there and finish the survey." Meantime the note of preparation had

The fleet passing out of Hampton Roads (MAGAZINE OF AMERICAN HISTORY)

been sounded throughout the fleet. The transports had been ordered to the rear and the decks of all the men-of-war cleared for action. At 1:00 P.M. on Tuesday the four flags that gave the signal to all the naval vessels—"cleared ship for action"—went fluttering to the masthead of the frigate *Wabash*. In a moment all was life and activity in the fleet. From the funnels of the steamships the smoke came in volumes, showing that all were awake to the importance of the occasion of the hour, while on board the sailing ships the busy topmen were aloft reeving preventer stays and braces, sending down the light spars and making everything snug aloft to engage in battle.

From the flagship we eagerly watched the movement of the *Mercury* and *Vixen* as they steamed around the harbor, casting the lead and taking angles, and anxiously waited their return in order that the signal for advance could be given. The commodore was ready for sailing at 2:00 P.M. The order of sailing had been issued as follows: "The flagship will lead the main column, composed of the ships of greatest draught of water, as follows: *Wabash, Susquehanna, Mohican, Seminole, Pawnee, Unadilla*, and *Pembina*. The remaining vessels will take position on the starboard side of the main column in the following order of sailing: *Bienville, Seneca, Curlew, Penguin, Ottawa*, and *Vandalia*. Other ships to follow as may be convenient."

At 4:00 P.M. the signal to get under way was given, but immediately recalled, for out of the clouds that lowered in the northwest a stiff breeze came down that set the white caps dancing on the bar and brought darkness before nightfall. The attack was postponed and many were the expressions of bitter disappointment and regret. At the council of officers held before sailing from Hampton Roads it had been arranged to attack at the moment the fleet arrived. In fact, the presence of the men-of-war was to be the signal for the Confederate forces that battle was at once to be had. But this was the situation. We had been off the coast three days, and the rebels had all the warning they could desire to call to their aid reinforcements and to strengthen their position. Whatever advantage we might have in the way of a surprise had been lost by the unavoidable delay caused by the gale.

Wednesday morning broke with continued heavy weather. The sea ran high and the wind blew a gale that rendered it impossible for the larger ships to cross the seething bar, and once more the signal of delay was sent to the masthead. Thursday morning dawned bright and beautiful. From our masthead with strong glasses we could plainly see that the enemy had not failed to avail themselves of the opportunity to strengthen their position. An extension of the Fort Walker water battery, the mounting of two more guns at Fort Beauregard, and the presence of two additional rebel gunboats that had come down from Beaufort, were the visible measures taken. The plan of attack was simple and effective being for the ships to steam in a circle or ellipse running close to Fort Beauregard, on the north side of the river, as they passed in and to continue in one direction until out of range, then drift slowly down on the other side of the river paying fiery respects to Fort Walker, on the south side of the river, as they went by.

By this means it was possible to engage both the starboard and port batteries at one time. The arrangement of the ships when once the signal was given was a work of speedy accomplishment. It was apparent to all that the great mission on which we had come was about to be realized, and every heart beat high with hope. We well know that the forts and batteries about to be attacked had been erected under the guidance of enlarged military experience and practical skill, and that behind these distant ramparts, so (clearly) visible in the gray light of the morning were men whose numbers were as yet unknown and who would defend with their lives any encroachment of the invader's foot upon the soil of South Carolina.

The ships made the entrance of the channel without a shot being fired. Between the forts the river is about 2,500 yards wide, and both columns had advanced to a point midway between the batteries when a wreath of smoke floated out from Fort Walker, a round shot ricocheted over the bow of the *Wabash* and fell just short of the *Bienville*. In an instant both batteries

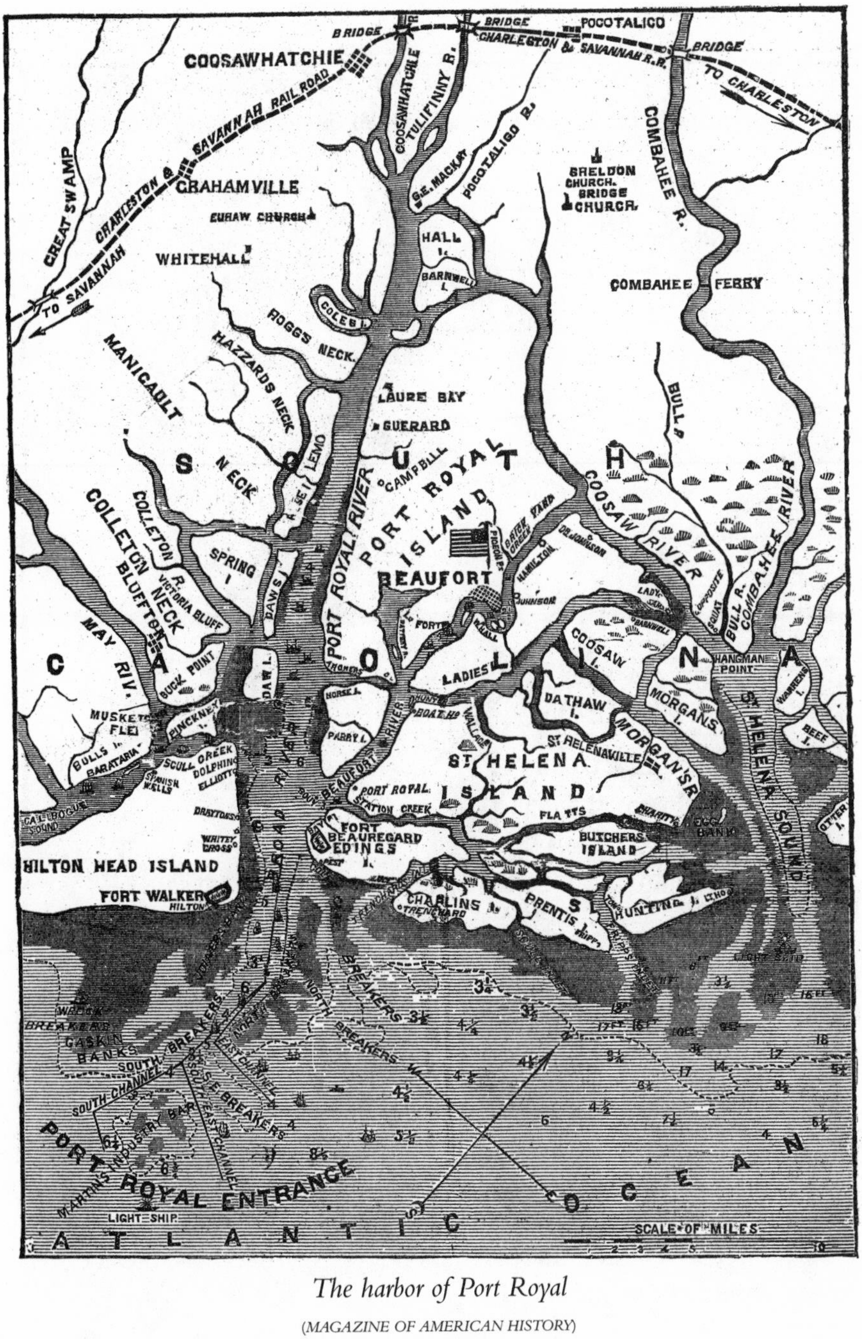

The harbor of Port Royal

(MAGAZINE OF AMERICAN HISTORY)

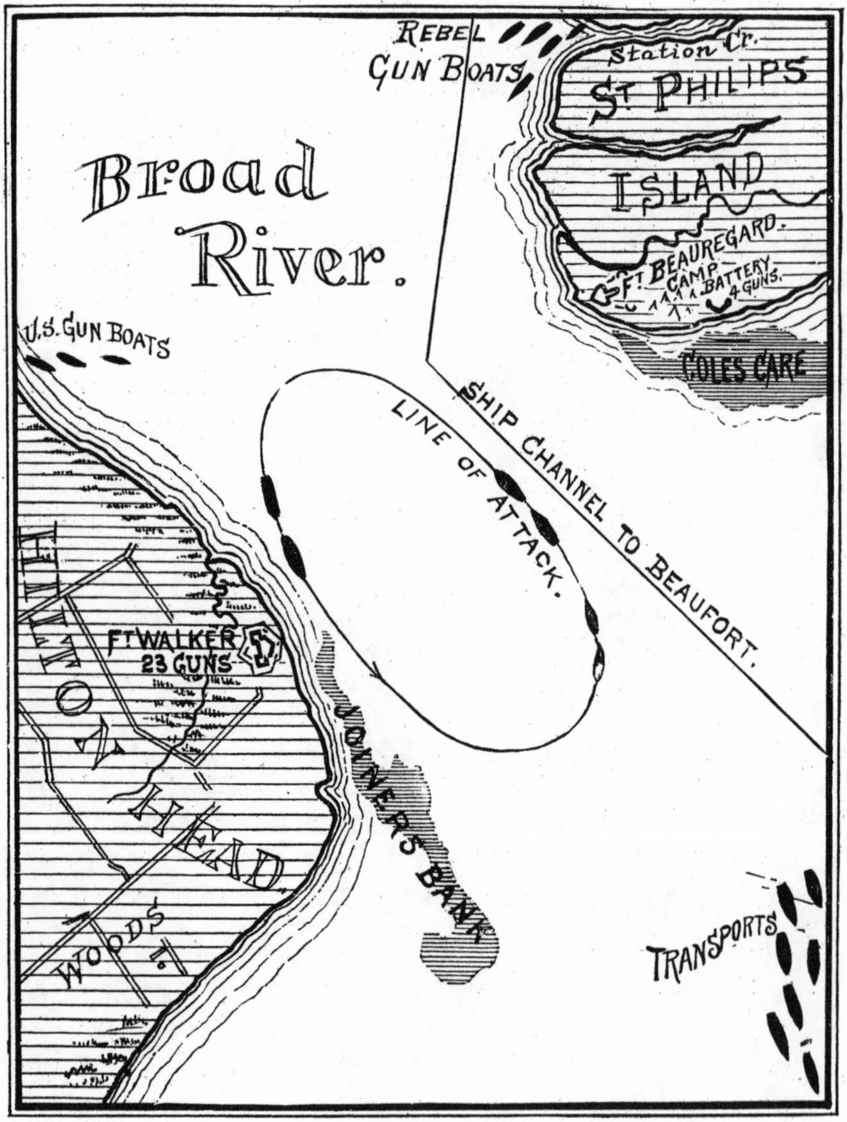

The fleet passing Fort Royal in the form of an ellipse

(*MAGAZINE OF AMERICAN HISTORY*)

opened fire with long range guns at the leading vessels, and the shot and shell rattled about us in a lively manner for a few minutes. Commodore Du Pont stood leaning over the capstan on which was spread a chart, talking calmly with Mr. [Charles] Boutelle, of the Coast Survey service, and did not seem in the least hurried to begin action.

From the position of the signal officer on the horse block the scene presented by the fleet was grand. Away to the eastward were the scars of transports black with troops, dancing on the blue waves. Around us were the men-of-war, moving silently and majestically into the harbor, their colors flying, their ports open, showing guns ready to belch forth the thunder of response to the smoking, frowning batteries. At ten minutes past ten the commodore turned his glass to the *Pembina* and *Vandalia*, bringing up the rear of the two columns, and said simply: "Begin firing."

In an instant both broadsides sent their storm of shell and shot at the two forts. Each volley fell a little short, and the commodore shouted: "Elevate your guns!" and the engagement was fairly begun. Broadside after broadside was fired in quick succession. In five minutes the action became general along the whole line. The scene was grand beyond description. Never before had so many ships been employed in a naval engagement in Western waters. The simultaneous booming of the broadsides, the quick flashing of the belching fires, the dense curling of the masses of smoke, accompanied by the whizzing of the enemy's balls and their destructive tearing of our masts and sides, gave an impress of danger and indications of the vastness of the engagement almost impossible to realize or adequately present in detail. Meantime, amid the roar of cannon could be heard the sharp, quick word of command, and as the smoke rolled upward from the deck of each vessel as it swung around to pass close to the other fort the men could be seen training and sighting their guns and displaying everywhere the most courageous and exciting activity. Of course eager eyes sought the forts and batteries of the enemy.

It was known that our firing must be producing terrible effect, and when a gust of wind rolled off the smoky canopy that hid them we saw the havoc our merciless fire had made. Guns were dismounted, and the neatly turfed sides of Fort Walker had disappeared to show great gashes and seams where our heavy shot had plowed its way. After the first circle had been described the order was issued for the smaller vessels to take positions at discretion, choosing such a point of attack as might seem to them the most effective. This they did, and the *Wabash*, leading the line of larger ships, continued to describe the ellipse, never ceasing her murderous fire—first one broadside and then the other, sometimes both together, but always raining in a stream of shot and shell. The complete second circuit was only made by the *Wabash, Bienville,* and *Susquehanna.*

At one time the *Bienville* ranged close into Fort Walker, and the enemy's fire was concentrated upon her, and she was struck many times. One shot killed several men. The third circuit was made by the same ships and the shot fell like a rain upon the damaged fortress. I have seen the most important of our naval engagements on the coast—Hatteras Inlet, Charleston, Fort Pulaski and Fort Fisher, but in one case was there such rapid or accurate firing from the men-of-war as continued from 10:30 A.M. until after 1:00 P.M. By that time the response from the shore was as if the demon of fight had been a little tamed, and our men were exhausted and worked less actively. They seemed to have concluded that a certain number of shot would reduce the batteries and it was only a matter of time when the task should be accomplished.

Two orders were issued from the flagship during the action: the one directing the smaller ships to take position at discretion, and at half-past two to send the one watch of each ship's crew to dinner.

Meanwhile the rebel gunboats, or at least three of them, composing a part of Cmdr. [Josiah] Tatnall's squadron, had steamed down the Broad River to engage in the fight. The *Wabash* ignored their presence, but the *Susquehanna* turned a broadside toward them, and at once they proceeded in inglorious haste to take themselves into safer position. They did not interfere any more. Before 3:00 P.M. the *Bienville* signaled that men were riding from Fort Walker. Afterwards the *Mercury* steamed gallantly into the bay, and at once returned with the tidings that the enemy were evacuating.

The order was at once passed to cease firing, and the commodore sent Captain [John] Rodgers in the third cutter, with a white flag floating at its bow, to the fort. As the boat pulled shoreward the thick smoke lifted and the word that Master Martin, of the *Mercury*, had brought was confirmed. The Palmette standard was not floating. The enemy had hauled down their flag. Captain Rodgers was temporarily attached to the staff of Commodore Du Pont, having come down in the *Wabash*, as a passenger, to take command of his own ship, on blockade off Charleston. He went, as did his boat's crew, unarmed. The visitors found no one to receive them. Under cover of the forest, to the westward, the enemy had withdrawn with their wounded and some of their stores, leaving, while executing the movement, a squad of gunners to keep up the appearance of defense. Simultaneously the batteries called Fort Beauregard, on the north shore of the river, were abandoned.

Fort Walker after the Battle (MAGAZINE OF AMERICAN HISTORY)

Not less exciting than the engagement itself were the moments that we waited for to see the flag of the United States go up over Fort Walker. Captain Rodgers, followed by a few of his boat crew, climbed upon the ramparts and gazed for a moment into the embrasure. Then he waved his hat and disappeared. A moment later a flag done up in a ball, as a sailor always hoists the colors, was run up to the top of the flag-staff, and instantly a sharp pull on the halyards disengaged its folds, and the Stars and Stripes was spread to the breeze, floating over a scene of desolation, but proclaiming victory to all the fleet. Then arose such a cheer as I never heard before or since. From thousands of throats there came a wild cry of triumph. It was borne out to sea by the wind and the soldiers on the transports caught it up and sent it back again, like a rich echo. The fight at Hilton's Head was over and the Northern foot had found holding ground on South Carolina soil.

After the battle the transports came gallantly into the mouth of the river. They were already inside of the bar, for I should have stated in defining the localities a narrow reach of sand makes a bar ten miles into the ocean, and a vessel once inside the bar is by no means inside of the harbor. The troops were landed, and the possession of the fort turned over to [Brig. Gen. Thomas W.] Sherman by Commodore Du Pont. After that the only

Raising the Stars and Stripes over Fort Walker

(JOHNSON, *CAMPFIRE AND BATTLEFIELD*)

service the navy did there was to second the river to Beaufort, ten miles above. They found the place deserted, and at once took possession. Port Royal never became a point of the strategic importance it had been expected it would. As a military and naval post for stores it was invaluable, but no incursions of importance were made into the rebel country from it. As a basis of operations against Charleston it assumed much importance, but the hopes that the great picture in the illustrated papers inspired, that by its capture the backbone of the rebellion was broken, found only a reward in disappointment.

Following close upon the occupation of Beaufort by the Union troops came the expedition to Savannah, the flanking of Fort Pulaski, at the mouth of the Savannah River, and its final capture. Port Royal fell into the hands of the Union forces in the early days of November. The succeeding weeks were spent in idleness and inactivity. The ships in the harbor swung idly at their moorings and the troops on the shore broke the monotony of drills and parade by lounging in the shade and fishing in the river. During that time, however, reconnaissances had been made through the creeks and sounds that encircle Hilton Head. Wassaw and Ossabaw Inlets had been explored by the light-draught gunboats and several batteries on their shores been found abandoned. This was only play, however, and it was not until Christmas day of 1861 that a reconnoitering party, commanded by Lt. [James H.] Wilson, chief of Topographical Engineers, was dispatched to the southward to ascertain the feasibility of entering the Savannah River at a point higher up than its mouth.

The ordinary map only shows the general direction of the Savannah River and offers but vague information as to the inland seas that surround the rich sea-island cotton lands on the east coast of Georgia and South Carolina. Lieutenant Wilson's expeditions put him in possession of the knowledge that an interior passage existed through Calibogue Sound to the Savannah River, which, if possible for gunboats, might lead to the cutting off of Fort Pulaski and perhaps to results still more important. His final reconnaissance carried him right under the guns of the fort with two boat crews, about seventy men of a Rhode Island regiment and the Negro pilots, who of all men only knew the intricate water of Calibogue Sound, New and Wright Rivers and the dozen or so of inlets that wind in and out through the marshes and lowlands of the coast.

Following the report that was made by Lieutenant Wilson, Maj. [Oliver T.] Beard, the provost marshal, led another adventurous excursion in the same direction with a party of volunteer engineers. He proceeded to Wall's

Cut to remove the obstructions placed there by the rebels. Piles had been driven into the ground and the hulk of an old bark had been moored so as to effectually prevent egress from the cut into the river without removing her. This was a task difficult of accomplishment. The guns of Fort Pulaski, only six miles below, and the frowning battery on the barbette Fort Jackson covered the entire country, but, obscured by the tall reeds and working only at night, the work was done and the passage opened.

It was rather a romantic operation, this working by night, as silently as death, to remove obstructions from the rebel stream quite within sight of the protecting forts and almost within hearing of the sentinels who walked up and down on the walls. On some nights the rain fell violently, but the work proceeded. The pickets were obliged to keep their dismal walk on this outpost, tramping in mud that came nearly to their hips and through the soaking reeds higher than their heads, a task solitary and cheerless enough, but not surpassed in importance by any in the command. It was well performed by a part of Major Gardiner's command of the 7th Connecticut Regiment.

When the report had been made Commodore Du Pont sent Captain Rodgers and Lt. [John S.] Barnes of the navy to examine and report on the feasibility of the passage; and here arose a little jealousy of feeling between the army and navy which, however, did not amount to anything serious. Captain Rodgers reported with a measured degree of enthusiasm. The passage, he said, was passable, but dangerous, yet he would be willing to lead a reconnaissance in force and it was so ordered. While preparations for this movement were going on, an incautious publication in a Northern paper made from an incautious army officer's letter, expressed the entire scheme to the rebels, and two nights before our forces arrived at Wall's Cut three Confederate gunboats appeared in Wright River, where they had not been seen before a month. The long concocted and carefully hidden plan had been discovered and all hope of a surprise frustrated. The scheme, however, was not abandoned, although sure to meet with opposition.

Meanwhile discoveries had been made of a new passage leading from Warsaw Sound through the Wilmington River and St. Augustine Creek to the Savannah, just below Fort Jackson. From St. Augustine Creek an inlet lets into the river above Fort Jackson, and as this had been discovered feasible by the navy the honors were easy, and the little ill feeling that existed between the two divisions of the services were smoothed away in the equality of achievement. It was resolved to use this upper passage, and [Brig. Gen. Horatio G.] Wright, with three regiments, was ordered by transports to follow in the wake of the gunboats *Seneca, Ottawa, Ellen, Isaac Smith,*

Potemeka, Westworld, and two armed launches, by way of Warsaw Sound in the rear of Fort Pulaski.

The expedition rested at night at a point where the rebels had obstructed the passage, and Captain [Charles H.] Davis, United States Navy, in command, with his aides reconnoitered the ground thoroughly in the morning. Captain John Rodgers, with the gunboats *Unadilla, Pembina* and *Henry Andrews*, appeared on the opposite side of the Savannah, in what may be known as the South Carolina waters, in fact, and passed through into Wright River. At this juncture the Confederates became alarmed at the magnitude of a demonstration that threatened to end in the capture of Savannah, and Commodore Tatnall, with five gunboats, came steaming down toward us. He was half way between the two divisions of the Federal naval force and distant from each of them about two miles. He had a double object in view—to drive me away and to convey a fleet of lighters, laden with prisoners and reinforcements to Fort Pulaski. He opened fire as soon as he came within range, and it was vigorously returned, both from the vessels commanded by Captain Davis, in Georgia waters, and by Captain John Rodgers, from the Carolina side, and the singular spectacle was exhibited of a triangular naval engagement in which the three parties concerned were each in a different river and each, in order to reach the enemy, was obliged to fire across land. Under the cover of the smoke of the action the lighters reached Fort Pulaski. Then the rebel gunboats steamed gallantly back to Savannah retiring and receiving our fire as they passed.

It was not until the month of April that Fort Pulaski was attacked. In the meantime the naval forces, with Commodore Du Pont's broad pennant flying at the truck of the "Mohican," had proceeded southward and occupied the ports of Fernandina, Brunswick and Jacksonville, and had control of the entire seacoast line, from Cape Sable to Hilton Head, except the mouth of the Savannah. The reduction of the forts, by virtue of which the rebels held possession, was left to the care of the army, General Hunter commanding. Protected by the gunboats in the cut, troops were landed on Tybee Island and the erection of batteries at once began. Eleven batteries were completed and equipped by the morning of April 11, and summons were sent to Col. Charles H. Olmstead, commanding the fort, to surrender. His answer was brief and pointed. It read simply: "I am here to defend the fort, not to surrender it." Immediately the firing began and all day long a stream of shot and shell rained down on the devoted fortress. At night firing ceased, with the exception of a gun fired every five minutes from one of the batteries.

At daylight the bombardment began again and continued with vigorous reply, until at 2:30 P.M. on the twelfth the Stars and Bars fluttered down from the flagpole and a white flag signifying surrender went fluttering up instead. It was just a year to the day since Sumter had been fired upon, and on the entire coast line south of Charleston the Confederates held not one position of strength.

Part Two

The War in 1862

Why Stonewall Jackson Resigned

Henry Kyd Douglas,
Major, C. S. A. (Staff of General Jackson)

Philadelphia *Weekly Times* 5, no. 21, July 16, 1881

Mr. Jefferson Davis is indebted to his enemies for making his book a great success, for although they have made every reader a critic they have assured an immense sale for the two volumes. While those whose predisposition was favorable to its kind reception were content to wait until they could read this new historical contribution, its predetermined foes hastened to anticipate public opinion by opening fire in the direction of its coming and before its appearance. I believe Mr. Davis ought to have written this book. It was not optional with him; it was his duty. He was the official head of the Southern Confederacy, a statesman of distinction before the war, who has held high office in the service of the United States, a man of very great ability as a writer and reasoner, whose candor, independence and courage were exceptional. The survivors of the armies of the South and the friends of her dead soldiers had a right to demand that Mr. Davis should present to the world and posterity the cause of the Confederate government, its rise and fall, as he understood it. This he has done. Whether he has done it wisely and well will appear before critics and reviewers have done with his work. But it is apparent from the first superficial glance at these volumes, whatever may be their other merits or defects as a defense of his cause, that this book is no apology; it is history. I am not disposed to write a panegyric on this book. I have no doubt it has faults of reasoning and conclusion, and grave defects of omission and aggression. It could not be otherwise with the work of a man of Mr. Davis' temperament and mental cast, of his positive and arbitrary opinion. Even were it possible

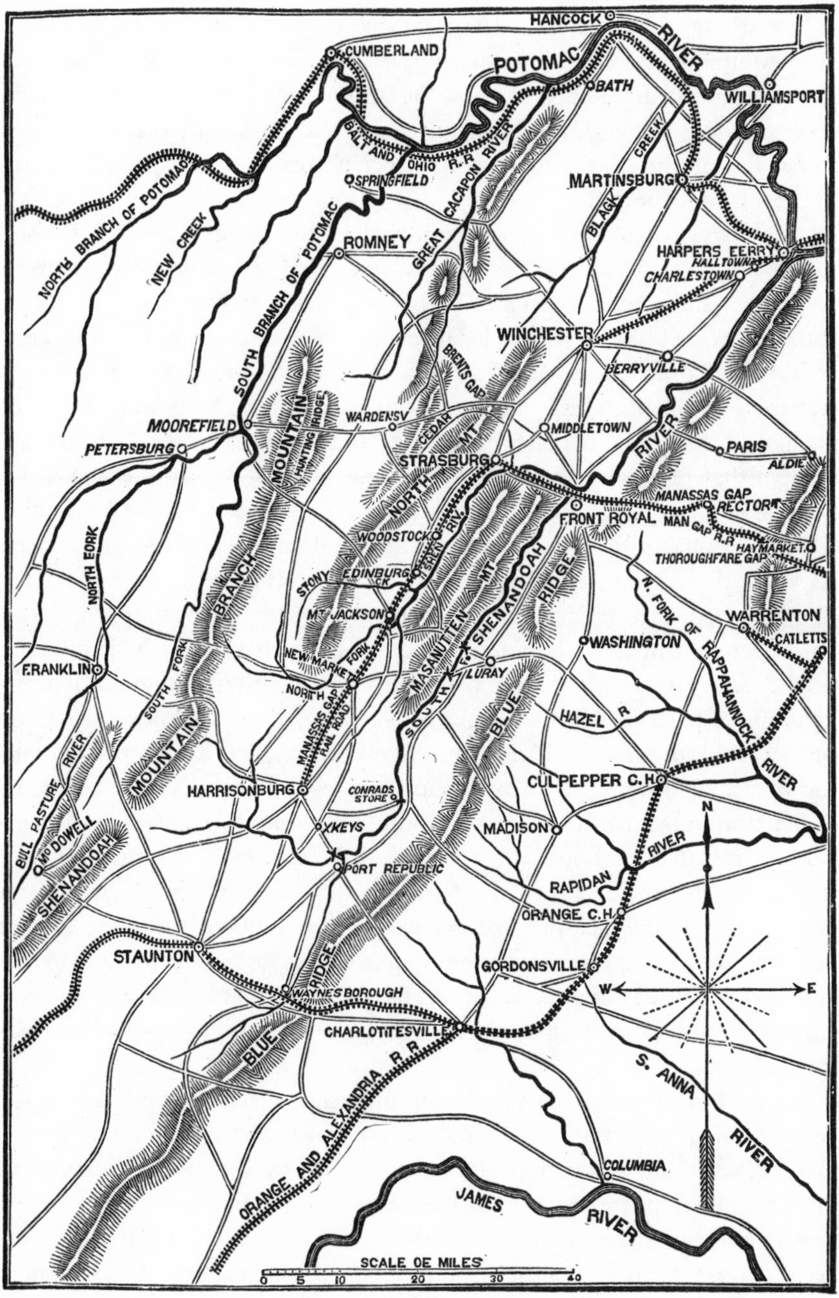

The Shenandoah Valley

(JOHNSON, *CAMPFIRE AND BATTLEFIELD*)

to be entirely accurate in the detail of facts, many of which he must gather from contradictory statements and hurried reports, Mr. Jefferson Davis was apt to magnify the ability of those he approved of and to underestimate anyone he did not endorse. His confidence was not lost by disaster, be this said to his infinite credit; nor was he surprised into unreasonable admiration by a brilliant achievement.

This is preliminary to an omission in the first volume, to which I desire to call attention. Mr. Davis has entirely ignored an event which it seems to me was of sufficient importance to have required explanation. In January 1862 [Thomas J.] Stonewall Jackson resigned his commission as major general in the Confederate army—an act not as startling to think of now as it was then, and one which Mr. Davis could not have forgotten. It is not needful to stop and speculate upon the consequences to the Confederate cause if that resignation had been accepted. It is safe to say the marvelous campaigns of 1862 in the Shenandoah Valley would not have been, that [Brig. Gen. Irwin] McDowell and his splendid corps would not have been stayed in their march against [Gen. Joseph E.] Johnston, to be bewildered then defeated, then eluded, that the campaign of the Chickahominy would have been fought under different conditions, and it is likely with different results, and Richmond might have fallen before the strategy and heavy columns of [Maj. Gen. George B.] McClellan. Mr. Davis knows the cause of General Jackson's resignation, and while treating of this matter and taking occasion in doing so to make public a letter in which he severely, by indirection, reprimands General Johnston, why does he omit even to mention the fact that the South then nearly lost the service of the most brilliant, if not the ablest, general in the field? It may be that Mr. Davis did not approve of General Jackson's course, and the general being dead, he did not care to appear in history as condemning it. If this be so it is a chivalric reason. But Mr. Davis might have stated facts without passing judgment; or, if his judgment is correct, history has a right to it let him express it as charitably as he might.

I think it likely Mr. Davis, having indorsed the error which led to the resignation of General Jackson, did not approve of that act. That General Jackson was right, I have never heard questioned by any military man, and I am convinced his prompt action then and there was subsequently of great service not only to himself but to other generals in the field. It taught the secretary of war that he must not undertake to manage Jackson's campaigns from his chair in Richmond. I think that Mr. Davis not only disapproved of General Jackson's resignation, but I have the impression now that prevailed in the Valley then, that our president much underrated the general's capacity as an officer—not only negatively underrated, but positively questioned it. In this he was not singular. Outside of the Valley of Virginia there were very few who had predicted for Stonewall Jackson the brilliant career he subsequently developed. I fear Mr. Davis then had sufficient distrust of our general's ability to make him unwilling to leave more to his judgment than could be understood at the War Department. When the president in his letter of November 10, 1861, tells General Johnston that General Jackson was selected to command the Valley army "for reasons well known to you" it is evident there were other reasons for the selection than the confidence in his military forces. But no one can complain that Mr. Davis has not in these two volumes given the general the benefit of his mature and unqualified admiration. And when we recall that at the time of which we speak, many other respectable gentlemen had been led to believe that "Old Jack was crazy," Mrs. Davis' doubts were not unreasonable.

When General Jackson took command of the Valley District in the fall of 1861 he could only collect at Winchester about three thousand untried and badly organized militia. With these he was helpless. He soon applied for and received, much against the wish of General Johnston, his own brigade, destined afterwards to share with him the name and fame of Stonewall, and the nucleus around which Jackson formed that incomparable little Army of the Valley that for a season monopolized the fighting and victories of the Confederacy in Virginia. Still with these, the general was not in condition for any effective movement, although he had already expressed his desire to clear Romney, Moorefield and that beautiful and fruitful portion of western Virginia of the enemy, and of relieving the Valley of the threat implied by the hostile occupation of these places. He laid his plans before the secretary of war in a letter dated November 20, 1861, and asked that all the troops under [Brig. Gen. William W.] Loring be ordered to his command. This was done, although General Johnston seemed to think General Jackson proposed to accomplish more than he was able to do. General Loring and the bulk of his command of three brigades did not reach Winchester until after Christmas, and on New Year's Day Jackson, with about nine thousand troops, started upon his celebrated "Bath trip." It was a terrible ordeal for new troops, making a winter campaign in the mountains, and for it the general was subjected to severe criticism. The long delayed severity of winter came down upon his little army with snow, ice, biting cold and all its accompanying hardships.

General Jackson was hardened in his determination by the resistance of the elements and he persisted in his undertaking until he had cleared that region of Virginia of the enemy and had planted his guns on the southern bank of the Potomac. Nothing but success saved him from irretrievable disgrace. The odds against him in military science were too great, and had he failed he would have disappeared from the history of the war. Having thus relieved the Valley of Virginia from threatened invasion he contemplated an expedition for the capture of Cumberland and the destruction of the Baltimore and Ohio Railroad at that point. But the continued violence of the winter and the damaged condition of the troops, especially of General Loring's command, resulting from their recent sufferings forbade that. Having with the approval of General Johnston placed General Loring and his command at Romney and dispersed other troops as the situation suggested, General Jackson returned to Winchester with the Stonewall Brigade.

Insubordination, incited by the officers, broke forth in the division General Loring commanded, and very soon produced a state of affairs which threatened to destroy the morale and organization of the little army of the Valley District. General Jackson was charged with favoritism and his old brigade was hooted at and taunted with opprobrious epithets, but the officers in command of the offending troops made no effort to stop this disgraceful state of affairs.

Many credulous and doubtless faithful soldiers honestly believed they were doomed to speedy disaster and ruin under a general who they were told was a religious fanatic. In this semi-insurrection were officers who afterwards followed Jackson with unfaltering devotion and faith, and soldiers who soon learned to believe him invincible and heaven-led, and shouted themselves hoarse whenever he rode along the line. Unrestrained criticism and invective were particularly active at the headquarters of General Loring, and one or more officers (it was said at the time a special committee) went to Richmond and arraigned General Jackson before the War Department. General Jackson knew of the feeling against him, but made no explanations, and when one of his officers was about to go to Richmond to counteract the effect of the Loring delegation the general peremptorily forbid it and all communication with the War Department on the subject. As a soldier, he reasonably supposed that if the report made to the president had any effect he would be notified and called upon to explain his action and the disposition of his command. But in this he was mistaken. Without consulting General Johnston or General Jackson, the secretary of war, on January 31, telegraphed to the latter to order General Loring back to Winchester. This was the crucial test of Jackson's character. I have said that only success in the Bath campaign saved him. But it had not saved him from this direct insult. At this moment General Jackson's future depended upon speedy action. If he submitted without protest his prestige and influence were gone and his future usefulness questionable. But he did not hesitate for a moment. He obeyed the order of the secretary of war and then, on the same day, resigned his commission in the army. He also, the same day, notified General Johnston and Governor [John] Letcher of his action and gave his reasons for it. In his letter to Governor Letcher, he said:

> As a single order like that of the secretary of war may destroy the entire fruits of a campaign, I cannot reasonably expect, if my operations are thus to be interfered with, to be of much service in the field. A sense of duty brought me here and has thus far kept me. If I have ever acquired, through the blessings of Providence, any influence over troops, this undoing of work by the secretary may greatly diminish that influence. I regard this recent expedition as a great success.

General Jackson's resignation startled the Valley like a clap of thunder. The excitement became intense in the army and out of it. The men of the Stonewall Brigade burst their dignified reserve and swore worse than the army in Flanders. Men of the different commands, even when confined in the guardhouse, came to blows in discussing the situation until separate quarters was provided for their confinement. The condition of affairs was indescribably critical and alarming. The excitement invaded the parlors of Winchester, although the feeling was all on one side. Bright eyes flashed fire, little fists were shaken in wrath, while prominent citizens sent hurried letters to Richmond, declaring that the acceptance of General Jackson's resignation would create a panic throughout the Valley. General Johnston retained General Jackson's letter of resignation for a few days. Laying aside all formality and addressing him as "My dear friend," he wrote:

> Let me beg you to reconsider this matter. Under ordinary circumstances a due sense of one's dignity, as well as care for professional character and official rights, would demand such a course as yours. But the character of the war, the great energy exhibited by the government of the United States, the danger in which our very existence as an independent people lies, require sacrifices from us all who have been educated as soldiers. I received my information of the order of which you have such cause to complain from your letter. Is not that as great an official wrong to me as the order itself to you? I regard you as necessary to the service of your country in your present position.

Governor Letcher—"Honest John"—swore a miscellaneous assortment of oaths when he heard that his general—for he always regarded General Jackson as under his especial care—was about to quit the army. He went straightway to the War Department, inquired into matters and made the request that action be reserved upon the resignation until he could communicate with the general. He then wrote a strong and earnest letter to General Jackson, pointing out the detriment which would inevitably result to the cause if he left the army under such circumstances, and insisting that he should authorize him to withdraw the resignation. Knowing the difficulty of moving General Jackson from his purpose, he sent this letter by his aid, Hon. A. R. Boteler, with directions to press it with his personal influence. Colonel Boteler had a long and earnest interview with the general at Winchester, and we may be assured that all the tact and persuasiveness of this accomplished gentleman were exerted in his behalf. General Jackson was persuaded at length and he gave his consent to the withdrawal of his resignation. In his letter to Governor Letcher, allowing his resignation to be withdrawn, General Jackson wrote, "If the secretary persists in the ruinous policy complained of, I feel that no officer can serve his country better than by making his strongest possible protest against it, which, in my opinion, is done by tendering his resignation rather than be a willing instrument in prosecuting the war upon a ruinous policy."

His protest was effective. He was never afterwards interfered with by orders from the War Department, and his prompt action doubtless saved other generals from like humiliations. On the February 12 General Jackson wrote to Colonel Boteler, "The enemy are in possession of Moorefield. Such is the fruit of evacuating Romney. General Loring should be cashiered for his course."

As I have objected, Mr. Davis, while referring to Jackson's Bath campaign and the subsequent order to remove Loring from Romney, ignores General Jackson's resignation and the complications consequent upon it. He only gives us his letter to General Johnston "in explanation of the act of the secretary of war," which I submit is not so much an explanation as a spur to General Johnston. An event of so much significance required more than this. I have noticed the devotion of the people of the Valley of reciprocal. As they stood by him in his first trial and always, he never for a moment forgot them, and on his death bed he asked to be buried "in Lexington, in the Valley of Virginia."

In this connection I desire to make some extracts from a letter written with the freedom of personal confidence to his intimate friend, Colonel Boteler, dated March 3, 1862, just before he began his famous campaign:

> I desire to hold the country as far as practical until we are in a condition to advance, and then with God's blessing let us make thorough work of it. But let us start right. I am delighted to hear you say that Virginia is resolved to consolidate all her resources, if necessary, to the defense of herself. Now we may look for war in earnest.
>
> I hope the Indians will come. I trust that General Lee will be made secretary of war. You ask me for a letter respecting the Valley. I have only to say this, if the Valley is lost, Virginia is lost.

General Jackson did not think the Confederacy had started favorably. He regarded with grave apprehension the inactivity which for a while so seriously injured the South after the battle of Manassas. I heard him say that battle had filled the people with false hopes, and he regarded this victory there gained as a great disaster to our cause. He was early in favor of strict laws being passed by Congress regulating appointments and promotions in the service and enforcing discipline in such manner as to get rid of the idea which some generals and many politicians had, that a volunteer soldier should be subjected to little restraint or inconvenience. He seemed to anticipate that want of discipline would be the ruin of the Southern armies. It had been proposed to send General Jackson a few Indians as scouts and "terrifiers." He believed that by discipline he could make them useful. It may well be doubted whether this was practicable, but the Indians never came. At the time General Jackson expressed the desire to see General Lee made secretary of war, that great commander was holding a position of honorary retirement in Richmond as quasi amanuensis to the secretary and President Davis. "If this Valley is lost, Virginia is lost." This was not prophecy, but the sound opinion of military sagacity. And when Virginia was lost how quickly the Confederacy tumbled to pieces.

I would like to place on record a letter of General Jackson in reply to one from Colonel Boteler, telling him that the people were beginning to use his name in connection with the next presidency, but I have not been able to get it. The general was very much astonished, for no great man so underrated himself or was so ignorant of his great reputation and popularity. He said he was unwilling to believe the people were so foolish, and declared with unmistakable emphasis that he never would be a candidate for nor accept the office of president. I do not believe he could ever have been induced to accept that position. His strategy was military not political, and he had no aspiration for civic honors. This will not commend him to some distinguished generals we know of, and it may be this idiosyncrasy caused General [Ulysses S.] Grant to express the opinion he has recently made public that Stonewall Jackson was not entitled to the position among military men to which he has been assigned by almost universal consent. Whatever estimate military critics may hereafter place upon the genius and abilities of General Jackson, there will be no dispute as to the correctness of the graceful tribute Mr. Davis pays to the man:

> In all his operations there conspicuously appears the self-abnegation of a devoted patriot. He was not seeking by great victories to acquire fame for himself; but always alive to the necessities and dangers elsewhere, he heroically strove to do what was possible, but the general benefit of the cause he maintained. His whole heart was his country's and his whole country's heart was his." And again to the soldier: "Of this great captain, General Lee, in his anguish at his death, justly said: 'I have lost my right arm.' As an executive officer he had no superior, and war has seldom shown an equal. Too devoted to the cause he served to have any personal motive, he shared the toils, privations and dangers of his troops when in chief command, and on subordinate positions his aim was to understand the purpose of his commander and faithfully to promote its success. He was the complement of Lee; united they had achieved such results that the public felt secure under their shield. To us his place was never filled.

The Battle of Shiloh

James S. Brisbin,
Brigadier General, U.S.V.

Philadelphia *Weekly Times* 3, no. 45, January 3, 1880

The battle of Shiloh is one of the disputed battles of the war. Many accounts of it have been written, each one giving, no doubt, what the author believed to be the true version of the battle. While it is not my intention to question what others have written about Shiloh, I intend to give my own account of that battle and at the same time invite the friendly criticisms of anyone who may think I err. The events immediately preceding Shiloh are of importance as showing relations to the conflict of April 6 and 7, 1862. The success of [Maj. Gen. Ulysses S.] Grant at Fort Donelson had unfortunately aroused the jealousy of [Maj. Gen. Henry W.] Halleck, who saw in the increasing popularity of Grant cause for alarm. Old, able and experienced as Halleck was, he allowed a feeling of envy to possess him and on March 3 he had telegraphed [Maj. Gen. George B.] McClellan, "Grant left his command without my authority and went to Nashville. His army seems to be as much demoralized by the victory of Fort Donelson as was that of the Potomac by the defeat of Bull Run. It is hard to censure a successful general immediately after a victory, but I think he richly deserves it. I can get no returns, no reports, no information from him. Satisfied with his victory, he sits down and enjoys it without any regard for the future."

This was most unjust, as Grant had been hard at work preparing to move against the enemy. On March 4, but one day after he had telegraphed McClellan, Halleck sent the following to General Grant: "You will place [Brig.] General C. F. Smith in command of the expedition and remain yourself at Fort Henry."

Taking these two dispatches in connection we cannot but believe the first dispatch was sent to prepare the way for the removal of General Grant, which had already been determined upon—in the mind of Halleck. Grant was relieved on March 5, 1862, and on the thirteenth following was restored. His disgrace and deposition was short-lived, but it shows no less the animus of his superiors at that time toward him. He bore his misfortunes with the quiet resignation which has since become so characteristic of the man and on being reinstated at once went to Savannah and began concentrating his troops for the great battle of Shiloh, or as it is more frequently called, Pittsburg Landing.

Brig. Gen. Charles F. Smith
(PETER COZZENS COLLECTION)

[Brig. Gen. Charles F.] Smith, who had temporarily relieved General Grant in command of the army, no sooner heard his old commander was restored than he made haste to write him, "I am glad to find that you were about to resume your old command from which you were so unceremoniously and, as I think, so unjustly stricken down." The relations between General Smith and Grant were of a somewhat peculiar character. When Smith was commandant at the military academy General Grant was a cadet in that institution. He often said he felt an awe when in the presence of his old commandant and that it was very difficult at first for him to give Smith an order. General Smith soon perceived this and one day said to Grant with great frankness, "General, I appreciate your delicacy, but I am now a subordinate and I know a soldier's duty. I hope you will feel no awkwardness about our new relations."

General Smith was sixty years old, a man of great military talent and from the first, understood Grant's worth as a soldier. The old veteran did all in his power to subordinate himself to his young chief, but despite his efforts General Grant never could or would assume any great authority over him. Soon afterward the gallant veteran sickened and died from disease brought on by exposure at Fort Donelson, and when Grant heard of his death it is said he wept like a child.

General Grant was now about to engage in the most important movement that had yet been made against the Confederacy, and that the rebels were thoroughly alive to the danger of his operations may be gathered from the speeches of their leading men and the publications of their journals at the time.

The Florence (Alabama) *Gazette* of March 12, 1862, had the following very significant article:

> We learned yesterday that the Unionists had landed a very large force at Savannah, Tennessee. We suppose they are making preparations to get possession of the Memphis and Charleston Railroad. *They must never be allowed to get this great thoroughfare in their possession, for then we would be crippled.* The labor and untiring industry of too many faithful and energetic men have been expended on this road to bring it up to its present state of usefulness to let it fall into the hands of the enemy to be used against us. It must be protected. We as a people are able to protect and save it. If unavoidable let them have our river, but we hope it is the united sentiment of our people *that we will have our railroad.*

General Grant arrived at Savannah on March 17 and established his headquarters. From this point he could best oversee his force and assist in getting up the reinforcements. The rebel forces were estimated at over sixty thousand men and were concentrated at Shiloh, [Gen. Albert S.] Johnston commanding and Gen. [Pierre G. T.] Beauregard second in command. The rebel army was divided into three corps and a reserve, as follows: Confederate Army—1st Army Corps, Lt. Gen. [Leonidas] Polk; 2nd Army Corps, Lt. Gen. Braxton Bragg; 3rd Army Corps, Lt. Gen. [William J.] Hardee; Reserves—Maj. Gen. [George B.] Crittenden. Union Army—Maj. Gen. U. S. Grant commanding; 1st Division, Maj. Gen. John A. McClernand;

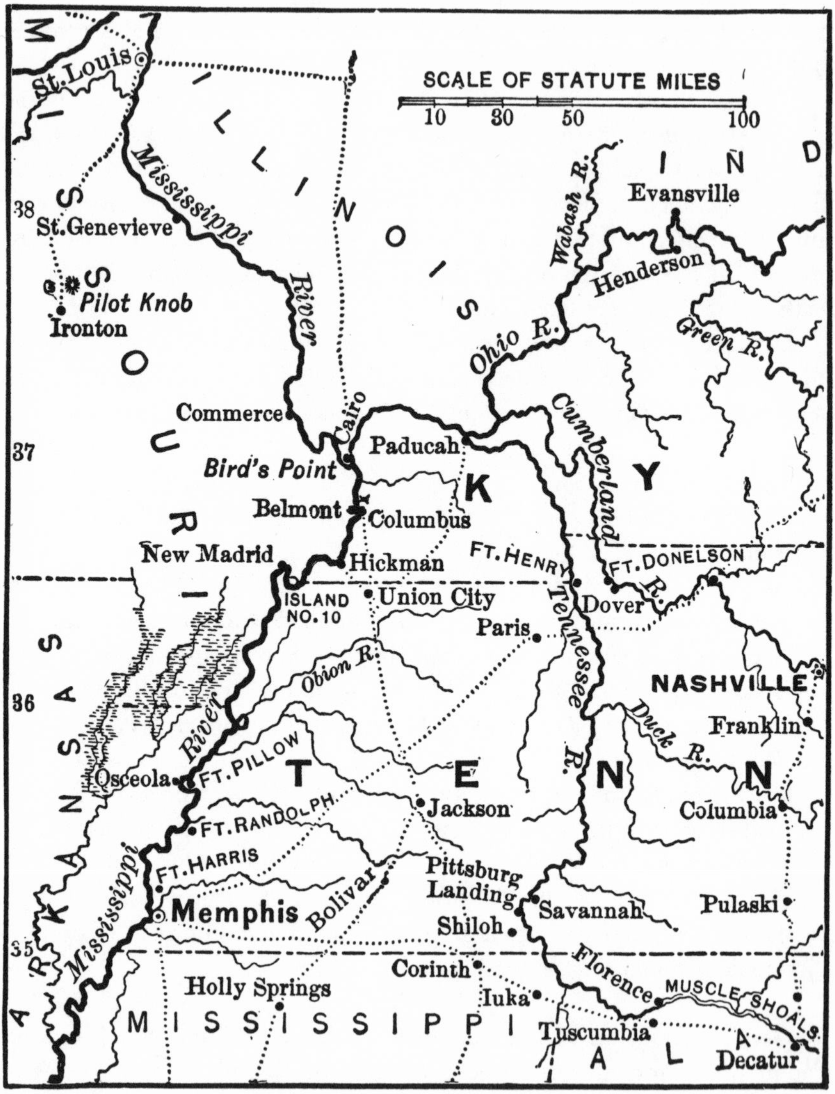

North Mississippi and West Tennessee

(*CENTURY MAGAZINE*)

2nd Division, Brig. Gen. [William H. L.] Wallace; 3rd Division, Brig. Gen. Lewis Wallace; 4th Division, Brig. Gen. [Stephen A.] Hurlbut; 5th Division, Brig. Gen. [William T.] Sherman.

The field on which the two armies were to contend was on the west bank of the Tennessee and for the most part densely wooded with tall trees and but little undergrowth. The landing is immediately flanked on the left by a short but precipitous ravine, along which runs the road to Corinth. On the right and left, forming a good natural flanking arrangement, runs Snake and Lick Creeks, which would compel the attack of the enemy to be made in front. The distance between the mouths of these creeks is about two and a half miles. The battle ground of Pittsburg Landing was selected by General Smith, and all writers agree that the position was admirably chosen. The locality where the fighting would take place was in easy range and protected by the gunboats *Tyler* and *Lexington.*

[Maj. Gen. Don Carlos] Buell's Army of the Ohio was coming up to reinforce Grant, and although the river lay in rear of Grant's troops, that was also the direction of Buell's advance. Grant had placed his five divisions as follows: Wallace's division—1st Brigade at Crump's Landing; 2nd Brigade two miles above it; 3rd Brigade at Adamsville, the whole division to be held in readiness to move down and join the main force whenever circumstances should render it necessary. [Brig. Gen. Benjamin] Prentiss held the extreme left of the line with [Lt. Col. David] Stuart. McClernand was at some distance on Stuart's right and facing southwest. Sherman was at Shiloh Church, on the right of McClernand and in advance of him. Hurlbut and W. H. L. Wallace a mile in rear of McClernand, in reserve—the former supporting the left and the latter the right wing. Grant's whole force consisted of about thirty-eight thousand men.

It was the evident design of the Rebel commanders to attack and overwhelm Grant's forces before the Army of the Ohio, under Buell, could come up to his support. While Grant was anxiously awaiting the approach of Buell's army a question of rank arose between McClernand and Smith, and to settle the matter Grant had to move his headquarters from Savannah to Pittsburg Landing and personally assume command of the forces in the field.

It was now April 6, 1862, and the first day of the great battle of Shiloh, or as it is more frequently called, Pittsburg Landing. Skirmishing had been going on since the second, and on the third the Rebel commander had issued the following stirring address to his army:

> Soldiers of the Army of the Mississippi: I have put you in motion to offer battle to the invaders of your country, with the resolution and discipline and valor becoming men fighting, as you are, for all worth living or dying for. You can but march to a decisive victory over agrarian mercenaries sent to subjugate and despoil you of your liberties, property, and honor.
>
> Remember the precious stake involved; remember the dependence of your mothers, your wives, your sisters, and your children on the result. Remember the fair, broad, abounding lands, the happy homes that will be desolated by your defeat. The eyes and hopes of eight million people rest upon you. You are expected to show yourselves worthy of your valor and courage, worthy of the women of the South, whose noble devotion in war has never been exceeded in any time. With such incentives to brave deeds, and with trust that God is with us, your general will lead you confidently to the combat assured of success.
>
> General A. S. Johnston,
> Commanding

On April 4 the enemy felt Sherman's front with such force that many thought a battle imminent. Grant rode out to the front and as he was returning after dark through the rain his horse in crossing a log slipped and fell on his rider, who received a severe contusion, and for over a week he suffered acute pains and was lame.

On the evening of the fourth Brig. Gen. Lewis Wallace reported eight regiments of rebel infantry at Purdy and an equal, if not larger force, at Bethel. Grant ordered W. H. L. Wallace to support Lewis Wallace's division, if necessary, and then returned to Savannah, promising to come up to the front early next morning.

On the fifth the Rebel cavalry had been very active, coming down boldly on Sherman's front and driving in the Union videttes. The same evening the head of [Brig. Gen. William] Nelson's column, belonging to Buell's army, arrived at Savannah and reported Buell rapidly coming up. Grant at once ordered Nelson to take position south of Savannah, five miles from Pittsburg Landing, and hold himself in readiness to reinforce the army on the left bank.

The morning sun rose bright and clear on April 6 and gaily shone on the tents of two great armies. The birds sang cheerily in the treetops and there was nothing to indicate the terrible tragedy that was soon to be enacted in those quiet groves. Who could have believed on that bright

April morning that the green sward beneath their feet would soon be crimsoned and slippery with human gore and the firm earth trembling under the charge of enraged thousands?

The Rebels had breakfasted at 3:00 A.M., and at early dawn laid aside their knapsacks and stripped for the bloody contest. Portions of the Union army were still wrapped in slumber when the battle began and others were lazily preparing their breakfast.

Neither Grant nor Sherman had expected a battle on the sixth, and it was, therefore, with some surprise the next morning Grant, while eating an early breakfast with his staff, preparatory to riding out in search of Buell, heard such heavy firing in direction of the landing as to convince him a severe action was in progress. Hastily dispatching Buell a note informing him a battle had begun and ordering Nelson to move his command to the river bank, Grant went on board a transport and hastened to the front. He stopped for a moment on his way up the river at Crump's Landing to see Lewis Wallace and instruct him in person as to what he expected to do in the battle.

The onset had begun by forty thousand Rebels precipitating themselves suddenly on Prentiss' little division and completely doubling it up. Sherman's division was next attacked and for a time held the rebels in check, but the troops being new and green soon gave way and were forced back through their camp, which fell into the hands of the rebels. McClernand promptly moved up to support Sherman's wavering left, and Hurlbut marched forward to the support of Prentiss. W. H. L. Wallace had taken position in rear of Sherman and was supporting the center and left of the line where the Rebel attack was most furious. Lewis Wallace had been sent for and ordered to come up and connect with Sherman's right, but he never came. Early in the action part of the brigade, composed of raw men and stationed on Sherman's left, broke and fled to the rear in great confusion. This necessitated a change of position and Sherman swung back his left—turning on the right as a pivot. Soon afterward Sherman's whole line was forced back, but he skillfully connected his left with McClernand's right, keeping his own right well out to prevent any flank movement of the enemy.

The Rebels never could get round Sherman's flank, and despite their efforts, he held until night the important crossing of Snake Creek bridge. Sherman was unceasing in his efforts to keep his men up to their work and beat the enemy. Although repeatedly wounded he refused to leave the field for a moment, even to have his wounds dressed. At 10:00 A.M. the battle was raging furiously, and Grant rode to Sherman's front and commended

The Confederate charge on the Union camps, morning of April 6

(FORBES, *LIFE OF SHERMAN*)

him highly for his skill in opposing the enemy. The cartridges were now giving out, but Grant, with careful foresight, had started Col. [George G.] Pride of his staff to the front with an ammunition train and this gallant officer, forcing his wagons over the narrow and crowded road, arrived just in time to supply the empty cartridge boxes of the Union soldiers.

At intervals all day Grant was engaged in sending forward deserters to their commands, forming new lines out of those who straggled to the rear, and putting them into action again. He was on every part of the field, constantly under fire and making unwearied exertions to maintain his position until Nelson and Lewis Wallace should come up. As hour after hour wore on and still Nelson and Wallace did not come, the Union forces fell suddenly back toward the landing, contracting their lines as they retreated. Nelson had been ordered to march at 7:00 A.M. but did not move out until after 1:00 P.M., although from the sound of the cannon he must have known a fearful struggle was going on in his front.

No sufficient excuse has ever been offered for this officer's conduct at the battle of Shiloh. Lewis Wallace, who had been personally instructed by General Grant to hold his forces in readiness to reinforce the troops on the left bank, when he was sent for set his column, it is said, in motion and marched five miles the wrong direction, although he had been on the ground a month and his men had helped to build a bridge over Snake Creek for just such an emergency as now occurred. When finally Col. (afterward major general) [James B.] McPherson reached him and set him right, it took him from 1:00 P.M. until 7:00 P.M. to march five miles in the direction of the battle, the cannonading being heard at the same time at Nashville.

On the evening of the fifth Grant had gone down to Savannah to meet General Buell, but that officer having failed to come up to the hour of the opening of the battle at the landing, on the morning of the sixth, Grant, before starting to the front, wrote and dispatched to Buell by courier the following note: "Heavy firing is heard up the river, indicating plainly that an attack has been made upon our most advanced positions. I have been looking for this, but did not believe that the attack could be made before Monday or Tuesday. This necessitates my forming the forces up the river instead of meeting you today as I had contemplated." Buell had written the general on the fifth, "I shall be in Savannah myself tomorrow with, perhaps, two divisions. Can you meet me there?" To which General Grant had replied at once: "Your dispatch just received. I will be at Savannah to meet you tomorrow. The enemy at Corinth are probably sixty to eighty thousand." This accounts for Grant being at Savannah instead of with his command when the battle commenced, a matter about which Grant's enemies have made many severe and unjust comments.

About 10:00 A.M. on the morning of the battle Grant, hearing that [Brig. Gen. Thomas J.] Wood, with the second division of Buell's army, had arrived at Savannah, sent him the following order: "You will move your command with the utmost dispatch to the river at this point (landing), where steamers will be in readiness to transport you to Pittsburg." Still later in the day another dispatch was sent to the commanding officer of Buell's advance forces, urging him to hurry up and closing with this sentence: "My headquarters will be in the log building on top of the hill, where you will be furnished a staff officer to conduct you to your place on the field."

At 3:00 P.M. Buell arrived on the field in person. He had reached Savannah in the morning with another division of his command and hearing a battle was raging at the front, had hastened on ahead of his troops. As he rode through the swarms of fugitives who had come back from the battlefield and crowded the landing or sheltered themselves under the banks of the river, Buell no doubt made up his mind that Grant's army had been defeated. Almost the first words he said to Grant when they met were:

"What preparations have you made for retreating, General?" "I have not despaired of whipping them yet," was Grant's quiet response.

Hurlbut's command was now slowly falling back, but raked the Rebels well each time they charged. On Hurlbut's right W. H. L. Wallace was gallantly fighting and repelled four desperate assaults, but was finally forced to fall back toward the landing. About four o'clock the troops on his right and left having retired, Prentiss stubbornly continued the fight with his shattered division until the Rebels swept around his flanks and captured him and four regiments. The Union line now lay in a semi-circle on the river, their flanks resting on Snake and Lick Creeks. With their backs to the river the soldiers knew it would be death and destruction to give way and they stood firm as a rock on their short line, hurling back the Rebels like waves from the shore. The Rebels came on again and again, but each time retired shattered and torn only to be brought up again by their officers and launched against the invincible line of Union soldiers.

A battery of guns had been admirably posted by Col. [Joseph D.] Webster, of Grant's staff, and mowed down the Rebels. The gunboats *Tyler* and *Lexington* had also opened fire and dropped their terrible missiles in the midst of the dense ranks of the enemy, where they exploded with fearful carnage. The Rebels, seeing they could not drive the Union line into the river, slackened their fire and sullenly retired as night crept over the hills and put an end to the contest for that day. When the battle began to wane General Grant was at Sherman's front and at once gave him orders to advance and renew the battle early on the following morning. He said, "The Rebel fury is spent; the turning point has been reached; whoever renews the fight will win." He told Sherman the story of Donelson; how at one time he saw that either side was ready to give way if the other showed a bold front; how he had advanced his jaded troops and the enemy had surrendered. The appearance on the field of Shiloh, he said, were the same, and the enemy would be beaten on the following day.

During the night of the sixth Buell busied himself in getting his troops up. Nelson's column and nearly all of [Brig. Gen. Thomas L.] Crittenden's and [Brig. Gen. Alexander McD.] McCook's divisions were ferried over the river and put in position. All night the gunboats dropped shells at intervals on the Rebel lines and the woods caught fire—lighting up the battlefield for miles. But for a merciful shower thousands of wounded soldiers would have been burned to death.

During the night Grant visited every division in his army and encouraged both officers and men by his example and presence to stand fast on the morrow. To each division he said: "As soon as it is light enough to see, attack with a heavy skirmish line and when you have found the enemy throw upon him your whole force, leaving no reserve."

The new line of battle now stood in the following order: Lewis Wallace's division on the right; Sherman, McClernand, and Hurlbut from right to left; McCook next, with Crittenden on his left and Nelson on the extreme left. The fighting began early and for a time was obstinate, but the Rebels were gradually pushed back until all the ground lost on the day before had been regained. By 2:00 P.M. the Union victory was complete and Beauregard in full retreat.

During the fighting on the seventh Grant met the 1st Ohio Regiment marching toward the northern part of the battlefield and immediately in front of a position which was important should be taken. The regiment on the left was fighting hard but about to yield, in fact, had given way, when Grant called upon the Ohio men to change direction and charge the rebels. The soldiers recognized their leader and with a cheer, obeyed—Grant riding along through the storm of shot and shell and cheering on the men. The retreating regiment, seeing what was going on, rallied and with loud shouts, drove the enemy from their strong position. General Grant rode through a piece of woods toward the left, where he met McCook and Crittenden. It was now late in the day, but Grant was anxious to push on after the beaten and retreating Rebels, but McCook and Crittenden reported their troops too much fatigued to continue the pursuit and so the Union forces encamped.

Grant's loss, including Buell's army, was 12,217; of those 1,700 were killed, 7,495 wounded and 3,022 missing. 2,167 of the losses were in the Army of the Ohio. Beauregard reported a total loss of 10,699 killed, wounded and missing; but, as the Union burying parties buried the bodies of four thousand dead Rebels, his loss must have been much larger. The New York *Herald*, which contained the first authentic account of the battle, said of General Grant and his staff in the battle:

> Grant and staff, who had been recklessly riding along the lines during the entire day amid the unceasing storm of bullets, grape, and shell, now rode from right to left, inciting the men to stand firm until reinforcements could cross the river.
>
> About 3:00 P.M. in the afternoon General Grant rode to the left, where fresh regiments had been ordered and, finding the Rebels wavering, sent a portion of his bodyguard to the head of each of the

five regiments and then ordered a charge across the field, himself leading; and as he brandished his sword and waved them on to crowning victory, the cannon balls were falling like hail around him.

There never had been a parallel to the gallantry and bearing of our officers from the commanding general down to the lowest officer.

General Grant and staff were everywhere on the field, riding along the lines in the thickest of the enemy's fire during the entire two days of the battle, and all slept on the ground Sunday night during a heavy rain. On several occasions General Grant got within range of the enemy's guns, was discovered and fired upon.

Lt. Col. James B. McPherson, of Grant's staff, had his horse shot from under him while riding by the side of his chief.

Captain Carson was near General Grant when a cannon ball took his head off and killed and wounded several others.

General Sherman had two horses killed under him, and General McClernand shared like dangers, as did also General Hurlbut, each of whom received bullet holes through their clothes.

The publication of the *Herald*'s account so soon after the battle created great excitement among the citizens of New York and during the day it was telegraphed to the national capital and to all parts of the Union.

Mr. James Gordon Bennett telegraphed the account to President Lincoln and both house of Congress, in which, it was read aloud. In the lower House, Mr. [Schuyler] Colfax, on asking leave to read the dispatch, was greeted on all sides of the House with cries of "To the clerk's desk." The previous noise and excitement subsided and as the House listened to the brief and pregnant details of the bloody struggle which preceded the glorious victory over the concentrated strength of rebeldom, all hearts were stilled and the very breathing almost suppressed till the last word of the dispatch was read. The rejoicing was great at the victory, though somewhat saddened at the price of blood with which it had been purchased.

On April 9 the War Department issued the following complimentary order to all concerned:

War Department
Washington, D.C. April 9, 1862

(Extract) . . . The thanks of the department are hereby given Generals Grant and Buell and their forces for the glorious repulse of Beauregard at Pittsburg, in Tennessee.

It has always been a mooted question whether Grant could have gained the victory of Pittsburg Landing without the aid of Buell's troops. Some have gone so far as to claim that Grant's army would have been utterly destroyed but for the opportune arrival of Buell. Without assuming to judge of what assistance Buell was to Grant at Shiloh, it is only fair to say Grant could have held his position between Snake and Lick Creeks and Beauregard could not have crushed him. Buell did help Grant gain the battle, but Grant's army would not have been destroyed or long held in check had Buell and his army been a thousand miles away.

The Peninsular Campaign: From the Slaughter at Seven Pines to a High Living in a Boston Prison

ALEXANDER HUNTER,
PRIVATE, 17TH VIRGINIA INFANTRY, C.S.A.

Philadelphia *Weekly Times* 6, no. 2, February 17, 1883

On May 30, 1862, I was detailed to go from the vicinity of Seven Pines into Richmond with strict orders to return that night. About noon it began to pour down rain, filling the streets and making the crossings nearly impassable. I waited patiently until the lamps were lit, shining dimly through the blinding showers, and then seeing there was no cessation I started to go and went several squares, when the storm became so violent that I halted in the Monumental Hotel for shelter. I waited until after 10:00 P.M. There was a large crowd of officers sitting around the big stove in the center of the room discussing the conduct of the war. While each had his own pet idea on that subject all agreed that the present rain would effectually put a stop to military operations for days to come. It was 11:00 P.M. when I rose to go; the tempest was at its height, but I was bound to get back to camp that night, so buttoning my overcoat tight around me I set off. It was as dark as pitch, but as I had to travel along a broad turnpike I could not get lost. Plunging on in mire up to my knees, with a big lump of mud on each foot and a stream of water from the hat rim pouring down my back, I struggled along. I felt a kind of delight in fighting the elements.

About midnight I reached camp and by instinct, I suppose, found my tent. Without trying to find my clothes in the dark I wrapped up in a blanket and lay down on the muddy ground and went to sleep, and the last thought that glimmered through my brain was that this deluge would put a stop to all drills and parades and that I could sleep all the next day in peace.

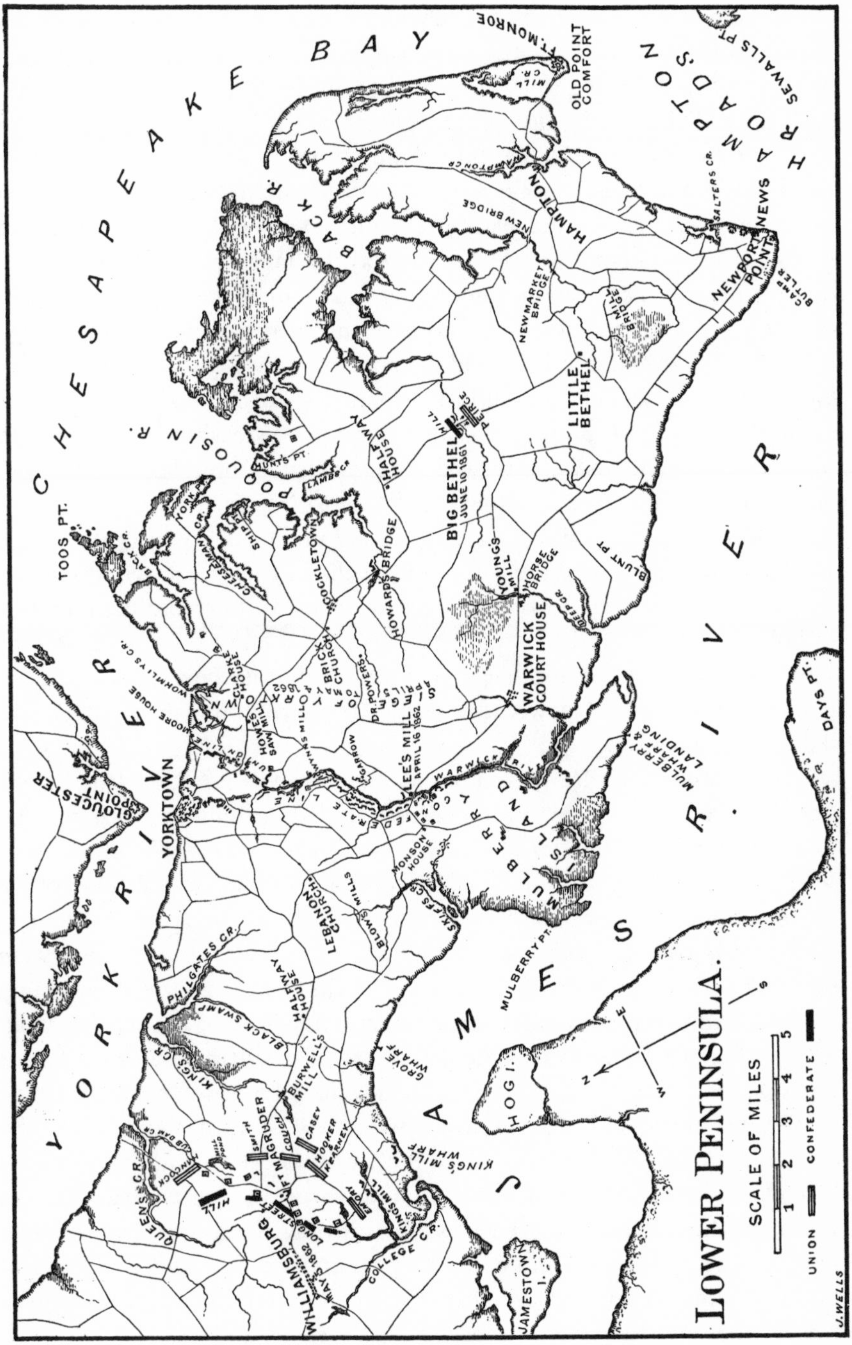

The Lower Peninsula (CENTURY MAGAZINE)

It seemed that my eyes had hardly closed before my comrade and myself were rudely awakened by having a lantern swung across our faces and Sergeant Stickley crying out: "Get up! Get up! Put on your accoutrements; pack up your knapsacks and fall in right away!" It was as dark as black air could be; from without came the warning drum beating the long roll. We had no light and had to grope about as best we could; but we packed up in five minutes and felt for our place in the forming line. The driving rain had given place to a gentle drizzle. As soon as the ranks were established and dressed the ordnance sergeant came along and by the light of the lantern distributed sixty rounds of cartridges to each man, forty to go in his cartridge box, which was all that it held, and the remaining twenty to be placed in his haversack. This looked like business. Following in his footsteps came the commissary sergeant, putting in each soldier's haversacks three days' rations. We were in for it now; every soldier knew that. Our work was cut and dried for us, and there was nothing to do but to face the music.

The marching to and on the Williamsburg road was fearful. Several small streams that crossed the road, now swollen by the torrent into rushing creeks, had to be forded. Some of them were breast high and the men had to hold their cartridge-boxes and haversacks away above their heads to preserve them from the water, but they did not mind it. There was some hot work waiting for us that would soon dry the wringing garments, and we did not complain.

About five miles from Richmond the brigade came to a halt. It was now broad day, but a fine, misty rain surrounded everything in a haze. The men sat along on the sides of the road, each improvising something for a seat, a stone, fence rail, anything to keep out of the wet. After moving down another hundred yards or so the regiment was again halted and orders were given to get breakfast. By hook and crook some few fires were started, but it required infinite patience to kindle a flame with everything steaming with dampness; however, by careful nursing and a steady blowing, enough fire was made to boil the coffee and fry the bacon. Then over our pipes we discussed the situation. Up to this time we had not heard a single gun, and we devoutedly trusted that it was a false alarm, yet knowing at the time what a vain hope it was. In an hour or two the rolling of the drums brought the soldiers into line, and continuing our march we halted about two miles further on and lay at rest. It was now high noon by the town clock, if we could have heard it strike; the rain had ceased; the fog had lifted, but the clouds still kept hanging, their somber curtains hiding the bright blue sky and making the scene appear dark and dismal.

At last it came. It was nearly 1:00 P.M.; a gun sounded on our left, then followed directly after a peal of artillery, and hardly had the roar died away when was heard the rattling of the small arms. Now battery after battery joined in the chorus, until it seemed as if everybody in the world were celebrating a Christmas day by shooting off firecrackers and bursting water pipes with powder, as all boys will do if they get a chance. Our regiment, the 17th Virginia, [Maj. Gen. James P.] Longstreet's Brigade, moved forward and bore to the right; we were evidently held in the reserve. A couple of hours passed; it was nearly 1:00 P.M. and the pounding was going on as heavy as ever. Still there were no signs of action on our part, and we then began to hope that there were men to spare on our side, when just at that time an aide to Col. [Heros] Von Borcke came up in a wild gallop his clothes spattered with mud from head to foot. He hardly stopped long enough to say some words to the commanding officer, when he was off like an arrow. "Fall in, men!" cried the colonel. "Steady, men; forward by the left flank, march, double quick!" and for a mile we went with a rush.

Our right wing had given away and we were sent for. As we approached the scene of action the crash of musketry was appalling. Long streams of wounded men made their appearance on their way to the rear, in every species of mutilation. Some were borne on stretchers, others swung in blankets, from whose folds blood and gore dropped in horrid exudations, staining the ground and crimsoning the budding grass. Others would be carried in their comrades' arms, every step they took extorting a groan of agony from the poor shattered fellow. Many were more slightly wounded and could walk, their hand pressed to the wound, or hobble slowly along with a musket for a crutch.

As we approached closer and closer to the scene of conflict, with its many terrors increasing at every step and the music of the bursting shells in our midst, we all beheld a sight that showed that there is but one step from the sublime to the ridiculous. We saw a broad farce enacting in the midst of the murderous tragedy with death in the air that caused the regiment to indulge in a peal of hearty laughter. The object came up; he was a soldier very slightly wounded in the arm, but he had kind, sympathizing comrades, two of whom supported him tenderly. But they were "making tracks" in order to get out of the reach of the shells that were falling in every direction; behind these came two more kind and sympathizing comrades, two able-bodied men, one carrying the wounded man's gun and the other his hat. As the stricken soldier passed he twisted his features in a look of supreme anguish, as if to seek compassion for his sufferings.

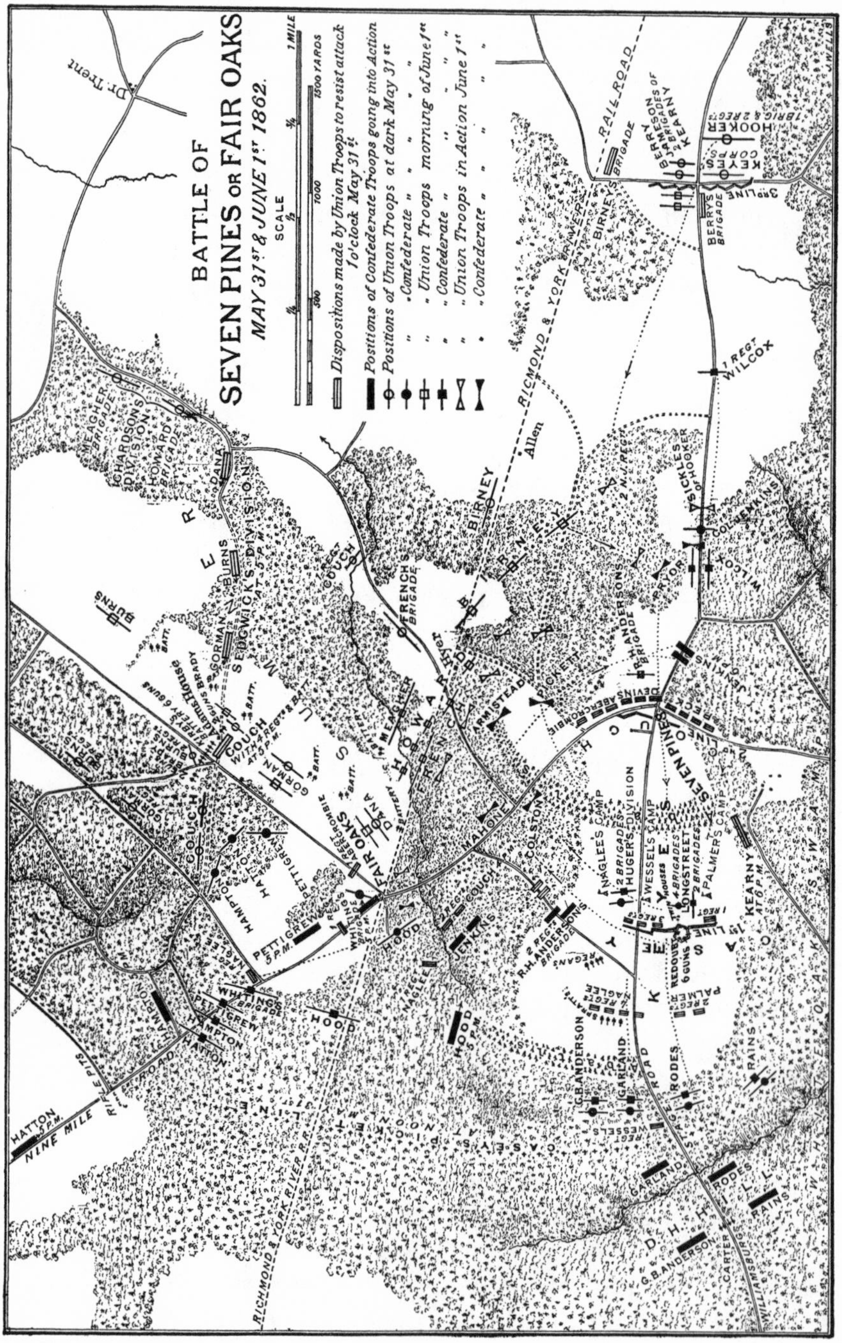

The battle of Seven Pines (CENTURY MAGAZINE)

As for the four comrades they were ready to fight for the honor of helping him. Never was such a sight seen before nor since, five strong soldiers leaving the battlefield to assist a man who only had a skin knocked off his arm. Of course they were arrant cowards and sought any pretext to get out of the seething fire just in our front. They went in a run as the jibes and contemptuous laughter from the whole line greeted them. Later in the war these fellows would have been seized and placed in front of the advancing line.

When we reached the vicinity of the woodpile where there was a big barn and several outworks that had been thrown up by the Federals, but which had been captured by our forces, we could see all the camp of [Brig. Gen. Silas] Casey's division not a hundred yards from us. The shelling was now terrific. As we had double-quicked across the field the enemy had plain view of our brigade and had trained their several batteries, located on the edge of the camp, upon us. Shell, shrapnel, and round shot screamed over us, fortunately a few feet too high. Then was the time to form in a line of battle; instead of that we kept on without changing our formation, which was in fours. In other words we pushed towards the enemy like a lance, instead of spreading out in a line. My company was in advance, the lance head of the column.

As we advanced close to the woodpile the musketry joined the artillery, and to go into that fire-swept camp seemed like entering the jaws of hell itself. "Why don't we form a line of battle?" was the rank and file cry, as the men began to drop, for in column as we were none could fire. We knew someone had blundered. The onward gait by the column was kept up. "Forward; forward!" cried the officers, waving their swords above their heads; "Don't stop, men, charge in the camp!" Into the camp we went with yells ringing high above the uproar of the guns. As we dashed in we passed a four-gun battery of ours which was deserted, every horse having been killed and the remnant of the men forced to seek shelter by the terrible concentrated fire that swept through the camp like an iron and leaden rain. I saw a little boy hardly sixteen years old, a "powder monkey," as they called him, cowering behind the wheel of one of the guns, his face wearing a look of humble affright, eyes protruding, hands clasped, teeth clenched—a face so white and startling that it haunted me days after, though I but glanced for a second at him.

As we passed the barn and got in among the tents the tempest of war was frightful; every deadly projectile which could take human life and maim and disfigure was showered upon us. The air was alive with their coming and shrill and shrieking with their passing. We could see no enemy,

"We knew someone had blundered" (BEYER, *DEEDS OF VALOR*)

but the whole of Casey's division, of some thousand men, formed around their camp in the shape of a half moon, poured a converging fire at the attacking column. Had our brigade (commanded by General [James L.] Kemper) been forced into action, we could probably have swept the enemy away by an irresistible rush, but by the incompetence and ignorance of our commanding officers we were allowed to pour like cattle upon a fortified foe. It sickens me at heart as I write what followed, a result that could not have been otherwise. Mixed up, mingled up, crowded up among the breastworks, barn and woodpile, the brigade got bunched in a lump, lost its organization, became a mob, and that splendid command, of some six hundred muskets, was forced to retreat.

From the half circle on the other side of the camp the enemy rained a constant fire upon the struggling mass. Order disappeared, discipline fled before that tempest. Within five minutes all was over. Men fell in groups, the noise of the Federal bullets ripping through the canvas of the tents added to the horrors of the moment. Men screamed as the balls struck them, the officers shouted out unmeaning cries, the flag went down; [Sgt. W. T.] Morrill, the color-bearer and the tallest man in the regiment, sank to the earth; Corporal [C. W.] Diggs caught the colors and he fell, too. A private grasped them. He raised the staff and in a second he sank face downward with a bullet through his heart. Another gallant private, named Harper, seized the staff from the dead man's hand and bore the colors the rest of the day. In five minutes seventy-four officers and men out of our regiment fell. Then there was a blind rush for shelter. Officers and men scrambled over the breastworks or hurried behind the woodpile. These rifle-pits, which were built by the Federals to protect their camp, proved now our salvation. But for them none save a few would have escaped alive. To have attempted running the gauntlet across the field in our rear would have been to have rattled dice with death. Few remember clearly the combined terrors of that useless massacre. I recollect, as I was rushing back to the protection of the redoubt, that I stopped to help the color-bearer, Morrill, and had raised him half up when two more balls struck him, passing through his body. He sank back with a groan and I left him, only stopping long enough to assist a soldier whose ankle was shattered by a bullet.

Being safe behind a good shelter I had time to look around and see how things looked. It seems that [Brig. Gen. Robert E.] Rodes' Alabama Brigade earlier in the evening had stormed Casey's Division camp with such vim and with such sudden dash that the Federals were driven out of their camp in a run, but they reformed on the outer edge behind an abatis, which, with wise precaution, they had constructed, and then they rained a torrent of fire upon every attacking force. They could not reoccupy their camp, but they could keep us from holding it, and when the old Longstreet (now Kemper's) Brigade came rushing towards them in column, occupying a small space, their whole line then converged their fire upon the struggling mass caught in this deathtrap and sent many, very many, to their last home. In this charge the 4th Alabama of Rodes' Brigade was forced to return and from the camp sought shelter behind the works. They witnessed our useless run and vain sacrifice, and had we charged in line of battle, as many of them as were in the vicinity would have rallied and advanced with us.

I have listened to some heavy firing and to the music of many missiles singing through the air, but I never heard the like of the noise made by shot and shell, as I lay securely behind that redoubt. They came so fast that at least twenty men were struck down by the overtaking balls as they were climbing over the works. They was a ceaseless pour of shot and shell, the bullets hissing like snakes, without a moment's cessation. Every second they would strike the work and bury themselves in the damp earth, or, hitting higher, scrape the top and send the mud spattering over us. As I glanced around I could see the soldiers of different regiments and brigades cowering beneath the parapet, but few daring or having curiosity enough to lift his head over the works to take aim at the running line of fire that showed where the foe lay concealed. Indeed, it was a dangerous experiment. I saw two men not a dozen feet from me, one [William J.] Higdon, from Alexandria, and the other an Alabamian, raise their heads above and both fell back dead, with their heads shattered by bullets.

The very sky seemed to be alive with little fiery devils who sang their song, each to its own tune, as they flew over the work. The canister sounded worse than all, and as the bits would strike against the earthwork it would make the bravest cower closer to the ground. I am sure if a life insurance agent could have come along just then he could have taken out many policies and done a rushing business. For fully an hour did this infernal fire keep up; for fully an hour did we lie there and listen to the sound of the projectiles striking the earthwork; for fully an hour did we congratulate ourselves upon hiding behind such friendly shelter and that fortune or good luck had protected us so far. A soldier's first thought at the close of the battle is always a selfish feeling of thankfulness at his own escape. After that other emotions can find place. Behind the works where we were the ooze and mire was so deep that it reached to our waist belts. Many of the Federals were killed here by Rodes' men and had found a grave without burial, for their corpses had sunk beneath the surface. We could feel that we were standing on their bodies, but the danger all were in prevented any remarks. All around the barn and breastworks the water lay in pools and several of our wounded, falling in these puddles, had absolutely drowned. One of my regiment that I examined was not mortally wounded, but dropping face downward in the water he had been suffocated; his mouth and throat were filled with liquid mud.

It was now late in the evening, the enemy's fire had gradually slackened and at last had died away. Col. [Montgomery D.] Corse then jumped in the open space and sang out for the 17th to form, and I don't think that any regiment in the army ever gave a more substantial proof of its splendid discipline than it did when the men responded with alacrity to the order. After such a terrible shock, a fearful loss, it yet regained its morale, and in ten minutes was formed into a long line. Then the order was given to guide by the colors, and we advanced again through the camp, no longer a mob, but a crack organization in line of battle. Free to return the foe's fire, our regiment went at a double quick, aiming to reach the shelter of the abatis. We arrived there panting and breathless, while not a hostile shot greeted us. Passing and breaking our way through the fallen trees of this obstruction we kept on some distance in the woods beyond, but saw no vestige of the enemy, who had retreated, carrying off their wounded, which must have been many, for Rodes' Brigade had it all their own way at first. We could easily detect where their line had stood that had fought us by cartridges, bloody rags, stretchers, with here and there a musket. It doubtless was fine fun to stand and shoot us crowding in between the forts and woodpile.

It was then nearly dark. We were halted just on the verge of the camp, and as this place was on the low grounds it was under water, and we remained for fully an hour up to our knees in the black mud. We suffered all the torture of Tantalus. After all the loss of men and the hardships we had been through to secure and capture this camp and to hold it, we were not allowed any of the spoils of war that was legitimately our due. It was enough to make a saint swear. There we were, just on the edge of the captured camp, with nothing to do, half buried in the mud, with the enemy gone, and instead of being allowed to get rations and clothing from the camp we had to stand passive and watch while some new troops, who had never been called upon to fire a gun, were brought in and let loose to help themselves at will. It seems that the Federals were at dinner when the storming party, the 3rd Alabama, burst in upon them, and the camp was filled with every luxury.

Hector Eches, a comrade, disappeared mysteriously that evening, and he did not turn up until the next morning, but with that instinct that marks the true soldier, with that intuition that induced Falstaff's company to take what they wanted, Hector had looked after the booty and the spoils. He spent the night in camp and joined us the next day, loaded down with articles, provisions, cloaks, swords, pistols and some fine old brandy. His report was interesting and showed us what we missed—barrels of flour, bags of fruit, boxes of meat, piles of clothes, while the sutler's tent was filled with luxuries. In the headquarter tent a fine dinner lay spread, but untouched, with luxurious surroundings and flanked by bottles of wine, some of which my comrade had seized and placed in a bag; hogsheads of sugar, rice and mess beef lay scattered around. In short it showed the beautiful system of the Yankee commissary. All that night the lucky troops camped in the captured place, luxuriated in the spoils; we could hear them singing and carousing around huge fires, while iron discipline kept us in ranks, not a hundred yards away. After waiting until it was dark the regiment marched back into the pine woods a mile or two to the rear, and without waiting to build fires, wet, hungry and utterly broken down, the soldiers threw themselves in the muddy, soggy ground and went fast to sleep.

A soldier after a battle is in a peculiar and self-complacent humor; he has escaped death and mutilation, so he loves to sit and recall the incidents

"In a peculiar and self-complacent humor" (MCCLURE'S MAGAZINE)

of the battle, narrate his narrow escapes and listen to his comrades' tales. Around the fires the next morning, for it was damp and cool, the whole campaign was discussed. The attack just after such a rain became clear to us all now. General Casey held the advanced post with his division on the south side of the Chickahominy River, the greater portion of McClellan's army being on the north. The sudden rain that deluged this low country and swelled the streams out of all bounds determined General [Joseph E.] Johnston to try and destroy Casey's, [Brig. Gen. Darius N.] Couch's, and [Brig. Gen. Philip] Kearny's divisions before reinforcements could cross the swollen Chickahominy. With this intention he ordered [Brig Gen.

Daniel H.] Hill, commanding a portion of Longstreet's Division, to strike them on the front, while he in person superintended the attack on the enemy's right. Our brigade was in D.H. Hill's attacking division, but held as a reserve. Rodes' Alabama Brigade led the attack, and carried, as related, the redoubts and works by a coup de main and then drove a portion of Casey's division across the Williamsburg or Seven Mile road, into the Nine Mile road, into the swamps of the Chickahominy. That our movement had failed to complete success we all know, and it was whispered that General [Benjamin] Huger was the cause by not attacking the enemy on the right.

Philadelphia *Weekly Times* 6, no. 3, February 24, 1883

It was in the Peninsular campaign on the morning of June 30, 1862, the 17th Virginia drew up in line of battle on Frazier's Farm. For the preceding week they had been on their feet night and day, and the men were well-nigh exhausted. It was the time when [Maj. Gen. George B.] McClellan with his splendid army was besieging Richmond, and would have certainly captured the Confederate capital had not Stonewall [Lt. Gen. Thomas J.] Jackson, hurrying from the scene of his triumphs in the Valley of Virginia, struck the right flank of the Union army at Mechanicsville and Gaines's Mill, doubled it up and, forming a junction with [Gen. Robert E.] Lee's army, forced McClellan to retreat to the protection of his gunboats, fighting every step of his way.

All day our regiment lay in a line, listening to the faint rattling of the musketry and the distant booming of the guns. Then came a long silence, until about five in the afternoon, when the order to fall in was given and [Lt. Gen. James P.] Longstreet's old brigade, consisting of the 1st, 7th, 11th and 17th Virginia Infantry, started in fine style across the field. On our way the serried line of the regiment was broken and almost stampeded by a swarm of bumblebees, that must have been good Union bees, for they charged the gray line savagely and set over a hundred of us "Rebs" in a mad flight towards the front. Our course lay straight for a dense woods about half a mile away. The enemy's skirmishers kept up a scattering fire, but the advance continued without our firing a shot. Reaching the woods, we climbed a Virginia snake fence and pushed our way steadily, the ground getting more and more swampy and the woods and slashes more dense. A few rods further we found ourselves in a regular morass and as we were laboriously plodding onward, all at once a volley was poured into us at pistol shot distance. It was too high. We returned it, the officers giving the only orders

I ever heard in the heat of conflict, "Fire low, men, fire low!" Then the command to charge rang out, and with the "Rebel yell" we dashed straight to the opening, which we could see through the trees. A sudden silence from the foe, and then came—there is only one word to express it—"hell." Solid shot, shell, shrapnel, grape and canister tore through the woods at point blank distance, and in a few seconds the 17th disappeared. I defy any participant in the ranks to give any sensible account of an engagement. I have been in fourteen pitched battles and only a few vivid pictures remain; the rest is only smoke, noise, cheers, a frenzied hurly-burly, that the memory holds without a single distinct impression. I only recollect turning to run and seeing my dear friend and comrade, Con Johnson, throw up his hands as he fell backward and heard some men cry out that we were flanked. Throwing myself flat on the ground, I saw the bluecoats swarming through the woods; and as soon as the first one got close enough, I told him I surrendered—and he started with me to the rear. Then my reason and my memory came back and I began to observe things and found my jacket and trousers wet with blood. A careful examination showed that my slim anatomy was not pierced by either iron, steel or lead; but when and how I became so ensanguined I never knew. Just on the edge of the woods I stopped and my heart felt like a stone, for there in the field lay another of my bosom friends, Dan Lee, stiff in death. There was no time to linger; the guard hurried us on and at last when we stopped out of reach of our own Confederate fire, we discovered what a terrible blunder had been made in sending one brigade against such a force as this—a six-gun battery in our front, one on each flank, with [Brig. Gen. George A.] McCall's whole Pennsylvania division in the advance, backed by a heavy reserve.

The wide road was filled with marching soldiers. Batteries of artillery dashed by, hardly discernible in the huge clouds of dust which they raised. Brigade after brigade was taking position, going in a double-quick, as if they had no time to spare. How soldier-like they looked—how distinguished in their uniforms! Used as we had been to the variegated shades of homespun and butternut, which were as ugly as unpretending, the spectacle of those bluecoats, with their gleaming arms and their high discipline, struck us with admiration.

The field was filled with stragglers, and the slightly wounded were coming out of the fight by hundreds. A brigade passed us on a run, to the front, each man with a spade strapped to his left hip. At that time we did not know the exact use of those implements so carried, unless it was to bury the dead; it never occurred to our minds that they were used to throw up rifle pits in case of need.

After a retreat of about a mile, our conductors halted where there were some prisoners seated on the ground, surrounded by a heavy guard. We were turned in amongst the throng and to our delight found others, ten or twelve, of the 17th Regiment. Misery certainly does love company. To our eager questionings they could make no reply, having been like ourselves scattered from the main body and gathered up singly or in groups of two or three by the enemy, who took them in just as a crack sportsman would pick up the dispersed partridges after the covey has been flushed.

The uproar was by this time deafening, while the mingled clouds of smoke and dust hung like a pall over where the Blue and Gray had locked horns. It was a great fight that was raging, and we sat there absorbingly interested. We had done all that our individual efforts could do. It soon becomes a soldier's philosophy to waste no time in vain longing or fruitless regrets; so we watched the denouement.

An hour had passed, and still the firing had not lessened. "Would their reserves never give out?" we asked each other, as brigades and divisions flowed onwards to the woods. "Can we ever face such a force as they have massed in column?" The answer came sooner than expected; for in one supreme moment the noise of the artillery and musketry reached such an infernal clamor that it seemed that the last day on earth had come and the sleepers were to be awakened from their graves. Every face was pale, both of prisoners and guards. A thousand stragglers were rushing frantically to the rear. The battle's thunder came closer. The bluecoats were falling back—who could doubt that? But there was nothing of a rout in those serried lines, only a giving of the ground inch by inch.

Again for the last time the storm of battle forced both guards and prisoners back. It was dusk when this occurred and the sounds of the battle died away with remarkable suddenness—only one rattling volley, then silence. "The same story over again," we thought—"a desperate struggle, blood flowing like water, and nothing decisive!"

The night was lovely. A full moon slowly rose from the horizon, and its light made the scene almost as bright as day. The soft rays covered the earth with a mantle of charity, hiding what was rough and unseemly and bringing out in greater beauty all that was fair and lovely before. They entered the soldier heart and softened it with thoughts of home. They breathed upon the air, so lately rent with the mad sounds of strife, a holy "Peace, be still!" They rested softly and solemnly on the faces of the dead, as would some farewell kisses, dedicating them lovingly to their future rest.

The prisoners could not sleep, but sat in a circle and talked over events of the day. The Yankees around us had claimed a victory; but we knew better than that. At the very best for them, it could be only a drawn battle. Our sole anxiety, therefore, was for our regiment and brigade. We knew the loss must have been very heavy; and we waited anxiously for news. Prisoners singly and in squads were being brought in every few minutes now.

Here we had conclusive evidence before our eyes that the accounts of the demoralization of the Yankees, which had been told and believed by our troops, had not the slightest foundation. These soldiers around us were full of enthusiasm; they actually claimed every engagement that had taken place within the last few days. When asked why McClellan was retreating and burning his stores behind him, they replied that he was merely consolidating his forces with the intention of taking Richmond in the rear. Never was an army in better plight than the Army of the Potomac on that evening of June 30, 1862. A murmuring sound in the distance attracted our attention; it came nearer, rising louder, until it swelled into a mighty shout, as thousands of voices rang out their enthusiastic cheers. Asking the meaning of this demonstration, a soldier pointed out a group of passing horsemen which he said were "Little Mac" and his staff. It was not quite light enough to distinguish the features of the commanding general, nor was he sufficiently near; but we could see that he held his hat above his head in acknowledgment of the tributes his soldiers paid him.

At last, overcome by fatigue, we lay down in the middle road, in the dust, for we had neither blankets nor overcoats, and like a litter of pigs nestled closely for comfort. Hardly had we fallen asleep before the cry of "Here comes the cavalry!" scattered guards and prisoners right and left. It was a false alarm, but it was some time before everything was serene again. How easy to have escaped during that stampede—especially as the dust had made it hard to distinguish friend from foe! None of us thought of it afterwards, except one, a member of the 17th, who had quietly stolen away.

About 10:00 P.M. the prisoners were formed into line for a long march. The officers in command told us that we should observe a perfect silence en route, that our lives depended on a strict obedience to this order, as the guard would bayonet any prisoner who might venture to offend by so much as a word. It is needless to say that the most talkative man in the squad soon became remarkably mute. Our faces were then turned towards the James River and we began our silent march. Not a syllable was whispered, nor did we stop at all, except to let troops pass us now and then, which they did without so much as the rasping of a gun or the jingle of a canteen against a bayonet resting within the scabbard. It was a weird scene, the moving of that noiseless host through the shadows which the pine trees cast beneath the moon, almost as if the disembodied souls from the Seven

Days' Battles had taken form again and were marching phantom wise to the sound of spirit music through the woods, joining forces and moving in one vast procession into the unseen world. We could easily see that this road was the open line of their retreat, which they were fearful might be closed; hence all this scenery and silence. It was apparent that this looked more as if the Yankees were escaping from a trap than like a victorious army taking a new position.

The march became very wearisome, and both guards and prisoners had hard work to keep their eyes open. A few of us started to escape several times, but wanted the nerve. It looked so easy to jump by the weary, unsuspecting guards into the dark recesses of the woods before they could fire. Indeed it is not certain whether under the circumstances they would have fired. Every prisoner there could have gotten away that night, had he only made the rush. The small procession was halted about 1:00 A.M. in a field on the edge of the swamp and were almost instantly asleep, all of them; but a dozen times were we aroused from our rest and made to fall into line and then drop down overcome, only to be aroused again and tortured until we prayed for the light, destruction, anything, rather than the darkness and disturbance.

The dawn came at last, faintly tinging the fog and resting on the swamp like a dark veil, heavy and damp; but when the sun arose above the treetops, it swept away its phantom foe with a few glancing beams and soon sat the earth simmering in a sickly heat. Falling into line, hungry, unwashed and unrested, still keeping the road, we soon overtook another squad of prisoners belonging to the 17th. In about three hours' march our captors came in sight of the James River and there halted for a time. The river shone like burnished silver in the sun. Before us lay broad, sloping meadows reaching away for miles, with not so much as a grove to intercept the view. On this immense plateau were two corps of McClellan's army, looking as fresh as if they had never fired a gun, nor marched a mile. One of our number said that he tried to count the regiments by the flags and had reached as high as twenty-five when he lost the tally. There could not have been less than twenty thousand men.

We soon reached Harrison's Landing and to our surprise and universal satisfaction saw sitting under the trees about seventy of the 17th Regiment, with Colonel [Morton] Marye at their head. There were three captains, nearly a dozen lieutenants and the balance rank and file. They were busily engaged in some discussion; and when we perceived each familiar face, a mutual shout went up and hand-shakings were liberally indulged in all around. Now for the first time we learned all about the battle and the extent of our loss. Nearly five hundred men were killed, captured and wounded in the brigade, fully one fourth of the whole number. The 17th had lost one-third of its fighting strength. Company A suffered severely—four killed outright, nine wounded badly, and thirteen prisoners. The color bearers of the command had gotten out safely with their flags, which was all the consolation we could manage to extract from such an accumulation of woes.

We remained in this cool, shady grove all day, for which we were duly thankful. We had rations issued, crackers, coffee, sugar, and meat of good quality and fair quantity. The rumbling of artillery in the vicinity of Richmond became more frequent as twilight drew towards night; and as we lay stretched at ease enjoying the glories of that exquisite summer evening, we could not help but remember that the contest of the Titans was now being enacted and that yonder setting sun was sinking behind a sea of blood.

The next morning it commenced raining, and we were ordered into ranks and marched one or two miles, only stopping when we had reached the marshiest bottom possible to find. There a square was marked out on the ground, around the edges of which the sentinels were posted; and we learned for the first time the meaning of a dead line. It was simply a line drawn upon the ground, a step beyond which was death. All that day we had literally to "stand it," for the ground was too wet to sit upon and the rainfall which always follows a great battle now came down in a continuous stream, just as if Nature had many ugly stains to wash away from the earth, or else was weeping for her children.

The space in which we were confined was not larger than a moderate sized sheepfold, and the mud trodden by many feet was soon a mire. The hours dragged by and then came the evening, but with no diminution of the rain nor of our misery. The hope of being removed to some place of shelter was doomed to disappoint; the painful truth forced itself upon us that we were to spend the night in this place. Dark, pitch dark, and a flood coming down. Some of the "Billy Yanks" showed us most disinterested kindness, sharing with us their hot coffee and doing all in their power to alleviate our woes. They were not at liberty to carry us to shelter nor to give us blankets; but we thanked them in our hearts for what they had done and would have done. It was very chilly and our teeth were chattering so we could scarcely eat our crackers; and how stiff, aching and numbed were our poor legs! In this manner we passed the greater part of the night. When at last fatigue had made us insensible to the mud and the rain, we crept close together and lying down with caps drawn over our faces, forgot the misery in the oblivion of sleep.

"The rain it raineth every day." It came down when it was time that any reasonable pour would have held up; the leaden sky did not show a rift in the clouds. The men were not allowed to move out of the narrow limits, not even to get water to drink. What they used was obtained from the little holes which they hollowed out with their hands in the mire. It was so brackish and filthy that nothing but the sternest necessity compelled them to drink it. Our pen was now changed from mud into a liquid slime. It was impossible for the men to become dirtier or more soaked, so they lay down in the filth. The Yankee guards and soldiers cried shame on our treatment and, noble fellows that they were, did the only thing that was in their power to alleviate the wretchedness, shared their hot coffee; but the officers took no notice of our complaints.

Towards evening the prisoners became desperate, for they saw it was impossible to spend another night in the quagmire, already up to the knees and in which none could have lain down without sinking beneath the surface. We shouted so long and loud for our colonel, that he came to us under guard and when he saw our condition, a more angry man it would have been hard to find in the two armies. He had to swallow his wrath; but he went to the officer in command and painted our woeful condition in such strong colors, that in an hour or two a large squad of men came bringing armfuls of hay, which they distributed lavishly to the prisoners. Then they brought rails and sticks of wood, which served as foundations for the beds. Though it rained hard all night, we managed to sleep through it comfortably.

The faint beams of the sun striving to dispel the mists showed us the worst was now passed. Under its warm rays we dried our clothes and the blood was sent circulating through the erstwhile numbed limbs. In the afternoon we were formed in rank and leaving our "wallow," though we carried away plenty of mud by way of a memento, were marched up the river and bivouacked for the night in a grove of trees. It was not until late in the evening of the next day that we stepped upon the wharf at Harrison's Landing, prepared to take passage on the steamboat en route for a most compulsory visit North. Marching single file across the gangway plank, then to the upper deck, we scattered in groups; the whistle blew, the ropes were cast off, the paddles revolved slowly and the boat, sluggishly turning prow in the direction of Old Point, steamed swiftly down the river.

Each man now received a blanket and also full rations and as the shades of night fell on the scene, the songs of the 17th's glee club, or what was left of it, floated through the air. They sang as men only can who have light hearts and full stomachs. Soldiers are but children at best. For them the past was gone, the future was hidden, the present only was theirs.

The "Glorious Fourth" of 1862 was clear and warm. No one ever saw a wet or cool Independence; it is always the sultriest day of the whole year. About nine in the morning we arrived in sight of Fortress Monroe. The waters shone beneath the sun like gold and broke into diamond sparkles at his touch, while its burnished surface rose and fell with a long, lazy swell that scarcely rippled the waters. Hundreds of vessels, from the stately man-of-war down to the little fishing smacks, lay at anchor, every one decorated with streamers, flags, and bunting, in honor of the day. Our steamer rounded the point swiftly, her prow seeming scarcely to cut the clear blue water. We passed the line of the battleship *Cumberland*, where it had been sunk by the *Merrimac* not many months before, its lofty masts appearing above the water, a splendid monument of American valor, whose crew went to the bottom sighting the guns. The *Monitor*, which gained a worldwide celebrity in her contest with the ironclad, was anchored not far off, an object of great interest. We were disappointed in the half-sunken, canal-boat-looking craft, with turret in the center, having had an idea that she was an immense structure. It was difficult to believe that this insignificant little vessel before us had been capable of whipping the mighty *Merrimac*.

The steamer was made fast to the wharf and the prisoners were marched into the fort. To us it was a splendid pageantry—the waving flags, the mounted guns, the showily dressed garrison, the officers in full uniform, the bands playing, and the booming cannon firing salutes. Our squad was halted at the barracks, and for the first time in many days we had the eating of a good dinner, to which we did full justice. As we were about re-forming, a Yankee lieutenant who had been drinking heavily came out with a canteen of whiskey.

"Boys," said he, "I will give you a pull if you will drink success to the Union."

A silence fell upon us. We wanted a drink. How could we indulge in a toast whose sentiments were so repugnant to our feelings? Yet we were very thirsty—so very thirsty! Not a drop of old rye had we touched for many a long day. It smelled delightfully fragrant and it kept on smelling, and—and—Well, Esau was not such a wretch after all! We blush to recall it. As many as could grasp that tin cup took the liquor and repeated the toast, "Success to the Union!" Some of our officers began to jibe us; but they were silenced with the reminder that they had been sleeping in a corn house, while we had paddled in a puddle.

The warning of the steam whistle hurried us to the wharf. Instead of our steamboats was a large steamship called the *Ocean Queen*, which was to carry us to New York. Just as the sun went down the steamer started and soon the last glimpse of Old Virginia faded from our view. The steamship carried no passengers except "deadheads"; besides the crew, prisoners and guards, there were no others on board. Our quarters were good. Yet men will rarely consent to let well enough alone; for within six hours of the start a plot had been started by one of the officers, Lieutenant Slaughter of Company K, to overpower the guard, seize the steamer, turn her prow towards Virginia, then beach the vessel on shore and make a way to Richmond. It would have been a comparatively easy task, fraught with but little danger. The guards were not many and scattered all about the boat, each generally surrounded by a group of prisoners conversing on the war. Really no attempt had been made to show us that we were under surveillance, for each man could roam at will over the vessel, even climb the shrouds and up the mainmast if he chose. The prisoners numbered some seventy-five or eighty; the guards all told were sixteen, under charge of one officer. The privates, with three exceptions, anxious for any excitement, eagerly joined the conspiracy, and faithfully promised to obey all orders and run all risks; and they would have done it. The plan only needed the sanction of our colonel to be put into instant execution. The plot was laid before Colonel Marye, who, after careful consideration, vetoed the whole scheme. In the first place, he said, there was no engineer or pilot on board who could take charge of the boat, in case the present crew should refuse to serve. Then the supply of coal was limited; while the gravest obstacle lay in the fact that it would be impossible to get beyond Fortress Monroe, either to go up the James or the Potomac. It was true that the prisoners could probably escape by going to New York and overpowering the guard as the boat steamed up the harbor; but then no one had any money and the risk would be too great. "Besides," the colonel reasoned, "we shall soon be exchanged; and so what will be the use of taking all this trouble, incurring all this risk, without a particle of necessity for it?"

The morning of the second day the boat passed Sandy Hook and made her way up the harbor amid a forest of shipping, steering towards Governor's Island. She stopped at the wharf and the prisoners were marched ashore, where the garrison under arms received us. We were the first Rebel prisoners to land there; and our appearance was such that it failed to make a favorable impression on our Northern friends. To heighten the effect, by way of contrast, we had the clean, natty men to offset our ragged, mud-stained garments and unkempt locks.

After standing several hours in the sun, going through roll call and arranging preliminaries until our patience was threadbare, we were marched by the demi-castle which stands on the edge of the island to a large row of tents that were pitched alongside the beach. Rations were distributed, consisting of crackers, coffee, rice, meat and potatoes—better than we had ever received at home. Then, the dead line having been marked and a guard stationed, we were left to our own devices. That evening we enjoyed a surf bath, and for the first time had a chance to wash off the Chickahominy mud that had stuck to us, through all adventures and travel, "closer than a brother." We stood sadly in need of underclothing, not one of us having had a change for nearly three weeks. Those we wore were grimy and black; but we washed them that evening after a fashion and at night some fifty men could have been seen clustered over the campfire, their bare backs shining in the glare, while each pair of hands held up before the blaze the steaming articles of wearing apparel. Lights were out at nine and then followed the first perfect restful slumber that had visited us since the twenty-fourth day of the month before.

Our stay at Governor's Island lasted only two or three days, during which we were in a high state of enjoyment, with as much rest, exercise, bathing and good rations as was consistent with our position. The only thing of which we had reason to complain was the brutality of our guards—militia of course. Veteran soldiers never ill-treated their prisoners—such was the experience on both sides; it was only those "dressed in a little brief authority," only those whose sole acquaintance with war was gathered from the daily papers, who gratified their malice by insulting defenseless men under their charge.

On the evening of the ninth of July, our squad, composed of 17th Virginia men, was started again on the tramp. A small steam tug carried us over to New York, whence we were transferred to the deck of one of the superb steamers that ply between New York and Fall River, Massachusetts.

"Where the mischief are you going to carry us?" asked one of our captains of the officers of the guard. "Turn us loose in Canada or send us to some watering place to improve our health?"

"You fellows ought to be very glad that you are going where you are," he answered, "instead of being sent to Fort Delaware. I have orders to carry you all to Fort Warren in Boston Harbor—and a fine place it is."

The steamer was filled with a gay company going to Saratoga, Canada and Niagara Falls. "Not much secesh in them!" remarked one of the guards to us confidentially. "See how spiteful they look." So they did. Their pretty noses went up and their red lips curled disdainfully, as they passed our ranks on the way the saloon. At this point one of the fair ones dropped her handkerchief and I, who loved the sex, was only too willing to pick up the dainty article and restore it to the owner, which I did with the most sweeping Sir Charles Grandison bow of which I was capable. The gentle dame received the handkerchief, but a fixed stony stare rewarded the bow and chilled me to the bone, while her escort, a little slim-waisted, dainty fellow, perfumed and yellow kidded, scowled like the humpbacked Richard when he ordered the princely Buckingham off to execution.

We had left the island in such a hurry that the commissary either forgot or neglected to issue the rations; at any rate we did not receive them, and after the steamer had got under way we woke to the fact that we were ravenously hungry. It happened that we were placed in an upper saloon, with steps leading down in the front and rear. In the center of the saloon was an open oval space, some twenty feet long, around which ran a railing and which, being directly over the dining room, commanded a complete view of all that passed therein. An appetizing odor and the clattering of knives and forks brought us to our feet and looking down, all sleep was banished from our famished eyes, while the pangs of hunger became intolerable. We felt like Dives looking up from his place of torment upon Lazarus, who was "being comforted." It was a long, luxuriously furnished apartment. In the center the long table was laid with snowy damask, glittering with cut glass and plate and decorated with brilliant flowers. Why attempt to particularize the viands, the fish, the fruits, and all the dainties, which passed before our eyes like the distempered visions of a dream? Bowls of crimson strawberries, piles of luscious raspberries, whose rich coloring grew more intense contrasted with the powdered sugar, the rich cream and sparkling ice, Malaga grapes whose look suggested a cool touch to the parched tongue, jellies, ices, cakes, salmon, mutton, ham, fried chicken, devilled crabs, salads, vegetables, a hundred dishes which we did not know, but whose combined odor filled our souls with longing unspeakable. We heard the popping of champagne corks, we recognized the long, slender bottles of Chamberlain, St. Julien, Medoc, while the steaming coffee rose as incense. We watched each mouthful which passed into blessed lips; we grudged every dish; nay, we could have fought over every cooling drop. Poor Johnnies! We sat there for two mortal hours, our jaws working spasmodically as we fathomed the very depth of a punishment which only Dante could have conceived for the souls of his Inferno.

The scene, however, had its fascinations. There were beautiful women, whose eyes outshone the diamonds which sparkled on their hands. Sitting near the center of the table was a bridal couple whom we watched—the groom, an old fellow with the love light in his ancient eyes and well got up; she fair as a lily, and young enough to be his grandchild. Another bridal couple not far off, going to Niagara, where all the newly married go—both young, both bashful, both radiantly happy. Indeed they were too ecstatic to eat; he, however, poured wineglass after wineglass of champagne down his throat. There sat a wounded officer, with his arm in a sling. Nobody seemed to take much notice of him; one of the servants cut up his food and attended him. "Ah, old fellow!" we thought, "if you only wore the gray and were in the South, every woman at that table would deem it an honor to wait upon you." At the head of the board was a general—of what especial rank and name we could not learn. He was exclusive; and it showed how great people gravitate towards each other, when the portly butler stood by him and paid him the most distinguished consideration. The butler we must not pass over, for though last, he was by no means least. He was a venerable gentleman of color, so bloated by rich living and a sense of his own importance that he could only waddle slowly across the floor. He never condescended to do any service except to pour out a glass of wine for some individual as high in the world as himself. He was evidently what we call down South "an aristocratic nigger." Attending in full dress, his big hands encased in white gloves, with marvelous studs and massive pinchbeck chain, he felt as great as the mighty Caesar. With a lofty wave of the hand he signalized his pleasure to a sable servitor, who flew to do his bidding. Surrounded by his crowd of satellites, he was a very sun of a system.

The gnawing pangs of hunger were growing every moment more intense; so several of us held a council of war, resolved to get something to eat by hook or crook. We counted funds. All told they amounted to twenty-six dollars—a goodly sum enough, but, woe the day! It was Confederate money. Tall, gaunt Jack Ballenger took the money, determined to try anyhow and slipped down two flights of steps to the dining room door; there, calling a waiter, he offered him the amount if he would manage to provide a supper for six. He seemed undecided; said he would go and see. Approaching the bloated old butler, he asked his consent; but that mass of flesh hated a "Rebel" with every pound of his swelled carcass and gave the waiter such overwhelming, withering rebuke that he slunk away and never came near us again. However, one or two hands on the boat took compassion on us and brought us a dish of cold tripe and bread. Ah that tripe! It hung as heavy on our souls as Meg Merrile's curse. It was true Union tripe and refused to give any aid or comfort to the enemy whatever—instead, many pains and many qualms. It is probable that not a man in that lot has ever eaten tripe since.

Early in the morning the steamer reached Fall River, where, leaving the boat, we were marched to the depot and took the train, a whole car having been allotted to us alone. Certainly, had we wished to escape, the guards allowed every opportunity. We were at liberty to stand on the platform of the cars by obtaining the permission of the officer of the day, who was disposed to be very friendly towards us. Passing through a long tunnel where the train went very slowly, it was debated among a few of us whether or not it were better to slip off; but we thought that in our gray uniforms, without a cent in our pockets and in the midst of bitter enemies, it would be only avoiding Charybdis to fall upon Scylla, and the idea was dismissed.

Boston and its suburbs, with villas, stylish county seats, neat farmhouses and grounds, seemed spick span and new, so different from the style to which we had been used. To be sure, there was nothing of age to be met with anywhere, not even so much as of the hundred years to which as a new country we are entitled; but on the other hand, there were no hanging gates, no tumble-down porches, no veteran pumps, nothing but what showed promptness in repair and energy opposed to our lazy plantation principle. The Southerner takes a pride in his old house, and will keep it intact as in the days of his great-grandfather—the same old portraits hanging on the wall, the same old furniture. He may add wings to the building and a porch here and there, but the old parental roof remains, like a chicken with her brood around her. The spirit of decay is not kept down on his grounds and rolling acres. He is in no hurry to improve things; he will tie and prop up where a nail should go; paint he does not hanker after; his very equipage is often wheezy; and so a flavor of age tinges his home, as it does the hair on his head and his wine. "What is good enough for my father before me is good enough for me!" becomes a maxim on his lips, to be handed down to his son after him.

The Northern spirit is essentially progressive, if not reverential. When the patrimonial mansion descends to a younger generation and increasing coffers are the reward of thrift, he says, "I will pull down my house and my barns and build greater"; and on the site of the old foundation stones arises a structure whose elegance and comfort are only limited by the length of the purse. Where money is no consideration, palatial residences are built for the nobles of the old world. Everything is modern, the more modern the better. His carriages are all glaze and shine; his furniture changes with the fashion; his grounds are laid out with mathematical exactness—the very trees grown to shape; the hedges are cut according to pattern; the lawns are sowed and rolled to velvet precision; and Nature is made to step back and yield to the aesthetic as it may be apprehended at the time. The Northern characteristic, however, is essentially that of cleanliness; the Yankee is obtrusively neat; he hates dust and dirt more than anything else, snakes and sin not excepted; in soap and scrubbing is his national faith. If he had his mother-in-law cremated, and the sacred dust were by accident to escape from the precious urn, a servant with soap and mop would wipe her up.

Early in the forenoon we left the cars and found ourselves in the spacious depot, in the ultra Union city of Boston—the first "Rebels" that ever pressed with sacrilegious feet its loyal streets; the first Rebels who walked under the shadow of Faneuil Hall. No; now that we think of it, a large gang of them passed its doors about a hundred years ago on their way to burn some British tea that a loyal tax had been placed upon; but then that was a long time ago and times have changed!

Boston, that city of furors, the Athens of America, the Hub of the Universe, the city of many titles, rarely enjoyed in those war times a greater sensation than was caused by the appearance of a hundred live genuine "Rebels" captured on the battlefields. The great sea serpent taken off the coast, the walking giant, nay, even a grand circus parade of wild animals with a hippopotamus and a giraffe heading up the thoroughfare, would not have collected a larger crowd in a shorter time. Had Bunker Hill monument stepped down from its stately perch and walked away on feet decorously wrapped in the American flag, bowing right and left to the multitude, it could hardly have excited more curiosity than did that line of simple gray jackets. A mob followed us up the street—a good natured mob, though, that only used its eyes. After having passed a square or two, the crowd became so dense, the pressure upon us so great, that further progress became impossible. The guards could not keep off the throng that hemmed them in; so we were halted while a heavy detachment of police formed an outer cordon and another squad in front opened the way; then we slowly made our progress through the streets. The pavements, the balconies, the very housetops were filled with an inquisitive, gazing multitude, while the little street Arabs swung like monkeys from the trees. Shops were suddenly emptied of clerks and purchasers; windows sprung open, shutters flew wide, heads were thrust out and eyes stared us in the face, whichever way we looked. The newsboys neglected to call their papers; the hack men pulled up on one side of the street, forgetting for a moment to lash their bony, lean horses; carriages came to a sudden halt. In fact, all business was as effectually suspended. Old men peered at us through spectacles; women stopped to watch us; boys gazed, and children, bless their innocent hearts, there is no knowing what tales those infant Bostonians had heard about the

Rebels that brought that look of fright into their young eyes. It was the same expression with which they gaze upon the man-eating lion in the menagerie; and they clung to their mothers and nurses as if they had been brought face to face with just so many monsters.

What the citizens thought of us we had no means of finding out; yet it must have been rather a disappointment. Each one of us, to accord with the popular idea, should have been at least seven feet high, with a villainous countenance, overshadowed by a wide brimmed hat. We should have had a shock of unkempt, flowing hair, and a beard like that of the giant in the fairy tale, who wore the seven league boots and ate a child at every meal. Bowie knives should have been our chief personal adornment and scowling our pastime. As it was, we were rather too commonplace, though our procession was quite imposing. First, the police at our head; next followed our officers, with our colonel leading—and a handsomer, more distinguished looking man to serve for our frontispiece would have been hard to find, North or South. Last came the privates, strung out in twos, with the guards on each side, the police escorting. Altogether the train stretched out for fully a square. A more reckless, daredevil set of boys—for nearly all those privates were no more than boys—was never before brought together by the fortunes of war. It may be safely surmised that they kept no decorous silence, as befitted *les miserables* on the way to prison. They scattered greetings right and left; they bowed to every pretty girl; they complimented every handsome woman in the same manner. So we went, making slow but steady progress. Not one rudeness nor insult was offered us during the whole route—which spoke well for the charity, the refinement, and good taste of the Bostonians.

Many onlookers tried to get inside the line to talk, but were repulsed by the police, the soldiers not caring one way or the other. Only the newspapermen joined our ranks; they can get anywhere. As they walked with us, they asked question after question.

It was an hour before we reached the wharf, where a steam tug lay in waiting. Going aboard and bidding our police escort a polite farewell, the little boat picked her way down the river, reaching Fort Warren at the mouth of the bay after a pleasant ride of eight hours. This fortification was an elaborate and massive work, commanding all the approaches of the city. From the upper tiers of guns a plunging fire of forty-five degrees could have sunk any vessel, ironclad or otherwise. Fort Warren well garrisoned was to our eyes simply impregnable.

After we had landed, a guard took us in charge, our former sentinels returning in the boat. We were left within the parade grounds, where we remained until arrangements were made for our comfort. We were soon surrounded by the political prisoners, who were of influence and had been incarcerated for their outspoken Southern sentiments or for some acts considered by the authorities as disloyal—whether justly or unjustly so remained to be proven. There were also some of our officers high in rank, Generals [Simon B.] Buckner and [Lloyd] Tilghman captured at Fort Donelson, Commodore [Samuel] Barron of the Confederate navy, Marshall Kane, and Dr. Margill of Maryland, and some other citizens of less note. There were none of the rank and file other than ourselves; and we blessed our stars that we had fallen into such a soft place.

The political prisoners had a splendid dinner ready for us—such a dinner as the Confederacy could not have given us in all its length and breadth, a dinner we had often dreamed over in our forced marches. It is needless to say that our onslaught was a heavy one; indeed, the amount of food that we consumed and the bottles of wine which we emptied in that one meal would have seemed incredible to any one not informed as to the expansive power of the Rebel soldiers' digestive apparatus. The donors watched our efforts with the liveliest delight.

After a good smoke the prisoners were assigned to their quarters, consisting of two long casemated apartments, one for sleeping, the other the mess room. In the former bunks were built one above the other, like berths in a ship. A blanket per man was issued, while the political prisoners presented each of us with a suit of underclothing. No rations were given, but instead the storeroom was open, to the contents of which the messes could help themselves as it might please them. Certainly no prisoners of war had ever been treated so luxuriously before, nor were they ever afterwards. Breakfast consisted of coffee—real, not ground rye or corn—fresh loaf bread, mess beef, hominy, broiled ham, and eggs *ad libitum*. Dinner was proportionally good. The mess room was a large vaulted apartment, cool even in the hottest part of the day, the casements allowing a refreshing ocean breeze to pass through. A large cooking stove was at one end, around which were hanging all the necessary utensils; and on one side was a temporary storeroom, with barrels of hard bread, flour, mess pork, beef, and groceries of various kinds.

Later in the day a few of us visited the Maryland prisoners. Their quarters were luxuriously fitted up, with Brussels carpets on the floors, mahogany furniture, and a fine library; at the same time, they had their own servants in attendance. The officers and citizens, with one exception, were not prisoners except in name, inasmuch as they had no guard placed over them. They had the freedom of the fort and were on terms of cordial intimacy with the family of the commandant. With such a pleasant mess, theirs must have been a regular clubhouse life, very enjoyable to look back upon in after years.

The authorities in Washington evidently entertained against our officer in rank, General Buckner, some bitter feeling; for by the explicit and positive orders of the secretary of war, he was kept in close confinement, the parole extended to all of his comrades in arms having been denied him, with the exception of a short walk every morning, which he took for exercise between two armed sentries. The commander of the fort was not responsible for this, for a kinder and truer gentleman, a more gallant or chivalrous officer, never lived than Colonel [Justin] Dimick. He was an old army officer, and had commanded at Old Point several years before, when that place was a fashionable pleasure resort. Some of us having met him in those happier days found no difficulty in recalling the erect, soldierly figure, the benevolent-looking face, and the kindly voice. In that large heart of his no bitterness, no malice, no sectional hate could find an abiding place. There was not a prisoner under his charge who did not learn to respect and love him, before a week had rolled over their heads. While doing his duty as a soldier, he did not sacrifice his humanity as a man.

Most of the first day our men spent in writing home to relatives and friends who lived within the Union lines. In their letters they were confined to business and family affairs, all political and war themes having been strictly forbidden. These communications were read by the garrison officers, and if there were found in them the slightest allusion to those subjects, the effusion was destroyed or handed back to the writer with an admonition to be more careful in the future.

A good many men were taken sick a day or two after reaching the fort. Several nearly shuffled off this mortal coil. Too much indulgence in rich food was the cause of it; though there were some who traced the primary cause back to "that tripe" eaten on the Fall River boat. Nothing but the skill and unremitting watchfulness of one of the political prisoners, Dr. Magill of Hagerstown, saved the lives of those who were so very ill that it was but touch and go with them. What a noble specimen of humanity that man was! Of Herculean stature, outspoken and fearless as a lion, yet with a heart and tender touch for the sick, as gentle as he was brave. Generally speaking, a Rebel private's life was considered comparatively nothing—only valued as so much finger power to pull a trigger, or as good food for powder. This good man sat up with those same worthless lives through the long hours of the night, watched the flickering pulses and nursed the wavering powers, with just the same fidelity and untiring devotion as if those poor soldiers had more than thanks with which to repay him, as if those lives were priceless.

A few days after our arrival, innumerable baskets, barrels, boxes, and packages of all sizes came pouring in for the prisoners, filled with clothes of all kinds, books, luxuries, indeed everything worn or eaten by man. Most of the freight was from Alexandria, Virginia, where the majority of the 17th had lived, though Baltimore, New York, and even Boston added a quota. We were overwhelmed with presents and were made the recipients of clothes sufficient to supply a brigade. All the fine citizen suits and underclothing left by the volunteers when they made their hasty exit from Alexandria were boxed up and forwarded promptly to Fort Warren. Several Dutchmen who had been taken prisoners found themselves appareled in broadcloth and fine linen such as they had never worn before. In fact, there was so much which the men could not use that they gave the garrison guards a good deal of clothing. Not only clothes were sent, but money, and some of us found our pockets full for the first time in many a long day.

The better class of prisoners who had funds formed a mess, and as there was a sutler at the fort, we lived like fighting cocks. The consequence was soon seen, as thin faces commenced to round out, stout figures began to change into fat ones; and in three weeks the difference between the hungry, gaunt crowd which made its way over the drawbridge and the well-dressed, lazy men sauntering about the fort was marked.

We find tares in all wheat—nothing is quite perfect in this world; and so in the Union loving, Hail Columbia, super loyal city of Boston there were actually Rebel sympathizers. They came on the steamer to visit us; but as such a procedure would have been contrary to military discipline, which permitted no visitors to enter the fort, their kind wishes took a more practical form in presenting each prisoner with a handsome gray uniform.

Those were halcyon days, those days of July 1862—light spots in a generally dark life. Our soldier prisoners so inured to hardship and want and suffering had now not a care on their minds, not a trouble in their hearts; they drew in long breaths of content, and could only sigh sometimes at the thought of the dark future, which was doomed to hold so marked a contrast to that perfect rest and satisfaction. It was too good to last long, that life of ours. Roll call in the morning at seven, breakfast at eight, cards, chess, conversation or reading until dinner, just as fancy listed; dinner at three, coffee and cigars at four; then came the post-prandial nap, at six an hour's stroll around the ramparts "en parole," or, if preferred, a bath in the briny deep; supper at eight, music until ten, then "taps." Such had been the order of our lives for three weeks, when the command was given to prepare to leave the next morning for Virginia.

Well, of course we were glad to go, and yet sorry. Two dry crackers a day washed down with parched corn coffee did not present quite an enlivening prospect. Then too everybody seemed to regret our departure. Our citizen prisoners would miss us dreadfully, for we stirred up the monotony of their quiet lives. The garrison guards would feel our absence, for many were the flasks of whiskey we had given them and clothes. The sutler who absorbed our money would gaze wistfully after our receding pockets, "all that was left of them"; while the Dutch girls employed by the garrison to do our washing and mending would cry their blue eyes out, we feared. They came to see us once more, poor Gretchens, and told us in broken English that they would think of us when we were across the rivers in that strange, dreadful country of Virginia. We swore as soon as the cruel war was over to return and marry every one of them, make them mistresses of a hundred slaves to do their bidding; and so they smiled through their tears.

Then the idea arose to celebrate the last night by giving those girls a dance. Colonel Dimick's consent was good humoredly accorded, with the proviso that the frolic should end at twelve. The mess room was selected for the scene of action. Word was sent to the Dutch maidens to come at eight exactly. The men were placed upon various committees, some to see the sutler and arrange about the supper, others to take down the stove and clear up the room, others yet to attend to the music. All worked with a will and promptly at the minute fun began. At ten supper was served, and in half an hour the dancing was renewed and kept up with a vim. Whiskey flowed like water, and the Dutch and English languages became so entwined thereby that it was an impossibility to distinguish one from the other. Every one talked enough and to spare, but no one understood any one else. As the fated hour approached, the revelry was at its height; the fiddlers played as only fuddled fiddlers could; the dancers shouted and swung each other; the lookers-on in excited tones urged them to renewed vigor; while the uproar made the rafters of the vaulted chambers fairly ring again.

Then the drum beat. "Lights out!" shouted the guard. The Cinderellas of the evening had touched the magic hour; the Prince's ball was over; not a moment's delay. Sad, tearful and hurried partings and protestations were sworn to in English and whispered in Dutch; when, presto, more quickly than the change of scene in a pantomime, the hall so brilliant in lights, so animated with moving figures, so resonant with music and joyous voices, was still, dark and empty, the banquet hall deserted.

Next day came the leave-takings. The Quartette Club, by sunlight, serenaded Colonel Dimick and his family, in that sweet farewell song of Schiller's, and afterwards every man of the "Rebel" line went up to the colonel, and out of a full heart and with dewy eyes thanked him for his undeviating kindness and generous consideration. He was touched by this gratitude and showed that he felt it. His sleep that night was not less sweet, doubtless, that so many Southern hearts held him in kindliest remembrance and had never the memory of one harsh act to bring against him in this world or the next.

Soon the farewell words were spoken and we went aboard the *Osceola*, a fine ocean steamship. The last we saw of the fort, the daughters of Dutchland, like so many black-eyed Susans, were still standing on the ramparts, waving their handkerchiefs. Gradually their figures faded in the distance and became invisible; and as the powerful strokes of the engine sent the boat surging ahead through the blue waters, Fort Warren looked like a speck in the horizon and then faded utterly away.

How We Resisted McClellan on the Peninsula

Allan B. Magruder,
Colonel, C.S.A. (General Magruder's Staff)

Philadelphia *Weekly Times* 3, no. 32, October 4, 1879

The unwritten history of the late war far exceeds in personal incident and in stirring interest aught that has yet appeared in official papers or in formal historical narrative. It is to rescue from oblivion and reproduce some historical events, characteristic incidents, personal reminiscences, adventures, scenes, and anecdotes that I write. The order of events naturally leads us to begin with some accounts of the Peninsular campaign in Virginia. Undoubtedly the hero of that campaign, from the Rebel point of view, was that gallant commander, the bold, eccentric, enterprising, and always brilliant general, John Bankhead Magruder, late of the United States Army and of high fame and gallantry in the Mexican War, and so well known throughout the country, especially to frequenters of Newport, Rhode Island, where he long commanded with his splendidly equipped battery attached to the First Regiment of the United States Artillery, stationed at Fort Adams. Early in the spring of 1861 General Magruder was sent by the Rebel military authorities at Richmond to take command of the new levies "raised and to be raised" for the defense of the Peninsula—that avenue to the Virginia capital which, it was justly supposed, the "enemy" would attempt to seize in their meditated march on Richmond. The writer was soon after ordered to report for service on General Magruder's staff. He well remembers the day on which he arrived, in obedience to orders, at Yorktown, then the "headquarters of the Army of the Peninsula." He found the general everywhere, directing, arranging, equipping, providing, organizing, and creating everything needed for efficient and thorough service in the impending campaign. Surrounded by a staff of young, ardent, active men, who, inspired by his presence and example, seemed willing, even to the highest point of emulation, to do everything in the great work of preparation for the stern strife impending. Their real inexperience kept them, notwithstanding, almost useless. Their ignorance and inaptitude sometimes sorely tried the patience of their chief, where long experience and training made him know everything and often led him personally, to do everything. Wearing a red fez cap, with a jaunty red-trimmed artillery fatigue jacket, with the inevitable pipe in requisition—sometimes mounted on a wiry, spirited sorrel charger which bore him gallantly during the whole war (a noble animal that knew and seemed to love his master, who actually took him with him subsequently to Texas and Mexico), supervising and energizing every department of his command, it was easy to see in our general one "every inch a soldier," in whom all recognized the "right man in the right place." The very presence of such a man was itself a perpetual reinforcement and was hopeful and inspiring in the extreme. Officers saw he was to be respected rather on account of his personal bearing and high qualities for command than for mere rank, and the men to whom he was always considerate and kind (though to support and maintain discipline he was firm even to sternness) were proud to obey him implicitly.

Many incidents in the campaign served to illustrate these qualities in our commander. Until officers and men are well known to each other, the personal bearing and manners of the former become like a good countenance in a stranger when first introduced to us—the best letter of recommendation. Subsequent acquaintance and experience may remove sometimes this agreeable first impression. It was never so with General Magruder. The qualities we admired in him at first were only intensified by subsequent observation of his military career. He combined above most men the opposite qualities of prudence and boldness in action. Nothing that intelligence, boldness, energy, resolution, and audacity could accomplish was too hard for him. Sent to guard the most vulnerable avenue to Richmond—the Confederate citadel—he was almost wholly unprovided by the government for this service. With no commissariat, no adequate transportation or organization in the Quartermaster Department, without cavalry—the "eyes and ears," as he was wont to say, "of an army in the field"—in the midst of a country without railroads or telegraphs, he seemed to be thrust forward into a position of great peril and responsibility, with no other resources than those he could himself create, or which might be drawn from a stout heart and a strong will.

The scanty preparations offered him for the impending campaign (consisting only of a few companies of raw troops, principally of the militia of Virginia and North Carolina, and a light battery of Richmond howitzers), was almost ludicrous. Nothing daunted, he commenced the efficient organization and equipment of his command and resolutely pursued and finally accomplished an active campaign, in which his faith and courage were rewarded by the achievement of the first field victory of the war against overwhelming odds at Great Bethel. This brilliant success inspired his small force with redoubled confidence in their chief, which suffered no abatement throughout his subsequent and successful strategic campaign against the grand army of [Maj. Gen. George B.] McClellan, splendidly equipped for service. It was his duty to defend that approach to Richmond. The enemy were to be kept back. How this was to be done the military authorities at Richmond seemed to think was no longer their affair after they had given the order.

We pass over the intermediate period from the fight at Bethel to the approach of the grand army of McClellan, which, landing at Fortress Monroe in April 1862, debouched from that point and marched, in all the assurance of conscious superiority, to overwhelm the little Army of the Peninsula, which presumed to dispute its advance. The perils of the situation at the time are well described in General Magruder's words as follows:

> Deeming it of vital importance to hold Yorktown, on York River, and Mulberry Island, on James River, and to keep the enemy in check by an intervening line until the authorities might take such steps as should be held necessary to meet a serious advance of the enemy in the Peninsula, I felt compelled to dispose my forces in such a manner as to accomplish these objects with the least possible risk under the circumstances of great hazard which surrounded the little army I commanded. I had prepared as my real line of defense positions in advance, at Harwood's and Young's Mills. Both flanks of this line were defended by boggy and difficult streams and swamps. In addition, the left flank, reaching to the York River, was defended by elaborate fortifications at Ship Point, connected by a broken line of redoubts, crossing the heads of the various ravines emptying into York River and Wormsley's Creek and terminating at Fort Grafton, nearly in front of Yorktown. The right flank was defended by the fortifications at the mouth of Warwick River and at Mulberry Island Point and the redoubts extending from the

The Army of the Potomac coming ashore at Fortress Monroe
(LIBRARY OF CONGRESS)

Warwick to the James Rivers. Intervening between the two mills was a wooded country about two miles in extent. This wooded line, forming the center, needed the defense of infantry in a sufficient force to prevent any attempt on the part of the enemy to break through it.

In my opinion this advanced line, with its flank defenses, might have been held by twenty-thousand troops. With twenty-five thousand I do not believe it could have been broken by any force the enemy could have brought against it. Its two flanks were protected by the Virginia on one side and the fortifications at Yorktown and Gloucester Point on the other. Finding my forces too weak to attempt the defense of this line, I was compelled to prepare to receive the enemy on a second line on Warwick River. This line was incomplete in its preparations owing to the fact that one thousand Negro laborers whom I had engaged in fortifying were taken from me and discharged by superior orders, in December last, and a delay of nine weeks consequently occurred before I could reassemble and reorganize the laborers for the engineers.

After two reconnaissances in great force from Fortress Monroe and Newport News the enemy, on April 3, advanced and took possession of Harwood's and Young's Mills. He moved in two heavy columns—one along the York Road and the other by the Warwick Road—and on April 5 appeared simultaneously along the whole front of our line from Minor's farm to Yorktown. I had no accurate data upon which to base an exact statement of his force, but from various sources of information I was satisfied that I had before me the enemy's Army of the Potomac, under the command of General McClellan (with the exception of the two corps d'armee of [Maj. Gen. Nathaniel P.] Banks and [Maj. Gen. Irvin] McDowell, respectively), forming an aggregate of certainly not less than one hundred thousand men, since ascertained to have been one hundred and twenty thousand men. On every portion of my lines he attacked us with a furious cannonade and with musketry, which was responded to with effect by our batteries and troops of the line. His skirmishers were also well thrown forward on this and the succeeding day, and energetically felt our whole line, but were everywhere repulsed by the steadiness of our troops. Thus, with five thousand men exclusive of the garrisons, we stopped and held in check over one hundred thousand of the enemy.

Every preparation was made in anticipation of another attack by the enemy; the men slept in the trenches and under arms, but to my utter surprise, he permitted day after day to elapse without an assault. In a few days the object of this delay was apparent. In every direction in front of our lines, through the intervening woods and along the open fields, earthworks began to appear. Through the energetic action of the government reinforcements began to pour in, and each hour the Army of the Peninsula grew stronger, until all anxiety passed from my mind as to the result of an attack upon us. The enemy's skirmishers pressing us closely in front of Yorktown, Brigadier General [Jubal A.] Early ordered a sortie to be made from the redoubts for the purpose of dislodging him from Palmentary's peach orchard. This was effected in the most gallant manner by the 2nd Florida, Colonel Ward, and 2nd Mississippi Battalion, Lieutenant Colonel [W. H.] Taylor, all under command of Colonel Ward. The quick and reckless charge of our men, by throwing the enemy into a hasty fight, enabled us to effect, without loss, an enterprise of great hazard against a superior force, supported by artillery, when the least wavering or hesitation on our part would have been attended with great loss. The Warwick line, upon which we rested, may be briefly described as follows: Warwick River rises very near York River, about a mile and a half to the right. Yorktown and Redoubts Nos. 4 and 5, united by long curtains and flanked by rifle-pits, form the left of the line, until at the commencement of the military road it reaches Warwick River, here a sluggish and boggy stream, twenty or thirty yards wide, and running through a dense wood fringed by swamps. Along the river are five dams—one at Wynn's Mill, one at Lee's Mill and three constructed by myself. The effect of these dams is to back up the water along the course of the river, so that for nearly three-fourths of its distance its passage is impracticable for either artillery or infantry. Each of these dams is protected by artillery and extensive earthworks for infantry.

After eleven days of examination the enemy seems very properly to have arrived at the conclusion that Dam No. 1, the center of our line, was the weakest point in it, and hence, on April 16 he made what seems to have been a serious effort to break through at that point. Early on that morning he opened at that dam a most furious attack of artillery, filling the woods with shells, while the sharpshooters pressed forward close to our lines. From 9:00 A.M. to noon six pieces were kept in constant fire against us, and by 3:00 P.M. nearly three batteries were directing a perfect storm of shot and shell on our exposed position. We had only three pieces in position at that point, but two of them could not be used with much effect and were rarely fired, so that we were constrained to reply with one six-pounder of the Troup Artillery, Cobb's Georgia Legion, Captain Stanley, under the particular charge of Lieutenant Pope. This piece was served with the greatest accuracy and effect, and by the coolness and skill with which it was handled the greatest odds against us were counterbalanced. By 3:30 P.M., the intensity of the cannonading increasing, heavy masses of infantry commenced to deploy in our front, and a heavy musketry fire was opened upon us. Under the cover of this continuous stream of fire an effort was made by the enemy to throw forces over the stream and storm our six-pounder battery, which was inflicting such damage upon them. This charge was very rapid and vigorous, and before our men were prepared to receive it several companies of a Vermont regiment succeeded in getting across and occupying the rifle-pits of the 15th North Carolina Volunteers, who were some hundred yards to the rear throwing up a work for the protection of their camp. This regiment immediately sprang to arms and engaged the enemy with spirit, under the lead of their brave but unfortunate commander, Colonel [Robert M.] McKinney, aided by the 16th Georgia Regiment; but when the gallant McKinney fell a temporary confusion was produced, which was increased by an unauthorized order to fall back. By this unfortunate mistake our men wavered, but at this critical moment, through the retreating North Carolinians, the 7th Georgia Regiment, Colonel [William T.] Wilson, of Anderson's Brigade, Toombs' Division, with fixed bayonets and the steadiness of veterans, charged the rifle-pits and drove the enemy from them with great slaughter, supported by the 8th Georgia, under Col. [Lucius M.] Lamar, and the companies of Captains Martin and Burke, under Major Norwood, of the 2nd Louisiana. Subsequently the enemy massed heavier bodies of troops and again approached the stream.

It was now evident that a most serious and energetic attack, in large force, was being made to break our center, under, it was believed, the immediate eye of McClellan himself; but Brig. Gen. Howell Cobb, who was in command at that point, forming the 2nd Louisiana, 7th and 8th Georgia, of Colonel Anderson's Brigade; the 16th and 24th Georgia and Cobb's Legion, in line of battle on our front, received the attack with great firmness, and the enemy recoiled with loss from the steady fire of our troops before reaching the middle of the water. Brig. Gen. [Lafayette] McLaws, commanding the Second Division, of which Cobb's command formed a part, hearing the serious firing, hastened to the scene of action and exhibited great coolness and judgment in his arrangements. The 10th Louisiana, 15th Virginia, a part of the 17th Mississippi and 11th Alabama were ordered up as reserves, and were placed in position, the 10th Louisiana marching to its place under a heavy fire, with the accuracy of a parade drill. The other regiments were assigned positions out of the range of fire. In addition, General McLaws placed the whole of his division under arms ready to move as circumstances might require. Colonel Anderson had led two of his regiments—the 7th and 8th Georgia—into action and held two others in reserve, while Brig. Gen. [Robert A.] Toombs advanced with his own brigade, under the immediate command of Brig. Gen. [Paul J.] Semmes, close to the scene of action, and by my order, having just arrived, placed two regiments of this brigade in action, retaining the rest as reserves. These dispositions rendered our position perfectly secure, and the enemy, suffering from his two repulses, and darkness put an end to the contest.

The enemy's loss, of course, cannot be accurately estimated, as the greater part of it occurred over on their side of the stream, but I think it could hardly have been less than six hundred killed and wounded. Our own loss was comparatively trivial, owing to the earthworks which covered our men, and did not exceed seventy-five killed and wounded. All the reinforcements which were on the way to me had not yet joined me, so that I was unable to follow up the action of April 16 by any decisive step. The reinforcements were accompanied by officers who ranked me and I ceased to command. I cannot too highly commend the conduct of the officers and men of my whole command, who cheerfully submitted to the greatest hardships and deprivations. From April 4 to May 3 this army served almost without relief in the trenches. Many companies of artillery were never relieved during this long period. It rained almost incessantly, the trenches were filled with water, the weather was exceedingly cold for this latitude; no fires could be allowed for fear of attracting the enemy's guns; the artillery and infantry played upon our men almost continuously day and night. The army had neither coffee, sugar nor a sufficiency of hard bread, but subsisted principally on flour and salt meat, and in reduced quantities, and yet no murmurs were heard. Their gallant comrades, the Army of the Potomac and the Department of Norfolk, though not for so long a time exposed to these trials, shared the hardships and dangers with equal firmness and cheerfulness.

I have never seen and I do not believe that there ever has existed an army (the combined Army of the Potomac, Peninsula, and Norfolk) which has shown itself for so long a time superior to all hardships and dangers. The best-drilled regulars would have mutinied under a continuous service in the trenches for twenty-nine days, exposed every moment to musketry and shells, in water to their knees, often without fire and without sugar and coffee or stimulants and with an inadequate supply of flour and salt meat. I speak of it in honor of these brave men, whose patriotism made them indifferent to suffering, to disease, to danger and death. Indeed, the conduct of the officers and men was such as to deserve throughout the highest commendation.

Riding Around McClellan's Army with Jeb Stuart

Richard E. Frayser,
Captain, 3rd Virginia Cavalry, C.S.A.

Philadelphia *Weekly Times* 7, no. 24, August 4, 1883

Near dawn on Thursday, June 12, 1862, [Brig. Gen. James Ewell Brown] Stuart, with portions of the 1st Virginia Cavalry, Col. [Fitzhugh] Lee; Jeff Davis's Legion, Colonel [William Thompson] Martin; 9th Virginia Cavalry, Col. [William H. F.] Lee, and two pieces of Stuart's horse artillery, started from camp near Richmond with the intention of making a reconnaissance in rear of the Federal army lying at that time on both sides of the Chickahominy River and menacing the Confederate capital.

The White House, situated immediately on the banks of the Pamunkey River, was in the possession of the United States forces and was held and used as their base of operations. This point of the Pamunkey is navigable for both steamers and sailing vessels and was admirably adapted for the purpose for which it was used. By an examination of a map of the Peninsula the reader will perceive that the distance from the White House to where the strength of [Maj. Gen. George B.] McClellan's army lay on the Chickahominy is about twelve miles. It will also give the reader a better idea as to the great peril in which Stuart placed himself after he began to penetrate the Federal lines, almost surrounded by navigable rivers and an alert enemy. The Richmond and York River Railroad passed at that time, as it does now, through the narrow strip of land lying between the Pamunkey and Chickahominy, which afforded the Federals all necessary transportation, but was not properly guarded.

Stuart was not only brave, but full of sagacity and vigilance. Before leaving camp he obtained some valuable information from scouts regarding the position and movements of the enemy and with respect to the condition of roads and fords. Little occurred of interest on the first day of the march which was bright and sunny with the foliage of the forest in full leaf and everything apparently propitious for the expedition. The command moved on the Brook Church Turnpike in the direction of the Rappahannock River. Reaching Winston's farm, near Taylorsville, Stuart, with his command, bivouacked for the night.

Near morning the firing of signal rockets announced the summons to horse and every man was quickly in the saddle. It was conjectured by many of the command that Stuart was en route to unite his forces with [Maj. Gen. Thomas J. "Stonewall"] Jackson in the Valley. But this notion was very soon dissipated by an attack on the enemy. Friday, the second day of the raid, opened with a cloudless sky, the air was soft and balmy and all nature had assumed a lovely aspect. In approaching Hanover Court House it was ascertained that it was in possession of the Federal cavalry. The pickets were driven in, and without stopping to make any resistance the whole force retreated on the road leading to Hawes' Shop. That daring leader, Col. Fitz Lee, by a flank movement, made an effort to capture this command, but failed.

The enemy halted near Hawes' Shop and formed in line of battle. But Fitz Lee very soon repulsed and scattered the Federals, who fled through forest and fields without much loss. It was there that Heros von Borcke, formerly in the Brandenburgischen Dragoons, Prussian army, who had very recently arrived and was serving as volunteer aide on General Stuart's staff, first attracted attention by his gallant bearing as an officer. And soon thereafter he won the esteem of all who witnessed his soldierly conduct. Drawing an immense saber he dashed forward in the midst of the charge upon the enemy. Some prisoners were captured in the skirmish, and the Confederates hastened on in pursuit of the retreating Federals, who never halted until after crossing the Tottapotomoy, a small stream spanned by a bridge and within a short distance of Old Church.

Passing through a deep ravine where the country road is narrow, with high and precipitous banks on either side and fringed with laurel and pine, Stuart found massed upon the summit of the hill the whole of the Federal cavalry; it was here he met a most determined resistance. A piece of artillery was placed in position and the road was shelled, but this failed in dislodging the enemy. Stuart, desirous of carrying this point, speedily ordered W. H. F. Lee forward with the 9th. The 3rd squadron of this regiment was composed of the Essex Light Dragoons, Captain [William] Latane and the "Mercer County Cavalry," L. Walker commanding. Captain

Latane charged at the head of the squadron and met the advancing Federals. As the two bodies clashed the Federal commander shouted, "Cut and thrust," and the gallant Latane yelled, "On to them, boys!" The 5th United States Regulars fought splendidly, but they could not long resist the 9th, which struck them like a thunderbolt. In this fight the brave and deeply lamented Captain Latane was killed while charging fifteen paces in advance of his squadron. The writer saw him after he fell in the road and while in the throes of death. A more daring and fearless spirit never drew saber. Captain [William B.] Royall, a gallant officer on the Federal side, was severely wounded.

The defeat and rout of the enemy at this point placed Stuart in possession of an immense camp, abundantly supplied with commissary and quartermaster stores, many of which were carried off by the Confederates. The rest, together with a large number of superb new tents pitched in the field near the roadside, were consumed by fire. Old Church had now been reached and the Federal cavalry had retreated in the direction of the Chickahominy and Stuart had penetrated far into the lines of the enemy, where he had cause to expect a most terrific attack at any moment. But he was cool and defiant.

Calling Capt. Richard E. Frayser, who subsequently became his chief signal officer and a member of his staff, General Stuart ordered him to take some men and go in advance of the column and report any movements of the Federals. Between Old Church and Tunstall's (the latter place is situated on the York River Railroad), some army wagons, loaded with stores, were captured, also teamsters, horses and mules belonging to them. As the command neared Tunstall's Captain Frayser reported a squadron of Federal cavalry drawn up in line of battle in a field and near the county road. The officer in command had evidently obtained some information as to the approach of Stuart and was on the qui vive. Taking his position in front of his command he hailed Frayser and interrogated him as to what command he belonged.

Captain Frayser being fully aware of the perilous situation of the officer and his command, and in order to detain both for capture, responded that he belonged to the 8th Illinois Regiment, said to be the finest in the Federal service at that time. Now this was a ruse to delay and entrap the Federal officer and his command and came near proving successful. But this truce was abruptly broken by the officer casting his eyes quickly to the right and discovering Stuart at the head of his column sweeping rapidly down upon him. He lost no time in giving the order, "Head of column to the right, wheel, march!" at the same time telling Frayser, in the most emphatic manner, to go to hell with his 8th Illinois Regiment. He moved off in a state of consternation with his command hurriedly on the county road leading to the White House.

Lieutenant W. T. Robins, with a detachment of the 9th Virginia Cavalry, charged an infantry force, consisting, perhaps, of more than one hundred men, occupying and guarding Tunstall's. After a very sharp and stubborn resistance the whole of this force was captured, together with all the military stores of the place. Before reaching Tunstall's, Stuart sent the Fourth Squadron of the 9th, under command of Captain [O. M.] Knight, consisting of the Lancaster Cavalry and Lunenburg Troop, with order to destroy some large transports with valuable cargoes at Putney Ferry, on the Pamunkey River; also wagons. This was done in the most satisfactory manner and they joined the column on its route. "Hab we got Richmond yet, boss?" asked a darkey, as he turned up his eye-ball in admiration of the cavalry; "if we ain't we soon shall, for McClellan and our boys is sure to fotch her."

It was late in the evening of the second day's march when Stuart reached Tunstall's, and as this was a very important point, he determined to inflict all possible injury upon the Federals. He halted his command and dismounted a large portion of it, although he was poorly prepared for the work before him. The cutting down of telegraph poles and tearing up of railroads without the proper implements is no holiday occasion. No sappers and miners accompanied Stuart on this expedition, so, in order to carry out his scheme of destruction, it became necessary for him to procure axes and picks from the neighboring farms, but the country had been so thoroughly pillaged by the Federals but few could be procured, and they were of the most inferior kind.

But with these the men went earnestly to work, and while engaged in it a train was discovered approaching from the direction of the Chickahominy with troops, and but a short distance off. The daring raider, ever ready for any emergency, quickly placed a large number of men armed with carbines on either side of the railroad and awaited in breathless silence for the train, which appeared as if reluctant to run the deadly gauntlet. It moved slowly, as if the captain of the train designed stopping it. Now putting on a full head of steam the train shot with the rapidity of an arrow through the heavy and destructive fire along the railroad and soon disappeared, going in the direction of the White House. Many of the troops on the train were killed, among them the engineer, who was shot by Capt. W. D. Farley.

Stuart being in a most perilous position could not long occupy Tunstall's, for he was within a few miles of the Federal base and not far removed from the head of McClellan's army. He had marched forty miles on this day and had whipped and demoralized the enemy in every encounter. About twilight his column was again in motion on the road leading to Talleysville. The burning of the transports and wagons illuminated the Northern horizon and rendered it a grand spectacle for an hour or more after nightfall. Col. W. H. F. Lee, after crossing the bridge spanning Black Creek, and who was in advance of the column, overtook an immense wagon train ascending Southern Branch Hill, which stretched out for miles on the road. The wagons contained commissary and quartermaster stores of every kind, which fell like ripe fruit into the hands of the Confederates, for there was no guard with it. The horses and mules were detached from the wagons and the latter, with all of their contents, were destroyed by fire. This was the most valuable capture made during this memorable raid.

Reaching Talleysville during the night, which is four miles from Tunstall's and about the same distance from the White House, Stuart halted for several hours to rest and put his column in proper shape. The raiders found some enterprising sutlers occupying Talleysville and carrying on a very profitable business, scarce as they supposed from the Confederates. All of their stocks, consisting chiefly of nice edibles, were quickly confiscated, and the sutlers were mounted on mules and informed that their destination was Libby Prison. This was a most opportune capture, for the men were nearly out of rations and just in the mood to appreciate such knick-knacks. At Talleysville, Stuart struck the old stage road leading from Richmond to Williamsburg, over which a large portion of the Confederate army had retreated in the evacuation of the Peninsula. After marching a mile or more on this road the head of the column filed into one leading to Providence Forge, a princely estate, a portion of which is situated on the Chickahominy River.

At Sycamore Springs, a contiguous plantation lying immediately above the one just mentioned, and which was noted for its great hospitality in the olden time, is a private ford, where the cavalry leader designed crossing the Chickahominy with his command into Charles City County, for he had been informed by reliable scouts before leaving camp near Richmond that the river at this point was fordable. But owing to heavy rains having fallen this ford was not in a condition to give such relief as the great exigency of the case required. On the approach of Col. W. H. F. Lee to the river he discovered an immense volume of water, which had overflowed its banks, rushing madly before him. This was, indeed a most startling surprise to the leader of the 9th. Here was an insurmountable barrier in the shape of a swollen river confronting him, with a powerful enemy menacing Stuart and his whole command with annihilation.

Capt. Jones R. Christian, of the 3rd Cavalry Regiment, who accompanied Colonel Lee as guide, and who resided at Sycamore Springs and was perfectly familiar with the locality and the ford, was unable to point out any relief, as he too was greatly disappointed in finding the river so high as to render it unfordable. This was, indeed, a most trying situation, but Lee determined on crossing the Chickahominy at this point at the peril of his life. After making a careful survey of the river and sounding the ford he, with others, plunged into the flood with the heads of their horses turned upstream. The effort to reach the opposite shore was a protracted one and came near resulting in the death of men and horses, for in swimming the river the feet of the latter became entangled in driftwood and roots of trees. Lee re-crossed the Chickahominy in the same manner and reported the scheme of swimming the river with the command as impracticable.

The next scheme was to construct a bridge at this point, if possible. Axes and other implements were procured and large trees standing on the banks of the river were felled in such manner that the tops might reach the opposite shore and thus form a substantial bridge.

But as they fell the current swept them down the stream as if they were reeds. This mode of escape was now abandoned and everything looked gloomy for the Confederates. At this juncture Stuart arrived. With eagle eye he at once saw his dilemma. The writer followed him from the time he began his campaigns in the Peninsula until he was cut down at Yellow Tavern, but never saw him the least excited under fire or elsewhere. When Stuart reached the ford he never dismounted. He sat erect in his saddle and occasionally caught hold of his long flowing beard, which was a habit of his when his schemes were not working smoothly. He did not long remain in this state of mind, for he very soon discovered a passage through which he and his whole command could escape. A mile or more below this ford on the Chickahominy, where the county road crosses the river leading from Providence Forge to Charles City Court House, were the ruins of Jones's Bridge, which had been destroyed by fire by the Confederates when this portion of the Peninsula was evacuated. The abutments and a few of the piers were all that remained of the old bridge, which Stuart at once determined to rebuild.

Working parties were organized and began to tear down an old farmhouse which stood in a field nearby, the timber of which suited admirably for the bridge. The great genius of Stuart was now fully evinced, and this was to be the grand achievement of the raid. Caesar-like, no trouble could abate his ardor or in the slightest manner affect his great presence of mind. The style of the bridge did not resemble the celebrated one of Caesar, over which youths sometimes rack their brain, but it was of sufficient strength for all to pass safely to the Charles City side. This impromptu structure did not exist long after being used by the Confederates, for the reason that [Col. Richard H.] Rush's Lancers, with other Federal troops, had followed in hot pursuit and were threatening Stuart's rear. The torch was applied, and the bridge was very soon consumed, which checked the advance of the enemy.

Among those who distinguished themselves in building the bridge, and whose names deserve to be recorded, are Captain [Redmond] Burke and Corporal [William H.] Hagan, who worked earnestly from the time the bridge was begun until it was finished. Without the services of these officers the column would have been long and dangerously detained, as it was in close proximity to the enemy. Corporal Hagan is deserving of more than a passing notice for his labors and justly merits all the praise and encomiums that can be given him. The corporal had won a name on the fields of Drainsville and Williamsburg for his coolness before the enemy, which had attracted the attention of Stuart, and he had already recommended him for promotion.

Stuart while at the ford at Sycamore Springs, already mentioned, sent a dispatch by Mr. Turner Dowswell, to General [Robert E.] Lee, giving him some account of his progress and of the important captures he had made. Mr. Dowswell had to pass through the Federal lines and he came near being taken prisoner. Stuart hurried on after reaching Charles City County, passed up on the north side of the Chickahominy, a distance of two miles, to Mr. Thomas Christian's residence; but although much fatigued he did not draw rein. He had now accomplished much in obtaining information as to the location and strength of the Federal army and was desirous of reaching the Confederate lines with all possible speed, and did not halt his column for rest until he reached the hospitable mansion of Judge Isaac H. Christian in the vicinage of Charles City Court House. Here he and his staff were received in the most cordial manner and entertained in princely style under some lovely shade trees in the yard. After partaking of some refreshments Stuart and his staff slept for several hours.

About twilight Stuart, after making all necessary arrangements with Colonel Fitz Lee, with whom he left his command at Buckland, the residence of Col. J. M. Wilcox, with instructions to follow at eleven o'clock that evening, left with Captain Frayser, his guide, and a courier for the headquarters of General Lee, near Richmond. The distance from Buckland to Richmond is about thirty miles, and the country through which he had to pass lay in the enemy's lines, and the route he took is known as the James River Road. While he was liable to capture by scouting parties he dashed over the road without the least fear.

At Rowland's Mill, about six miles from Charles City Court House, Stuart drew rein to quaff a cup of strong coffee, a favorite beverage of his, and to rest fifteen minutes or more; then springing in the saddle he galloped off in the direction of Richmond.

The writer never saw this dashing officer on an inferior horse, although he had been with him on many a long and weary march. As Stuart approached the neighborhood of White Oak Swamp with his guide and courier, he was in great danger of being captured or shot, for it is but a short distance from White Oak Swamp to the road upon which he was traveling at the time, and this was occupied by [Brig. Gen. Joseph] Hooker, with his command, who could have intercepted the bold raider without the slightest difficulty had he known of his approach. At this point he had the James very near him on the south and General Hooker on the north in uncomfortable proximity. But this never delayed Stuart a minute in his important mission. He moved rapidly on and arrived at Gen. R. E. Lee's headquarters before sunrise the following morning.

Before this he had given orders to Captain Frayser to see Governor John Letcher, for whom he had great esteem and admiration, and to report to him all he had done in making his reconnaissance. Captain Frayser, on his arrival in Richmond, repaired at once to the Executive Mansion; the servant, who met him at the door, informed him his Excellency was in bed and that he could not be seen at such an early hour; that later in the morning, when his toilet was made, he could be seen. Now Captain Frayser was under orders to report in person without delay and he insisted on an interview. He told the servant to tell the governor that a soldier from General Stuart's command was at the door with important dispatches and desired to see him. When this announcement was made all ceremony was at once waived and Captain Frayser was soon ushered into the presence of the governor.

On entering the bedchamber Captain Frayser had hurriedly communicated all that had been done; he arose to take leave, when the broken condition of his saber attracted the attention of the governor, and after learning how it happened in the raid he very kindly said to Captain Frayser, if he would call that day or the next he would give him an order on the officer in charge of the state arsenal for a superb one. Now a good saber is always prized by a cavalryman. The generous impulse which prompted this officer was duly appreciated, and Captain Frayser called and received the order from his Excellency and made his own selection out from a large collection of superior sabers at that time in the arsenal.

This raid was full of exciting incidents and will never be forgotten by those who participated in it. Col. Fitz Lee, with whom Stuart had left his command at Buckland, arrived within the Confederate lines in due time with all the prisoners and other captures that had been made on the expedition. This brilliant achievement of Stuart was heralded by the press throughout this country and Europe. The great military genius of this daring leader was at once recognized by the Confederate authorities by making him major general of cavalry, and who subsequently became one among the most distinguished leaders of the Army of Northern Virginia and a great friend of General R. E. Lee.

How McClellan, with a grand army, allowed Stuart to ride around him with only fifteen hundred cavalry is a mystery to the writer. In less time than two hours he could have thrown a sufficient number of troops into Tunstall's by the York River Railroad to intercept and crush the Confederates. Instead of having five thousand men here he only had the use of one hundred. Again, when Stuart passed into the Confederate lines between White Oak Swamp and the James, McClellan could have closed the only avenue of escape by ordering General Hooker, who occupied White Oak Swamp, the extreme left wing of his army, to extend his lines to the James. This would have closed the doors upon Stuart, and he and his whole command would have inevitably been captured or killed. McClellan had been on the Chickahominy but a short time when the raid occurred and must have been somewhat ignorant of the geography of the country through which Stuart passed, for he could have intercepted him at Tunstall's, and if Stuart had been compelled to retrace his steps from this point by the way of Old Church, his command would have been in great peril.

But McClellan never acted as if he understood the situation. He was struck so suddenly and with such violence at a vulnerable point that apparently he knew not how to act, and this stunning blow afforded Stuart a golden opportunity to prosecute his foray. If the reader will take a map of the Peninsula and examine it carefully he will at once see the many difficulties the Confederates had to overcome and the great peril to which they were exposed during the reconnaissance. The command, as it passed over the country roads, presented a most formidable appearance, and to persons unaccustomed to witnessing military displays its strength was estimated at five thousand men.

Stuart, on his return to camp at Braxton's, near Richmond, issued the following general orders:

> Headquarters Cavalry Brigade,
> June 16, 1862
>
> General Orders, No. 11
>
> The general of cavalry, profoundly grateful to Divine Providence for the signal success attending the late expedition to the enemy's rear, takes pleasure in announcing in orders his appreciation of the bravery and cheerful endurance of the command. History will record in imperishable characters and a grateful country remember with gratitude that portion of the 1st, 4th, and 9th Virginia Cavalry, the Jeff Davis Legion, and the section of the Stuart Horse Artillery engaged in the expedition. What was accomplished is known to the public and to the enemy, but the passage of the Chickahominy under existing difficulties furnishes a separate chapter of praise for the whole command.
>
> The general will despair of no enterprise when he can hold such guarantees of success as Colonels Fitzhugh Lee, W. H. Fitzhugh Lee, Martin, with their devoted commands. The loss of the gallant and heroic Captain Latane, leading his squadron and successful charge, was a severe blow to us, but the enemy, routed and flying before him, will bear witness to a heart intrepid and a spirit invincible, whose influence will not be lost after death, while his regiment will want no better battle cry for victory than "Avenge Latane!" Proud of his command, the general trusts that it will not lose sight of what is at stake in this struggle and the reputation its province to maintain.

In General Stuart's official report to Gen. R. E. Lee, dated June 17, 1862, he says, "Although the expedition was prosecuted farther than was contemplated in your instructions, I feel assured that the considerations which actuated me will convince you that I did not depart from their spirit and that the boldness developed in the subsequent direction of the march was the quintessence of prudence. The destination of the expedition was kept a profound secret (so essential to success), and was known to my command only as the actual march developed it."

At Old Church Stuart conferred with his officers as to the expediency of prosecuting the expedition farther. In his report he says:

> Here was the turning point of the expedition. Two routes were before me, the one to return by Hanover Court House, the other to pass around through New Kent, taking the chances of having to swim the Chickahominy and make a bold effort to cut the enemy's lines of communication. The Chickahominy was believed by my guide to be fordable near Forge bridge. I was fourteen miles from Hanover Court House, which I would have to pass if I returned. The enemy had a much shorter distance to pass to intercept me there; besides, the South Anna river was impassable, which still further narrowed the chances of escape in that direction. The enemy too, would naturally expect me to take that route.
>
> These circumstances led me to look with more favor to my favorite scheme, disclosed to you before starting, of passing around. It was only nine miles to Tunstall's Station, on the York River Railroad, and that point once passed I feel little apprehension beyond. The route was one of all others which I feel sure the enemy would never expect me to take. On that side of the Chickahominy infantry could not reach me before crossing, and I feel able to whip any cavalry force that could still be brought against me. Once on the Charles City side I knew you would, when aware of my position, if necessary, order a diversion in my favor on the Charles City road, to prevent a move to intercept me from the direction of White Oak Swamp. Besides this, the hope of striking a serious blow at a boastful and insolent enemy, which would make him tremble in his shoes, made more agreeable the alternative I chose. In a brief and frank interview with some of my officers I disclosed my views. But while none accorded a full assent, all assured me a hearty support in whatever I did.

In the Richmond *Dispatch* of June 16, 1862, we find the following in reference to this expedition:

> What, then, was the result? asked we of a wearied, dusty trooper, watering his jaded and faithful animal by a roadside spring. "The result?" We have been in the saddle from Thursday morning until Saturday noon, never breaking rein for breakfast. We have whipped the enemy wherever he dared to appear—never opposing more than equal forces. We have burned two hundred wagons laden

> with valuable stores, sunk or fired three large transports, captured three hundred horses and mules, lots of arms, etc., brought in one hundred and seventy prisoners, four officers and many Negroes, killed and wounded scores of the enemy, pleased Stuart and had one man killed, poor Captain Latane. This is the result, and three million dollars cannot cover the Federal loss in goods alone.

This raid gave General Lee the information he desired, for it disclosed McClellan's position on the Chickahominy and the advantages derived from it enabled him to strike that terrific blow which resulted so disastrously to the Federal arms in the Seven Days' fighting around Richmond, driving McClellan to Harrison's Landing, on the James, where he sought refuge under his gunboats, which raised the siege of Richmond and gave the people of that city temporary relief and much encouraged the Confederate forces.

The Second Battle of Manassas

HENRY KYD DOUGLAS,
MAJOR, C.S.A. (STAFF OF GENERAL JACKSON)

Philadelphia *Weekly Times* 2, no. 8, April 20, 1887

In closing his second article on Gettysburg ["Lee's Invasion of Pennsylvania," *The Century* 33, no. 4, February 1887], General [James P.] Longstreet mentions a little incident of the battle of the Second Manassas, which I find also in my notes of [Lt. Gen. Thomas J.] Jackson's campaigns. General Longstreet has done himself no more than justice, if that much, in his brief reference to it, and his article has suggested this. Soon after General [John] Pope took command of the Army of Virginia his famous military order from his "headquarters in the saddle" was republished in the Richmond papers. It gave rise to many comments not altogether complimentary. When it was read one day to General Jackson, he did not utter the questionable joke which is attributable to him by tradition, but at first a smile and then a strange expression went over his face—as one would say, "there's grim work ahead."

In the vicinity of Jeffersonton, during the artillery duel near Warrenton Springs, was held the council at which Jackson's movement across the Rappahannock was determined upon. A plain table was placed in the middle of an open field, with not even a tree within fifty yards to overhear the conversation. A map was spread upon the table, at which sat General [Robert E.] Lee, with Longstreet sitting on his right, Jeb [Maj. Gen. James Ewell Brown] Stuart sitting on his left, and Jackson standing opposite and in front of him. A group of staff officers were lounging on the grass of an adjacent knoll, and there was not an orderly present at the discussion. The council was brief. General Jackson called me, and as I drew near General Lee asked him if he

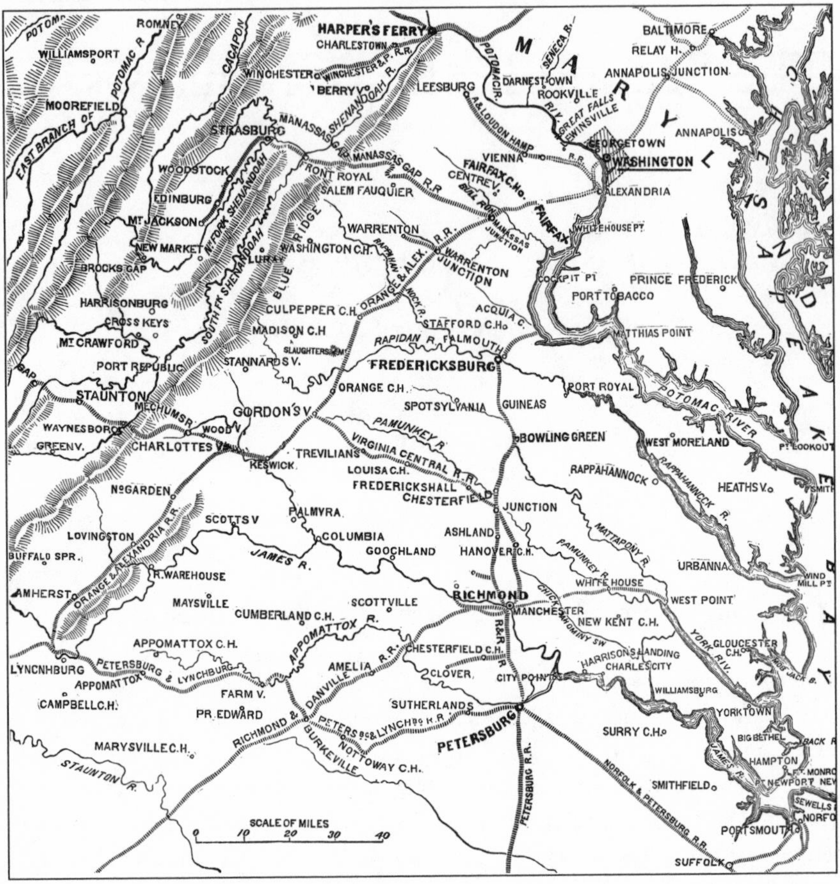

The seat of war, from Harper's Ferry to Suffolk, Virginia

(JOHNSON, *CAMPFIRE AND BATTLEFIELD*)

could start that afternoon. "In an hour," was the response, and he began to give me his orders for the command—to see each of the division commanders, to indicate the order of their march, to put the leading division in motion, and to direct its movements. Within the hour the corps was on the march, and in the distance might have been heard the bugle notes of Stuart calling his horsemen to the saddle.

It is not a part of this paper to follow Stuart's little dash at the enemy's center, which resulted in the capture of a train and General Pope's wagons. I remember the light of amusement on Stuart's face as he came galloping up, next day, to where General Jackson was sitting on a fence. As he drew up his horse and threw himself from the saddle, he unrolled a bundle which was tied behind it, and displayed a beautiful uniform coat, on the inside of which was marked, "John Pope, Major General." Stuart proceeded to report that about a week before a squad of Federal cavalry had surprised him in a house, had captured his hat and plume and nearly captured him; and then added with a jolly laugh, that he had a proposition to make to General Pope. Hunting up an appropriate piece of paper, he with assumed gravity wrote a communication substantially as follows:

> Headquarters Cavalry
>
> Major General John Pope Commanding,
>
> General: Your cavalry have my hat and plume; I have your best coat. I have the honor to propose a cartel for the exchange of these prisoners.
>
> Very respectfully,
> J. E. B. Stuart
> Major General
> Confederate States Army

The note was submitted to General Jackson for approval and amused him greatly. It was sent through the lines, and, I suppose, reached General Pope, who may or may not have been just then in the mood to appreciate its humor.

Nor do I desire now to repeat the movement of Jackson through Thoroughfare Gap, which had been left unguarded, nor the surprise of Bristoe Station, nor the night attack so handsomely made under Brigadier General [Isaac M.] Trimble and the capture of Manassas Junction with its immense collection of stores, nor the details of strategy by which Jackson forced the wedge of battle into the Federal lines until its point reached the old battlefield of Bull Run, where it was held in fearful pressure until relieved by Lee and Longstreet.

On the night of August 27, 1862, having distributed to the troops as many of the captured stores as they could carry, General Jackson destroyed the rest and moved out upon the plains of Manassas. The appearance of the marching columns was novel and suggestive. Commissary, quartermaster, and sutler stores enough for an army and for a campaign were carried along on the backs of soldiers wearied with marching and battle. Here one fellow bending beneath the weight of a score of boxes of cigars, smoking and joking as he went, another with as many boxes of canned fruits, another with coffee enough for a winter's encampment, or a long string of shoes hung around his neck like beads. Following Jackson, and with battle and sudden death near at hand, what did this martial masquerade mean?

On the morning of the twenty-eighth General Jackson put his corps in position near Sudley's Church and Groveton. He had no desire to bring on an engagement, for it was the obvious policy of the Federal commander to force one on him before he was reinforced by Longstreet. Consequently, after some preliminary shuffling of troops on both sides, an attack was made by General Pope late in the afternoon. A tough fight for several hours followed and the attack was repulsed, but not without a loss which we could not afford. Major General [Richard S.] Ewell, one of the best division commanders the war produced, was disabled, and his efficiency permanently impaired by the loss of a leg. Generals Trimble and [William B.] Taliaferro were badly wounded. On the same evening General Longstreet was engaged in forcing his way through Thoroughfare Gap, which, after Jackson passed, had been occupied by the enemy. It was vital that Longstreet should force a passage that day and he did it.

On the morning of the twenty-ninth the position of General Jackson was perilous in the extreme. His corps was strongly posted chiefly along a projected railway fronting the main position of the enemy, with its back toward its anxiously expected friends. The position was independent but not defiant; not inviting, but not avoiding an engagement. Having been reinforced during the night General Pope's policy was to attack at once. The morning passed away, but in the afternoon the assault was made handsomely and in great force. It failed again. Three or four times the solid columns of blue, gallantly led, came charging against our lines with staggering violence and were thrown heavily back. Each attack was weaker and each repulse more difficult—the Federals dispirited, the Confederates worn out. The situation grew more critical, and next to Longstreet, the most desirable thing was night. For the first time in my life I understood what was meant by "Joshua's sun standing still upon Gideon." No one knows how long sixty seconds are, nor what length of time can be crowded into an hour, nor what is meant by "leaden wings" unless he has been under the fire of battle and compelled to stay there and hold on with his teeth—so to speak—hour after hour and minute after minute, waiting, hoping and praying for reinforcements which will not come. On that day the sun would not go down; it stood still high over the field of Manassas, blazing and motionless.

During the afternoon I had an occasion to visit the line occupied by Major General [Alexander Powell] Hill. The last two attacks had been directed particularly against him, and the last one had been barely repulsed. One of his brigades was out of ammunition, and details from each regiment

Maj. Gen. John Pope
(PETER COZZENS COLLECTION)

were out on the field collecting cartridges from the boxes of the dead and wounded—friend and foe. His situation was a desperate one, for his command was not even afforded the protection of the railway embankment. He requested me to go to General Jackson and explain the situation of his force—worked down and out ammunition—and to say that if another attack was made he would do the best he could, but could not hope for a favorable result. These were weighty words when spoken by a man as bold and tough as Hill himself. I found the general [Jackson] and delivered the message. He was pale, serious, and calm, appreciating the responsibility he had taken and the peril of his situation. His eyes were cast longingly to the rear; they seemed to look into the distance, as if they would, like lodestones, draw Longstreet forward. All about him seemed to know the burden of his thoughts and wishes, but he gave no utterance to them. The silence in the group was oppressive and painful. The message from General Hill seemed to deepen the shadow on the general's face, but he answered promptly and sternly, "Tell him if they attack him again, he can and must beat them." As I started off he followed. We soon met General Hill coming to see General Jackson, and he repeated what he had said to me. They both glanced at the sun—it was slowly moving downward. Jackson then said calmly, "General, your men have done nobly. I hope you will not be attacked again; but if you are you will beat the enemy back." As he spoke a sharp fire of skirmishers broke along Hill's front. "Here it comes," he said, and, as he dashed away, Jackson called after him, "I'll expect their repulse." The attack was rapid and fierce, but soon over. In a few minutes we heard our well-known yell, and knew the work was done. And then came a staff officer, saying the attack had been repulsed. "Tell him I knew he would do it," said Jackson, gently, with a smile. This was the spot where a year ago before he had won the name of "Stonewall"; on this day the title was confirmed.

Just as the last attack was made on Hill's Division, Longstreet's advance (the headstrong Hood in front) marched with rapid and steady stride upon the field, and were quickly thrown into line on Jackson's extreme right. Hood, always hot for battle, pushed forward his skirmishers and prepared to turn loose his Texans upon the enemy. The line became engaged, but not severely. I believe General Lee at first intended to assume the offensive from Longstreet's front, but doubtless, at the suggestion of the latter, as he says, the commanding general abandoned the intention, and only ordered a forced reconnaissance. With this reconnaissance the day's fighting ended, and the sun had gone down at last.

Saturday morning, August 30, was clear and warm. The stillness was as the repose of the thousand dead and the resigned silence of the thousand doomed. The morning passed and noon also, with nothing to disturb the peace except an occasional picket shot and the constant marching and counter-marching of the Federal infantry. General Lee remained on the defensive, but impatiently, for he believed in offensive strategy and bold tactics. Jackson himself was not more aggressive than General Lee. Today General Jackson did not believe the battle would be renewed, for he did not think General Pope would hazard a general attack. Between 1:00 and 2:00 P.M. he was sitting on the ground with his back against a straw stack, writing a note to General Lee, in words like these, "Notwithstanding the threatening movements of the enemy, I am still of the opinion, expressed this morning, that he does not intend to attack us. If he does—" and here the note ended. Just then there was a shot of artillery and some skirmish firing. General Jackson arose hastily and handing over the unfinished note, said, "That's the signal for a general attack." We mounted and rode rapidly to the position occupied by his old division (General [William E.] Starke) against which he expected the chief assault to be made. Before reaching the line the roar of artillery and musketry told us that the battle was joined in earnest. Just then the general's horse, a little bay, captured the day before, refused to go forward against his old friends. Spurs could not overcome his loyalty or his cowardice. Dismounting quickly, the general said, "Let's trade horses and you ride rapidly to General Longstreet and ask him for a division." He climbed into my saddle by stirrups one-third too long for him, and left me to mount his horse by stirrups equally too short for me.

As the general disappeared in the wood I turned my new steed in the direction of General Longstreet. The wretched beast at once ran off with me, and I cannot believe the war furnished an instance of an order carried with such velocity. But the sight of it was more ludicrous than heroic. The stirrups were of no use to me and I had been happier on the horse's bare back. But away we went like a shot, over bushes and ditches and fallen trees and dead horses, along the rear of Lee's and Crutchfield's artillery, amid bursting shells, which made my brute more frantic and my situation thereon more precarious. The distance was soon done. I found General Longstreet on the left and in front of his line watching the attack and making his dispositions. The assault was entirely against Jackson's Corps, and principally against Starke's Division. When I delivered Jackson's message, "Certainly," replied General Longstreet; "but before the division can reach him that attack will be broken with artillery." General Longstreet says he received a similar message from General Lee by a courier. This must have been after I delivered that of General Jackson. At any rate he hurried off a staff officer for [Maj. Gen. David R.] Jones's Division and just then two batteries came galloping up the hill. He requested me, while waiting for Jones's Division, to direct the firing of one of them.

The position taken by these batteries being still more on the flank of the enemy than the artillery of Crutchfield and [Stephen D.] Lee, was a very favorable one. They were soon at work sending a storm of shell crashing through the thickets and into the front and flank of the assaulting columns. The diversion was most timely. The charging Federals had rushed through the destructive fire up to the very bank of the railway, from which the decimated lines of the old division were pouring such a fire upon them as their scanty ammunition permitted, and Starke's Louisianans, out of cartridges, were hurling clubs and rocks upon their assailants. But this demoralizing attack of artillery did its work effectively. The assaulting line halted, was thrown into confusion and then fled. In their place came another line with the same disastrous result. And then again a splendid column of attack, compactly formed, came grandly on their determined work. By this time, Longstreet's artillery well in position, with that of Lee and Crutchfield awaited the angry onset. When the blue line was within proper range, these hoarse hounds of war were unleashed and the destruction they did was fearful. Deep rents were torn in the ranks, colors went down, the charge was utterly broken and the retreat which followed was soon a wild rout. The avenging shot and shell pursued and overtook the fleeing mass, scattered them and added to the panic of the flight. The dead strewed the field and now the thin line of Jackson's Corps, revived by their success, became the pursuers and added their scattering but careful fire to the destruction made by the artillery.

As the enemy's line was broken Jones's Division arrived on the hill occupied by General Longstreet, was promptly thrown into line and moved against the retreating foe. I had joined General Jackson as soon as I saw General Jones's Division would not be needed. General Longstreet advanced his whole line to the attack, and a little while after a staff officer came from him to General Jackson, congratulating him upon the result and offering troops. "Tell General Longstreet," he replied, with a smile, "I am obliged to him, but I don't need assistance; if he gets hard pressed I'll send him some reinforcements." Where he would have found them is more than I can tell. The pursuit was continued until long after dark and the enemy driven beyond Bull Run.

The Fifth Corps at Manassas

J. S. Slater,
Corporal, 13th New York Volunteer Infantry

Philadelphia *Weekly Times* 8, no. 30, September 13, 1884, and no. 32, September 27, 1884

When [Maj. Gen. Fitz John] Porter reported to [Maj. Gen. John] Pope for duty the V Army Corps lay near Warrenton Junction, at the end of a hard day's march. [Maj. Gen. Nathaniel P.] Banks, with his corps, was then supposed to be on the road from Fayetteville in the direction of Bealeton; [Maj. Gen. Irwin] McDowell's Corps and [Maj. Gen. Franz] Sigel's Corps were along the Warrenton Turnpike in the direction of Gainesville; [Maj. Gen. Joseph] Hooker and [Maj. Gen. Jesse L.] Reno, with the remainder of the troops then serving under Pope, were along the Orange & Alexandria Railroad in the vicinity of Bristol and Manassas Junction.

The Confederate [Maj. Gen. Richard S.] Ewell, with his division, was near Bristol, where he had been engaged with Hooker in the afternoon, after which he retired in the direction of Manassas, where were [Maj. Gen. Ambrose P.] Hill's and [Lt. Gen. Thomas J.] Jackson's divisions. The fact that Ewell fell back, after having been attacked, led General Pope to suppose that he had been defeated (when the fact was that he was simply maneuvering for position) and hence Pope's order of 6:30 P.M., August 27, to General Porter, directing that the V Corps should start at 1:00 A.M. so as to be upon the ground (at Bristol) by daylight. At the same time Porter was informed that the enemy had been driven back, but were retiring along the railroad.

The object of the movement, as stated, was to drive the foe from Manassas and clear the country between Manassas and Gainesville, where McDowell was supposed to be. Orders were also sent to [Maj. Gen. Philip] Kearny, Reno, and McDowell to hurry to the same point (Bristol) to aid in

Maj. Gen. Fitz John Porter
(RAY D. SMITH COLLECTION, SEYMOUR LIBRARY, KNOX COLLEGE)

"bagging" Jackson (who was not there), and all were required to be on hand with Porter at daylight. Porter had about ten miles to march over a road blocked up with wagons, the trains of Pope's army; the others (Kearny and Reno) but four or five miles through an unobstructed country. Owing to the fatigue of his men, the excessive darkness, and the obstructed roads, Porter, acting upon the advice of his division and brigade commanders, changed the hour for starting from 1:00 to 3:00 A.M., at once notifying Pope of the fact and of the reasons for so doing, the latter taking no exception at the time. At 3:00 A.M., then, the V Corps started and reached Bristol between 7:00 and 8:00 A.M., almost simultaneously with the commands of Kearny and Reno, which had marched only half the distance, while McDowell, for some reason, failed to get up at all, as ordered.

The movement proved unnecessary. In fact, the concentration of troops at that point was just what ought not to have been effected, for it withdrew the last Federal soldier from the very position which Jackson, who had been joined by Ewell, had selected for his prospective battlefield and where he intended to await the arrival of Longstreet. General Pope charged Porter with disobedience of the order in question. He apparently forgot that the V Corps marched ten miles while Kearney and Reno were marching five under equally imperative instructions, and forgot also that McDowell neglected to obey the order at all.

Marching by torchlight (an advantage Porter's men lacked) (CENTURY MAGAZINE)

It was alleged by Porter that nothing could have been gained by starting at 1:00 A.M.—that the intense darkness would have prevented his troops from reaching the designated point in proper condition to meet an enemy. But Pope maintains the night was not dark. [Major] General John F. Reynolds, however, who was a witness on the court-martial of General Porter, said of that night: "It was a very dark night, so was the succeeding night. I recollect both of them distinctly from having been about a good deal until after midnight on each night."

The afternoon of the twenty-eighth Pope was hunting for Jackson in the vicinity of Centreville, where the latter had been, while some of the choicest Union soldiers were being cut in pieces in the direction of Groveton and Gainesville. On this same day McDowell, who had been ordered to move with his whole corps on Manassas Junction as expeditiously as possible, so far violated the order as to detach one division (James B. Ricketts') to Thoroughfare Gap to oppose Longstreet, who was reported as coming through. But Pope appears to have tacitly accepted the idea of this movement, for McDowell was never censured for directing it.

On the morning of the twenty-ninth, after sunrise, Porter, still at Bristol, received the following:

> Headquarters Army of Virginia,
> Near Bull Run, August 28, 1862, A.M.
>
> General: McDowell has intercepted the retreat of Jackson. Sigel is immediately on the right of McDowell. Kearny and Hooker march to attack the enemy's rear at early dawn. Major General Pope directs you to move upon Centreville at the first dawn of day with your whole command, leaving your trains to follow. It is very important that you should be here at a very early hour in the morning. A severe engagement is likely to take place and your presence is necessary. I am, General, very respectfully, your obedient servant,
>
> George D. Ruggles
> Colonel and Chief of Staff
> Major General Porter

Very soon after the above was dispatched Pope found out two very important facts, viz: First, that McDowell had not intercepted the retreat of Jackson, but that Ricketts, in falling back from Thoroughfare Gap, without orders, after he had been sent there, had opened that mountain gateway for

Longstreet who was rapidly pushing eastward along the Warrenton Turnpike to the support of Jackson. Second, Pope learned that if the enemy had a "rear" it was so securely concealed that he was unable to discover, much less attack it. The truth is that when the order above quoted was issued Jackson's command, reunited, lay north of and nearly parallel to the Warrenton Turnpike, from near Sudley Springs westward in the direction of Groveton, along the line of the abandoned Independent Railroad. He had no more idea of retreating than had the mountains looking down upon him.

Such being the real situation, any soldier can readily perceive how important it was to send the Fifth Corps seven or eight miles away from the scene of action, when it could be of no possible use in case of battle.

General Porter, immediately upon receipt of the order, although greatly wondering at its requirements, put his troops in motion, leaving Pope squat, as before the hole of a groundhog, waiting for the animal to come out and be caught.

The head of column of the corps had already passed Manassas Junction some distance on the way to Centreville, where its commander received the following, first verbally, subsequently, after he had begun the required movement, in writing:

> Headquarters Army of Virginia
> Centreville, August 29, 1862
>
> Push forward with your corps and King's Division, which you will take with you, upon Gainesville. I am following the enemy down the Warrenton Turnpike. Be expeditious, or we will lose much.
>
> John Pope
> Major General Commanding

When the foregoing reached General Porter, [Rufus] King's Division, that had really been on Jackson's right, near Groveton, had by some strange fatality been permitted to leave that position and was at Manassas Junction, and Ricketts, with McDowell's other division that had been hunting after the enemy's rear, was falling back from Thoroughfare Gap in a southeasterly direction, while [Brig. Gen. John F.] Reynolds, with the Pennsylvania Reserves, the remaining division of the III Corps, was upon the left of Sigel, south of the Warrenton Turnpike and a little south of west from Groveton, forming the extreme left of Pope's line which extended eastward towards Centreville, parallel to Jackson's and mostly north of the pike.

Porter at once countermarched and set his troops in motion upon the road to Gainesville. Returning to Manassas Junction the corps halted long enough to obtain a fresh supply of ammunition (but no food) and heading westward pushed on, leaving King's Division to follow. It was no wonder that General Porter should have been surprised at the conflicting orders received.

The day previous Pope had ordered McDowell first to Manassas Junction, then to Centreville, then to Gum Spring, Jackson having all the time been elsewhere than at either of those places, and on the morning of the twenty-ninth, at about the time the 3:00 A.M. order was being written, McDowell (who was alleged to have intercepted Jackson's retreat) was leaving the immediate scene of hostilities and on the march with one of his divisions (King's) for Manassas Junction. Ricketts, with another division, was floating around loose, nobody but himself knowing his exact whereabouts. Reynolds, in command of the remaining divisions of the corps, continued to hold his position near the Warrenton Turnpike, west of Groveton, upon the left of Sigel, but even he was not in a condition to have intercepted Jackson had the latter attempted to retreat in the direction of Thoroughfare.

The distance from Manassas Junction to Gainesville is eight miles, from Gainesville to Thoroughfare Gap six miles, and from Gainesville to Groveton, which lies eastward on the Warrenton Turnpike, about three miles. The V Corps, moving south of the Manassas Gap Railroad, which intersects with the pike at Gainesville, pushed forward beyond Bethlehem Church (where a road turns off northward towards Sudley Springs) and a little before noon reached Dawkin's Branch, an insignificant water course, one and one-half or two miles from the church, or about halfway between Manassas Junction and Gainesville, the point aimed at.

As the advanced regiments ascended a gentle rise of ground overlooking towards the west the small narrow valley of the stream, they were fired upon by the enemy, whose skirmishers occupied the opposite heights, and first a small howitzer, then two rifled guns were run up and opened, the shells striking in the first brigade of [Maj. Gen. George W.] Morell's division, killing and wounding several of the men. Considerable bodies of the enemy's troops were distinguishable, infantry as well as artillery and there was every indication of a large force in that vicinity. My own regiment (the 13th New York) happened to be at the extreme front of the brigade and was put in line immediately after the firing began, a short distance down the slope, the other regiments and batteries being in the rear upon and just over the crest.

We had scarcely assumed this position when General Porter directed our Colonel [Elisha G.] Marshall to advance us beyond the branch and deploy as skirmishers. The movement was expeditiously made; we crossed the bed of the water course (which was then dry, or so nearly so that water could not be found to fill a canteen), and there the colors and reserves remained while the skirmishers were sent out covering our front. Meanwhile the guns, which had opened upon us from our right front, had been silenced by one of our own batteries; but other pieces began a fire upon us from yet further on our right, and the 62nd Pennsylvania, of [Brig. Gen. Charles] Griffin's Brigade, was deployed as skirmishers in that direction, joining their line with ours.

Such was about the situation when General McDowell made known to Porter the terms of the joint order, which reads as follows:

Headquarters Army of Virginia,
Centreville, August 29, 1862

[General Order, No. 5]

Generals McDowell and Porter:

You will please move forward with your joint commands towards Gainesville. I sent General Porter written orders to that effect an hour and a half ago. Heintzelman, Sigel and Reno are moving on the Warrenton turnpike and must now be not far from Gainesville. I desire that as soon as communication is established between this force and your own the whole command shall halt. It may be necessary to fall back behind Bull Run, at Centreville, tonight. I presume it will be so, on account of our supplies. I have sent no orders of any description to Ricketts, and none to interfere in any way with the movements of McDowell's troops, except what I sent by his aide-de-camp last night, which were to hold his position on the Warrenton pike until the troops from here should fall upon the enemy's flank and rear. I do not even know Ricketts' position, as I have not been able to find out where General McDowell was until a late hour this morning. General McDowell will take immediate steps to communicate with General Ricketts and instruct him to rejoin the other divisions of his corps as soon as practicable. If any considerable advantages are to be gained by departing from this order it will not be strictly carried out. One thing must be held in view, that the troops must occupy a position from which they can reach Bull Run tonight or by morning. The indications are that the whole force of the enemy is moving in this direction at a pace that will bring them here by to-morrow night or next day. My own headquarters will be for the present with Heintzelman's Corps, or at this place.

John Pope
Major General Commanding

When this order reached General Porter, with McDowell, the former, as has been shown, was already carrying out the previous instructions to move on Gainesville; in fact, he had progressed so far as to bring his command in actual contact with the enemy and to impel McDowell to say, "Porter, you are too far out; this is no place to fight a battle." The two generals held a consultation, and after they had ridden towards the right and returned, McDowell left, subsequently sending back the message, "Give my compliments to General Porter and say I am going to the right and shall take King with me. He (Porter) had better remain where he is, but if necessary to fall back; can do so on my left."

Now, it must be remembered, that the main requirement of the "joint order" was that the corps of Porter, with King's Division, should form a junction with the extreme left of the army under Pope, and which, as already stated, consisted of the Pennsylvania Reserves under General Reynolds. Between Reynolds and the V Corps (both being south of the pike) there was a gap of two and one-half or three miles, the intervening country being impracticable for the direct movement of troops across it. This was the opinion of General Reynolds himself, who, on the twenty-eighth, had ridden over it to ascertain its character. He says: "On the morning of the twenty-eighth, after passing Gainesville for a short distance—less than a mile—my column was directed to the right to march on Manassas. I intended to march in as open order as possible, but found the country such that I put my command in three columns, one brigade in each column, with the artillery in the interval, and marched in that formation for probably a mile or mile and a quarter in the direction of Manassas. The country there became so broken, wooded and obstructed that I had to turn into a road leading along the railroad from Gainesville to Manassas Junction, and finally marching on that road, in one column, around to Bethlehem Church, towards the old battle-field of Bull Run, late in the evening."

When McDowell left Porter he started with the intention of placing King's Division in the interval between the V Corps and the Pennsylvania Reserves. This is made evident not only by his instructions to Porter that if found necessary he should fall back on his (McDowell's) left, but by his subsequent movements King's Division (the cross country route being impracticable, as stated by General Reynolds) was marched by way of the Bethlehem Church road north towards Sudley Springs, until it reached the Warrenton pike at the "Old Stone House," where the two thoroughfares intersect at a right angle, and then the head of column was turned westward.

Regarding the further movements, General McDowell, in his report to Pope of operations says: "Immediately on my arrival with King's Division I directed it to move forward and take place on the left of Reynolds, then still engaged on the left of Sigel's Corps, and some of the brigades went forward to do so, when I received your instructions to order the division over to the north of the turnpike to support the line held by Reno, which had been hotly engaged all day, and the division was recalled and brought back to the Sudley Springs road for that purpose."

Thus it appears that Pope himself was responsible for the failure of his own plans. His order to McDowell to take King's Division north of the pike not only prevented its being put in on Reynolds' left as the joint order contemplated, and where it would have been able, in connection with the V Corps, to have assumed the offensive with some prospects for success, but took it so far away that it could not be used in support of either Porter or Reynolds, who occupied the extreme left.

During the afternoon, after McDowell left, taking with him more than half the force deemed necessary for Pope to successfully attack the right and rear of Jackson, the V Corps held its position on Dawkin's Branch, making such demonstrations as were essential to keep the enemy in check and prevent Longstreet from precipitating his command upon the Union soldiers confronting Jackson. Just before sundown we heard the sounds of a sharp engagement on our right, but some distance away. The firing continued for probably an hour, finally ceasing shortly after night cast over the earth her mantle of darkness.

We did not know at the time whose troops were engaged, but subsequently learned that a portion of King's Division, under [Brigadier] General [Edward] Hatch, piloted by McDowell, under Pope's order to move north of the pike and, subsequently, to "pursue the enemy" (Jackson) who was supposed to be in retreat, had come in contact with a part of Longstreet's force near Groveton, but considerably to the right of Reynolds and been driven back with severe losses.

There is the conflict (against bringing on which Hatch protested), for not taking part in which the V Corps, through its commander, has been so severely censured by Pope. But had we been given an open country and smooth, broad roads and been pushed to the uttermost, we should have arrived too late even had we started at the first sounds of the guns.

McDowell had demonstrated the impracticability of the cross-country route by not attempting it; but more important still, we were confronted by a force superior to our own, to have attacked which would have been folly, under the circumstances, and to have withdrawn from before which would have brought on the very disaster we were helping to avert. A movement to the rear, such as had been made by McDowell, would also have laid us open to the accusation of Pope that we retreated to the sounds of the enemy's cannon. Further, had we marched to the assistance of our comrades on our right, who were at least three miles distant, it would have taken us away from the enemy's flank and placed us nearly opposite his center, thus uncovering Reynolds and leaving open the country between him, Gainesville and Manassas Junction for Longstreet's passage to our rear.

It is now generally conceded that Longstreet was in our front that day, but was his presence known at the time? Pope denied and to this day denies that he was there, upon what grounds it is difficult to understand. He knew or ought to have known that the Confederate right wing, with Lee himself personally present, had passed through Thoroughfare Gap on the day previous, the twenty-eighth, and this fact was doubtless reported by General Ricketts of McDowell's Corps, on the evening of that day. He says, "On the twenty-eighth, being ordered to assist Colonel [Percy] Wyndham, who at 10:15 A.M. reported the enemy passing through Thoroughfare Gap, marched from New Baltimore through Haymarket, where the troops were relieved of their knapsacks to hasten the movement, but before reaching the Gap, about 3:00 P.M., met Colonel Wyndham's skirmishers retiring before the enemy, already in possession."

Now, it is only six miles from the Gap to Gainesville, and early on the morning of the twenty-ninth General John Buford, of our cavalry, had reported to General McDowell, who informed General Porter, when they met at Dawkin's Branch, that seventeen regiments of infantry, one battery and five hundred Confederate cavalry (the advance of Longstreet's command) had passed eastward through Gainesville that morning before nine. More convincing still, a number of Longstreet's men had been captured by scouting parties from the V Corps, all of which went to satisfy Porter and every man under him that the enemy, in force, was in his immediate presence. That such was in fact the case is shown by abundant testimony.

General John F. Reynolds, who, it is to be remembered, was on the extreme left of Pope's line and nearest Porter, said in his testimony given

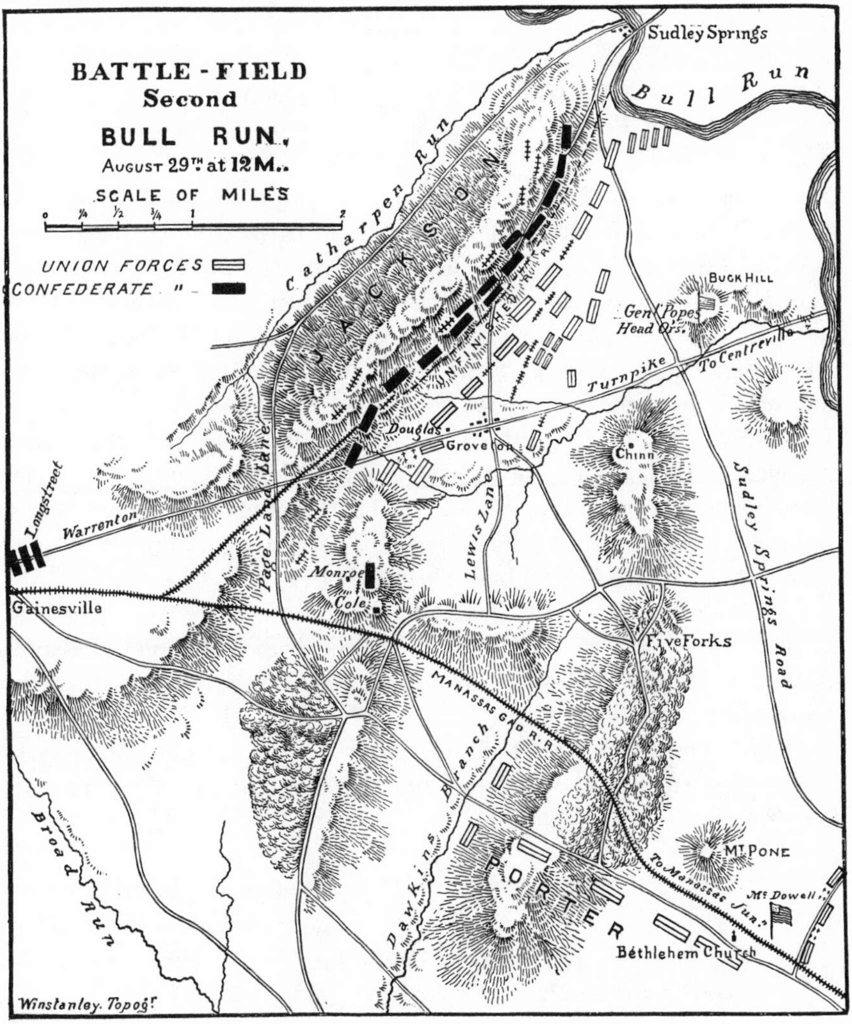

Situation at noon, August 29 (CENTURY MAGAZINE)

before the court-martial that between noon and 1:00 P.M. in the day (the twenty-ninth) he was compelled to change from front to rear on the right to meet the enemy coming down the pike from the direction of Gainesville. And again: "I think his (the enemy's) position was partially between myself and the position occupied (by Porter), as far as I can judge." And the same authority states that the force of the enemy he considered a pretty heavy one, and that it extended beyond his (Reynolds') left flank, across the pike, the movement having begun between noon and 1:00 P.M., when the Confederate leader began throwing troops out on Jackson's right as they came up and extending them right out along the ridge and across the pike towards Porter's position on the one he was supposed to have occupied.

General Lee, the Confederate commander-in-chief, says: "Longstreet's command arrived within supporting distance of Jackson on the twenty-ninth of August, 1862, and his line was formed by noon, General [John Bell] Hood's Division crossing the Gainesville turnpike and General D. R. Jones' Division the Manassas Gap Railroad." And again: "It was after 12 M. when General Stuart reported the approach of a column of troops which threatened our right (Brig. Gen. D. R. Jones), and [Brig. Gen. Cadmus C.] Wilcox, with his three brigades, was sent to reinforce it." Still later General Lee wrote: "Porter could not take Jackson in flank while he was attacked in front. He could do nothing of that sort. I was there then. I saw Porter approach. I went out and reconnoitered his corps and made proper dispositions to meet it. We flanked him. He could not flank Jackson."

Generals Longstreet, Wilcox and others confirm the foregoing statements of their chief, all of which goes to clinch the testimony of General Reynolds and other Union officers who sustain Porter in his assertion that Longstreet was in his front that day.

About dusk, while the conflict between Hatch and Hood was progressing on our right, General Porter received the famous 4:30 P.M. order, which reads:

Headquarters in the Field,
August 29, 1862—4:30 P.M.

Your line of march brings you in on the enemy's flank. I desire you to push forward into action at once on the enemy's right flank, and, if possible, on his rear, keeping your right in communication with General Reynolds. The enemy is massed in the woods in front of us, but he can be shelled out as soon as you engage their flank. Keep heavy reserves and use your batteries, keeping well closed to your right all the time. In case you are obliged to fall back do so to your right and rear, so as to keep you in close communication with the right wing.

John Pope,
Major General Commanding
Major General Porter

Before this reached Porter, however, he had ordered an attack, upon receipt of information from the right that the enemy were retreating, as follows:

> General Morell: I wish you to push up two regiments, supported by two others, preceded by skirmishers, the regiments at intervals of two hundred yards, and attack the party with the section of artillery opposed to you. The battle looks well on our right and the enemy are said to be retiring up the pike. Give the enemy a good shelling when our troops advance.
>
> F. J. Porter,
> Major General

General Morell began to execute this order, at the same time expressing his opinion that the news of the enemy being in retreat was erroneous and that an action brought on under the existing state of affairs could but result disastrously to the Union arms.

General Porter made a personal examination of the situation in his front, and satisfied of the impropriety of bringing on an engagement, completely isolated as he then was from all supports, having, moreover, learned that the information upon which he had acted was untrue, directed the troops to be put in position for the night so that they would be prepared "to resist anything." This order had scarcely been complied with when the 4:30 P.M. order above given came to hand and arrangements were at once begun to assume the offensive. Before these could be perfected darkness intervened and the troops were again placed in position for the night according to the previous instructions which had been countermanded.

Had a battle ensued we should have been obliged to contend against the bulk of Longstreet's force, which occupied the Warrenton pike in our front and could have been easily massed against us, and beyond the reach of assistance, as we were, with both flanks fully exposed, there could have been but one result for us—defeat. Seeing this, Porter adopted the best possible course. He did not fight, but he accomplished more by remaining passive than did Hatch by his bloody encounter.

It has been charged against General Porter that he not only disobeyed the 4:30 P.M. order by not attacking Jackson's right flank, but that he also retreated from the field to the sounds of the enemy's cannon at a time when a fierce and bloody battle was raging in which his command was sorely needed. The regiment to which I belonged was on the extreme front from about noon on the twenty-ninth until about 3:00 A.M. of August 30, first as skirmishers and after nightfall on picket, in actual contact with the foe. My recollections are very distinct. I know there was no retreat nor any movement in my division in that direction during the above period.

From my position I could look back and discern the locality of every regiment of my division lying but a few hundred yards in the rear while the daylight lasted and when darkness came there was constant communication between them and us, so I know that they remained there until the command came for us to march to Bull Run. It is utterly impossible that any portion of Morell's Division could have been moved in retreat without my knowledge. There was no retreat—Pope himself knows there was none as well as does every man of the V Corps present that day; but yet he persists in his false accusation in utter disregard of the precepts of truth and in violation of the divine attributes of an honest manhood.

The troops that the brush-dragging Confederate cavalrymen saw, upon whose statements Pope bases his assertion that we retreated, was doubtless a portion of Banks' Corps, which, as the records show, mistook the road and subsequently withdrew.

In order to magnify the enormity of Porter's alleged offense, Pope insists that Porter not only retreated, but left the field while a fierce conflict was raging. In other words, General Pope asserts that a hard battle was fought on August 29, lasting from morning until nightfall, within hearing of Porter. There was fighting on that day, occasional severe skirmishes, chiefly on our extreme right, near Sudley Springs, and the usual pounding of artillery; but there was no conflict having the importance of a battle within hearing of the V Corps prior to that between Hatch and Wood, near Groveton. [Maj. Gen. Samuel P.] Heintzelman, with a portion of his corps, had a sharp engagement in the afternoon, winning some slight successes, which he was compelled to yield to the enemy after nightfall. We could hear nothing of that outside the cannon, the sounds of which were not unusual along our front.

Regarding a battle on the twenty-ninth, General J. F. Reynolds testified before the Porter court martial as follows:

> "On the twenty-ninth, before 4:00 P.M., what was the character of the battle, artillery or infantry?"
>
> "Principally artillery."
>
> "About what time did the infantry fire commence in force and volume?"

"As near as I can recollect it must have been between 4:00 and 5:00 P.M.—that is, I refer to the part near me. There may have been infantry firing on the right which I could not hear."

"Was there not considerable and heavy infantry firing about 11:00 A.M. on the twenty-ninth and at intervals from that time to 3:00 P.M.?"

"There was some firing at intervals, but I do not recollect any very heavy infantry firing."

The reader may find it interesting in this connection to look at the following outline of facts concerning those who had to do with Porter's conviction. Judge Advocate General [Joseph] Holt was appointed colonel and judge advocate general September 3, 1862, the day Pope reported in person to Secretary [Edwin M.] Stanton after the Bull Run battle, evidently for the purpose of enabling him to be judge advocate of a court of inquiry on Porter dated September 5. He was judge advocate of Porter's court-martial, during the sessions of which his nomination, made December 10, was not acted upon, for what reason does not fully appear; but does anyone at all familiar with the facts suppose that he would have been confirmed February 6, 1863, very soon, only seventeen days, after he had furnished the president with such a summary or review of the case as to induce him to confirm the findings and sentence if he had been just to Porter, so that an acquittal instead of conviction had followed instead?

Colonel Holt's nomination went to the Senate December 10, 1862, while he was assisting Pope in the prosecution of General Porter; but the action of the Senate was delayed. January 10, 1863, the findings and verdict were rendered; January 19 Holt completed his review; January 21 the matter was acted on by the president (the short time intervening showing that he could not have read the testimony, but depended upon Holt's version of it), and February 6 the colonel and judge advocate (Pope's attorney) was confirmed in the rank to which he had been nominated.

Now as regards the members of the court-martial. Ricketts and King, two division commanders of McDowell's Corps, were themselves under a cloud for having fallen back, without orders, from the Warrenton pike on August 28, opening up the way for Longstreet to reinforce Jackson.

Ricketts was especially blamable, for he had been sent to hold Thoroughfare Gap early in the day and withdrew in advance of the enemy's arrival, almost and without making any ordinary effort to oppose him.

Both of these officers probably saw as clearly as did Pope, Stanton and [Maj. Gen. Henry W.] Halleck the fix they were in.

N. B. Buford, Silas Casey and B. M. Prentiss entered as members of the court according to their then rank of brigadier generals. Within less than a week (I think it was the next day) after the sentence was known these three judges were appointed major generals. When their names reached the Senate some of Porter's friends then in that body called attention to the fact that such action had the appearance of a reward for their verdict and the nominations were withdrawn and not renewed until March 6, 1863, after Porter's friends had left.

John P. Slough was nominated as brigadier general on the same day with the above, about January 22, but his confirmation was also held over till sentence was secured.

General [David] Hunter had been relieved from command at Charleston, S.C., for cause, and it was generally understood he was not to be returned there. He was looking for some assignment in New York. Immediately after the sentence was secured his offenses were condoned and he was ordered to Charleston, thus putting him upon a par with Casey, whose major general's commission was the plaster covering his dereliction of duty at Fair Oaks.

Lt. Col. Thomas C. H. Smith, the chief witness against Porter, was made a brigadier general at the same time that the judges who condemned him were promoted to be major generals or otherwise compensated for their services.

General Reynolds, as already observed, was two and one-half or three miles east of Porter, McDowell having failed in getting King's Division in the interval, leaving them thus widely separated, which Pope did not realize, else he would not, in the 4:30 P.M. order, have required Porter to keep his right in communication with Reynolds' left, which was an impossibility. However, Reynolds was in position where, if a fierce battle had been fought anywhere along Pope's line to Sudley Springs, he would have heard something of it.

It was 3:00 A.M. on August 30 when we were called in from picket and in pursuance of orders from General Pope, took up the line of march for the battlefield of that day. We retraced our steps to Bethlehem Church and thence moved northward on the road to Sudley Springs, reaching the high ground overlooking the Warrenton Pike at an early hour in the morning. Unfortunately, in the darkness, but through no fault on the part of General Porter, the 2nd Brigade (Griffin's), 22nd Massachusetts, of the 1st Brigade and Martin's Battery (C, 1st Massachusetts), with General Morell, of the 1st Division, moved on to Centreville, Pope's great objective point during the

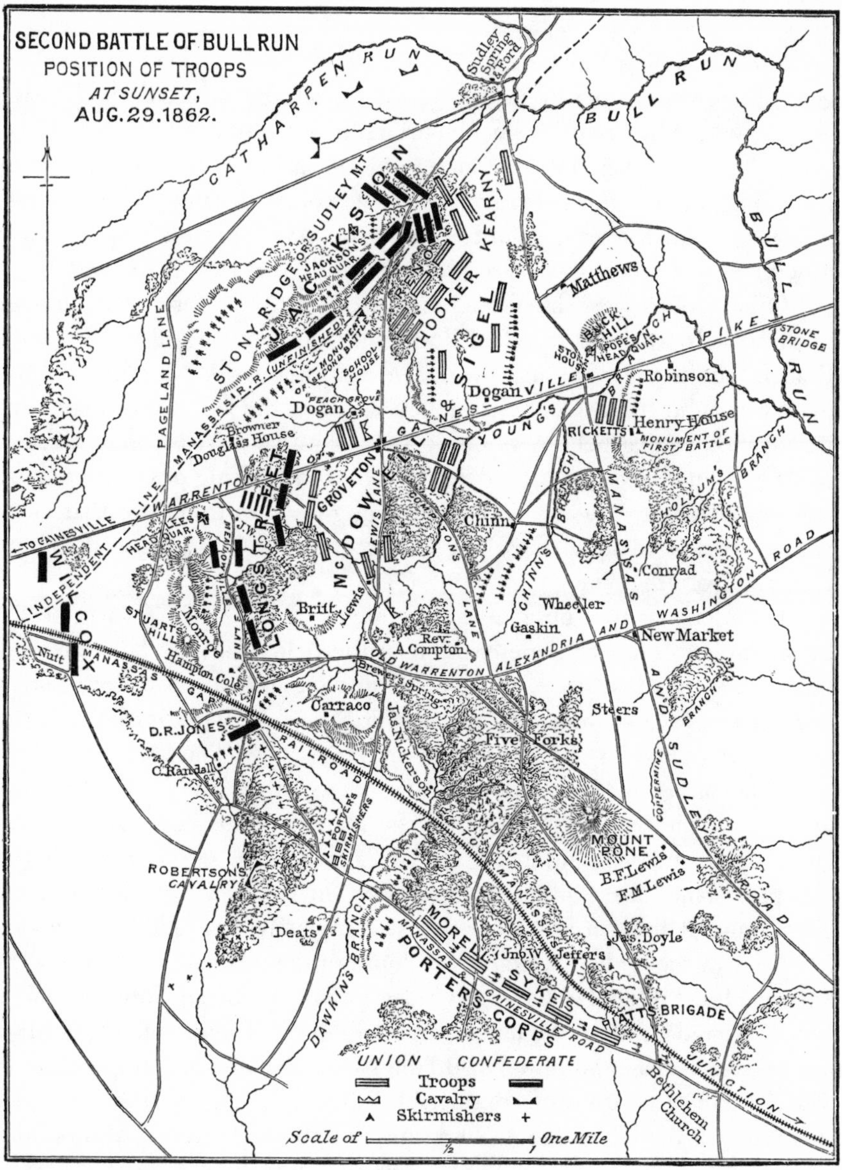

Positions at sunset, August 29

(CENTURY MAGAZINE)

campaign, thus reducing the strength of the corps to about seven thousand men of all arms.

Upon reaching the Henry House Hill we were enabled to trace the general alignments of the opposing forces, already arrayed against each other, by the white puffs of smoke curling from the muzzles of the guns on either side. Shells were bursting high in the air, over the heads of foemen or exploding among the moving masses of troops dotting the landscape. Below us in the foreground, just north of the Warrenton Pike, upon which its left rested and facing westward towards Groveton, was Sigel's Corps.

Other troops were distributed over the field, but before we could take in the details we were marched down into the narrow valley of Young's Branch, across the pike and formed in front of Sigel, Morell's Division upon the right, [Brig. Gen. George] Sykes' upon the left, occupying a similar position to that held by the I Corps except that we were in advance of it. After a little we were moved yet farther ahead, taking position partly in rear of a piece of woods, upon the sloping ground in front of our artillery, which was posted upon the ridge or succession of hills just north of and rising up from the pike.

In order that the subsequent movements of the V Corps may be the better understood a brief description of the field will now be attempted. The Warrenton Pike runs nearly east and west and the road from Sudley Springs to Manassas Junction intersects it at a right angle in the valley of Young's Branch, close by the Old Stone House, well known to every soldier who served in that section of Virginia. South of the Warrenton Pike and east of the Sudley Springs road the Henry House Hill rears its commanding summit; some distance east of it on the same side of but nearer to the pike stands the Robinson House, on an elevated plateau. Both the Henry and Robinson farms are almost completely surrounded by woods.

West of the Sudley Springs road, south of the pike and confronting the Henry House Hill, Bald Hill, its sides heavily timbered, looks down in gloomy grandeur upon the quiet hamlet of Groveton reposing, just north of the pike, at its base. South of Bald Hill, some little distance in the midst of Hazel Farm, a clearing of considerable extent, sloping from a high ridge eastwardly, is the China House, also situated upon high ground overlooking, as does Bald Hill, the Henry House elevation and adjacent country towards the north and east. West of the China House is heavy timber, extending almost unbrokenly to the Warrenton pike, and east of it, skirting the Sudley Springs Road, is a strip of woods intervening between it and the Henry House Hill.

Proceeding north of the Warrenton road, from the narrow valley of Young's Branch, which follows the pike from Groveton eastward until it crosses it diagonally a little east of the Old Stone House, the ground ascends at first gradually, then more abruptly forming a sort of ridge of rolling country or range of hill, chief of which, just east of the Sudley Springs road, is Buck Hill, thickly wooded. North of this stands the Mathews House in the midst of cleared fields, upon lower ground. West of the Stone House, a little over a mile and directly on the Warrenton Pike, the village of Groveton is located. About one-fourth of a mile or less, a little to the west of north from the hamlet, upon Dogan's Branch, a small tributary of Young's Branch, stands the Dogan farmhouse, surrounded by an orchard of peach and apple trees, and eastward but nearer the pike, two-thirds of the distance from it to the Stone House, in the middle of an open, rolling, but somewhat elevated country sloping towards the north and northwest, is the residence of the Widow Dogan.

From Groveton, at first having a direction a trifle east of north and further on tending more towards the east, extends the Groveton and Sudley Springs wagon road, a continuation of Lewis' Lane, which crosses the Warrenton Pike at Groveton at nearly a right angle. Upon this thoroughfare, not much more than half a mile from Groveton, is located a schoolhouse, on the western edge of a thick strip of woods that borders the roads or through which it passes for a mile and a quarter or thereabouts on its way to Sudley Springs. In the angle formed by this road and the Warrenton Pike, east of the former and north of the latter, lay the bulk of the Union army, its right resting near Bull Run, south of Sudley Springs. A portion of it, however, was west of the Groveton and Sudley Springs road, near Groveton and yet another small force south of and nearly parallel to the Warrenton Pike west of the hamlet.

The lines followed generally the contour of the country, the artillery being mostly posted upon the ridges and commanding positions in rear of the troops. From the front of the Union army north of the pike the country sloped gradually away into the meadows and cleared fields of the Dogan estates and then gradually ascended until it terminated in what is known as Stony Ridge or Sudley Mountain, which overlooks all the intervening landscapes and Groveton, perched upon its eastern slope, where the Warrenton Pike cuts through on its way west. From the pike, west of Groveton, this ridge by a gentle curve extends around in form of an irregular crescent to Sudley Springs, and along its inner (southern) slope just below the crest until it reaches a point about two miles from the place last named lays the graded bed of the abandoned Independent Railroad, having a generally southwesterly direction until it meets the Manassas Gap Railway at Gainesville.

A little west and about five hundred yards in front (north) of the schoolhouse already referred to as standing in the edge of a tract of woods, the grade of the Independent road turns quite abruptly more towards the northwest, forming an elbow, the angle pointing southerly to avoid a ravine grown up with scrubby trees and bushes in the line of its general direction. This roadbed which presented the usual succession of cuts and fills, was held on the thirtieth by Jackson's wing of the Confederate army, consisting of Jackson's old division, under General W. E. Starke, on the right, next Ewell's Division and last upon the extreme left, near Sudley Springs, the division of A. P. Hill, about twenty-thousand men in all.

Upon the right of Jackson and a short distance in rear, but not too far for ready support, Longstreet's command, aggregating about 25,000 men, pointing eastward, stretched along and across the Warrenton pike west of Groveton, considerably beyond the extreme left of the Union line. There was an interval of about a quarter of a mile between the two wings of Lee's army, but along the ridge which overlooked the ground in front for perhaps two thousand yards, were posted twenty-six pieces of artillery, eighteen of them under Col. Stephen D. Lee, which could, with their fire, sweep along parallel to the front of Jackson's right, securely defending that flank from being turned. The country towards the west in rear of the guns and of Longstreet, was diversified by considerable tracts of timber, interspersed with bare knolls and small clearings.

For some time the V Corps lay in the position first taken upon reaching the field, without cover, in front of our batteries and under the enemy's bursting shells, and those of us who cared were enabled, by the general character of the country and our location, to take in a pretty extensive view of our surroundings.

About noon General Pope issued the following order:

Headquarters Near Groveton,
August 30, 1862, 12 M.
[Special Order]

The following forces will be immediately thrown forward in pursuit of the enemy, and press him vigorously during the whole day:

Major General McDowell is assigned to the command of the pursuit; Major General Porter's corps will push forward on the

Warrenton turnpike, followed by the divisions of Brigadier Generals King and Reynolds.

The division of Brigadier General Ricketts will pursue the Haymarket road, followed by the corps of Major General Heintzelman. The necessary cavalry will be assigned to these columns by Major General McDowell, to whom regular and frequent reports will be made.

The general headquarters will be somewhere on the Warrenton turnpike.

By command of Major General Pope.

Geo. D. Ruggles,
Colonel and Chief of Staff.

And General McDowell the following:

Headquarters Third Corps,
Army of Virginia, August 30, 1862

Major General McDowell, being charged with the advanced forces ordered to pursue the enemy, directs me to inform you that your corps will be followed immediately by King's Division, supported by Reynolds. Heintzelman, with his corps, preceded by Ricketts's division, will move on your right, on the road from Sudley Springs to Haymarket. He is instructed to throw out skirmishers to the left, which it is desirable you should join with your right. General McDowell's headquarters will be at the head of Reynolds' Division, on the Warrenton road. Organize a strong advance to precede your command and push on rapidly in pursuit of the enemy until you come in contact with him. Report frequently. Bayard's Brigade will be ordered to report to you. Push it well to the left as you advance. Very respectfully, your obedient servant,

Ed Schriver,
Colonel and Chief of Staff.

Major General Porter, commanding, &c., &c.

When the foregoing order from General McDowell was received by General Porter, General Reynolds, with the Pennsylvania Reserves, was south of the Warrenton Pike, near the Henry House, his command in column by company at full distance, with all his artillery on the left. His divi-

Maj. Gen. Irvin McDowell
(RAY D. SMITH COLLECTION, SEYMOUR LIBRARY, KNOX COLLEGE)

sion was to have formed the pivot of the attack which the V Corps was to make upon the enemy, who were then supposed by Pope to be retreating.

The intention was that General Porter should push his command forward (west) on the Warrenton Pike (north of it, the country there being more open) followed by King's Division and that of Reynolds in the order mentioned, while Heintzelman, with his corps, preceded by Ricketts' Division of McDowell's was to move upon Porter's right, sweeping around westward upon the road from Dudley Springs to Haymarket, which was parallel to but some distance north (in the rear) of the position then occupied by Jackson. If the enemy had, in reality, been retreating, as Pope when he issued his order of "pursuit" assumed was the fact, the plan adopted would have served admirably, for it would have interposed his army squarely between the fleeing Confederates and Washington. But, as already shown, the situation was altogether different.

As affairs were ordered Porter's command was destined to be driven into a cul-de-sac against Jackson's right, the Confederate center (and from which, as it turned out, he was to have no substantial help to extricate his troops), instead of making an attack upon the rear of a defeated and disorganized foe, only intent upon getting to a place of safety. More than this, in pursuit of a mistaken idea instead of a fleeing enemy, Pope was about to expose his entire left flank to the impetuous assaults of Longstreet's veterans, who were west of the Chinn House, awaiting the moment when they might with the certainty of success enter the conflict.

It therefore happened that, so soon as General Porter put his troops in motion to carry out McDowell's orders, he became involved upon his right to such an extent that he was compelled, instead of following along the Warrenton Pike westward, to turn more towards the north and engage in a pitched battle with Jackson. But he nevertheless continued his movement towards the left so far as practicable and had he been properly supported, might have eventually succeeded in breaking the enemy's line in two.

Immediately upon discovering that the foe were not retreating General Porter notified General McDowell of the change in the situation and received in response the following:

> Headquarters Third Corps, A. of Va.
> August 30, 1862
>
> Major General Fitz John Porter commanding etc.:
>
> General: Major General McDowell directs that you push on the movement suggested in your note to him on the left, and General Heintzelman, now here, will attend to the front and right. You have at your disposal to reinforce you King's division and Reynolds'.
>
> Ed Schriver,
> Colonel and Chief of Staff.

Appended to the foregoing, however, was a note, viz:

> The enemy having shown indications of advancing by the right, Reynolds has been withdrawn from your column and put over on our left. It is still thought you will be strong enough to effect your purpose with King; if not, General Pope will send you Sigel.

This note, informing Porter that nearly one-third of his entire force had been taken from him, rendered necessary a new disposition of some of his troops, which was speedily accomplished, and knowing the desperate undertaking he had in hand and desiring to know if King's support was certain, he communicated with General McDowell, receiving in reply the following:

Headquarters Third Corps,
Army of Virginia, August 30, 1862

Major General Porter, Commanding etc.,

Major General McDowell is now busy attending to our left. He directs me to inform you that you must use your discretion in reference to the employment of King's Division in connection with the services you are to perform. Very respectfully,

Ed Schriver,
Colonel and Chief of Staff.

Meantime, under a severe fire from the Confederate artillery, the V Corps was formed in column of attack a short distance west from and at a right angle to the Manassas and Sudley Springs roads, in the following order: The 1st Brigade, Col. Charles W. Roberts commanding, of the 1st (Morell's) Division, under [Brig. Gen. Daniel] Butterfield (Morell being absent), occupied the extreme front, about half a mile to the eastward of the ground held by King's troops the day previous, the line being formed in the strip of woods south of and parallel to the Groveton and Sudley Springs wagon road, which runs along the edge of the timber and divides it from a cleared field stretching up to the railroad cuts and embankments occupied by the enemy.

This brigade was expected to charge the heights in front, capture the guns and then sweep around towards the left in the direction of Groveton. The regiments composing it were disposed as follows: The 18th Massachusetts, Captain Thomas, was in line of battle directly in rear of the reserve of the 25th New York, Col. [Charles] Johnson, thrown out as skirmishers; the 13th New York Volunteers, Colonel Marshall, in a line of battle in rear of the 18th Massachusetts; and the 1st Michigan, Colonel H. S. Roberts, and 2nd Maine, Major Sargeant, were in echelon of the other regiments, respectively, ready to promptly relieve them, provided they were obliged to give way. The 1st United States Sharpshooters, Colonel [Hiram] Berdan, occupied the extreme front. (The 22nd Massachusetts was absent and did not take part in the fight.)

On the left of the 1st Brigade, a section of Battery K, 5th United States Artillery (Smead's) was posted.

Then came the 3rd Brigade, under Colonel H. A. Weeks, of the 12th New York Volunteers, in column doubled on the center, the 17th New York, Major W. T. C. Grower, deploying and forwarding the line of battle, followed by the 44th New York, Col. Freeman Connor; 83rd Pennsylvania,

Captain De Witt C. McCoy; 12th New York Volunteers, Captain Root; and 16th Michigan, Captain Ransome, which latter regiment joined its right with the left of the 2nd Maine of the 1st Brigade.

The 2nd Division of the corps under General Sykes was further yet towards the left, facing west, occupying the open field in front of the Dogan House, with its left resting on the Warrenton Pike. The 1st and 2nd Battalions of the 14th Infantry of the 1st (Buchanan's) Brigade, which was most advanced, were deployed in a cornfield, with the 12th and 4th Infantry covering them in their rear in columns of battalions. The 3rd Infantry was advanced to the front and right under cover of a wood about a thousand yards distant, where it was deployed as skirmishers.

The 2nd Brigade, Colonel William Chapman, consisting of the 2nd and 10th Infantry, Major C. S. Lovell, commanding; 6th Infantry, Captain L. C. Bootes; 11th Infantry, Major D. L. Floyd Jones; and 17th Infantry, Major G. L. Andrews, was formed in columns of division, as a reserve, in rear of the 1st Brigade. The 3rd Brigade, composed of the 5th (Duryea's) and 10th New York Volunteers, under General [Gouverneur K.] Warren, with the three batteries of the division, were held in reserve.

South of the pike, nearly in alignment with Sykes, but somewhat in rear of his left, were other troops which the scope of this narrative renders it unnecessary to particularize.

King's Division of McDowell's Corps, under Hatch, was posted partly in and south of the timber, on the right of the 1st Division of Porter's Corps, also confronting the railroad grade, in seven lines, with fifty yard intervals between, Hatch's Brigade constituting the first and second, Patrick's Brigade the third and fourth, Gibbon's the fifth and sixth and Doubleday's Brigade the seventh line. The 2nd United States Sharpshooters were thrown forward as skirmishers.

Extending from the right of King's Division and continuing the line towards Bull Run Creek, came Heintzelman, preceded by Ricketts' Division. The I Corps, under Sigel, was held in reserve.

Between 3:00 and 4:00 P.M. the attack was finally ordered and almost simultaneously Reynolds, with his Pennsylvania Reserves, was taken from the left and moved further away, exposing Sykes' flank. General Warren, quick to perceive the dangerous opening thus made for the enemy, took his two regiments south of the pike, occupying the ground Reynolds had vacated, but correspondingly depleting the forces of Porter. At the word "attention" the men of the 1st and 3rd Brigades were on their feet; but for some reason King's Division, which had been ordered to attack with us, had not yet gotten into proper position to assist in carrying out the intended movement.

"Forward! March!" The line began moving towards the open field. Reaching the Groveton and Sudley Springs wagon road the troops were uncovered from the protection which had been afforded by the timber, and as the leading regiments of the 1st Brigade began tearing down or scaling a six or seven rail "stake and rider" fence bordering the farther side of the road, the hostile guns opened upon them at ranges varying from six hundred to twelve hundred yards.

The fact that King's Division did not come up promptly as directed by General Porter left a considerable gap on the right of the 1st Brigade, which was partly filled by the 1st Michigan and 13th New York Volunteers, the latter coming into line with, instead of in rear of, the 18th Massachusetts, so that these two regiments "took the fence" at about the same moment. As we reached the obstruction the hostile guns opened and immediately the air was full of splinters, flying rails and all the dread missiles of war. There was a little temporary crowding in the ranks at the first owing to this slight modification in the formation of the attacking column; but before twenty steps had been taken the men took elbow room, the lines were straightened and advanced rapidly in fine style toward the heights, where death lay waiting to welcome multitudes out of the thousands destined to fall there within the next half hour.

For the first hundred yards the ground over which my own brigade (the First, of Morell's Division) passed inclined quite gradually to a narrow strip of level land, beyond which it as gradually inclined for another hundred yards or so, after which it rose quite abruptly to an elevation of perhaps thirty feet, then sloped slightly upward for a distance of twenty-five or thirty feet more to the edge of the cut, along the breast of the ridge, which latter, from the right, where the embankment ended, to the ravine on the left was about two hundred or two hundred and fifty yards in extent, as nearly as can now be remembered.

My own regiment, the 13th New York Volunteers, was just about halfway between the ravine on the one side and the termination of the fill on the other, into which depressions the ground sloped from either flank after approaching to within twenty or twenty-five yards of them respectively. On our left, with its left slightly advanced and resting on the eastern edge of the ravine, was the 18th Massachusetts, and on our right, extending down into the hollow heading at the embankment and across it far enough to reach the edge of the woods, stood the 1st Michigan. Just west of the ravine first mentioned, partly in the scrubby timber growing there, rested the right of the 3rd Brigade, only a short space intervening between the two commands. This much I saw as we dashed up the slope.

The air was heavy with flying missiles, shot, shell, shrapnel, spherical case, grape and canister and leaden bullets, as we made our way towards the crest, each messenger of death having its own peculiar music set in harmony with the scenes transpiring; but as yet our rifles were silent. Stormed at from right, left and front, we could see no number of foemen worthy of a volley. As we appeared above the brow of the elevation we had been climbing, however, the fearful tempest swept through our ranks with redoubled violence.

The guns, planted on slightly higher ground, their black throats just showing above the crest not more than a hundred yards distant, opened with terrific violence. We used our weapons then and to those of us who had hasty glances through the curtained smoke it seemed that the gunners immediately in our front left their pieces. A wild cheer went up from a thousand throats as we dashed onward—we, some of us at least, thought the day was already won.

Suddenly in our faces—so close that the sheet of flame almost blinded us—burst a volume of musketry, and men went down like stubble before the reapers. Peering through the sulphurous vapor following the discharge, I discovered that my regiment was not more than fifteen or twenty feet from the railroad cut, of which, up to that time, none of us had any definite idea. The ditch was full of Confederates, three or four lines deep. The effect of their volleys was awful. Our line melted away like steam discharged into the atmosphere. But we pushed ahead and the flag of the "Old Thirteenth" was planted within ten feet of the barricade of fire. On the right and left of us the colors were equally well advanced. To add to the desperation of the situation in which we found ourselves Jackson's reserve came dashing from behind his guns to the front, formed upon the edge of the cut opposite to us within fifty feet and opened upon us over the heads of their comrades below them.

Such deadly work could not long continue. Flesh and blood were never made to withstand the tempest of lead hurled at us and yet for twenty minutes or more—it seemed a lifetime—we held possession of the narrow strip of nearly level ground leading up to the brink of the excavation in which lay the enemy, the muzzles of whose muskets we could have almost touched with our own. Again and again we endeavored to advance and take possession of the cut, but the merciless fire that greeted us proved too

"Jackson's reserves came dashing to the front" (BEYER, *DEEDS OF VALOR*)

severe—we could neither overcome nor pass through it. Meantime our ranks were thinning rapidly. Men were falling by scores. The dead and wounded covered the slope, but the harvest was not over.

In the midst of the smoke and hurly-burly of the conflict it was impossible to catch more than now and then a momentary glimpse of what was going on at any distance, yet during the melee I took occasion to give one or two hasty glances on either side and beheld how well our comrades of other regiments were helping to sustain the honor of the corps. Joining the 13th (New York) on the left, with its left thrown slightly in advance and resting on the edge of the ravine south of the elbow in the roadbed, the 18th Massachusetts was hotly engaged, and across the ravine, in the scrubby growth bordering its western edge, the gallant 83rd Pennsylvania was holding its own against overpowering numbers. The remainder of the brigade to which it belonged I could not see, but the steady roll of musketry in the direction where they ought to be showed they were there.

In front of the embankment on the right the men of the 1st Michigan were bravely breasting the storm, being, in addition to the direct fire of the enemy, subjected to a severe crossfire from the Confederates, who had

The fight at the Railroad Cut (CENTURY MAGAZINE)

secured a lodgment in the woods upon their right flank. The 1st United States Sharpshooters (Berdan's), 25th New York and 2nd Maine were in the midst of the fray, as their losses verify, but I did not get a view of their standards.

We had been engaged about fifteen minutes when I was wounded, the ball, a large Minie, entering the neck just to the left of and grazing the windpipe, about five inches below the ear, passing directly through, inside the jugular and carotid veins, and finding an exit at the back a little lower down to the left of and between the fifth and sixth cervical vertebrae, fracturing the spinal processes, several fragments of which were subsequently removed.

At the time of being struck I was less than ten feet from the edge of the cut in which the enemy lay and the flags of my regiment (I was with the color guard) were close beside me. One or the other of the standards had already gone down once or twice and one of them, the state flag, went down again a second before I did, so that my head fell upon one corner of it. As I was reeling to my fall I heard one of the Confederates cry out, "There goes their flag!" Just then the ensign was jerked abruptly from

"The flags of my regiment were close beside me" (BEYER, *DEEDS OF VALOR*)

under me, giving my head another bump, and one of our boys, I know not who, for I could not see him and failed to recognize the voice, shouted back, "Yes, damn you, but it's up again!" And so it was.

Two or three times while I lay there, the flags of my regiment went down, but there were strong and faithful hands ready each time to lift them up, and they were not dishonored, though sadly riddled and torn by the deadly storm of bullets hurled at their defenders.

The feelings experienced during the next five or ten minutes after I was hit are beyond adequate description and yet I remember wonderfully well every incident succeeding the impact of the leaden messengers. I never lost consciousness for an instant; on the contrary, the mental faculties seemed abnormally keen.

I was temporarily blinded, but only until I struck the earth, and my eyes seemed to have closed upon a vision of the man who, as I believe, shot me. I could recognize him today were I to meet him. I saw him to his shoulders through a rift in the smoke cloud, a big, bushy, whiskered man with long neck, thin face, and whose large upper teeth projected, so that they showed through his long, straggling sandy moustache, and I recollect, too, as I was going over backwards, hearing a comrade say, "There goes——," mentioning my name, and of myself thinking, "Not only going, but gone."

The shock from the bullet was severe. I was paralyzed longitudinally, the left half of me, and the right side was stricken with such sudden sympathy that physical control was for a season beyond my best endeavors. But I experienced no pain. The chief sensations were of being violently throttled with a grasp of iron, of having my head suddenly thrust into a stream of swiftly flowing water, a roaring in the ears as if a hurricane were sweeping past, and a brief moment of suffocation as I fell over backwards, my head first reaching the ground, where it rested lower than my feet, and the hot blood gushed in jets, filling my eyes, covering my face, saturating my garments and getting into my mouth as I gasped for breath. The power of speech was gone at first, and although I endeavored to cry out, not a sound came from my lips.

Tom Harvey, of Company E, however, as he was reaching down to pick up a rifle instead of his own that had been disabled, and in response to a motion made with my right hand, dropped upon one knee beside me in the midst of that awful place, lifted me to a sitting posture and laid my head upon his other knee. I had in one of my pockets a "housewife" for needles, etc., which also contained a small package of lint, scraped and given me by a kind mother when I went to the war (the greater portion of her gift had been used for gun wipes), and this I managed to get out and stuff into the yawning wound. Then partially recovering my speech, I asked Tom to get me over on my knees, so I could crawl back out of the direct and crossfire that swept the position where I lay.

He did so and re-entered the fight, but when I attempted to move I fell prone, the blood gushing forth freely in spite of the lint, which, when compressed, made a ball nearly as large as a hen's egg. Yet I persevered and at last, like a hurt animal, succeeded in dragging myself to the shelter of a rock about ten feet down the slope, against which I reclined with my back towards the enemy, somewhat protected from their fire, although but a few steps in rear of our line of battle.

Then I took an account of stock, as it were, to learn what capital I had to live upon. The hemorrhage was still profuse and I took a handkerchief and crowded it after the lint, but grew so weak that death was momentarily expected. My pulse was scarcely discernible. Curious to see what might be my personal appearance, I took a small mirror which I carried and gazed into it. The face looking into mine startled me. My countenance, in spite of the sunburn and grime of conflict, was ghastly pale; my hair, rather long, was clotted with blood, and the same sanguinary ornamentation clung to the incipient down—forerunner of a beard—giving to my otherwise boyish features a most hideous expression.

Meanwhile, just as I was completing this survey, Captain Savage, of Company F, came back with both hands clasped over his abdomen and fell close beside me. He recognized me.

"You here?" he inquired.

"Yes, Captain, I've got my billet," I replied, "Where are you hit?"

"Oh my God! I can't live," he groaned in intense agony, and opening his clothing showed the fatal mark. It was an insignificant looking wound, about an inch below the navel, the circumference not greater than that of half a dime. A purple mark, with a bluish rim surrounding it, but no more blood than would come from the prick of a pin, was all I saw; but death was there, none the less. Noticing the canteen by my side he asked for water. I gave him it to drink. He died in less than twenty minutes and with my one hand I closed his eyelids.

From the place where I lay I could look over the field where a portion of the 3rd Brigade of my division was engaged and also take in the view towards Groveton and south of the Warrenton pike for some little distance east of Bald Hill. Sykes' troops had entered the conflict, having been ordered to support Butterfield, the 14th Regulars, of Buchanan's Brigade, occupying the strip of woods vacated by the 3rd Brigade, of the 1st Division, when it advanced. The 3rd Regulars, which had been advanced about one hundred and two hundred and fifty yards in front of and to the left of the woods, held possession of two houses located there until all the troops were withdrawn from the center.

Chapman's Brigade of regulars was advanced when a portion of Buchanan's entered the woods, deployed its columns and formed a column of regiments in line, but later on, before the close of the contest, was ordered south of the pike to reinforce the left, where Warren had been for some time previous hotly engaged.

Just after Captain Savage died, from near Groveton, Longstreet's artillery, with some of Jackson's, some twenty or more guns in all, opened an enfilading fire, sweeping the Union troops already engaged and others approaching to the attack from left to right of their lines. One of the shells burst near me and a piece tore the clothing from my left hip, inflicting, however, but a slight injury. It was terrible, the iron tempest under which the unhurt fought and the dead and wounded lay upon that fatal hillside, and could not, for any time, be withstood, even by veteran soldiers. The retreat was ordered, and covered by Buchanan's Brigade of regulars, the remnants of the 1st Division bore back their tattered flags, marching under the uplifted hand of death to the rear.

"The men in blue who fell back so steadily were my comrades" (LIBRARY OF CONGRESS)

It was with an indescribable feeling of anguish that I saw the Union lines recede and yet I felt an honest pride in knowing that the men in blue who fell back so steadily were my comrades. The withdrawal, so far as I could see, was conducted in good order, considering the fearful ordeal through which they had passed, the deadly artillery fire directed upon them and the heavy masses of the enemy pressing hard upon their rear. They were subsequently reformed in rear of Sigel's troops, who ought to have been sent to their support, but were not, except perhaps a brigade, and even that did not get up in season to afford substantial aid.

As Jackson's vacated the cut and started in pursuit of their late assailants, physically exhausted and wearying of studying military strategy under such disadvantageous circumstances, I closed my eyes, scarcely expecting to open them again to the light of day. The advance of Jackson had then passed me. I had fallen into a half-drowsy state when I heard footsteps near, and next a rough voice saying, "Bayonet the Yankee son of a bitch!" I opened my eyes and saw two of the enemy standing over me, one with his bayonet fixed and held ready to thrust. I supposed it was all up with me and shut my eyes, just as the injunction to bayonet me had been repeated, not desiring to be a witness to my own execution.

I was holding what little breath remained in my body, anticipating the entrance of the sharp steel into my vitals, when I heard quick footsteps and a commanding voice cry out, "What in hell are you doing here?" followed by a thwack as if something solid had come in contact with somebody's cranium. This gave me courage to take another peep and I saw a Confederate lieutenant, who had just struck my intended executioner on the head with the flat of his saber. "Get out of here," he continued, and they left, he following after them.

To avoid the artillery fire, which was quite severe upon the exposed hillside, I crawled with great difficulty up to the edge of the railroad cut, but in my weakened condition, in endeavoring to get into it, lost my balance and tumbled heels over head, like a turtle off a log, to the bottom. The fall (about eight feet) set my wound bleeding afresh and I lay for a few seconds too faint to move. I had just gotten into a sitting position when Jackson, the great Confederate chieftain, rode up on the edge of the excavation from the rear where his reserves had been posted and remained sitting on his horse within a few feet of me for several minutes. Then he went his way following in the footsteps of his victorious men. But he saw as he sat there what I had already perceived, that the ditch was lined with his own dead and wounded. He had won the battle, but at terrible cost, considering the advantageous position occupied by his troops.

The fury of the contest had been transferred south of the pike almost contemporaneously with the opening of Longstreet's guns upon the columns attacking Jackson's. Warren's Brigade, of two regiments, of Sykes' Division, had felt the brunt of Longstreet's impetuous assault as he swept over Bald Hill and down from the direction of the Chinn House, and before the 1st Division of Porter's Corps had been extricated from its perilous situation; Reynolds, with his Pennsylvania Reserves, Tower, Schenck, McLean and Milroy, with their respective commands, together with fragments of brigades from various sources, were steadily opposing the Confederate right, which was endeavoring to envelop the Union left. Jackson, pressing on in a southeasterly direction, made the situation even more critical. But the gallant men who were meeting this combined assault were undismayed. Forced from Bald Hill by overwhelming numbers, they were speedily marshaled upon the plateau surrounding the Henry and Robinson houses, where, facing south, west and partly north, they held their own and the waves of conflict were stayed. The gray ranks could proceed no further.

On withdrawing south of the pike, Buchanan's, with the remnants of Warren's Brigade, of Sykes' Division, was formed immediately in rear of the plateau upon which the Henry and Robinson houses stand, deployed in line of battle, the right of Buchanan resting upon the Henry House. Later the 12th and 14th Regulars were sent to the left front to support [Brig. Gen. George G.] Meade's Brigade of Pennsylvania Reserves, then severely pressed, and speedily it was found necessary to order up also, the

3rd and 4th Regulars to their assistance. After about an hour's unequal contest, the enemy greatly outnumbering them, these troops, their ammunition being nearly expended, were retired in regular order, resuming their former position on the plateau, where they remained until ordered to Centreville, late at night.

The 2nd Brigade of Sykes' Division had been sent south of the pike to assist in defending the left flank earlier in the engagement. The 17th Infantry led the advance, followed by the 11th, 6th, 2nd and 10th and occupied the edge of a wood through which a heavy force of the enemy were advancing. The line was formed with the 6th Infantry advanced a little way in the woods. For nearly an hour this brigade withstood the repeated assaults of the foe and retired under orders only after Buchanan, with the 1st Brigade, had been ordered up to its relief. It subsequently rejoined the rest of the 2nd Division near the Robinson House.

The battle continued until late in the evening, the Union phalanx holding the enemy at bay on the high plateau overlooking Bull Run, thus preserving a line of retreat, which was taken advantage of during the night.

(I may add in this connection that since the war I have visited the field and clearly identified the ground whereon the corps fought. The monument erected in commemoration of the battle now stands about thirty feet in rear and about ten or fifteen feet westward from the spot where the colors of my regiment were placed at the furthest advance.)

Throughout all the trials of that long, hot, summer's day the V Corps acted well its part. Every company passed through the baptism of fire again and again, and there were few skulkers from the ranks. It lost in that engagement in proportion to the numbers taken into action more men than did any other corps of Pope's army, and yet, after the fight was over, after the wounded had been counted and the dead had been buried, after blood had been given time to cool and uncertain intellects afforded opportunity to get settled, Pope, major general commanding, in the face of more than two thousand men killed and wounded out of seven thousand taken into the fight, said deliberately that "the attack of Porter was neither vigorous nor persistent, and his troops soon retired in considerable confusion."

But what say our enemies, those against whom we fought? They unanimously agree that the assault and the succeeding contest for the heights were among the most persistent of the war. Stonewall Jackson says, "The Federal infantry, about 4:00 P.M., moved from under cover of the wood and advanced in several lines, first engaging the right, but soon extending its attack to the center and left. In a few moments our entire line was engaged in a fierce and sanguinary struggle with the enemy. As our line was repulsed another took its place and pressed forward as if determined by force of numbers and fury of assault to drive us from our position. So impetuous and well sustained were these onsets as to induce me to send to the commanding general for reinforcements, but the timely and gallant advance of General Longstreet on the right relieved my troops."

Brig. Gen. Bradley T. Johnson, who commanded a brigade in front of the 1st Division of Porter's Corps says, "Before the railroad cut the fight was most obstinate. I saw a Federal flag hold its position for half an hour within two yards of a flag of one of the regiments in the cut and go down six or eight times, and after the fight one hundred dead were lying twenty yards from the cut, some of them within two feet of it. The men (Confederates) fought until their ammunition was exhausted and then they threw stones."

General Cadmus Wilcox says: "About 3:30 P.M. the enemy's infantry, Morell's Division, V Corps, was seen emerging from a wood upon an open field in line of battle, the wood and field being in front of Jackson's extreme right, to the left of and near Featherstone's Brigade. This field was about five hundred yards wide and terminated one hundred and fifty yards from Jackson's line, the ground here rising rather steeply for a short distance and then level to the railroad, behind the embankment (or in the cut) of which at this point were Jackson's men. Seeing this advance of the enemy I repaired at once to the interval between Pryor's and Featherstone's Brigades.

"From this point there was an excellent view of the field and not more than four hundred yards distant. The first line advanced in fine style across the open field. There was but little to oppose them. They were fired upon by our pickets and skirmishers, but they continued to advance, and ascending the rise above referred to, came within full view of Jackson's line and were here received with a terrific fire of musketry at short range. They hesitated for an instant, recoiling slightly and then advanced to near the embankment (or cut). Twice did I see this line advance and retire, exposed to a close and deadly fire of musketry.

"Seeing a second line issuing from the woods upon the field, I was in the act of ordering a battery to be placed in position to fire upon them, when a battery was directed by the Major General commanding (Longstreet) to fire upon them—this battery being near the turnpike in an excellent and commanding position."

General Longstreet, in speaking of the matter, says, "Just after reaching my front line I received a message for reinforcements for General Jackson, who said he was severely pressed. From an eminence nearby one portion of the enemy's masses (the V Corps) attacking General Jackson were immediately within my view and in easy range of batteries in that position. It gave me an advantage that I had not expected to have and I made haste to use it. Two batteries were ordered for the purpose and one placed in position immediately and opened. Just as this fire began I received a message from the commanding General informing me of General Jackson's condition and his wants. As it was evident that the attack against General Jackson could not be continued ten minutes under the fire of these batteries I made no movement with my troops."

Col. Stephen D. Lee in his report says: "My station August 30 was on a ridge between Jackson and Longstreet, about a quarter of a mile in extent and overlooking the ground in front for some two thousand yards. This ground was occupied by several farms, orchards, fences etc. and was undulating. Opposite the top of the ridge and some thirteen hundred yards distant was a strip of timber with a fall of ground behind it. Between this strip and Jackson's right along an old railroad excavation was an open field."

He then describes how stubbornly Jackson was assailed by the troops issuing from the strip of woods and closes by saying that for half an hour he had the fire of his eighteen guns directed upon them, taking them squarely in flank.

Each one of the foregoing extracts from the official reports of the Confederate leaders has reference to the V Corps and none other. No other troops were put into that open field against the railroad cut where rested Jackson's right.

The V Corps took into the fight, according to the most careful estimate, not exceeding seven thousand men of all arms, including officers. I even doubt if we had that number present on the field. According to the official return of "present for duty," September 1, the second day after the battle, Morell's (the 1st) Division showed an aggregate of 3,867 men, but the acting assistant adjutant general, in certifying to them appended a note in which he stated that full returns of casualties had not then been received. If we add the losses on the thirtieth, 1,233 officers and men, to the figures given it will make the strength of the 1st Division at that time of the conflict 5,100 men. But from this aggregate must be deducted Griffin's Brigade, 1,717 men; the 22nd Massachusetts, of the 1st Brigade, 166 men; and Martin's Massachusetts Battery, 234 men, which by some misunderstanding went on to Centreville, thus leaving actually present on the field only 2,983 officers and men.

On September 1 Sykes' (the 2nd) Division aggregated "present," 3,489 men; losses August 30, 970, making the actual strength 4,459 men on the day of the battle, or, with the 1st Division, giving the corps an aggregate of officers and men present August 30 of 7,446.

But these figures were not large enough to suit Porter's enemies and therefore, in order to give him a larger force than he really had and thus add to the enormity of his alleged offense in not engaging Longstreet, someone changed or caused to be changed the date of an official return, made by General Porter on and dated August 21, to 31st of August 1862, thus giving no credit for the dead and wounded at Groveton, and deceiving many, as was doubtless intended, into the belief that the V Corps numbered ten or twelve thousand men on August 30, instead of the actual strength present of about seven thousand or less. But however shrewdly conceived, the trick failed to work as satisfactorily as it was expected it would. When the figures were made public by Pope, or through some of his friends, General Porter wrote to the Adjutant General of the Army requesting copies of the returns in question, and received the following reply:

Headquarters of the Army,
Adjutant General's Office,
Washington, November 5, 1878

General F. J. Porter, New York City, N.Y.:

Sir: In reply to your letter of the first instant requesting to be furnished with copies of the returns, etc., from which the information dated the eleventh ult. was compiled, I have the honor to enclose herewith the copies referred to. The morning report of the 5th Corps dated Newport News, Va., August 31, 1862, it is believed should be August 20 for the following reason: The date has evidently been changed from August 20 to August 31, by whom it is not known. The headquarters of the corps left Newport News August 21, and they could not, therefore have been there on August 31. This fact was not discovered at this office until the 1st inst., when copies of the papers were furnished Major Gardner.

E. D. Townsend,
Adjutant General.

The losses of the V Corps were as follows:

First Division.	Killed.	Wounded.	Missing.	Total.
First Brigade	103	374	99	576
Third Brigade	70	357	163	590
First U.S.S.S.	5	41	15	61
Artillery	–	5	1	6
Total First Div.	178	777	278	1,233
Second Division				
First Brigade	31	189	65	285
Second Brigade	19	159	40	218
Third Brigade	102	235	75	412
Artillery	1	2	–	3
Total Second Division	153	585	180	918
Grand Total	**331**	**1,362**	**458**	**2,151**

Thirty officers were killed, including Colonel H. S. Roberts, Captains Pomeroy, Alcott, Wendell and Whittlesey, of the 1st Michigan; Major W. T. C. Grower and Captains Blauvelt and Demqarest, of the 17th New York; Captain Ransom, 16th Michigan; Captain C. W. Carroll, 18th Massachusetts; Captains Savage and Hassler, 13th New York Volunteers; Captain Reed, 12th Regulars; Captains Lewis and Huger, 5th New York (Duryea's); Captain Smead, Battery K, 5th U.S. Artillery.

Comparing the figures above given with those showing losses in other corps it will be found that the casualties in the V Corps were nearly one-third as great in that one battle as were those of the whole of Pope's Army of Virginia, consisting of the corps of Sigel, Banks and McDowell, in all the engagements fought by them between August 16 and September 2 inclusive—eighteen days, and that they exceeded by 64 men the losses in Sigel's Corps during the same period. They only lacked about 500 men of being one-half of the aggregate of losses in McDowell's Corps, consisting of King's, Ricketts' and Reynolds' Divisions, about twenty thousand men in all, which did the bulk of the fighting except what was done by the Army

The retreat over Stone Bridge (CENTURY MAGAZINE)

of the Potomac (Heintzelman's Corps) and Reno prior to August 30. And from what I saw on the field, I am satisfied that among the 458 men reported as missing from the V Corps there were not 100 unwounded prisoners. Of the ten reported missing from my own regiment all but two were wounded.

The losses in Pope's army from August 16 to September 2 were:

Corps	Killed	Wounded	Missing	Total
1st Sigel	295	1,361	431	2,087
2nd Banks	23	80	238	341
3rd McDowell	595	2,835	2,021	5,451
5th Porter	331	1,362	458	2,151

Going a step further it will be found that the First Brigade of Morell's Division, V Corps, lost as many men killed and wounded on the thirtieth of August as did Hatch's Brigade of King's Division in all its fighting between August 16 and September 2, and with the exception of Gibbon's Brigade, more than any brigade in King's Division—Gibbons' losses in killed and wounded alone having aggregated 776 men—and the same brigade of the V Corps also lost more men in killed and wounded than did either of the brigades under Duryea, Tower and Hartsuff, of Ricketts' Division, and exceeded the similar casualties in Reynolds' Division of Pennsylvania Reserves—three brigades (thirteen regiments and four batteries)—by eighteen. The 5th New York (Duryea's) of Sykes' Division, V Corps, lost in killed and wounded alone 240 men out of 490 taken into the fight. Only the 2nd Wisconsin of Gibbon's Brigade, King's Division, exceeds these figures, that regiment having lost between August 16 and September 2, 266 men by similar casualties, and my own (the color) company, of the 13th New York, out of 39 officers and men lost 5 killed and 17 wounded.

I do not make this showing for the purpose of disparaging other commands, but simply to prove how unjust is the charge that the V Corps failed in its duty on the thirtieth of August. Men could not have been killed and wounded as they were under General Porter's command without first getting in pretty close proximity to the enemy and then remaining there for a season. No. The V Corps was loyal. So was its commander. The fault was with Pope. I thought so when, a lad of eighteen years, I lay for three days and nights with not one drop of water nor one morsel of food, my wounds festering with maggots, upon the field where I fell. I believe the same today and my conviction has only grown stronger during the more than twenty years that have elapsed.

Incidents of the Battle of South Mountain

BY HENRY T. OWEN,
COLONEL, 18TH VIRGINIA INFANTRY, C.S.A.

Philadelphia *Weekly Times* 4, no. 23, July 23, 1880

Brig. Gen. [George E.] Pickett was wounded and his brigade had suffered very heavy losses in the battles around Richmond, and a report of all the casualties made soon after the last battle—Second Manassas—showed an aggregate loss in killed and wounded up to this time of over fifty per cent. During the Maryland campaign the brigade was placed temporarily under command of General [Richard] B. Garnett, and on September 13, 1862, encamped in a body of woods a little south of Hagerstown. The baggage had been left behind at Brandy Station, in Virginia, about three weeks before, and not having a change of clothing the soldiers were now dirty and ragged and many were barefooted. Soon after sunrise on Sunday morning the fourteenth there came trembling along upon the bosom of the sultry air that low, whispering, dull, heavy sound of a distant cannon. Several minutes elapsed and then again in quivering echoes came that long, rolling sound repeated and prolonged and the veteran soldiers' experienced ear recognized at once the signs of a distant battle somewhere far back in the rear toward Frederick City.

General Garnett promptly issued orders "to roll up blankets, refill canteens and be prepared to march at a moment's notice"; but as the hours rolled on and the sun rose higher and higher, the atmosphere became more rarefied, the sound of the distant battle grew fainter and appeared to recede, until by 10:00 A.M. it had ceased altogether. About 11:00 A.M., however, a courier, mounted on a large, blood-bay horse, came tearing along on a mad gallop, in front of a cloud of dust, and dashed through camp like a shooting meteor straight on toward headquarters.

His orders were soon delivered, and back again he swept through the camp, looking neither to the right nor left and disappeared like a fleeting shadow upon the dusty course he had come. The long roll was beat, the lines were rapidly formed, heading towards Boonsboro, and off we went, at a double-quick, down the long, sandy lanes, with clouds of hot, suffocating dust floating around us and drifting away in heavy volumes across the fields on the roadsides. Many of the men, overcome by the dust and heat, fell out of the ranks and were left scattered by dozens along the roadside, yet on swept the column at a tremendous pace. The perspiration welled out at every pore and ran down the neck and arms and back in little rivulets; the clouds of dust settled upon the clothes and hands and face until the hair and whiskers were so changed in color that the soldier could hardly recognize his messmate.

Every three or four miles there was a halt and rest of ten minutes allowed and the canteens were refilled several times at the branches and wells along the line of march. On the road couriers were sent in hot haste down the dusty lanes to hurry up the weary column and at long intervals could be seen, among those who came and went, that fierce rider upon the blood-bay steed, whose color had changed to a darker hue, while flecks of froth from the champing bit had fallen like snowflakes here and there in white spots upon the flowing mane and smoking flanks where they clung like locks of cotton. These outriders, hovering around a moving column and dashing along the lines, were ever recognized by the veteran soldiers like "Mother Cary's chickens," or the "stormy petrel," to the mariner upon the rolling billow, as the precursor of a gathering tempest.

Reaching Boonsboro the column turned to the right upon the road towards Sharpsburg and, going a mile or more, turned to the left and advanced up the mountainside. Just over the top of the mountain a fierce battle was going on and our lines were quickly formed and advanced until under a shower of ball, when it was found that we were needed on some other part of the field and we were counter-marched down the hill and back towards Boonsboro. About half a mile from Boonsboro there is now, or was then, a little cottage on the left of the road to Sharpsburg. There was a grove of trees. A little yard of perhaps ten feet extended from the cottage door to the paling fence along the roadside. On the opposite side of the road there is a hill, up which ran a footpath. Along the road in front of this cottage the line was halted, extending, perhaps, a half mile each way, and the men were ordered to load their muskets. As usual upon such occasions, there was a great noise created by the popping of caps and the ringing and jingling of the ramrods in the musket barrels. Standing at the head of a company just in front and facing the gate to the little cottage, the writer saw a man rush out of the house, terribly frightened, and run around the cottage and across the fields towards the mountains. He was in his shirt sleeves, without a hat, and must have been terribly alarmed at the sudden halt of the tramping line of men in front of his quiet dwelling, and the loud command given to "load," followed by the rattling and ringing of five hundred ramrods and the bursting of caps up and down a line half a mile long.

A few minutes later a woman came out of the cottage door with a child in her arms and approached the little gate. Her head was bare, her eyes glazed with fright, her bloodless face whiter than the driven snow, and her parted lips were dry, ashen blue. She reached the gate, tried to lift the light latch, but her strength had failed, she attempted to speak, but her voice failed, and reason was fast going as she stared wildly and trembled like an aspen leaf and would have fallen but an officer stepped quickly to the gate, opened it, touched her lightly on the arm and spoke in the mildest accents he could possibly command, "Come this way, madam, and do not be alarmed," and he led her across the road through the ranks that opened a space for them to pass to the little pathway upon the opposite side, and then said to her, "Take that path and go to the rear." She now said, "Oh, tell me where I must go to be safe." The line was again moving and as he rushed to fill his place, he replied, "Take that path over the hills; get with your neighbors, and go as far toward the rear as you can, and may God protect you." Long afterward Major [George C.] Cabell, who witnessed this incident spoke of it, and said, "The deathlike pallor of that woman's face exhibited more alarm and dread than he had ever before seen depicted upon any human countenance," and through all the changes of after years that woman's frightened face has haunted my memory like a dreadful nightmare and troubled me like a revengeful ghost.

Moving up into Boonsboro we turned to the right and took the road toward the gap. It was now about one o'clock and the men were going at a trot up the side of the mountain, led by the guide upon the dark bay horse, whose pace was still an unbroken gallop. By the time the top of the mountain was reached at least half of the command had succumbed to the heat and fatigue of the long forced march, and a hasty count in the five regiments showed only four hundred and seven men present, being an average of eighty-one to the regiment. At the hotel on the top of the mountain the guide turned to the left and led us perhaps half a mile along a rough path, then across some open fields to the right of the road, the enemy's batteries, stationed on an eminence to the front and right of our course, opening upon the line a terrible fire of shot and shell as it crossed the open fields. There was a fence across the field and as the command passed over it, going at a double-quick, a bursting shell struck the fence just behind the writer and placed hors de combat the four men following next behind him, but on went the command to a wooded ridge, which appeared to be the position intended for us to hold, as the companies were aligned along this sharp, rocky ridge and came to a rest. There was no enemy in view and we had rested about five minutes when a soldier, looking at the mountainside in front, where there was very little undergrowth, saw between the large trees a Federal soldier moving toward us and said, "Major Cabell, yonder is a Yankee." Major Cabell looked in the direction the man pointed and sung out very loudly, "Come in here and surrender, you blue-bellied rascal, or by gums, I will have you shot." Then a man in the line said, "He is coming." And another man said, "There are two Yankees down there." And another man said, "Who-e-e! just look at 'em!" And sure enough there was a skirmish line a mile long moving in our direction, while behind could be seen in a few minutes the serried ranks of a dense column coming sternly on.

A heavy fire was soon opened upon the enemy, but they neither paused nor faltered, and a brief, fierce contest took place along the ridge until the enemy brought up a second line of reinforcements, when the Confederates, being greatly outnumbered, suddenly gave way and rushed back down the hill and out in the open field. There was great confusion, and the broken ranks were hard to rally and re-form, so that had the enemy followed up closely behind they could have taken the gap without any difficulty, as this brigade were the only troops at that time on that side of the gap; but the enemy halted on the ridge to cheer and yell for half an hour, and this gave the Confederates time to rally and re-form in separate squads and detachments behind the rocks and fences and re-open a brisk fire. Conspicuous among those who encouraged the men to rally and re-form, and infused a spirit of resistance, was a man that had been found by the rearguard a few days before straggling in the wake of the army. His haversack was empty and his feet were blistered. He proved himself a brave and gallant soldier. Still falling back and fighting as we retreated, we reached the fence across the field, and although half of the brigade had disappeared, the survivors made a stand along the fence and endeavored to hold the enemy back until reinforcements could be brought up.

There were now, probably, not more than two hundred men left in the brigade, and these were fighting in squads of a dozen or more, with great gaps between them, and were scattered along behind the fence and bushes for half a mile, while the enemy had a strong line in front and outflanked our position on both the right and left. On the right of our line Col. Eppa Hunton, with some thirty or forty men, was trying to keep the enemy back, then a gap in the line, perhaps of fifty yards, and a dozen men were found together, and then another gap and another squad, then a gap of two or three hundred yards, and on the other side, but in line came Major Cabell and General Garnett with perhaps a hundred men more. The sun was now behind the mountains and the somber shadows of night were settling down over the smoky, bloodstained field. The groans of the wounded and dying rose above the slacking fire of the thinning ranks, while the exultant cheering of the victorious foe in front made the welkin ring and echoed along the defiles and dark mountain gorges for miles away. In the midst of this uproar I heard a soldier, about fifty yards to my left, calling me by name, and on answering his call, he said, "Come up here. General Lee is up here and wants to see some of you officers." I passed the message down to my senior, Colonel Hunton, on the right, and when he came up we went up the line and found General [Robert E.] Lee on his horse "Traveler" in the open field, in full view of the enemy, about two hundred yards off, and in a situation exposed to a shower of balls. My first impulse was to take his horse by the bridle and lead him out of danger, but just as we came up in front he asked Colonel Hunton, "Where is General Walker?" Hunton replied, "I don't know." "Where is General Jones?" "I don't know." "Then who commands these troops here?" Hunton replied, "This is Pickett's Brigade, commanded by General Garnett," and added, "The enemy are driving us back." General Lee answered, "I will have reinforcements here in time to check them. Where is General Garnett? I want to send him a message to get these troops out of here as quick as he can."

Colonel Hunton pointed up to the left where there was heavy skirmishing and said, "General Garnett is up that way somewhere."

A pause of a minute ensued and General Lee then asked Hunton, "How many men have you here?" and he replied, "About thirty or forty." General Lee then said, "Get your men together and form them out there on that road (to the rear) facing toward the mountain on the left. I have no troops out in that direction and I am afraid those rascally Yankees are going to try to flank us. If you hear any troops coming from that way, fire on them, for you may know it is the enemy. I have a picket down at the gap that has collected several hundred stragglers. Get them up here and strengthen your lines." He then rode off slowly across the open field in full view of the enemy, to where he could hear the guns of Garnett on the left, and Hunton collected his men on the right and took us all down to the gap to bring up the stragglers. On the way we met a brigade coming at a double-quick, with their muskets upon the "right-shoulder shift," and at their head rode their commander in a gallop, with that ubiquitous courier on the dark bay horse, directing and pointing out the course. We had to give the road to let them pass, and there was a roar and rush of trampling feet as they swept by. Soon after passing us they entered the open field and the commander, in front, rose in his saddle and gave the order, "By brigade, right wheel!" and by the time the command had been commenced on the head of the column he shouted, "Forward, charge bayonets!" and the two movements were executed together. There was a roar of musketry, a wild yell, a rush, and the enemy was driven by the sudden shock and surprise over the hill and down the mountain side. These were the reinforcements that General Lee had spoken of to Colonel Hunton. The fighting continued into the darkness of the night, and the flashing of thousands of muskets, the bursting of shells along the brows and sides of the mountains, mingled with the cheers and yelling of the combatants, made a sublime but awful picture never to be erased from the memory of the participants nor of the witnesses.

Upon reaching the gap we found several hundred stragglers in front of a strong picket across the road, and Colonel Hunton proceeded to organize these stragglers into line along the middle of the road. Some of them came into line promptly when ordered, but others, lying by the roadside, had to be shaken up, and each individual made to get into line. After arousing some dozen or more the writer came to a soldier by the roadside, lying down, who refused to get up. He said he had been fighting ever since sunrise and was barefooted. He had charged and fought and retreated all day. His feet were blistered and he had nothing to eat. He was tired fooling with the Yankees for one time, and if they would let him alone he would let them off until the next morning. When told the Yankees would take the gap if he did not get up and keep them back, he replied, "There's no use talking that way, for they are as tired of fighting tonight as I am, and if they come fooling around here they will find that I am going to stay right here tonight." I threatened to stick my sword in him if he did not get up, and he deliberately turned over on his back and, laying his hand on his breast, said, "Well, captain, if you think it right to do so, you can stick me right here."

Now this placed me in a dilemma and I left the man where I found him, and a few minutes afterward Colonel Hunton tried all sorts of appeals and threats on that man, but he positively refused to get up and was left in his recumbent position. While engaged in getting up the soldiers on the roadside those already in line would fall out about as fast as we could get others in. Much time was lost and we did not go back to the place designated by General Lee. Later in the night the wagons and artillery passed through the gap, and the infantry, followed by the cavalry, brought up the rear, and taking the road toward Sharpsburg, encamped some two or three miles south of Boonsboro until day and then continued the retreat to Sharpsburg.

Protecting the Charleston and Savannah Railroad

JOSEPH BLYTHE ALLSTON,
CAPTAIN, 1ST BATTALION SOUTH CAROLINA SHARPSHOOTERS, C.S.A.

Philadelphia *Weekly Times* 3, no. 25, August 16, 1879

An important engagement—important principally for the disparity of the forces engaged and the successful protection of the line of the Charleston and Savannah Railroad—occurred on October 22, 1862, between Mackey's Point and Old Pocotaligo, about midway between Charleston, S.C. and Savannah, Ga., in what, in colonial days, was known as the Yemassee country. [Brig. Gen. Ormsby M.] Mitchell, then commanding the Federal forces at Hilton Head, thus states the objects of the expedition: "to test practically the rapidity and safety with which a landing could be effected; to learn the strength of the enemy on the mainland, and to accomplish the destruction of so much of the Charleston and Savannah Railroad as could be effected in one day."

The force embarked for this purpose amounted (according to the reports of [Brig. Gen. John M.] Brannan and of General Mitchell) to 4,418 men. It consisted mainly of Brannan's and [Brig. Gen. Orris F.] Ferry's brigades of infantry and two sections of artillery, three boat howitzers and 108 cavalry. There were also some detachments of other infantry organizations and of engineers. Of these, about four hundred, under Col. [William B.] Barton, were directed to make a diversion in the direction of Coosawhatchie, leaving a force of four thousand, or, allowing for the delay of some of the detachments in disembarking, at least 3,500 men for the main advance on Pocotaligo.

General—then Colonel—[William Stephen] Walker, an officer who had served with distinction in the Mexican War and who was, at its close, appointed to a command in the 1st Cavalry, United States Army, was in command of the Confederate forces, with his headquarters at McPhersonville, about twelve miles distant from the point at which the Federal troops landed. General Brannan, in his report, says, "Facts tend to show that the rebels were perfectly acquainted with all our plans as they had evidently studied our purpose with care and had two lines of defense—Castor and Frampton—referred to hereafter as Hutson's—before falling back on Pocotaligo where, aided by their fieldworks and favored by the nature of the ground and the facility of concentrating troops, they evidently purposed making a determined stand; and indeed, the accounts gathered from prisoners leave no doubt but that the rebels had very accurate information of our movements."

This is a mistake. The landing was effected at 6:00 A.M. on the morning of the 23rd of October, 1862. We received information of it at 9:00 A.M. Colonel Walker telegraphed at once to Charleston, to Savannah and to General [Johnson] Hagood, commanding the next military district, for reinforcements; notified the command near Coosawhatchie to expect an attack and sent a section of artillery to their assistance; directed that the main body of his pickets be withdrawn and brought up to reinforce him and with his whole available force (475 men) marched down to meet the enemy. The command consisted of two sections of the Beaufort Artillery and the Nelson (Virginia) Artillery, portions of eight companies of mounted riflemen and two companies of foot. We met at 11:30 A.M. in an open field, seven miles from our camps and only five from the point at which General Brannan had landed.

It was my first battle. My company (thirty-nine enlisted men and three officers, including myself) had out-marched the other infantry company and Colonel Walker did me the honor to request me to open the fight by supporting, in connection with two companies of mounted riflemen, two pieces of [Capt. William W.] Elliott's Battery, while he placed the rest of his troops in position on the edge of a marsh near Dr. Hutson's residence—mentioned in General Brannan's report as "Frampton." We were deployed as skirmishers to the right of the guns and could see the long lines of Federal troops marching up the road and deploying to the right and left as they came into the open field. A heavy line of skirmishers was thrown forward and bullets began to whistle past our ears. Our two guns had kept up an active fire and the enemy's line of skirmishers was comparatively near before the order to limber to the rear was given by their commander. It was not until this order was given that a single shot was fired by our riflemen. We then fired two volleys—one from the front and one from the rear rank—and the guns being then well in rear, marched in retreat, firing alternately by each rank falling back through the woods on our main position.

While I was superintending the destruction of the bridge across the causeway the mounted guide who had been assigned me reported to me for orders and received a shot in the forehead. His horse, which was also hit, carried him off on three legs and the firing soon became general on both sides. An energetic commander, with one-third of the force at the disposal of General Brannan ought to have carried the position at once, for the marsh, though somewhat boggy, was practicable for infantry. We held it for three-quarters of an hour and retired then, not in consequence of any bold movement, as General Brannan asserts and doubtless imagines, but because, in consequence of the short range across the narrow marsh, the artillery were suffering severely in men and horses.

I have a vivid recollection of the light of battle in Colonel Walker's eyes as he told me that he intended to withdraw and desired me to cover the retreat with my own company and a portion of Company I, 11th South Carolina Infantry. This consisted mainly in holding the ground with a handful of men until the rest of the troops had withdrawn from the field. About this time the Federal troops turned our left flank occupying Dr. Hutson's residence and at the same time advanced in front across the marsh. This compelled me to withdraw my men from the bushes which border the marsh—in doing which Lt. Middleton Stuart, of Beaufort, S.C., the only officer with me, for the other had gone to the rear early in the action, was sharply wounded in the arm.

We continued to fire in retreat in the open field, some fifteen or twenty of the men retaining their formation as skirmishers. One of these was passing by me, off the field, when I told him to rest his rifle on the topmost rail of a fence near by and take another shot. He obeyed readily, fired, and turning, said, "Captain, I have got one!"—when a bullet struck him and he fell dead, nearly touching my feet. His rifle and accouterments were brought off, but we were compelled to leave his body on the field and another man shot in the leg, whom we were too hard pressed to remove. A sergeant of Company I and myself were the last to leave the field, and a large portion of the Federal troops were then fairly across the marsh.

One of the teams of the Virginia battery had run away with a limber early in the action and broken it. The caisson was, consequently, left on the field. Its capture seems to have afforded General Brannan great satisfaction and by the time it reached Hilton Head, General Mitchell had multiplied it into two caissons and lays some stress upon the circumstance in his report to [Maj. Gen. Henry W.] Halleck. We know that the enemy greatly outnumbered us, but had no idea that the disparity was so great as the reports indicate. It is inconceivable that with so large a force no attempt should have been made earlier in the action to turn our position, or carry it by a front attack, or what would have been still better, to combine both. One or perhaps two attempts to form column and charge across the causeway were made, but Elliott, the same who afterward commanded Fort Sumter, with his own guns and those of the Virginia battery completely covered this point and the enemy were compelled to retire in confusion.

Walker retired upon Pocotaligo and to cover his movement the troops under my command were re-formed as skirmishers on the edge of an old field, about a quarter of a mile from Hutson's, where we waited about fifteen or twenty minutes. As the enemy advanced we retired, intending to fire upon them from the woods. The dense jungle which borders the road prevented this, for we could neither see nor fire through it, though the tramp of the enemy's horses could be distinctly heard. We were compelled, therefore, to retire upon a line nearly parallel with the advance of the Federal troops to the Coosawhatchie turnpike, which crosses the Mackey's Point road at right angles.

So close was it that as I entered the turnpike with the last of my men and passed the head of the Mackey's Point road, we were hailed at a distance of about twelve yards by a party of mounted men, whom I took to be cavalry formed by fours, with the order to halt and surrender. The soldier with me did so, but I ran on, greeted with a few scattering shots from the enemy and gained the causeway leading into old Pocotaligo. In front were Elliott's guns covering the road along which I was advancing, the men at the lanyards. Behind me were the enemy. There was nothing for it but to plunge into the marsh. There I found two of my men lying flat on their faces within thirty yards of the line on which the Federal troops were forming, but holding their rifles upright. These I struck down and, directing the men to remain where they were, made an effort to cross the marsh to our forces under a pretty sharp fire from both sides. This I found impossible and was compelled to lie down during the whole engagement, which as nearly as I can judge, must have lasted for more than four hours, during which time I received two slight flesh wounds, one from either side.

During all this time no effort was made to turn our position, which might have been easily done by a prompt and decisive extension of the Federal left through the woods between our position and Pocotaligo Station. Such a movement would have compelled Walker to fall back on the Salkehatchie, leaving the station, its supplies and the line of railroad between that point and the Salkehatchie bridge in the hands of his adversaries. A few mounted men appeared in this direction and completely foiled such a movement, if it was ever contemplated. [Brig. Gen. Alfred H.] Terry speaks of them as "a considerable body of cavalry." Nor was any attempt made to destroy the railroad, the avowed purpose of the expedition, nor to connect themselves by the turnpike with the detachment sent to Coosawhatchie. They simply stood in the woods and fired at us.

General Brannan says, "The bridge across the Pocotaligo was destroyed and the rebels from behind their earthworks continued on the only approach to it through the swamp. Night was now closing fast and seeing the utter hopelessness of attempting anything further against the force which the enemy had concentrated at this point from Savannah and Charleston, with an army of much inferior force, unprovided with ammunition and not having even sufficient transportation to remove the wounded who were lying writhing along our entire route, I deemed it expedient to retire to Mackey's Point, which I did in successive lines of defense, burying my dead and carrying our wounded with us on such stretchers as we could manufacture from branches of trees and blankets; and receiving no molestation from the rebels, embarked and returned to Hilton Head."

A paragraph could hardly be penned more full of inaccuracies. Captain [W. L.] Trenholm had joined Walker at Pocotaligo with the men withdrawn from picket duty and probably thus replaced those who had been killed, wounded or cut off during the day. The only reinforcements which arrived in time to take any part in the action was a battalion of two hundred men sent by General Hagood, who commanded the west military district. They arrived almost an hour or so before the fight ended. Their regular fire by files on the right of our line, which could be readily distinguished from the irregular fire of the men who had been engaged all day, was the first intimation that he was reinforced. One piece of Elliott's Battery was withdrawn during the engagement at Pocotaligo and posted three hundred yards on our right. It was retired by a crossroad unseen by the enemy and had all the effect of a reinforcement from its new and unexpected position. Another ruse was resorted to of withdrawing Captain Rutledge's company and ordering them up with a shout to produce the impression of reinforcements.

General Brannan, too, is mistaken in saying that we fired from siege guns. There were some earthworks at Pocotaligo, but no guns in them. The only artillery were light batteries already mentioned which had been engaged at Hutson's and which suffered severely in both actions. Lieutenant Meade, of the Virginia battery, could bring only one piece into action, owing to the original smallness of his company—now greatly reduced by deaths and wounds. Two pieces of Elliott's Battery were silenced by the disabling of the gunners, the remaining two keeping up a fire to the close of the fight.

General Terry is correct, I think, in saying that our position at Pocotaligo could not have been forced by an attack in front across the marsh. Such an attempt would certainly have been extremely hazardous. The marsh is not only much wider than that at Hutson's, but the stream which intersects it is deeper at high water and very muddy at all times. Fortunately for me the tide was out. The mistake was in not attempting at once to move higher up the stream, cross it, and turn our right. An attack in front across the causeway was not impossible to daring and gallant troops, for the timbers of the bridge were standing though the planks had been torn off; and if General Terry was correct in saying that he silenced our artillery, it might have been accomplished. But in this he is mistaken. Some of the guns were silenced, but three at least of them kept up an active fire to the last.

In General Mitchell's report to General Halleck the following sentence occurs: "One bayonet charge was made over causeways with the most determined courage and with veteran firmness." This is pure fiction. No such charge could have occurred without my seeing it, and it is due to General Brannan and Terry to say that no such incident is mentioned in their reports.

About 6:00 P.M. the fire of the Federal troops slackened and I could hear, though I could not very plainly distinguish, the commands of their officers. The whizzing of Parrott shells overhead from the boats in the river confirmed me in the conclusion that the enemy were retiring. My relief may be better imagined than described as, rising from the marsh, I gained the causeway and walking over one of the timbers of the bridge, reported to Colonel Walker at Old Pocotaligo. The Federal command marched back to Mackey's Point and re-embarked the next day under cover of their gunboats, whose commanding position prevented our troops from approaching nearer than two miles. The detachments which had been sent to Coosawhatchie displaced a couple of rails on the railroad track, an injury which was repaired in a few minutes, and cut the telegraph wire, when they were driven off by the troops sent from Pocotaligo Station and there stationed in the neighborhood. In the hurry of their retreat one of their barges was left in our hands.

The results of the expedition may be thus summed up: The line of the railroad was thoroughly protected against a force nearly ten times greater than our own. Our loss consisted of fourteen killed, one hundred and two wounded and nine missing. We also lost one caisson. General Mitchell reports the Federal loss at about fifty killed and three hundred wounded. They also lost one barge, nineteen rifle (3-inch) shell, loose, five boat-howitzer cases containing ammunition, and from fifty to one hundred small arms. Forty-six were reported by W. W. Elliott, ordnance officer. Captain Hartstene, formerly of the United States Navy, served as aid to Colonel Walker during the day and acted with courage and efficiency, but his whole heart seemed to be with the boat howitzers on the other side. I know of no instance which so strongly illustrates the yearning of the old officers for their own arm of the service. For weeks afterward whenever reference was made in his presence to the events of the day he would be certain to dilate on the excellent practice of the navy howitzers.

The fight made Stephen Elliott a communicant of the Episcopal Church. He said that while sitting on horseback behind his guns he found himself more than once praying and reflected on the cowardice of doing that under the pressure of danger which had not been habitual with him. On more than one occasion afterward when, after a night on the parapet I reported to him as commandant of Fort Sumter, have I found him and Captain Johnson, of the engineers, on their knees. A braver man and a better soldier never lived.

Too much credit cannot be accorded Colonel Walker for promptness and decision of his movements and the skill and tenacity with which he conducted the flight. Credit, too, is due to him and to the command for the efficiency of their condition. The officers were not only men of courage but of education, and an efficient officer could always count upon a liberal support from headquarters in all measures looking to the comfort and discipline of his men. The men, too, were well disciplined, well trained and composed of excellent material. The Beaufort Artillery, especially, had marched off to Port Royal Island leaving behind them all they owned in the world save their training as gentlemen and their pay as Confederate soldiers.

The Battle of Tazewell

DANIEL R. HUNDLEY,
COLONEL, 31ST ALABAMA INFANTRY, C.S.A.

Philadelphia *Weekly Times* 7, no. 17, June 16, 1883

As far as my reading extends, little is known about the battle of Tazewell, fought in East Tennessee on August 6, 1862, and the subsequent siege of Cumberland Gap by the division commanded by [Brig. Gen. Carter L.] Stevenson. It is my purpose in this article briefly to lay before the readers such information on the subject as I can vouch for as of my own knowledge. When it had been decided by the Confederate authorities to move the forces under Bragg into Kentucky, while he and [Maj. Gen. Edmund] Kirby Smith sought their way to the "dark and bloody ground" by different routes, the command to which I belonged was ordered to open a way through Cumberland Gap. General Stevenson commanded our division, which at the time was camped near Rogersville in the mountain country of East Tennessee. In the main our command was composed of raw troops but recently mustered into service. We had been stationed at various places in East Tennessee for a couple of months, most of the time in camps of instruction; but we had already satisfied ourselves that fully one-half the citizens of that region were by no means friendly to secession.

We left our camp near Rogersville on July 29, 1862, marching that day fifteen miles to Lee's Springs, not far from Blain's Crossroads. We remained at Lee's Springs four days. On Sunday, August 3, we left Lee's Springs, marched across Clinch Mountain, bivouacking at night five miles from Clinch River. The following day we advanced cautiously to Capp's Ford on the Clinch, leaving our baggage behind us. We had with us neither cavalry

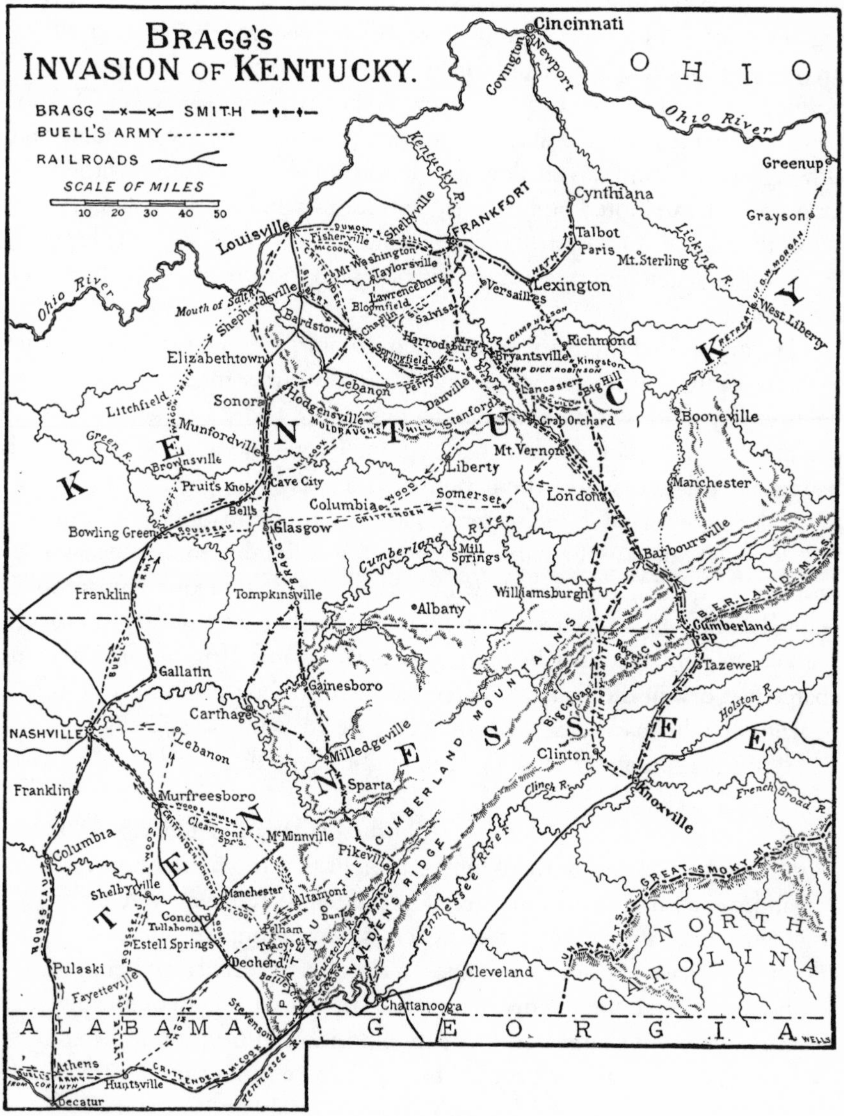

Bragg's invasion of Kentucky

(CENTURY MAGAZINE)

nor artillery. Upon reaching Capp's Ford we learned that the enemy were in force at Tazewell, only ten miles distant, on the other side of the river. During the succeeding day General Stevenson busied himself getting all the information possible from trustworthy citizens in regard to the strength and position of the Federal force at Tazewell. Just before dark we crossed the Clinch, the men wading it. The current proved to be swift and strong, although the stream was shallow and it was quite laughable to witness the long lines of barefooted and bare-legged troops winding their slippery way across the stream. Occasionally some luckless fellow tripped and fell sprawling into the water, and every such mishap called forth roars of laughter from his comrades.

Having crossed the river we marched late into the night, advancing with extreme caution and silence, resting at last on our arms, without fires or lights of any kind, within a mile and a half of the Federal pickets. Knowing the number of Union men in that region, I have often wondered how it happened that not one of them ventured to make our presence known to the Federal commander. He seems to have had no intimation of it whatever. On the following day the battle of Tazewell was fought—only a heavy skirmish, in fact, with few casualties on either side; but to our raw troops it seemed to be a hotly contested engagement. I remember running up against a smoke begrimed soldier belonging to our Alabama Brigade just after our charge had driven the Federals helter-skelter from their position, when, recognizing me, he exclaimed valiantly, "Oh, we Alabamians are hell!"

I find the following account of the fight in my diary:

> On the battlefield, August 6, 1862
>
> My heart is full of thankfulness tonight that the battle is over and we are the victors and my life has been spared. We were up before light and cautiously crept across two mountain spurs and through dark and somber ravines, trackless and heavily timbered, hoping to take the enemy by surprise. In this we were completely successful. We found him in a strong position in front of Tazewell, attacked him with fury, routed him and drove him back two miles. What his strength was I have no idea—certainly not so great as ours. It has been a day long to be remembered. The dead and dying, the roar of musketry, the boom of cannon (for the enemy had a battery in position) the smoke of battle sulphurous and black and all the incidents of the deadly strife are things never to be forgotten. Tonight we are resting on the field with the dead and

wounded around us. War certainly wears a horrid front and yet I find that harlequin follows close upon his rear.

While penning these lines by the light of a flaming torch, not twenty paces from where I sit, the Negro servants belonging to my field and staff are discussing the events of the day with great animation. It is their first experience of the sterner realities of the tented field and their grotesque descriptions of the fight and comments on it are almost enough to make one forget the pale faces of the dead and the groans of the wounded scattered around him.

"Willis," old Uncle Frank has just been saying to my Colored servant, "dar ain't no use a talkin' but white folks ain't niggers, shuah! Niggers nebber could a stood all dat gustament, nebber! Fo' God, I thought ebery body was kilt; I did for a fac'."

"Tubbe sho' Uncle Frank," replied Willis, "I thought so too. Laws amassy! How dem big guns did boom! Boom! Boom! I tell yer, man, dey fa'rly shuck de yearth! An' dem muskits—whew! Hit seem to me as how dem bullits was a flyin' in de a'r same as bees in swarmin' time."

They then both sagely concluded that their young masters had reaped glory enough already and about the best thing they could do now would be to go home at once and "stay dar." Willis has already supplied himself with a complete Federal outfit, overcoat, new uniform, knapsack and all. Uncle Frank, it seems, has not been so fortunate as yet, but on tomorrow promises to "sarch aroun'" to see whether he too cannot meet up with the same luck.

The day following the battle was devoted to burying the dead. Among the Federal dead the captain of an Ohio company especially attracted my attention. He was apparently some thirty years of age, extremely handsome, with light curly hair and a face and head indicative of a man of education. He was buried on the spot where he fell, just in the edge of a small copse of cedars on the side of a steep hill. Often afterwards during the war did I recall the calm, cultured face of my dead enemy and wondered to myself how soon the fortunes of war would consign me also to such a lonely and neglected grave.

The Federals continued their retreat to Cumberland Gap, their base of supplies, although we did not pursue them immediately. Had we a good cavalry force with us I believe we could have captured their entire command, for so completely were they taken by surprise they retreated precipitately, throwing away guns, knapsacks and other accouterments in their flight. Among the trophies brought to me by one of my soldiers was a vest ingeniously lined with steel plates—a vest of modern breastplate, in fact, the like of which I had never seen before. I dare say, however, it would have offered small resistance to a well-aimed Minie ball at the distance of even one hundred yards.

We remained at Tazewell ten days waiting for our baggage and commissary stores. Leaving Tazewell at 10:00 P.M., Saturday, August 16, we marched until daylight, by which time we reached Cumberland Gap, our destination. We began immediately to reconnoiter the place, which we soon discovered to be very formidable; a natural fastness in fact, and not assailable by such a force as we had. The enemy shelled us for several hours, so soon as he became aware of our presence, wounding two men, but otherwise doing no damage. General Stevenson very soon decided to invest the place closely and make no effort to dislodge [Brig. Gen. George Washington] Morgan, the Federal commander, by a direct assault. It was thought that General Kirby Smith would soon be in his rear on the other side of the mountain.

[Brig. Gen. Seth Maxwell] Barton's Brigade, to which my regiment was at the time attached, was placed on the extreme right of our line. We were bivouacked in a stately woods on the mountainside, the dense shade of the trees screening us entirely from the hot rays of the August sun. At every turn ice-cold springs bubbled up from underneath moss-covered rocks and altogether, at no time during the war did I find my lines fall to me in such a pleasant place as at the beginning of our siege of Cumberland Gap. Still it was not without its drawbacks, as I soon discovered, and as witness the following leaf from my diary:

Camp of Investment, August 20, 1862

The enemy in the Gap continue to keep quiet. We are shut out from news of all kinds where we now are, but we hope for a change in a day or two. Besides, we sleep on the ground in the woods and are glad to get a flour hoecake and a rind of bacon to eat. I am faring a little better myself, from the fact that I have an old Union man by the name of Scott under my protection and he furnishes me buttermilk and butter every morning in exchange for flour.

This Mr. Scott is certainly an odd character. He is one of the most nervous and excitable men I have ever met. The soldiers have nearly ruined him and would doubtless have ruined him completely had I not placed a guard over his premises. Even now, however, there is hardly a day passes but some new outrage is done him, when he comes rushing immediately to my quarters, his eyes large as saucers, his hair standing out all over his head like Mr. [John C.] Calhoun's and his hands in such a furious motion it is impossible to tell which one holds his hat. So soon as he catches sight of me, no matter how far off he may be, he begins to proclaim his losses in a tone loud enough for a political stump speaker or a camp-meeting exhorter. His first exclamation usually is, "Colonel! Colonel!" several times repeated. Then he continues without waiting for me to put in a word, "Oh, sir, I'm a ruined man! My wife and children will starve. I tell you, Colonel, I am a ruined man. I know you do all you can, Colonel, but the soldiers, the soldiers! Colonel, all I have is yours. Come to my house, Colonel, come! Come and see for yourself what they have done to my property. Really, really, really, Colonel, I am a ruined man!"

Some of the more thoughtless of my men make themselves merry over the sorrows of this poor old man and truth to tell, at times it is hard not to laugh at his extravagant demonstrations of rage and grief, but in the main he has my pity and sympathy. I call to mind that I have an aged father myself, who is at this time inside the enemy's lines in North Alabama, and how do I know but he is daily being subjected to like indignities with this unfortunate Unionist of East Tennessee? This thought has led me to do all in my power to protect Mr. Scott's property from injury, as well as his gray hairs from insult; but alas! Soldiers will be soldiers and I grieve to think we have some serving under the stars and bars who would do no discredit to [Maj. Gen. John] Pope's or [Maj. Gen. Benjamin F.] Butler's legions.

From August 18 to September 18 I was present with the army of investment. During that time the enemy shelled us repeatedly, but did us little or no damage. We patiently waited for him to evacuate the place, for we knew that both Smith and [Gen. Braxton] Bragg were already in his rear, making it imperative for him to leave or be captured. How soon after September 18 the Federals did evacuate Cumberland Gap I do not now recall, for on that day a sore domestic affliction called me away from my command. After we had been investing the Gap about two weeks my wife came from Alabama to see me, bringing with her our little son Oscar. He was only three years old, but a bright, brown-eyed, beautiful little fellow, who had during all the time the Federals were in possession of North Alabama been pining once more to see his "Sojer Papa." Mrs. Hundley had taken lodging in Tazewell at the house of Mr. Graham, an elderly gentleman, over eighty years of age, with a companion nearly as old—both of them models in every respect of the purer and better days of the republic. They lived in a large brick mansion, with extensive grounds and were as kind to my wife and child as her own parents could have been. But our little boy, fresh from the sunny skies of Alabama and still wearing his light linen clothes, was soon stricken down with pneumonia and after a few days' illness, died. Alas! Even after the lapse of twenty years, I cannot recall, without a heartache, the beautiful moonlit night, when those caressing little arms were stretched out to me for the last time and when the light of a love unutterable faded forever from the soulful eyes.

Although it was evident that the Federals were on the eve of evacuating the Gap the commanding general gave me a short leave of absence to accompany my wife back to Alabama, taking our dead with us. I crave pardon of the reader for the introduction here of this, to me, melancholy episode, but I found he would not otherwise be enabled clearly to understand what follows.

Owing to the condition of the railroads in North Alabama I did not reach Knoxville on my way back to my command until October 2. I learned then that my regiment was already in the heart of Kentucky and further, that it would not be safe to attempt to reach it unless protected by a sufficient escort. I was also informed that such an escort would be furnished me, together with other officers belonging to Bragg's army, in a few days. I whiled away the interim in the society of old and new acquaintances, for I found many such in Knoxville. Among them were some persons more or less famous, as may be seen from the following leaf from my diary:

> Knoxville, October 3, 1862
>
> Met [Maj. Gen. John C.] Breckenridge today for the first time since I was introduced to him at the Galt House in Louisville last year. He is a splendid looking man, but has aged somewhat during the past twelve months. His division, or a part of it at least, is now here on its way to join Bragg. I have also just had an interview with [Champe] Ferguson, [Col. John Hunt] Morgan's pathfinder, as he is called. He intends leaving for Kentucky tonight. I have sent a letter by him to General Barton, informing him that I will rejoin my regiment as soon as it is possible for me to do so. I was introduced to Ferguson by [Brig. Gen. Samuel B.] Maxey and also

at the same time to Col. George St. Leger Grenfell, the eccentric Englishman, who has figured so much of late with John Morgan.

Colonel Grenfell still carries his hand in a sling from a wound received somewhere in Kentucky. He is about my height, six feet two inches, as erect as a Maypole and tells me that he has been in the English service over thirty years and that he wonders to see men so young as myself in command of a regiment. He served a long time in India and although he is quite dark and lean and very sociable, still no one would take him to be other than an Englishman. He is a soldier every inch and fighting is his pastime. Ferguson is also a tall, dark-haired, dark-skinned man, but somewhat stooped in his broad shoulders and more ungainly in his carriage than his dashing looking English comrade. He has small, quick, furtive eyes, a retreating forehead and a mouth and chin which stamp him as a character it would not be safe to meddle with on the highway. He carries a large, white-handled bowie knife in his belt, which, with his pistols, gives him a very brigandish appearance. He usually travels by himself and is said to possess an accurate knowledge of all the paths through the mountains of Tennessee and southern Kentucky. He is quite reticent and has little to say, but Grenfell entertains one by the hour with the incidents of his strange career.

After a few days' longer delay our escort declared itself ready to serve us. We left Knoxville October 11, and from this time on I will let my diary tell its own story of our adventures. After the lapse of twenty years no man's memory can be relied on as much as the record of events written down at the very time of their occurrence:

In Bivouac, October 11, 1862

We did not leave Knoxville until 1:00 P.M. and in consequence have only traveled about ten miles today. Our escort consists of twenty men, exchanged prisoners, just from Camp Chase, who formerly belonged to Colonel Morgan's original band, now so famous. They, with their Captain Austin, who is also with us and commands the squad, were captured at Lebanon, Tennessee and are a noble-looking set of fellows. I am certainly not afraid to take chances with them among the Union jayhawkers and bushwhackers who now infest the mountain fastnesses all the way from Cumberland Gap to the open region of Kentucky.

Besides our escort, most of whom are gentlemen, there are several officers in our company. Major [James] Nocquet, Bragg's chief of engineers, a little, polite, black-bearded Frenchman, has with him his ambulance, which carries most of the provisions of myself and brother officers. The escort has two wagons along to carry our forage etc. Major [John D.] Wickliffe, a tall, free and easy Kentuckian, son of the Union congressman of that name, with Adjutant Purth, of Louisville, a nephew of Judge Purth, are accompanying us on a visit to their homes, in advance of Breckenridge's command, to which they belong and which is expected to leave Knoxville soon. Captain Steel, of the engineers, accompanies Major Nocquet. My old friend, Captain Henderson, is also with us, being on his way to rejoin his regiment. Altogether we are a very pleasant company and around our campfire tonight have had some lively discussions of the situation of affairs, both in Tennessee and Kentucky, as well as in other portions of the South.

We traveled some twenty-five miles today (October 12) in spite of the rain and succeeded in crossing the Clinch River soon after dark. The more I see of my traveling companions the better I am pleased with them. They are certainly a lively crowd, full of anecdotes of stirring adventures by flood and field. We took dinner today (the 13th) at the mansion of my old friend, Mr. Graham. During the dinner hour we had a very animated discussion as to the future of our new republic. Major Nocquet maintained, with his foreign shrug, that so far democracy had proved itself a failure and that nothing but a monarchy can ever heal our dissensions. I grieve to say some of my brother officers inclined to agree with him, but the discussion served to rouse me from gloomy reflections and I combated their ideas to the best of my ability. I am for a republic today, tomorrow and for all time to come. We crossed the Cumberland Gap just before dark and are now in camp at the foot of the mountain on its Kentucky side. We learn that there has been some hard fighting in Kentucky; also, what concerns us more, that Major Thomas' Indians, the same that accompanied us to Chattanooga last June, have pretty well put a stop to bushwhacking through all this region. So we do not anticipate any bloody adventures on tomorrow, but collect about our blazing fires and fight over again our former battles, while Major Nocquet favors us occasionally with a snatch of that marvelous song, "Allons enfants de la patrie, le jour de glaire est arrive."

We are stopping tonight (the fourteenth) about five miles from Barboursville, in one of the most notorious Union settlements in Kentucky. Our ride today was through a country rugged, picturesque, even grand at times, with overhanging cliffs, with many fertile valleys lying between. Tonight we have had bad news. It is said that Bragg's army is retreating from Kentucky! We can hardly credit this report, but we fear it is only too true. I am the only one of my fellow travelers who sustains Bragg in this unexpected move and I do so because I think it is better to be on the safe side and to have our army south of the mountains during the rapidly approaching winter. The Kentuckians with me are exceedingly sorrowful, however, and refuse to be comforted, while Major Wickliffe is swearing worse than "our army did in Flanders." We made no move today (the fifteenth) except to take up our quarters in a country church, since it is evident we need to go no further, for there can be no longer any doubt about Bragg's army being on the retreat. The advance of his wagon train reached here early this morning and has been passing by us all day, the wagons loaded down with the stores captured by our forces while in Kentucky. We learn from the officers in charge that there was a bloody fight at Perryville, in which we were the victors and they express themselves as unable to account for the order to retreat. As the day advanced the evidences of a grand "skedaddle" became more and more conspicuous. Besides the wagons there have been passing all day immense trains of mules, great herds of fat oxen, regiments of stragglers, together with thousands of fleeing citizens, male and female, old and young, some of them in carriages and all of them evidently in a hurry to get out of the way as fast as possible.

The great army of wagons, mules, horses, stragglers and fleeing citizens has continued all of today (the sixteenth) to pass by us like a great caravan. The spectacle certainly surpasses anything I ever before witnessed. Meanwhile we ourselves have not been idle. John Morgan's men have already proven themselves to be his true followers. In the first place there is an old farmer living near us, the owner of a fine apple orchard, but not an apple would he allow us to touch. This fact becoming known, in a little while after an officer was seen, posting sentinels around the orchard and loudly instructing them to allow no one to enter the orchard. After a reasonable delay a respectful message was sent to the cross-grained old farmer, informing him that "the colonel" would like to get a few apples for his own consumption. "Certainly," replied the old fellow, suspecting no evil, "I have nothing too good for the colonel." In less than an hour afterwards his trees were all stripped of their luscious burden, the sentinels were quietly withdrawn and are now assisting their comrades to dispose of their apples, all of them laughing merrily at their practical joke.

While his men were thus entertaining themselves Captain Austin, who is a Texan, a tall, stout, square-built man of some thirty years, dressed in a fanciful buckskin Indian hunting shirt, was also busy. He had found out by some means that an old Union man in the neighborhood had made his house a sort of headquarters for some time for a band of mounted guerrillas. His house was ordered to be searched in consequence, when lo! We discovered it to be a perfect arsenal. We have drawn from its hidden recesses nearly a hundred splendid United States sabers, with rifles, muskets, cartridges, etc., until our country church tonight looks like an arsenal indeed, bristling as it is with so many weapons of war.

There was another noteworthy incident of the day. We arrested an old Unionist, taking him to our church under guard. We kept him durance vile until nearly dark, hoping to make him tell us where the band of jayhawkers lay concealed to whom the arms we had captured evidently belonged. He persistently refused to tell anything and Captain Austin suggested that we dispose of him summarily as a spy. This was done after consultation with myself and others, simply to frighten him. The old fellow seemed greatly concerned for a while and begged to be permitted to send for his wife and little children. They soon put in an appearance and I do not know when I have been as much moved. I could withstand his wife's entreaties with dry eyes, knowing as I did that we designed bringing her husband to no harm; but when one of his little boys crept up timidly to his father's side, the big tears rolling down his cheeks and took from his pockets a couple of large red apples which he tremblingly handed to his parent, saying artlessly, "Father, I thought you might be hungry," I could resist no longer. I wiped the mist from my eyes and bade the old man go home, to which decision there was not a dissenting voice from any of the stern men around me.

Captain Austin and his men, as well as Major Nocquet, Major Wickliffe, Captain Steel and Adjutant Purth, left early this morning (the seventeenth) from our late stopping place, Austin taking with him the captured arms, leaving me alone with Captain Henderson and my servant Willis. Soon after my friends left me I rode over to the house of our late captive, who is a thrifty and well-to-do farmer. I found his premises invaded by the hordes of stragglers who still continue to pour along the public highway in advance of the army. I certainly never witnessed such straggling before. How they managed in such numbers to get so far ahead of their commands passes my comprehension. What is more, from what I saw of their conduct during this visit to the house of the old Unionist, they are about as hard a set as one could find anywhere. What they could not buy with Confederate money they took with much unblushing impudence. I looked on in perfect amazement. Chickens, turkeys, ducks, geese, pigs, sheep—everything, in part, that could walk or fly was soon shot down and some of the more ragged and dirty of the unscrupulous party even seized hold of live pigs and bore them off squealing over their shoulders. It was certainly to me a most humiliating spectacle. What must the Union citizens of Kentucky think of such soldiers? We will certainly gain no new friends where these loafers and bummers have had a chance to rob peaceable and law-abiding citizens in such a dastardly manner. While these reflections were passing in my mind the advance guard of the army of Bragg came in sight and hastening to the public road to meet it, I was informed that Kirby Smith's forces, with whom is my command, had taken a different road, which forks with the main Cumberland Gap road at Flat Lick. Consequently, Captain Henderson and myself, with Willis, left immediately for Flat Lick, where we now patiently await the arrival of our respective commands.

Kirby Smith's wagon trains passed by on yesterday and today (the eighteenth) and after the last wagon had passed came the veteran legions of Bragg's army. It is a sight one sees but seldom, such an army passing in review before him. For hours and hours I sat in the dust, looking on with a sort of fascination, while regiment after regiment moved past me, waving their bloodstained banners, many of them torn and riddled with the balls of many a hotly contested fight, officers and men all covered with dust and tramping along in a sort of sullen silence. Occasionally an officer stopped long enough to say that they have all suffered from hunger, thirst, exposure and forced marches, but most of all from

> hunger and thirst. For several days they have had to subsist on parched corn and to drink water out of filthy pools in which lay the carcasses of dead mules. The stragglers who had preceded them had pretty well cleaned up all the farmyards and farms lying along their line of march. This I can well believe from what I myself witnessed yesterday.

Thus for my diary. The army continued to pass at Flat Lick on the nineteenth. I saw Captain Berry, my regimental quartermaster, and from him learned that the regiment would pass Cumberland Gap in a few days. I went to the gap, therefore and waiting for it to come up rejoined the command, weary then with toilsome marches.

The Battle of Fredericksburg

ST. CLAIR A. MULHOLLAND,
COLONEL, 116TH PENNSYLVANIA VOLUNTEER INFANTRY,
AND BREVET MAJOR GENERAL, U.S.V.

Philadelphia *Weekly Times* 5, no. 18, April 23, 1881

In the early days of November 1862 the mountains of the Blue Ridge looked down upon one of those scenes of martial pageantry, a display of force and arms and men in battle array that happily our country but seldom witnesses. For hours and days the great Army of the Potomac, masses of gallant men, infantry, cavalry and artillery, more than one hundred thousand in number—veterans of the Peninsula, victors of Antietam—swept by in serried ranks, with faultless step and perfection of discipline. Old hero [Brig. Gen. Edwin V.] Sumner was there with [Maj. Gen. John] Sedgwick, whom the men called father. And [Maj. Gen. William B.] Franklin and the brilliant [Brig. Gen. William W.] Averell, and [Maj. Gen. John F.] Reynolds, and [Maj. Gen. William F. "Baldy"] Smith, [Maj. Gen. Darius N.] Couch and [Brig. Gen. George D.] Bayard, who was so soon to fall; [Maj. Gen. George G.] Meade and the superb [Maj. Gen. Winfield S.] Hancock, [Maj. Gen. Daniel E.] Sickles and [Maj. Gen. William H.] French, and [Brig. Gen. Thomas F.] Meagher, the orator-soldier from the Emerald Isle, and the impetuous [Lt. George A.] Custer, whose golden locks were to fall in the Black Hills, and so in review they all passed by, but although the army had only a few short weeks before gained a glorious victory, the greatest and most important, as yet, of the war, a victory that had saved the national capital and checked the march of the Southern army towards the North, yet the occasion was one of the deepest sorrow. The saddest hour that ever the Army of the Potomac knew; every heart beat with a subdued throb, every eye was moist and tears wet alike the cheek of white-haired Sumner and the youngest drummer boy—for the great soldier who had organized and made this an army; the general that possessed the absolute confidence and love of every man there was taking his farewell of those corps that he had formed and taught and led so well; it was the last review of the noble army by the only general who had, as yet, shown the ability to lead it and who had just relinquished the command and who had been relieved at the moment when he had made another victory a certainty and the destruction of the army of Northern Virginia almost assured.

The order relieving General [George B.] McClellan from command was received on the evening of November 7, and a most ungracious moment was selected for his sudden removal—a moment pregnant with hope for our army and our cause. Never had his genius flashed forth with such luster. By the celerity of his movements and admirable handling of the army he had accomplished a most important strategic advantage. Leaving Harper's Ferry on the twenty-eighth of the previous month he had, by forced marching and a series of the most brilliant cavalry battles and skirmishes, seized the passes of the Blue Ridge and masked so well the movements of the main army as to completely deceive General [Robert E.] Lee as to our whereabouts and purposes, and on the evening of November 7, when he had concentrated our army in the vicinity of Warrenton, he had succeeded in practically severing the two wings of the Army of Northern Virginia—[Lt. Gen. James P.] Longstreet, with his corps, was at Culpeper, and [Lt. Gen. Thomas J. "Stonewall"] Jackson, with the remainder of the army, was at Millwood, west of the mountains and more than two days' march away. It was General McClellan's intention to strike Longstreet, and the early dawn of the following day would have found every corps in motion with that end in view, and with our forces of one hundred and twenty-seven thousand men, full of fight and hope and reliance on their leader, who could doubt the result? Longstreet would have been crushed before help could have reached him and then we could have taken our own time to finish the work and Jackson.

But, says someone, Longstreet would not have fought, but would have retired and formed a junction with the remainder of Lee's forces. Admit this and still we had the advantage. In order to connect with Jackson's Corps Longstreet would have to fall back upon Staunton, uncovering Richmond and leaving the road to that city open and clear. McClellan would then have promptly moved in and our flag would have floated over the rebel capitol. But then says the Comte de Paris, "Jackson and Lee certainly projected some bold movement upon McClellan's rear." This is not at all probable, for we now know, beyond a doubt, that General Lee had no such intention, and was not even aware of our position or whereabouts. Yet admitting the surmise of the Comte de Paris as correct, I assert that General McClellan would have welcomed any such movement on the part of the enemy with delight. It would have more effectually separated their forces and rendered the final triumph more certain. General McClellan had certainly succeeded in placing the Army of the Potomac between the two wings of the army of General Lee, and we could fail now only by the most lamentable blundering. But the great advantages secured by General McClellan to the army and the nation must be sacrificed and forever lost, in order that a political object might be gained, and the great soldier of Antietam had to fall.

So at noon on November 11, with the torn battle flags drooping to do him honor and the most enthusiastic demonstration of affection by all the troops, General George B. McClellan, bidding us adieu and saying, "We shall ever be comrades in supporting the Constitution of our country and the nationality of our people," left us and the soul of the army seemed to go with him. Not, indeed, that victories were not afterwards gained, or that the army ever failed to nobly respond to every call. Under [Maj. Gen. Ambrose E.] Burnside the men marched to death in a most hopeless contest, without a murmur. With [Maj. Gen. Joseph H.] Hooker they fought in a way that would have earned success had the head not failed. With Meade they hurled back the enemy from Gettysburg and covered the battalions with new glory, and under [Lt. Gen. Ulysses S.] Grant they stood up day after day, in battle after battle, with stubborn, unflinching courage, while brigades, divisions and corps were literally wiped from the face of the earth; but never again from that day until the end did the hearts of all the members of the army beat in sympathetic unison with that of the commander. Then General Burnside, the gallant soldier and honorable gentleman, protesting against the responsibility forced upon him, with unsteady hand gathered up the reins and inaugurated the campaign that was to terminate in the impotent, useless and sanguinary disasters of Fredericksburg. General [Henry W.] Halleck came down and visited us. The six corps were formed into three grand divisions under Sumner, Franklin and Hooker, and with Sumner and the Second Corps in the lead we marched for the Rappahannock.

On the evening of November 17 the head of our column struck the river near the old Virginia town of Falmouth. On the opposite bank we could see a battery of four guns which promptly opened upon us. General Sumner ordered Pettit's Battery to the front and in just eight minutes from

Maj. Gen. Ambrose Burnside
(PETER COZZENS COLLECTION)

the time that Pettit fired his first shot the graybacks had closed up shop and retired from business. Their four guns stood silenced and abandoned. Sumner, whose seventy-two years had not dampened the ardor of youth, carried away by the enthusiasm of the moment, called for troops to ford the river, seize the guns and occupy the city. The Irish Brigade had bivouacked in a field near by and were cooking coffee and resting after a hard day's march, but in three minutes after receiving the order the brigade was going to the river at a run. Then Sumner, remembering that he had orders not to cross and being too old a soldier to disobey, stopped the movement and sent back to General Burnside asking permission to occupy the city and the answer came, a peremptory "No!" So we were compelled to look at the prize without grasping it. How very odd the official report of this affair by General Lee when read along with the plain facts. He says: "The advance of General Sumner reached Falmouth on the afternoon of November 17 and attempted to cross the Rappahannock, but was driven back by Colonel Ball with the 15th Virginia Cavalry, four companies of Mississippi infantry and Lewis' Light Battery." Why we did not cross the river and push on for Richmond has been often told; blundering by somebody and no pontoons. A general feeling prevailed that the year's campaign was ended and winter quarters were next in order. The pine-covered hills and undulating slopes of meadowland, broken up by running brooks and rippling streams, furnished the most inviting sites for pleasant camps, and soon the dark woods were lit up by campfires. Campfires fifty feet long—whole trees cut down, piled up and forever kept cheerfully crackling and burning—around which the whole company would gather, and with their faces ruddy with the pleasant glow, spend the long evenings in uproarious fun, the day being filled up with marching, drilling, inspection and reviews, without limit. Thus passed the three most agreeable weeks I ever remember in the army. By and by the pontoons arrived, but too late. Lee and Jackson and Longstreet had also put in put in an appearance, and from the bluffs we could see them busy, very busy, indeed. Every day gave us new evidence of their industry. Every hour saw new earthworks rising in our front; redoubts, lunettes and bastioned forts, rifle pits, epaulements for the protection of artillery arose in rapid succession until the terraced heights which ran parallel to the city and two miles below and nearly a mile in the rear of it, were crowned with artillery, bristling with bayonets and so formidable as to make an attempt to carry the place an act of insanity. The coming fight was to be an assault upon an entrenched position rather than an open battle.

Some time about the first week of December a council of war was held at headquarters, at which General Burnside and the grand division and corps commanders were present. It is difficult at this day to tell just what was determined at this council, as one of those present afterward remarked, they talked to General Burnside at arm's length. There would seem to have been a total absence of that harmony and unity of purpose so necessary to success between the commanding general and his lieutenants; a painful uncertainty, a vagueness of purpose hangs over these meetings; but it is evident, however, that a flank movement by way of Skinker's Neck, twelve miles below the city, was discussed and determined upon and the council adjourned, believing this to be the program. A few days after this General Burnside sent for one of the corps commanders and invited him to ride with him along the high bluffs, Stafford Heights, that skirted the river in front of the city. He there told him that he (Burnside) had determined to change the order of battle and to cross and fight at the city, and gave as one of his reasons that Colonel [Henry J.] Hunt had called his attention to the excellent opportunity that Stafford Heights offered for the employment of all our artillery. The general officer in question, after being warned by General Burnside not to communicate the fact of the change to anyone, left him with a sinking heart and dark forebodings of the coming storm. General Burnside, in a letter to General Halleck, dated December 19, 1862, a few days after the battle, confirms the idea that the original intention, known to not only the grand division and corps commanders, but also General Halleck and the president, was that of turning Lee's flank, and in this letter he magnanimously takes all the responsibility for the change and failure upon himself. He says: "I have the honor to offer the following reasons for moving the Army of the Potomac across the Rappahannock sooner than was anticipated by the president, the secretary of war, or yourself, and for crossing at a point different from the one indicated to you at our last meeting at the president's."

This contemplated flank movement was discovered by the enemy, and General Lee, to be prepared for it, had sent General [Daniel H.] Hill's Division to the vicinity of Skinker's Neck and the balance of Jackson's Corps was stationed so as to support him. The fact of Lee's army having been partially separated seems to have been the only reason for General Burnside's altering, unknown to any of his subordinates, the plan of operations.

He thought that by rapidly throwing the whole army across at Fredericksburg and striking a vigorous blow he could pierce the extended and weakened line and divide the forces of the enemy which were down the river from those on the crest in rear of the town. So the night of December 10 found us in motion. The roads leading to the front were filled with troops, in silence marching to the fray, camps deserted, the campfires burning dim, the woods pouring out their thousands, everyone, everything moving towards the river, the infantry massing in rear of the bluffs by the stream and the chief of artillery, Colonel Hunt, covering those heights with one hundred and forty-seven cannon. The pontooneers were hurrying the boats, planks and bridge material to the water's edge.

Working rapidly, swiftly, but so noiselessly that those within one hundred yards of the enemy's pickets, who were lined on the opposite shore, were not heard, the pontoons were brought down and quietly let into the water, great piles of planking arose, a multitude of spectral men were hurrying to and fro, cannon was got into position, more than one hundred thousand cavalry and infantry massed at hand. Yet no confusion, no clashing, so perfect the discipline; the silence so profound, no sound save the lapping of the waves on the prow of the pontoons, the moaning of wind in the forest trees. The night wore on. Two regiments of engineers, the 15th and 50th New York, stood prepared to build the bridges, and two regiments of Hancock's Division, the 57th New York, Colonel Chapman, and the 66th New York, Colonel Bull, were on hand to cover and support them. Towards dawn the work began—swiftly fastening the boats to the bank, getting others in position, lashing them together, putting down the planking, so the work, for a few minutes, went on; then the sharp crack of a rifle broke the stillness of the night, a pontooneer dropped his burden, fell forward into the dark, cold water, and went floating down with the tide; the first victim, the first corpse of the fight; then more shots and balls went whistling through the fog. Then two loud reports of heavy ordnance peal from Marye's Heights, echo along the Valley of the Rappahannock, reverberate among the hills, the signal for the concentration of the Army of Northern Virginia; the battle of Fredericksburg begins. The firing becomes heavier, volleys of musketry, the rifle balls rattle on the flanks and the boats are riddled. Many, very many, of the pontooneers fall and go floating away.

It is so dark and the fog so dense that we can see but a few yards from the edge of the shore. Men go out on the bridge in the darkness and never return. The fire is hot and deadly—but the men stick to their work most gallantly—but every moment the numbers of the artificers become less. Bull and Chapman return the fire, but they shoot at random and into the dark, while the enemy know by the sound of the bridge building where to throw their iron. Colonel Bull falls mortally wounded and the losses are so great that the engineers fall back and for a time give up the attempt. Again they try it and again they fail, and a third time they rush at the work but find it an impossibility to continue, and the brave little band falls back, leaving the bridge half-finished, slippery and saturated with blood. Then daylight is upon us. The work must be pushed. The bridge must be finished. The riflemen that checked our work must be driven out of their shelter, and for that purpose General Burnside decides upon treating us to one of those rare and magnificently grand spectacles of war, the bombardment of a city, so the order went forth to batter down the town, and about 10:00 A.M. our twenty-nine batteries, one hundred and forty-seven guns, opened. Then for an hour or two the fire was incessant, the sharp crack of the rifled guns, the heavy boom of the larger ordnance mingled with the echoes from the woods and hills until we could no longer distinguish separate sounds, and the roar became continuous; clouds of sulphurous smoke rolled back from the massed artillery, the air became loaded, suffocating, with the odor of gunpowder.

The fog still lay heavy in the river; the water margins and the lowlands and the city was almost hidden from our view. One of the church spires shot up through the mist, glittering in the morning sun and a few of the tallest chimneys and buildings struggled into sight. Tons of iron were hurled into the town; shells, solid shot, shrapnel and canister raked and swept the streets. We could not see yet. We could hear the walls crumbling and timbers crashing; then a pillar of smoke rose above the fog; another and another, increasing in density and volume, rose skyward and canopied the doomed city like a pall. Flames leaped high out of the mist—the city was on fire. Again the engineers make an attempt to finish the bridge, but they find Barksdale with his Mississippians still at their posts and their fire still as accurate and the effort is finally abandoned.

Then Colonel Hunt drops an idea that a party be sent over in open pontoon boats to drive the sharpshooters from the opposite shore. Strange that the simple device was not thought of before. But better late than never. A dozen of the boats lie by the river bank and plenty of volunteers are ready to man them. The 7th Michigan and 19th and 20th Massachusetts rush down the steep bank, launch the boats and are off. The oarsmen pull lustily, the Southern marksmen redouble their fire, many in the boats are killed and wounded, but in a few minutes the shore is reached, our boys leaping out form in line and dashing through the smoke and fire drive the sharpshooters from their shelter. Soon more boatloads of our men come over, the river front is in our possession, and the work of building the bridges progresses to completion. But we have not yet captured the city. The first troops that cross over the bridges thus constructed had to fight for every foot of ground, and it was not until dark and after a sharp contest through streets, lanes and alleys, met at every step by the fire of Barksdale's men from windows, roofs and every available point, that our line finally halted for the night on Caroline Street. The dead were everywhere, in the street, on the cellar doors, in the yards of the houses, in the gardens by the river. Some few of the citizens had remained during the bombardment, taking refuge in the cellars, and two of them were killed, a man named Jacob Grotz and a Negro woman. On the left, where Franklin was to cross, half a mile below the city, but little difficulty had been met, and he finished his bridges early in the morning.

It was now more than twelve hours since the signal gun of General Lee summoned his divided army to concentrate, and as the sole hope of success on the part of General Burnside rested on being able to cross the river in force and take the enemy by surprise, it would look as though our cause had already sustained a heavy blow in this unfortunate delay. Moments now were precious, yet the whole night of this day was suffered to pass without a move on our part, and our troops did not begin crossing in force until the morning of the twelfth, and by 5:00 P.M. of that day the grand division of Sumner had crossed on the lower bridges. It was now thirty-six hours since the movement against Fredericksburg began, giving General Lee ample time to get his corps together, destroying any virtue that might have existed in General Burnside's plan of attack and rendering it absolutely abortive. Owing to the delay in forcing the passage of the river the enterprise had been stripped of its only hope and our failure was complete, our only alternative to withdraw the army or adopt an entirely new plan of battle.

To retire was not thought of, fight we must; the evil genius of General Burnside seemed to irresistibly beckon him on to destruction. The silver lining of the cloud that was gathering over us was a suggestion that originated with General Franklin: that the battle should be fought on the left; that a column of thirty or forty thousand men should be formed and at daylight on the morning of the thirteenth make the main assault on the Confederate right with this body. This idea had no doubt also occurred to General Sumner, for during the afternoon of this day he had directed General Hancock to build bridges over Hazel Run, a creek that ran between our right and left wings. In preparation for this movement General Burnside visited the left at 5:00 P.M. and discussed with Generals Franklin, Smith and Reynolds this order of battle and at dark left them with the full understanding that it was adopted by him, promising to send the orders for carrying it into execution before midnight, thus giving time enough to General Franklin to get troops into position during the night. Had this attack in Franklin's front been carried out it would most likely have been successful and General Burnside would have gone down to posterity as a great general; but it was not to be, and instead of pushing the preparations for the only movement that contained a ray of hope General Burnside went back to his headquarters and went to bed, leaving Franklin, Smith, and Reynolds anxiously waiting the orders that were to insure a victory—and how patiently they waited together with their respective staffs, sitting up all night, thinking, wondering, trying to conceive what important event must have happened to prevent the arrival of the expected orders.

In the city the troops bivouacked in the streets. Sleep was impossible, it was so cold and chilly. Groups of officers occupied the parlors of the fashionable residences, spending the night in song and story and Reb pianos played accompaniment to "Hail Columbia" and the "Star Spangled Banner." Fires still lit up portions of the town, the firmament was aglow with a magnificent Aurora Borealis, the artillerists strove to rival the glories of nature and illumined the sky with scores of shells whose trailing fuses filled the air with streams of light. The long hours slipped away, morning came and at 7:30 A.M. General Hardie handed to Franklin orders for a new plan of battle—not which was discussed and determined upon the night before, but the most remarkable, incongruous, disjointed plan of action, with the least possible hope of success, that ever emanated from the brain of a commander. "That Franklin should keep his whole command in position for a rapid movement down the old Richmond road. That he should send out a division, at least, to seize the heights at Captain Hamilton's, on the extreme right of the enemy's line. He also orders another column of a division or more from the command of General Sumner to seize the heights in the rear of the town." Two isolated attacks by light columns, on distant positions, rendered almost impregnable and held by the flower of the Rebel army.

Franklin selected the Pennsylvania Reserves for the almost superhuman task and for the reason that that division at the moment lay nearest the point of attack. General Meade, their commander, was one of the most discreet and able officers in the service and the division was one of the most reliable, and indeed for other reasons the selection was most admirable. The line of march to reach the heights to be carried was across a level plain, over which hung a thick haze; the Reserves had been encamped here for some time the year before when attached to McDowell's forces and knew every inch of the ground to be marched over and fought for. So having got his instructions, Meade started the division into the fog and into a fight that was to cover with glory himself and his command, though at the cost of nearly half their number—the objective point, the heights at Hamilton's, in a direct line two miles away. The division was formed with the First Brigade on the right, the Third on the left and the Second in support. Hardly had the march commenced when the enemy began firing; although they could not see our lines, yet they seemed to feel that something was going on; solid shot and shells went flying over the fog shrouded plain. Meade rode along the lines giving words of encouragement to each regiment. As he passed Colonel McCandless he said, alluding to a possible promotion: "A star this morning, William"; to which McCandless replied: "More likely a wooden overcoat," then a shell passed through the horse ridden by McCandless and he did the rest of the fighting for that day on foot. And so for a half hour the march went on; then young Major Pelham, of Stuart's Horse Artillery, from a point on the Port Royal road, opened a telling fire on Meade's left flank, enfilading his whole line and becoming so annoying as to cause him to pause. The line halts and the four light batteries of the Reserves return Pelham's fire and so vigorously as to cause his sudden withdrawal. Stuart, with his cavalry, makes threatening demonstrations and General Doubleday is deployed on Meade's left to check him.

Franklin instructs Gibbon to support Meade's right and again the column moves forward. To meet the attack General Lee has arranged Jackson's corps in the woods at Hamilton's, with A. P. Hill's division composing his second line and D. H. Hill's division in reserve. The division of A. P. Hill, forming the advanced line, was composed of the brigades of Archer, Lane and Pender, with the brigades of Gregg and Thomas directly in their rear. As Meade neared the enemy's lines the fog suddenly lifted, giving the Confederate artillerists a clear view of our advancing lines. Three batteries—those of Weeder, Braxton, and Carpenter—that had been pushed out on the skirmish line in front of Lane's Brigade and the five batteries of Lieutenant Colonel Walker's command opened on our ranks, using shell and canister, damaging our alignment considerable; but Meade pushes on, the four light batteries of the Reserves reply energetically. General Smith (Baldy), seeing the trouble from afar, directs the fire of his Sixth Corps guns upon the three batteries first named and compels their withdrawal. The cloud of skirmishers that cover our advance strikes and drives in those of the Confederates.

The battle waxes hot, but Meade, oblivious to the roar, impetuously pushes on; with a great crash our infantry strike that of the enemy; the fighting for a few moments is extremely earnest. Our men vie with each other in acts of noble daring. Many prisoners are taken and one regiment—the Nineteenth Georgia—is captured entire, Corporal Jacob Carl, of the Seventh Reserves, tearing from the hands of the color bearer the flag of that regiment. Our men drive Lane's Brigade back across the railroad into

The fierce fighting on Meade's front (BEYER, *DEEDS OF VALOR*)

the woods, and crashing through the interval between the brigades of Archer and Pender flank both their lines and compel them to fall back, then up the wooded crest with a rush so sudden that General Maxcy Gregg, the Confederate commander on the second line, cannot believe that the advancing troops is the Union line and falls dead while trying to prevent his South Carolinians from firing upon us. But his men pour a withering fire into our line. At this moment the divisions of Generals Early and Taliaferro sweep forward at a double-quick, striking Meade with irresistible force and overpowering numbers, enveloping his flanks and endangering his whole command. The situation becomes most critical, the surroundings awfully grand. The woods echoed and re-echoed every shot until the roar is appalling. Great shells go screaming through forest, cutting down giant trees and the crash of the falling timber adds to the deafening sound. In the midst of the tumult the Reserves fall back and are soon out again on the open plain. In one short hour our men had known both the thrilling ecstasies of victory and disastrous defeat. Meade halted after recrossing the railroad and reformed the division, but he was not allowed much time to rest. Early pushed after him and the brigade of Atkinson and Hoke struck with vigor at the shattered ranks, forcing him to fall back rapidly and with some confusion. Franklin, foreseeing the difficulty, had ordered Birney's Division to the front and just in time he arrived to check the advancing enemy and save what was left of the Reserves.

While Meade was moving on Hamilton's, the troops in the city were prepared to strike. Under arms, listening to the sounds of the fight on the left and waiting patiently for their turn to share in the strife, [Brig.] Gen. Thomas Francis Meagher, mounted and surrounded by his staff, addressed each regiment of his (the Irish) brigade and in burning, eloquent words besought the men to uphold in the coming struggle the military prestige and glory of their native land. Then green boxwood was culled from a garden near and Meagher placed a sprig in his Irish cap. Every officer and man followed his example and soon great bunches of the fragrant shrub adorned the caps of everyone. Wreaths were made and hung upon the tattered flags and the national color of the Emerald Isle blended in fair harmony with the red, white and blue of the Republic. At noon, Meade not yet having reached Hamilton's, General Couch ordered French and Hancock to the assault. French moved first, closely followed by the superb. As we wheeled into the streets leading towards the enemy we were in full view of the frowning heights and the march of death began. Nearly a mile away arose the position that we were expected to carry and though not yet clear of the city we felt the pressure of the foe, the fire of whose batteries concentrated to crush the heads of our column as they debouched upon the plain. Solid shot, fired with light charges, ricochet on the frozen ground, caromed on the pavement and went tearing through the ranks, traversing the entire length of the streets, bounding over the river to be buried in the opposite bluff.

Shells began dropping with destructive effect. One striking in the 88th New York placed eighteen men hors de combat. I will ever remember the first one that burst in my regiment—wounding the colonel, cutting off the head of Sergeant Marley and killing two or three others. I was struck by the instantaneousness of the deaths. The column had halted for a moment, a sharp report, a puff of smoke and three or four men lay stark dead, their faces calm, their eyes mild and lifelike, lips unmoved, no sign of pain or indication of suffering. Marley had not fallen, but dropped upon his knees, his musket clasped in both hands and resting upon the ground. After getting into the open and crossing a millrace a rise in the ground hid us from the enemy, giving an opportunity to dress the ranks and prepare the column of attack, which was by brigade front, General Kimball's Brigade in the lead, followed by those of Col. J. W. Andrews and Colonel Palmer. Hancock's Division came next, with the brigades of Zook, Meagher, and Caldwell in the order named. Here the thought struck me: "How different is the real battle from that which our imagination had pictured. After the reading of our boyhood, with heads filled with Napoleon and his marshals and harrowing tales of gory fields of yore, with what realistic feeling we can see the wild confusion of the storm-swept field—charging cavalry, hurrying artillery, the riderless steeds madly rushing to and fro, their shrill neighing mingling with the groans, screams and shrieks of the wounded." Here there is no disorder. The men calm, silent, cheerful. The commands of the officers, given in a quiet, subdued voice, are distinctly heard and calmly obeyed. The regiments maneuver without a flaw.

In this trying moment the guides are ordered out and the alignment made as perfect as on dress parade. The destruction of human beings is done with order and system. Yet it is terrible enough; the very absence of confusion and excitement but adds to the dreadful intensity of the horror. As for the screams and shrieks, I have never heard anything of that kind either on the field or in the hospitals. It may be that the soldiers of other nations indulge in cries and yells; our men took their punishment without a complaint or a murmur. Just before morning from this spot one of my young officers, a brave boy from Chester County, Pennsylvania, Lieutenant Seneca G. Willauer, was badly torn by a shell, which stripped the flesh from his thigh and left the bone for four or five inches white and bare. He came to me and holding up the bleeding limb for inspection, said, with the most gentle manner and placid voice: "Colonel, do you think that I should go on with my company or go to the hospital?" No doubt had I told him to go on he would have done so. Then the advance is sounded. The orders of the regimental commanders ring out clear on the cold December air. "Right shoulder, shift arms," "battalion forward, guide center, march!" The long lines of bayonets glitter in the bright sunlight. We have no friendly fog, as Meade had, to hide us from our foes, and as we advance up the slope we come in full view of the Army of Northern Virginia. All their batteries open upon us. We can trace their line by the fringe of blue smoke that quickly appears along the base of the hills and we see that we are marching into an arc of fire. And what a reception awaits us! Fire in our front, from our right and our left. Shells come at us direct and oblique and drop down from above; shells enfilade our lines, burst among us in front, in rear, above and behind us. Shells everywhere; a torrent of shells; a blizzard of shot, shell and fire. The lines pass on steadily. The gaps made in the ranks are quickly closed. The colors often kiss the ground, but are quickly snatched from the dead hands and held aloft again by others who soon in their turn will bite the dust. The regimental commanders march out far in advance of their commands and they, too, fall rapidly, but others run to take their places. Still in good order, we push forward until five hundred yards of the long half mile that lay between us and Marye's Heights is passed, then the sharp whiz of the minie joins the loud scream of the oblong bolts.

Soon we forget the presence of the shells in the shower of smaller missiles that assails us. The hills run fire, and the men advance with heads bowed, as when walking against a hailstorm. Still through the deadly shower the ever-thinning lines press on. The plain over which we have passed is thickly spotted with the men of the Second Corps, dead, in twos and threes and in groups. Regiments and companies have now their third or fourth commander and the colors are borne to the front by the third or fourth gallant soul who has raised them. The gaps in the line have become so large and so numerous that we have to make continued efforts to close them and the command "Guide center" is frequently heard. French nears the entrenchments of the Confederates' first line, and the enemy redouble their efforts. The storm rises to greater fury. The struggle is hopeless. His lines wave like corn in a hurricane, recoil, then break, and the shattered mass falls back amid the shouts and cheers of Cobb's and Kershaw's brigades that line the trenches in our front. Now Hancock, with the division that never lost a gun or a color, sweeps forward, and being joined by many of the gallant men of French's command makes the most heroic effort of the day. Passing the furthest point reached by the preceding troops, he impetu-

The attack on Marye's Heights (LIBRARY OF CONGRESS)

ously rushes on, passes the brick house so conspicuous on the field—on, on, until his flag waved within twenty-five paces of the fatal stone wall. Then with a murderous fire everywhere around us we realized the full absurdity of the attempt to accomplish an utter impossibility. We had not yet fired a shot. We had only reached the spot where our work was to begin. Forty percent of the force had already fallen. No support within three-quarters of a mile. In our front line after line of works followed each other up the terraced heights to the very crest, which was covered with artillery. To carry the assault further would be extreme madness. Should we take and occupy the first line, it would simply be to meet the fire of the second and third. To fight the host in front was not possible. We were here only to be shot down without being able to return the blow. So the division, or rather the half of it that still existed, began falling back; but Hancock would not be driven from the field, and halting where the formation of the ground afforded some shelter to his hard-tried command, he remained until relieved at nightfall. And now the long, long, dreadful afternoon that awaited the thousands wounded, who lay scattered over the sad and ghastly plain.

The only place of cover was the brick house out near the stone wall. To this hundreds of the wounded dragged themselves and a great mass of sufferers huddled together and struggled to get nearer the house, that they might escape the fire. All around the great heaps of dead bore testimony to the fierceness of combat. Near by a color sergeant lay stark and cold with the flag of his regiment covering him. Just in front of the stone wall lay a line of men of the Irish Brigade, with the green boxwood in their caps, and the two bodies nearest the enemy were those of my beloved friends, Major William Horgan and Adjutant John R. Young, both of the 88th New York. It was not yet 1:00 P.M. when the assaulting column retired and we had nearly five hours to wait for darkness. We heard the clock in the Episcopal Church in the city strike the hours that seemed so long. The sharpshooters of the enemy soon got a position from which they could enfilade the house, and when anyone moved among the mass of bleeding men it was the signal for the rifle balls to whistle around. Few of us expected to live until night, and but few did. Keeping very quiet, hugging the ground closely, we talked together in low tones. The bullets kept whistling and dropping, and every few moments someone would cease talking never to speak again. How quietly they passed away from the crimson field to eternity, their last gaze on their waving flag, the last sound to reach their ears the volleys of musketry and their comrades' cheers.

What a cosmopolitan crowd these dead and wounded were—Americans from the Atlantic Coast and the Pacific States, from the prairies, from the great valleys of the Mississippi and the Ohio; Irishmen from the banks of the Shannon and Germans from the Rhine and the blue Danube; Frenchmen from the Seine and Italians from the classic Tiber mingled their blood and went down in death together that our cause and the Union might live. Every little while we could see other columns emerge from the city, deploy upon the plain, march forward, but never get so far as the brick house. The appearance of these troops would draw the fire of the batteries on the hills above us and hundreds of deadly projectiles would go screaming over us and we could see them bursting in the midst of our friends. Evening came at last; the sun went down behind the terrible heights and we anxiously watched the shadows lengthen and steal across the field of blood, creeping slowly over the plain, through the houses of the city in the shade, then up the church tower until the only object that reflects the rays was the cross of burnished gold, which sparkled a moment against the purple sky and then twilight was upon us and deepened until it was difficult to discern objects. We thought the battle ended, when through the darkness loomed up the division of Hooker. Nobly they came to the work, with empty muskets and orders to carry the position with the bayonet. The dark mass passed the brick house and almost to the point that Hancock had reached. They had come up through the gloaming unseen and surged against the base of Marye's Heights.

Again the hills flashed fire, shook, rocked, roared, and belched forth more tons of iron on the red plain, more minutes of useless carnage. The somber wave rolled back, the last and most absurd attempt of the disastrous day had come to naught and seventeen hundred more had been added to the ponderous list of casualties. Clouds overshadowed the skies, and guided by the lurid fires still smoldering through the ebony darkness, the immense crowd of wounded began crawling, struggling, dragging themselves towards

Cobb and Kershaw's Confederates behind the Stone Wall (CENTURY MAGAZINE)

the city, those who were slightly hurt assisting others who were more seriously injured; those with shattered limbs using muskets for crutches, many fainting and falling by the way. And when in the town how hard to find a spot to rest or a surgeon to bind up the wounds. More wounded than the city had inhabitants, every public hall and house filled to overflow, the porches of the residences covered with bleeding men, the surgeons busy everywhere. In the lecture room of the Episcopal church eight operating tables are in full blast, the floor is densely packed with men whose limbs are crushed, fractured, and torn. Lying there, in deep pools of blood, they wait so very patiently, almost cheerfully, their turn to be treated; there is no grumbling, no screaming, hardly a moan; many of the badly hurt smile and chat and one, who has both legs shot off, is cracking jokes with an officer who cannot laugh at the humorous sallies, for his lower jaw is shot away.

The cases here are nearly all capital and amputation is nearly always resorted to. Hands and feet, arms and legs are thrown under each table and the sickening piles grow large as the night progresses. The delicate limbs of the drummer boy fall along with the rough hand of the veteran in years, but all, everyone is so brave and cheerful. Towards morning the conversation flags; many drop off to sleep before they can be attended to and some of them never wake again. The only sound is the crunching of the surgeons' saws and now and then the melancholy music of a random shell dismally wailing overhead. Few the prayers that are said, but I can yet hear the soft voice of a boyish soldier as he is lifted on to the table, his limbs a mass of quivering, lacerated flesh, quietly say, "Oh my God, I offer all my sufferings here in atonement for the sins by which I have crucified Thee." Outside the members of the Christian Commission are hard at work relieving all within reach, the stretcher carriers hurrying the wounded from the field; and a few priests and the chaplains were quietly moving among the suffering thousands, shivering, giving them comfort and soothing their dying hour. Out on the railroad at Hamilton's lays the body of the fearless commander of the 3rd Brigade of the Pennsylvania Reserves, [Brig.] Gen. C. Fager Jackson, and at the Bernard House, where he had been carried, died at midnight the youngest general officer and one of the most beloved of all that fell, [Brig.] Gen. George D. Bayard of the cavalry. While conversing with some other officers early in the day a shell struck the group, passing through the overcoat of Captain H. G. Gibson, destroying his saber. It crushed General Bayard's thighs and carried away a portion of his abdomen. He lived fourteen hours after being hit and passed the time in quietly giving directions and in dictating letters to his friends. In one to Colonel Collum he said, "Give my love to General McClellan and say my only regret is that I did not die under his command." He was to have been married on the following Wednesday. The bride awaited her cavalier, who never came. Bayard, *sans peur et sans reproche*. The losses in some of the commands were unusually severe. The 11th Pennsylvania Reserves lost six color-bearers inside of a few minutes and Company E of that regiment had but three men left unhurt. Company C, 12th Reserves, lost forty of the forty-nine present, and among the wounded was the captain, H. S. Lucas.

But the most appalling loss was in the division of General Hancock. Of the five officers composing his personal staff, three were wounded and four horses were killed under them. The general himself was struck by a rifle ball but not seriously hurt. Of the sixteen officers of the 69th New York, every one was killed or wounded, and the regiment lost seventy-five percent of the enlisted men and left the field with its fourth commander, three having been disabled. The 5th New Hampshire lost seventeen out of twenty-three officers and had five commanding officers during the fight. The 116th Regiment Pennsylvania Volunteers had all the field and staff and many of the line officers killed or wounded and was taken off the field by the fourth officer in command during the fight. The first color-sergeant, William H. Tyrell, held up the flag until hit with five rifle balls. The 81st Pennsylvania lost twelve out of sixteen officers and seventy-five percent of the enlisted men. The fourth commanding officer brought the regiment off the field. The 57th New York lost nine out of the eleven officers present. The 66th New York had four commanders during the battle, the three first having been killed or wounded. Many other regiments of the division suffered almost as severely, yet, notwithstanding the great loss, on the morning of the following day, when ordered to support the IX Corps, the command fell in, ready and willing, and the contemplated assault with the IX Corps, led by General Burnside in person—from which he was happily dissuaded by Generals Sumner and Hooker at the moment that all was ready to make the attack—was the last attempt of the campaign.

The day of December 14 passed without a renewal of the contest, but was made remarkable by an episode very unusual on such occasions. The flags of the regiments of the Irish Brigade had been torn to ribbons during the many contests in which it had participated, and the citizens of New York had procured others to present in their place. The standards arrived during the battle, and with them came a committee who brought a very generous supply of the good things of earth wherewith to celebrate the presentation, and a banquet was determined upon. A concert hall in one of the upper streets was selected for the feast. Here the tables were spread and decorations improvised. Invitations were sent out, and at noon two or three hundred officers seemed to do honor to the event and toast the new banners. For two or three hours the hall teemed with wine and rang with wit and eloquence and the flags were baptized amid speeches by Couch, Hancock, Sturgis, Meagher, and many other distinguished and gallant officers. The enjoyment and festivities ran high, the enthusiasm great, but the loud cheers drew the fire of the Southern batteries and the enemy, envying perhaps the good times our friends were having, sent their compliments in the shape of shells; one of them passing through the ceiling of the room knocked the plaster down among the viands and was suggestive of an early adjournment; so the company separated with rather unceremonious leave-taking—not on account of the shell, certainly not, but as some of the gentlemen remarked, it being Sunday they thought it well to close the feast a little early that they might attend Divine service. During the night of this day and on Monday, the fifteenth, the troops lay on their arms waiting the next event. After dark a rumor spread that the army was to move to the left and strike the enemy again the following morning, but soon the columns began marching over the river and through the storm and gloom back to their camps. Shortly after daylight on the sixteenth the last regiment, the 69th Pennsylvania Volunteers, filed across the pontoons. With sturdy blows the pontoniers severed on the city side the lashings of the bridge, which swung around with the current of the stream, landing on the other shore, leaving to the mercy of God and the enemy the killed and many of the wounded of our gallant army. The battle was over; the result, a graveyard. Save one regimental flag, no trophies of the fight were ours. Yet the field was redolent with acts of noble daring. No troops that marched on Marye's Heights but equaled in the grandeur of their bravery the gallant six hundred immortalized by the poet laureate, while by this sacrifice, though they did not gain a victory, they raised a monument more enduring than marble or brass to the valor and heroism of our times and our people; and in other ages, when the memories of the contest will have been mellowed by the lapse of centuries, in the bloodshed will be seen a holocaust at the altar of freedom, in the smoke of the battle sweet incense at the shrine of human liberty. We failed—so did Leonidas of Sparta, yet what son of Hellas but shares even to this day in the glory of old Thermopylae and what American even to the most remote period of the future but will share in the glories that cluster around the plain of Fredericksburg. These fields resplendent with the great deeds of our people, where the verdure and every blooming flower is nurtured and enriched by martyr blood, will ever be hallowed places in our land, around which will crystallize the warm, full gratitude of a nation saved.

The Rout of Rosecrans

W. R. FRIEND,
LIEUTENANT, 8TH TEXAS CAVALRY, C.S.A.

Philadelphia *Weekly Times* 9, no. 31, August 9, 1885

The principal fighting around Murfreesboro was done on Wednesday, December 31, 1862. On the twenty-sixth of that month [Maj. Gen. William Starke] Rosecrans began to advance from his fortifications in the vicinity of Nashville. On that day the Confederate cavalry pickets on the Nolensville Turnpike were driven in. After much desultory skirmishing on boggy ground and in long muddy roads, on the afternoon of the twenty-ninth [Brig. Gen. John A.] Wharton's Cavalry Division, two brigades, commanded by Colonels [Thomas] Harrison, of Texas, and Crews, of Georgia, there being in all eleven regiments, aggregating about four thousand effective men, were escorted by the bluecoats into Gen. [Braxton] Bragg's lines, where the reception was warm and by no means cordial. They struck [Maj. Gen. John P.] McCown's Division on Bragg's left, in front of which was a battery commanded by Capt. Felix W. Robertson, a youthful Texan, a little beyond his majority. This battery, mistaking Wharton for the enemy, let loose on his advance with painful accuracy, dispersing it for the time being and killing and wounding a few men and horses.

Wharton sent forward an orderly to inform our side of the error. This orderly was a German, who spoke in broken English, but riding forward impetuously he stirred up a hornet's nest in the way of a skirmish line in front of Robertson's Battery, which, mistaking him for a Federal, instantly put an end to his Confederate enthusiasm by riddling him with bullets. It took an hour or so to recover from the confusion occasioned by this fire in the rear.

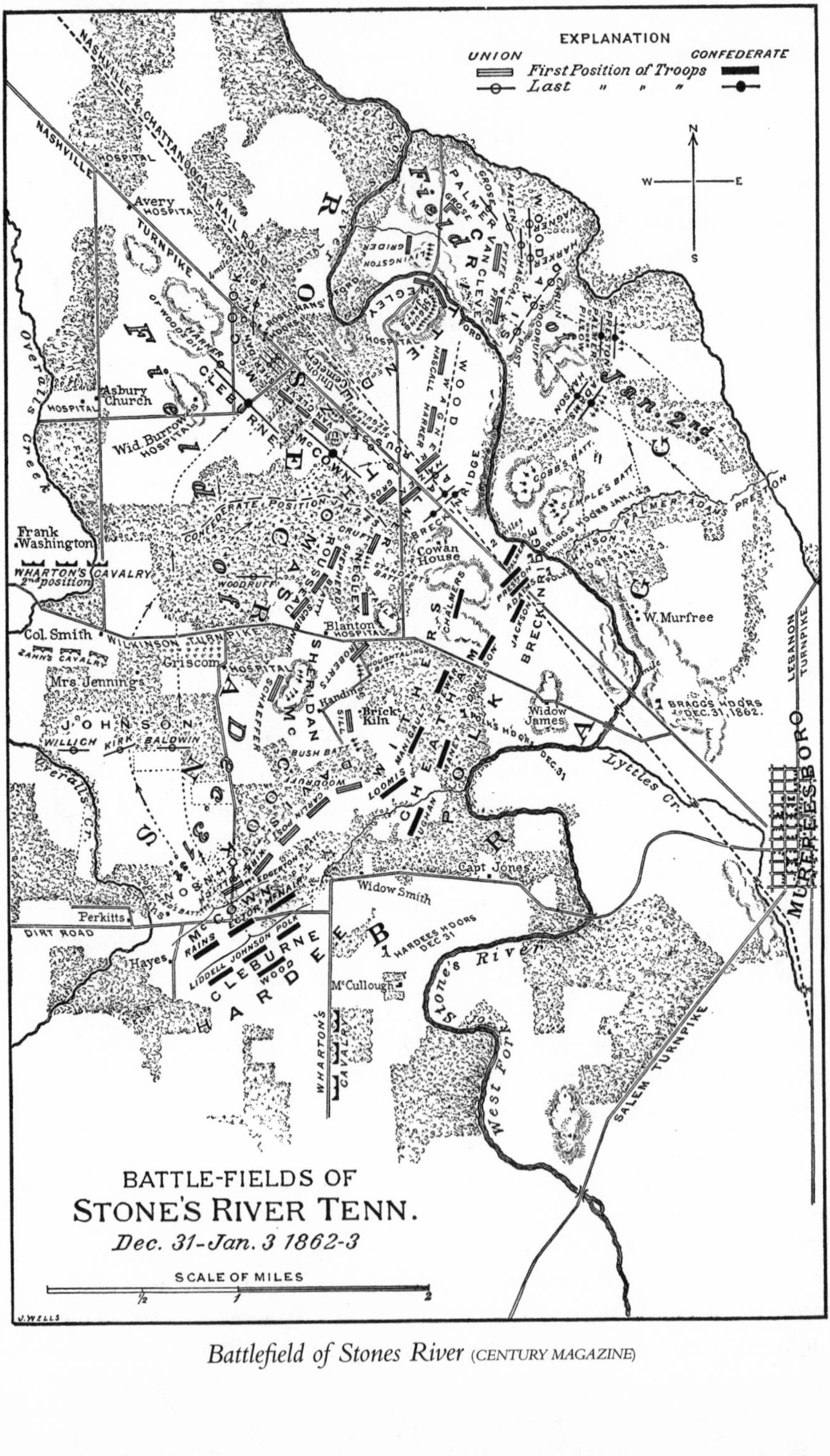

Battlefield of Stones River (CENTURY MAGAZINE)

Before sunset, however, Wharton's Division was pretty well established in line on the left of McCown, his division covering and protecting about five miles on Bragg's left. This position was occupied during Tuesday. Towards night the artillery performances, which had been casual during the day, became the center of attraction. The enemy threw forward several batteries, while Bragg utilized but one, that of Robertson, the others being masked in reserve, as I afterwards learned. [Brig. Gen. Wiley B.] Ector's Texas Brigade was on the left of McCown's Division, Harrison's Cavalry Brigade was next on the left of Ector, with the 8th Texas Cavalry, known in the Army of Tennessee as the Terry [Texas] Rangers, on Harrison's right. This was the order of battle on the afternoon of the thirtieth.

About sunset the writer's company was sent some four miles in the direction of our left to picket. The night was passed without anything to note, but at daylight, a clear cold morning, it was evident to the ear that something beyond a skirmish was taking place. Soon the roar of a great battle was heard and it was plain that somebody was getting hurt.

A courier soon reached me, ordering that we should close to the right with all speed and report to Colonel Harrison. This was done with promptness, and about sunrise we joined the brigade on the left of our army and found Ector's Brigade of infantry immediately on our right. Here a scene seldom seen was presented. As far as the eye could reach the fields and open places were covered by more men than I ever before, at one time, beheld. The enemy was routed and retreating, some running apparently for dear life. There would be seen squads, companies, and fragments of regiments in measurably good order, doggedly falling back, and while doing so, wheeling and firing on the advancing Confederates, who soon became a mixed mass of cavalry and infantry. The Terry Rangers on horses and Ector's infantry on foot were whooping, screaming and yelling, hungry and dirty. The game was noble and the pursuit was so exciting that the veriest coward on earth could not have skulked to the rear.

The killing and capturing lasted about an hour, when approaching the Nashville Pike a shell or two from a battery of the enemy checked the excitement for a while and disabused our minds of the impression that Rosecrans' army was entirely routed and in full retreat. The bugle brought the 8th Texas to a halt, when it was rapidly reformed, fronting the battery. I think about two hundred men were rapidly gotten into line. There was a delay in making a charge on the battery as had been ordered by the brigade commander, Colonel Harrison, which, being observed by him, he hastened up and ordered Capt. Gustave Cook to assume command and to charge. This order was promptly responded to by him and at his heels the regiment dashed forward and two pieces of the artillery were captured. The other two pieces running off and falling back on an infantry support escaped. Here all were drawn off and for an hour or so kept still and out of range of hostile guns.

The result of the morning's work so far was a receipt to the division commander for about 1,500 prisoners and two pieces of artillery. The casualties in killed and wounded did not exceed twenty. General Wharton here remarked that our regiment in the charge on the battery had approached within a quarter of a mile of General Rosecrans' headquarters near the Nashville and Murfreesboro Pike and complimented the regiment for its dash and gallantry, but his compliments fell on empty stomachs, for we had eaten no supper or breakfast and the morning exercise had generated a taste for something more substantial than compliments from the general commanding.

The compliments ending and empty stomachs continuing, we soon found ourselves in a line of battle, beyond the reach of my eye to the right and left. The Rangers were about the center of the division, which fronted north and was parallel with the turnpike. The division had been advanced from the woods in which it had been formed into open fields in sight of the pike, on which, to my eye, seemed a flying mass of wagons as compact as the space would permit. About one hundred yards this side of them was a blue line of cavalry, looking as if, on full rations, they breathed nothing but hatred and defiance.

Here let me say that Wharton's Division, with the exception of the Terry Rangers, was nothing more than mounted infantry, their only arm being the Enfield rifle, a weapon wholly unfit for fighting on horseback, for after the first volley they could not well be reloaded in the excitement of battle. The Rangers were armed with from one to three six-shooters and breech-loading carbines, easily reloaded and readily slung to the horn of the saddle when the six-shooter was desired; hence, for true cavalry performance, the Texan was in arms, as well as in horsemanship, proudly eminent. The enemy's cavalry, while well-armed and mounted, were the poorest horsemen I ever saw. They were entirely ignorant of the capacity and power of the horse. In fact, I was told by their prisoners that they had but recently been instructed in a riding school how to ride and manage a horse. These troopers, when brought in contact with the Texan cowboy, could not bear a comparison.

Down the line came the order to move forward. This was obeyed first in a walk, but soon full speed was attained. When within one hundred yards of the enemy a blue line of smoke from their carbines obscured them from our view. All of the division, except the Rangers, came to a halt. They impetuously dashed ahead, broke the line in their front, drove the enemy through their trains and beyond the pike, and for the time being had possession of the trains; but not being supported by their comrades, who, having discharged their Enfield rifles and being unable to reload, were receiving a galling fire from the enemy in their front, wavered and gave way, and the enemy, seeing the situation, charged and in driving them back, the Rangers were drawn into the vortex and conscious of the situation, as well as appreciating how much more agreeable absence of body would be over presence of mind, exercised their only available privilege and that was to run out of the scrape, which maneuver was performed with energy and zeal under a heavy fire on each flank.

The entire command was soon reformed out of range of the enemy's fire. Had the enemy followed up our repulse with a vigorous charge the result must have been disastrous in the extreme. It was not done, however, and soon they disappeared from our front and the immense trains were apparently unprotected in their rapid movements toward Nashville. After a short rest, seeing the great prize, what appeared to be the entire transportation of General Rosecrans' army, unprotected and within his grasp, General Wharton ordered another attack. This was done in column of companies, the Terry Rangers leading, striking the train obliquely, and finding that the cavalry which had repulsed us a few hours before were not on hand, it was child's play to outride the wagons, shoot down the drivers and lead mules and destroy or carry off the train. The Rangers being ahead I saw but little behind me.

Certain it is that for three or four miles we had this undisputed possession of the "block" of wagons spoken of by the writer on the Federal side in a former number of the *Weekly Times*. The whole Confederate force was turned loose upon it and it was ours—but instead of by regular detail, burning the wagons or compelling the teamsters to turn off the pike and drive in a southward direction, instead of utilizing the advantage, nothing was actually done beyond rushing on, regiment after regiment becoming mingled in a confused mass, and when the opportunity presented a gratification of the insatiate lust of plunder, the bane of an army, the Rangers dashed along, shooting and banging away without restraint. The teamsters, so far as I observed, were Germans and could not understand English; anyway, in the excitement they were too badly demoralized to halt when told to do so and many were shot who perhaps would not have been had they made an attempt to check up.

Rushing on our advance came on several hundred stragglers from the rout of the enemy's right in early morning, unarmed, though among them was a battery of artillery. They were huddled together in a confused mass on the banks of a deep stream, checked in their flight by the destruction of the bridge across it. Upon our approach an officer stepped forward and formally surrendered the entire party, handing me his sword and pistol. Soon the Confederates who had been in the charge gathered to the point, ranks broken, without order, elated and excited at the result. It seemed to me that they covered two acres of ground. I could see no one to give orders, and had an order been given, there was no one to obey. In this confusion I endeavored with the assistance of one or two men whom I recognized to start the prisoners and the artillery in the direction of our rear and had partially succeeded. I was particularly anxious to secure that battery to the cause of Dixie and felt that time was precious.

But the fates were against us, for just here, from the north side of the pike, came thundering down on us about a thousand Federal cavalry. Maj. Pat Christian, of the Rangers, assembled about thirty of the regiment and endeavored to check the advance until something in the way of order could be brought out of the mob, but it began to move off. No order could be heard, much less obeyed. On it went like stampeded cattle. Christian's little force availed nothing and all was lost, and before getting out of sight a few rounds from the battery added momentum to the disorderly retreat. The entire train was left to itself, without injury beyond the killing of a few drivers, mules etc. It is plain that this result could have been avoided by retaining two regiments in order; in fact, one regiment would have sufficed to capture all the train, for it was without a guard.

This was the end of the cavalry operations on General Bragg's left on this great day. Night coming on we were encamped till morning. During the day General Rosecrans right having been turned, it fell back on the railroad between Nashville and Murfreesboro, making an angle upon which the Confederates lashed all their fury, but failed to carry the position. Night put an end to the contest.

The Regulars at Stones River

ALEXANDER S. JOHNSTONE,
FIRST SERGEANT, COMPANY H, 4TH U.S. ARTILLERY

Philadelphia *Weekly Times* 8, no. 8, April 12, 1884

In the narrative that follows I submit to the readers of the *Weekly Times* a description of scenes that came under my notice at the battle of Stones River, near Murfreesboro, Tennessee on December 31, 1862. I was then a member of Company H, of the 4th United States Artillery. The 4th was attached to [Col. William] Grose's brigade of [Brig. Gen. John] Palmer's division of [Maj. Gen. Thomas L.] Crittenden's corps, which formed at the time the Left Wing of the Army of the Cumberland. During the previous summer and fall that army had trod the soil of four states. It was composed of fine material with excellent discipline; its good qualities were always conspicuous, whether in bivouac, march, or battle. [Maj. Gen. William S.] Rosecrans, who had lately assumed command of it, had a fine record as a man of warm and generous nature, possessing indomitable courage, a witty strategist, and a tenacious fighter. We had some regiments with us which had served with him in West Virginia. These regiments never failed to cheer their old commander when he passed them.

The morning of December 26 saw the army strike tents, sling knapsacks, and file out on the different roads that converged towards the Confederates. Crittenden's corps marched out on the Murfreesboro Pike, Palmer's division in the advance. We had not been long on the march when the rain began to fall in torrents and the army received a severe drenching. When within half a mile of Lavergne, some twelve miles from Nashville, we saw the first evidence of a conflict with the enemy—a horse belonging to the

Maj. Gen. William S. Rosecrans
(PETER COZZENS COLLECTION)

Anderson cavalry lying on the roadside, its head being severed from its body. At this point Palmer's division filed to the left and went into bivouac for the night. About sunset I was the eyewitness of a gallant charge made by the Anderson [15th Pennsylvania] Cavalry and the 21st Ohio Infantry on the right of Lavergne. They drove the Confederates out of their rifle pits, Maj. [Adolph G.] Rosengarten, of the Anderson Cavalry, being killed in the charge. Twenty-one years have passed since then, but I have seldom seen such a happy body of soldiers as those who then stood in groups around their campfires. Merry songs, jovial laughter, and boisterous merriment pervaded the entire camp. The lighthearted Major [Frederick C.] Jones, of the 24th Ohio, was conspicuous by his ringing merry laugh as he interchanged repartee and witticisms with our officers. Little did he know that night that one week hence he would be writhing and groaning piteously, suffering from a mortal wound and calling upon his Maker to end his misery. Numbers of those who sang their gay songs around the fires that night are now moldering in the National Cemetery at Stone River.

On the twenty-seventh [Brig. Gen. Thomas J.] Wood's division was in the advance. Our battery was with it. Several times during the day [Brig. Gen. Joseph] Wheeler's command would open with a battery upon the head of our column to impede advance, but our battery would soon brush it away. The last time his battery opened upon us our battery of eight guns unlimbered in a field to the right of the pike. The captain gave the command, "Load by battery, load! Battery, ready, aim, fire!" And eight shells went straight for the Confederate battery. They fell in and around it, hissing and bursting, making the fence rails gyrate above and tumbling down among the cannoneers. Not liking the compliment, the enemy's battery limbered up and galloped away to trouble us no more. At Stewart's Creek we went into bivouac. On the opposite side of the stream the Confederates had their pickets finely protected by a belt of timber, while our pickets were in an open field sheltered at intervals by stumps of trees.

The twenty-eighth being Sunday no advance was made. During the morning a unique specimen of a picket made his appearance among the Confederates; he wore a stovepipe hat and a white duster, which reached to his heels. His appearance put our pickets in the best of humor, as they eyed him with curiosity. "Oh, what a hat!" yelled one of them. "Does your mother know you're out?" came from another. The Confederate pickets evidently enjoyed the bantering he received, judging from the laughter that could be heard along their line. But the man in the duster was not to be trifled with. He came there on business and he meant it, too. None of our pickets could expose themselves in the least. His tactics were as unique as his dress. No sooner did he fire than he would run to the next tree, so that the smoke from his gun would not expose his position. He never thought that his white duster disclosed his whereabouts. For over an hour he kept shooting at our pickets. Then he found out he had got himself in a scrape. About a dozen of our infantry who had been silently watching him slipped back to their regiment for their muskets and ammunition. When they returned they took position behind a worm fence, some forty yards in rear of our pickets, to catch the conspicuous picket on the fly.

In a few minutes that person fired. He ran to the next tree as usual, his duster flying horizontally behind him like the tail of a kite. Instantly a scattering volley from a dozen of muskets went for him. The Confederate pickets took in the situation at once, as was shown by the hearty laugh that came from their line. Half an hour elapsed before he essayed another shot, but being of a persevering nature and thinking he saw an opening, he fired again. Another volley went for him and the Confederate pickets cheered him as he ran to the next tree as usual. His duster could be seen gently swaying from behind the tree where he had last taken refuge, and behind the worm fence still lay those to whom he had become an object of interest. While waiting patiently for another opening they passed their jokes. An interested spectator myself, I waited to see the end of it, but the Southerner was not to be bluffed. Finally he ran to a log cabin on the edge of the creek, some forty yards off. Our men blazed away at him. With a few long leaps of desperation he dashed into the building apparently unhurt. It was evident that he became disgusted at the warm civilities extended to him. He remained a recluse for the rest of the day. Our soldiers got tired waiting for him, and with laughter at the fun they had met with they returned to their companies.

The advance was continued on December 29 with little opposition until we came close to the Confederate lines, when heavy skirmishing took place. The 6th Ohio particularly received strong opposition when attempting to drive the Confederate skirmishers back. Taking refuge in a brick house the enemy defied the 6th for some time, firing out of the windows till the Ohioans charged and drove them out. Then they stationed themselves behind a slight breastwork, in proximity to the Confederate lines. Palmer deployed his division in line of battle to the left of the pike, with the exception of the regular battery, which took position in an old cornfield to the right. The 84th Illinois, the 6th and 24th Ohio served as its support. Four hundred yards to our front was a three-story brick house, called the Cowan House. At that time it was in flames. [Brig. Gen. James S.] Negley's Division, of [Maj. Gen. George H.] Thomas' Corps, had now arrived. It marched by our battery and deployed in line on the right of it. The situation of these four divisions was dangerous in the extreme. We were only seven hundred yards from the Confederates, and from the lay of the ground on our front they could have marched in line of battle to within four hundred yards of our position without being discovered. There was a looseness as well as a want of caution in Crittenden, which, as far as my personal observation went, amounted to extreme rashness. Soon after dark it began to rain, and the campfires blazed cheerily along the line.

Though we evidently were on the eve of a battle the usual nonchalance of soldiers was everywhere visible. Songs were sung around the fires with no thought of the morrow. Hearing the sounds of a fiddle coming from Negley's division, I strolled along the line until I came across the fiddler. He belonged to the 79th Pennsylvania. He had a crowd around him listening, which were in the best of humor. The fire was blazing in the center of the group. The fiddler sat on a cracker box, with an oilcloth over him to protect the fiddle from the rain. A rabbit, which had become bewildered, ran toward the fire, leaped over it and landed on the top of the fiddle, breaking one of the strings. It was seized by the fiddler, who held the little creature aloft by the ears while it kicked for liberty. There was no more music there that night, but stewed rabbit instead. The rain fell in torrents during the

Bring up the artillery (HEARST'S MAGAZINE)

night, and the morning of the thirtieth broke bleak and chilly. No visible preparations were being made for battle. The soldiers collected in groups around their campfires, cooking and smoking.

About 8:00 A.M. Crittenden, with anxious looks, rode along the lines and rectified his position. Wood's division held the extreme left of our line. [Brig. Gen. Horatio P.] Van Cleve's division was in reserve. Only one division of Thomas' corps was in line (Negley's). The other three divisions had not arrived. [Maj. Gen. Alexander McD.] McCook's corps was expected to arrive during the day. Coxe's Ohio Battery took position one hundred yards in front of our line and to the left of the pike and opened fire on the Confederates, a piece of foolhardiness which was inexcusable. The enemy soon responded with their batteries, shelling that part of our lines close on the pike. This might have brought on a general engagement, which would have been disastrous in the extreme to the Union forces. That morning I had the honor of being put in command of the left section of the battery. We had not replied so far to the shelling of the Confederates, although the cannoneers were standing at the guns looking for the command to open every moment. A shell entered between the two guns I commanded, wounding me severely, mortally wounding a private by the name of John Mayberry, and killing a horse. Mayberry and I were placed in an ambulance and hurried to the rear, amid the hissing and bursting of shells. My companion, whose legs were shockingly mangled, groaned piteously.

The ambulance halted about half a mile from our lines, when we were transferred to the cold charity of a field hospital. My sole companion in misery when I entered was Corporal Riehl, of the 6th Ohio Infantry. He had received a flesh wound across the breast the night previous on the skirmish line. In a few minutes another cripple entered, a private of the 84th Illinois, and then another, also from the 24th Ohio. Stretched on the bare floor we patiently waited for the sound of battle, which we expected would soon open, but the day passed quietly away, darkness came and with painful wounds we quietly slept the night away. The morning of December 31 broke clear and chilly. About eight we could hear faint sounds of musketry far to the right, but we looked upon it as being only heavy skirmishing and paid little attention to it. About 10:00 A.M. I was startled by Riehl exclaiming, "By God, Sergeant, look here! I believe our whole army is retreating." Looking on the pike to which my attention had thus been called, I saw it crowded with wagons and artillery, galloping to the rear, with Confederate cavalry shooting at the drivers. My impression at the time was that our army was in full retreat. Corporal Riehl, who had his musket with him, seized it and, drawing it to his shoulder, said to me, "I have a good shot at one of them," at the same time taking aim through the window. I ordered him to stop, explaining to him the consequence of firing from a hospital.

As far as the eye could reach on the pike there was one mass of wagons and artillery. The Confederates made the drivers turn the wagons around with the intention of driving them into their own lines. Not satisfied with what they had captured, they dismounted, tying their horses to the fences and began plundering the hospital. Blankets, overcoats, hospital rations, and the doctors' horses fell into their hands. "Now you will see some fun," exclaimed my friend Riehl, "here comes the 4th Regular Cavalry." Looking out I saw them forming in line about fifty rods away. The bugle of the Confederates gave the alarm. The sound of the bugle had scarcely died away before our troopers were in their saddles. In a quick, ringing voice Captain McIntyre, of the Regulars, gave the command, "Unsling carbines! Draw sabers! Forward! Trot! March! Gallop! Charge!" Two of the enemy, afraid and bewildered, ran in among the wounded for safety. There was a few minutes of fighting, but the enemy, unable to stand the dash of the Regulars, broke and fled through a cedar brake with the cavalrymen in hot pursuit till the sound of the carbines died in the distance. In about an hour they returned with prisoners and horses which they had captured.

Hints from one of the Regular cavalry gave us the first intimation that our right wing had been driven back; but we did not know the extent of the disaster; we did not know then that McCook's corps was a disorganized mass of fugitives and that the divisions of Thomas' corps, vainly striving to hold their own against the exultant Confederates, were also being driven back in confusion. The battle surged to our left until it struck Crittenden. Palmer's division received the first shock, which smashed Grose's brigade in pieces. In the midst of the confusion the Regular battery attached to the brigade was charged upon by the Texas cavalry and only saved from capture by the heroic courage of the 4th Cavalry, who had a hand-to-hand contest with the Texans. The Texans captured a cannoneer belonging to the battery and took him away with them. The prisoner was [taken] before [Maj. Gen. John P.] McCown, of the Confederates. When McCown found that he belonged to Company H, of the 4th Regulars, he exultantly exclaimed to the officers around him, "By God, I told you it was my old battery that was on the pike; no other battery in the service could have done such execution." McCown formerly was captain of Company H, but resigned to enter the Confederate service. He sent the cannoneer back to his company.

If we in the hospital did not know how disastrous the day had been to our arms we had practical evidence of it when a battery of the 5th Regulars in command of Capt. [Francis L.] Guenther unlimbered his guns alongside of the hospital and opened on the advancing enemy with double-shotted canister. The bullets of the Confederates crashed through the wooden building, creating consternation among the inmates. In spite of the strain and anxiety which my system had undergone, and though I was at the same time suffering from a painful wound, I involuntarily went to sleep with the roar of Guenther's guns ringing in my ears. During the night I awoke to find the room I was in crowded with mutilated humanity, eighteen men lying on the bare floor, besides three others in cots. Two of those who occupied the cots were Confederates. The other was a sergeant of the 24th Ohio. One of the Southerners was a lieutenant of the 2nd Arkansas Infantry; the other belonged to a Texan regiment. Each of them had a foot amputated. "Look a-here!" said the Texan, pointing to his trousers that were ripped along the seams all the way to the thigh; "my wife made these pants at the head of the Red River, one year ago. What would she say if she could see them and me now?"

The sergeant of the 24th Ohio was badly wounded. He was raving and cursing in his wild delirium. He imagined he was on the field of battle waving his hands wildly in the air and calling on his company to charge. Then his delirium changed to a terrible calm. He gradually grew weaker and before the sun had set another had been added to the long list of dead. A boy of fourteen years attracted my attention. His hand had been amputated at the wrist. He was also seriously wounded in the groin. Holding up his delicate arm to me while his large liquid hazel eyes filled, he asked me if I thought he would get well. I said I thought he would. He replied, "Well, if I don't, I suppose it is all for the Union"; but his eyes could not hold the moisture longer, for the large tears trickled down his cheeks. Wiping the tears away he looked at me earnestly for a moment and said, "I could not help it, Sergeant." The rough but warmhearted surgeon called the attention of one of the attendants to the boy, saying, "Give that boy anything he asks; that boy is a hero!" Night came at last and amid the groans and misery of the wounded around me I went to sleep.

January 2 broke clear and cold. Close to our line of battle the stillness that prevailed was remarkable; not even the shot of a picket could be heard. I looked upon this quietness as portentous and I felt uneasy. I would rather have listened to the roar of battle and awaited the result. The Arkansas lieutenant and the Texan were well aware that the battle had yet to be decided, that Rosecrans had concentrated his forces and had also thrown up works of defense and that he was even calculating on assuming the offensive. "Yes," said the lieutenant, looking towards the Texan, "if it had not been for the cowardice of the Texas brigade when we were charging the Yankee batteries on the thirty-first in the afternoon we would have been in possession of the Nashville Pike and would have been in the rear of the Yankees and would have taken Nashville again." The Texan resented the charge in very abusive language. "Why," said the Texan, "you Arkansas soldiers are only a lot of sardines." "Oh, you'd better go back to Texas and herd cattle again; that is all you are fit for," replied the lieutenant. As both were cripples it ended in a war of words.

It was getting late in the afternoon and a drizzling rain began to fall, when as sudden as a clap of thunder the battle opened. The roar of artillery and the crash of musketry was deafening. So close were we to our line of battle that it shook the building we were in. We listened and waited in suspense. The rain fell heavier and heavier, but still the battle raged with such fury that to the ear it was one perpetual roll of musketry and artillery. It had lasted, perhaps, more than [an] hour when cheers were heard, now here, now there, till the cheering became continuous along our line. I made the remark to the lieutenant, "We are beating you; do you hear those cheers?" He said, "How do you know that it is your men cheering?" I replied, "You Rebels never cheer; you yell like a pack of coyotes." "I'm afraid so," he answered. As the cheering ceased so did the sound of battle. About two minutes after a solitary shot could be heard and all was still. The rain continued to fall. Soon the dull rumbling sound of ambulance wheels came as they bore in their freight of wounded. I asked a surgeon who had just come from the front how the battle had gone. "Glorious, glorious victory!" he exclaimed; "captured the celebrated Washington Battery and a thousand prisoners in the last charge and drove the Rebels into Murfreesboro." Ambulances were busy all night carrying in the wounded from the field. Every place of shelter was occupied and hundreds of the dying and wounded lay exposed on the wet ground to the pitiless storm of rain that continued during the night.

Major Jones, of the 24th Ohio, had just been carried in from the field mortally wounded. I could hear him moaning in the adjoining room. A fine-looking young fellow entered the room I was in and stated that the surgeon sent him there to get a place to lie down. As he was so spry in appearance I had my doubts whether he was wounded. I said to him that he could see for himself that there was no room for him. "Anyhow," I said, "this is for the wounded." "The reason I was sent in here," he answered, "was because I was badly wounded." Unbuckling his sword belt and unbuttoning his overcoat and blouse he showed where he had been shot through the right breast, the bullet coming out through the back. He was first sergeant of Company A, of the 51st Illinois Infantry. I soon found a place for him to lie down. The two wounded Confederates were terribly chagrined at the defeat of [Gen. Braxton] Bragg. Previously cheerful, they became morose, sullen, and spiritless. The lieutenant was very restless. I asked him if his leg hurt him. "The pain from the leg is nothing," he said; "it is the damned bullet in my side that worries me." He had never mentioned having a bullet in his side before.

I passed a miserable night. Sleep was impossible. I was kept awake by the groans and sharp cries of pain which came from all parts of the room. The morning of the third broke bleak and gloomy, as if it were in sympathy with the horrible sights to be seen on all sides. Rows of dead that had passed away during the night lay at intervals outside of the hospital, having been exposed to the pelting rain which fell steadily during the night. The surgeons had been busy all night amputating legs and arms. I had never seen the horrors of war so vividly before. I fairly shuddered at the sight. The road to Nashville was now clear and during the day long trains of wagons halted in front of the hospital to receive the wounded to take them to the Nashville hospitals. I went in the first. On arriving I was placed in the Broadway Hospital, in which I received the best of treatment and in a few weeks was able to fight for Uncle Sam again.

A few words on the battle of December 31 and I am done. Historians of the battle state that McCook's corps was surprised. I will say that I have conversed with intelligent officers and soldiers of McCook's corps and not one of them spoke of a surprise. They said that they saw the Confederate lines advancing towards them, that the corps was in line of battle waiting for them, but that McCook and some of the division generals were not present when the battle opened. The line when broken became disorganized and could not be rallied. As a general, McCook was loose and careless. He took too many chances. He lacked that military acumen necessary in a successful general.

PART THREE

The War in 1863

Ironclads Against Fort Sumter

SAMUEL JONES,
MAJOR GENERAL, C.S.A.

Philadelphia *Weekly Times* 8, no. 31, September 20, 1884

Among the United States war vessels which were destroyed or partially destroyed by the Federal officers on the eve of their evacuation of Norfolk and the Gosport Navy Yard, April 20, 1861, was the United States steam frigate *Merrimac* which was burned to her copper line and berth-deck, scuttled and sunk. Subsequently she was raised by Confederate naval officers, reconstructed on a novel model, encased in iron plates, armed with heavy guns and an iron prow, and soon became famous as the Confederate States steam ram *Merrimac*. The report went abroad that she was invulnerable to any guns then in use, and could readily overcome and destroy any vessels then in the navy with which she might come in collision.

The knowledge of the existence of this novel engine of war caused no little apprehension in the North, which was greatly heightened by the ease with which she and her consorts sunk the United States ship *Cumberland* and destroyed the *Congress* in Hampton Roads on March 8, 1862. Excitable and imaginative people even apprehended that New York City and Philadelphia would soon be under the fire of her guns. It became therefore a grave question how the steam ram could be destroyed.

To that end an ironclad steamer designed by Capt. John Ericsson on a new model was speedily constructed, and was the first of the class of war vessels since known as monitors. Seven of them were hastily constructed, armed with the heaviest guns ever before used and sent to Port Royal, South Carolina, to operate against Charleston. Early in January, 1863, several of them were on their way to Port Royal. The original *Monitor* foundered at sea off Cape Hatteras, and two others, the *Montauk* and *Passaic*, narrowly escaped the same fate.

While awaiting the arrival of the full number, Admiral [Samuel F.] Du Pont deemed it prudent to test the power of those that had arrived, and selected as the object on which to make the experiment Fort McAllister, an earthwork at Genesis Point, on the Ogeechee River near Savannah, and if possible destroy or capture it. On January 27, and again on February 1, the *Montauk*, aided by several other less formidable vessels, engaged the fort. On March 3 the *Montauk*, having been joined by three other monitors, the *Passaic, Patapsco*, and *Nahant*, and aided by other vessels, again engaged the earthwork. The attack and defense of Fort McAllister do not come within the proposed limits of this narration. Suffice to say that after a bombardment of eight hours, in which the fire of the fort was directed exclusively on the *Passaic*, the monitors withdrew.

No injury was done to the fort says Captain [Daniel] Ammen, who commanded the *Patapsco*, that could not be readily repaired during the night. The gunboats and mortar schooners, which fired at the distance of about four thousand yards, did neither good nor harm. On March 6 the monitors were taken in tow to Port Royal. The *Passaic* had been so damaged in the bombardment that she required three weeks of repairs to be put in serviceable condition.

By April 1 the whole monitor fleet was in North Edisto Inlet—an admirable harbor, about twenty miles from Charleston bar—and as thoroughly provided as they could be for the attack on Charleston. Such a fleet had never before been seen. Its capacity for destruction and resistance was unknown. In the North it was looked to with confidence, hope, and expectation for the accomplishment of an object so ardently desired, the reduction of Charleston, while in the South it unquestionably excited grave apprehension.

Maj. Gen. [David] Hunter, commanding the Department of the South, with an aggregate land force present of a little over twenty-three thousand men, moved up a large part of his force and occupied Folly and Seabrook's Islands and other points on or near the Stono, and prepared to follow up the expected success of the fleet and occupy Charleston.

The concentration of such formidable land and naval forces at Port Royal, Hilton Head, and North Edisto had warned General [Pierre G. T.] Beauregard, then commanding the Department of South Carolina and Georgia, that the long expected attack on Charleston was immediately impending, and he prepared to meet it. The troops nearest the city were distributed as seemed best to meet the coming storm, and arrangements

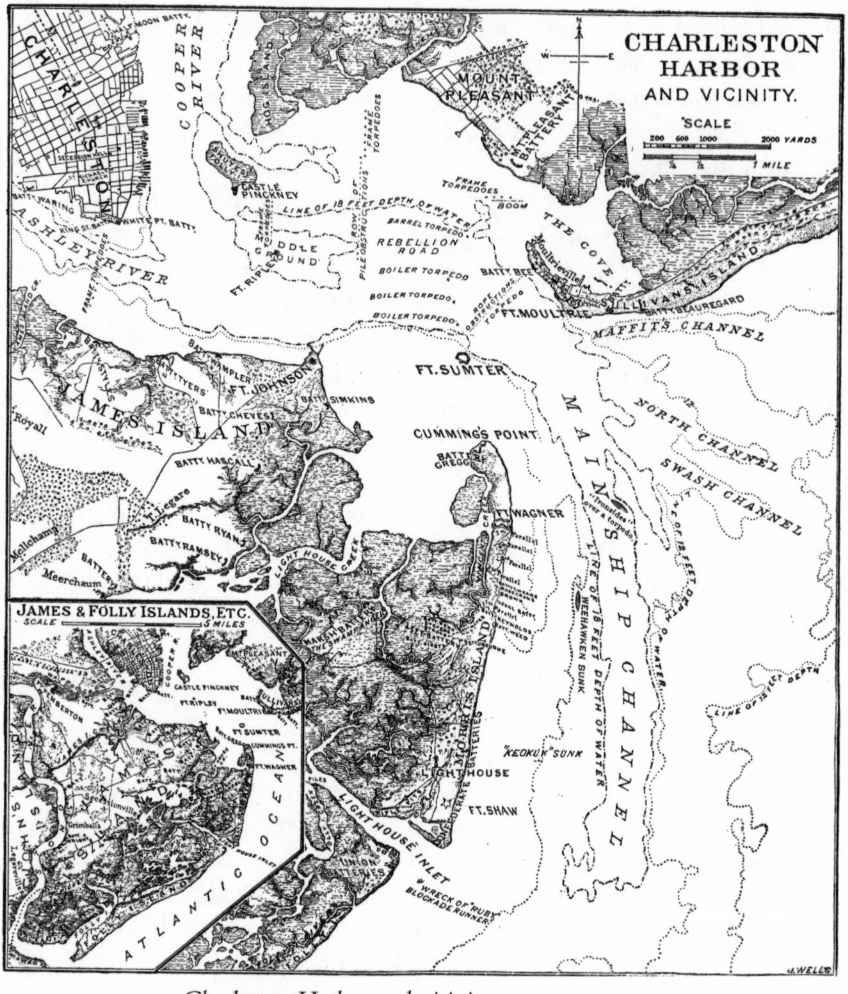

Charleston Harbor and vicinity (CENTURY MAGAZINE)

made to draw reinforcements quickly, if required, from other points in his department.

The First Military District of the department which embraced the defenses of Charleston was commanded by Brig. Gen. Roswell S. Ripley, an officer of distinguished ability, great energy, and fertile in resource; no more accomplished artillery officer could have been found in either army. He was especially charged with the defenses of the harbor, and the completeness of the preparations was in a great measure due to his skill and energy. Brig. Gen. James H. Trapier commanded the second subdivision of the district, which embraced Sullivan's Island. The defensive works on that island, Fort Moultrie and Batteries Beauregard and Bee, were under the general direction of Col. Lawrence M. Keitt.

Fort Sumter, the chief object of attack, was commanded by Col. Alfred Rhett, of the 1st South Carolina Regular Artillery, and was garrisoned by seven companies of that regiment. Lt. Col. J. A. Yates and Maj. Ormsby Blanding, of the same regiment, had general charge, the first of the barbette, the latter of the casemate batteries.

Brig. Gen. [States Rights] Gist commanded the first sub-division of the district, which embraced James Island and St. Andrew's. It was known that General Hunter had concentrated the mass of his force on Folly Island and its vicinity, and it was supposed would cooperate with the fleet by an attack either on James or Morris Island. The responsible duty of meeting the enemy in that quarter was confided to General Gist.

Col. [Robert F.] Graham commanded the small force on Morris Island, on which were the very important works, Batteries Gregg and Wagner.

On the morning of April 5 Admiral Du Pont on his flagship, the *New Ironsides*, having joined the ironclads, as they were generally called, at South Edisto, the whole fleet streamed towards Charleston harbor, the monitors in tow of suitable steamers. That evening, the *Keokuk* having sounded and buoyed the bar of the main channel, the *Patapsco* and *Catskill* passed the bar and anchored within. The next morning the admiral, his flag flying on the *New Ironsides*, crossed the bar, followed by the other ironclads. It was his intention to proceed the same day to Charleston, attacking Fort Sumter on the way, but the weather was unfavorable and the pilots refused to proceed further.

At midday on the seventh, signal was made for the whole fleet to move forward to the attack. The order of battle was "line ahead," the vessels moving in the following order: the *Weehawken*, Capt. John Rodgers; the *Passaic*, Capt. Percival Drayton; the *Montauk*, Capt. John L. Worden; the *Patapsco*, Cmdr. Daniel Ammen; the *New Ironsides* (flagship), Cmdr. Thomas Turner; the *Catskill*, Cmdr. George W. Rodgers; the *Nantucket*, Cmdr. Donald McN. Fairfax; the *Nahant*, Cmdr. John Downs; and the *Keokuk*, Cmdr. A. C. Rhind.

The *New Ironsides* carried fourteen eleven-inch guns and two 150-pounder Parrott rifles; the *Patapsco*, one fifteen-inch and one 150-pounder Parrott rifle; the *Keokuk*, two eleven-inch guns; the others, one fifteen-inch and one eleven-inch gun each.

Commanders were ordered to pass the Morris Island batteries, Wagner and Gregg, without returning their fire, unless specially signaled to do so by the admiral. They were directed to take positions to the north and west of

Sumter, within about eight hundred yards, and open, firing with great care, low, and aiming at the center embrasures. The admiral's order of battle adds: "After the reduction of Fort Sumter it is probable that the next point of attack will be the batteries on Morris Island." A squadron of vessels, consisting of the *Canandaigua, Housatonic, Huron, Unadilla,* and *Wissahickon*, Captain J. F. Green commanding, was held in reserve outside the bar and near the entrance buoy, in readiness to support the ironclads in the proposed attack on the Morris Island batteries.

The *Weehawken* was handicapped and encumbered by a raft attached to its bow to explode torpedoes. (It was called the *Devil* and was cut adrift and floated ashore on Morris Island.) In weighing anchor her chain became entangled in the grapnels of the raft, delaying the line nearly two hours. About 1:15 P.M. the whole fleet was under way, but the raft attached to the *Weehawken* delayed her and the ironclads that were following, causing wild steering along the whole line, the monitors "sheering every way" when their engines stopped, so that it was impossible to preserve the ordered interval of one hundred yards between the vessels. The weather was calm and the water as smooth as could have been desired for naval firing. Reports had gone abroad of the extent of the obstructions and number of torpedoes in the harbor. Whilst moving into action a number of buoys were observed, unpleasantly suggestive of the presence of torpedoes, one of which exploded near the *Weehawken*, lifting her somewhat, but without disabling her.

Just before the leading vessel came within range the long roll was beat in Fort Sumter, "the garrison, regimental, and Palmetto flags were hoisted and saluted by thirteen guns, the band playing the national air, 'Dixie.'" A few minutes before 3:00 P.M., the leading monitor having approached to within about two thousand yards of Fort Moultrie, the action was opened by a shot from that fort fired by its commander, Col. William Butler. Three minutes later the leading monitor, when about fifteen hundred yards from Sumter, fired two guns simultaneously. Then Sumter opened, firing by battery. The action became general and for more than two hours nearly a hundred guns on land and water, many of them of the heaviest caliber ever before used, were in rapid action.

It was a calm and balmy day in spring—the season of greatest natural beauty and luxuriance in that wild region. It was the season at which Charleston had been wont to present its most attractive phase, when the wealthy planters and their families had not yet been driven by the heat from their city houses and when the hotels were most crowded with visitors from the North. In strong contrast with the picture of tranquil pleasure and enjoyment in a mild, delicious climate which the city had formerly presented at this season, was the scene of strained excitement and anxiety on this day of the attack on the harbor defenses of Charleston. From every point of view in the city the eyes of the many thousands of spectators were riveted on the grand and imposing spectacle. The church steeples, roofs, windows, and piazzas of houses on the "Battery" were crowded with eager, breathless witnesses of this bombardment, the precursor of a siege which was to arouse in the people there assembled and those whom they represented every high and patriotic hope, every reserve of courage and endurance, the sublimest exercise of patience and submission.

From the blockading fleet and transports off the bar, this trial of strength and endurance between forts and ships, the latter brought to the highest point of precision and destructive power, was witnessed by other anxious spectators who confidently anticipated a brilliant victory for the fleet, with feelings scarcely less intense than those of the people in the city, who fully realized the importance to them of the events which hung upon the issue.

Through the thunder of artillery ran the heavy thud of the huge shells as they pounded the brick walls of Sumter and the sharp metallic ring and crash of the shot and shells as they struck the iron turrets and casings of the monitors, tearing away the iron plates, crashing through the sides and decks or shivering into fragments by the concussion and falling in showers about the deck or into the water.

The ironclads came into action in succession, and though it lasted about two hours and twenty minutes, from thirty to forty-five minutes' exposure to the fire of the forts and batteries sufficed to put them hors-de-combat.

The *Weehawken* fired twenty-six shots and was struck fifty-three times. A part of her side armor was so shattered that it hung in splintered fragments, which could be pulled off with the hand, thus exposing the woodwork. Her deck was pierced, making a hole through which the water poured, and her turret was so shaken by the pounding to which it was subjected that it revolved with difficulty, thus greatly retarding her fire.

The *Passaic*, Capt. Percival Drayton, was even more roughly handled than the *Weehawken*. She succeeded in firing only thirteen shots and was struck thirty-five times. At the fourth discharge of her eleven-inch gun the turret was struck twice in quick succession, bulging in its plates and beams and forcing together the rails on which the gun-carriage worked, rendering the gun wholly useless for the remainder of the action. An instant later the turret was so jammed that it could not be moved, thus effectually ending its fire. The turret was again struck by a heavy rifle shot which shattered all of the eleven plates on the upper edge, then glancing upwards struck the pilot house with such force as to mash it in, bend it over, open the plates and press them out and lifting the top, exposing the inside to such a degree that another shot would, it was thought, knock the top entirely off. Under the terrific fire to which his vessel was exposed Captain Drayton could not examine it to ascertain the extent of the injury. He could not fire a shot, and signaled the admiral for permission to withdraw, but receiving no answer he did not stand on the order of his going, but went at once out of range. He could not discover then nor the next morning when he had a good view of the exposed face of the fort that it was in the least injured, and he was satisfied that under the circumstances then existing, "the monitors were no match for the forts."

The *Montauk* suffered less than her predecessors, but the chief engagement convinced her commander, Captain Worden, "that Charleston cannot be taken by the naval force now present, and that had the attack continued it could not have failed to result in disaster."

The *Patapsco* opened fire on Sumter with her one 150-pounder rifle at fifteen hundred yards. At the fifth discharge the 150-pounder was disabled for the remainder of the action. The commanders of the leading vessels apprehending entanglement by drifting with the rope obstructions which could be seen ahead, turned their prows seaward. The *Patapsco*, endeavoring to follow their lead, refused to obey her helm and was determined sufficiently long to receive the concentrated fire of Sumter and the Sullivan Island batteries. She was struck forty-seven times and her turret was so battered as to prevent or greatly retard its turning, thus rendering her only remaining gun next to useless, when she retired out of range.

The turning back of the four leading monitors and their moving seaward threw the line into much confusion, the vessels becoming somewhat entangled, so much so that the flagship came into collision with two of the monitors and was obliged to anchor twice to prevent running ashore. She could not fire on Fort Sumter without great risk of firing into the monitors, but was detained at the distance of about a mile from Fort Sumter; subjected to a heavy fire, all the more galling because it could not be returned, she only fired eight shots at Fort Moultrie.

The Confederate account says she was struck sixty-three times at the distance of between seventeen hundred and eighteen hundred yards, and then moved to the distance of two thousand yards—out of effective range. She was less injured than the monitors, probably because she was, for want of sufficient depth of water, at a greater distance than they. One of her port shutters was shot away and Commander Turner, in his official report to the admiral, says, "My impression is, had you been able to get this ship into close position, where her broadsides would have been brought to bear, that not one port shutter would have been left under the fire of such enormous projectiles as were thrown from the enemy's works multiplied on every side of us."

For several minutes she was in greater peril than any on board perhaps knew. She was directly over a torpedo, which from some unknown cause failed to explode.

Finding his own ship blocking the way the admiral signaled, "Disregard the movements of the commander-in-chief," and the rear vessels passed ahead, and coming under fire shared substantially the same fate as those that preceded them. Commander Fairfax, of the *Nantucket*, says that having approached close to the obstructions thrown across the channel he opened fire on Sumter:

> We were then under the fire of three forts, and most terrible was it for forty-five or fifty minutes. Our fire was very slow, necessarily, and not half so observable upon the walls of the forts as the rain of the rifle shots and heavy shells was upon this vessel. Certainly their (the Confederate) firing was excellent throughout; fortunately, it was directed to some half dozen ironclads at once. Our vessels could not long have withstood the concentrated fire of the enemy's batteries. I must say that I am disappointed beyond measure at this experiment of monitors overcoming strong forts. It was a fair trial.

His fifteen-inch gun fired but three shots when it was disabled for the remainder of the action and his eleven-inch fired twelve times.

Commander Downs gives a lamentable account of the experience of his monitor, the *Nahant*, under a fire "of one hundred guns," as he erroneously supposed, which he describes as terrific, and he believed almost unprecedented. The blows from heavy shot very soon so jammed the turret that it could not be turned, which effectually stopped his fire. The concussion of a heavy shot on the pilot house forced off on the inside a piece of iron weighing seventy-eight pounds, and drove it with such violence that in its course to the other side it came in contact with the steering-gear, bending and disarranging it so that it could not be worked.

Bolt heads were forced off and driven in showers about the pilot house and turret, one of them mortally wounding the quartermaster, Edward Cobb, and others knocking the pilot, Mr. Sofield, senseless, leaving the commander himself alone in the pilot house. His vessel was struck thirty-six times, the iron plating was broken in several places, and in some stripped from the wood backing, which was broken. He describes the effects of the shot more minutely than the other commanders to draw attention to the weak points of the monitors for the benefit of future builders of such vessels. After repeated futile efforts to train his guns on the fort and renew the action he abandoned the effort and withdrew.

The *Keokuk* was the rear vessel of the line. Her commander, A. C. Rhind, becoming impatient of the long delay, passed not only the *Ironsides* but the vessels ahead of him and defiantly directing his prow towards Sumter, approached nearer than any other vessel had done, firing as he advanced and drawing on the *Keokuk* the concentrated fire of Sumter, Moultrie, Bee and the battery on Cummings' Point. But he was permitted [to] fire only three shots. Commander Rhind's daring gallantry in carrying his vessel into action was equaled only by the frankness and brevity with which he officially reported the result. He says,

> The position taken by the *Keokuk* was maintained for about thirty minutes, during which period she was struck ninety times in the hull and turrets. Nineteen shots pierced through at and just below the water line. The turrets were pierced in many places; one of the forward port shutters shot away; in short, the vessel was completely riddled. Finding it impossible to keep her afloat many minutes more under such an extraordinary fire, during which rifle projectiles of every species and the largest caliber, as also hot shot, were poured into us, I reluctantly withdrew from action at 4:40 P.M., with the gun carriage of the forward turret disabled and so many of the crews of the after gun wounded as to prevent a possibility of remaining under fire. I succeeded in getting the *Keokuk* to an anchor out of range of fire and kept her afloat during the night in the smooth water, though the water was pouring into her in many places.

In the morning, the water becoming a little ruffled, she sunk, leaving only her smoke-stack out to show her position. Her crew, with the killed and wounded, were rescued.

About half-past four Admiral Du Pont signaled the fleet to withdraw, intending to renew the attack the next day. By 5:00 A.M. the monitors were under way, following the flagship seaward and soon anchored out of range, but within the bar, the fire of the forts gradually ceasing as the fleet receded.

The fire of the fleet had been directed mainly against Fort Sumter, but little attention being given to the other batteries. The flagstaff of Fort Moultrie was shot down, killing in its fall Private Lusby, of the 1st South Carolina Infantry. There was no other casualty on Sullivan's Island. When the flagstaff fell, Captains [W. H.] Wigg and Wardlaw and Lieutenants King and Calhoun quickly sprang to the top of a traverse and on the parapet and displayed the regimental, garrison, and battle flags in conspicuous positions.

Fort Sumter, though not seriously damaged, was more injured than the Federals seem to have thought, but not as much as might have been expected from the impact on brick walls of the heaviest shot ever before used in war. The walls were struck by about thirty-six of those heavy shot. Two fifteen-inch shells penetrated the eastern face near an embrasure of the second tier, one exploding in the casemate, the other in the middle of the fort. One eleven-inch shot also penetrated the wall. The carriage of the ten-inch Columbiad was demolished and a forty-two pounder was dismounted, both of which were promptly remounted and made ready for action. Five men were wounded by fragments of masonry and wood in Fort Sumter; three were killed and five wounded in Fort Wagner by an accidental explosion of an ammunition chest.

The Confederates had sixty-nine guns of various caliber in action, but only forty-one of them (exclusive of mortars) were above the caliber of thirty-two pounders. The armament of the fleet was thirty-two guns (eight of which, it seems, were not fired), of eight, eleven and fifteen-inch caliber, which at a single discharge could throw nearly as great a weight of metal as could the land batteries.

The Confederates fired in all 2,229 shots and consumed 21,093 pounds of powder. The fleet fired 142 (the Confederacy say 151) shots and consumed nearly 5,000 pounds of powder. The two combined fired upon an average of seventeen shots, varying in weight from thirty to four hundred pounds (or about 1,300 pounds of iron), and consumed about 185 pounds of powder per minute, during 140 consecutive minutes, the heaviest fire ever before delivered in so brief a bombardment.

The Confederate fire seems to have been much more accurate than the Federal. About an equal proportion of the shots fired on each side struck the objects at which they were aimed, but there was a very wide difference in the sizes of those objects. A monitor afloat is "in appearance not inaptly likened to a cheese box on a plank," the "plank" representing the deck and the "cheese box" the revolving turret in which are the guns. Its apparent length is two hundred feet and beam forty-five feet. The hull, however, is but one hundred and fifty-nine feet in length. The turret is twenty-one feet and ten inches in diameter and nine feet high. It is surmounted by a pilot house nine feet four inches in diameter and seven feet high. From bow to stern the deck varies from two and a half to one and a half feet above the water. An exceedingly small part, therefore, of the hull was exposed above water to fire. They were in motion also during the action.

Such an object in motion presented but a small mark at which to fire at the distance of from one thousand to fifteen hundred yards. Fort Sumter on the contrary was a very large and stationary object, presenting fronts of three tiers of guns at which to aim. The accuracy of the Confederate fire was due in a great measure to an ingenious contrivance of Lieutenant Colonel Yates, which enabled five men to hold the heaviest guns trained on the ironclads when in motion.

The little damage that Fort Sumter suffered was promptly repaired during the night and the weak points in the walls which the fire had disclosed were reinforced by sand bags. The Confederates confidently expected the engagement to be renewed the next day, and the forts and batteries were as well prepared to receive an attack on the morning of the eighth as they had been on the morning of the seventh. But it was not renewed. "The enemy was beaten," says General Ripley, "before their adversaries thought the action had well commenced."

During the evening of the seventh the commanders of the ironclads went on board the flagship and verbally reported to the admiral the incidents of the engagement and the condition of their respective vessels. Their reports decided him not to renew the attack and he promptly forwarded to the secretary of the navy a dispatch, in which he says,

> I yesterday moved up with eight ironclads and this ship and attacked Fort Sumter, intending to pass it and commence action on its northwest face, in accordance with my order of battle. The heavy fire received from it and Fort Moultrie and the nature of the obstructions compelled the attack from the outside. It was fierce and obstinate and the gallantry of the officers and men of the vessels engaged was conspicuous. This vessel could not be brought into such close action as I endeavored to get her. Owing to the narrow channel and rapid current she became partly unmanageable, and was twice forced to anchor to prevent her going ashore, once owing to her having come into collision with two of the monitors. She could not get nearer than one thousand

> yards. Owing to the condition of the tide and an unavoidable accident, I had been compelled to delay action until in the afternoon, and toward evening, finding no impression made upon the fort, I made a signal to withdraw the ships, intending to renew the attack this morning.
>
> But the commanders of the monitors came on board and reported verbally the injuries of their vessels, when without hesitation or consultation (for I never hold councils of war) I determined not to renew the attack, for in my judgment it would have converted a failure into a disaster, and I will only add that Charleston cannot be taken by a purely naval attack, and the army could give me no cooperation.

In reply to a complimentary letter from General Hunter, who had witnessed the action in a transport steamer, the admiral says, "I feel very comfortable, General, for the reason that a merciful Providence permitted me to have a failure, instead of a disaster."

Captain Ammen, who commanded the *Patapsco*, says in his recently published book, *The Atlantic Coast*,

> The result of the attack was mortifying to all of the officers and men engaged in it. Had any loss of life been regarded as likely to render another attempt successful there would have been few indeed who would not have desired it. The opinion before the attack was general, and was fully shared in by the writer, that whatever might be the loss in men and vessels blown up by torpedoes or otherwise destroyed (and such losses were supposed probable) of all events Fort Sumter would be reduced to a pile of ruins before the sun went down.

General Beauregard had confidently expected every man of his command to do his duty and he was not disappointed, for their hearts were thoroughly in their work. Confederate and Federal officers alike bear testimony to the accuracy of the Confederate fire, and the monitors themselves bore mute but more expressive evidence of its effects.

All that professional skill and gallantry could do had been done by the officers and crews of the vessels to achieve success. They had fought the united ironclads to their utmost capacity. The result had proved that these novel engines of naval warfare on which such high hopes were built had not materially changed the military relations between forts and ships. It had also given another striking proof of the fallacy of the belief that, ceteris paribus, ships can reduce forts. Just two years previously, less one week, Confederate land batteries had opened fire on Fort Sumter, newly constructed by United States engineers at greater distance than that which the monitors had attacked and with greatly inferior guns had compelled its surrender. A few months later, Federal land batteries on Morris Island, at more than double the monitors' distance, had demolished the exposed walls of Fort Sumter.

This attack also illustrated what was conspicuous throughout the war, the great difference in the relative numbers of killed and wounded in battles on land and those between forts and ships. In this engagement between the Federal ironclad fleets and the forts and batteries at the entrance to Charleston, the casualties on the Confederate side were one killed and five wounded. On the Federal side, one killed and twenty wounded. Little less than a year before in a battle on James' Island in sight of Fort Sumter, nearly nine hundred men had been killed or wounded in less than half an hour.

The fleet remained within the bar but out of range, repairing and refitting, until high tide on the evening of April 12, when it passed out, the *New Ironsides* taking her place with the blockading fleet, and the monitors were towed southward to Port Royal for repairs, leaving only the *Keokuk*, sunk with her smoke stack out of water marking her position. In a few days the Confederates dived into her and lifted out her heavy guns, flags, swords and smaller articles. Her guns were soon mounted in the Confederate batteries.

When the news of failure reached Washington, President [Abraham] Lincoln dispatched Admiral Du Pont:

> Executive Mansion, April 13, 1863
>
> Hold your position inside the bar near Charleston, or, if you have left it, return to it and hold it until further orders. Do not allow the enemy to erect new batteries or defenses on Morris Island. If he has begun it drive him out. I do not herein order you to renew the general attack. That is to depend on your discretion or further orders.
>
> A. Lincoln

The following day, April 14, he dispatched to the admiral and General Hunter jointly:

> This is intended to clear up any inconsistency between the recent order to continue operations before Charleston, and the former one to remove to another point in a certain contingency. No censure upon you, or either of you, is intended; we still hope by cordial and judicious co-operation you can take the batteries on Morris Island and Sullivan's Island and Fort Sumter. But whether you can or not, we wish the demonstration kept up for a time for a collateral and very important object; we wish the attempt to be a real one (though not a desperate one) if it affords any considerable chance of success. But if prosecuted for a demonstration only this must not be made public or the whole effect will be lost. Once again before Charleston, do not leave till further orders from here. Of course this is not intended to force you to leave unduly exposed Hilton Head or other near points in your charge.
>
> Yours truly,
> A. Lincoln

Replying through the Navy Department, the admiral assured the secretary that he would urge forward the repairs of the serious injuries sustained by the monitors and return within the bar as soon as possible; he thought, however, that the move would be attended with great risk to the monitors from gales and the fire of the enemy's batteries, which "they could neither silence nor prevent the erection of new ones." He would, of course, obey with fidelity all orders he might receive, even when entirely at variance with his own judgment, such as the order to reoccupy the unsafe anchorage off Morris Island, "and on intimation that a renewal of the attack on Charleston may be ordered, which in my judgment would be attended with disastrous results, involving the loss of this coast." He was painfully struck by the tenor and tone of the president's orders, which, he thought, implied censure and requested the secretary not to hesitate to relieve him by an officer who might be thought "more able to execute that service in which I have had the misfortune to fall—the capture of Charleston."

In Washington, and in the North generally, it had been confidently believed that the attack would result in the fall of Charleston. So confident was the Navy Department of a successful result that on April 2 orders were issued and dispatched to Admiral Du Pont to send a number of the ironclads, which the fall of Charleston would render available, to the Gulf of Mexico for service in that quarter and in the Mississippi. The failure was a grievous disappointment in the North, while in the South the vague but serious apprehension of danger from the ironclads was dispelled, and in Charleston especially it was felt that the city had nothing to apprehend from the fleet alone.

Of course the failure was sharply criticized in the Northern press. Whoever relies on the newspapers of the period for correct information in regard to the battles of that war will inevitably be led into grave errors. In regard to this naval attack, some of the papers severely censured the administration for ordering or permitting it without providing ample means to insure success, and the causes of the failure were fully explained. The ironclads, it was said, while moving up to the attack had become entangled in the rope obstructions which were well known to be in the channel and, whilst so hampered, had been exposed to the fire of three hundred guns, many of them supplied from England and of the heaviest caliber ever before used in war, and at short range, in some instances three hundred yards.

The secretary of state, Mr. [William H.] Seward, seems to have obtained some of his information on the subject from the newspapers rather than from the official reports. In a printed circular letter signed by him and addressed to the diplomatic agents of the government abroad he says,

> An attack by the fleet on April 7 last upon the forts and batteries which defend the harbor of Charleston failed, because the rope obstructions in the channel fouled the screws of the ironclads and compelled them to return, after passing through the fire of the batteries. These bore the fire of the forts, although some defects of construction were revealed by the injuries they received. The crews passed through the unexampled cannonade with singular impunity. Not a life was lost on board a monitor.

None of the ironclads approached the rope obstructions nearer than six hundred yards except the *Keokuk*, which, after being disabled, drifted to within about three hundred yards of them before she could be got under way again. The rope obstructions were therefore not encountered by any of the vessels. They had not passed through the fire of the forts, for some of the heaviest batteries had not been brought into action. The *Keokuk*, as has been stated, was not nearer Fort Sumter than nine hundred yards and none of the other vessels were so near any of the forts or batteries. The ranges varied from nine hundred to about two thousand yards.

Instead of three hundred three were but seventy-six Confederate guns of all kinds of action. Some of these were mortars, the fire of which on so small a target as a monitor and at such long range is so inaccurate as to be practically ineffective. Of the other guns only forty-one were above the caliber of 32-pounders, and guns of this latter caliber were of little avail against the ironclads. The most effective fire was from ten ten-inch and nineteen eight-inch Columbiads, three nine-inch Dahlgrens, and two seven-inch Brook guns, and they were American, not English guns. Judging by the effects of the fire from the guns actually engaged, and at such long range, it is hardly extravagant to suppose that if, during the two hours and twenty-five minutes the action lasted, the ironclads had been exposed to the fire of three hundred guns, at distances of from three to nine hundred yards, every one of them would have been sunk or irreparably disabled.

General Hunter had held his troops on Folly, Cole's, and Seabrook's Islands in readiness to follow up the expected naval success. On the morning after the attack all was in readiness to cross Light House inlet to Morris Island, "where," says the general, "once established, the fall of Sumter would have been as certain as the demonstration of a problem in mathematics." But the active cooperation of the navy was deemed necessary to insure the success of the movement. The crossing, however, was suspended because of the announcement of the admiral that he had resolved to retire. The general sent an officer of his staff to represent to the admiral his readiness to make the movement, the great importance of making it promptly when the enemy was unprepared to dispute it successfully and to urge him to cooperate actively with the fire of his fleet. But to all of these considerations, says the general, "earnestly and elaborately urged, the admiral's answer was that he would not fire another shot."

The intended movement was therefore abandoned or indefinitely suspended. The land as well as the naval expedition had come to naught and further movements for the capture of Charleston were deferred.

The Battle of Chancellorsville

WILLIAM T. FORBES,
LIEUTENANT COLONEL, 102ND NEW YORK VOLUNTEER INFANTRY

Philadelphia *Weekly Times* 5, no. 13, May 21, 1881

Of all the great battles of the late war that of Chancellorsville has been least explained and is least comprehended. Nor is this lack of understanding confined to civilians. Among military men and critics there has never yet been a clear solution of the riddle why [Maj. Gen. Joseph] Hooker, after doing so well at the outset, allowed himself to be beaten by inferior numbers. Whatever can be written that may contribute to this solution is of value and should be placed on record before the actors pass away. Especially is this of importance, as this battle was not only one of the hardest fought on the part of the troops actually engaged, but also was pre-eminent among all the battles fought by the Army of the Potomac for brilliant strategic success on the part of Hooker, overmatched by more brilliant tactical success on the part of [Gen. Robert E.] Lee.

I was a staff officer in the XII Army Corps and an active participant in that battle from beginning to end. The most of the fighting after the rout of our right wing took place under my own observation and I received from General Hooker probably the last order given by him at the Chancellor House before he was disabled. I kept a careful journal of all that came within my knowledge and have taken pains to verify or correct my own records and recollections by official reports, both Federal and Confederate. During the Chattanooga and Atlanta campaigns, while serving as a staff officer under General Hooker, and again after the war, I had repeated conversations with him upon the battle of Chancellorsville and know what his own opinions were upon the subject.

Before proceeding with the narrative it is proper to say that I have taken unusual pains to avoid inaccuracy of statement. Whatever I state as fact is derived either from my own journal or from official reports of both sides, and when these differ I have consulted current accounts and the recollection of living actors in the battle, with the purpose of reaching carefully the truth before rushing into print.

The two armies confronted each other on the Rappahannock; Hooker's right near Stafford Court House and his left facing Fredericksburg; Lee's right at Skinker's Creek, ten miles below Fredericksburg and his left at United States Ford, fifteen miles above. The lines of each army were not continuous, but were a series of encampments, established with reference to the comfort of the troops and the protection of salient points. Hooker had present for duty as per official returns, April 29, 1863:

Infantry and artillery	119,661
Cavalry, about	12,000

There were reductions from various causes, and after careful comparison of returns and other accounts, I reach the following estimate:

I Corps, [Maj. Gen. John F.] Reynolds, three divisions, say	16,000
II Corps, [Maj. Gen. Darius N.] Couch three divisions, say	16,000
III Corps, [Maj. Gen. Daniel E.] Sickles, three divisions, say	18,000
V Corps, [Maj. Gen. George G.] Meade, three divisions, say	15,000
VI Corps, [Maj. Gen. John] Sedgwick, three divisions, say	22,000
XI Corps, [Maj. Gen. Oliver O.] Howard, three divisions, say	15,000
XII Corps, [Maj. Gen. Henry W.] Slocum, three divisions, say	11,000
Total infantry and artillery	113,000
Cavalry under [Brig. Gen. Alfred] Pleasonton, three regiments	1,500
Total effective battle of Chancellorsville	114,500

These figures, I feel assured, are closely approximate in the aggregate. Individual corps may be slightly over or under estimated for the sake of giving round numbers.

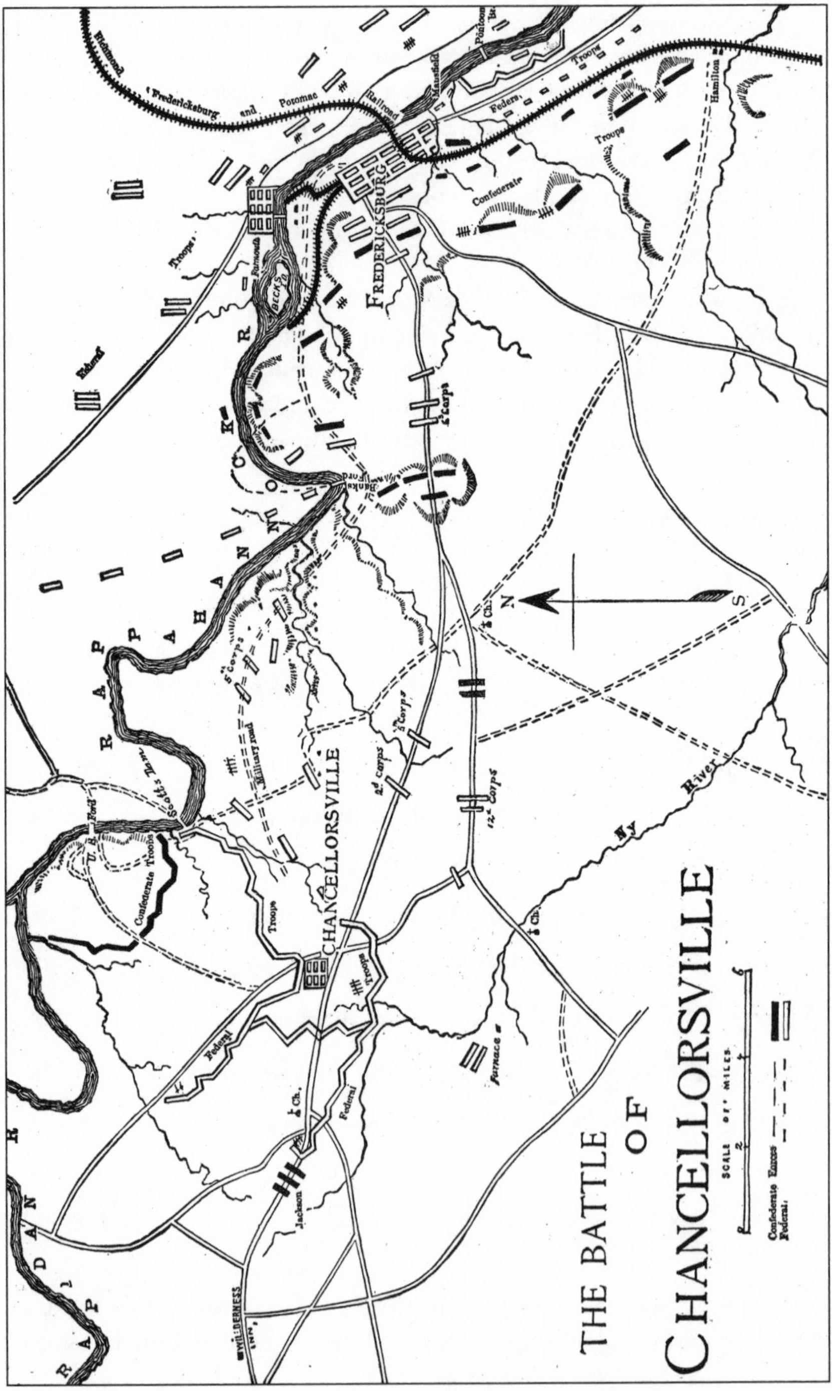

The battle of Chancellorsville (JOHNSON, *CAMPFIRE AND BATTLEFIELD*)

The Confederate authorities differ as to Lee's strength. The latest official returns on file seem to be those of March 31, showing 57,112 total effective. Meantime there were daily additions. After much comparison I adopt the statement of Capt. [Jedediah] Hotchkiss, of Jackson's staff, as follows:

1st Corps, [Lt. Gen. James P.] Longstreet.	
Muskets	
[Maj. Gen. Richard H.] Anderson's Division, five brigades;	
[Maj. Gen. Lafayette] McLaw's Division, four brigades	17,000
2nd Corps, [Lt. Gen. Thomas J.] Jackson.	
[Maj. Gen. Ambrose P.] Hill's Division, six brigades	11,000
[Maj. Gen. Daniel H.] Hill's Division, five brigades	9,000
[Maj. Gen. Isaac R.] Trimble's Division, four brigades	6,000
[Maj. Gen. Jubal] Early's Division, four brigades	7,400
[Brig. Gen. Fitzhugh] Fitz Lee's brigade	1,800
[Maj. Gen. James E. B.] Stuart's Cavalry.	
[Brig. Gen. Wade] Hampton's (absent)	
[Brig. Gen. William H. F.] Lee's	900
Artillery, 170 pieces	5,000
Total muskets	58,100

Total effective, say 62,000

General W. H. F. Lee's Cavalry Brigade remained absent attending to [Brig. Gen. George] Stoneman on his raid.

Lee's position was practically impregnable to attack on the front or right flank. Hooker with great secrecy matured and put in operation once of the most brilliant movements of the war, in which the left rear of Lee's army was his first objective and his own right the attacking force. For several days the cavalry corps had attempted to cross the Upper Rappahannock, but without success, the rains having made it too deep to ford. On April 27, Hooker became impatient of Stoneman's delay and decided to make his infantry campaign without further reference to the operations of his cavalry. Early that morning (Monday, April 27) the XI and XII Corps broke camp and marched by way of Stafford Court House and Hartwood, concentrating by the afternoon of the next day (April 28) near Kelley's Ford, twenty-seven miles above Fredricksburg.

The V Corps by another road reached that point about the same time. The troops carried on their persons eight days' rations and forty rounds of ammunition. One battery accompanied each division; also, pack trains of mules laden with extra infantry ammunition. Few wagons were allowed—the regular supply trains, under charge of the division commissaries and ordnance officers, being parked near Banks' Ford in expectation of that being the next point of supply for the right wing. Upon reaching Kelley's Ford, Stuart's cavalry pickets were at once driven back and a bridge was laid upon canvas pontoons. Early the next morning (the twenty-ninth) all three corps were across and marched for Chancellorsville—the V by the Ely's Ford road and the XI and XII some distance on the right by the road crossing the Rapidan at Germanna Ford, without waiting to repair it, waded the stream more than breast deep, capturing 150 of the enemy who were rebuilding the bridge and bivouacked for the night on the other side. While the advance troops waded the stream others hastily made a passable crossing with the timbers the enemy had collected for repairs, and the rear of column crossed dry shod.

Stoneman having severed communication with the right wing on the twenty-eighth and gone on his Richmond raid, the only cavalry retained by Hooker comprised three small regiments under General Pleasonton. These moved with our column and were handled most efficiently, being always where they were needed, in the advance and on the right flank of the infantry. Stuart had retained one brigade of cavalry, under Fitz Lee, and the two bodies repeatedly exchanged compliments after leaving Kelley's Ford, Stuart's object being to learn our numbers and probable designs, and Pleasonton to keep him at a respectful distance. From Stuart's official report I learn that he took a few prisoners from all these corps, and finding on them forty rounds and eight days' rations (signs that this march meant business), late on the twenty-ninth he informed General Lee, who first comprehended Hooker's intention. These prisoners were doubtless stragglers after the passage of the rear guard, as none were captured from our main body during the march.

Early on April 30 the two columns marched, Slocum in the advance on the Germanna road, brushing aside the enemy's cavalry with trifling loss and reaching Chancellorsville by 4:00 P.M., where the V Corps had already arrived from Ely's Ford. This concentration at Chancellorsville completely uncovered United States Ford, [Brig. Gen. William] Mahone and [Brig. Gen. Carnot] Posey's Brigades of Lee's army retiring before the V Corps and Stuart before the XII. By 3:00 P.M. Hooker had a bridge across at United States Ford (four and a half miles due north from Chancellorsville), and Couch, with two divisions of the II Corps, crossed, and leaving [Brig. Gen. John] Gibbon's division at Falmouth, joined us that evening. Hooker also arrived and fixed his headquarters in the Chancellor House, and all hands had a love feast before we laid down for the night without tents under the moonlit canopy.

Upon our arrival that afternoon the troops and artillery were at once placed in line, covering the approaches to the Chancellor House. This temporary line was the same that afterwards became our battle front on May 2 and 3. Slocum occupied the center, Meade the left and Howard the right, with Couch in reserve for that night. Slocum, immediately on forming line at 4:00 P.M., placed [Capt. Joseph M.] Knap's Battery at the apex on the plank road, 250 yards in front (south) of the Chancellor House, posted strong pickets well in advance, and set the pioneers at work felling the half grown timber in front, falling the trees outward, thus forming abatis along the entire front. I believe similar work was done by the corps on the right and left wherever the line lay in the woods. A few logs were roughly piled here and there in front of the line of troops, but without special orders or concert of action, and no regular breastworks were erected, except at the salient points, where artillery was posted to sweep roads or other open approaches.

The Chancellor House was in the region known as the "Wilderness," within about one mile of its eastern limit. From it diverge the following roads: north to United States Ford, northwest to Ely's Ford, northeast to Banks' Ford, east the old turnpike and the plank road to Fredericksburg, and west the plank road to Orange Court House and Germanna Ford. Two miles west of the Chancellor House the plank road and old turnpike separate, the former running to Orange Court House, the latter to Germanna Ford. At the house the turnpike continues due east, the plank road diverges southward for half a mile, then obliques sharply to the left, and again unites with the turnpike five miles east of Chancellorsville, near Tabernacle Church. From Fredericksburg to Chancellorsville is ten miles, one easy day's march for infantry. For one mile to the east, five miles or more west and about one mile in front of Chancellorsville, there was little cleared ground save one large field in the rear of Slocum's line. This field extended south of the plank road from the Chancellor House, about half a mile west, and at its widest point may be three hundred yards across. The woods in front were half-grown timber, with almost impenetrable underbrush.

On the left the forest was of larger growth and rather more open. Not far in front of Slocum's right and Howard's left was a small clearing, and what looked like a young orchard on a hill that overlooked our line and [was] known as Hazel Grove. Howard's line extended west by north from Slocum's right and crossed the plank road near Talley's House. In this position by dark on April 30, Hooker had by my estimate 51,000 effective troops. Everything thus far had exceeded beyond expectation, and we held this most important strategic position with a total loss thus far of six men, two mules, and one wagon. We were directly in the rear of Lee's army and only nine miles away.

Before proceeding farther with the direct narrative let us understand what Sedgwick and Lee, the other two factors in the problem, have done up to this date. Hooker had placed Sedgwick in command of his left wing, comprising the I, III, and VI Corps and Gibbon's division of the II—in all say 61,000 troops. Gibbon had been left to maintain a show of strength in the field works at Falmouth, facing Fredericksburg, and during the twenty-seventh and twenty-eighth the other three corps were massed near Franklin's Crossing, three miles below the town. Before daylight on the twenty-ninth, Sedgwick had laid his pontoon bridge at that point, having first ferried across a small force and captured the enemy's pickets. Under cover of the morning fog he laid another bridge one and a half miles below. [Brig. Gen. William T. H.] Brook's division (VI Corps) crossed on the upper bridge and [Brig. Gen. James S.] Wadsworth's division (I Corps) on the lower, and entrenched their positions. Late on the thirtieth he received orders from Hooker for the III Corps to join the right wing. Sickles marched and reached Chancellorsville on the morning of May 1.

Until now, Lee with his main body remained at Fredericksburg awaiting the further development of Hooker's plans. He had learned from Stuart of the advance of our right wing to the Rapidan, but Lee was well informed as to the organization of our army, and he knew that more than one-half of Hooker's army was probably still in his front with its advance across the river on his right. All day on April 30 Stuart was busy ascertaining Hooker's movements and force. Having satisfied himself on these points, as stated in his official report, late that night he reported in person to Lee at Fredericksburg. Lee lost not a moment. Seeing Sedgwick passive in his front and Hooker active in his rear, he decided promptly and correctly. He had but two options, either at once to retreat toward Richmond by the line of the railroad, or leaving a small force in Sedgwick's front, to march with the bulk of his army and attack Hooker before the latter could collect more troops.

Ordering Anderson's three advance brigades (Mahone, Posey and [Brig. Gen. Cadmus M.] Wilcox) to retire to near Tabernacle Church and Jackson to march his corps in the same direction, Lee placed Early's Division (of Jackson's Corps) with [Brig. Gen. William] Barksdale's Brigade and the reserve artillery—altogether nine thousand—to oppose Sedgwick, and ordered McLaws to march by the plank road, join Anderson and oppose Hooker. By daylight of May 1, McLaws joined Anderson at the designated position and their commands commenced entrenching. At 8:00 A.M. Jackson arrived at the head of his column, assumed command, stopped entrenching and ordered a general advance and attack.

About 10:00 A.M. on that day Hooker advanced from Chancellorsville, with two corps, by three roads: Slocum on the right by the plank road; Meade, with [Brig. Gen. Charles] Griffin and [Brig. Gen. Andrew A.] Humphrey's Division, on the left by the Banks' Ford road and [Maj. Gen. George] Sykes' Division in the left by the Banks' Ford road and Sykes' Division in the center by the old turnpike—[Maj. Gen. Winfield S.] Hancock's Division of the II Corps in support of Sykes. The XI Corps and [Maj. Gen. William H.] French's Division, II Corps, remained near Chancellorsville, under arms, awaiting orders. One battery of artillery accompanied each division. The orders for this movement were most specific and contemplated a general advance (without, if possible, showing his whole strength) to a line with Banks' Ford for his left and Tabernacle Church his right center and key point of advantage. This he expected the army to complete not later than 2:00 P.M. He was not aware that before his troops moved from Chancellorsville Jackson had ordered a general advance from Tabernacle Church to find and attack Hooker. Thus the armies met each the advance of the other two and a half miles from Chancellorsville. Griffin and Humphreys met no opposition and advanced five miles until in sight of Banks' Ford.

Sykes met the troops of McLaws' Division one mile east of Chancellorsville and pushed them back with some loss on both sides, but no serious fighting, about one mile farther, where McLaws was reinforced by Anderson and gave Sykes a lively fight, flanking him on both sides. Hancock then moved up in readiness to support Slocum, advanced over two miles and was there met by the advance of Jackson's column and had some skirmishing. Here his column halted, awaiting orders, every moment expected, to connect with Meade and attack the enemy—the presumption being that Hooker would bring the rest of his army to our support. Sickles with his III Corps had arrived at Chancellorsville during the forenoon.

The ridge we occupied extended generally across the roads toward the river and was a good point from which to attack. It was entirely out of the Wilderness, generally cleared and with an open country in front and on our right flank. Slocum's front consisted of [Brig. Gen. John W.] Geary's 2nd and 3rd Brigades, deployed in line, with the left resting on the plank road and the right on a high, cleared ridge, from which the country could be viewed for miles to the right. [Brig. Gen. Alpheus S.] Williams' division of the XII Corps was in hand either for support or protection to the right flank. I have never seen troops on the eve of battle more enthusiastic and confident in their commander and their advantage of position than were ours. There were then in that commanding position at 1:00 P.M. 31,000 more, making 60,000 available with which to attack Lee, who with 45,000 was about to attack us. The three columns of the advance did not connect, but after getting out of the Wilderness could communicate "across lots"; and if the reserves had been promptly brought up the general line would have been sufficiently connected to have advanced with strong columns of attack.

From the Confederate official reports I learn that Anderson and McLaws formed the column that engaged with Sykes and Hancock, while Jackson was in Slocum's front. McLaws reported to Jackson that the force in his front was heavy and asked for aid. Jackson sent some assistance and ordered other troops on a flanking expedition, to gain our right, meantime halting his own advance, and merely opening upon Slocum from a battery and skirmish line. This explains the fact that we had no serious engagement on the right, and amused ourselves skirmishing and dodging Jackson's round shot, while a mile or more on our left where the ridge was not so high we could hear Sykes' volleys of musketry. The relative positions were unchanged, while our men lay in line awaiting the order to advance for nearly an hour. Knap's Battery, which had moved on the plank road with the advance of our troops, replied to the enemy, the only loss on our side being Captain Knap's horse, which was killed under him by a round shot.

Our troops had passed in line of battle through a piece of woods and laid flat in the further edge ready for the word. The enemy seemed to be in a belt of woods half a mile in our front, where their battery was posted, but we saw very little of them, and I do not think they saw much of us. After half an hour of sluggish artillery exchange the order came, "Retire to Chancellorsville." General Slocum and his subordinates hesitated, and before yielding the splendid position so easily gained word was sent to Hooker explaining the advantage of remaining and respectfully asking if we had not better fight where we were. A second and imperative order to withdraw was the reply.

Dissatisfaction was stamped upon the faces of the troops as we faced to the rear, and passed again through the woods and the Wilderness, Knap's Battery keeping the advancing enemy at a respectful distance and [Brig. Gen. Thomas L.] Kane's brigade covering the rear. A squadron of the enemy's cavalry made a dash on our rear guard, but a round shot from our battery brought them to their senses and we were not further molested. Some very forcible utterances fell from the lips of general officers of Slocum's corps during this retrograde movement. I remember taking the order to Kane, whose brigade was on the extreme right. I had to take it a third time before he would move from his position. This general, whose brain and pluck were enough to supply three times his size (he was small and crippled with wounds), fairly danced with insubordinate excitement.

"Go back," said he, "and tell the general that I can whip the whole Rebel army with my brigade in this position. I can't give it up without a fight."

The third order had to be given somewhat curtly before he would move his brigade to the rear, and by that time the rest of Geary's division were out of sight and he was in danger of being surrounded, but by good management came in rapidly in good order without serious loss.

For reasons that will be discussed hereafter, Hooker had suddenly changed his original intention, and finding Lee close at hand, had decided to fight a defensive battle, with United States Ford as his point of supply, instead of an offensive, with Banks' Ford in his rear. The army was at once placed in line of battle in its position of April 30, with few minor changes. On the right Howard, his right refused across the plank road and old turnpike, near Talley's, two miles west of the Chancellor House, his left connecting with [Brig. Gen. David B.] Birney's Division, near Dowdall's and not far in front of the plank road. His line was partly in the thicket, with some clearings in his front and around Talley's and Dowdall's. Slocum's line extended from Birney's left and crossed the plank road 250 yards in front of the Chancellor House. At that point the center of the army line was held by Geary's Division, whose batteries were quickly entrenched upon and near the plank road to sweep the approaches. At no other point on Slocum's line could artillery be used to advantage, as his line of battle was entirely in dense thicket, except two regiments on the left of the road, supporting the batteries.

Next on the left came Hancock's division, along Mott Run, his left curving to the rear, and beyond him Meade, whose V Corps, well refused toward the river, formed Hooker's extreme left. In this formation on May 1, about 3:00 P.M., [Brig. Gen. Amiel W.] Whipple's and [Maj. Gen. Hiram

G.] Berry's divisions (III Corps), French's division (II Corps), were held in reserve. Hooker, with his staff, retained his headquarters in the Chancellor House.

During our withdrawal that afternoon McLaws followed closely, skirmishing with Hancock, who had relieved Sykes in the front, and Anderson followed Geary by the plank road and formed line in our front as far as Catharine Furnace. About dusk the enemy felt Geary's lines by a reconnaissance in force, driving in his pickets and advancing with sharp firing on both sides of the plank road. They were driven back by artillery and musketry and the picket line was re-established in the woods, well to the front. McLaws also felt strongly of Hancock's lines, but was easily repulsed by the picket line. At the same time Hancock's and Geary's lines were shattered by artillery, which the enemy had posted on the high ground one mile to our left. All night we heard the axes of the enemy at work in our front and knew that they also were entrenching. Hooker this night sent orders for Reynolds' (I) Corps to join him the next day. He expressed himself perfectly satisfied with his position and arrangements for battle, positive that Lee must either attack at once or retreat, and confident that in case of attack our army would whip.

The next day (May 2) the operations of the forenoon were of little moment. There was some skirmishing and feeling of lines along Slocum's and Hancock's front, and occasionally the batteries on our left opened a lively fire upon us. These batteries could be plainly seen and the guns counted on a cleared hill, from which Hancock had been withdrawn the day previous. It was about a mile from our batteries at the plank road, and too far for their fire to be effective except with solid shot; but as they enfiladed Geary's line he trained Knap's and Muhlenberg's batteries on them and made them a little more respectful. All day from early morning there were indications that the enemy was marching towards our right; but as their line of march, owing to the Wilderness in our front, deflected southwest from our points of observation, Hooker inclined to the opinion that they were moving in retreat. Still, as they might be gaining on our flanks, he cautioned Howard and Slocum to guard well their front and flanks and to keep feeling the enemy's line.

This column of the enemy was Jackson's and kept mostly out of sight and range from our front line, but about 1:00 P.M. a column of their troops by mistake followed the plank road until within eight hundred yards of Geary's front, where, at the head of the road, they came into plain view, and Muhlenberg gave them a few rounds of canister, which sent them back to their main body.

At the Furnace, two miles in front of Birney's position, about noon, Birney saw the rear of Jackson's column, his wagons and artillery passing the Furnace. His infantry had already passed without detection, leaving the 23rd Georgia Regiment and a body of Stuart's Cavalry as guard at that exposed point. J. Birney, under orders from Hooker, advanced to pierce the moving column, Sickles giving personal supervision to the movement. Advancing a mile he had a skirmish and captured prisoners. The enemy showing increased force at the Furnace, Whipple's division (III Corps) was sent to his support on the left, and [Brig. Gen. Francis C.] Barlow's brigade (XI Corps) on the right. Williams' division (XII Corps) also advanced on the left and rear of Whipple in readiness to support if needed. Pleasonton, with about one thousand cavalry, accompanied Birney and aided in the attack. Whipple and Barlow having come up, Birney advanced a mile further and gained Jackson's road at the Furnace, capturing the 23rd Georgia Regiment.

Meantime Pleasonton, finding the ground too rough and woody for cavalry movements, left one regiment with Birney, and taking the other two returned towards the main line. It was now dusk, and on the way he met an aide-de-camp, who reported the rout of the XI Corps. So rapidly had Jackson moved in his charge that his advance was already in Pleasonton's front. Reaching the open ground near Howard's left of line, Pleasonton found the enemy surging through the woods without organized opposition. With a single glance he took in the position, which, for our army, was perilous beyond measure. Something must be done on the moment to give them a check until infantry and artillery could be brought to the near front.

Turning to Maj. [Peter] Keenan, commanding the 8th Pennsylvania Cavalry, he ordered him to charge. With 450 men Keenan charged ten thousand. It was into the jaws of certain death. Keenan, two officers and fifty-six men were killed, but ten minutes of time were gained. Pleasonton's horse artillery galloped into battery, unlimbered and opened fire, and other batteries in the vicinity, twenty-two pieces in all, were brought on the run to the same position. Hooker had mounted his horse and swept down the field, facing the enemy's fire, and gathering on his way the only troops close at hand—Berry's division (III Corps) and [Brig. Gen. William] Hays' brigade (II Corps), placed them on the right of the batteries, near the plank road, where they instantly engaged the enemy and held their ground. Thus within a few minutes was formed the nucleus of a new line on our right and Jackson's assault was stayed. But we must return a little in the narrative.

Jackson had bivouacked on Friday night on the plank road, two miles east of Chancellorsville. Marching early next morning (May 2) with wonderful secrecy, while Stuart with his cavalry screened the movement and Lee demonstrated on our left and center, he passed Catharine Furnace, turned to the right by the Brock road and halted briefly near Wilderness Church, on the plank road, down which he sent Fitz Lee with cavalry to examine Howard's lines. Quickly ascertaining that he had not yet reached Howard's flank he pushed on, cutting his way through the woods to the old turnpike, where he soon found that he was in Howard's right and rear. There he formed his column of attack with his three divisions (26,000 strong), [Brig. Gen. Robert E.] Rodes in front, [Brig. Gen. Raleigh F.] Colston next, and A. P. Hill in the rear. Each line was separated by 200 yards distance and was deployed with full division front, the turnpike being the center line of the column. His front line extended nearly a mile on each side from the turnpike. A section of horse artillery on this road advanced with the first line. Each brigade and regimental commander was ordered to move forward to the aid of those in front whenever needed or called for, without awaiting superior orders. It was 5:30 P.M. and all along our front was quiet, except where Sickles was skirmishing near the Furnace.

Everything conspired toward Jackson's success. Howard's Corps (16,000 strong) was in one long line, without reserves, and Jackson, with 26,000, was in his right and rear. Between Howard and the Chancellor House, on the line of the plank road, we had nothing except Berry's division in reserve. Between Howard and Slocum was a gap in our front line, left when Birney, Whipple, Barlow, and Williams advanced toward the Furnace. French's Division was in reserve, two miles away, behind the Chancellor House. Geary held the center, his right in air, unconnected with any other troops, Hancock and Meade on his left. Reynolds with his I Corps had just reached United States Ford, five miles away. Lee's demonstrations on Hooker's left and center had all day shown his presence there in force, and Hooker dared not detach troops from those positions in mere anticipation of a possible attack on his extreme right. Everything depended upon Howard holding his ground. So unsuspected was Jackson's attack that Howard himself had gone about 3:00 P.M. with Barlow's brigade to reconnoiter the enemy from Sickles' advanced ground and returning reached his corps after the attack began.

At half-past five Jackson advanced. His proximity was unsuspected, and the troops of [Brig. Gen. Charles] Devens' division had stacked arms and were chatting around their campfires over their hardtack and coffee. No

Bringing up reinforcements to meet Jackson's flank attack (HEARST'S MAGAZINE)

warning seems to have been given by their pickets. They only heard the bugles sounding the charge and Jackson was upon them. Many of them had not time to take their muskets from the stack and panic took almost complete possession. Devens was wounded, Howard was among them exerting all his power to check the retreat, but Jackson's men were upon their rear and both flanks, and on they broke in a confused mass that nothing could arrest, Stuart's and Jackson's artillery adding to their panic by rapid firing of solid shot that came ricocheting down the plank road to the Chancellor House. Near Dowdall's, [Brig. Gen. Adolph Von] Steinwehr, with [Col. Adolphus] Buschbeck's brigade and fragments under [Brig. Gen. Alexander] Schimmelfennig, made a brave stand, but they were a handful and were soon forced to retire by the enemy on both flanks. Now came that heroic charge of Keenan, and the enemy in a few minutes met the fire of Berry's division and the twenty-two guns that Pleasonton wheeled into bat-

Union guns answering Jackson's batteries (HEARST'S MAGAZINE)

tery. Rodes' Division (Jackson's front line) was checked within half a mile of the Chancellor House, in the edge of the thicket, and Colston surged to the front and recoiled from the deadly fire.

It was 7:00 P.M. and growing dark. At that time Lee made active demonstrations on Hancock and Geary, advancing in force through the brush with the double purpose of keeping our forces busy on center and left, or of making a charge if Jackson's assault was not arrested. He was promptly driven back and our pickets and troops retained their old position. But no troops were at hand to join Berry on the right, and upon the artillery now depended the salvation of the army. Capt. [Clermont L.] Best, Slocum's chief of artillery, was entrusted with this duty. He hastily collected all the available field artillery of the XII and III Corps, in all between forty and fifty guns, and posted them on a slight rise in the open field south of the plank road and six hundred yards west of the Chancellor House, near to and fronting the thicket in which Jackson had halted to reform his lines. This ridge was called Fairview. He shelled the woods and the turnpike at short range with terrible effect.

This gave breathing time, which Hooker actively employed. He had previously ordered Sickles to return from the Furnace and attack Jackson's right flank. Sickles returned, pushing back the enemy's right during the night and placed Birney on the left and in advance of the artillery. Williams formed in the rear of Birney and Whipple in the rear of Berry, across the plank road on the right. In front of Sickles' left was Hazel Grove, the commanding position before referred to which threatened Jackson's right and commanded the Chancellor House. Sickles held this position till towards morning, but Hooker deeming it too far isolated from our line ordered its abandonment. In the next day's battle the enemy's artillery massed at that point aided them most effectively.

By 10:00 P.M. these new dispositions of troops were mainly completed. In the stillness of the night Jackson's officers could be heard as they reorganized and formed their shattered columns. Jackson had ordered Hill to relieve Rodes in the front line and intended to push the attack at once and cut Hooker off from United States Ford. He only awaited Hill's arrival in front. Meantime Hooker at 11:00 P.M. made a counter on Jackson's right, with [Brig. Gen. J. H. Hobart] Ward's brigade of Birney's division, Best at the same time opening a rapid fire from his fifty guns. This attack was terrific, driving the enemy back half a mile and retaking some of Howard's lost artillery.

Shortly after, Jackson was mortally wounded by the fire of his own men. A. P. Hill took command and was soon disabled by a piece of shell. Rodes succeeded in command, but was displaced by Stuart, whom Lee sent to the vicinity of Ely's Ford, of which, with his cavalry, he was then trying to gain possession. Thus between 11:00 P.M. and 2:00 A.M., the charging column changed commanders three times, and their farther advance was postponed till morning.

The rapidly changing events of that evening and the next day, around and to the right of the Chancellor House, are photographed on my memory with greater distinctness than almost any other battle of the war. A little after 5:00 P.M. Geary had just returned from making a reconnaissance in force in his front. He had advanced about four hundred yards on both sides of the plank road through the thicket, and stirred up a heavy fire both of artillery and musketry in his front, and had returned with considerable loss in killed and wounded. We were just taking our coffee on the open ground near Knap's Battery, when the terrific road of Jackson's charge brought every man to his feet, staff officers in the saddle and troops into line ready for action.

The charge seemed to advance like a prairie fire, sweeping before it a confused mass of troops, wagons, ambulances, caissons, beef cattle, etc. Such a sight I never saw elsewhere in battle. Hooker mounted at once, and galloped to meet the storm, taking with him Berry's division. The general staff officers, and those of Slocum and Geary, mounted, and with drawn sabers formed line across the field to halt the fugitives, who had become thoroughly panic-stricken. Down the plank road, through this mass, came plunging shot past the Chancellor House. Suddenly we saw Berry come into action and heard Pleasonton's artillery at work, and the field took on a new face. The troops of the XI Corps passed to the rear, in fifteen minutes more every man was at his post, the field once more cleared for action. The disaster thus far was most serious, but not irreparable.

The artillery discharge at 11:00 P.M. was probably the finest display of the sort during the war. Fifty cannon, firing by battery for half an hour, riveted the gaze of all who were not actively engaged. There were few slumberers that short night.

Hooker rearranged his forces for battle in the form of a "V," Geary holding the apex, Sickles on his right having Best, with forty pieces of artillery, in rear of his center; Birney to the left of Best and Williams in support of Birney, Berry on the right of Best across the plank road, with Whipple in support. Williams' left was near Geary's right, the two lines forming a right angle. Sickles and Williams faced Jackson's Corps. To the right of Berry was Meade's V Corps, and prolonging his line farther to the right was Reynolds' I Corps, who had reached his position after dark and whose right stretched well toward the Rapidan, along Hunting Creek; on the left of the apex, joining Geary, was Hancock's division, and prolonging his line Howard, who occupied Meade's former position on the extreme left of the army. During the night Howard got his troops well in hand again, and he and his officers were anxious to redeem their failure of the day previous.

In the rear of the Chancellor House was Couch with French's division in reserve. Hooker's headquarters at the Chancellor House were 250 yards in rear of Geary. The relative positions of the armies were now as follows: Stuart, with Jackson's Corps (26,000 before the attack), confronted Sickles, and Williams (23,000 before the attack) and Best's artillery, equal to another division, within ready call for action on Stuart's flank were Meade, Reynolds, and Couch (37,000). Lee, with McLaws and Anderson (15,000), confronted Geary and Hancock and Howard's right, say 20,000 effective. Lee did not connect with Jackson by a space of over a mile. It was clear to all that the issue of battle was on our right. Neither Geary nor Hancock could leave their positions unless an entirely new line was established in the rear. Sickles, with Best's artillery, was about equal to Stuart. Reynolds, Meade, and French were the trump cards to be played at the proper time.

Having relieved himself from immediate pressure, the evening of May 2 Hooker sent orders to Sedgwick to advance, seize the heights in the rear of Fredericksburg and unite with the main army at Chancellorsville by daylight. He hardly expected the literal fulfillment of such an order, but thus indicated his wishes and hopes. The distance was fourteen miles. Sedgwick received the order at 11:00 P.M., and had barely time to make such a march if no enemy had been in his front. He advanced, with some skirmishing, before dawn and occupied Fredericksburg, but not the heights, which were held by Early.

At daylight Stuart opened the ball. Advancing two brigades on his right he took possession of Hazel Grove, from which Birney's rear was withdrawn after some fighting. There he posted thirty pieces of artillery and opened upon us a most distressing fire, raking Sickles, Williams, and Best at an acute angle, completely enfilading Geary's breastworks and reaching effectively every part of our lines to the plank road and Chancellor House.

At the same time his infantry and that under Lee charged, and from 4:30 until 10:00 A.M. the battle raged without cessation. Sickles and Best held their ground, fighting bravely and incessantly and bringing Williams and Whipple to the front early in the action. Up to 8:00 A.M. Stuart had made five distinct charges and each time was repulsed with heavy loss and constant fighting on both sides [and] counter charges by Sickles. About this time [Col Samuel S.] Carroll's brigade (French's division) advanced in front of Meade's left and assaulted Stuart's flank, gaining the plank road and taking some prisoners, but Stuart promptly dispatched a strong force to the point of danger and with the aid of artillery on his flank drove Carroll's unsupported force back until the broken line was re-established.

No other attack on Stuart's flank was made during this battle, although that was clearly the point where the day should have been won.

About half-past eight Sickles' left flank was pushed somewhat to the rear, and Lee succeeded in connecting his line with Stuart's by a general "squeeze" on the angle formed by Geary and Williams and a thin extension of Anderson's left. All the morning Sickles and Best had suffered severely from the enemy's thirty guns on their left at Hazel Grove, and by this time many of his troops were out of ammunition, and the artillery had to take a new position in the rear; many of the guns had also become too hot to work. The losses had been heavy, but those of the enemy probably heavier. The enemy, gaining new ardor by the weakening of Sickles' left and their own junction with Lee, now forced the fighting with fresh vigor. Sickles and his allies resisted with all in their power, calling and hoping every minute for reinforcements and the expected attack on Stuart's left flank, but no aid came from that quarter except the resultless attack by Carroll's brigade, which had now been repelled.

There was no help for it, and Sickles and Williams were forced to the rear across the plank road. Such of the artillery as remained effective was posted around and in rear of the Chancellor House, and the full force of the attack now fell on Geary from front, right, and rear. Since 5:00 P. M. Lee had attacked in front of Hancock and Geary, steadily moving his forces towards his left to join Stuart. This movement gradually weakened the attack on Hancock and increased the pressure on Geary. All the morning Geary's lines were enfiladed both ways with solid shot from the enemy's batteries on his right flank at Hazel Grove and those on his left a mile away in Hancock's front. On his front Anderson's troops pressed through thicket and abatis to his very breastworks, and were repeatedly driven back.

At 8:30 P.M., when Sickles' left was turned, the enemy reached Geary's right rear. He had already faced two regiments on that flank to the right, perpendicular to his breastworks, and by the aid of his artillery firing at short range, with desperate fighting, held his ground nearly another hour. All this time, with the exception of Hancock's partial engagement, no other body of Hooker's infantry was actively occupied, and Geary had less than six thousand men. The contest here was as closely fought as I have ever witnessed. I myself saw an officer grapple the flag of the 12th Georgia and contest its possession in hand-to-hand struggle. Men of both sides seized each other and disputed as to which was prisoner. There were grim touches of humor in the midst of carnage.

Geary's right brigade faced and fired in three directions—south, west, and north. About 9:00 P.M. Geary received orders to withdraw his right and center and form a new line perpendicular to the breastworks. It was

Repelling the Confederate attack of May 3 (FRANK LESLIE'S ILLUSTRATED NEWSPAPER)

understood that his left was to remain where it was and the rest of his troops wheel to the rear and re-engage the enemy in the new position. This would carry his right brigades into the woods east of and in rear of Chancellor House. While executing this movement, Geary himself being near the Chancellor House, Hooker came up and said in loud, clear tones, within my hearing:

"General Geary, face your command about, charge and retake your old position and hold it. I will advance on the right to your support."

Officers and men caught the spirit of the order instantly, and without awaiting more definite formation or the regular transmission of the order to brigade commanders, caps were swung in the air.

"Right about, double quick, charge!" rang along the line and Geary, with 1,500 men, regained about two-thirds of his original position. The distance passed over in this charge was not more than four hundred yards, and on the way we found two regiments of [Brig. Gen. George S.] Greene's brigade, 102nd New York and 109th Pennsylvania, who, not having heard the first order to retire, had remained fighting and had taken a flag and thirty prisoners. Now we found that Geary had with him only

[Col. Charles] Candy's brigade, and these two regiments of Greene's, in all less than two thousand men. The other two brigades had passed on to the rear, having received no order to halt and not having heard Hooker's command. In the excitement and hurry of the charge they were overlooked, and Geary neither knew their precise location nor had time to recall them. Geary had sent his horse to the rear out of danger and was on foot among his troops, without his hat, his face blacked with powder smoke, his voice gone by the windage of a shell that knocked him down early in the fight.

As we charged, the enemy, wearied and shattered with their long contest, had somewhat slackened their musketry fire, but their artillery at short range redoubled its fire from three sides upon the Chancellor House and vicinity. There were then not less than sixty cannon, whose fire converged in that point and Geary's and Hancock's positions. It was red hot. Their infantry gave way before our impetuous charge, but soon closed again with us, and for half an hour, while Geary held his ground, they concentrated upon him such a fire from front and right as I never again saw men withstand. From end to end of his division came solid shot in quick succession, often three or four at once, cutting off saplings and knocking men in the air, while Anderson and Stuart pressed upon him with volleys of musketry at short range. Yet our men stood their ground, repelling several successive charges, our officers anxiously looking to the right and rear for Hooker's promised attack. Immediately upon regaining our ground Geary had discovered the absence of his other brigade, and, judging that there was no time to recall them, sent me to Hooker to report his condition and ask immediate support. I was still mounted, my horse bleeding from two wounds, and it took but a few minutes to reach the Chancellor House, where I found Hooker. His reply was:

"Tell Geary he is doing splendidly and to hold his position. I will soon be on Jackson's flank."

At that time, immediately succeeding our charge, there was something of a lull in the fight, but it was still hot enough. I took this word to Geary. The enemy had now renewed their furious attack upon him. Turning to me he said:

"Go back and tell Hooker I can't stand this. My men can't stay here fifteen minutes longer."

I hurried back and near the Chancellor House met General Couch with troops massed and lying down to the left of the house. I asked for Hooker. Couch replied: "He has been disabled and I am in command." I gave him Geary's message. His reply was in effect that Hooker had not informed him of his plans and disposition of forces. I explained Geary's position and Hooker's last order and returned to the front (for that matter, it was all front around there then). Once more Geary sent me back. I could not find Couch and presumed he had then, as stated in his narrative, gone to confer with Hooker. A few minutes more and Geary's half hour of desperate fight was ended. The enemy came on the run across his right and rear, and to save his little remnant from capture he faced to the rear and came out by the left flank in quick time. All through this fight Lieutenant Muhlenberg, with six pieces of artillery, had held his position on the plank road, near Geary's front line, changing his fire to front, right, left or rear, as most needed. When we withdrew all his gunners were killed or wounded and many of his horses killed. By the aid of our infantry his guns were all taken off safely, the enemy closing upon our right, left and rear, as we rapidly filed into the ravine and gave him our parting volley, in rear of Hancock's position.

The loss of the plank road rendered Hancock's position untenable, and we saw him then withdrawing on our right. The troops that I had seen twenty minutes before massed at the Chancellor House were no longer in sight and had doubtless been withdrawn to the new line. During Geary's last struggle the Chancellor House took fire from the enemy's shells and was burning as we passed. Several ladies belonging to the family there were escorted to the rear by Major Dickerson, of Hooker's staff, after their house was in flames. So ended the battle of Chancellorsville.

The new line fixed upon and partly fortified on the night of the second was at once occupied and held until Tuesday night, May 5, when in a heavy rain storm, and across a swollen river and shaky bridge, the army recrossed the Rappahannock at United States Ford. As Geary and Hancock withdrew the enemy rushed forward and soon occupied Hooker's old position, establishing their line with the ruins of the Chancellor House as its center. Our new line was still in the form of a "V," with the II and III Corps massed and artillery in position at the apex, near Bullock's House, less than a mile in rear of Chancellorsville; the V and I Corps extended on the right to the Rapidan, and the XI and XII on the left to Scott's Dam. United States Ford was, as before, in rear of our center. Lee's purpose was to attack Hooker again without delay, and he opened upon our center with artillery, but before resuming the offensive received a dispatch announcing Sedgwick's advance to Salem Church.

To meet this new danger he lost no time and at once dispatched McLaws with three brigades to reinforce Early, and the next day (May 4) followed in person with Anderson's division. Sedgwick had, we have seen, in obedience to Hooker's order, advanced at midnight, May 2, from Hamilton's Crossing, three or four miles below Fredericksburg, and by dawn had possession of the town, where he threw across a bridge and Gibbon joined him. After two unsuccessful efforts on each flank he carried the heights by storm at 11:00 A.M., losing one thousand men in the assault, and driving Early two miles southward, he changed front and advanced by the plank road. His progress was necessarily slow, with the enemy on his front and flank. During the afternoon he met the enemy, reinforced by McLaws, at Salem Church, five miles west of Fredericksburg, and after hard fighting lost a little ground.

The next day, May 4, Lee came up with Anderson's troops and while Early retook the heights from which Gibbon had, under order, withdrawn to Falmouth, and moved on Sedgwick's rear and right to cut him off from the river, Lee attacked in front, and with hard blows the combined forces pushed him back to Banks' Ford. There, by the morning of the fifth, he had recrossed the river. In all three fights Sedgwick lost five thousand men. I have thus briefly sketched his operations and as necessary to a just criticism of the battle of Chancellorsville. The details of Sedgwick's movements and battles I leave to be told by some one who participated. The losses in the battle of Chancellorsville were officially reported as follows:

Federal

I Corps	292	XII Corps	2,883
II Corps	2,025	Engineer Corps	2
III Corps	4,039	Signal Corps	2
V Corps	699	Cavalry Corps	143
VI Corps	4,601		
XI Corps	2,508		
Total	**17,197**		

Of these General Lee reports he captured non-wounded 5,000, having killed and wounded 12,197.

The heaviest percentage of loss was in the XII and III Corps, upon whom fell the weight of the battle.

Confederate

Early's Division	851	McLaws' Division	1,379
A. P. Hill's Division	2,583	Artillery Division	227
Colston's Division	1,868	Cavalry Division	11
Rodes' Division	2,178		
Anderson's Division	1,180		
Total	**10,277**		

This does not include prisoners captured by us, which should be 2,500 more, making the total Confederate loss 12,777. Lee reports the loss at Fredericksburg of eight pieces of artillery and capture at Chancellorsville of thirteen, making a net gain of five. Also the capture from us of 19,500 muskets, seventeen standards and a large quantity of ammunition. I believe these reports on both sides to be accurate.

Until Friday morning, May 1, Hooker's campaign was not only the most brilliant of its kind during the war, but it was faultless in plan and execution. Thus far it had been purely strategic, and the strategy was bold and effective. The desired purpose had been accomplished, and it was the purpose most to be desired. Lee's position was no longer impregnable, it was simply untenable. Hooker's utterance that Lee must either fight or retreat at once, though couched in boastful phrase, was true. But the superior tactics of Lee and Jackson soon reversed the advantage and their marching and fighting were conducted with a rapidity upon which Hooker had not calculated.

During May 1 and 2 Hooker was fairly outgeneraled, but still had ample opportunity to recover lost ground and turn reverse into overwhelming victory. On Friday, May 1, he of his own choice changed his tactical plan from the offensive to the defensive. The strong conviction among his generals was that the high, clear ground gained by Slocum and Meade should be held, and the II, III and XI Corps brought to that point, and the enemy attacked in force without giving him the advantage of more time to concentrate, mature his plans, and attack us. After much consideration and comparison of the numbers and movements of both armies I am still of the same opinion. Other considerations influencing Hooker that day were that the supply trains were not yet up and the troops would soon be out of rations and with only a limited supply of ammunition. If he had advanced to the attack with all his infantry, his rear and supply trains would have been exposed to the enemy's cavalry, and of their strength he was not informed. Just here he felt the need of his own cavalry. Had he retained even half the cavalry corps with him to scout and protect his right and rear, he would doubtless have taken a bolder course.

At all events Lee forced him to decide at once, and Hooker chose the defensive. Having taken this course the position chosen was in my opinion the best. The advanced ground of May 1, while admirable for prompt attack, must have been hazardous for defense. There has been much fault found with Hooker's choice of position at Chancellorsville, but with one exception I do not see that it is open to serious criticism as a defensive line.

The one weakness in Hooker's line was his right flank. Although this was refused, probably half a mile to rear of the center, and the extreme right brigade faced west on pretty high ground, yet the position was one of great danger, poorly guarded and without any body of infantry reserves. Everything depended upon Howard's holding his position, yet it was the poorest guarded point of the entire army line. Precisely why this was so has never been publicly explained. Some one of Hooker's subordinates was grievously at fault. The following order, issued May 2, 9:30 A.M., to Generals Slocum and Howard, shows that Hooker did not overlook the danger on his right:

> I am directed by the major general commanding to say that the disposition you have made of your corps has been with a view to a front attack by the enemy. If he should throw himself upon your flank he wishes you to examine the ground and determine upon the position you will take in that event, in order that you may be prepared for him in whatever direction he advances. He suggests that you have heavy reserves well in hand to meet this contingency. The right of your line does not appear to be strong enough. No artificial defenses worth naming have been thrown up and there appears to be a scarcity of troops at that point, and not, in the general's opinion, as favorably posted as might be.
>
> We have good reason to suppose that the enemy is moving to our right. Please advance your pickets, for purposes of observation, as far as may be safe, in order to obtain timely information of their approach.
>
> James H. Van Alen,
> Brigadier General and A.D.C.

When the XI Corps was routed, between 6:00 and 7:00 P.M. on May 2, the situation was one of instant peril to the entire army. The only right thing then to do was whatever could be done most quickly, and Hooker fully met the demand. The disposition of troops and artillery here on the night of May 2 were, I think, made to best advantage and in sufficient strength. Hooker has been criticized for not retaining Hazel Grove, the occupation of which with artillery by the enemy was so disastrous to us the next day; but on this point I think his judgment was correct.

I think Hooker erred in the position assigned that night to Meade, and especially to Reynolds. These two corps were now his strong cards to play and should have been placed well up on the enemy's flank, with orders to assault with at least one-half their force at early dawn. That Hooker intended something of the sort is clear to my mind, and I have never been able to ascertain why the order was not given, or, if sent, was not delivered. Throughout the morning of the third those two corps, 31,000 men, lay behind their breastworks, from one to three miles distant from the fight, expecting the command to advance, which for some unexplained cause never came. There and then was the battle of Chancellorsville lost. Up to the last Lee was in greater peril than Hooker. All the next day (May 4) Sedgwick was fighting, no longer to aid Hooker, but to save his own corps. Then again should the army at Chancellorsville have assumed the offensive in earnest.

But Hooker, though in command, was mentally oppressed if not prostrated by all that had happened and by his personal injury, and nothing was done. The idea often expressed that "Hooker was drunk" at Chancellorsville may as well be dismissed. I know to the contrary, and so do all who saw him during the battle of May 2 and 3. His habits were convivial, but neither on this occasion nor in any other battle did I ever see him unduly affected by liquor. This was his first experiment as commander of a large army, and up to the morning of the third his management had been prompt, clear and without serious fault. Yet Lee outgeneraled and outfought him.

Milroy at Winchester

Robert S. Northcott,
Lieutenant Colonel, 12th West Virginia Volunteer Infantry, and Brevet Brigadier General, U.S.V.

Philadelphia *Weekly Times* 4, no 41, December 4, 1880

Never having seen in print any history of Maj. Gen. Robert H. Milroy's gallant defense of and final defeat at Winchester, Va., in June 1863, I deem such a history worthy of a place in the "Annals of the War." Before commencing this history it will not be improper to state that from the commencement of the War of the Rebellion the possession of Winchester had rather rapidly alternated between the belligerents. In the autumn and early winter of 1861 the Confederates occupied it, but early in 1862 they were driven from it by the Federal forces under Maj. Gen. [Nathaniel P.] Banks, who, early in the following spring, was forced to yield possession of the place to the Confederates under [Lt. Gen. Thomas J.] "Stonewall" Jackson, who, after retaining possession of it for a time, evacuated it and it was subsequently occupied by the Federal forces under Brig. Gen. [Julius] White, who in turn evacuated the place upon the approach of a Confederate force. The latter remained but a short time when they evacuated. In December 1862, General Milroy, who was in command of a Federal force at Moorefield, West Virginia, was ordered to remove his forces and occupy Winchester. His advance, under Brig. Gen. [Gustave P.] Cluseret, reached Winchester on Christmas Day 1862, and a few days thereafter the remainder of his troops arrived. General Milroy's forces consisted of the 2nd Division of the VIII Army Corps, commanded by Brig. Gen. [Robert C.] Schenck, whose headquarters were in Baltimore. General Milroy's forces at Winchester were kept intact until February 25, 1863, then three regiments and a battery of artillery were sent to Berryville, a small town ten miles east of Winchester, under the command of Colonel [Andrew T.] McReynolds, of the 1st New York Cavalry. The Confederates, during the spring of 1863, made several feints in the direction of Winchester and Berryville, but nothing more serious had occurred to June 1 than some slight skirmishes between cavalry scouts. In fact, these feints had become so frequent and amounted to so little that the commanders of the Federal forces had almost ceased to apprehend any serious demonstration by the enemy. It was thought that the Confederates would not try during that summer to repossess the lower Shenandoah Valley. In the meantime, General Milroy had strongly fortified his position near Winchester. He had built a very strong fort a few hundred yards from the northwestern boundary of the city which was surrounded by rifle pits and manned by siege guns. Northwest of this large fort two smaller ones were built, which were also manned by siege guns.

On Monday morning, June 8, a company of the 1st Michigan Cavalry from the Army of the Potomac appeared in Winchester, having made a daring reconnaissance from Culpeper Court House to that place. The captain of this company brought intelligence that from all he was enabled to learn a heavy cavalry force under Brig. Gen. [James Ewell Brown] Stuart had commenced a raid in the direction of the Baltimore and Ohio Railroad and would probably pay Winchester a visit. This caused little apprehension of danger, for the reason that the Federal position was deemed impregnable against a cavalry attack, it mattered not what the force might be. General Milroy, in order to prevent surprise, kept the surrounding country well scouted. On the evening of the tenth rumors of the approach of the enemy in large force were brought in by citizens and scouts and every precaution taken by General Milroy to prevent surprise. On the eleventh rumors were prevalent that the force of the enemy approaching Winchester was small and it was supposed had entered the Shenandoah Valley for the purpose of foraging, but the sequel will show how fallacious these rumors were.

On the morning of June 12, Colonel [John W.] Schall, of the 87th Pennsylvania Infantry, was ordered to take his regiment and two companies of the 13th Pennsylvania Cavalry and reconnoiter on the Staunton Turnpike south of Winchester, the direction in which it was supposed the enemy would approach. When this force had advanced about half a mile beyond Newtown—a village eight miles from Winchester—Colonel Schall learned that a large cavalry force was advancing so as to meet him. He immediately made such a disposition of his infantry and artillery as to make them available and then ordered his cavalry to advance and attack the enemy as soon as they came within the proper distance and then retreat to the infantry. The cavalry had not proceeded far before they came in contact with the Confederates and, discharging their carbines at them according to directions, soon began a rapid retreat and were as rapidly pursued by the Confederates, who were thus led into the ambuscade prepared for them before they were aware of it. The infantry, when they approached sufficiently near them, opened upon them with musketry. The Confederates stood this fire but a few minutes, when they retreated, leaving sixty of their comrades killed, wounded and captured.

During the day it became known in Winchester that a large force of both cavalry and infantry were approaching. In order to be prepared for any emergency, General Milroy ordered all the tents to be struck and with the baggage to be laden in wagons before the next morning and took additional precautions in guarding against surprise during the night. But morning came and all was quiet and many began to believe that the report of the approach of the enemy was unfounded and that there would be no attack. Some of the soldiers re-pitched their tents and officers and men began their usual routine of camp life, such as they were employed in when no enemy was near. The scene, however, soon changed. The day which opened so calmly and peacefully was destined to witness scenes of blood "ere set of sun."

Notwithstanding the peaceful surroundings of Winchester on the morning of the thirteenth, General Milroy, in order to ascertain whether there were any grounds for arriving at the conclusion that no enemy was approaching, ordered Colonel [Joseph W.] Keifer, of the 110th Ohio Infantry, to take his own regiment, the 123rd Ohio Infantry, a detachment of the 13th Pennsylvania Cavalry, and two companies of the 3rd West Virginia Cavalry and make a reconnaissance on the Staunton Turnpike south of Winchester. Colonel Keifer had not proceeded more than two miles when he learned that the Confederates were approaching in large force. He halted and, placing his command in a favorable position for receiving an attack, sent the intelligence which he had received to General Milroy, who about the time that Colonel Keifer's messenger arrived, received the further information that another large force was approaching Winchester on the Front Royal road, which road enters Winchester on the southeast. Colonel Keifer was ordered to retain the eligible position he occupied on the Staunton turnpike and the 87th Pennsylvania, the 5th Maryland, the 18th Connecticut and Washington Battery were ordered to take position on the Front Royal road two miles southeast of Winchester. The 12th West Virginia Infantry and Carlin's (Wheeling) Battery were ordered to join Colonel Keifer.

About 10:00 A.M. cannonading commenced between the Washington Battery and the Confederates, and a spirited artillery duel was continued for two hours. In the meantime, the Confederate infantry coming within range of that portion of the Federal infantry stationed on the Front Royal road, a very brisk engagement took place, which lasted for some time. At noon the Confederates withdrew their forces on the Front Royal road. Colonel Keifer's forces on the Staunton Turnpike still had not been attacked. From noon until 2:00 P.M. the time was spent by the Federals in maneuvering and selecting the best positions.

After the engagement had commenced on the morning of the thirteenth, General Milroy dispatched an order to Colonel McReynolds, who was in command of the Federal forces at Berryville, directing him to evacuate that place and join him at Winchester. Colonel McReynolds received this order just as a large body of Confederates were seen approaching Berryville, and apprehensive of being cut off by a superior force if he traveled the direct road, he marched his command off immediately upon a circuitous route. After all his precaution his rear was attacked as he was crossing Opequan Creek, but owing to the bravery and promptness of the 87th Pennsylvania, 5th Maryland, and Captain Alexander's (Hartington) Battery, the Confederates were repulsed, and Colonel McReynolds proceeded to Winchester without being further molested, at which place he arrived with his command at 10:00 P.M.

But to return to the further operations around Winchester during the day (the thirteenth). At 2:00 P.M. the Confederates were discovered approaching in force on the Staunton Turnpike. Colonel Keifer, who was then in command of the 12th West Virginia, 110th Ohio, and Carlin's (Wheeling) Battery, and a small force of cavalry, disposed of his forces so as to give the enemy as warm a reception as possible. Skirmish firing soon commenced, and by 3:00 P.M. the engagement became general, and a continuous firing of musketry and artillery was kept up from 3:00 to 6:00 P.M. The Confederates engaged were what was known as the old "Stonewall Brigade" and were experienced soldiers, brave and thoroughly disciplined. The Federals under Colonel Keifer were mostly new troops and this was the first time they were ever under fire, but they stood their ground well, and for three hours the engagement lasted without any apparent advantage to either side. At 6:00 P.M. the Federals retreated in the direction of Winchester, about one half-mile across a small stream. They retired in good order and shortly they halted for reorganization. The Confederates advanced, and the battle was renewed and continued until dark. In this engagement both sides lost rather heavily. Capt. John Carlin, an old soldier of the Mexican War and commander of Carlin's Battery, did gallant service in this engagement. He was said to be one of the best volunteer officers in the artillery service.

At dark the firing ceased, and shortly after nightfall the Federal forces were withdrawn into Winchester. As it was anticipated that the Confederates would attack the large fort at dawn the next morning, the infantry were ordered into the rifle pits surrounding it two hours before daylight. Contrary to expectations no attack was made. Early in the morning the Federal forces were so disposed of as to encircle the city of Winchester, and very soon skirmishing began and was kept up continuously until 3:00 P.M.

On this day (June 14) the Confederates used no artillery until 3:00 P.M. This led many to believe that the Confederate artillery force was weak. This illusion was dispelled between 3:00 and 4:00 P.M., when they opened twenty guns on the large fort from an eminence northwest of it and four from another on the one south of it, and the cannonading from that time until dark was incessant. Very soon after the cannonading began all the infantry regiments were ordered into the rifle pits surrounding the forts to be in readiness to repel any attempts to take them by storm. The Confederates at length succeeded in driving a small Federal force from one of the smaller forts and in capturing the artillery belonging to it. They made several abortive attempts to capture the other small fort. Notwithstanding the immense cannonading but two or three casualties happened to the Federal soldiers in the large fort and the rifle pits surrounding it. At dark the firing ceased, and the infantry ordered to remain in the rifle pits.

At 10:00 P.M. that night General Milroy called a council of war. The result of the deliberations of this council was a determination to evacuate the position at 2:00 A.M. the next morning and if possible to reach the Baltimore and Ohio Railroad at Harper's Ferry. This step was deemed advisable from the fact that it had been ascertained that the force of the enemy around Winchester then amounted to more than twenty-five thousand, and added to this the ammunition and provision in the fort was almost exhausted. At the time designated the Federal forces took up their march, but owing to the darkness of the night they made slow progress and by dawn of day had advanced but four miles to a point at which the Harper's Ferry road diverged from that leading to Winchester. Here they were attacked by a division of Confederates, aided by a large artillery force which was awaiting them in ambush.

When the fire of the Confederates opened the Federal forces were soon thrown into position and maintained the action determinedly for some time, but evidently at great disadvantage, owing to the artillery of the enemy, the grape and canister of which dealt fearful havoc on the Federal forces. After maintaining their ground for some time they gave way, but the brave and intrepid Milroy succeeded in rallying the larger portion of them and made three desperate charges upon the Confederate artillery; but notwithstanding their determined bravery they were repulsed each time. Upon retiring the third time the brigade commander of Milroy's 2nd Brigade, Colonel [William G.] Ely, of the 18th Connecticut, displayed a white flag in token of surrender.

Besides the brigade surrendered by Colonel Ely, one other regiment was captured at another point. Captain William Martin's company of the 14th Massachusetts Heavy Artillery had been left in the fort for the purpose of spiking the guns. This company was also captured. The loss of the Federals in the four days' engagements (June 12–15) in killed and wounded was about five hundred. About four thousand, including the wounded, were surrendered as prisoners of war. This was considerably above half of Milroy's command. It was said that the Confederate loss in killed and wounded was more than one thousand; but for the correctness of this the writer does not vouch.

General Milroy was censured in certain quarters for his conduct during these engagements in and around Winchester, but a court of inquiry, after a labored investigation, acquitted him. The cause of the censure was that he remained at Winchester too long and thus suffered the greater part of his forces to be captured. He was ordered by General Schenck to hold Winchester as long as he possibly could. It is very probable that General Milroy rendered the government very valuable services by his obstinate resistance of the Confederates at Winchester. The Confederate forces that attacked Milroy at Winchester was the advance of Lee's army that was then on its way into Pennsylvania. Milroy's obstinate resistance delayed them several days in their advance and consequently gave General Meade longer time for preparing to receive the Confederates. General Milroy's bravery stands unquestioned among those who served in the army with him.

Marching in Clover: A Confederate Brigade's Tramp from the Rappahannock to Gettysburg

FRANK H. FOOTE,
48TH MISSISSIPPI INFANTRY, C.S.A.

Philadelphia *Weekly Times* 5, no. 33, October 8, 1881

During the first week in June, 1863, [Brig. Gen. Carnot] Posey's Mississippians, [Maj. Gen. Richard H.] Anderson's Division, began the march which culminated a month afterwards at Gettysburg. In the outset of this march we were braced by a consciousness of superior valor and contempt for our foe, which in the end proved our ruin. The idea of making the North feel some of the rigors and hardships of war was uppermost in our minds and we contemplated with satisfaction the green and pleasant Valley of Pennsylvania, teeming with abundance for man and beast, in the event of our occupancy. Thus, with light hearts and feet, we began the march, the first night's bivouac of which was on the battlefield of Chancellorsville. The recollections of that terrible battle were yet fresh in our minds, and as we spread our blankets under the sheltering trees for rest there came floating from around the notes of the disturbed whippoorwill, causing many of us to refrain from mirth and jesting out of place. Each of us could recall a friend or relative who had gone down in that fierce engagement only a few weeks before. The very place seemed hallowed to our memory, and we reverently invoked their departed spirits and recalled to mind their virtues and gallantry.

We felt the absence of water, and parties went in search of it, but found only a stagnant pond, which was of such a peculiar flavor that none of us could use it. Betimes next morning we were up and went in search of better water. At the far end of the marsh or pond, we solved the mystery of the peculiar smell and taste of the water, for there we found floating around the body of a Federal soldier in the last stages of decomposition. His body was dragged ashore and a fine gold ring taken from his finger, the flesh of which cleaved from the bones. His body was then buried, and we went into camp, sick and disgusted at the very idea of water, none of which we would touch until we reached the Rapids at Germanna Ford. Traces of the conflict of May 2–3 were still visible in many shapes. One poor fellow's skull—of friend or foe, we knew not nor cared not it seemed which—lay beside the turnpike and was for some distance kicked about as a football and finally, to cap it all, was pierced by a sword-point through the eye and carried further along as a banner, when for very shame some one hurled it out of sight in the bushes.

In the march up the Valley of the Shenandoah the abundance of blackberries offered substantial repasts that did us much good. One evening a vast field of them attracted our attention, and the whole division of Anderson were stopped perforce, because there were none left in the ranks to move up, and went in to "fill up." [Brig. Gen. Cadmus M.] Wilcox facetiously remarked to one of his colonels to "turn out your cattle to graze," and when he thought they had a surfeit ordered the colonel to "drive on his cattle." Passing through the town of Charlestown, Va., the ladies of the place in their fervor caused General Posey to dismount and "kissed him for the Mississippi Brigade" and would not let him off lightly. Sharpsburg was reached and a rest given us for several hours, which some of us occupied in reveries of the battle fought there nearly a year previous.

While sitting on the porch of a cottage with a comrade a door behind us was partly opened and a lady quietly asked us if we did not wish for something to eat. Assenting, we were told to go through the gate to the rear of the house, so as not to attract much attention, which we did. The lady soon appeared with bread, milk and butter and a delicious lunch it was. After disposing of it we thanked her for her kindness and started away. She called us back and said, in a quiet, dignified manner: "I have given freely to you men such as I have to give, but I assure you it is not done for any sympathy for your cause, for it is one I abhor and detest, but because I thought you were tired and hungry. I hope to see the Union preserved and pray it may be without any more battling, for I have dear ones in the Union army fighting for its preservation." The quiet dignity and patriotism of the lady made a deep impression on me, one that I shall not forget. One evening, while quietly trudging along near Berryville, an aged Negress, leaning on a fence, put the query to us:

"Is dere any more sojers to hind youn's?"

Replying in the affirmative, she broke out again, "Fore God, I nebber seed so many people afore. Tree days dey've bin passin, and now here's more. Jes think, all dese people in de wurl, and dey's all got mammies."

The "wurl" she then knew was little bigger than her owner's plantation. Near Hagerstown, Md., one evening, as [Brig. Gen. Ambrose R.] Wright was riding leisurely along in the rear of his brigade, a couple of shots from bushwhackers admonished him of the uncertainty of life, for one of the shots cut off some of his long, black, curly hair. Instantly a dozen men sprang from the ranks and started in pursuit of the assassins. A few shots and suppressed yells told the tale; but the men reported that they found no one. We knew what it meant, though. We afterwards found out that it was an old, gray-headed man and a youth who attempted the crime. As we trudged the stony pikes or tramped the mud of the neighborhood roads perhaps our thoughts were far away in sunny Mississippi, but the spirit of all was there. The merry jests that invoked the gibes and provoked taunting retorts bespoke feelings not preoccupied of danger, death, or wounds ahead. That set of veterans passing in review, as it were, presented a scene unequaled in the annals of war hitherto. Not a full uniform was to be seen except of the staff. A whole coat or unpatched pantaloons would have been a treat indeed to the veterans. A solid shoe unventilated for the comfort of the toe or an original skin of the blonde or brunette would have been met with taunts as the thought suggested the owner a "bomb proof" or "hospital rat," yet beneath those ragged, dirty garments beat many a chivalrous heart—gallant both in field and poetry, and ever ready for deeds that would rival the old-time champions for liberty's cause. While they presented a rough uncouth appearance, a glimpse of a rifle and bayonet as bright as the polished mirror attested the gallant fact that in it the owner dared all for the cause so near at heart, and believed in the homely but trite expression, "Trust in God, but keep your powder dry."

From Sharpsburg to Chambersburg one meets with many little villages along the turnpike. In one of these, Greencastle, I think, the village population were out to see [Gen. Robert E.] Lee's veterans pass, gazing sullenly and flaunting little flags of the Union at us; conspicuous in numbers were the young girls of the place, each one sporting bunting of the stars and stripes, some waving them and wearing them crossed on their breasts. Two of the young girls were particularly zealous in flaunting their colors at us, all of which afforded us merriment only. A rough, uncouth specimen of a veritable "Reb," happening along, straggling outside the line of march, foot sore and weary, got tired of their persistent efforts and vented his ire by saying: "Look hyar, gurls, youn's had better take off those durned flags fur we

Rebels are hell on breastworks." The good-natured laugh that greeted the discomfiture of the "girls" was joined in by some of the citizens while the girls beat a hasty retreat.

Citizens of the neighborhood of the line between Pennsylvania and Maryland point out the invisible boundary, and when reached and crossed an old-fashioned, prolonged yell attested the fact and vented our joy. The first night in Pennsylvania we had whisky served out as rations, which was about as foul as the average Northern estimate of Jeff Davis and his cause. Two drinks of it, I knew, caused a Negro man attached to our command to buck against a barn door full tilt, splitting a plank and knocking himself senseless. In one of the little hamlets we passed through one of our command conceived the idea that a bait of onions would be wholesome and fragrant, from recollections of the family garden at home, quietly went into a garden patch and began helping himself, to the annoyance of the old German lady, the owner. She ordered him out, which order he never noticed, whereupon she seized a broom or picket and put out after him. The "bummer," to avoid anything unpleasant, which might expose him to the jests of the boys, beat a retreat towards a gap in the fence. The place of exit was too small for the man and his knapsack, and there he stuck, while the old woman gave him several whacks, to our merriment and his disgust. Chambersburg was reached, and we bivouacked in the suburbs.

While passing through the city some of those irrepressible boys who can see and have fun out of anything concluded to exchange hats with the citizens as they met them on the streets. Espying a citizen with a good looking hat on, they would unconcernedly edge up to him, and before the hapless victim knew it his tile would be snatched from his head and a forlorn looking specimen of a ragged, dirty, rebel hat would be substituted in lieu of his. His appeals for restoration only met with ridicule and cries of "come down out of that hat!" "I see your legs sticking out!" etc.

The morning after the occupancy of Chambersburg a detachment of one officer and eight non-commissioned officers and privates were detailed to proceed some three or four miles out into the country and gather supplies for the regiment to which we were attached. Being assigned as one of the "bummers" has since always been regarded by me as a piece of good luck, for two of the most enjoyable days I ever spent happened there. Our captain, Coffee, had instructions to purchase supplies such as were needed, giving an order on a designated officer in Chambersburg for payment.

We left camp early, lightly equipped but fully armed. A double team accompanied us for the supplies. We took a direction I am unable to locate from Chambersburg, but it finally led us to a little village called Orrstown.

One scout was thrown well forward and every precaution taken to escape capture if any enemy were near, which we doubted. In the best of spirits, we set out like schoolboys turned loose and made a delightful day of it. The first farmhouse we stopped at, some four miles out, we secured some substantial supplies. The farmer gave us a hive of bees, but requested us not to rub it near his house. Two of the men undertook to carry it away, when a sharp sting from one of its inmates caused him to drop his hold, and in a second that swarm of bees had us cleaned out of sight, stinging our horses and causing them to break away and nearly ruining both horses and wagon. Some of the men, to escape the "varmints," ran into the house and while there espied in a room, prone on the floor, the figure of a man, evidently hiding.

Communicating his discovery to the captain he ordered two men into the house to bring the man out, which was done. He was in a fright and a bad one at that. Quietly assuring the farmer that we intended no harm to the young man, we marched him off with us determined to extract some fun out of his fears. About a half mile beyond the farm we halted, formed a circle around the unhappy young man, and gave him to understand that we were conscripting the young able-bodied men of Pennsylvania for Lee's army and that when we came across the Federal army we would exchange all such as him for our men held as prisoners by the Union forces. After a torture of suspense to him in which we really pitied the man, at our solicitation to the captain he was sworn into the "services of the Confederate States and loyalty to Jeff Davis" in a solemn oath on the face of a pocket dictionary. We turned him loose after a hearty cheer for Jeff Davis, and told him to pack his duds, and we would call for him that night on our return to camp. He left, and we quietly watched him for a few minutes as he took the direction of home. Suddenly he darted in a run into a piece of woods and was lost to sight.

Several other farmhouses were visited and necessaries purchased. At one an aged lady, assisted by two comely maidens, were busily engaged in seeding cherries. They kindly invited us to eat what cherries we wanted and questioned us as to what state we were from. On replying Mississippi, she showed some interest and asked "if any were from Vicksburg." Replying in the affirmative, she again asked if we knew anyone by the name of Grammer living there, whose relative she was. We told her yes and furthermore that a man by that name was in camp from Vicksburg. When we returned Grammer got permission and went out to see the old lady, who proved to be his grandmother and the maidens his cousins. An overflowing knapsack and haversack attested as to his reception. The first night out was an enjoyable one, as we were free from the restraints of camp duties. Some of us were up early and repaired to a spring near by for a bath. A dairy attracted our attention, and finding it was open we thought it no harm to try a little cream and milk, which we skillfully confiscated, taking a little only from each crock, so as to have it appear that it was undisturbed, and then quietly returned to camp. Further along in the day we paid dearly for the "appropriation" by a lot of stinking canteens, as all old soldiers will attest.

Approaching the village of Orrstown we noticed several of the people leaving rather hurriedly. Imagining that they were frightened, we concluded for fun to overtake one, so off started several after a party that were making their way up the mountain slope. They managed by separating to head off a young man and unknown to him concealed themselves behind a clump of bushes, and as he came panting by they suddenly sprang out with leveled rifles, and in a trice that unhappy young fellow was on his knees begging most piteously for mercy. Speaking our contempt for such arrant cowardice, we swore him also in the C.S.A. service in the usual formula and with the dictionary. Entering the village we found one store open and bought for Confederate money many little articles we were sadly in need of and a quantity of flour, sugar, molasses, and soap for the command. For ourselves hair oil, combs, brushes, needles, and pins stood no show. Fine combs ("search warrant" in soldier's parlance), in exchange for our notes, were soon exhausted. I asked the shopkeeper why he sold so readily for Confederate money. He replied he could get it exchanged for good money in Baltimore.

That night we stopped at a farmhouse to go into camp. Receiving permission from the farmer to occupy his barn on the condition that we would build no fires near it we did so, and soon in fragrant new mown hay we forgot our sorrows and country's cause in sleep, oblivious of the Federal army, of whom at that date we had not heard a word. An early rise and preparations were made for breakfast. Hot, steaming coffee was furnished by our host. Strolling into the orchard in quest of cherries, the different species of which were explained by our farmer host, who feared we would break the branches of his trees.

Suddenly we heard the sound of cannon. Again it was borne to our ears. Asking the direction we were told that it was Gettysburg. Receiving directions as to distance, eight miles, I believe, we set out about nine o'clock for the turnpike between Chambersburg and Gettysburg, knowing well that if a fight was up in all likelihood we would sooner overtake the command by trying to intercept it ahead than by following its wake. We rejoined our command on the march, and as we neared Gettysburg the sounds of battle went on increasing. The steady roll of musketry was heard, and the rapid firing of artillery told that "something was up." All thoughts that it was only a cavalry engagement were dispelled by that sullen roar. We had an intimate acquaintance with such sounds, and we knew that our old foe, the Army of the Potomac, was in the neighborhood.

Ambulances of wounded were passed and after a while prisoners under guard appeared. A set of Pennsylvania state colors was seen and assurances were given that it was only militia from Harrisburg who were in our front. A wounded soldier, whose serried cheek showed how he was shot, told us that old soldiers were there against us, and we believed him. The firing began to slacken just as Anderson's Division arrived upon the battlefield. Orders arrived to file to the right, take position, and stack arms. Fatal order that was, for there were five fine brigades in that division, over eight thousand strong and a forward march would have place them in thirty minutes on the very ridge for which the next two days both sides struggled so hard to possess. A few stray shells and bullets only greeted us, and we bivouacked that night in peace, while the enemy were working like beavers bringing up troops, so that when the morning of July 2 broke the startling sight of the heights opposite bristling with guns and bayonets was presented. During the morning we were moved to a position across the turnpike, nearer Gettysburg itself. Our trains were parked in the town.

The following incident reveals the vicissitudes of life and its changes to a remarkable degree. In the good old days of antebellum a favorite teacher of ours in Port Gibson, Mississippi, was one D. J. Benner. We knew he was from Gettysburg, for he often spoke of his home in the mountains of Pennsylvania. One of his former pupils made inquiries concerning him, and his father stated that his son, with the rank of major, was in the Federal army, then investing Vicksburg, Mississippi. Thus by war came changes. Pupils and teacher were separated by sectional animosities. The teacher was in the Federal army occupying his pupils' home; his pupils in a hostile army occupying his home; his family in our lines, our families in his lines; each of us flushed with victory and seeking to conquer on each other's land.

After much shifting of position we were finally stationed in support of a battery occupying a slight elevation, beyond which in a wheat field stood a red barn; in our rear was a two-story house with a marsh or pond of water in front of it. The day waned and no general attack was made. Sharpshooters made things lively. Being old soldiers we knew the value of any sort of protection we could improvise, so at it we went and soon had a little trench excavated to shield us from their aim. The forepart of July 2, as far as we were concerned, passed without anything of moment. After a while by the excited career of orderlies we began to "sniff a fight." [Lt. Gen.

Ambrose P.] Hill and Anderson halted near us for a while and took a look over the field. Soon after they left we received orders to shelter ourselves as best we could. The signal gun boomed out that sounded the death knoll of many a one, and the carnival of death in the pleasant vales of Gettysburg was again begun. The signal was answered by a tremendous uproar of the batteries in our front and in the height our regiment, the 48th Mississippi, was advanced to the picket line, with instructions to lie off the flank of the attacking column of General Wilcox, but not to join in the attack with them. The brigades of Wright, Wilcox, and Posey, under the command of General Wilcox, advanced in splendid order, Wright being next to Posey. By the time the line reached where the 48th Regiment was lying down we had by sharpshooting silenced the Federal battery in the immediate front. As Wright's Georgians came up they began yelling at us to "Get up and fight," to "Come forward, Mississippians."

The effect was felt and the entire regiment left its place in the flank and went into action against the earnest efforts of Col. [Joseph M.] Jayne to stop them. Our adjutant was killed in making the same effort, but everything rushed forward to the charge. Wild with enthusiasm and ardor, on we pressed, while every instant the enemy thundered their shot and shell in our midst. Shells amongst us, shells over us, and shells around us tore our bleeding ranks with ghastly gaps. A comrade shrieks and falls. A hasty glance shows that his right leg was torn off by a shell. Many of us saw the shell just before it struck. Another comrade falls, and the third drops by his side. A shell comes bouncing along, skips one of the two friends lying side by side in agony and strikes the other and tears him in two. The ground roared and rumbled like a great storm, and the shower of minie balls was pitiless and merciless. We pressed on, knowing that the front was safer now than to turn our backs and with a mighty yell, we threw ourselves upon the batteries and passed them, still reeking hot.

An attempt was made to reform the line, but before it could be done a heavy column of infantry in blue came up at double quick; we were too detached to cope successfully with them, and in a moment we were hurled, bleeding and crippled, from our hard-won trophies. Wright's men, with whom we still were, began to fall back, and then came the dreadful part of the whole matter—a falling back across the wide, open fields, with an exultant enemy thundering at our heels with every contrivance of death.

The attack had failed for want of support and no matter how good, tried and true the soldiers of Wilcox were, they could not bear that storm of iron ball unsupported and then, like the Old Guard of Napoleon at Waterloo, they broke and fled with the cry, "Save yourselves who can." We rallied behind the other regiments of the brigade, who looked on our struggle without participating. They had no orders to attack and saw with grieving hearts the cruel havoc made in our ranks. After the firing ceased, which was late in the night, we crawled out to gather up our wounded. Flitting forms a few feet off showed us our foe engaged in the same task. A whisper above the breath would call forth a shot from our foe on picket, a shot called for a volley, and a volley meant death. So in quietness, disturbed only by the groans of the stricken wretches, we finished our work.

Morning broke brightly on July 3. A few shots only as pickets were fired by us, and the day waned and passed and night settled down in woe and disaster to our right. The harvest of death, so far as Gettysburg was concerned, for us had been gleaned. A fearful reckoning we paid for our attempt, so reckless, so gallant, but unwarranted and in disobedience to orders to assault at all.

July 3, in the heavy attack of [Maj. Gen. George E.] Pickett, we did not participate. That night we spend on picket, and could distinctly hear the tramp of the Federals and rumble of the wagons and artillery as they shifted positions. Daylight revealed to us, to our great surprise, our comrades gone, whither for some time we knew not. We followed as best we could in midst of rain and mud, and finally caught up with the command. We had in charge some thousand odd Federal prisoners taken in the campaign, and we soon got on good terms with them. We recall one evening, as we neared the Maryland line, that while our bands were regaling us with some stirring airs and among others they played a piece known as "Dixie Doodle," part of it being the notes of "Way Down in Dixie" and the other "Yankee Doodle." When the "Dixie" part came on a general yell would attest our humor and spirits; and when the "Doodle" part was reached, a corresponding sentiment arose from our captives.

At Hagerstown, Md., we halted for rest and rations; also to wait the subsidence of the Potomac River, so as to cross it, our pontoon bridges having been destroyed just before our arrival. We lay here for several days and then passed into Virginia at Falling Waters by pontoon. Thus ended a most stirring campaign, in which a most overweening confidence of our great leader in his army had come to naught, and the strains of "Carry Me Back to Ole Varginny" had more inspiration for us than those of "Maryland, My Maryland," to the tune of which we forded the Potomac on the onward march of invasion.

Pickett's Charge at Gettysburg

WILLIAM W. WOOD,
COLONEL, 14TH VIRGINIA INFANTRY, C.S.A.

Philadelphia *Weekly Times* 1, no. 24, August 11, 1877

In 1863, when General [Robert E.] Lee's army crossed the Potomac on what is generally spoken of by the survivors of that army as "The Gettysburg Campaign," two of the five brigades which made up the full complement of [Maj. Gen. George E.] Pickett's Division were left behind in Virginia for reasons satisfactory to the general in command. The brigades left behind were [Brig. Gen. Micah] Jenkins' and [Brig. Gen. Montgomery D.] Corse's, numbering about four thousand muskets. The brigades participating in the campaign and which made the charge on the third day of July in Gettysburg were [Brig. Gen. Lewis A.] Armistead's, [Brig. Gen. Richard B.] Garnett's, and [Brig. Gen. James L.] Kemper's, all comprised entirely of Virginians and numbering, rank and file, about 4,500 men. These three brigades, each led by its regular brigadier, were under the immediate command of Major General George E. Pickett, a graduate of West Point and a captain in the infantry branch of the United States Army at the break of the war. The division, shorn of nearly half its strength as stated above, constituted the rear guard of the army on the whole march from Virginia to Pennsylvania. Armistead's Brigade, to which I belonged, was the provost guard, and General Armistead, a captain of infantry in the old army, appointed from civil life, was provost marshal general.

The division was halted at and south of Chambersburg on June 27, and for several days thereafter was engaged in the uncongenial work of tearing up the railroad, destroying bridges, collecting provisions, etc. I have purposely used the term "uncongenial" because, never having "brought up the rear" before, the men of the division were unaccustomed to the performance of such duties. They considered their selection for such services rather a reflection than otherwise upon their past brilliant record, and their murmurs against "Old Mars" (as they fondly designated General Lee) for keeping them behind were loudest and deepest when, day after day, couriers and wounded men arrived from the front and told wondrous tales of how the remainder of the army, under [Maj. Gen. Jubal A.] Early, and [Lt. Gen. Richard S.] Ewell, and their own beloved corps commander, "Old Peter" [Lt. Gen. James P.] Longstreet, was sweeping everything before it. They did not know what great honor for them, and what wholesale slaughter of them, were in the immediate future.

On the night of July 1 orders were received to cook three days' rations and to march for Gettysburg at 4:00 A.M. next day. All knew that this meant business, and preparations for the march and the fight were made with alacrity. At the designated hour the march began, Armistead's Brigade bringing up the rear, and passing through Chambersburg between daybreak and sunrise. The line of march was thence toward Cashtown by a pass through the South Mountains, in which were situated the iron works of the Hon. Thaddeus Stevens. The fire which had destroyed them was still smoldering when we passed, and from the mountainsides adjacent "bushwhackers" fired a few revengeful shots at the division, without, however, inflicting any damage. At about 3:00 P.M., having made a march which was estimated to be fully thirty miles, the command arrived in sight of Gettysburg and the battlefield of that day—July 2. Arms were stacked, and the men rested while a staff officer went to headquarters to report the arrival of the division. In a little while information was brought back that the division would not be wanted that day, but would be held in reserve for special and distinguished service on the morrow. A little later we were bivouacked near a stone bridge on the Cashtown road, where we remained all night, putting arms in order and conjecturing vainly one to another what special service we would be call upon to perform next day.

Before daylight on the morning of July 3 the division moved from its bivouac across fields, to the right and southeast of the Cashtown road, and thence up a valley, the head of which is just opposite Cemetery Ridge, to a point called Bream's Mills. At this point the division was halted, arms inspected, extra ammunition making each man's complement sixty rounds issued, and knapsacks and blankets were piled. The field hospital was also established here, and canteens were filled for the last time. Line of battle was formed also, but in a little while the division marched by the right flank

Maj. Gen. George Pickett
(CENTURY MAGAZINE)

perhaps a mile further to the southeast, where it took its final position before the charge.

The march from Bream's Mills to this position must have been entirely concealed from the enemy's view by a low range of hills parallel to and not over half a mile distant from Cemetery Ridge. For, during the whole time it took to execute it, not a shot was fired at the division, nor was there heard in that part of the field a sound indicative of the approaching battle. The little valley up which the movement was made, and at the head of which rested the right of the division, was but a very slight depression in the earth's surface even at its greatest depth. Coming into line Kemper's and Garnett's Brigades were placed half way up the gentle ascent of the hill, while the Confederate artillery, numbering more than one hundred guns, was already in position immediately in their front and just near enough to the crest of the hill for their shot to clear it. The configuration of the ground was such that Armistead's Brigade could not be placed on a line with the other two without fatal exposure and then it was posted some one hundred yards to the right and rear of them, with orders to catch up when the advance should begin. Even as thus placed the very slight elevation in its front afforded the right of the brigade scarcely any shelter from the furious storm of shot and shell that soon afterward swept the field.

After the line of battle had been formed, the commanding officers of regiments were sent for to brigade headquarters to receive instructions, which had already been given to the brigadiers by General Lee in person. After they returned to their regiments all company officers were assembled at regimental headquarters, and then explicitly and carefully told what work the division had to do, and how it was expected to do it. These instructions were in turn communicated by the company officers to the men, and this before a shot was fired. The humblest private knew the plan of battle and the surroundings as well as the commanding general himself. No disguises were used, nor was there any underrating of the difficult work in hand. All were informed that Cemetery Ridge, naturally a very strong position and heavily defended by the enemy's infantry and artillery, were situated directly in our front and only some half mile from the crest of the hill behind which we then were; that it had been stormed and taken the day before by Confederate troops but could not be held, and that General Lee regarded it as the key to the enemy's positions, which, if taken, ended the war. We were to remain where we were until scouts could burn up the houses and stacks of straw in our front which might impede or disorganize the advance, and after that was done a signal of two guns would be fired, and then all our artillery would open on Cemetery Ridge, and continue firing on it until the batteries there were silenced. When they were silenced our guns would cease firing, and thereupon every man, without further orders, was to go forward. We were told also that long lines of infantry, which we could see were in line to the right and left of us, and somewhat to the rear, would advance in echelon to our support, at the same pace and time with us, and thus all possibility of an attack on our flanks would be prevented. This information was especially gratifying to the Fourteenth Virginia Regiment, to which I belonged, and which that day was the extreme right regiment of the line.

If I remember correctly, Pickett's Division and the artillery were all in position by 11:00 A.M. The battle, however, did not begin for some hours later. The day was clear and bright. There was not a cloud in the sky, and the sun, from whose rays there was no shelter, shone intensely hot. There was no water near us, and not knowing how soon the battle might begin, no details could be sent for any. The canteens, which had been filled at the last water we passed, were soon emptied, and there was great suffering from thirst. But there was no help for it. It had to be endured. While waiting for the expected signal, we saw Generals Lee, Longstreet, and Pickett riding up and down the line, and occasionally approaching the crest of the hill to take

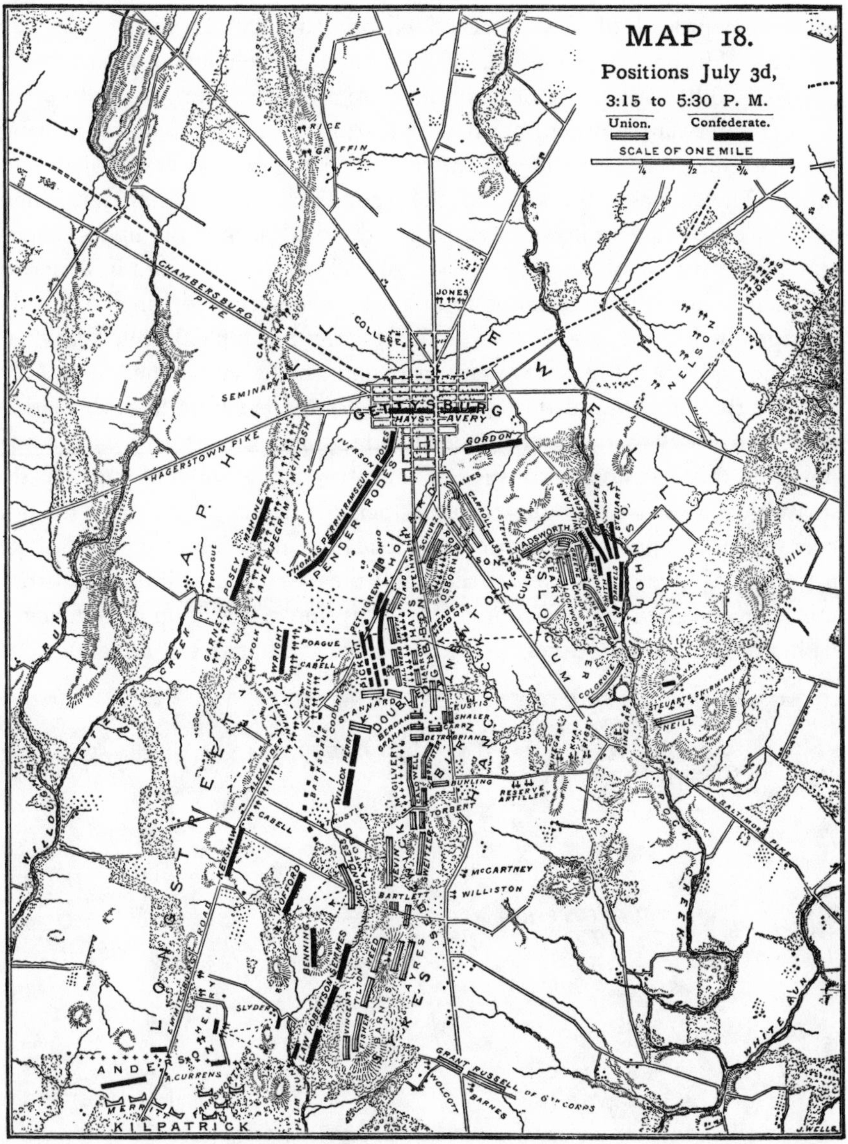

Positions July 3, 3:15 to 5:30 P.M.

(CENTURY MAGAZINE)

a look at the enemy's position. It was then whispered among us that Longstreet disapproved of the proposed charge and had earnestly protested against it. His protest was heard, but overruled by the council of war.

At 1:00 P.M. a single shot was fired from a Confederate gun, and in two minutes afterward another. It was the pre-concerted signal, and on hearing the first gun every man threw himself flat on the ground in obedience to orders. The echoes of the sound of the second gun had not died away when all the Confederate artillery at that part of the field opened fire upon Cemetery Ridge with a salvo the like of which had never been heard in America till then. The Federal batteries must have been surprised, or else greatly damaged by it, for it was several minutes before they replied to it. Yet when they did reply their fire was very effective and deadly, and seemed to be fully equal to that of the Confederates. I am not going to attempt to describe that duel, so to speak, between the Federal and Confederate artillery, each composed on this occasion, so it was said, of more than a hundred guns. To do so would be to fail. I confess that my pen is unequal to it, and I do not believe that any pen could convey an adequate conception of it. The smoke from the Confederate batteries, although they were but a little ways from me, soon obscured them from my sight. This smoke was lit up by red, angry flashes of flame as the successive discharges left the muzzles of the guns. The

Confederates waiting for the end of the artillery duel (CENTURY MAGAZINE)

firing was so rapid and continuous that the report of a single gun could not be distinguished. Over the space intervening between the infantry and artillery frequently passed some mounted officer and his staff—notably once General Lee, and several times Generals Longstreet and Pickett. The Federal batteries were returning the Confederate fire with great vigor, and when General Lee passed over the ground it was being swept with a deadly hail of every missile known to the nomenclature of artillerists. His appearance at a place of such imminent danger both thrilled and horrified the line, and the men shouted to him to go away to shelter. Always regardless of himself when duty called, but mindful of the lives of others, he had but one attendant with him. When the men yelled to him to go away, he took off his hat in acknowledgment of their affectionate solicitude, and then rode on without quickening the pace of his noble gray.

Maj. James E. Dearing, chief of artillery of Pickett's Division, had boasted that the flag of his battalion should not on that day touch the ground. Accompanied by his flag-bearer, he galloped incessantly from one end of the line of guns to the other, cheering the cannoneers by his presence, and giving them directions where to direct their fire. While galloping along the line, at full speed, a little in advance of the color-bearer, a round shot struck and killed the horse of the latter, and threw him to the ground. Major Dearing turned and saw his flag falling, but so quick was he that before it had actually reached the ground, he seized it from the standard-bearer, and throughout the remainder of the battle carried it himself. This gallant act, performed in full view of the line of battle, was greeted with such a Confederate yell as not even the infernal roar of the guns could drown.

General Pickett, while tarrying unnecessarily long, as some of his staff thought, at a point where the death missiles came thickest, was urged by a captain of his staff to move to some other portion of the field where the danger was not so great and operations could be equally as well directed. The captain said to him: "General, I don't believe that even a fly could live here two minutes." Strange to say, that although throughout the artillery combat and the subsequent charge General Pickett most recklessly exposed himself, yet neither he nor any member of his staff was struck. The general afterward said to me that on the day after the battle he felt that he would have no right to resent the insult if someone should accuse him of cowardice, because he was not among the killed, wounded, or captured. "For" said he, "when men hear that almost my entire division perished, and that I escaped harm, they will be loath to believe that I did my duty." The charge was never brought against him.

The combat between the artillery of the two armies must have been two hours in duration. Throughout all of it the officers and men of that portion of the line where I was were stretched flat upon the ground, with their heads toward the firing. The water in our canteens had long been exhausted, and no more could be had until the battle was over. Not a breath of air was in motion, and the sun shone down on us intensely hot. The bursting of innumerable shells added to the heat. My company, numbering about fifty men present, lost four killed and some fifteen wounded while in this position. The enemy's shot hurtled among us and clipped off the clover heads by our sides. The fire was so terrific that when a man sang out "Wounded!" the ambulance corps would not go to his relief. To have taken anyone to the rear while that firing was in progress would have been almost certain death.

At last the Federal batteries began to slacken their fire, and not long afterward they ceased entirely. Soon the Confederate guns ceased firing, too, and then all knew that the supreme moment had come. Each surviving commandant of a company sprang to his feet and ordered his men into line. All who could got into line, but there were many dead and wounded and sun-stricken poor fellows left upon the ground. The order to go forward was given and obeyed with alacrity and cheerfulness, for we believed then that the battle was practically over, and that we had nothing to do but to march unopposed to Cemetery Ridge and occupy them. The ascent to the crest of the hill, which had hitherto concealed us from the enemy's view, was made speedily and in good order. While making the ascent it was seen that the supports to our right and left flanks were not coming forward, as we had been told they would. Mounted officers were seen dashing frantically up and down their line, apparently endeavoring to get them to move forward, but we could see that they would not move. Their failure to support us was discouraging, but it did not dishearten us. Some of our men cursed them for being cowards, but sill our charge was kept up, and no man fell out. Soon we were past the crest of the hill and out of sight of them. Before us stood Cemetery Ridge, of which we could get occasional glimpses through rifts in the cloud of powder smoke which enveloped them. We could not see whether or not there were troops there to defend them against us.

Somewhat further on, perhaps a hundred and fifty yards beyond the crest of the hill we had just passed, a post-and-rail fence some five feet high was encountered. This fence was quickly mounted, and at a little distance beyond it my regiment, and I suppose the whole line of battle, was halted for the purpose of rectifying the alignment. From the time the charge began up to this moment not a shot had been fired at us, nor had we been

Pickett's Charge as viewed from the Union lines (CENTURY MAGAZINE)

able to see, because of the density of the smoke which hung over the battlefield like a pall, that there was any enemy in front of us. But directly afterward, just as the line started forward again, a shot, fired from somewhere to our left, struck the center company of my regiment, and, enfilading its right wing as it did, killed and wounded a large number of men and officers. The smoke now lifted from our front, and there right before us, scarcely two hundred yards away, stood Cemetery Ridge in awful grandeur. At their base was a double line of Federal infantry and several pieces of artillery posted behind stone walls, and to the right and left of them both artillery and infantry supports were hurriedly coming up. We fully realized then that Pickett's three little brigades, already greatly reduced by heavy casualties, was making, alone and without possibility of support, a desperate charge against the whole power of the Federal army.

The situation now was indeed appalling, though it did not seem to appall. The idea of retreat did not seem to occur to any one. Having obtained a view of the enemy's position, the men now advanced at the double-quick, and for the first time since the charge began they gave utterance to the famous Confederate battle yell. The batteries to the right and left of Cemetery Ridge now began to rain grape-shot and canister upon us, and the enemy's infantry at the base of the ridge poured volley after volley into our ranks. The carnage was indeed terrible, but still the division, staggering and bleeding, pressed on toward the Ridge they had been ordered to take.

Of course such terrible slaughter could not last long. The brave little division did not number men enough to make material for prolonged slaughter. In a few brief moments more the left of Armistead's Brigade, led by himself on foot, had passed beyond the stone wall and were among the guns of the enemy posted in rear of it. General Garnett had before then been instantly killed, and General Kemper had been severely wounded. The survivors of their brigades had become amalgamated with Armistead's. The line of battle was now not one-third of its length when the crest of the hill was passed. Our line of battle was not parallel to the ridge, and the left of the diminished line reached the ridge first. The right of the line never reached them. The men of the right, however, were near enough to see General Armistead shot down near a captured gun as he was waving his sword above his head, and they could see the men surrendering themselves as prisoners. Just then a detachment of Federal infantry came out, flanking our right, and shouted to us to surrender. There was nothing else to do except to take the chance, which was an extremely good one, of being killed on the retreat back over the hill. There was a general laying down of arms; but a few, myself among the number, rightly concluding that the enemy were weary of carnage, determined to run the risk of getting back to the Confederate lines. Our retreat was made singly, and I, at least, was not fired upon.

The survivors of the division gathered that night at the field hospital at Bream's Mill. There all through the night the ambulance corps kept bringing such wounded men as a relaxation of vigilance on the part of the enemy's pickets enabled them to take from the field. The few who were not hurt assisted about the hospital and prepared meals for the wounded. The morning of the Fourth of July dawned upon us still there. There was no roll-call that morning. There were not enough non-commissioned officers left to make the usual morning report of companies. Of the three brigadier generals who led their brigades into battle, Garnett and Armistead were killed and Kemper was desperately wounded. Of the twelve colonels who led their regiments, seven were killed and five wounded. Of the six lieutenant colonels, three were killed and three wounded and captured. Only one field officer of the fifteen regiments composing the three brigades escaped unhurt. Of my own regiment, the colonel and major were killed and the lieutenant colonel wounded. I was third captain of my regiment on the third. On the Fourth of July I was entitled by seniority to the office of lieutenant colonel, a promotion which I received soon afterward. When the retreat commenced on the night of the fourth, the nearly three hundred men of the division who had been confined in the various brigade guard-houses were released from confinement, and they and their guard permitted to return to duty in the ranks. The ambulance corps were disbanded also, and returned to the ranks, and many detailed men were treated the same way. On the morning of July 5 the report of the division showed not quite eleven hundred men present. Eleven hundred from forty-five hundred leaves thirty-four hundred, and that was the number of casualties suffered by Pickett's little division of Virginians in its famous charge at Gettysburg.

Pickett at Gettysburg

HENRY T. OWEN,
CAPTAIN, 18TH VIRGINIA INFANTRY, C.S.A.

Philadelphia *Weekly Times* 11, no. 9, March 26, 1881

In February 1863, while the ground was yet covered with snow, the river locked in ice and chill, [and] wintry blasts swept over the hills and howled through the forests of Northern Virginia, [Maj. Gen. George E.] Pickett's Division was ordered from Fredericksburg on a foraging expedition. It marched down through Richmond and Petersburg into the South Side counties, while a part of the command was sent as far south as Tarboro, the snow still falling for several weeks. The command reconnoitered around Greenville, Plymouth, and Washington, North Carolina, and skirmished occasionally with the enemy until the month of May, when it returned to Suffolk in time to start upon the memorable Pennsylvania campaign.

Selected by General Lee as rear guard of his invading army, Pickett's Division was detached from [Lt. Gen. James P.] Longstreet's Corps to perform the arduous duty of keeping open the communication with Virginia and to guard all the roads, mountain passes, and fords in the rear. The division was ever on the alert while others slept (or on the march while others rested), to meet some real or rumored advance of the enemy, and the men often retraced their steps for many miles and then by countermarching passed over much of the same ground three times or more. Thus climbing over the Blue Ridge through Snicker's Gap and wading the Shenandoah River breast deep at Castleman's Ferry, the division moved on down the Valley, but was recalled and detained several days to be in supporting distance of [Maj. Gen. James Ewell Brown] Stuart's cavalry that was skirmishing along the eastern side of the mountains. A part of Pickett's command crossed and recrossed the Shenandoah River no less than six times before the enemy disappeared and then had to hurry forward by long forced marches to overtake Lee's army, now far in advance toward Pennsylvania. On the night of June 30, 1863, Pickett's Division bivouacked in the woods about two miles south of Chambersburg. The men were footsore and weary and went into camp from an almost continuous march of more than a thousand miles.

The bright uniforms and braided caps of earlier days were now gone and had given place to the slouched hat, the faded, threadbare jacket, and patched pantaloons. The veterans' faces were tanned by summer's heat and winter's storms and covered with unkempt beard. Boys who enlisted in their teens appeared with long tangled locks, changed and weather-beaten, now, apparently into men of middle life. Their tents had been destroyed early in the war and their baggage had been reduced from time to time, until the men often marched for weeks together without a change of raiment. They waded rivers, climbed mountains, shivered beneath a single ragged blanket as they slept or watched upon the frost-clad hills or tramped barefoot stony turnpikes and tangled swamps.

The missiles of war had plowed their ranks, and fallen comrades, left thickly strewn on many fields, pointed as landmarks the track of the division and the course of battle. Heavy losses in many battles and still greater losses by disease, besides various recent details, in addition to the two largest brigades being left behind in Virginia, had reduced the division now to about one-third of its former strength. But though its numbers were lessened its prestige was still unbroken; each bloody conflict that thinned its ranks had spread a wider fame and forced confidence in the terror of their name. Upon the long rapid march the weak, the feeble, and the sick had fallen by the way and been left behind and those now answering to roll-call were the strong on the march and the stout in battle, who paused at no obstacle, quailed at no danger, and to whom scenes of carnage had grown familiar.

Strict military discipline, regular drill, and the proper handling of these troops in the first two or three engagements, when victories were gained, soon converted the raw recruits into efficient soldiers, and as the flush of successive victories followed, these soldiers had become in time almost invincible. A reputation once acquired by a corps or division is easily retained and hard to break, as each single soldier, if not himself a hero, thinks every other upon his right and left is one, and he is soon converted by association into a reliable veteran.

Maj. Gen. George E. Pickett was a graduate of West Point, had passed through the war with Mexico, and was bronzed by long service in the old army upon the distant frontier from the Rio Grande to the mouth of the Columbia, and among the officers of lesser grade were many graduates of military schools, while all, from the highest to the lowest in rank, had seen very arduous service and possessed a vast and varied experience in all the perils and hardships of war long before they reached the memorable "Heights of Gettysburg." Scattered through the different regiments was a sprinkling of restless, roving adventurers, seekers after excitement, whose passion, pastime and pleasure had been war and revolution for the last quarter of a century—some who had fought under Sam Houston at San Jacinto, others with the celebrated British Legion through the Don Carlos War, others with [William] Walker in Nicaragua, and others with [Maj. Chatham Roberdeau] Wheat and [Giuseppe] Garibaldi in Italy. There were men who fought under Zack Taylor from Palo Alto to Monterey and with [Gen. Winfield] Scott from Vera Cruz to the City of Mexico, while their later experience may be summed up as with Longstreet at Bull Run and with [Gen. Pierre G. T.] Beauregard at Manassas; some with [Brig. Gen. Simon B.] Buckner at Fort Donelson, and some with [Gen. Joseph E.] Johnston at Williamsburg and Seven Pines and with [Gen. Robert E.] Lee around Richmond, at Second Manassas, at Chantilly, South Mountain, Sharpsburg, Fredericksburg, and Chancellorsville. Each regiment had now inscribed on its torn and tattered banners all the noted fields over which it had been borne to victory.

Wednesday morning, July 1 was hot and sultry; scarcely a zephyr breathed to stir the loosened beef, and the birds, awed by the unusual sights and strange sounds amid their quiet bowers, had sought the denser shade and ceased to sing. Through camp, scattered over wooded hill and dale, the jest, the laugh, and snatches of Southern song kept up a busy hum, while the ragged Rebel mended his tattered garment or wrote a message to distant friends and loved ones at home, the last, perchance, he ever sent—to be received and read after the hand that penned the lines was cold. The morning wore slowly on to noon, when stragglers returning into camp reported that out upon the hills beyond the noise of camp there could be heard heavy distant cannon firing. The ball had opened, the play had begun, and a bird's-eye view would then have disclosed every road in Southern and Central Pennsylvania filled with clouds of dust and long dark columns of infantry, cavalry, and artillery rushing along to unite in the bloody conflict going on in and around the village of Gettysburg.

About four o'clock General Pickett received a message from [Brig. Gen. John D.] Imboden that a column of the enemy was moving in the direction of Chambersburg, and Pickett moved his division out upon the road above Greencastle and drew up in line of battle to await the threatened attack upon the rear of Lee's army. During the evening a storm of wind and rain and loud peals of thunder passed over the battalions, and the men were drenched in the shower, but the tempest was over in an hour and the sun went down bright and clear. The night came and rolled along over the long hours until dawn to find the division still drawn up in line of battle, watching under arms for the approach of the enemy.

The rumor turned out to have been a false alarm, but about one o'clock at night a courier came clattering along in search of Pickett, and at daylight on Thursday morning, July 2, the columns of wet, worn, and sleepless men were put in motion on the road to Gettysburg. The sun rose bright and clear, raindrops sprinkled on every twig and blade of grass, a cool refreshing breeze, laden with sweet perfumes of summer flowers, lifted the tangled lock upon the heated brow and fanned the care-worn cheek, until along the long lines of rough and rugged veterans, tramping rapidly forward could be heard here and there some humorous jest or joyous laugh, but before noon the day was hot and sultry.

At three o'clock the division reached the crest of the hill that overlooks Gettysburg and in sight of the distant battlefield beyond, having come since daylight twenty-seven miles. Here the division was halted, and a rumor circulated along the lines that General Longstreet, apprised of Pickett's approach, sent him this message, "Bring your division around on the right at once. [Maj. Gen. John B.] Hood is about to attack and I want you to support him." To which General Pickett replied, "My men are exhausted and must have rest before going any farther." General Lee replied to Maj. Walter Harrison, who reported to him the approach of Pickett's Division, "Tell General Pickett I shall not want him this evening; tell him to let his men rest and I will send him word when I want them." And soon afterward meeting General Pickett, General Lee said, "I am glad you have come; I shall have work for you tomorrow."

General Hood relates a conversation that occurred early in the morning, in which he said to General Longstreet, "General Lee seems a little nervous this morning." To which Longstreet replied, "He wishes me to attack. I do not wish to do so without Pickett. I never like to go into battle with one boot off." When the division came in sight of the battlefield at three o'clock it was halted by Pickett and he, accompanied by his aide, Capt. [Edward R]. Baird, rode forward and reported in person the arrival of his division to Longstreet, who upon learning the jaded condition of the men, ordered them into camp where they had been halted. Many of the officers and men of the division came out upon the hill to view the distant battlefield and to listen to the uproar of that fierce onset of Hood and [Maj. Gen. Lafayette] McLaws, which began at precisely [3:30 P.M.] and lasted until about [7:30 P.M.].

General Longstreet says these two divisions combined numbered scarcely 13,000 men and that for four hours they contended for the disputed field against more than 50,000 of the enemy, and their grand and headlong charge overthrew the III Corps, the II Corps, the V Corps, the XI Corps, a part of the XII Corps and were only prevented by the darkness of night and the arrival of [Maj. Gen. John] Sedgwick with the VI Corps of 15,000 fresh troops from gaining the most brilliant victory of the whole war.

Hood and McLaws fell back at dark, leaving upon the field 4,529 men, being a loss of more than one-third of their numbers carried into action. General Lee says, "It being now about dark General Longstreet retired and determined to await the arrival of Pickett." Pickett's Division was silent, within sight and hearing of this sanguinary conflict, and perhaps the opportunity to change the course of history was lost. For had Pickett's Division, upon its arrival on the field at 3:00 P.M., been led straight into battle, or had it supported the assault of Hood and McLaws at any time after an hour's rest, it is possible the battle of Gettysburg would have ended there without a third day's bloody sequel, for history is filled with instances of long forced marches, fierce conflicts, and great victories gained by the wearied troops, until the truth is established that while some armies have fought well when rested, all armies have fought better when taken into battle from a long, rapid, tiresome march. The most successful general of the late war was [Lt. Gen. Thomas J.] Stonewall Jackson, whose victories were due to his rapid forced marches, sudden surprise, and fierce onset. His infantry will live in history as "the foot cavalry of the Valley." But no better instance is wanting of the timely arrival of troops upon any field than that of Sedgwick at Gettysburg on July 2, from a forced march of thirty-two miles, made night and day, to reach the field just in time to check the victorious career of Longstreet and save the Union army from defeat.

On Friday morning, July 3, Pickett's Division left its bivouac at dawn of day and moving around to the right reached the position assigned it in the ravine behind Cemetery Ridge soon after six o'clock. Long dark lines of infantry were massed along the bottom, concealed from the enemy's view, and orders were given "to lie down and keep still to avoid attracting the attention of the enemy." About 8:00 A.M. Generals Lee, Longstreet, and Pickett, in company, rode slowly along up and down in front of the long lines of prostrate infantry, viewing them closely and critically as they rode along. They were not greeted with the usual cheers, as orders had preceded them forbidding this, but the men voluntarily rose up and stood in line with uncovered heads and hats held aloft while their chieftains rode by.

This review over, strong detachments were thrown forward to support the artillery stationed along the crest of Oak Ridge and Cemetery Ridge, composed of about one hundred and twenty cannon and stretching along the brow of these ridges for a mile. The supporting detachments were placed about a hundred yards in the rear of this line of batteries and lay down in the tall grass with a cloudless sky and a bright July sun pouring its scorching rays almost vertically upon them for five long, weary hours, while they listened and watched in painful suspense for some sound or some movement to break that profound stillness which rested over the vast battlefield and depressed the spirits like a dreadful nightmare.

At 1:00 P.M. this awful stillness was suddenly broken and the men startled by the discharge of a couple of signal guns fired in quick succession, followed by a silence of half a minute and then, while their echo was yet rolling along the distant defiles and mountain gorges, an uproar began as wonderful as had been the previous silence. Lee's one hundred and twenty guns opened at once with a crash and thunder sound that shook the hills for miles around from crest to base and were instantly replied to by about eighty guns ranged by [Maj. Gen. George G.] Meade along the front of Cemetery Ridge, about one mile in front.

No sound of roaring waters, nor wind, nor thunder, nor of these combined, ever equaled the tremendous uproar and no command, no order, no sound of voice, could be heard at all above the ceaseless din of thousands of shrieking shot and shell falling thick and fast on every side and bursting with terrific explosions, while others by thousands came bounding, skipping, racing and chasing each other over the hill and down the slope, hissing, scoffing, spitting and moaning like relentless demons as they dashed through the detachments and went onward to crash among the reserves far back in the rear. The bursting shell in mid-heaven or upon the earth scattered death wherever its fragments flew, and the shrill shot overhead or bounding madly across the field would both alike dip through a line of prostrate men and tear away with a wail to the rear, leaving a wide track of blood behind. The air was filled with clouds of dust and volumes of sulphurous, suffocating smoke rolled up white and bluish gray like frightful storm clouds and hung like a pall over the field, through the rifts and rents of which the sun with dim light looked down upon the ghastly scene.

After two hours the firing suddenly ceased and silence again rested for half an hour over the battlefield, during which time the Confederates were rapidly forming an attacking column just below the brow of Seminary

Pickett's Confederates forming for the charge (LIBRARY OF CONGRESS)

Ridge. Long double lines of infantry came pouring out of the woods and bottoms, across ravines and little valleys, hurrying on to the positions assigned them in the column. Two separate lines of double ranks were formed a hundred yards apart, and in the center of the column was placed the division of Pickett, said to be "the flower of Lee's army"—4,481 privates, 244 company officers, 32 field officers and four general officers, making 4,761 all told. In the front line was placed [Brig. Gen. James L.] Kemper and [Brig. Gen. Richard B.] Garnett's Brigades side by side, covered by [Brig. Gen. Lewis A.] Armistead's Brigade in the second line.

The column of attack, composed of [Brig. Gen. Cadmus M.] Wilcox's Brigade, Pickett's and [Maj. Gen. Henry] Heth's Divisions and several other commands, detached for this duty, had been variously estimated, but probably numbered about 13,000 troops, the command of the whole line given to General Pickett, a brave and fearless officer and a fit leader of this forlorn hope, thrown forward to retrieve disaster or turn by fierce conflict the waning fortunes of a dying cause.

Riding out in front, Pickett made a brief, animated address to the troops and closed by saying to his own division, "Charge the enemy and remember old Virginia." Then came the command in a strong, clear voice, "Forward! Guide center! March!" and the column, with a front of more than half a mile, moved grandly up the slope. Meade's guns opened upon the column as it appeared above the crest of the ridge, but it neither paused nor faltered. Round shot, bounding along the plain, tore through their ranks and ricocheted around them; shells exploded incessantly in blinding, dazzling flashes before them, behind them, overhead and among them. Frightful gaps were made from center to flank, yet on swept the column and as it advanced the men steadily closed up the wide rents made along the line in a hundred places at every discharge of the murderous batteries in front.

A long line of skirmishers, prostrate in the tall grass, firing at the column since it came within view, rose up within fifty yards, fired a volley into its front, then trotted on before it, turning and firing back as fast as they could reload. The column moved on at a quick step with shouldered arms, and the fire of the skirmish line was not returned. Half way over the field an order ran down the line, "left oblique," which was promptly obeyed and the direction changed forty-five degrees from the front to the left. Men looking away, far off toward the left flank, saw that the supporting columns there were crumbling and melting rapidly away. General Pickett sent his brother, Maj. Charles Pickett, galloping swiftly to rally, if possible, the wavering lines, saying to him, "Unless they support us on the left my division will be cut to pieces." Major Pickett and other officers rode among the breaking battalions and vainly attempted to restore order, but hundreds and thousands of fugitives from the front could be seen fleeing from the field and went rushing pell-mell toward the rear like dry leaves before a gale. Order was not restored upon the left and Pickett's support there was gone excepting some brave Tennesseans and North Carolinians, who never wavered in the storm, but closing up by the side of Pickett's Virginians went as far, fought as long, bled as freely, and fell as thick as Pickett's men.

The command now came along the line, "Front, forward!" and the column resumed its direction straight down upon the center of the enemy's position. Some men now looking to the right saw that the troops there had entirely disappeared, but how or when they left was not known. The enemy in front, occupying an elevated position and watching closely every movement of the advancing columns, say "the right gave way first, then the left broke up and fled the field, but the massive center, composed of Pickett's veterans of firm nerve, wounded in scores of battles, were coming sternly on." Guns hitherto employed in firing at the troops on the right and left sent a shower of shells after the fleeing fugitives and then trained upon the center, where the storm burst in tenfold fury, as converging batteries sent a concentrated fire of shot and shell in, through and around the heroic column.

The destruction of life in the ranks of that advancing host was fearful beyond precedent, officers going down by dozens and the men by scores and fifties. Kemper had gone down terribly mangled, but Garnett still towered unhurt and rode up and down the front line, saying in a strong, calm voice, "Faster, men! Faster! Close up and step out faster, but don't double quick!" The column was approaching the Emmitsburg Road, where a line of infantry, stationed behind a stone fence, was pouring in a heavy fire of musketry. A scattering fire was opened along the front of the division upon the line, when Garnett galloped along the line and called out, "Cease firing," and his command was promptly obeyed, showing the wonderful discipline of the men, who reloaded their guns, shouldered arms and kept on without slackening their pace, which was still a "quick step."

The stone fence was carried without a struggle, the infantry and the skirmish line swept away before the division like trash before the broom. Two-thirds of the distance was behind and the one hundred cannon in the rear were dumb and did not reply to the hotly worked guns in our front. We were now four hundred yards from the foot of Cemetery Hill, when away off to the right, nearly half a mile, there appeared in the open field a line of men at right angles with our own, a long, dark mass, dressed in blue and coming down at a "double-quick" upon the unprotected right flank of Pickett's men, with their muskets "upon the right shoulder shift," their battle flags dancing and fluttering in the breeze created by their own rapid motion and their burnished bayonets glistening above their heads like forest twigs covered with sheets of sparkling ice when shaken by a blast. Garnett galloped along the line saying, "Faster, men! Steady! Don't double quick. Save your wind and your ammunition for the final charge!" and then went down among the dead and his clarion voice was no more heard above the roar of battle.

The enemy were now seen strengthening their lines where the blow was expected to strike by hurrying up reserves from the right and left, the columns from opposite directions passing each other double along our front like the fingers of a man's two hands locking together. The distance had again shortened and officers in the enemy's lines could be distinguished by their uniforms from the privates. Then was heard behind that heavy thud of a muffled tread of armed men that roar and rush of trampling feet as Armistead's column from the rear closed up behind the front line and he (the last brigadier) took command, stepped out in front with his hat uplifted on the point of his sword and led the division, now four ranks deep, rapidly and grandly across that valley of death, covered with clover as soft as a Turkish carpet.

There it was again! And again! A sound filling the air above, below and around us, like the blast through the top of a dry cedar or the whirring sound made by the sudden flight of a flock of quail. It was grape and canister and the column broke forward into a double quick and rushed toward the stone wall where forty cannon were belching forth grape and canister twice and thrice a minute. A hundred yards from the stone wall the flanking party on the right, coming down on a heavy run, halted suddenly within fifty yards and poured a deadly storm of musket balls into Pickett's men, double-quicking across their front, and under this terrible crossfire the men reeled and staggered between falling comrades, and the right came pressing down upon the center, crowding the companies into confusion. But all knew the purpose to carry the heights in front, and the mingled mass, from fifteen to thirty deep, rushed toward the stone wall, while a few hundred men, without orders, faced to the right and fought the flanking party there, although fifty to one and for a time held them at bay. Muskets were seen crossed as some men fired to the right and others to the front and the fighting was terrific—far beyond all other experience even of Pickett's men, who for once raised no cheer, while the welkin rang around them with the "Union triple huzza." The old veterans saw the fearful odds against them and other hosts gathering darker and deeper still.

The time was too precious, too serious for a cheer; they buckled down to the heavy task in silence and fought with a feeling like despair. The enemy were falling back in front, while officers were seen among their breaking lines striving to maintain their ground. Pickett's men were within a few feet of the stone wall when the artillery delivered their last fire from guns shotted to the muzzle—a blaze fifty feet long went through the charging, surging host with a gaping rent to the rear but the survivors mounted the wall, then over and onward, rushed up the hill after the gunners who waved their rammers in the face of Pickett's men and sent up cheer after cheer as they felt admiration for the gallant charge.

On swept the column over ground covered with dead and dying men, where the earth seemed to be on fire, the smoke dense and suffocating, the sun shut out, flames blazing on every side, friend could hardly be distinguished from foe, but the division, in the shape of an inverted "V" with the point flattened, pushed forward, fighting, falling, and melting away, till halfway up the hill they were met by a powerful body of fresh troops charging down upon them, and this remnant of about a thousand men was hurled back out into the clover field. Brave Armistead went down among the enemy's guns, mortally wounded, but was last seen leaning upon one elbow, slashing at the gunners to prevent them from firing at his retreating men. Out in front of the breastworks the men showed a disposition to reform for another charge, and an officer looking at the frowning heights, with blood trickling down the side of his face, inquired of another, "What shall we do?" The answer was, "If we get reinforcements soon we can take that hill yet." But no reinforcements came, none were in sight, and about a thousand men fled to the rear over dead and wounded, mangled, groaning, dying men, scattered thick, far and wide, while shot and shell tore up the earth and minie balls flew around them for more than a thousand yards.

High Tide at Gettysburg

(*SCRIBNER'S MAGAZINE*)

Col. [Arthur J. L.] Fremantle says, "General Lee rode among Pickett's men after the repulse and with a few kindly words rallied the broken troops and that he saw many men with an empty sleeve seize a musket and turn readily into line; that there was less noise and confusion than on an ordinary review." Here are the facts of this rally of Pickett's Division. An attempt was made on the brow of Cemetery Hill, in front of the Confederate batteries, by a couple of officers to rally the fugitives, but the effort (under a heavy cross fire from both sides now) failed, and then commenced a rout that soon increased to a stampede and almost demoralization of all the survivors of this noted charge, without distinction of regiments or commands.

A few hundred yards behind the Confederate batteries there is a ravine, along which runs a country road that makes at one place an abrupt angle by turning or bending to the left. At this point there is a bluff on one side and a slight swamp on the other, creating a narrow pass, through which the fugitives without distinction of rank, officers and privates side by side, pushed, poured and rushed in a continuous stream, throwing away guns, blankets and haversacks as they hurried on in confusion toward the rear. Here another effort was made to rally the broken troops and all sorts of appeals and threats made to officers and men who turned a deaf ear and hurried on, some of the officers even jerking loose with an oath from the hand laid on their shoulders to attract attention. At last a few privates, hearkening to the appeals, halted and formed a nucleus around which about thirty others soon rallied, and with these a picket was formed across the road as a barrier to further retreat, and the stream of stragglers dammed up several hundred strong.

General Pickett came down from the direction of the battlefield weeping bitterly and said to the officer commanding the picket, "Don't stop any of my men. Tell them to come to the camp we occupied last night"; and passed on himself alone toward the rear. Other officers passed by, but the picket was retained at this point until Maj. Charles Marshall came galloping up from the rear and inquired, "what this guard was for and who placed it here"; and finding the officer without orders, he moved the picket back a few hundred yards and extended the line along the stream or little creek found there. Here the guard did duty until sundown, arresting all stragglers from the battlefield, and Colonel Marshall took them forward himself, with no other help, to where General Lee was on the field, and it was to these men that Colonel Fremantle heard General Lee address his kindly words, but none of them had empty sleeves, as all the wounded were allowed to pass to the rear. When Colonel Marshall first came up to the picket across the road he had come from a point still farther in rear, where he had been sent by General Lee to rally the stragglers, if possible, and failing to do so was returning to report to General Lee. Colonel Marshall came down several times before sundown after the stragglers collected by the picket and carried up to the field probably a total of four or five hundred men during the evening.

The Comte de Paris makes a mistake in estimating the strength of Pickett's Division at Gettysburg at 5,500, as he includes [Brig. Gen. Montgomery D.] Corse's Brigade, which had been left behind in Virginia and was not with Pickett in this campaign. The total loss in the battle is given by Col. [Walter] Harrison, [adjutant and inspector general] of the division as 3,393. General Armistead and Garnett were killed, and Kemper wounded and captured. Colonels [James G.] Hodges, [Edward C.] Edmonds, [John B.] Magruder, [Lewis B.] Williams, [Walter T.] Patton, [Robert C.] Allen, [John C.] Owens and [William D.] Stuart were killed and Colonels [Eppa] Hunton, [Joseph] Mayo, [William R.] Terry, [Henry] Gantt and [William R.] Aylett were wounded. Three lieutenant colonels were killed—[Alexander D.] Callcote, [Benjamin H.] Wade and [John T.] Ellis. Seven lieutenant colonels were wounded—Swindler, [Kirkwood] Otey, [Norborne] Berkley, N. Cannyton, [William] White, [Powhatan B.] Whittle and [Rawley W.] Martin.

Of nine majors one was killed, seven wounded, and one escaped unhurt, being the only field officer left out of thirty-two that went into the battle. The 8th Virginia Regiment went into battle with 173 privates and lost 157, leaving one captain and 16 privates. The 18th Regiment carried in 281 privates and 28 commissioned officers and lost 246 privates and 26 commissioned officers.

Cavalry Raiding in 1863

John D. Imboden,
Brigadier General, C.S.A.

Philadelphia *Weekly Times* 4, no. 12, May 15, 1880

[Maj. Gen. George B.] McClellan's appearance on the Chickahominy, within less than ten miles of Richmond, in June 1862, with a magnificently appointed army of 120,000 men, menaced the Confederate capital and authorities with such great peril that their military defenders felt the necessity of adopting every possible means of ascertaining the plans, purposes, and position of the enemy and by harassing, to confuse and delay his operations. It was to these ends that [Brig. Gen. James Ewell Brown] Jeb Stuart, with a single brigade of cavalry, performed the brilliant feat of sweeping rapidly and entirely around the Union army, cutting all its communications and temporarily, at least, interfering with the harmony of its aggressive movements. This exploit of General Stuart's suggested to both sides the employment of large bodies of cavalry in a class of auxiliary operations remote from the supporting army, appropriately and expressively called "raids," in which the aim was not to encounter the enemy in force and fight him, but rather to avoid serious conflicts of arms and expend all possible energy in the destruction of lines of communication and depots of military supplies within the enemy's lines, and then get safely back to base again.

The year 1863 was noted for great raids on both sides, the story of any of which would, if carefully and truthfully written by the leaders in them, furnish instructive entertainment to the future generations of our country, to whom the War between the States will be a topic of absorbing interest for hundreds of years to come; and even the minor details, which had no marked effect on the general result, will possess a local interest inseparable

Brig. Gen. John D. Imboden
(CENTURY MAGAZINE)

from the districts of country where these stirring scenes transpired. As I possess a complete knowledge of two of these raids—one on our side and one on the other—both made in the mountain regions of Virginia in 1863, and both successful in the attainment of their objects, it is probably due to the cause of truthful history that they should be recorded in the *Weekly Times'* "Annals of the War." My chief embarrassment lies in the fact that circumstances gave me a personal prominence in connection with these operations that renders it scarcely becoming to me to be their historian, nor would I venture upon the narrative but for the reflection that my relation to the events is matter of official record in the formal reports of the time and therefore, what I now write may be taken as simply the filling in of the skeleton outlines of reports to superior authority.

From Staunton, in the Shenandoah Valley, to Parkersburg, in West Virginia, the State of Virginia more than twenty years before the war constructed a very finely graded turnpike road. When hostilities began it was the great artery of communication between a large number of counties lying between the Valley and the Ohio River. Both sides used it from opposite ends in the operations of 1861 about Beverly, Philippi, and Rich Mountain, till the Confederates were driven east as far as the Valley, which, by the genius of [Lt. Gen. Thomas J.] Stonewall Jackson, they held against all odds in 1862. About twenty-two miles northwest of Staunton this "pike" crosses its second high range, called the Shenandoah Mountain. The crest of the mountain here had been fortified by Gen. Edward Johnson, in 1861, when he fell back from his fortified camp on the Allegheny Mountain, and after his failure to capture the Federal fortified camp on Cheat Mountain, an impregnable position in the face of so small a force as General Johnson commanded. At the close of the year 1862 I was ordered to occupy during the winter the strong position of Shenandoah Mountain, which thus became an outpost against such forces as the enemy might have on the line of the Staunton and Parkersburg pike.

From December till late in April we had a dull, quiet time at our mountain camp, which was located at the eastern base of the mountain, the top being too cold and destitute of water. I had a small brigade of a mixed character, consisting of the 62nd Virginia Mounted Infantry, Col. George W. Smith commanding; the 18th Virginia Cavalry, Col. George W. Imboden—my brother—commanding; the 23rd Virginia Cavalry, Col. Robert White, commanding; Captain McLanahan's six-gun Light Artillery; and Capt. John McNeil's company of Partisan Rangers, together with Maj. Henry Gilmor's and Major Davis' Maryland Battalion, these three latter detachments being almost constantly employed in the lower valley and on the south branch of the Potomac, scouting. The nearest body of the enemy was a brigade at Beverly, some fifty or sixty miles from me. The intermediate country was debatable ground, small parties often meeting and fighting when on scouting service.

Many of my men were from the northwestern counties of Virginia and so familiar with all the roads and mountain passes and acquainted with the political and partisan feelings of the people that I had no difficulty in sending small parties of these brave and indomitable mountaineers fifty or one hundred miles to my front—on foot—to gain information. This they would obtain from our friends or their own families, who had access to the Federal camps. Thus during the winter, it was ascertained that the Federals had considerable detachments at Beverly, Buchanan, Clarksburg, Weston, Bulltown, Sutton, Summersville, Fayetteville Court House, and Charleston and were accumulating stores at all these points for the evident purpose of aggressive movements in the early spring against the Confederates in the Shenandoah Valley and in Southwestern Virginia. During the winter—in February, I think—General [Robert E.] Lee had sent Brig. Gen. William E. Jones to Rockingham County, in the Valley, with a fine brigade of cavalry to be convenient to abundant supplies of forage. General Jones went into camp at Lacy Springs, eighteen miles north of Harrisonburg. [Maj.] Gen. Samuel Jones was at Dublin, on the Virginia and Tennessee Railroad, with some

1,500 or 2,000 men, wintering. Finding that the entire Federal force at all the points above named did not aggregate over 12,000 men; that they were so widely scattered and had not, since the departure of General [William S.] Rosecrans the previous season, maintained a very rigid discipline, nor close communication between their posts and above all, that they had shown but little enterprise during the winter to find out anything about our condition, it occurred to me in March a successful raid could be made very early in the spring by the two Joneses and myself acting in concert and moving on different lines—that is, for William E. Jones to move by the Northwestern Pike and to strike the Baltimore and Ohio Railroad at Rowlenburg, destroy it there and on up to Fairmount and Grafton, and then follow the Parkersburg branch as far as he safely could, while I, moving on Beverly and Buchanan and threatening Clarksburg, would cover his left flank; and as I expected to capture or drive off the troops at Beverly and Buchanan, the way would be open for Jones and I to form a junction at Weston and thence move southward toward the Kanawha in cooperation with Gen. Samuel Jones moving from southwest Virginia. That in addition to breaking up all the posts mentioned and destroying the stores we could collect a large number of horses for General Lee's army in those remote counties.

This plan, in all its details, I laid before General Lee. He did not approve of it as promptly as I had hoped, but after the interchange of several letters he gave it his hearty sanction and sent me the 22nd, 25th, and 31st Regiments of Virginia Infantry (as fine veteran troops as he had in his army) and also ordered to join me Col. William L. Jackson's command and Lt. Col. [Ambrose C.] Dunn's South Carolina battalion, thus giving me an effective force of between 3,000 and 3,500 men before I left camp to cross the Alleghenies. About the last of April the snow on Cheat Mountain having so far melted that the pike was practicable, General Lee directed me to be at the telegraph office in Staunton on a particular evening at eight o'clock. At the same time Gen. Samuel Jones was at his telegraph office at Dublin and William E. Jones at his in New Market—General Lee being at the Richmond office. The wires were all connected; General Lee was informed accurately by each of us of every fact he desired to know and within an hour all the details of our respective movements were arranged and our orders given by General Lee as clearly and distinctly as if we had been sitting in the same room. I went out to my camp that night and next morning set out across the mountains. William E. Jones moved at the same time. Samuel Jones was not to move till a few days later, having so much less distance to go. We knew that after we started we should hear nothing of each other for a week or more, owing to the wilderness nature of the intervening country and the hostile feelings of many of the sparse population, who would shoot down any supposed bearer of dispatches.

We began the march the last week in April or the first in May. The weather had been good, but the very day we set out it began to rain and poured down for nearly two weeks. The first night we bivouacked in Crab Bottom, at the eastern base of the Allegheny Mountains. Next day we crossed the mountain in torrents of cold rain and bivouacked on Greenbrier River. By daybreak of the third day we were putting a rude bridge across the river and early in the day began the ascent of Cheat Mountain. It is here eighteen miles across it to Tygart's Valley. In places we found the snow two feet deep on top of the mountain, and being wet and slushy, it was very trying on the infantry, but not a murmur of complaint was heard, as most of my men were marching toward their homes in the remote counties and hoped soon to see dear ones from whom they had been separated nearly two years. Just as night was closing in we reached some open land near Huttonsville, on Tygart's Valley River, twelve miles from Beverly, and bivouacked for the night in the pitiless storm. We had no tents—not one in all our wagons, as I deemed it more important to haul food and ammunition than even officers' tents and but few of those had any before we started and the men none. I recall but few nights, if any, of more discomfort than that. Where we lay for the night were no buildings save a dilapidated cabin, in which some hogs had wintered. These were driven out and perhaps some thirty or forty shivering men took their places. We were now within twelve miles of the enemy and hoped to surprise him early in the morning. I sent a small scouting party two or three miles down the road toward Beverly to guard it all night. But the weather had been so horribly bad for three days that we afterward learned that the commanding officer at Beverly had not even sent out a single scout toward Cheat Mountain. The enemy was, therefore, totally ignorant of our approach.

As the morning dawned on our fourth day the storm increased in fury to such a degree that a man could hardly be seen at a distance of a hundred yards. This favored the plan to surprise the enemy, which we should undoubtedly have done but for the—to us—misfortune that a Mr. Phares, sheriff of Randolph County, lived four miles from Beverly, on our road, and having risen very early, had mounted his horse to go to town when our advance guard came in sight. He fled rapidly toward Beverly, hotly pursued and frequently shot at and badly wounded by the advance, and escaped, taking in the news of our approach. As he had only seen a few men his report created no great alarm. A company of cavalry, mostly Germans, was sent out to see what this attack on Phares meant. These we captured almost to a man, but some got away and reported an "army" advancing. The long-roll was beat, a line of battle formed on a high bluff overlooking the road we were on, and a battery put in position to rake it for more than a mile. Discovering these preparations for our reception, the 18th Virginia Cavalry, Colonel Imboden, was sent by an obscure road to cut off retreat toward Buchanan, and all our other troops, except Col. [George S.] Patton, with his splendid regiment (the 22nd Virginia), were moved through the woods and alongside of the mountain, east of Beverly, to turn the enemy's strong position.

Patton was ordered to keep out of range on the road and await the dislodgment of the enemy by the flank movement and then close down rapidly on him. With much labor two of McLanahan's guns were dragged to the top of a wooded hill commanding the enemy's position and fire opened to divert his attention from the flank movement. But no sooner did our guns open fire than the enemy seemed to surmise his danger and began a rapid retreat, first firing all the storehouses on the edge of the town. Being cut off from the pike leading across Rich Mountain to Buchanan, he took the road to Philippi, and having gained full two miles start before our flanking forces could come down out of the densely wooded mountain and the roads being almost impassable for man or beast, trampled and cut up as they were by the retreating force, we did not attempt active pursuit, but went early into bivouac to rest the weary troops.

The rain ceased toward noon, and by the next day the men, refreshed by a good night's sleep and abundant rations, were in fine plight. The march was resumed the following day across Rich Mountain to Roaring Run, a tributary of Buckhannon River in Upshur County. Here one whole day was lost by me in the futile attempt to get across the country by an obscure road and intercept the Beverly refugees between Philippi and Buchanan, believing that if I could do so William E. Jones would prevent their reaching Grafton or Rowlesburg and we should thus capture the whole force. The cross road, bad at the best, was literally impracticable for wagons, artillery, or cavalry in consequence of the late storm.

We had to come back to Roaring Run next day and move on to Buchanan. On reaching it we found the place evacuated by the enemy, the stores destroyed, and the bridge across the river burned. As the stream was not fordable we had to extemporize a bridge, which we did by floating a raft of logs into position until their buoyancy would support a causeway, on which we crossed. We were now in a fine cattle country and improved the opportunity of our delay in crossing the river to collect several hundred head, which I sent back under guard to the Valley. I may here mention that about half the men of the South Carolina battalion deserted at Roaring Run in consequence of my threat to have some of their number shot for participation in the robbery of the house of some Union families in the neighborhood. It was reported to me that the deserters alleged that adherence to the Union side by any Southern man forfeited all his rights and any Confederate soldier could not only shoot such people on sight but had the undoubted right to take their property wherever found; and as I did not entertain these views and threatened them with death for exercising their clear rights, they "would be d——d if they would serve under me another day." It is just to the better part of the battalion to say that they did not sympathize with the deserters and were greatly mortified when detailed to go back as cattle guards.

The morning we crossed at Buchanan General Jones appeared with his brigade. He had had a rough time of it. In Hardy County he had to storm a blockhouse that covered his only way across the mountains. It was vigorously defended and he lost some men and officers before he took it, which he could only accomplish by getting a keg of powder under the floor, when the garrison surrendered before the match was applied. He reached Howlesburg late in the evening—too late, he thought, to attack it—and during the night heavy reinforcements were brought by rail to the garrison and forbade the attempt to capture the place without artillery, and he had none. So he went to Fairmount and destroyed the magnificent railroad bridge there and then came to Buchanan.

We decided to move together to Weston, as we heard the enemy was concentrating his forces at Clarksburg and at Weston we could give him a good fight and have two ways of retreat open if we were worsted—one by the route I had marched over and the other by the Weston and Gauly pike, which was in the line of our intended march to form a junction with Gen. Samuel Jones at Kanawha Falls. We remained two days at Weston, only annoyed by one or two feeble attacks on our pickets near Jane Low, on the Clarksburg road. We also gathered up some horses and cattle around Weston, and I furloughed a good many of my men to visit their families in the counties around. With the exception of two or three who were discovered and either shot or captured, they all returned within the few days allowed them. It still continued to rain nearly all the time, and the roads were little better than a quagmire.

It was manifestly clear to us that whatever force the enemy might concentrate at Clarksburg it would be physically impossible for him to follow us along any road we might take and trample and cut to the conditions of a brickyard or mortar bed. So we concluded to separate again, Jones going westward far enough to get on the line of the Parkersburg branch of the Baltimore and Ohio Railroad and damage it as much as possible and then give his attention to the oil works on the Little Kanawha—I to go forward on the Gauly Pike to break up the military posts at Bulltown, Sutton and Summersville and drive the enemy before me to Kanawha.

That march surpassed any I ever undertook in respect to the difficulties to be overcome. Language cannot convey to the mind a true idea of the condition of the roads. Horses sunk in the mud to their breasts; the axles of wagons and gun carriages would roll up the mud before them; muzzles of cannon would drag in the mud and leave a trail as though a log had been dragged along the road. Horses could not pull the guns and wagons—it had to be done by men with ropes, they walking on the roadsides. The day I left Weston, with all the energy I could bring to bear and the most ceaseless exertion of the men working in shifts and relief gangs every half hour, we accomplished but two and a half miles with the wagon train and battery.

The next day, with similar efforts, we made but five miles. I then threw away half of my ammunition and part of the contents of the wagons and after that could accomplish ten or twelve miles a day. But we suffered much for bread. The people were either destitute—as they alleged—of flour and meal or had hidden what they had, so that for a week we went without bread, though we had an abundance of meat all the time. At Bulltown and Sutton the enemy had destroyed their forts and blockhouses and burnt their stores on our approach. Our sufferings for bread were now so serious that the continued inclement weather began to tell on the physical condition of the men.

It was evident the enemy knew our logistic difficulties and made little haste to get away before we came. So when we reached Powell's Mountain and had a little firmer ground to stand upon, it was resolved to make a dash on Summersville and capture something to eat. Colonel Imboden was ordered, with all the cavalry, to make a night march and surprise the place and take it if he could. If this was impracticable, to pass beyond it and prevent a retreat till I could come up next day with the infantry and artillery. The colonel accomplished the march during the night and was on the ground just in time to see the rearguard of the enemy leaving on the road to Kanawha, whither they were retreating with a large train and all their stores. He gave chase; they fled at top speed, passing the train and imparting such a panic to the drivers that they all fled to the mountains and in a few minutes the long train of new wagons and over one hundred and sixty of the finest Kentucky mules I ever saw were ours.

The colonel wisely decided to let the enemy push along toward Kanawha under the fright he had given them, while he secured the much coveted commissary stores by turning and moving the train back to Summersville, some four miles distant, keeping his troops well in hand to resist any attempted recapture till I could come up. His success was reported to me and the infantry early in the day and caused the liveliest marching we had had so far on the raid to reach the hardtack awaiting us. This was the best piece of luck we had met with and made the cavalry immensely popular with the rest of the command. But for the great celerity of this movement and the determination with which the coup de grace was given, we should have suffered very greatly for six or eight days more and would have found great difficulty in getting back to the east, as our artillery and wagon teams were nearly worn out, and were incalculably relieved by the big, fat Kentucky mules, all as fresh as a daisy.

Gen. William E. Jones came up to Summersville that night and his "boys" were as happy as mine over the replenished commissariat. He had inflicted serious damage on the railroad and literally destroyed the oil works on the Little Kanawha. He set fire to all the rigs and tanks he could find for miles around, and his description of the scene was exceedingly graphic, winding up with the climax, "Why, sir, when the burning tanks gave way and poured their thousands of barrels, all hissing and seething, down upon the river, it looked like the gable end of hell itself had been knocked out and the fire let loose around us."

From Summersville we expected to have moved on Kanawha, but we had not heard one word from General Jones and learned that the Federal troops were still at Fayette Court House. We, therefore, feared to venture into the Kanawha Valley, where we might be entrapped. General Jones decided to take the road by Carnifex Ferry, on the Gauly, for Lewisburg and the east. I undertook to work my way in the same direction by a long abandoned road, known as the "Cold Knob route," into Greenbrier County. It was a formidable undertaking, but was accomplished after much labor, not the least of which was the construction of an artificial ford in the Gauly, at the mouth of Cranberry River, in Nicholas County. This was done by setting five hundred men to rolling down large stones from the mountainside and as many more to placing them in the riverbed till it was thus raised to within two feet of the surface of the water. On this submerged causeway we crossed and on going into camp that night a messenger from General Sam Jones reached me with the information that he was at Lewisburg, waiting to hear from William E. Jones and myself before moving on Fayette Court

House. It was then too late. This courier brought me a copy of the Richmond *Enquirer* newspaper in deep mourning lines. I opened it and found the calamity it recorded was the death of Stonewall Jackson, giving all the details. My men assembled around me that night to hear the paper read. Under a large sugar-maple tree, by the light of a pine torch, I read the sad story of his death. Strong men wept like children when it was ended. The men went off in groups to lie down and sleep on that mountain top and not one loud word was heard around their fires that night; no boisterous laughter; no fun or joking peculiar to the camp was there. It was a solemn night to us all. I heard one soldier say he would rather have heard that Jackson's whole corps had perished than that he had died, so far as our success in the war was affected by the event.

It was the second week in June when we reached Buffalo Gap, in Augusta County, eight miles from our old camp on Shenandoah Mountain. We had been gone thirty-seven days—most of the time cut off from all communications with our friends and in a hostile country. The fruits of the raid was the immunity of the Shenandoah Valley that year from West Virginia incursions of the enemy for the destroyed posts were not soon reestablished. We also got a large supply of cattle and horses. After two or three days' rest we moved northward to take part in the Gettysburg campaign, then just begun.

Up to near the close of the year 1863 the Federal cavalry operating in Virginia had not inspired the Confederates, civil or military, with any serious dread of that arm of the colossal forces opposed to them. True they had fought very well on several fields when in close proximity to the supporting masses of their infantry and artillery. But as a self-dependent arm of the service little had been attempted and less accomplished by the Federal cavalry during the first two years of the war. [Jeb] Stuart, [Nathan B.] Forrest, [John Hunt] Morgan, and [Wade] Hampton on our side had done much to prove that even poorly armed and equipped mounted men, vigorously handled by enterprising commanders, could inflict great damage on an enemy in the open field and dependent on long lines of communication for his supplies. The year 1863, however, brought prominently to the front several able cavalry officers in the Union army, to one of whom history will probably assign a place in the foremost rank on his side in that arm of the service. I refer to Gen. [William Woods] Averill, whose official career was cut short for some reason by the civil authorities at Washington (which I never have fully understood) just about the time he was inspiring us with admiration for his abilities and dread of his power and capacity to deal our cause the deadliest blows.

A cavalry skirmish (BEYER, *DEEDS OF VALOR*)

It is the purpose of this article to give a brief account of his celebrated raid from New Creek, on the Baltimore and Ohio road, to Salem, on the Virginia and Tennessee Railroad, in December 1863. We were aware that General Averill was in command at New Creek and had a considerable force under him late in the fall. For some months military operations in the Shenandoah Valley had been so inconsiderable that a period of comparative repose was enjoyed by that region.

After the retirement of our army from Pennsylvania, I was on July 21 assigned by General Lee to the command of the Valley district. Excepting an occasional dash at the Baltimore and Ohio road, we had little of moment to vary the monotony of camp life during the fall months. To be near abundant supplies of forage I had in November established my camp at Kratzer's Spring, a few miles north of Harrisonburg, sending to the Lower Valley numerous small parties of active, intelligent men and officers to watch and report appearances on the border. There were many citizens of that region living at home who performed most useful "outpost" duty for us. They observed everything going on near them and reported confidentially whatever excited their suspicions. Many ladies were, in this regard, very useful to us. I often received information from them sooner than my scouts could report it, as they would frequently have to hide in the daytime and travel only at night, while a lady or male citizen would go about as they pleased. I was, therefore, not much surprised when, early one morning in December, a sealed note was handed to me, addressed in a dainty but familiar female hand, from Moorfield, in Hardy County. It was handed to me by a wounded soldier, whose arm was still in a sling. He said he had ridden hard all night to bring me the note, as he had promised the writer to do. It was but a few lines and no name signed to it, but its contents made me spring from my seat and call my staff and order out the whole command to move in thirty minutes, the wagons to follow with supplies as quickly as possible. The little note was to this effect, and as nearly as I can recall it, in these words:

> I was visiting in Petersburg today. General Averill passed toward Franklin with an army. I hid upstairs and watched them through the window slats; counted till I was tired; am sure there were over 8,000 cavalry, as many infantry, some artillery, and over two hundred loaded wagons. They did not halt, and as soon as all had passed I got my horse and hurried home to send you word. None of your scouts are here. A wounded man who is here will take you this, riding my horse. What does it all mean?

The writer of this important note was a beautiful, accomplished girl, whose brother was an officer in my command. Petersburg is twelve miles west of Moorfield, directly on the road from New Creek through Franklin, in Pendleton County, to Monterey, in Highland County, where it intersects the Staunton and Parkersburg Turnpike, forty-four miles from Staunton. I therefore had no difficulty in answering to myself my fair young friend's question, "What does it all mean?" It meant that General Averill was off on a big raid and was taking along large supplies under an infantry guard till he reached a point from which to dash forward with his cavalry and its attendant light battery. Of course, he knew that no troops but my command were in the Valley, and if, under cover of the North Mountain and Shenandoah Mountain, he could get nearer to Staunton than I was, he would dash upon it, destroy the stores and railroad there, and then, with his fleet-footed command—larger than mine—get the start along the Valley to Lexington, possibly to Lynchburg, but certainly to Salem, on the Virginia and Tennessee Railroad and do an incalculable amount of mischief before an adequate force could expel him from the country, which he would leave at his good pleasure in safety toward the Ohio River when danger should thicken around him. Small parties of his men for several days had been riding through Hardy County and had made it too hot for my little squads, so that when he came to move the chances were I would not hear of it till he was near Staunton. However, I did gain information of his movements from my scouts, but it was half a day later than the above note had reached me—some of them having discovered his camp the night of the day he passed through Petersburg.

In half an hour after I got this note we were in rapid motion to reach the top of Shenandoah Mountain, nearly forty miles distant, before daybreak next morning. At Harrisonburg I telegraphed General Lee the danger and as fast as additional information reached me I sent it to him and called for assistance. We reached Shenandoah Mountain in the nick of time. Averill had struck the pike and was at McDowell when his scouts discovered us on the mountain. He made no attempt to dislodge us. If he ever had aimed at Staunton he gave it up. At McDowell he supplied his cavalry with all they could carry and left General [Jeremiah C.] Sullivan there with the train and infantry to menace my position and himself set forward on his march to Salem, via the Warm Springs and Covington. I kept a single company on his flanks as far as the Warm Springs, to report to me his progress and route.

General Lee fully appreciated the danger on receipt of my first dispatch and ordered General [Jubal A.] Early to Staunton with Thomas' and Walker's infantry brigades by rail and Gen. Fitz Lee's division of cavalry to cross the Blue Ridge into the Valley by Swift Run Gap, some twenty-five miles northeast of Staunton. I was directed to meet General Early in person at Staunton, report fully everything to him, and receive his orders. He accompanied me out to my camp, which was then in the little valley between the North and Shenandoah Mountains, on the Valley Pike. Sullivan was still at McDowell, but of course would not advance, but the next day began to fall back toward New Creek with his train.

After supper General Early went to Buffalo Gap, ten miles west of Staunton, to spend the night. About ten o'clock he ordered me to bring my command across the mountain to Buffalo Gap. The weather had been very dismal. It was raining and sleeting and turning very cold. A little before midnight we reached the gap, when General Early informed me that from the latest intelligence of Averill's movements he was making his way rapidly to Salem; that we could not possibly precede him there, but that he had decided to send Fitz Lee and me after him to inflict what injury we could upon him. He, therefore, ordered me to move at once to Lexington, thirty-five miles distant, where Fitz Lee would join me in the morning and, being superior in rank, would assume command.

It was an awful night for men to be out. Our clothes and beard were loaded down with ice. The roads were very rough and freezing rapidly, but in many places not yet hard enough to bear the horses and gun carriages. Through all the dreary hours we pushed on. I heard that two of Fitz Lee's men froze to death that night, and just before daybreak one of mine was reported frozen to death. Many of my men had no overcoats and only ragged blankets. Fearing more would freeze I halted in a rich man's lane, two miles long, and ordered the men to make piles of the rails on either side and set fire to them, thaw the ice off their clothing and get themselves warm. The owner of the place, aroused by the light, got up and dressed and found and threatened me with the vengeance of the law for ruining his farm. I knew him well. He was old and gray-headed; had no living child; was very rich and lived on his large estate surrounded by his well-fed and warmly-clad Negroes. I kept my temper; told him my men were freezing and hungry. He replied that we should have gone to the woods and found old logs to burn. This was more than I could stand. I requested him to go and get his smokehouse and corncrib keys, otherwise we should break in; that I must have hams enough for my men to broil a meal by his rail fires and corn to feed the horses before daylight. He was very angry, but men and horses got a good feed, where we had only hoped for a good warming at his expense. I, however, ordered him to be paid for all we got and have never seen him since. He died soon afterward.

We reached Lexington about 9:00 A.M., and in a short time Fitz Lee arrived. A conference was then held with the leading citizens familiar with all the roads Averill was likely to avail himself of in falling back. I recall to mind as present [Brig.] Gen. Francis H. Smith, superintendent of the Virginia Military Institute; ex-member of Congress S. McD. Moore, James D. Davidson, and Judge John W. Brockenbrough. All concurred in the opinion that Averill must go back via Covington. General Lee and myself decided that to be the point we must reach without delay. He assumed command and, as I had a battery, ordered me to move out that night to Collierstown, at the foot of the North Mountain range, and remain there till daybreak next morning and then push on to Covington, he intending to follow close after me.

It had quit raining and sleeting and turned intensely cold. It must have been twenty or thirty degrees below the freezing point. We had a hard night at Collierstown, but as soon as dawn appeared we were in motion. The road up the mountain was a solid sheet of ice. It seemed at one time impossible to get the cannon up, but patience and toil accomplished it and we were well down on the other side when a courier overtook me with a written order from General Lee to turn back and follow him with all haste to Fincastle, south of the James River, in Botetourte County. I was so well advanced on the way to Covington that I should have reached it long before night.

This order astounded me. I directed the retrograde movement and, leaving my men to follow, hastened to overtake General Lee and ask what it meant. In a couple of hours I came up with him. He was as much disturbed as I was, and drew from his pocket an order received that morning from General Early, saying in substance that Averill had burned Salem and started to retreat toward Covington, but had changed his plan and was returning again toward the Valley, wherefore General Early peremptorily ordered Lee toward Fincastle. After I had read the fatal document, Lee remarked, "Now you understand it. A soldier must obey orders." We discussed the situation and I think neither of us had the slightest doubt that Averill was safe so far as we were concerned—that we should never see him.

The morning we reached Lexington, General Early went back to Staunton from Buffalo Gap, and during the day he received a telegram from a demoralized operator in the railroad office, at Bousack's I believe, a few miles from Salem, with that cock and bull story of Averill's return to the railroad. I have since learned that Averill, finding how much he would be delayed in getting down Craig Creek and up Jackson River to Covington on account of ice and high water, did send a squad of ten or fifteen men back to spread the news that they were his advance guard and that he was returning, and he took good care that this intelligence should reach the railroad and have its effect.

The trick saved him, for if General Early had not changed Lee's movement, his division and my command would have reached Covington twelve or thirteen hours ahead of General Averill and have captured him and every man and horse he had. Escape was impossible, for his men were nearly frozen to death, his guns were unserviceable, their bores being solid full of ice, both cannon and small arms. We would have been in position waiting for him with an equal force, our men rested and fed and with a splendid six gun battery covering the bridge over Jackson River, his only possible means of passage.

As it was we went on to Fincastle, and just as we expected, he was then well on his way to Covington, with the high range of Rich Patch Mountain between us, which we found it almost impossible to cross on account of the great masses of ice in the road. When we did get to Covington it was to learn that General Averill had passed there the night before and was beyond pursuit. And there we heard of the horrible sufferings of his men and the easy task we should have had in bagging them all. A very small force under Col. William L. Jackson, that reached Jackson River, did capture a considerable portion of one of his regiments by cutting them off at the bridge.

In a couple of days we got back to the Valley near Staunton, weary and worn, and with nothing to show for all our laboring and suffering. Averill got back to New Creek weary and worn, too, but rewarded by the complete success of his brilliant raid.

Through Tennessee and Around Rosecrans' Army

ISAAC W. AVERY,
COLONEL, 4TH GEORGIA CAVALRY, C.S.A.

Philadelphia *Weekly Times* 3, no. 11, May 10, 1879

After [Maj. Gen. William S.] Rosecrans had pushed [Gen. Braxton] Bragg out of Tennessee in the summer of 1863, there was a lull in active operations in the Western department for a while. Our cavalry spent a month or two recuperating in camp. The Chickamauga campaign followed, resulting in Rosecrans retiring pell-mell into Chattanooga with a badly beaten army, the Confederates hopeful of sweeping him back into Middle Tennessee. As an effective agency in dislodging him, Bragg planned and [Maj. Gen. Joseph] Wheeler executed an extensive cavalry raid around Rosecrans' army to cut his railroad communications and capture his wagon trains of supplies and thereby force him out of his stronghold. To give the details of this raid, the greatest of the war up to that time, will be the purpose of this paper.

General Wheeler had three divisions of cavalry, with artillery under Maj. Gen. [John A.] Wharton, [Maj. Gen. William T.] Martin and [Brig. Gen. Henry B.] Davidson. His command was neither well organized nor well equipped, well armed nor well mounted. A large portion of the force consisted of troops from [Maj. Gen. Nathan B.] Forrest's command, who were not well disposed to Wheeler. Forrest, that incomparable fighter but most intractable of independents, was not liked by Bragg—a martinet in his generalship—and there had been trouble between them which resulted in Forrest's transfer to West Tennessee and the placing of a considerable part of his men under Wheeler.

Maj. Gen. Joseph Wheeler, who thus became the chief cavalry officer of Bragg's army, was a gallant, valuable young officer, whose rise had been something exceptionally swift and brilliant. He was a West Pointer, had entered the war as a lieutenant of infantry, became soon a cavalry general, and had shown so much activity and capacity that his promotion and fame were both remarkable. At the age of twenty-six he had achieved this high distinction of heading the cavalry of a great army. In charge of the advance, rear, or flanks of a movement, Wheeler had no superior. His vigilance was sleepless, his enterprise untiring, his audacity bold. He covered a retreat with rare skill. His energy and resources were unlimited. He was both a fine scout and a vigorous fighter. And withal, there was never a more modest, unpretentious, polite little gentleman. General Wheeler was so young and unassuming that his very extraordinary rise in rank made him the envy of some of his ambitious subordinates, who did not always give him the hearty support a leader should have from those under him.

General Wharton and Martin were both experienced and gallant officers. Wharton was a Texan, a brilliant, ambitious, dashing soldier, the idol of his rollicking, hard-fighting Texan followers. Martin, a Mississippian, less brilliant than Wharton, was a steady, game, capable officer. The three divisions aggregated about six thousand troops. The expedition started on the last day of September, crossing the Tennessee River near Cotton Port Ford, not far from Charleston, Tennessee. The Federals were on the opposite side of the river—three brigades strong. Wheeler here exhibited some creditable generalship. He cut a new road about a mile below the ford, crossed the river at night with Wharton's division, in which the writer commanded a regiment (the 4th Georgia Cavalry) and, moving down on the opposite side of the river on the main ford, attacked and drove off the enemy's pickets there and crossed over Martin's and Davidson's divisions with the artillery and ordnance wagons. A cold autumnal rain set in which continued heavily all night and the next day. It was an almost freezing fall of steady drenching rain-pour. We rode in it without sleep and fire. Occasionally the column was stopped by some impediment for a short while, and the troopers would fall asleep upon their horses or some would dismount and stretch upon a convenient log to snatch a moment of rest and slumber in the descending flood. It was one of those nights of unspeakable discomfort that illustrated the dark side of the soldier's life.

About dusk the next evening we camped on the opposite of Walden's Ridge, in Sequatchie Valley, near Foster's Crossroads.

Here the command divided. General Wharton, with the body of the force, proceeded directly across the Cumberland Mountain to attack

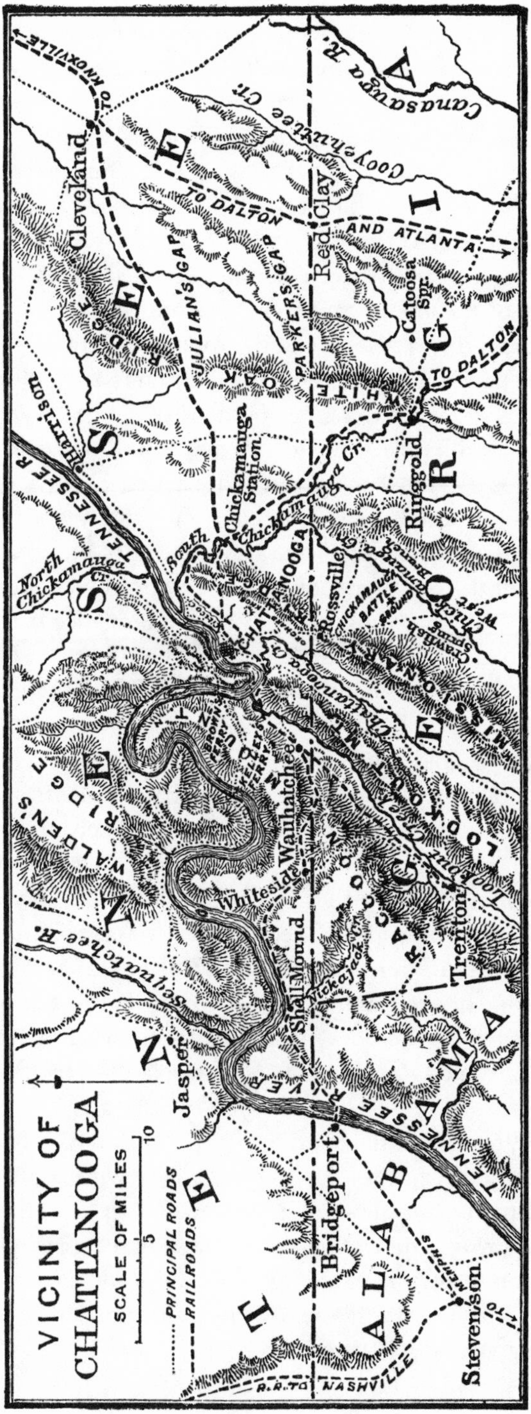

Chattanooga and vicinity (CENTURY MAGAZINE)

McMinnville. General Wheeler took two picked brigades, one from General Martin's Division, under immediate command of the writer, and went down the valley after a large wagon train on its way to General Rosecrans at Chattanooga. Our detachment, under General Wheeler, left at 3:00 P.M. We struck the wagon train about 9:30 A.M. near Dunlap, at the foot of the mountain, and went for it with a rush. The resistance was brief but spirited. We captured six hundred prisoners, eight hundred wagons, and three thousand mules. A part of the wagons were parked at the foot of the mountain while the rest of the train wound its serpentine length up the mountain ascent. The surprise was perfect and the capture complete.

The larger part of the train contained commissary and ordnance stores for the army, but there was a large number of sutlers' wagons filled with everything delightful to eat and drink and comfortable to wear. Such a bonanza had not greeted our starved and patched Confederates in a seeming age. Crackers and breads, canned meats and vegetables, wines and brandies in profusion substituted the hard rations of bacon and dodger that made the fare of the Southern soldier. The wagons were burned, and such a terrific cannonading as took place when the ordnance wagons were consumed has not been heard during the war. The mountainsides echoed and reverberated the loud and continuous explosions. 1,500 mules were killed, and the rest were sent back under guard over the mountain. The stores destroyed were valuable. There were sixty wagons of ordnance.

By four o'clock in the afternoon the work of destruction was complete, but the men were in a bad condition. Officers and men to a large extent were unfitted for fighting. They had indulged too freely in the unwonted luxuries to which they had access. Just then, too, came the word from scouts that two brigades of Federal cavalry were coming swiftly down the valley. Fully half of our detachment had been sent back with mules and stores. A third of the remaining half was on picket in the rear and on the flanks. The enemy reached us and the retreat began. The fighting was desperate and determined. Colonel [A. A.] Russell, of Martin's command, was captured at the wagons.

General Wheeler retired with a part of the force to reach the mountains and secure our captures, leaving the writer with about three hundred of his brigade (part from the 4th Georgia and a part from the 1st Kentucky) to bring up the rear. The enemy pressed vigorously. They charged a dozen times in the course of a mile, killing, wounding, and capturing fully a third of the rear guard. Their force was so overwhelming that General Martin and Col. [Isaac W.] Avery were both nearly taken—the latter's horse being shot. Lt. Col. [J. W.] Griffith, of the 1st Kentucky, was wounded; Captain

Jones, 1st Kentucky, killed; Captains Stewart and May, 4th Georgia, captured; Captain Johnson, 4th Georgia, wounded; and Lieutenant Dave May, 4th Georgia, killed. Maj. [Duff Green] Reed, of Wheeler's staff, was captured.

When near the foot of the mountain—it being dusk—the writer was cut off from his men and escaped with a soldier named Thomson by making a detour around a neighborhood road and riding over a creek on a bridge with loose plank on it a foot apart. We reached the reserve with General Wheeler a little after dark, and about 9:00 P.M. the entire force was up the mountain and marched until 3:00 A.M., rested until daylight, when the march was resumed and we camped at the opposite foot of the mountain about midday.

General Wharton, with the main body of the force, crossed the mountain and his advance guard, under Lt. Col. [Ezekiel F.] Clay, attacked the enemy's pickets in front of McMinnville about 11:00 A.M. of October 3, drove them in, and gallantly secured the outer works. His artillery was put in position commanding the town and a flag of truce sent in to demand the surrender of the garrison, which was promptly made. Six hundred troops were taken and a large quantity of commissary and sutlers' stores were captured, consumed and destroyed.

General Wheeler left our detachment under command of General Martin and hurried on the main body under General Wharton, at McMinnville. General Martin, with his two brigades, marched more leisurely. The enemy were after us. About 9:00 P.M., [Col. John T.] Wilder's Lightning Federal Brigade, with repeating rifles, struck our rear. The writer has a vivid recollection of that night fight. Our men were dismounted save the regimental officers. The night was densely black. Our line ran through woods with thick underbrush. The stillness was oppressive. A rustling, faint at first but growing in volume, was distinctly heard. The writer called out loudly, "Who comes there?" Immediately a clear, ringing voice in front responded, "God damn you, we'll show you! Charge men! Fire!" The next instant a vivid sheet of continuous flame blazed and lit up the woods some thirty yards in front of us, while a deafening, continuous, rolling volley thundered upon the night and broke the silence with startling effect. The writer was on his horse, and the dense stream of bullets whizzed above his head harmless. The firing line over shot us. Had it aimed low it would have swept our line out of existence. As it was, not a man was hurt in all the terrific firing. The effect of the night shooting was singular upon the writer's horse—a veteran animal, insensible to the loudest clamor of the guns in the day. The horse acted like a crazy animal. He was wholly unmanageable, plunging and rearing and wild with terror, so that the writer was compelled to dismount and send the animal to the rear in charge of an orderly.

The writer instantly ordered his men to fire low. Our fire must have been effective, for the charge was [repulsed], and in several minutes the firing entirely ceased. We remained in position a half hour, when our men were quietly withdrawn, mounted, and we marched all night, joining the main force at McMinnville the morning of the 4th, when we received a supply of the palatable rations captured at that place.

Our entire force reunited, marched all day and reached Woodbury that night. The Federals were after us in force and pushed vigorously. In the afternoon they charged three companies of the Texas Rangers acting as rear guard and dispersed them, but Col. [Thomas] Harrison, of Wharton's Division, formed his brigade and checked the attacking force. Here General Wheeler, after consultation with his division commanders, determined to give the enemy battle with his entire command, and the men were delighted. But upon further reflection it was determined to be impolitic, and the intention was abandoned.

The next morning, October 5, the main body of the force made a rapid march to Stones River, above Murfreesboro, burned some valuable bridges, tore up and destroyed a good deal of railroad track, and then joined the wagons at Fosterville. A small force of Federals at Christiana was captured in a stockade. At daylight on the morning of the sixth the Texas Rangers, under Lieutenant Colonel Cook, charged into Shelbyville, but the cavalry guarding the place had left during the night. Large quantities of sutlers' stores were here captured. General Martin, with his division, proceeded to Wartrace, burned all the bridges on the railroad, tore up and destroyed a lengthy line of track, and rejoined the command by a night march. General Davidson's Division camped below Shelbyville, on the southern side of the river, and General Wharton's Division camped the same distance from Shelbyville on the northern side of the river.

With the command thus scattered the opportunity was too fine for a wily enemy not to attempt to take advantage of it. General Davidson's Division below Shelbyville, on the south side of the river, was vigorously attacked by a heavy Federal force early on the morning of the seventh and pushed back after a sturdy resistance on the Shelbyville and Lewisburg pike. One of his brigades was driven in considerable disorder. There was in this sudden emergency a stiff race by General Wheeler with Wharton's and Martin's Divisions for this pike. His object was to strike it at Farmington before Davidson's Division, in rapid retreat, should be pressed to that point. Davidson had some rough fighting. The Federals struck him repeatedly with increasing vigor, emboldened by his evident disorder and eager to reap the full advantage of his defeat. Colonel Montgomery, commanding Scott's Brigade, in this division, was wounded in this running engagement while Major McDonald was killed.

It was close work and by swift marching that, in the very nick of time, General Martin's Division arrived and was thrown into position on the pike, just where the road enters the pike, and the rest of the command marched into the pike under a warm fire from the enemy. This was General Wheeler's order, and the gallant soldiers obeyed it with admirable coolness and steady nerve. It was here that a fierce fight ensued. The Federals, elated with their success in driving Davidson, fought with magnificent spirit. Our own troops, realizing their danger, stood up with undismayed pluck. The Texas Rangers were ordered to charge down the pike, and they did it with their accustomed spirit. The commanding officer of that regiment, Lieutenant Colonel Cook, Major Christian, and two lieutenants were wounded. General Wharton's horse was killed. The charge was repulsed and our line broken, and we had the misfortune to lose three pieces of artillery. The 4th Tennessee, 11th Texas, and 1st Kentucky were cut off and had to move across the country to regain the command. Our loss at this point must have been fully 150.

The enemy pressed their advantage, but the Georgians of Wharton's Division and a part of Martin's Division rallied, reformed the line and stood so firm and administered such punishment to the Federals that their onward advance was checked and the fighting ceased.

During that night our force marched to Cornersville and then through Pulaski to Sugar Creek the next day, where we camped. Men and horses were much jaded. All the possibilities of harm to the enemy had been accomplished and our object was to get the command safely over the Tennessee River. The Federals in the fight on the pike had been handled severely enough to make them cautious. Had they have pushed us with boldness and vigor they could have given our wearied force a great deal of trouble and made our passage of the Tennessee River humiliating.

At Sugar Creek a rear guard was left composed of the 2nd Georgia, a gallant little regiment under Lieutenant Colonel Iron and a battalion of General Morgan's men, under Captain Kilpatrick. Colonel Iron was a brave officer, but one distrustful of his ability for separate command. The rest of our force proceeded through Rogersville and reached the Tennessee River at Muscle Shoals. The rear guard was attacked by a heavy force and resisted sturdily, but a good disposition of the men was not made, and the line was broken by the charge and badly scattered. Lieutenant Colonel Iron, Lieutenants Lunceford and Davergne, and thirty men from the 2nd Georgia, and several officers and forty men from the battalion of Morgan, were captured. The Federals did not follow up their advantage, and the force made a leisurely, safe passage of the river without loss or danger, all getting across on October 10.

The raid was a success. Our loss out of the 6,000 troops engaged in the movement was not over 400, while the loss of the Federals was fully 1,500. The destruction of 800 wagons, 3,000 mules, and the immense quantity of commissary, ordnance, and other stores was a valuable result. The burning of a large number of valuable bridges and the tearing up of much railroad track was another good result. Our men were well remounted and armed. The successful passage of our force through the State of Tennessee, garrisoned at every point with strong bodies of troops, our command pursued and environed by superior bodies of the enemy, with railroad and telegraphic facilities for concentrating at various points, is a crowning demonstration of Wheeler's generalship and a superb testimonial to the fighting qualities of his command. Our military authorities were well satisfied with the movement.

The Battle of Missionary Ridge

I. E. NAGLE,
SURGEON, ARMY OF TENNESSEE, C.S.A.

Philadelphia *Weekly Times* 2, no. 27, August 31, 1878

When the administration at Richmond received the news of the success of [General Braxton] Bragg's army on the field of Chickamauga, September 20, 1863, orders were sent to follow up the advantages with the utmost rapidity. But, during the night, our advance was obstructed by the insurmountable obstacles that our troops had exhausted their ammunition and strength during the battle and [Maj. Gen. George H.] Thomas defended the Union retreat so effectually that it was impossible to take his position at Rossville until [Maj. Gen. William S.] Rosecrans' entire army was safely entrenched in Chattanooga and its impregnable fortifications. Those of us who were situated so as to know the condition of affairs readily understood the fact that we had gained a victory beyond all estimate, barren of good results, for the battle was more disastrous to us than it was to the enemy. But a wild excitement was agitating the country, and the people and authorities were very eager that our supposed advantages should be improved.

Under this pressure orders came from the War Department urging Bragg to move promptly and rapidly onward toward Nashville, to flank Rosecrans out of Chattanooga. But he prudently stopped on Missionary Ridge and proceeded to examine into our capacity for performing the service so urgently demanded. We soon learned that the late battle had nearly annihilated some of the commands, destroyed our wagon trains, left us very short of provisions, the supply of ammunition totally exhausted, or inadequate to the requirements and the army too much wearied and worn to make any further demonstrations. The bridges throughout the section to be traversed were destroyed, the fords impassable and the probabilities of being delayed by heavy rains that usually fall in autumn in that region, all served to prevent any movement from the position occupied on Missionary Ridge.

Having decided on remaining there, we proceeded to repair the railways and quickly established communication with our sources of supplies. The troops were located in healthy situations; sickness almost entirely disappeared; convalescents were kept close to the army, and accessions made by receipts of conscripts and recruits from hospitals and those who had long been absent from various causes. A general feeling of hopefulness, characteristic of our mercurial soldiers, and a general sense of security pervaded the Confederate camp. We occupied strongly entrenched positions and were confident of holding with ease and few numbers all of the apparently insurmountable passes and heights from which we beheld every movement of the enemy.

On October 16 we discovered that something of unusual interest had occurred in the Federal camp and soon afterward learned from signals, given by those whom we kept employed in the enemy's service, that [Maj. Gen. Ulysses S.] Grant had been placed in command of the Union army. That evening our emissaries signaled particulars stating that the territory of the Western army was called the "Military District of the Mississippi" and comprised the "Departments of the Ohio, Tennessee, and Cumberland," with a force of over 150,000 available men in the field. Thomas [was] in charge of the Army of the Cumberland; [Maj. Gen. William T.] Sherman of the Army of the Tennessee; [Maj. Gen. Ambrose E.] Burnside at Knoxville; [Maj. Gen. Joseph] Hooker, with his command from Virginia, in position in the vicinity of Walden's Ridge.

From these active preparations and changes it was evident that sharp and decisive action was intended by the enemy. Hence we were aroused from the comparative apathy that had fallen like sleep on us during the soft and deliciously balmy weather which prevailed during the delectably sweet Indian summer season of that lovely autumn. Bragg became restive, dissensions occurred between him and his generals, many foolish changes were made in the organizations by taking commands from the corps, divisions, and brigades to which they had made reputation and fame; regiments, companies, and squads were transferred to fill up bodies, with which they had no affiliation, sympathy, or community of feeling or state pride. Every part of the army was disrupted. The men became maddened at such want of consideration of their feelings, and a sullen spirit of dissatisfaction was manifested in the deep and bitter curses that were cast on the author of the obnoxious changes. All the counsels of subordinate officers were of no avail to bring about a better feeling, and so an ominous cloud hung over the army.

On the heels of this dissatisfaction in rank and file it was discovered that some of the principal officers had no confidence in Bragg's capacity, luck, etc. It became known also that [Lt. Gen. James P.] Longstreet was ambitious of having command of the army. Finally the cabals became so bitter that a council was called and held in Bragg's quarters to decide on a plan for the prospective campaign. That meeting was one of the stormiest scenes ever held in a commanding officer's presence—one that the survivors who witnessed it and participated in the debate will never forget. The private resentments, bitter recriminations, and exposures of ambitious designs uttered and developed there requires that the secrecy which has been held inviolably concerning it should be kept sealed forever. The conference decided that to settle all dissensions and give Longstreet opportunity to exhibit his merits and capacity as an untrammeled commander, President [Jefferson] Davis and Bragg arranged to send him into East Tennessee, whither he proceeded early in November, taking eight thousand infantry and five thousand of [Maj. Gen. Joseph] Wheeler's cavalry.

They were not a half day's journey away when our emissaries signaled that the movement was known and prompt action had been taken by the Federal authorities to meet the case. It was reported, too, that the enemy was ordered to immediately prepare for an active campaign and we quickly saw that new life and spirit was enthusing those men whom we had driven into the entrenchments a few weeks before. There came upon us an indefinable and pervading sense of insecurity. We felt that the taking off of such a large body of our troops at that critical moment boded evil to us, was a virtual abandonment, and insured disaster and inevitable defeat to our army. The reading of the news to the men sounded like a death-knell. The soldiers began with furtive looks and with guarded words to speak of the matter and anxiously seek the rear for safety. Suspicion, alarm, distrust, and fear came over many who had never before felt anything but cheerfulness and courage that made them invincible. Discontent with the new arrangements of their commands and being placed under strange officers caused a mutinous resentment to appear and break out into querulous complaints. The hospitals in the pleasant places in the South were very soon filled, many took furlough without permission and there seemed to be a feeling extant that if Bragg was defeated the army would be well rid of an unpopular officer, who was too strict in enforcing severe penalties for light infractions of discipline while he permitted great wrongs to go unpunished and unheeded.

My experience with him was that he was just, so far as his knowledge of a case went. But the misfortune was that he seldom knew the real condition or circumstances of the cases which he decided upon. He kept too much isolated from his men and hence having no idea of the estimate in which he was held by them, as a matter of course was often duped into doing injustice by means of the influences that were used by his favorites, who safely vented their malice against those who fell under their displeasure or happened to be in the way of their ambitious designs. Many of the officers exhibited very plainly in their conduct that they unwillingly served under this general, in whom they had no confidence and who was personally odious to them. With such demoralizing influences prevailing the soldiers became mere machines and performed their duties sullenly, without hope of success.

On November 23 we learned that Grant had fixed his headquarters on the first knob north of Cemetery Hill. The location gave him a complete and almost unobstructed view of every portion of the positions and lines occupied by both armies. There he was completely beyond range of our guns and on that incomparable outlook he remained during all of the active and strategic operations that were maneuvered on that and the succeeding day. The code of Federal signals were changed, and hence several hours elapsed ere our emissaries were able to send the key. In the meantime several important changes were made and advantages gained by the enemy that made our evacuation and retreat only a question of time.

Early in the morning of the twenty-third our pickets between Citico and Chattanooga Creeks were driven from their posts and obliged to take refuge in the first line of entrenchments. There were no prisoners taken in this skirmish, an event which surprised us, for we had an arrangement by which, whenever a conflict of that character occurred, certain men in the enemy's ranks fell into our possession and with them the object of the attack as well as other secrets that were sent from Grant's headquarters. On that occasion, however, the sphinx had been silent, and we did not learn anything concerning the object of the movement.

Having been thrown off guard and not suspecting any danger, the Confederates lay idly looking on and admiring the handsome appearance of Thomas' Corps as it advanced in full view in the open fields. The command was in bright uniforms and marched into position as if for review, almost within long range of our sharpshooters. As they formed in a hollow square and then into lines, front face to our view, we though the spectacle was a dress parade or inspection for the delectation, perhaps, of some notables who were visiting the Union army. The movement at that hour of the

The attack on Orchard Knob (JOHNSON, *CAMPFIRE AND BATTLEFIELD*)

day was suspicious, but the object did not seem to occur to Bragg, who looked on the scene as if it had a fascinating interest to him. The day was unusually beautiful, the sky nearly clear, a few vagabond clouds drifted over its smiling face and vagrant puffs of mist and rifle shots only gave passing shadows over the scene. The light of the meridian sun shone exquisitely golden on the autumn-tinted hills, which lay bathed in a delusive haze of soft blue mist. The air was balmy and seemed filled with opiate influences and we were as deliciously lazy as the most indolent could desire. But at 1:00 P.M. we were aroused from all this dreaminess by the sudden appearance of [Maj. Gen. Philip H.] Sheridan's and [Brig. Gen. Thomas J.] Wood's divisions of [Maj. Gen. John M.] Palmer's corps, which drove in and captured several pickets and reserves. Before our surprise permitted us to know what it all meant, the enemy secured possession of Orchard Knob. Directly we learned from prisoners that [Maj. Gen. Gordon] Granger's troops were entrenched on the knob and the advances of the wings on his right and left were made to obliterate and cover from view the front line of the works, behind which nearly all of Thomas' command was placed. We were now thoroughly alive to the emergency and appreciated the fact that a battle was imminent.

During the night Bragg ordered [Maj. Gen. William H. T.] Walker's Division to leave its position on the west side of Lookout Mountain, and after a long march it was placed in the north part of the valley between Citico and Chickamauga Creeks. He also ordered every encumbrance to be sent to the rear, and in accordance thereto all the sick, wounded, and surplus of all kinds were shipped by railway from the tunnel and other stations with as much speed as our motive power and transportation facilities could effect. Numerous half-sick and many malcontents took leave without permission and straggled off into every part of the country, knowing that as our cavalry was far away they could do so with impunity.

At daylight on the morning of the twenty-fourth the surgeons' and adjutants' reports exhibited the startling fact that the army consisted of 27,362 men who were fit for active service. Bragg was evidently shocked at this showing, for he supposed he had at least ten thousand more men who would be available in battle. In a few minutes he arose from his reverie and took on a look that meant a fearful struggle to maintain his position or fight to the bitter end of annihilation, for he knew that on the coming battle was staked all that was dear to him as a military chief.

Early in the morning of the twenty-fourth Walker discovered that [Maj. Gen. Oliver O.] Howard's Corps was in his front and moving in the vast cornfields of the valley to make connection with Sherman. A disagreeable rain and thick mist almost constantly covered the enemy from view, and under the veil Sherman occupied the hills north of the East Tennessee and Georgia Railroad tunnel, which position he quickly strengthened with entrenchments and fortifications, without making any notable demonstrations. The fighting of that part of the line during the day consisted chiefly of desultory exchanges of shots between pickets. During the night of the twenty-third the enemy discovered the disappearance of Walker from the west side and sent [Brig. Gen. John W.] Geary's command from Wauhatchie (on the Nashville and Chattanooga Railroad) to proceed around and under the point of Lookout Mountain, which march they effected by remarkable toil and courage as well as admirable strategy. During the movement the Federal batteries on Moccasin Point were constantly employed against the Confederate guns situated on the top of Lookout and which responded without intermission all through that eventful night.

Hooker had been ordered to make a demonstration against the east side and north point of the mountain and having succeeded in getting Geary's troops into his line, advanced up the slope to make the assault. The highest altitude of Lookout is about twelve hundred feet above the plain. Two-thirds of the way up there is a considerable farm clearing and white building,

Missionary Ridge, as viewed from Orchard Knob (JOHNSON, *CAMPFIRE AND BATTLEFIELD*)

called the halfway house, to which a comparatively good road extended, also above and beyond, along the base of the cliff. From this highway radiated numerous wagon roads which had been made and temporarily used by woodsmen for hauling timber on and by these the ascent to that point was comparatively easy. The artillery duel which occurred during the night before and the morning of the twenty-fourth caused a vast quantity of smoke and produced thick, vaporous clouds, which hung and drifted halfway down the mountain, obscuring its sides, but leaving the valley below and top of Lookout comparatively clear. Beneath this thick veil Hooker's command slowly and successfully toiled up the heights to startle the Confederates, who saw them emerge like an apparition from the clouds.

Before this advance the line contracted until the total defense at the foot of the palisade of rocks was chiefly occupied by Georgia conscripts and recruits, who fought like veterans for a long time, but were finally driven back until sustained by [Maj. Gen. Benjamin F.] Cheatham's invincibles, who occupied the line on the east bank of Lookout Creek. [Maj. Gen. Carter L.] Stevenson's Division also occupied a part of that line and was ordered to operate against Hooker's advance, but failed to do so. General Bragg was furious at the time at what he considered a dereliction of duty and hence it was not surprising to find in his report the statement that "Major General Stevenson had six brigades not used, and having sent for assistance, another brigade was given to him, and if he had sustained General Walthall, as per orders, the loss of Lookout Mountain would not have occurred." The soldiers of that division were brave beyond all question, and had made themselves famous for their courage on numerous hard-fought fields and certainly would have done as Bragg says if they had been employed as their general was ordered to use them.

After Hooker captured the white house our troops were ordered to evacuate the crest of the mountain during the night of the twenty-fourth, and to cover their retreat constant firing was kept up by various batteries along the entire line of the west wing. The view along the side of Lookout and part of the crest of Missionary Ridge presented a brilliant and thrilling scene that night, when continuous artillery flashes sprang out in long red and yellow lines of fire, seeming like tongues of flame darting from the mouths of deep-sounding monsters. The heavy discharges of cannon, mingled with fusillades of musketry, explosions of bombs and brilliant lights of both signal corps, mingled with the roars and reverberations that echoed from the sides and rocky recesses of that vast mountain, lasted from early evening until near midnight and gave singularly exciting interest to the occasion.

As that eventful night was filled with more important events than any other of the campaign, the memorable incidents will never be forgotten by those who saw and participated in them. Under cover of the display, the Southern troops were withdrawn from the top and sides of the mountain and moved by quick marches and without any losses of men or munitions into other positions, by which the appearance of the field and plans of battle were totally changed. The weak points were strengthened and all necessary precautions used for defense against those flank movements which were favorite tactics of the enemy. The lines very soon made evident the fact that our latest positions were taken with the object of having clear passageway for retreat along the line of the Western and Atlantic Railroad (State Railroad). By this new disposition of the forces the Confederates occupied the crest and western slope of Mission Ridge. At many points the line was very thinly manned, the defense consisting of skirmishers, who were stationed from thirty to a hundred feet, and at some of the least accessible places a hundred yards apart. [Maj. Gen. John C.] Breckenridge's gallant and famous command, consisting of [Brig. Gen. Patton] Anderson's and [Maj. Gen. Alexander P.] Stewart's splendidly officered and remarkably brave men, were overwhelmed in an engagement which occurred early on the twenty-

Raising the flag on Lookout Mountain (FORBES, *LIFE OF SHERMAN*)

fourth, and being ordered to retreat, their abandonment of the position at Rossville left the valley open to the Federals, who quickly occupied the place, but did not push their advantage.

The extreme right was held by [Lt. Gen. William J.] Hardee's Corps, which on that day consisted of [Maj. Gen. Patrick R.] Cleburne's Division, occupying the extreme northern part of the line, the right of and near the tunnel; Walker's (under [Brig. Gen. States Rights] Gist), Cheatham's, and Stevenson's Divisions all extending in this order along the crest and side of Missionary Ridge northward, making a line about seven miles in length. General Bate had command of the center and left of Bragg's headquarters. His own force was very small, but his instructions were to gather and control all stragglers as they fell back in retreat. With the latter unreliable means he was expected to make a determined stand at all points in that vicinity that presented opportunity for resisting the onset of the enemy. When our left abandoned Rossville and retreated eastward and northward Bate intercepted the fugitives and used every endeavor to arouse the stragglers to a sense of their duty, but all appeals to their pride, honor and courage were without avail. He found the double work of fighting the enemy [and] rallying our flying squads a most Herculean task, but that he did his duty bravely I can attest from observations. When, however, the enemy pushed into the immediate vicinity of our central headquarters and the battle was waged with special fury, Bragg, seeing his army fleeing past without paying heed to Bate or any other officer, became frenzied, and his usually swarthy countenance was livid with rage and despair. Dashing furiously upon the men he urged them to stand and do their duty as soldiers, but they derided and cursed him as they fled.

In this moment of peril, the turning point of his march to ruin, Bragg exhibited more humanity than he had credit for. Under the malign waning of his star he might have used the guns of convenient batteries against his panic-stricken deserters and quickly stopped the increasing rout which Bate was using superhuman efforts to check; but the stragglers increased with formidable numbers and continued to rush to the rear. In this critical hour and extremity, fortunately for the safety of the left wing of the army, the Fifth Company of Washington Artillery (Capt. Cuthbert Slocomb) came to the rescue. During the night before this famous battery of two Napoleons and four rifle guns had been placed in field position on the top of the ridge, a short distance north of Bragg's headquarters and almost in rear of the place it occupied the previous day in the vineyard in the valley. The evening before it had been detached from the command with which it had fought from Shiloh to Chickamauga and moving by way of Rossville, took position at 9:00 A.M. on the twenty-fifth, where they fought without defenses or support through the battle.

At 3:00 P.M. the enemy made a heavy assault on this position and continued to advance until, like a wave of blue, they rolled over the rocky edges of the hills and under clouds of smoke from their own rapid discharges of musketry and artillery, rushed on the battery with a gallantry and courage that elicited admiration and applause from every Southern soldier who witnessed the attack. I regret that the name of the command is unknown to me, for it would give me pleasure to make for them, in this report, a record of one of the most daring episodes of the war. Their assault in storming the center in the face of the terrible, galling and destructive fire of canister discharges from the battery, was recognized by the company as one of the very bravest acts they had ever looked on.

At this critical moment [Brig. Gen. Alexander W.] Reynolds' Brigade of Tarheels, composed of Virginians and North Carolinians, appeared and were urged by the officers of the Fifth Company to support the guns. But when that flying brigade saw the long lines of blue advancing they prudently did what they had seldom done before—took long and rapid strides rearward. The officers of the battery, finding that a disastrous shot had almost completely disabled them and the enemy was within twenty yards of their guns, assaulting on three sides, they cut loose and escaped with the horses and limbers, but left their guns captives. This was their first disaster in the war, though they were consoled with the knowledge that they never defended or fought them more bravely and effectively.

Having succeeded in securing some stray guns, they came to the rescue of the routed left wing and with the support of Major Austin's sharpshooters made a stubborn stand, which prevented the enemy from cutting Bragg's army into irretrievable ruin, while they covered its retreat across the inadequate pontoons over the swollen Chickamauga. After the abandonment of our left and center, the brunt of the battle devolved on the north end of the line. All afternoon of that bitter day in November Hardee's Corps and Cheatham's troops were kept busily employed and suffered severe losses in the great contest that decided the evil fate of Bragg's army.

Suddenly, about 4:00 P.M. there appeared on the banks of Citico Creek and extending into apparently interminable space, long lines of reserves—legions of men in blue—who steadily tramped forward and formed into thick masses and irresistible assaulting columns. The movement was watched with strange feelings of wonder and thrilling interest by our troops, for it seemed as if myriads of armed soldiers had dropped into the keeping of Grant and his victorious generals. One of our gallant officers in his peculiar exaggerating way, said he could hear Sherman issuing orders, "Nations fall in line! By states, form columns! By worlds, march! Universe, charge!"

Hurrying to the tunnel I found Cleburne's command making most desperate resistance against fearful odds. His men were shooting with foul and unreliable guns and the artillery almost useless. Many of them were short of ammunition, others who had none were fighting in hand to hand combats, throwing stones and striking the advancing foes with whatever things they could get and use for defense. The vast army in blue came steadily on up the heights and it soon became evident that our defeat was inevitable. The roads, fields, and forests back of the ridge were covered with fugitives, whose flight sounded like the rushing of heavy rain, and whose retreat could not be stayed by the most energetic efforts of the officers' commands; whose tattered standards showed they had been in numerous battles were seen flying, not so much in panic as with a conscience that resistance would be unavailing against the hordes that were displacing them. Therefore they sought self-preservation in retreat, and where everyone seemed bent on securing safety in the Southern fastnesses, the action of the routed army did not seem to be disgraceful.

The enemy captured many of our guns, but found the caissons empty; they gathered many muskets, but no ammunition; they reaped a harvest of clothing, but in its worthlessness learned that we were as ragged and poverty-stricken a set of tatterdemalions as ever disappeared from a battlefield. But with the indomitable pluck that had urged the victorious foe to the top of the bastions and rocky crests of Missionary Ridge, they found strength and means to bring ordnance with them, under the explosions of whose shells and beneath the screaming, whistling and crashing paths of their shot, we felt indescribably uncomfortable as we fled in all directions that were not in possession of, or would fall into the hands of, the victorious enemy.

At 5:00 P.M., receiving orders to get away to the hospitals with all wounded and sick that could be carried from the ambulance and Chickamauga stations, with regret I left Pat Cleburne withdrawing with his usual skill and success, my old comrades and favorites fighting steadily as they slowly retreated while bringing up the rear. Hurrying from the scenes of defeat, in the dusk of evening I took out the last train of cars that left the army, and kind fortune favored us in making the transit to Dalton with a heavy load of wounded, but under a strain of anxiety that I hope may never occur again in my experience.

In my next interview with Bragg he appeared to be a galvanized dead man; his face was old-looking, parchment-like, and wearied; his form shrunken and feeble. His star of hope was eclipsed. The cabals against him had proved successful. His want of popularity had left him without sympathy. The remnant of his brave army obeyed orders mechanically, but seemingly ever with a hope that another general would soon take his place. He knew that his career as commander of the Western armies was at an end, and so he retreated sullenly, in an aimless, wearied, spiritless manner, animated only by a hope that death or release from his burden would come quickly. He never had any magnetism in his companionship, never thrilled the men with eloquent words, nor led them with the dash of a Bayard. He seemed rather to have no community of feeling with his soldiers, or disposition to recognize any fraternity, such as made Cheatham, Cleburne, and others very popular. Hence the army estimated him as an icicle, a mere brute force machine or overseer, and when disaster came they had no sym-

Federal units sweep across Missionary Ridge (LIBRARY OF CONGRESS)

pathy for him in his misfortune, even though the great loss was to their beloved Confederacy.

The summary of the battle of Missionary Ridge is that the defeat of Bragg's army was primarily caused by being weakened by the loss of Longstreet's forces; by the foolish action of reorganizing on the eve of active hostilities, under which arrangement commands that had fought side by side with confidence in each other were separated and attached to others whom they knew not and perhaps detested. Again, the army was always short of ammunition and provisions at the very moment they were required and most necessary. The ordnance stores were closed out in a manner that was often not only insulting to the applicants but also totally inadequate to the emergency. The chiefs of the ordnance and commissary departments were the most unpopular and incompetent persons that could be found to entrust with the important service of furnishing such supplies, while many of the subordinates in those branches were very popular and genial. The small army that was left after the departure of Longstreet was daily treated by the enemy to spectacles of review, in which the earth seemed to give birth to legions of armed soldiers as they trampled over her brown bosom. The marshaling of those hosts in plain view caused the dullest among us to calculate their strength, and it was no wonder that the estimate enumerated them at a half million.

Against these, we knew we had a very small force to operate with and consequently were considerably scared ere active work occurred; in fact, were prepared to run away on the least provocation that gave excuse, and so a large number did so with as little display of grace and valor as the enemy could desire. We had been effectually demoralized by all sorts of adverse influences, long ere the realities of battle began, and hence were easily routed by an army that was too much exhausted by its efforts in reaching the heights to advance or follow with sufficient speed our flying squads. Herein is the reason why so few of the Confederates were wounded and very few taken prisoners. Our loss in small arms and cannon was very large, but they were quickly supplied from the reserves in the rear, a large amount and number of which quickly came to the front and saved us from annihilation, which would have otherwise happened at Ringgold.

From Chattanooga to Knoxville with Longstreet's Corps

WILLIAM M. ROBBINS,
MAJOR, 4TH ALABAMA INFANTRY, C.S.A.

Philadelphia *Weekly Times* 4, no. 43, December 18, 1887

After the battle of Chickamauga, in September 1863, the Federal army in Chattanooga was closely besieged for several weeks and, although in possession of the country north of the Tennessee River, was reduced to great straits for supplies, the Confederates having seized all the railways leading into that place. From the top of Lookout Mountain Federal foraging parties could be seen cutting and hauling into the town for horse feed the dry cornstalks of October, and this showed the Confederates how "hard up" [Maj. Gen. William S.] Rosecrans' army was and gave them hopes of soon reducing the place by starvation.

The impossibility of driving out the Federal army by assault without fearful loss was too evident to be attempted till all other means were tried. By scouts sent north of the river it was learned that General Rosecrans brought his supplies from Sequatchie, thirty miles away and beyond the mountain ridges which shut in Chattanooga on the west; that his wagon trains had but two roads through these mountains and that one of these roads ran for a considerable distance immediately along the north bank of the river some miles below the town.

Those who have stood on the top of Lookout Mountain remember how the river at its foot, after rounding Moccasin Bend, trends away northward for miles, passing Brown's Ferry and disappearing as it curves round the farther end of Raccoon Ridge, which runs up from the south. Winding its romantic way through these wild gorges, the river forms at its northernmost curve what is called Raccoon Bend. Here the mountain on the south bank abuts closely upon the water's edge and on the north bank there is just room enough for the road between the river and the overhanging cliffs for about two miles. The river is about three hundred yards wide. Here, then, through this defile ran one of Rosecrans' two roads, and we could command it with our Enfield rifles.

Having discovered this, [Lt. Gen. James P.] Longstreet sent the 4th and 44th Alabama Regiments to occupy the south banks of the river at this place; and before daylight on Sunday morning, October 11, these troops were deployed along the margin of the stream for about two miles in skirmishing order, the men being concealed among the rocks and shrubbery.

Soon after sunrise a long train of wagons drawn by a six-mule team was seen entering the pass, the teamsters whistling and cracking their whips in merry mood, entirely unsuspicious of the impending danger. They were allowed to drive on unmolested till the foremost wagon neared the outlet of the defile and the train, two miles long, was exposed, broadside to us, without a chance of extrication, when bang went a Whitworth rifle and brought down the two leading mules of the front team. This, of course, at once stopped the whole train, and the Confederates opened fire upon it with their Enfields along the entire line. Our orders were to kill all the mules. The teamsters at the first alarm sprang behind their wagons for shelter; but seeing soon that no random sport but serious work was on hand, they left their teams to our tender mercies, scrambled up the cliffs, and disappeared. But we paid no attention to them—it was mules we were after, foes, it must be confessed, not very worthy of our prowess at four hundred yards distance, however they might have been at close quarters.

The Enfield rifle is of long range, but not suited for accurate marksmanship, and those who never tried the experiment cannot realize how many chances there are to miss a mule with that arm at four hundred yards. What with our inaccurate shooting and the flouncing and prancing of the poor animals when stung by our bullets, it took us the whole day to finish the job; and indeed, here and there a mule seemed to bear a charmed life and stood in sleepy composure all day untouched, and when the darkness of evening shut out the view, still remained a lonely survivor of hundreds dead. It looked pitiful, this wholesale slaughter of the patient, unresisting brutes. But we reflected that it was far better to kill mules than men—not to say a good deal safer.

About noon a Federal force came down and returned our fire during the rest of the day in a lively style; but we being on the shady side of the river and among the rocks were nearly invisible to our opponents, and they could not seriously hinder our operations. One of our men got hit by uselessly exposing himself. Every participant, no doubt, will always remember that singular and not very pious Sabbath day's work. During the following night the wagons and a few living mules were carried off by the Federals, but of course no more trains could travel that road, and the situation of the army in Chattanooga thus became so much more straitened that without some new resources its commander must have soon relinquished that town.

But just at this crisis, most opportunely for the beleaguered army, General Grant and [Maj. Gen. Joseph] Hooker's Corps appeared upon the scene. By a night attack and surprise, Brown's Ferry, which crossed the river above Raccoon Bend, was seized, while Hooker, marching up the railroad from the west, formed a junction with the forces at that ferry and thus a new line of communication, principally south of the river, was secured for the besieged.

Our brigade in Raccoon Bend had a lively time getting out of there by slipping between the jaws of the two Federal armies that were coming together like a steel trap across the isthmus behind us. But we made the trip by dint of a little bold skirmishing and a good deal of tall walking.

This whole maneuver of Grant and Hooker must have been unexpected by the Confederate commander, for Brown's Ferry was weakly guarded and easily taken, and on the other hand, Hooker's Corps from down the river seemed to come into our presence with the suddenness of apparition. For surely, had his approach been known (if a soldier of minor rank may venture an opinion on such a point), Hooker should have been met by the Confederates and beaten before he arrived in operating distance of the army in the town, which meanwhile might have been kept at bay for a short period by a fraction of the Confederate forces.

The next movement which the Confederate generals did make, however, was an attempt to break the line of junction between Hooker and the Chattanooga army before it became firmly cemented. This attempt was made in the night of October 27 and led to some desperate fighting and a few incidents worth noting. The wagons of Hooker, with some artillery, were packed in camp near the railroad about two miles west of Lookout Mountain and defended by a portion of his troops, while the rest of his men were in position about Brown's Ferry, two miles off. These two parts of his corps were connected only by an indifferent country road which, about the halfway point between, ran for some distance along the base of a very steep little mountain ridge.

[Brig. Gen. Micah] Jenkins' South Carolina Brigade was ordered to make an attack—by surprise, if possible—upon Hooker's aforesaid camp near the railroad. [Brig. Gen. Evander M.] Law's Alabama Brigade, to which the writer belonged, was directed to take up a position on the steep little ridge above mentioned, in a line parallel with the road connecting the two parts of Hooker's Corps and near enough to that road to command it, so we might intercept any reinforcements sent from about the ferry to the aid of the camp when attacked by Jenkins. Only these two brigades were employed on this occasion, for the reason, as was said, that in a night attack large forces are in danger of confusion and mutual collisions; and so, also, each of these brigades was assigned to a separate duty and point of action.

Having made our way with much toil, but in profound silence, across the creek which skirts the western base of Lookout Mountain and through rugged and wooded ravines for about a mile further, the Alabama Brigade reached its allotted position about midnight and formed line along the brow of the ridge, in easy range of the road we were to guard. We utilized the few minutes allowed us in throwing up along our front a breastwork out of old logs and other available materials. It was not more than knee high and looked like a poor job, indeed, but old "Rebs" and "Yanks" both know how much help there is sometimes in works which scientific engineers would laugh at. The old moon in a hazy sky shed a dim ray upon the scene soon to be illuminated by fiercer lights. Suddenly, away to our left, burst out the loud crash of Jenkins' musketry and the wild charging yells of his men. But more quickly than I can write it came the answering boom and shout from Hooker's camp like the roaring of an old lion roused in his lair. Fierce and terrible was the din in this encounter and the night air trembled with "the thunder of the captains and the shouting." Its sublimity was enough to rouse the coldest blood, and the Alabamans stood and listened to it with the impatience of war horses longing to mingle in the fray.

We had not long to wait. In a very few minutes, indeed, the Federal columns from about Brown's Ferry came rushing along the road to aid their comrades at the camp, and as soon as they came in our front a terrific fire was poured down the slope upon them from our whole brigade. At once they halted and turned upon us, charging up the steep hill again and again. Much of our fire probably went over their heads while far down the slope, but when they came near it was deadly, and being breathless with climbing and no doubt disordered by the charge through the woods, our opponents recoiled from the leaden storm which met them and to which, while charging, they could make but small reply.

So they retired to the base of the hill many times, but as many times they came again to the charge, like [the] magnificent American heroes they were. We could hear them, after each repulse, call the rally and reform the line for a fresh onslaught, while we loaded our rifles and fixed our bayonets to receive them. Oh! That such men should ever have met in hostile ranks! Several times the Federal flags were seen within five paces of our line by the flashes of our guns. Once the two lines came into actual hand-to-hand collision with the bayonet at a place a few steps to the right of where I stood. I can never forget the horrid commingling of yells, shouts, shrieks, and imprecations which burst out for a few moments from that spot where cold steel was doing its work, while balls came zipping down the line by the handful as well as from the front. In this crossing of bayonets several men on each side were slain, and among these was Orderly Sergeant Byington, belonging to a company in the 44th Alabama, who fell with a bayonet in his breast, having transfixed his assailant in like manner. In this as well as every other attack so gallantly made upon it that night, the Alabama Brigade succeeded, by strenuous exertions, in holding its ground and repelling its adversaries. We should have been overwhelmed, I suppose, after a while, and perhaps surrounded and captured by the superior forces opposed to us. But after an hour or more of the kind of work I have described—during a lull in the fighting—word came to us that Jenkins' attack had failed of any useful result and that he had retired. Our action being merely subsidiary to his, we also were ordered to withdraw to our camps, which was done without further conflict or danger. Our loss was not very heavy. Our assailants must have suffered severely, but I never learned how much. This night fight of infantry, fierce and persistent as it was and at such close quarters, was one of the most thrilling experiences of the war.

Early in November, Longstreet's Corps, of which we formed a part, left Chattanooga with orders to advance on Knoxville and drive [Maj. Gen. Ambrose E.] Burnside from that town and out of East Tennessee. It must have been expected that Longstreet would do this promptly and return with his corps in time to take a hand in the great conflict which was brewing and which did occur so soon on the heights of Lookout Mountain and Missionary Ridge, with such unfortunate results to the Confederates. What influence the presence of Longstreet's veteran corps might have had on the events of that day, who knows? History has very imperfectly recorded the reasons why he failed to overwhelm Burnside and get back quickly to Chattanooga. Other and better reasons might perhaps be given, even by a soldier of humble rank and limited means of observation like myself, and at some time hereafter I may possibly devote a few sheets of paper to this subject. Suffice it to say now that opportunities were lost on the way to Knoxville (not by Longstreet's fault), which, had they been improved, would have put such a face upon affairs that the town would certainly have been taken at a dash as soon as he arrived there on November 17. But from the appearance of things on his arrival, Longstreet deemed an immediate assault too hazardous, which was afterward, when too late, ascertained to have been a mistake, as the town would have fallen if it had been attacked at once and boldly. Not knowing this, Longstreet sat down to a regular siege, the result of which is known to all. I mention this siege of Knoxville now merely for the purpose of giving a single incident which occurred at it.

Upon the hill on the western or southwestern outskirts of the town stood Fort Sanders, flanked by strong earthworks, forming part of the continuous line of defenses around the place. Our besieging lines of pickets and rifle pits were pushed forward closer to the defense works, from time to time, as was found practicable. It so happened that about November 20, the writer, commanding the 4th Alabama Regiment, was in charge of the picket line fronting the western face of Fort Sanders and the adjoining earthworks. During the night we were ordered to move our line up and dig rifle pits much in advance of our former position and within about three hundred yards of the fort and its flanking works. By daylight we had a large number of rude, square holes dug waist deep in the ground (the best we could do with the time and tools we had) in a line running parallel in the main to the face of the Federal works, but, nevertheless, curved considerably forward at the left and concealed in that part by shrubbery. These pits were occupied by the men of one battalion of the 4th Alabama, while the other battalion was placed in reserve in a piece of woods a little to the rear. The ground in front of our new pits, especially on the right of our line, was an open, smooth lawn, sloping upward (to the Federal works) at a considerable angle of inclination.

As soon as daylight revealed to the Federals our new line of rifle pits, suddenly we beheld springing over their earthworks and dashing impetuously down the slope towards us a body of men about two hundred strong, which we soon afterwards found was the 2nd Michigan Regiment, led by Major [Cornelius] Byington and sent to dislodge us from our new position. I hurried up in a moment the reserve battalion of the 4th Alabama to reinforce the men in the pits. And then ensued for a few minutes one of the fiercest and deadliest combats of the war. These two veteran regiments, both having come to the field at the first sound of the tocsin, as their names show (2nd Michigan and 4th Alabama), thinned now by hard service and many battles to about two hundred men each, but every man of them utterly fearless, splendidly daring and knowing all about war, grappled with each other as in a death grip. If courage, such as makes an old soldier's hair stand on end to think of, could have won against equal courage and superior position, the gallant Michigan men would have triumphed. But the Alabamians had the advantage of shelter in their pits, which, shallow as they were, afforded much protection. It so fell out, too, that the curve in this line of pits on the left proved of great service to us, for as our assailants charged in line parallel to and square against our right, they were enfiladed with terrible effect by the fire from our pits on the left, which, hidden by bushes, had not been noticed. This circumstance quickly decided the contest in our favor. Many having fallen or been captured, a remnant only got back to their works, some bearing on their shoulders wounded comrades. As it looked too cruel to fire on these, the Alabamians were ordered not to fire on anyone who was carrying a wounded man, and the Michigan men, hearing this order, shrewdly availed themselves of its protection by shouldering wounded comrades, so that several made good their escape by this means. But the grassy slope remained thickly strewn with the dead and wounded. Alas! For the high hearts that were stilled there forever.

Major Byington displayed a heroism worthy of the leader of such men or of any men. He came in, sword in hand, in front of his line, exhorting them to follow him to victory and rushed to the very brink of our rifle pits, where he fell desperately wounded within a few feet of me. The fight being quickly over, I had him carried back to the little piece of woods in our rear and made as comfortable as possible till he could be sent to the hospital. His leg was broken and he was shot also in the side, but bad as those wounds were he seemed to suffer little pain. While lying there he inquired the name of my regiment, and on being informed, said quickly: "I have, or had lately, a brother in your brigade—Orderly Sergeant Byington, of the 44th Alabama." How he knew so well the brigade of his brother and the regiments composing it, I did not think to ask and do not know. Said he: "My brother is a Northern man by birth, but went South some time ago and became a 'secesh' and he is now in your brigade," and he added that he would like much to see him, and begged me to send for him. The reader may imagine how it pained me to have to tell him that his brother of the 44th Alabama had been killed three weeks before in the night fight near Chattanooga, under the circumstances already related.

If any surviving relative of Major Byington shall read this sketch, I can say for their consolation that every possible kindness was shown that gallant gentleman and that he bore the double pain of his wounds and sad bereavement with the fortitude of a brave soldier and Christian philosopher. He survived but a few days, and when his wounds proved mortal and he was no more, no heart mourned over him more sincerely than that of the foeman who met him in his last battle. Let me add, alas, that no better or braver soldier than Sergeant Byington, of the 44th Alabama, ever served in the Confederate army. Peace to the ashes of those two noble brothers who fell on opposite sides!

Part Four

The War in 1864

The Battle of the Wilderness: The Fourth Alabama in the Slaughter Pen

PINCKNEY D. BOWLES,
COLONEL, 4TH ALABAMA REGIMENT AND BREVET BRIGADIER GENERAL, C.S.A.

Philadelphia *Weekly Times* 8, no. 33, October 3, 1884

We had come out of our winter quarters in East Tennessee and by easy stages on cars and marches reached Gordonsville, at the junction of the Virginia Central and Alexandria Railroads. We there spent several days in regimental and brigade drill. In the meantime the men had received new uniforms, and our ranks had been doubled by the late furloughed men coming in. General [Robert F.] Hoke had just captured Plymouth, N.C., and a good supply of rations had been sent to us fresh from Uncle Sam's commissariat. May 3 the sun rose clear and after inspection in the morning the brigade was ordered out for drill, which lasted something over one hour, when we were marched back to camp. It being a warm day, both officers and men had disrobed themselves, when to our surprise orders came to prepare three days' rations and be ready to march in one hour. A part of the rations was sixty rounds of cartridges.

We left Gordonsville about 3 P.M., not knowing in the least in what direction we were to go. But after marching out and halting in the edge of a large plain, we saw that the whole corps was in motion. General [James P.] Longstreet and staff soon came in sight across the field and slowly rode down the road leading in the direction of Spotsylvania, which we afterwards found was called the Catharpin road. It was night before we came to the main line or road, and only went a short distance further before we bivouacked. The fourth was spent in going at a slow pace in the same direction, and at night we bivouacked in a grove near the road we had marched during the day. We quit camp at sunrise the next morning and still

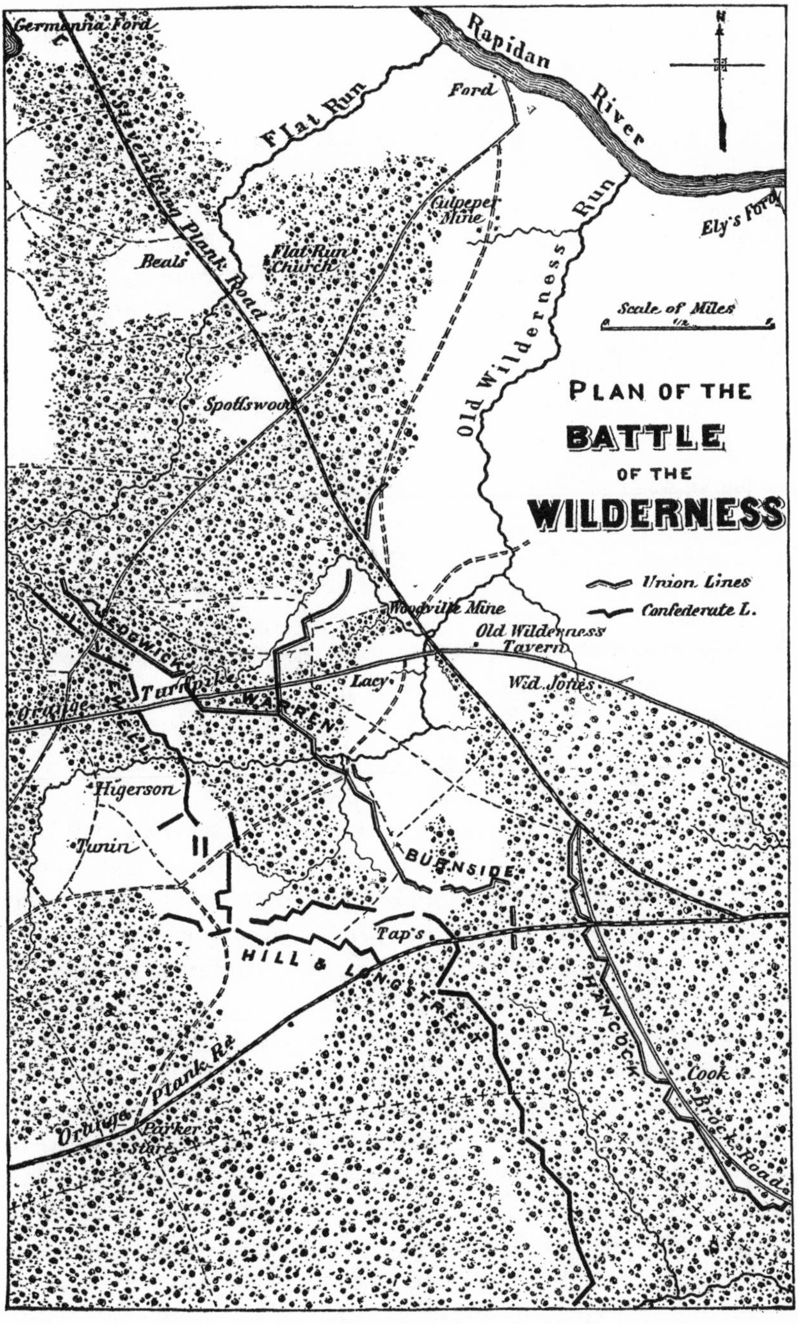

Plan of the battle of the Wilderness

(JOHNSON, *CAMPFIRE AND BATTLEFIELD*)

marched slowly as on the day before, until about 1 P.M., when we heard distant artillery firing in our front, which seemed to grow nearer as we continued to advance.

After going a few miles further we met a squad of about thirty Yankee prisoners. In the squad was a captured colonel. From the officer in charge of those prisoners we learned that a brigade of Federal cavalry had come into our lines and that our cavalry was in hot pursuit. Every few hundred yards we would pass a house with from two to five wounded or dead Federal soldiers. We also passed a squad of Confederates digging a grave to bury one of their comrades, who, they said, had only joined them that morning and was killed in the first charge.

It was about this time that the news was passed down the line that General [Ambrose P.] Hill was at that time engaged in a pitched battle with General Grant in the Wilderness. Further on we learned that Hill had driven the Federals several miles and had taken six thousand prisoners. This caused loud cheers for Hill and seemed to revive the spirits of the tired men, who marched on as if they had been imbued with new life. We halted about 10:00 P.M. and slept until 2:00 A.M. in the morning of the sixth, when we were awakened by the sweet notes of the Palmetto Sharpshooter's Band serenading General [Micah] Jenkins. I never could find out why they should have chosen that inopportune hour for music, unless they had some kind of a presentiment that it would be the last time they would ever have the chance, as he was killed the same day.

The band was cheered, and in a few minutes orders came to break camp, and we continued our march down the Catharpin road, which was nearly parallel with the Wilderness plank road. At this point every few minutes orders came to quicken our steps, and we were not long in coming in full hearing of Hill's musketry on our left front. After going in this direction for a mile or two our head of column diverged to the left. I saw that we were making a bee line for the heavy firing, when a dashing courier came in sight, with orders for me to bring the command up at double-quick. So on we went over dew-wet fields, across branches and creeks, until our proximity to the firing suggested that we, too, had better prepare for action. So the column was halted and ordered to load, and then march on to the plank road.

The command had to pass through Hill's field hospital, where we saw hundreds of men who had been wounded the night before and that morning, and the reader may imagine that those hideous sights, fractured limbs and bloody clothing, did not add much to our courage. At this time there was also a continuous stream of wounded meeting us as we advanced, and each one was eagerly questioned as to how the fight was progressing. If it was a private who was questioned he would say: "They are sorter driving us back." If it was an officer he would say: "Well, it's about a stand on both sides." We continued to move, expecting every moment to be hotly engaged, while the men were busy destroying letters and playing cards. Many of the former were tender missives from loved ones far away, which they determined should not run any risk of falling into the hands of either friend or foe. So in a very short time the line of march was strewn with bits of paper.

The increased nearness of the firing and the long faces of the wounded were having a dampening influence upon "Old Bull's" (General Longstreet's) boys, but the change was not long in coming. We soon met a private holding up his wounded hand with a smile on his face, who almost hallooed it out: "Longstreet's boys are driving them like sheep." Then came such an expression of joy to the men's faces that I could see it at once. The whole line moved off at a quick step and soon passed out of the thick woods into the edge of an old field to the left of the plank road. Here we saw signs of desperate fighting all around.

General [Robert E.] Lee was riding his horse up and down the column and calling out to the men: "Go on my brave Alabamians, and drive them back." This is the memorable time at which it is said he offered to lead [Lt. Gen. John B.] Hood's old Texas Brigade in person, but was prevented by some of the 5th Texas taking his horse by the bridle and leading him to the rear against the protest of the general. At this time the 5th Alabama Regiment, under the command of the gallant [William C.] Oates, present member of Congress from the Third Alabama district, was just in my front, and there was a corpulent captain (the old hero, Captain Hatcher) of that regiment some fifteen paces in the rear of his company and trying to get up at a good run, and when he passed General Lee the latter called out: "Go on, my brave Alabama captain, and drive them back!" I must confess that this was one of the times that I thought things were getting a little squally.

After passing General Lee something over two hundred yards we came to the crest of the hill, where we were halted and ordered to form line right forward. By the time this was done General [Charles W.] Field came down the line in person and called out to me to throw forward a good skirmish line and at the word "advance" to place the right of my regiment on the plank road and keep it there. During this time wounded Texans were coming out of the wood, while my skirmishers were halted at the edge of the dense undergrowth, which was so thick that you could not see ten feet in front of you. Soon the whole line was ordered to advance. The

4th Alabama went forward at a double-quick, my right still resting on the plank road, and as my skirmish line was fired upon before they had gone fifty steps in the wood, they halted until my main line came up.

By this time the first or advance line of the enemy opened fire on us, and without a halt I ordered a charge, which was responded to by the whole line. On advancing some seventy-five or a hundred yards we came upon a breastwork, which consisted of logs piled up here and there sufficiently arranged to satisfy me that the enemy had just reached it and here hastily erecting it from logs lying indiscriminately in the woods. At the time of reaching this point we could see a few retreating Federals in front. So I ordered the command to lie down and sent forward a few videttes, who kept firing for some time only a short distance in my front. The 47th Alabama was supporting me on the left and was under my supervision, the colonel being absent. I knew these were Confederate troops on the right of the plank road by the heavy firing, and that they were well up with their portion of the line. For a while, then, these few scattered logs constituted my outer line.

Soon the Federals began firing and driving in my scouts, while they slowly advanced. When they came in sight I ordered my command to fire, which stopped the onward movement for a short time. Soon, however, the enemy began to advance the second time and in larger numbers than before, and as they advanced they fired very low, so that their shots were having a very perceptible effect on my line. I then ordered a charge over our low works, which was obeyed with alacrity, and the column continued to advance until we came to their second line of works, which was well built and some three feet high, the Federals retiring slowly as we came up. The Confederates at once took a sheltered position behind the same and opened a fire to the front, which the enemy slowly returned.

After remaining in this position some ten or fifteen minutes I discovered by the balls coming from the right of the plank road that we had passed beyond our supports and were receiving a flank fire. I discovered, also, that the 47th Alabama had fallen back in a few minutes after we had reached the second line of the enemy's defenses. It was also reported that a large body of Federals was on our left. So I at once ordered the command to fall back to our first line. The enemy saw all this immediately and began to shower their leaden hail upon us just as we began the retrograde move, but the retreat was made in good order and continued until we reached our first line of works, when we turned and opened fire upon their advancing lines. My wounded were then taken to the rear.

In the meantime, the enemy were continuing to advance through the thick underbrush until they came within about thirty yards of my line, when I ordered a second charge, and again the hillsides echoed to the valleys the "Rebel yell," and for the second time the Federals were driven beyond their second line of works. At this time the 20th Georgia came up and took position on my right, but parallel and facing the plank road. The loud commands of the Federal officers could be heard above the din of the musketry. It was a terrible moment. The Union lines began another advance. On they came, again and again, to meet a fearful slaughter and to be hurled back upon their supports with terrible loss, while their ranks were decimated at every advance.

During this time a Federal officer came dashing up almost to my right. Whether this was a mere act of bravado or because he could not manage his horse I do not know, but just as he reached the opening on the plank road and was near a large tree, one of the men in my command shot him off his horse. General [James S.] Wadsworth was found mortally wounded at this point that night after the fight and properly cared for by the direction of General Lee.

We discovered soon that we were opposed at this point by a valorous foe—one every way worthy of our steel. They continued their advance, firing as they came, while my men were falling by the dozens before their well-directed aim. It was here that Major [William M.] Robbins (late Con-

Wadsworth's division in action in the Wilderness (LIBRARY OF CONGRESS)

gressman from the Seventh North Carolina district) was by my side and my adjutant, [Robert T.] Coles, called out that Major Robbins was dead. Turning around I saw that the major had fallen upon his face. On being turned over he opened his eyes and asked to be taken to the rear, but I well knew that to grant his request was to have two or three men riddled with bullets, and it was discovered that the major only had a severe but not dangerous scalp wound.

The Georgians during the time had retreated back to our first line, and for some cause the enemy had ceased to fire, so I took advantage of the brief lull in hostilities to get the wounded off the field and at the same time ordered a retreat to our first line. When we began to fall back the Federals fired several volleys after us, but did not follow. On reforming I found that my command had suffered terribly. The gallant Captain Baylus Brown, of Company B, and his no less heroic comrade, Lieutenant Coonsy, were among the killed; Lieutenant J. S. Stearnes, of Company E, and Major Robbins were wounded. The enemy did not follow and seemed to be satisfied. So, after forming and waiting for some time, General Field came up and ordered me to march my regiment by the left flank, while [Gen. Robert E.] Rodes' Alabama Brigade took our old position on the plank road. My command moved to where I found the remainder of the Alabama troops building works. We assisted at this work until about 3 P.M.

For some time no enemy appeared in our front, but very heavy firing could be heard on both our right and left most of the time. At this time Colonel [William F.] Perry, of the 44th Alabama Regiment, was commanding the brigade and ordered the command to advance by regiments in echelon—the 4th, being on the right, was naturally in the rear some distance. This move was to support Brigadier General Perry's Florida Brigade, which was being hard pushed in our front. Our left front did not advance very far before they came up with the Floridians, who were retreating slowly. We were soon hotly engaged and had arrived just in time to prevent a disaster on that part of the field, as General Perry was certainly outnumbered by the Federals. The general and some of his color-bearers had just passed around my right, calling out that they were out of ammunition.

There were two or three clay banks or roots of trees that had been torn up by the wind in my front, behind which two or three Floridians were stationed and firing at the enemy at a distance of not more than forty steps. Finally they left this ambush and had not gone more than a few steps when one of them fell, shot in the leg. His comrade deliberately walked back, squatted down, and the wounded man put his arms around his neck while he walked off with him before the whole Federal line, and if a single hostile shot was aimed at the two it passed wide of its mark and the wounded man was carried in safety from the field. It was one of the most heroic acts I ever witnessed.

Here for a short time we were as hotly engaged as we had been at an earlier hour in the day. Every shot from the Federal lines seemed to tell on my already badly thinned ranks. The air was full of leaden hail, and why the whole of my line was not swept away seems a miracle. I had determined, however, to breast the storm until I saw one regiment of the brigade on the left had marched to the rear, leaving a gap in the line to which the Federals were moving forward to occupy and thus cut off our retreat.

It was then stay and be captured or go. We went. As soon as we had ceased firing the line in my immediate front charged. We moved off to the right, the enemy following rapidly and calling out at every breath: "Halt! Halt! Halt!" Their guns were either empty or their supply of cartridges was exhausted, as they fired only a few shots at our retreating lines. Looking back I saw a Federal officer with a long duster on and not less than one hundred sergeants and corporals, each one trying to capture a prisoner, for which they were promoted, as will be seen in my description of Spotsylvania hereafter.

We soon came out of the wood and marched slowly up the hill in an old field, some three hundred yards from where we had formed in the morning. After forming with the remainder of the brigade in line, with the right front to the enemy, I went over to talk to Colonel Oates. He pointed out to me one of his men who was lying down by a Federal soldier and said: "You see that fellow over there by that wounded Yankee? Well, he has just brought him out of the woods on his back so as to get his boots as soon as he dies." Just about this time we heard three loud huzzas from the Federals in our front, but their joy was soon turned to grief by General [Joseph R.] Davis' Mississippi Brigade firing into them from the rear, when off they went like frightened sheep to the right, throwing away guns, hats, blankets, and knapsacks by the hundreds.

We then marched over the same ground from which we had been driven only a short time before and took a position several hundred yards in front and remained until night awaiting the enemy, who failed to advance again. After dark we marched by the right flank across the plank road and took up a position about four hundred yards to the right and spent the night in building log works. The time passed quietly until morning, when I walked over the field and on the right of the plank road, where General [Lafayette] McLaws' Brigade had been engaged the previous day. I stepped seventy yards square in two or three paces and counted ten dead Federals to one dead Confederate, and on the left where our brigade had been engaged I counted six dead Federals to one Confederate. I also counted twenty-seven bullet marks on one small hickory bush. On the morning before the fight it was impossible to see twenty yards in any one direction, but then I could see for two hundred yards and leap my horse with ease.

The 4th Alabama went in on the morning of May 6 with two hundred muskets and seventeen commissioned officers. During the day ninety men and ten officers were disabled, among the number Captain James Brown, Company I, and Lieutenants Jones and [William O.] Newsome, and others whose names I do not remember, but I know that many a gallant soul on both sides went out on that awful day.

Fighting Under Forrest at the Battle of Brice's Crossroads

John W. Morton,
Captain, Chief of Artillery, Forrest's Cavalry

Philadelphia *Weekly Times* 7, no. 30, September 15, 1883

Headquarters Forrest's Cavalry,
Tupelo, Miss., May 29, 1864

General Order No. 21.

Captain Morton, Chief of Artillery, will hold the batteries ready to move to-morrow morning with five days' rations, cooked, and three days forage prepared. He will see that he is supplied with three hundred rounds of ammunition to the piece. By order of Brigadier General Crowder, A.A.G.

[Lt. Gen. Nathan B.] Forrest being temporarily absent, the order just noted put Forrest's Cavalry on the march for North Alabama to meet a hostile raid threatening that region. After three days' march, on reaching Russellville, a dispatch from Lt. Gen. Stephen D. Lee recalled the force to Tupelo, to meet a heavy column moving out from Memphis. We reached Tupelo on the evening of June 5, having marched and counter-marched one hundred and fifty miles.

This countermarch to Tupelo was one of the most trying of the war. [Capt. John W.] Morton's Battery had just traveled the breadth of the State of Mississippi, having marched from Columbus across to West's Station and returned to Tupelo, a distance of 225 miles. It had rained incessantly for more than a week, the sloughs and low grounds were filled with water and mud, and it seemed that the artillery could not possibly pass back over the roads, so cut up by the repeated passages of Forrest's Cavalry and trains. On reaching Tobytuby Bottom the water was found to be from one foot to three feet deep over the road for more than a mile. The rails and poles forming the road were floating in many places. The cavalry passed with great difficulty. General Forrest, anticipating trouble in getting the artillery across, sent a courier back to Morton to know if it was possible to bring the artillery over. Morton said, "Tell the General we are following him." The cannoneers waded in water and mud waist deep very often. A man would press on either end of a floating rail to hold it down until the gun carriage could pass over, the cavalry carrying the ammunition in their arms.

Late in the night Tupelo was reached, but only to halt and feed, when the march to Boonville was ordered, as trusty scouts had reported the enemy, some 13,000 strong—infantry, cavalry, and artillery—at or near Salem, and moving in the direction of Baldwyn. The streams brim-full were unfordable, bridges generally swept away, and the roads in that part of the country had not improved on the roads just passed in returning from Alabama. After a most necessarily fatiguing march to both men and horses, we reached Boonville on the eighth.

Boonville was a small station town on the Mobile and Ohio Railroad, containing, perhaps, three or four groceries and as many private residences. Looking in any direction the eye could rest on nothing but dark forests and tangled underbrush, an old dry sedge field excepted, a short distance west of the railroad, where, on the ninth, two deserters found in the enemy's ranks knelt down in front of their newly-made graves and received their reward. A third was pardoned on account of his extreme youth.

In the afternoon of the ninth we received orders to draw three days' rations and hold the artillery ready to move at daylight the next morning. Various were the conjectures as to the probability of an engagement. [Brig. Gen. James R.] Chalmers had been ordered with [Col. Robert] McCulloch's and [Col. James. J.] Neely's Brigades and [Lt. Edwin S.] Walton's Battery to Monte Vallo, Alabama, to protect the iron works in that region. [Col. William A.] Johnson's Brigade had been ordered from Cherokee, on the Memphis and Charleston Railroad, across to Rienzi, eight miles north of Boonville, where [Col. Tyree H.] Bell's Brigade camped the night of the ninth. [Col. Edmund] Rucker, meanwhile, had been ordered from Oxford, Mississippi, and after striking the Federal cavalry at New Albany and driving them for some distance, joined Forrest at Boonville on the ninth. [Col. Hylan B.] Lyon's Brigade was bivouacked at Boonville on the night of the ninth, which gave Forrest the following force, brought into action the next day:

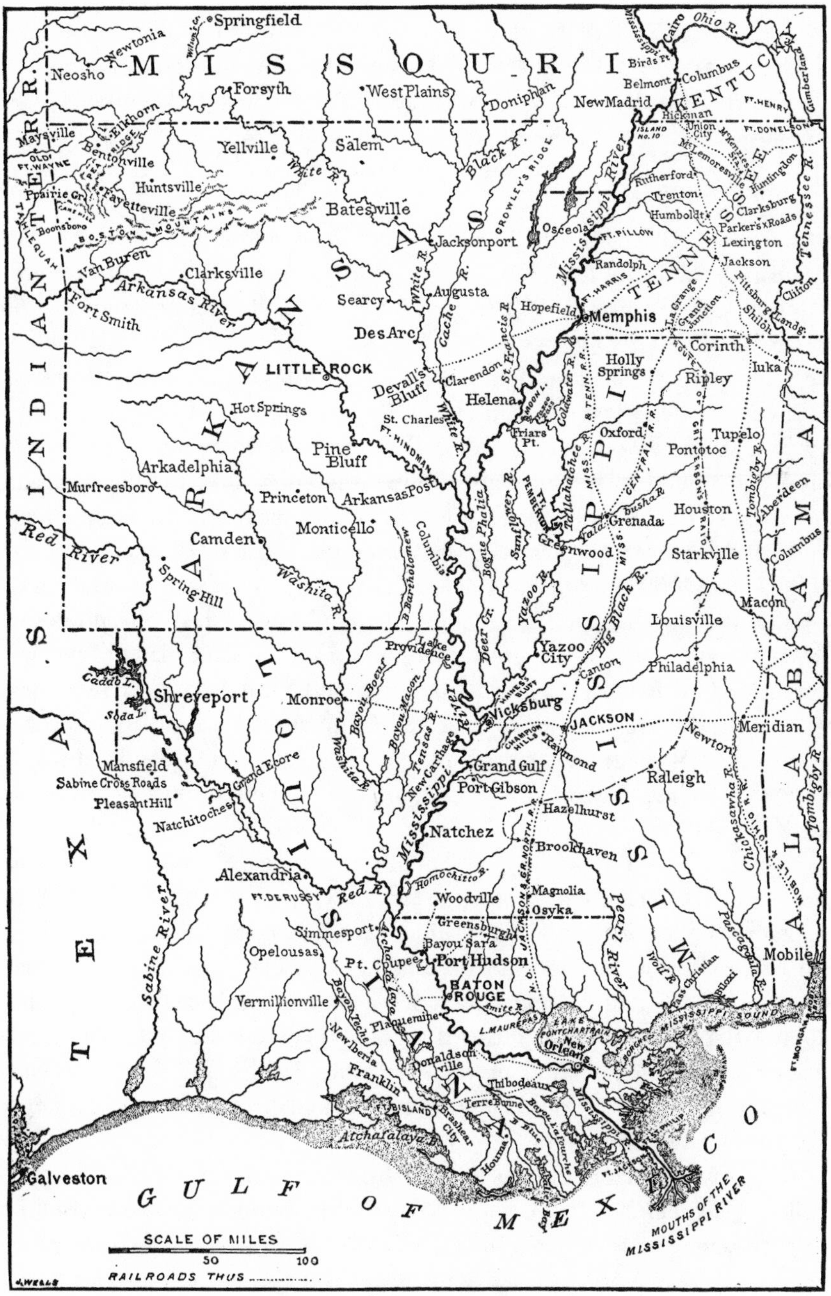

Campaigns of the Mississippi Valley

(*CENTURY MAGAZINE*)

Bell's Brigade: [Col. Clark R.] Barteau, [Col. A. N.] Wilson, [Col. John F.] Newsom and [Col. Robert M.] Russell's Regiments, 950 rank and file.

Lyon's Brigade: 3rd, 7th, 8th and 12th Kentucky Regiments, 800 strong.

Rucker's Brigade: 18th and 19th Mississippi and 7th Tennessee regiments, 700 strong.

Johnson's Brigade: 4th Alabama Regiment, and [Lt. Col. F. M. W.] Moreland's, Williams' and Warren's Battalions, 500 strong; Forrest's escort and Gartrell's Company, 100 strong; Morton's and Rice's Batteries, 165 strong. Total, 3,215.

Reliable scouts had brought information to the Confederate generals at Boonville that the Federals had passed Ripley and were moving on Guntown, a small station twenty-five miles south of Boonville. The Federal force was now estimated at eight thousand infantry, four thousand cavalry and six batteries. A conference was held at Boonville on the night of the ninth, at which were present Generals S. D. Lee, Forrest, Rucker and Lyon and Captain Morton. After discussing the probable direction of the Federal column and the disparity in numbers of the Confederates concentrated at Boonville, and they [being] greatly fatigued from constant marching, it was determined to fall back toward Okolona, and with Chalmers, who had been ordered there and troops expected from Mobile, Meridian and other points below, a successful stand could be made at Prairie Mound, a strong point for defense, just on the border of the prairie country, a few miles north of Okolona.

General Lee ordered all the supplies and baggage train, with Thrall's and Ferrill's Batteries, sent southward by rail with all possible haste. He proceeded in the like direction and manner the night of the ninth, while General Forrest was ordered to move with the available command mentioned westward of the railroad and pass south between the Federal column and Guntown. No engagement was anticipated by General Lee short of Prairie Mound, but this little band of veteran cavalry well knew that they, with Forrest at their head, could never pass in close proximity to the enemy without "feeling him a little."

At early dawn on the tenth Lyon took the advance, with Morton's artillery close behind, Rucker and Johnson following. Meanwhile, Bell, as we have stated, at Rienzi, eight miles further north, was ordered to move up at a trot. The roads, soaked with water from recent continuous heavy rains and so much cut up by the previous passage of cavalry and trains, greatly retarded the progress of the artillery, so that Rucker and Johnson soon passed us. On reaching Old Carrollville five miles northeast of Brice's

Cross Roads, heavy firing could be heard just on ahead. Forrest, as was his custom, had passed to the front of the entire column with his escort.

He had, however, ordered Lt. [Robert J.] Black, a dashing young officer, temporarily assigned to his staff, to take a detachment of men from the 7th Tennessee Cavalry and move forward and develop the enemy. Black soon reported that he had met the advance of the Federal cavalry one and a half miles from Brice's Cross Roads and there was skirmishing with them. General Forrest ordered Lyon to press forward with his brigade. A courier hastening back to the artillery said, "General Forrest says, 'Tell Captain Morton to fetch up the artillery at a gallop.'" Lyon in the meantime had reached the enemy's outposts, dismounted his brigade and thrown it into line and had warmly opposed a strong line of infantry or dismounted cavalry, which, after stubborn resistance, had been driven back to within half a mile of Brice's Cross Roads.

Lyon was now ordered to strengthen his position, which was on the Baldwyn and Pontotoc road, by making fortifications of rails, logs, and such other material as presented themselves, Johnson being on his right and Rucker on his left. A heavy skirmish was kept up until about twelve o'clock, when [Brig. Gen. Abraham] Buford arrived with Bell's Brigade. General Buford says that he and General Forrest held a short conference. Forrest asked him, "What do you think of the situation of the two armies, General?" "Our troops are nearly all up," Buford replied, "the artillery will soon reach us; the enemy is scattered; the only thing for us to do is to fight and damn quick!"

General Forrest directed General Buford to open vigorously when he heard Bell on the left, and taking with him his escort and Bell's Brigade, moved rapidly around southeastward to the Guntown-Ripley road. He formed Wilson's and Russell's Regiments on the right of the road, extending to Rucker's left and placed Newsom's Regiment on the left of the road; [Col. William L.] Duff's Regiment, of Rucker's Brigade, was placed on the left of Newsom; Captain H. A. Tyler, commanding Company A, 12th Kentucky, was ordered by Lyon and subsequently by Forrest to take his company, with Company C, 7th Kentucky and keep mounted on the extreme left of the line. The escort, under Captain Jackson, moved around the extreme left of the line and on striking the Baldwyn and Pontotoc road about two miles south of the crossroads had a sharp skirmish and pressed the enemy's cavalry back to where Tishimingo Creek crosses that road; here it was joined by Captain Gartrell's Georgia Company and a Kentucky company. By mutual agreement Captain Jackson, of the escort, was placed in command of the three companies and Lt. George L. Cowan in command

"Our cannoneers were greatly enlivened" (HARPER'S NEW MONTHLY MAGAZINE)

of the escort. Meanwhile General Buford had ordered Barteau's 2nd Tennessee Cavalry to move across the country and gain the Federal rear and if possible destroy their trains and then strike them in flank.

Bell now opening, a roar was heard along the entire line. This continuous peal of musketry was singularly affecting, as we put forward every effort to speed the batteries along over the swollen streams and rugged roads. Orders were continually arriving to stimulate a gait almost up to the gallop. Our cannoneers were greatly enlivened and seemed to realize the importance of their presence in the unequal contest now raging with doubtful results in the front. Soon the greeting of the horse holders, ambulance drivers, and "Company Q," with an unencumbered road for our passage, clearly showed that we were rapidly approaching the line of battle. Maj. [Charles W.] Anderson, of Forrest's staff, dashed down towards us and directed Morton to place his artillery in an open field to the right of the road, just in rear of Lyon's position. This was quickly done, when a concentrated fire was plied with spirit and execution upon the Federal infantry and artillery confronting Rucker and Lyon.

This position was reached by the artillery about 1:00 P.M. A continuous fire with shell and solid shot was kept up for half an hour. General Buford says he was often asked by officers and men in passing down his lines if those were our guns they heard. When answered, "Yes, don't you hear them?" a wild yell of confidence would go up from the ragged Confederates. The entire line was now hotly engaged and pressing forward. Lyon had already taken the offensive and gallantly drove the enemy for three hundred yards to the edge of an old field, where they had thrown up temporary works. Johnson's Brigade, under the intrepid Colonel W. A. Johnson, had held its position against great odds. Rucker, with his characteristic courage and valor, led his Tennesseans and Mississippians, breasting the fire of rifles and artillery that swept the bare field over which they advanced and established his line within half a mile of the crossroads. Bell on the left was sorely pressed and at one time was flanked and compelled to fall back, but, rallying his valiant troopers with pistol in hand, drove back the enemy and held his ground on a line with Rucker.

It was at this critical moment an officer of Bell's staff dashed up to General Forrest, very much excited and said, "General Forrest, the enemy flanked us and are now in our rear. What shall be done?" Forrest, turning in his saddle, very coolly replied, "We'll whip these in our front and then turn around, and won't we be in their rear? And then we'll whip them fellows!" pointing in the direction of the force said to be in his rear. Jackson and Tyler, charging on the extreme left, drove back two colored regiments of infantry upon their main line at the crossroads. In this charge the gallant Captain Tyler was severely wounded.

Meanwhile the Federals, with desperation, hurled a double line of battle, with the four guns at Brice's house concentrated upon Rucker and Bell, which for a moment seemed to stagger and make them waver. In this terrible onslaught the accomplished adjutant, Lieutenant W. S. Pope, of the 7th Tennessee, was killed and a third of his regiment was killed and wounded. Soon another charge was sounded. Lt. Tully Brown was ordered, with his section of 3-inch rifles, close on the front at the Porter house, from which position he hurled a thousand pounds of cold iron into their stubborn lines. A section of 12-pounder howitzers, under Lieutenant B. F. Haller, pressed still further to the front and within a stone's throw almost of the enemy's line. Mayson's section of 3-inch rifles were quickly placed in line with Haller's. Just then, General Buford, riding up and seeing no support to the artillery, called General Forrest's attention to the fact, when Forrest remarked, "Support, hell; let it support itself; all the damn Yankees in the country can't take it."

Now rose the regular incessant volleys of musketry and artillery. The lines in many places were not over thirty paces apart and pistols were freely used. The smoke of battle almost hid the combatants. The underbrush and dense blackjack thickets impeded the advance of the dismounted cavalry as the awful musketry fire blazed and gushed in the face of these gallant men. Every tree and brush was barked or cut to the ground by this hail of deadly missiles. It was here the accomplished and gallant William H. Porter, brother of Maj. Thomas K. and Governnor James D. Porter, fell mortally wounded. This promising young officer had not attained his manhood. He was a cadet in the regular Confederate States Army and had been ordered to report to General Bell, who assigned him to duty as A.D.C. Captain J. L. Bell, General Bell's assistant inspector general, had just been killed from his horse and almost at the same moment young Porter lost his own horse and just mounted Captain Bell's when he received the fatal shot. Lt. Isaac Bell, aide-de-camp of Bell's staff, was severely wounded. Capt. Ab Hunt, a mere boy, who commanded Bell's escort, rendered most efficient service at this critical juncture and Maj. Tom Allison, the fighting quartermaster of Bell's Brigade, was constantly by the side of his fearless commander and in this terrible loss in staff officers his presence was most opportune.

Like a prairie on fire the battle raged and the volleying thunder can be likened in my mind to nothing else than the fire of [Maj. Gen. Patrick R.] Cleburne's Division at Chickamauga, on that terrible Saturday at dusk. At length the enemy's lines wavered. Haller and Mayson pressed their guns by hand to within a short distance of Brice's house, firing as they advanced. Bell, Lyon and Rucker now closed in on the crossroads and the Federals gave way in disorder, abandoning three guns near Brice's house. [Brig. Gen. Samuel D.] Sturgis in his official report of the fight says, "We had four pieces of artillery at the crossroads. . . . Finding our troops were being hotly pressed, I ordered one section to open on the enemy's reserves. The enemy's artillery soon replied and with great accuracy, every shell bursting over and in the immediate vicinity of our guns." A shell from one of the

Confederate guns struck the table on Brice's porch, which was used by General Sturgis, stunning that officer.

Lieutenant Brown, having refilled his ammunition chests, dashed forward with his section, and as Sergeant Brady caught a glimpse of one of the captured guns—a three-inch rifle Rodman—he ordered his old iron piece unlimbered, limbered up the captured gun, and pressed it forward into action. This completed Morton's Battery with three-inch steel rifled Rodman guns, all captured from the enemy. One was captured at Lexington in West Tennessee, two at Chickamauga, and this one at the crossroads, and poured a torrent of shell and double-shotted canister upon the fleeing enemy as they huddled infantry, cavalry, wagons, and ambulances in an almost inextricable coil in the valley approaching Tishomingo Creek.

Forrest's ignorance of artillery drill and a well-known trait were shown here. He was always greatly displeased at seeing anyone turn his back upon the enemy during an engagement. When going into action at the crossroads the command, "Action, front!" was given the gun was unlimbered, pointing to the front. The limber was moved rapidly to its position in rear of the gun. When the general saw the limber moving to the rear he drew his sword and started for the drivers, yelling out, "Where in the hell are you going with that little caisson?" and it was only the prompt facing to the front again that saved their scalps.

Lt. Tully Brown, pressing his section down the road by hand as he advanced, soon silenced the Federal battery on the hill at Brice's Quarter. Over 800 Federal and 640 Confederates fell dead and wounded within a short radius from Brice's house. Here Corporal C. R. Temple was wounded and Jimmie Moran, a lead driver of Brown's guns, although shot through the arm and ordered to the rear said, "No, captain, I'll stay with you as long as I can sit up," and right nobly did he drive his gun team throughout the fight, with one hand in a sling, showing his fortitude and bravery. It affords me pleasure to testify to the uniformly good conduct in the camp and on the march and heroic bravery on every battlefield of this gallant young soldier. At Dr. Charlton's, a few miles from Nashville, Jimmie now sleeps his last sleep in a flower garden, with the ivy and jessamine covering his grave. When [Lt. Gen. John B.] Hood was investing Nashville we attacked a blockhouse on Mill Creek and having several cannoneers wounded, Jimmie, with his accustomed promptitude and valor, turning his gun team over to the next driver, came forward to one of the guns and while standing with lanyard in hand ready to fire the piece, was shot through the heart and instantly killed.

Johnson, pressing his brigade forward upon the enemy's position at Brice's Quarter, with Lyon supporting the artillery in the road below Brice's house, the position was soon captured with many prisoners and three pieces of artillery. Haller's and Mayson's sections were moved up at a gallop and established on the hill at Brice's Quarter and opened a destructive fire with double-shotted canister upon the enemy's fleeing columns and wagon trains. The bridge over Tishomingo Creek, still standing, was blocked up with wagons, some of whose teams had been killed. Finding the bridge thus obstructed the enemy rushed wildly into the creek, and as they emerged from the water on the opposite bank in an open field, our artillery played upon them for half a mile, killing and disabling large numbers. Forrest's escort, under the dashing Lieutenant Cowan, having become detached in the meantime, had pressed around to the west side of the creek and south of the Ripley Road and here made one of its characteristic charges across an open field near the gin house, upon the enemy's wagon train, capturing several wagons.

Lieutenant Cowan, in a letter to me says, "Just at this moment, your battery, having gained an elevated point and mistaking us for the enemy's reinforcements, opened fire on us, and I can assure you your range was good. One of your shells took off the rear end of one of the wagons in our possession, but General Forrest, recognizing his own colors through his field glasses, soon changed your fire from us to the enemy; this was a great relief, as your fire worried us more than that of the enemy."

Meanwhile Barteau was not idle. He had moved his regiment, as we have stated, across to get in the enemy's rear and in his own language says, "I took my regiment across the country westward, to reach the Ripley road, on which the enemy was moving, and being delayed somewhat in passing through a swampy bottom I did not reach that road, at Lyon's gin, three miles from Brice's Cross Roads, until probably 1:00 P.M. I then learned that the last of the Federal regiments, with all their train, had passed by rapid march and as there was now a lull in the engagement (for I had been hearing sharp firing in front), I greatly feared that Forrest was defeated and that the Federals were pushing him back, so I moved rapidly down the road till I reached the open field near the bridge."

This could not have been the Ripley–Guntown road, as that road was filled with Federal troops, wagons, and artillery from Dr. Agnew's house to the crossroads, a distance of two miles. "Having placed some sharpshooters, whose sole attention was to be directed to the bridge," he continues, "I extended my line nearly half a mile and began an attack by scattering shots at the same time. Sounding my bugle from various points along the line, almost immediately a reconnoitering force of the enemy appeared at the bridge and being fired upon returned. This was followed, perhaps, by a regiment, and then a whole brigade came down to the creek. My men taking good aim, fired upon them coolly and steady. Soon I saw wagons, artillery, etc., pushing for the bridge. These were shot at by my sharpshooters. I now began to contract my line and collect my regiment, for the Federals came pouring in immense numbers across the creek. Your artillery was doing good work. Even the bullets from the small arms of the Confederates reached my men. I operated upon the flank of the enemy until after dark."

The wagons blockading the bridge were soon removed by being thrown into the stream, and a section from each battery was worked across by hand, supported by the escort and brought to bear upon a Negro brigade with fearful loss; the other two sections were quickly to the front, ahead of any support for the moment and drove the enemy from the ridge back of Holland's house across Dry Creek. The cavalry in the meantime had halted, reorganized, and soon joined in the pursuit. The road was narrow, with dense woods on each side, so that it was impossible to use more than four pieces at a time, but the number were kept close upon the heels of the retreating enemy and a murderous fire prevented them from forming to make a stand.

The ridge extending southward from the Hadden House offered a strong natural position for defensive operations. Upon this ridge the Federals had established a line of battle, but a few well-directed shots from the artillery stationed near the Holland House and a charge by our cavalry across Dry Creek readily put them to flight. A section of each battery was ordered at a gallop to this ridge, which was reached in time to open with a few rounds of double-shotted canister upon their demoralized ranks as they hastily retreated through the open fields on either side of Phillips Branch. Our cannoneers were greatly blown and well nigh exhausted from excessive heat and continuous labor at their guns for full five hours. We noticed a number drink with apparent relish the black powder water from the sponge buckets.

It was soon evident that another strong line had formed behind the fence in the skirt of woods just westward of Phillips Branch. General Forrest riding up, dismounted and approached our guns, which were now plying shell and solid shot. With his field glasses he took in the situation. The enemy's shot were coming thick and fast; leaden balls were seen to flatten as they would strike the axles and tires of our gun carriages; trees were barked and the air was laden with the familiar but unpleasant sound of these death messengers. Realizing General Forrest's exposure, we involuntarily ventured the suggestion that "You had better get lower down the hill, General." Instantly we apologized, as we expected the general to intimate that it was none of our business where he went. He, however, stepped down the hill out of danger and seating himself behind a tree seemed for a few moments in deep study, but soon the head of our cavalry column arriving he turned to me and said, "Captain, as soon as you hear me open on the right and flank of the enemy over yonder," pointing to the enemy's position, "charge with your artillery down that lane and cross the branch."

The genial and gallant Captain [T. W.] Rice, coming up at this time and hearing the order, turned to me and said, "By God, whoever heard of artillery charging?" Captain Rice's Battery had been stationed at Columbus, Mississippi and other points on local duty and only a few months previous had been ordered and assigned to our command. He accepted his initiation into the ways and methods of horse artillery with much spirit and good grace.

Meanwhile, watching Forrest at the head of the cavalry moving through the woods and across the field in the direction of the enemy's right, I directed Lieutenants Tully, Brown, and H. H. Briggs, whose sections had been held in the road below the Hadden House for an emergency, to be ready to move into action at a moment's notice. The enemy observing our cavalry passing to their right began to break and retire through the woods. Forrest seeing this dashed upon them in column of fours. At the same moment Lieutenant Brown passed his section down the road, even in advance of the skirmish line and opened a terrific fire upon the enemy, now breaking up and in full retreat. Lieutenant Briggs also took an advanced position and got in a few well-directed shots. Brown's section and a section of Rice's Battery were pushed forward across Phillips Branch and up the hill under a sharp fire, the former taking position on the right of the road and the latter in the road just where the road turns before reaching Dr. Agnew's house.

Our skirmishers had driven the enemy's skirmishers upon their main line, when we were about to make another artillery charge, but distinctly hearing the Federal officers giving orders to their men to stand steady and yell, "Remember Fort Pillow." "Charge! Charge! Charge!" rang along their lines and on they came. Our right was pressed back on the "Negro avengers of Fort Pillow." They steadily moved upon our guns and for a moment their loss seemed imminent. Our cannoneers, standing firm and taking in the situation, drove double-shotted canister into this advancing line. The cavalry rallying on our guns sent death volleys into their ranks which staggered the enemy and drove them back, but only to give place to a new line that now moved down upon us with wild shouts and got almost within handshaking distance of our guns.

Lyon coming up opportunely at this moment formed his brigade on our right and springing forward with loud cheers, hurled them back with so stormful an onset that their entire line gave way in utter rout and confusion. Lieutenant Brown's horse was shot under him. The gallant young soldier, Henry King of Rice's Battery, fell with his rammer staff in hand, mortally wounded. His grave now marks the spot where he fell. Several members of the artillery were wounded, and a great many battery horses were killed. The reason for this desperate stand was soon discovered. The road was filled with their wagons, ambulances, and many caissons, the dying and wounded. Cast away arms, accouterments, baggage, dead animals, and other evidences of a routed army were conspicuous on every side. The sun had set, but the weary and over-spent Confederates maintained the pursuit for some five or six miles beyond and until it became quite too dark to go further. A temporary halt was ordered, when a section from each battery was directed to be equipped with ammunition and the best horses from their respective batteries and be ready to continue the pursuit at daylight.

It is just as natural for a soldier to "prowl" when the chance is offered as it is fun for him to follow a whipped foe. Weary, exhausted, and hungry as the men were, no sooner had the horses of the artillery been cared for than they made a general break for the captured wagons filling the road near camp. Great quantities of ammunition, both for small arms and artillery, were found; but this wasn't what the boys wanted just then. Sugar, coffee, tea, savory bacon, as it was broiled on the coals, was greatly enjoyed and made us almost forget the dangers and fatigues of the day. One of our gallant lieutenants, who never lost a chance to go into a fight or "take a drink," remarked, as he shook a canteen high above his head, "There's just enough left, boys, for your lieutenant's night cap." A most exemplary soldier, as modest as he was brave, was seen going in at one end of a wagon duly serene and in a little while he emerged from the other end with a lady's dress on, a canteen of "fire water" around his neck, singing, "The girl I left behind me."

Long before daylight found us moving rapidly to overtake the flying foe. We had changed positions. The cavalry, now being in the advance, overtook the enemy at Stubb's farm; a sharp skirmish ensued, when they broke, leaving the remainder of their wagon train. Fourteen pieces of artillery and some twenty-five ambulances, with a number of wounded, were left in Little Hatchie bottom, further on. The discomfited Federals were badly scattered throughout the country. Forrest, therefore, threw out his regiment on either side of the roads to sweep the vicinity. A number were killed and many prisoners captured before reaching Ripley, twenty-five miles from Brice's Cross Roads. At this point two strong lines were formed across the road. After a spirited onset the Federals broke, leaving one piece of artillery, two caissons, two ambulances. Twenty-one killed and seventy wounded were also left on the field. Colonel G. M. McKeaig, of the 120th Illinois Infantry, was among the killed; also [Capt. William J.] Tate, 7th Tennessee Cavalry. This was accomplished just as the artillery reached the front.

Lt. Frank Rodgers, of Rucker's staff, the night previous, with a small elect detachment of men, assisted by Captain Gooch, with the remnant of his company, hung constantly upon the Federal rear, with a daring never surpassed. Their series of attacks greatly harassed and annoyed the enemy, numbers of whom were killed and wounded. The artillery followed to Salem, twenty-five miles distant from Ripley and although moving at a trot most of the way and killing outright fifteen horses and breaking down many others from the heat and fatigue of the march, was never able to overtake an organized body of the enemy. As Private Moore, of the 7th Tennessee, was straggling on the flank, a little detached from his command, he suddenly came upon twenty Federals. He threw up his hands to surrender. Moore thought they were trying to play some trick off on him, each insisting, however, on the right to surrender, when the officer of the squad directed Moore to conduct them into Ripley and turn them over to the proper authorities. This was done with great pomp and display. Moore says, "he was the hero of the hour, the lion of the town—one man, all alone, capturing and bringing in twenty prisoners." The joke was too good to keep and Moore would tell it on all occasions.

Before reaching Salem, General Forrest fell from his horse from sheer exhaustion and for more than an hour lay in a state of stupor by the roadside. On the morning of the twelfth the artillery was recalled from the pursuit. General Forrest, in passing our guns on his return from following the scattered Federals—pardon this personal allusion—struck Morton familiarly on the shoulder and said, "Well, John, your artillery won this fight." Morton replied, "General, you pressed us up pretty closely at times," when Forrest remarked, "Yes, artillery is made to be captured and I wanted to see if they could take yours." General Buford soon coming along, remarked that "the artillery had saved the day." Generals Bell and Lyon were equally complimentary in speaking of the conduct of the officers and men of the artillery.

Ever since Alexander led the Macedonian horse at the battle of Arbela, he has been ranked the first of cavalry generals of all times—his tactics outflanking the enemy's wings, dividing the enemy's forces, rallying, attacking the rear, supporting the menacing points and his wonderful pursuit of seventy-five miles in twenty-four hours has never been approached until this battle fought by Forrest. Starting from Boonville at 5:00 A.M. on the tenth, at 5:00 P.M. on the eleventh his artillery had marched to Salem, fighting six hours at and around the crossroads, with seven hours' rest on the night of the tenth, making seventy-three miles in twenty-nine hours. Probably there is no artillery march on record to surpass this in endurance, efficiency, and distance. Bell's Brigade moved from Rienzi on the morning of the tenth and at 7:00 P.M. on the eleventh camped at Davis' Mill, on the LaGrange road, having marched and fought eighty-six miles in thirty-one hours.

General Forrest, in his official report, says, "My available force in the engagement was three thousand five hundred." This had been controverted by a number of his own officers. 3,315, the number we give, comes nearer the truth. But admitting that his force was 3,500, take off one-fourth for horse holders, would leave 2,625 actually engaged, with two batteries of light guns. Forrest further says, "From reports of prisoners captured, corroborated by official documents captured on the field, the enemy had in the engagement 10,252."

Since the war I have met a number of Federal officers who were in the fight. They unhesitatingly say that the cavalry, under Grierson, numbered 4,000, with 8,000 infantry and twenty-two pieces of artillery. The entire command was especially selected and equipped for this expedition. Thus the reader will see that the Confederate force was a little more than one-fourth of the Federal army.

The victory was as decisive as it was brilliant. General Forrest further says, "The loss of the enemy in killed and wounded is not less than two thousand. The whole number captured and in our hands is not less than two thousand." General Sturgis, in his official report, gives his loss in killed at 223; wounded, 394; total killed and wounded, 617; missing 1,571. This is far from correct, as we buried 400 Federals in a trench a short distance north of Bethany Church and over two hundred in a ditch northeast of Brice's house. General Forrest further says, "We captured 250 wagons and ambulances and eighteen pieces of artillery."

In this statement, so far as the artillery is concerned, he is again in error. I had charge of the captured artillery. We secured twenty-one pieces; the one remaining was probably buried or hid in the swamps. General Sturgis places his artillery in his official report at twenty-two guns, and we have never seen from written or published accounts of where a single gun was saved. Forrest further says, "Five thousand stands of small arms, five hundred thousand rounds of ammunition and all his baggage and supplies were secured." Chief Surgeon Cowan reported our loss in killed and wounded at 493, though it was always believed we lost 640 in killed and wounded. The Federals claim that after defeating their cavalry at the crossroads we whipped their infantry in detail.

An extract from a letter to me by Col. Arthur T. Reeve, who commanded the 55th Colored Infantry in this fight reads, "Our (the Federal) command having been moved up on double-quick—a distance of about five miles—immediately before their arrival on the field and the consequent fact that this arm of our force went into the engagement very seriously blown, in fact, very nearly exhausted by heat and fatigue, with their ranks very much drawn out, were whipped in detail and overwhelmed by the very brilliant and vigorous assaults of your forces. When the engagement first began I was at the rear of the Federal column, in command of the train guard, and hence passed over the ground on the way to the battlefield after the balance of the army had passed and am able to speak advisedly of the extreme exhaustion of the infantry, as I passed large numbers entirely prostrated by heat and fatigue, who did not reach the field of battle and must have fallen into your hands after the engagement."

The entire Confederate force was brought into action at once. We kept no reserves; every movement was quickly planned and executed with the greatest celerity. A potent factor which made the battle far bloodier than it would have been was it being reported, and with some degree of truth, that the Negroes had been sworn on their knees in line before leaving Memphis to show "no quarter to Forrest's men," and badges were worn upon which were inscribed, "Remember Fort Pillow."

[Maj. Gen. Cadwallader C.] Washburn, commanding the District of West Tennessee, distinctly admits that the Negro troops with Sturgis had gone into this fight with the declared intention to give no quarter to Forrest's men.

General Forrest wrote General Washburn on the subject June 14 as follows, "It has been reported to me that all of your colored troops stationed in Memphis took on their knees in the presence of Major General Hurlbut and other officers of your army an oath to avenge Fort Pillow, and that they would show my troops no quarter. Again I have it from indisputable authority that the troops under Brigadier General Sturgis on their recent march from Memphis, publicly, and in many places, proclaimed that no quarter would be shown my men. As they were moved into action on the tenth they were exhorted by their officers to remember Fort Pillow. The prisoners we have captured from that command, or a large majority of them, have voluntarily stated that they expected us to murder them, otherwise they would have surrendered in a body rather than have taken to the bushes after being run down and exhausted."

General Washburn replied to this letter June 19, 1864, as follows, "You say in your letter that it has been reported to you that all the Negro troops stationed in Memphis took an oath, on their knees, in the presence of General Hurlbut and other officers of our army, to avenge Fort Pillow and that they would show your troops no quarter. I believe it is true that the Colored troops did take such an oath, but not in the presence of General Hurlbut. From what I can learn this act of theirs was not influenced by any white officer, but was the result of their own sense of what was due to themselves and their fellows who had been mercilessly slaughtered."

Col. Arthur T. Reeve, who commanded the 55th Colored Infantry in this fight, tells me that no oath was taken by his troops that ever he heard of, but the impression prevailed that the black flag was raised and on his side was raised to all intents and purposes. He himself fully expected to be killed if captured. Impressed with this notion a double effect was produced. It made the Federals afraid to surrender and greatly exasperated our men, and in the break up the affair became more like a hunt for wild game than a battle between civilized men.

General Forrest says in his official report that "my obligations are hereby returned to Brigadier General Buford, commanding division. He was prompt in obeying orders and exhibited great energy, both in assaulting and pursuing the enemy. The high praise he bestows upon his brigade commanders, Colonels Bell and Lyon, is truthful and just. They exhibited coolness, skill and ability." General Forrest also in this report speaks in high terms of the gallant and efficient service of Colonels Rucker and Johnson and of his staff, which he calls by name and further says, "Thus did my troops in the hour of need rally to the defense of their country. They deserve well of her gratitude. Notwithstanding the great disparity in numbers, they repulsed the foe and achieved a victory as imperishable as it is brilliant."

General Sturgis in his official report says, "I need hardly add that it is with feelings of the most profound pain and regret that I find myself called upon to record a defeat, and the loss and suffering incident to a reverse at a point so far distant from base of supplies and reinforcements. Yet there is some consolation in knowing that the army fought nobly while it did fight, and only yielded to superior numbers. The strength of the enemy is variously estimated by the most intelligent officers at from fifteen to twenty thousand men. A very intelligent sergeant, who was captured and remained five days in the hands of the enemy, reports the number of the enemy actually engaged to have been twelve thousand and that two divisions of infantry were held in reserve," and General Sturgis further says, "It may appear strange that so large a force of the enemy could be in our vicinity and we be ignorant of the fact." It would have been "strange" indeed. No doubt the Federal commander believed that Forrest's force greatly outnumbered his own and was consoled at the last to when he "only yielded to overwhelming numbers." The greatest commander might sometimes be mistaken, when, forsooth, the palliative defensive is resorted to. Sooy Smith at West Point, Streight at Rome, and Campbell at Athens are examples.

Where all acted so well as the officers and men of the two batteries it would be invidious to discriminate. Adjutant Blakemore and Lieutenant S. K. Watkins, ordnance officer of the battalion of artillery, deserve special mention for prompt discharge of duty. Lieutenants J. C. Barlow and W. J. D. Winton, of Thrall's Battery, on learning that their battery would likely not be in the engagement, volunteered their services and were conspicuous throughout the engagement for gallantry. My presence being with the artillery I, of course, know more of its service and I hope to be understood that it is not my intention to detract in the slightest from the well-earned laurels of any part of the cavalry command. Each regiment and every company, if written up, would make a chapter of interesting history.

The Battle of Tupelo

William S. Burns,
Captain, U.S.V. (Staff of Maj. Gen. Andrew Jackson Smith)

Philadelphia *Weekly Times* 2, no. 24, August 10, 1878

Upon the death last fall of General [Nathan Bedford] Forrest, late of the Confederate army, various accounts of his military career were published in the newspapers both North and South. Properly understood, it was one that has considerable interest for the student of military affairs, and it was one often understood at the North, where he has been generally spoken of as a guerrilla. It is unnecessary to recall historically the attempts made from time to time by different nations to combine in one soldier the advantages of infantry and cavalry, nor to show how it produced the dragoon who was neither an efficient cavalryman nor an effective infantryman. It was the fortune of General Forrest to make a similar attempt and to bring into military existence an excellent force of mounted infantry—the country in which he conducted his movements and the men under him were both adapted to such service. It was his special merit to use his horses simply to move his men to the place of engagement, where they were then directed as infantry, armed only as such, and no effort was made to combine cavalry duty with infantry service.

It is believed that a somewhat brief account of the battle of Tupelo, fought in July 1864, near the line of the Mobile and Ohio Railroad, in Mississippi, will disclose some of the characteristics of such troops and of their general, and which made their success so often possible and prevented disaster from following upon defeat. It is the more satisfactory to recall this engagement because it is one of the very few in which Forrest was more than checked—it is one in which he was defeated. It will be remembered that [Major General William] Sooy Smith, with an excellent cavalry command, had been ordered in February 1864 from Northern Mississippi to the line of [Maj. Gen. William T.] Sherman's intended march eastward from Vicksburg across the state and that at Okolona this cavalry command was met by an inferior force under General Forrest and forced to retreat. Not even the severity of General Sherman's report in this connection sufficiently condemns the weakness and incapacity of General Sooy Smith's management. Fortunately it produced no disaster to Sherman, but it left the fertile region of North Mississippi under the control of Forrest and this was deemed reason sufficient to justify an expedition against him. Accordingly, in May, a force of about 13,000 men, chiefly infantry, commanded by [Brig Gen. Samuel D.] Sturgis, moved from Memphis eastwardly. On June 10 they were met by Forrest, with scarce half that number of men and so utterly defeated that they were pursued the night and day following the battle a distance of over twenty-five miles. It is the story of want of generalship and its disastrous consequences unto defeat and rout.

It was at this time, when Forrest was flushed with two such victories and when his horsemen might ride where they would, that [Maj. Gen. Cadwallader C.] Washburn, then in paper command of the large department of which Forrest had entire control, except the headquarters at Memphis, ordered the expedition which resulted in the battle of Tupelo.

The humiliation from the defeat of Sooy Smith, followed by that of Sturgis, was bitter. And notwithstanding the difficulty of sending infantry in pursuit of a mounted force and of the fact that the troops in numbers were scarce equal to those of Sturgis, it was the general conviction that Forrest would not balk the wishes of the intended expedition and the belief as general that the result would differ from those that had gone before. The infantry had been trained in two years of successful war and was fresh from the service of holding at bay the enemy which, for many days, pursued [Maj. Gen. Nathaniel P.] Banks upon his retreat from the Red River; and they were commanded by [Brig. Gen. Andrew Jackson] Smith, of the Regular army, whose services had been such that he had inspired not only the troops of his command, but those with whom it was associated, with an enthusiastic faith and a belief that he could not be beaten, as it had been theretofore his fortune (perhaps his military genius) not to have been. At this time he was somewhat past middle life, with a thoughtful student-like air, emphasized by his use of glasses, looking, in fact, far more like a college professor than a man of sieges and battlefields.

The forces under General Smith's command were as follows: There were two divisions of the right wing of the XVI Army Corps, Army of the

Tennessee—1st and 3rd; the 1st Division was commanded by [Brig.] Gen. Joseph A. Mower, and the 3rd by Col. [David] Moore, 21st Missouri Infantry (who had lost a leg at the battle of Shiloh) and consisted chiefly of Iowa, Minnesota, Wisconsin, Illinois, Indiana, and Ohio troops. In addition to the above was a brigade of Colored troops, commanded by Col. [Edward] Bouton, and a brigade of cavalry commanded by [Brig. Gen. Benjamin H.] Grierson. In all about twelve thousand troops with twenty guns.

On July 1 this command assembled at LaGrange, Tennessee. On the fourth General Smith sent the writer with a flag of truce, escorted by a few men of the 7th Kansas Cavalry, to convey to General Forrest a copy of the congressional report of the investigation of the massacre at Fort Pillow, asked for by him in a letter to General Washburn. That night was passed with two of Forrest's officers inside of his lines. From their conversation it was apparent that Forrest knew he now had a general to fight, of whom he must be, to say the least, very wary. The fights with Generals Sooy Smith and Sturgis were lightly spoken of, but it was admitted that in General A. J. Smith they had an antagonist worthy of their own commander.

Upon returning to LaGrange next day the troops were met marching southeastward into Mississippi. Starting each morning at three, they were pushed on day after day with Forrest hovering on their front and flanks, but not making a stand, seemingly afraid to strike as usual. On July 11, after a sharp skirmish, General Smith entered Pontotoc, driving Forrest's command through and beyond the village. The weather at this time was intensely hot, and the command was rested in Pontotoc on the twelfth. It had now arrived within striking distance of the Mobile and Ohio Railroad. During the evening of the twelfth a consultation was held between Generals Smith, Mower and Grierson and Colonel Moore and next morning at five the troops were moving eastward as if to strike the railroad at Tupelo, nineteen miles distant, thereby "flanking" General Forrest, who, with his army, numbering a little over 12,000 men, was in a good fighting position about ten miles south of Pontotoc, on the Okolona road, awaiting General Smith.

Of course General Forrest soon discovered this move and started in a northeasterly direction to strike General Smith before he reached the railroad, which he did about six miles of Tupelo. Forrest's first attack fell upon General Mower's division in the rear. But he was soon repulsed. About an hour later he made a similar attack upon the same division, but was again repulsed, Mower's men charging upon the enemy and driving them in confusion, capturing some prisoners and the battle flag of the 19th Mississippi. This last attack was as violent, with as equally furious a counter-charge, as is often witnessed.

About dark the troops encamped at Harrisburg, a small hamlet, one mile from Tupelo, which ground proved to be the battlefield of that name. General Smith was now in a position to compel an attack from Forrest.

Next morning at a very early hour General Grierson was sent to Tupelo with orders to destroy the railroad, north and south, and General Smith placed his troops for the battle that was impending. They occupied a knoll almost clear of trees, for a mile or more to the south, west, and northwest and beyond which was a growth of timber. The road over which the troops had marched the day before led into the center of the position. General Mower, with his division, was stationed on the right or north of this (Pontotoc) road, looking west and Colonel Moore on the left, or south. Colonel Bouton's Colored brigade was on the extreme left. About 6:00 A.M. General Forrest made his attack, the brunt falling upon Colonel Moore's division and the left wing of General Mower's. The onset was made with Forrest's characteristic impetuosity, but it was impossible for his men to reach our lines. General Smith's command were in the open and without any protection excepting a part of Colonel Moore's division, in front of which there was a worm fence; beyond this was a wide gully and here the attacking force was rallied. Four times they attacked and each time without success.

Between the attacks General Forrest's artillery was very active and one battery was handled with great accuracy, throwing its shot and shell into the 21st Missouri, 58th Illinois, and 89th Indiana until the Illinois and an Indiana battery engaged their attention. These batteries so annoyed the enemy that Col. W. W. Faulkner charged upon them for their capture, but he was met by an enfilading fire from the 21st Missouri, 58th Illinois, and 89th Indiana, the 122nd Illinois charging to the right, and in the confusion Faulkner's line broke and fled, leaving many of the men dead upon the field, among them their leader, who fell in front of the 21st Missouri.

For an hour and a half the struggle continued. At length they were driven from the front of Colonel Moore's division, leaving the ground covered with their dead and dying. Instead of retiring to the woods (where their horses were held in reserve) as soon as they retreated, they moved in what at first appeared a confused mass to their left, crossed to the north of the Pontotoc Road, turned and in good line of battle swept down upon General Mower's division, the men of which (under orders) reserved their fire until the enemy were quite near, when they opened upon them with musketry and canister. Human beings could not stand such a storm and the attacking line fell back, but only to return to some seemingly exposed part of Moore's line, and for two hours and a half the battle raged on this part of the field—the enemy attacking and our men keeping their positions and repelling all attacks. At the end of that time General Mower ordered his division to advance, which they did, capturing many prisoners and driving the enemy across the fields and into the woods. It was useless to pursue them further; they mounted the horses there awaiting them and moved off.

The victory was complete. As the prisoners were brought in by General Mower it was reported that General Forrest was killed—that he had been seen to fall from his horse. He had, in truth, been wounded right through the foot—the only wound I believe he received during the war. After this repulse of the enemy General Smith's ambulances went upon the field gathering the wounded of both armies and the dead of our own. The writer counted one general, four colonels, and two hundred seventy-one dead of the enemy on our outer line. General Smith had defeated Forrest's army as it had never been defeated before. His cavalry, under Grierson, was destroying the railroad. His rations and ammunition were low; he could, in a military point of view, do no more, and he determined to move next morning (the fifteenth) in a northwesterly direction toward LaGrange. The afternoon was spent bringing in and caring for the wounded and burying the dead. The loss sustained by General Smith was about six hundred and fifty. That of General Forrest could only be estimated—of his dead alone there was left on the field between three and four hundred.

About 9:00 P.M. Forrest again attacked, this time on the extreme left, where was Colonel Bouton's Colored brigade and the 14th, 27th, and 32nd Iowa, and 24th Missouri; but it was rather a feeble attempt and in half an hour it was repulsed. Next morning the enemy made his appearance and advanced from the cover of the woods, but as they did not come with much energy General Mower's division advanced upon them, when they fled to their horses. In the meantime troops were seen advancing upon the scene of last night's attempt, where the Colored brigade was still in position.

General Smith hurried to the spot and for two hours there was some artillery firing and then, under cover of his artillery, Forrest advanced, determined to have a parting blow at the colored troops who, by command of General Smith, held their fire until he gave the word, which he did, and then ordered them to charge—himself leading them. The charge was made with spirit and in excellent order, the enemy breaking and fleeing in disorder to their horses. Believing that this was the last of the foe, General Smith moved slowly northward and at the end of five miles' marching went into camp at "Old Town Creek." The men were comfortably settling themselves for the rest they needed when the sound of artillery was heard at our rear and a few shells fell and burst in our camp. General Mower, with one of his brigades, quickly repelled this attack of a few horsemen and a piece of artillery and no more was seen of them. LaGrange was reached on July 21.

Perhaps no better instance of the implicit confidence of the men in Maj. Gen. A. J. Smith can be given than the conduct of the teamsters during the battle. The little army on its southward march subsisted upon the supplies in the large wagon train which accompanied it. Each wagon was drawn by a team of six mules, driven sometimes by a soldier unable to march and oftener by civilians, white and black, hired for that purpose. This and the other wagon trains, consisting of over two hundred wagons, was parked in the rear of the line during the engagement and sufficiently close to enable the train guard to be reduced to its smallest number. Before the main attack upon Colonel Moore's division the enemy (who had twenty-two guns) opened a vigorous artillery fire, and many shells from the guns passed over the line and burst among the wagons. The teamsters showed all the coolness possible, holding the mules and doing what was possible to keep order, and no exception to this conduct was noticed. To those who have seen the confusion usually made by shells exploding among the wagons of a train and who have seen the conduct of the drivers, bound by no sense of discipline or even pride, the conduct of those at Tupelo can only be explained upon the theory of a faith in their general, more severely tried, but as enthusiastic as that of the men in action.

The movement of General Smith from the direct march after Forrest toward the railroad at a point selected for the advantages it offered as a battlefield, compelling him to leave his selected position and to attack, was one which could have been much more readily effected had Forrest's troops been composed of infantry. Being mounted he was enabled to strike the marching column before it had reached the point selected. It is true he did not prevent its occupation, but what was done indicates the rapidity with which his troops (relatively to infantry) could be and were moved. It will be remarked also that the retreat to their horses by Forrest's infantry after a repulse prevented altogether any pursuit by the victors and the rout which such pursuit causes the fleeing troops. It may well be doubted, in view of the character of the late battlefields east and west and the uselessness of cavalry upon the field unless well trained, whether mounted infantry, for all the purposes of independent operations, as well as for those for which the cavalry in the late war was used, was not its superior in efficiency.

The Crater Battle

THOMAS H. CROSS,
SERGEANT, 16TH VIRGINIA REGIMENT, C.S.A.

Philadelphia *Weekly Times* 5, no. 29, September 10, 1881

The morning of July 30, 1864, was bright, but the air was filled with an intense heat that brought little refreshment to the soldiers of the opposing armies which occupied the lines around Petersburg. Few save the generals of the Federal army knew and certainly few save the generals of the Confederate army suspected that beneath one of the Confederate batteries which formed a *re-chirant* in the Confederate lines lay the dormant power of many tons of powder which would soon rend the earth and air and bring death to many a sleeping soldier. At the point selected for the explosion the lines were so near to each other that during the night a desultory fire was kept up on each side to prevent a surprise from the opposite party, and the Confederate line just here formed an angle which was covered by a fort. To blow up this fort and thus cause a breach in the lines seemed a comparatively feasible plan of gaining the crest of the hills in rear of the Confederate line and distant from the Federal lines about five hundred and fifty yards.

In executing any movement in which co-operation of many persons is essential there is, of course, unavoidable delay, and the explosion of this mine was no exception to the general rule. So, what by prearrangement should have occurred at half-past four took place just twelve minutes after, when the defective fuse, having been repaired or replaced, brought the spark to the powder, and the event for which thousands of eyes and ears were watching and waiting proclaimed itself to the world as an accomplished fact amid fire, smoke, death, and desolation.

The first division of Federal troops, under command of Brig. Gen. [James H.] Ledlie, was assigned by lot to the hazardous duty of filling the deadly breach, and immediately following the explosion they leaped their own defenses, swept across the short space dividing the lines and gained the Confederate lines before the latter troops could fully realize what had occurred or could rally from the inextricable confusion into which the event had thrown them. Ledlie was supported by Generals [Robert] Potter and [Orlando B.] Wilcox, but the troops seemed to look upon the chasm which had been rendered by the explosion rather as a place of refuge than as an initial point for making further assault upon the town now almost within their power.

It is needless here to attempt to describe the dull, heavy thud produced by the explosion of many tons of powder down in the bowels of the earth. The earth yawned as if just awaking and shaking off the sleep of centuries, a heavy rumbling noise pervaded space, a perceptible quaking told those at a distance that some untoward event was happening, the ground immediately covering the mine lifted and was thrown more than a hundred feet into the air while the lurid flames shone from below through the awful fissures in the earth and lit up a scene at once grand and appalling. A heavy veil of smoke stood for a moment over the wreck as if reluctant to disclose the destruction which the hand of man had caused, and then, stirred by the early morning breeze, it floated slowly away in the great mass of smoke which was now pouring from the throats of all the available guns in both armies.

The grand chorus of artillery which immediately succeeded the explosion was such a roar as would fitly herald the introduction of fiends from the lower regions, and was played by an orchestra that combined in its awful diapason all the notes from the shrill treble of the whistling shell to the heavy bass of the Dahlgren or mortar. On the Confederate side men quietly sleeping were hurled into eternity, no moment of waking, reflection, or preparation, while their places were filled by the legions of invading soldiery. But with the Federals what was apparently plain sailing soon began to be a difficult problem, and as the latter line of troops pressed into the breach, confusion naturally followed, and an unmanageable mass of men huddled behind the very works which were intended only as a place to rest upon their laurels and seek safety and enjoy honor in the accomplishment of this easy and unresisted assault. The Stars and Stripes defiantly floated from earthworks that had been built by Confederate hands, a panic had seized upon the Confederates immediately adjacent to the crater and nothing apparently was between the Federals and their coveted prize but the hills of Blandford Cemetery.

Every effort was made by Federal officers to align and reform the troops for a further advance, but confusion grew worse confounded, and a sort of selfish fate had ordered a delay which proved fatal to the whole enterprise. In the meantime the dawn of day had been supplanted by that light which marks Virginia's July weather, and the sun looked with a burning eye through the sulphurous cloud down upon a scene of sickening carnage.

The artillery duel had fully aroused all who had failed by that sound—sweet sleep which none but the thoroughly tired can know—to hear the explosion, and there was hurry, hot haste, and wild speculation rife amid the boys who wore the gray. Statements vague, contradictory and doubtful, were readily told and as readily believed, but soon all gave way to the brief recital of the fact that the Federals had blown up and taken a part of our lines and that somebody had to retake them. This fact was speedily confirmed by Thomas Bernard, the courier of General [William] Mahone, then in command of the division of which his old brigade formed a part. Bernard soon found Brig. Gen. [David] Weisiger's headquarters and delivered his order. Then came that peculiar rat-ta-tat of the kettle drum; "fall in!" was passed down the line, and soon what was a sleeping camp became a line of soldiers ready for any duty and prepared for any danger.

To avoid as much as possible a concentration of artillery fire we repaired to a valley just in our rear by squads, and there the line was formed. After marching a short distance, possibly half a mile, we were ordered to "unsling knapsacks," and soon a mingled pile of Yankee blankets and tents showed with what a Confederate soldier's knapsack was packed. Our baggage was soon disposed of, the line of march was resumed, the steady, regular tramp of the veteran line told of determination to do the task assigned us, let the hazard be ever so great. Wright's Georgia Brigade, commanded by Lt. Col. [Matthew R.] Hall, was also detailed to take part of this day's work, but Mahone's old brigade had reached the line before the Georgians had deployed, and then they were twice met by a fire so galling that not even Georgia valor could face the storm or achieve their purpose. Mahone's Brigade, numbering about eight hundred guns, was the first to strike the enemy and from that blow, struck by a veteran soldiery, the enemy never recovered.

When we first set out on our expedition we did not know that we should be called upon to "lock horns" with Negro troops, and that they had leaped our works "no quarter!" The information gained, a stranger would perhaps have noticed a quickening of the step, each eye burned with a brighter glow, and each gun received more than a casual examination to see that it was properly loaded and ready for action. We had never met Negro

A scene from the fighting near the Crater (BEYER, *DEEDS OF VALOR*)

troops. We did not know whether we should be met by a sort of savage ferocity or whether we should meet that cool, imperturbable bravery which characterizes men fighting for freedom. But we did know that behind us lay the town of Petersburg with its inhabitants looking to us for protection; we knew that this was the key to Richmond. We knew that an enemy who had proclaimed "No quarter!" was before us, and we determined to spare neither ourselves nor the enemy till the earthworks were retaken and the city was saved.

A ditch dug by the former occupants of the lines to secure safe passage to and from the lines enabled us to approach near them with comparative safety. From this ditch we deployed in a little valley and then came the final preparation for the assault. The tops of fifteen flagstaffs could be seen over the hill, and fifteen hostile banners flaunted defiance in our face. The order was passed in the subdued tone which denotes a stern purpose to "fix bayonets," and by those to whom the thought occurred an extra turn was taken in the little screw which holds the bayonet shank on the gun. The thought of having his bayonet "unshipped" flashed across the writer's mind, and his right hand instinctively sought his cartridge-box and the possibility was provided against.

Some said that Generals [Robert E.] Lee and [Pierre G. T.] Beauregard would witness the charge, and thus another incentive was given to us to do our work well and faithfully. Orders were given to the commanders of regiments to withhold the fire until the works were reached, and we were cautioned against unnecessary and exhaustive speed until the top of the hill was gained, when we would be exposed to the heavy fire of five lines of infantry which had been gathered in our front. All was now ready. "Forward," came down the line as a movement among the enemy was noticed and the counter-charge was successfully made before their lines could be arranged. Slowly and deliberately we came to the top of the hill, and here, as we became more exposed, our step was quickened and the lines were gained, but not taken. Guns were emptied in the face of the foe and then the bayonet was relied on, as it was then almost impossible to reload. The blood of whites and blacks, of friend and foe, combined to form rivulets which should bear down to future generations the testimony that men can forget mercy and that human wrath is stronger than human love. The earth then drank to satiety, while every dripping bayonet, every flashing sword and every kissing ball told that the sacrifice was not yet done.

Maj. [John T.] Woodhouse, of the 16th Virginia Infantry, was the first man whom the writer saw fall, but soon the field and trench were covered with the dead and wounded. The first line which we encountered was a traverse running parallel with the main line of breastworks, the interval between the two being honeycombed by sleeping apartments, so constructed as to insure the greatest possible safety to the occupants. This traverse was about seventy-five feet in rear of the main line, was about ten feet from the bottom of the ditch to the top of the embankment, and commanded the line of works which was nearest to the enemy. All of this space, more than one hundred feet, was occupied by the enemy, and when they had realized the fact from the impetuosity of our charge that their attack was a failure they incontinently sought refuge in these little "bomb proofs" and in the "Crater." But the Confederates followed close on their heels, and here the hand-to-hand fight continued until the work of recapture was fully and irrevocably accomplished. All this happened in much less time than it takes me to tell it; some say it was twenty minutes, but certain it is that before the sun had reached meridian some of those who had escaped the dangers of assault and the wounds of conflict had yielded to the heat, which was well nigh intolerable. Then we began to realize the fact that several thousand dead and festering bodies would soon force an abandonment of the lines, but still more must be added to the list before those already dead could be buried.

The "Crater" had by this time become a place of retreat for the crouching foe, and while a part of the line was assigned to the task of keeping up a fire on the enemy in our front, in their own lines, the remainder of the line was called upon to prevent the escape of Brig. Gen. [William F.] Bartlett and several hundred men who had gathered in the "Crater." To do this more effectually we took advantage of the many guns lying about us, and loading all of them, when the enemy would make a rush for their lines we would give them such a volley as would force them back within the pit. Then came in the Alabamians with a rush, a yell, and a volley, and Bartlett, with his disheartened troops, was marched to the rear as prisoners of war, their number being estimated at about five hundred.

As an evidence of the number killed in the "Crater," the writer remembers keeping count for Corporal Shepherd, of Company A, 16th Virginia Infantry, who had charge of the burial of the bodies within the "Crater," and knows that one hundred and forty-two white and black Yankee soldiers were buried in the bottom of the pit, being covered by the loose dirt from its sides. In the adjustment of the troops after the surrender of Bartlett, a portion of the 16th Regiment was assigned to the "Crater," a banquet-tread having been constructed in the sides of the pit. It became necessary to bury the dead here as soon as possible, and Corporal Shepherd was assigned to that duty on Sunday morning, the banks protecting the squad from the fire of the enemy.

Where all did well it were invidious to say who did best, but the writer is certain that no man who took part in the battle of the "Crater" and lives today to tell the tale would exchange his proud recollections for a coronet, while of the dead who fell there it may be truly said that their death in defense of a cause and country which they dearly loved is their highest encomium. Of instances of personal prowess, of hair-breadth escapes, of instances of devotion on the part of soldiers to officer or friend, the writer could recount not a few, for deeds of valor were not wanting. Nor need I recount them here to make good the boast that every man there had witnessed a baptism of fire equal to Balaclava. Many an old Confederate, who had drawn a nice bead on a Yankee in more than a score of battles and skirmishes, could then swear to his man, and could swear to a bayonet crimsoned when before it had served only to glitter on dress parade. Bradbent, of Company E, 16th Virginia Infantry, who commanded the detail of sharpshooters, here met his fate. The victory was with us, but dearly had we paid for it, for every company left more than half of its numbers among the dead or wounded. The company to which the writer belonged, Company A, 16th Virginia Regiment, out of twenty-eight men who went into action, lost in killed and wounded fifteen men, while his regiment, with only seven companies, lost twenty-one killed and twenty-one wounded. Other regiments, numbering ten companies each, lost in like ratio.

Among the Negroes captured and sent back to the lines on Monday morning to assist in burying the dead was one who could scarcely speak English. But in a conversation with the writer, in broken English, he told me that he was born in the West Indies, came to New York on a Spanish ship, got leave of absence to go on shore, got drunk, and when he recovered consciousness he was well on his way to Virginia, snugly buttoned up in a blue uniform and cooped up with a number of his race similarly conditioned. He lamented his fate in piteous tones, mingling English and Spanish in due proportion, and with the most emphatic language he declared that if he ever got out of this scrape the American Negro could work out his freedom without hope or expectation of further help from him.

Sunday was intensely hot, and the condition of the unburied bodies, the danger and difficulty of getting water and the fatigue of the day before made it a memorable day in the calendar of our sufferings. The day was spent in watching, if not in praying, and night again called upon us to resume the irregular fire upon the enemy, which served to keep us awake and to keep him in his works. Monday, by an agreement between our respective generals, witnessed the burial of the dead by both sides, and that night we returned to our old camp ground at Wilcox's farm, bearing with us regrets and tears for the untimely death of many brave comrades and friends.

The Battle of Trevilian Station

NOBLE D. PRESTON,
CAPTAIN, 10TH NEW YORK VOLUNTEER CAVALRY

Philadelphia *Weekly Times* 4, no. 27, August 28, 1880

On June 6, 1864, while acting as assistant commissary for subsistence of [Brig. Gen. Henry E.] Davies' brigade of [Brig. Gen. David McM.] Gregg's division [I] left the command at Bottom Bridge and proceeded with a few wagons, several pack mules, and a detail of men to White House to obtain a supply of rations. I reached White House late in the afternoon and from the infantry officers and soldiers there learned that "the cavalry was to start on a raid early in the morning." It was common camp talk with them, but was news to us. So little credence did I give the rumor that I made no unusual haste to return, finally leaving White House a little before dark to rejoin the command at Bottom Bridge.

The route lay through wilderness and broken country most of the distance for five or six miles, and it was quite late and very dark before we reached the place where we expected to find our comrades encamped as we had left them. Before reaching the place, however, we encountered quite a number of stragglers, from whom we learned that the cavalry had all but left, but there appeared to be no Moses among them whom we could safely follow, and we therefore struck boldly out in the intense gloom of the night in search of the trail.

Wandering about until next morning and meeting with only an occasional straggler, several of my own men having become separated from the command and lost, hungry, tired, and dispirited as most of the men were, I resolved to halt until daylight and rest. A clean little copse of underbrush in the forest was selected and the horses unsaddled, and without much ado the

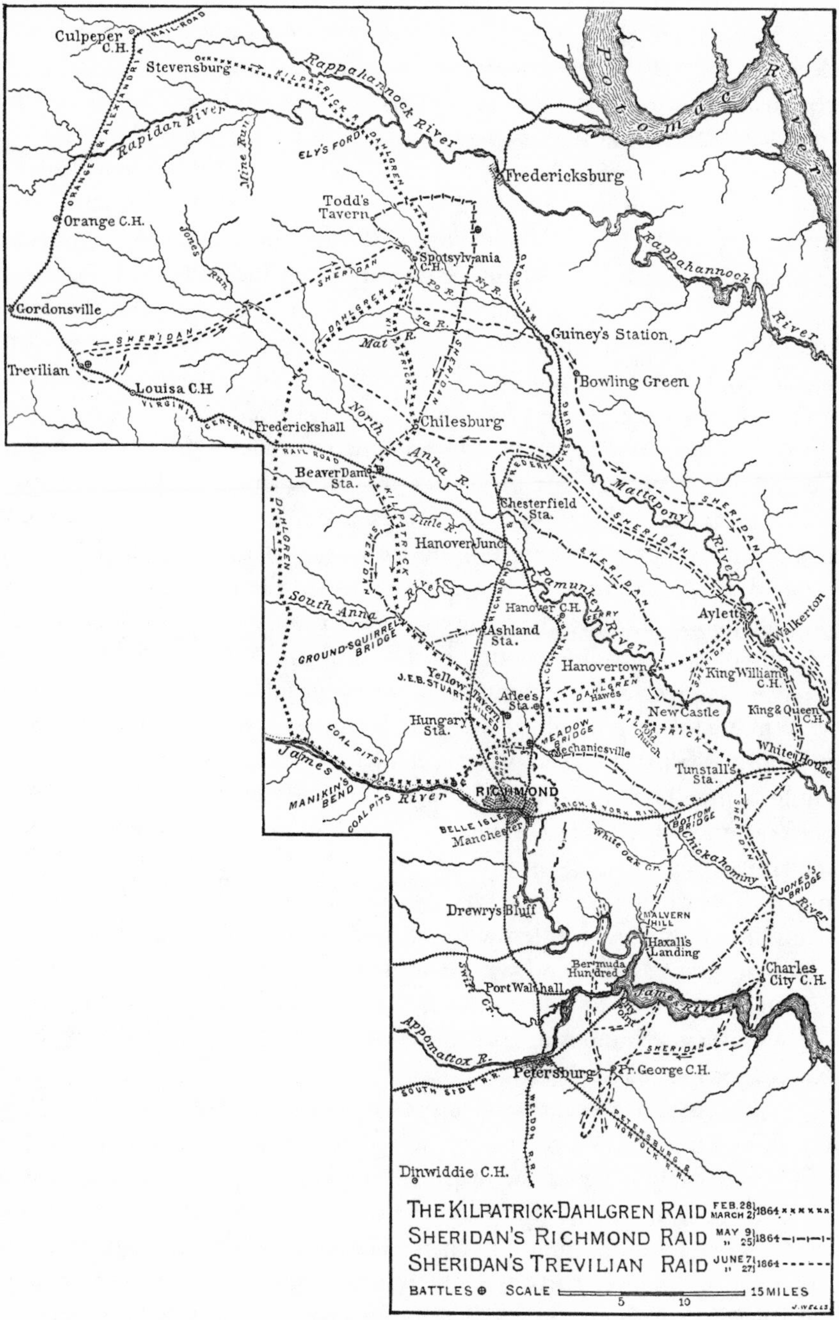

Sheridan's Richmond raid

(CENTURY MAGAZINE)

men threw themselves down on the bed of leaves and were soon enjoying sleep. For myself I could not close my eyes, for my anxiety to find the command was so great as to almost lead me in search of them while the men were asleep. What if we had wandered inside of the enemy's lines in our midnight traveling? Daylight would surely reveal us to them, and we would be marched to Richmond as prisoners of war. Or, if we were not actually inside the lines of the enemy, we knew not which way to move in the morning and we were as liable to march into the embrace of foe as of friends. However, the few hours of daylight soon sped, and with the coming of light came the murmur of many voices not far away. Horses were saddled and all put in readiness for a move rather lively. A reconnaissance in force, i.e., two men—the writer and a trusty orderly—was made in the direction of the hum of noises. On reaching the edge of the wood, away in our front, we beheld our cavalry in the broad open fields, where their horses were eating the rank clover, others saddling up and part of the command on the move and crossing the Pamunkey at New Castle. Marching forward, we found our own brigade had crossed the river and we hastened on and joined it while they were formed in an open field awaiting the crossing of the remaining portion of the command.

We now received a verification of what our infantry friends had told us at White House and which we had listened to with such indifference because we felt that so important a matter would hardly be known to the entire army. The movement fairly commenced about 10:00 A.M. The weather was oppressively hot and the dust arose in such clouds as to render it at times impossible to discern the person in the immediate front line of march. The irrepressible foragers soon spread out upon either flank, and in many instances their recklessness was paid with their lives, as during the entire march the command was environed by guerrillas. We encamped the evening of the seventh near a village, in the center of which stood the ruins of several rather imposing brick structures, which had evidently been erected for manufacturing purposes.

While here I accompanied my own regiment—the 10th New York Cavalry—on picket. As the pickets were being posted a small party of one of the other regiments of the brigade, mistaking us for the enemy, essayed to drive us from our position by a saber charge. We in turn, supposing them to be "Johnnies," met the charge and repulsed them, the result being one man of our own party wounded in the leg and three of the opposite party wounded, one mortally. The unfortunate affair caused considerable gloom to spread over the command.

Near our picket post was the plantation of a wealthy but ignorant and licentious old man named Scott. On our approach he fled, but his slaves, in great numbers, some of them young girls of very pretty faces and but a slight brunette tinge to their complexion, being mixed in the crowd of black, greasy, and repugnant countenances, came down the road and gazed upon us, apparently quite bewildered at the sight of so many Yankees. Almost all the literature found in the house of this man Scott was of the most obscene kind.

The morning of the eighth the pickets were called in and the march resumed. Learning that a Rebel mail had passed us on a parallel road during the early morning hours, General Davies dispatched Lt. Col. [Benjamin F.] Sceva of the 10th New York Cavalry with a small force to intercept and capture it. Meeting with a small Rebel escort to the mail, Sceva charged, losing his hat in the melee. He failed to get the mail and started on the return march. To protect himself from the scorching rays of the sun, Colonel Sceva was compelled to do a little foraging to obtain a covering for his bare head and succeeded in finding a silk hat of very ancient construction and style. Under its shade he presented something of the appearance of William Penn, as illustrated in the old-time schoolbooks. Hastening forward at the head of his little command, he passed General Davies, commanding the brigade, who viewed with apparent disgust the apparent departure from the regulations in the head gear of the lieutenant colonel. The ridiculous appearance caused by the venerable hat had not occurred to Sceva, whose dignity would not for a moment have tolerated the exhibition. With him it was a matter of necessity. Imagine his surprise and consternation at being placed in arrest by General Davies for a breach of discipline. He hastened to explain matters and was released with the admonition that he should make a change in chapeau to more nearly conform to the army regulations at as early a moment as possible. This day's march brought us to a point near Polecat Station, where we encamped for the night.

On the ninth the march was resumed southward. Guerrilla bands continued to hang upon the flanks and rear of the command, and fighting between them and the foragers was continual. Near evening, as we emerged from a piece of woods, we espied away to the right quite a large body of Negroes congregated, who were seemingly viewing us with something of indifference. Presently the 1st New Jersey Cavalry, following us, emerged from the woods, bearing its designation flag—the Stars and Stripes. No sooner did the darkies behold its beautiful folds than the air was rent with their joyous songs and shouts. The crowd that but a moment before seemed

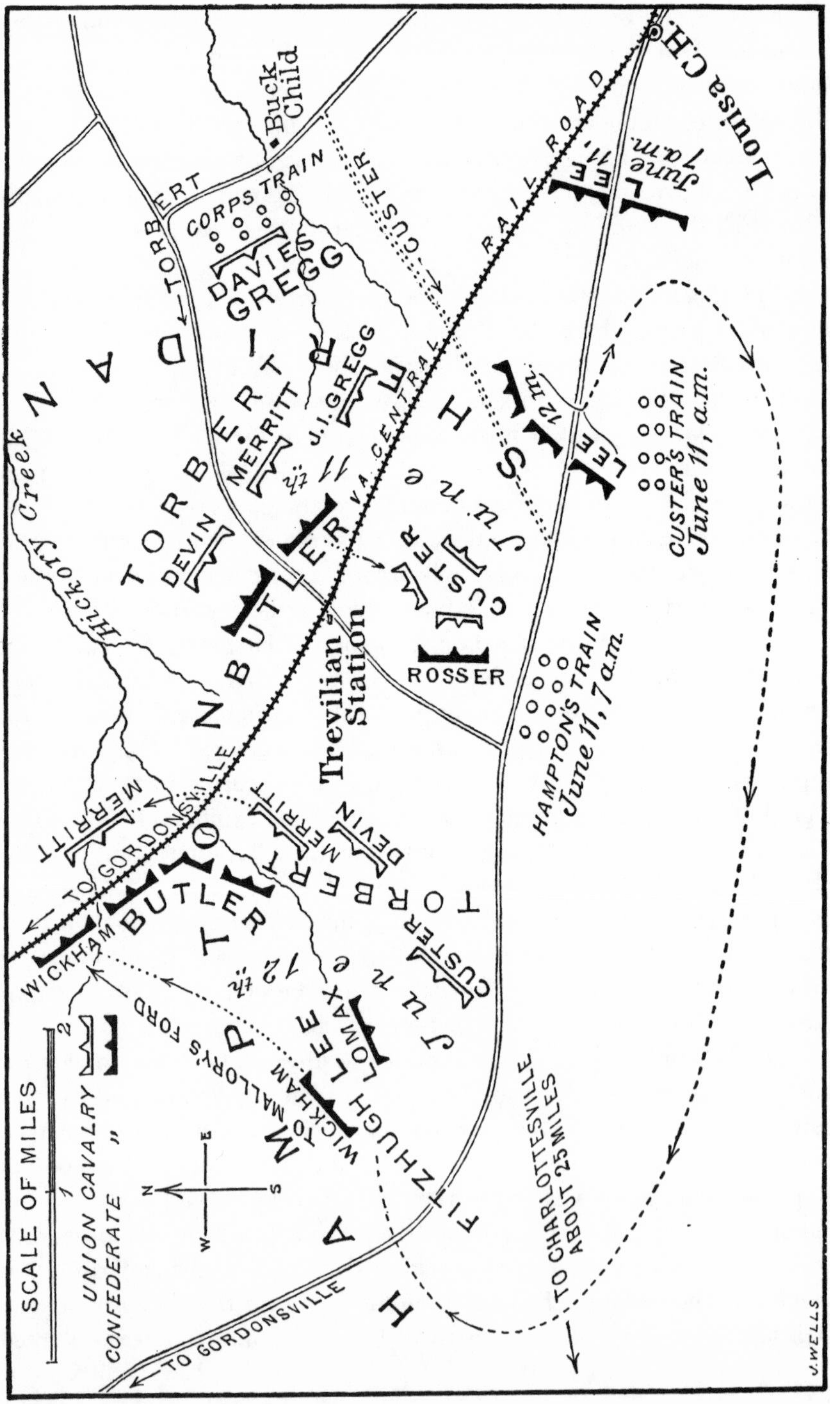

Battle of Trevilian Station (CENTURY MAGAZINE)

so stoical and indifferent was changed as if a bomb had descended in their midst. The dust had so covered our uniforms that they were unable to distinguish whether we were Johnnies or Yankees, but the sight of the Stars and Stripes dispelled all doubts. Said one of the blacks, "Golly, Mass'r, when we seed dat flag we know'd we'se all right!" The day of jubilee had arrived, and the whole force fell into line in the rear and commenced the tramp, they hardly knew whither.

During the day we passed through Childsburg. In vain did the crafty cavalryman look for plunder in the town. Frugal Ruth would have starved to death had she depended on her gleanings from the town for a meal. We passed New Market and encamped near a bridge over a small creek.

On the tenth we marched on through Andrews' Tavern and Lieman's Store. During the day [Brig. Gen. George A.] Custer caused his troopers to march dismounted a portion of the time to give the horses rest. In the evening of this day I made a request of the A.C.S. of the division to be relieved, that I might accompany my own regiment, as I was tired of the monotony of moving with the trains. The request was denied. Mounting my horse I rode to brigade headquarters and with the intercession of Col. [M. Henry] Avery, commanding the 10th New York Cavalry, obtained my release from General Davies.

The morning of the eleventh we were astir early and marching in the direction of Trevilian Station, on the Virginia Central Railroad. Custer's Brigade of Torbert's Division was in the advance. Considerable hilarity was manifested among the troops as we plodded along through the dust, when lo! The discharge of a piece of artillery in our front put a quietus on all merrymaking. Anxious looks were exchanged between officers and men. The first shot was quickly followed by the second, the third, and the fourth, each succeeding shot seeming to still further hush the noise in the ranks and set each individual to communing with himself. It was plain that we were on the eve of a battle, the nature and extent of which no one could forestall, but in which we felt that the messenger of death would be sure to make his selections from among our number. Quickly following the report of the cannon came the sharp rattling of the carbines. A moment later and an aide came galloping back with instructions for our regiment to move out of line to the left and guard the wagon train, which was already parked there.

While the regiment was being marched into position I obtained leave from Colonel Avery to go forward and see what was going on. Pushing through the underbrush to the side of the road, which was filled with troops, I emerged into an open field just in time to witness a line of dismounted troops charge into the opposite wood, where the Confederates were posted. Away to the right was a Confederate battery in plain view, which was pouring a murderous enfilading fire into our charging column. Turning to go, I espied the head of a column of my regiment, which had been relieved and ordered to report to Col. J. Irvin Gregg, commanding the second brigade of Gregg's Division, just issuing from the wood I had passed through. Moving with Colonel Avery at the head of the regiment, we were guided by a staff officer to Colonel Gregg, who left his brigade and advanced down the road to meet Colonel Avery and give him instructions. Colonel Gregg informed Colonel Avery of the relative position of the Rebels and his own brigade; that they lay facing each other in a piece of woods in our front, on either side of the road on which we then were.

By the conformation of the ground between us we were unobserved by the enemy. We were dismounted and moved up and took position behind a rail fence, smothered with weeds and small trees, which run at right angles with the road and directly across the flank of the enemy's position and not more than twenty rods from it, the intervening space being a newly plowed field. No sooner had we fairly got into position than Gregg's brigade with a cheer charged the enemy's line. Then followed the din of cheers and rattle of carbines, anon drowned by the heavy roar of artillery. As for the moment the result of the charge was in doubt, our hearts heaved and swelled as we lay behind the fence, unable to see the contending parties who were in the timber.

We were not left in doubt. The dying down of the cheers from our side, the desultory firing and the confusion of voices from the Rebel line, indicated too plainly that Gregg had been unable to drive the enemy from their position. To us it had been assigned to charge across the open field and assist in taking prisoners should Gregg be successful in forcing the rebels out of the woods. Knowing that the Rebel line must be broken up from Gregg's charge, lying across their flank as we did and our regiment being fresh, I recognized the opportunity offered us making a glorious record for ourselves by immediate action. I left my position in the center of the regiment and hastened to the right, where I found Colonel Avery and in an enthusiastic manner proposed to charge the enemy before they could complete their formation again or change front so as to receive us. Colonel Avery, so brave and sagacious an officer as graced the service, did not like to assume so great a responsibility. He had no authority; Gregg, with his entire brigade, had failed to drive them from their positions, etc. I urged that our position across their flank gave us a great advantage, and if we could charge at once they would not get re-formed in season to make a successful resistance. Receiving from him permission to lead the charge, I hastened back,

The battle of Trevilian Station (JOHNSON, *CAMPFIRE AND BATTLEFIELD*)

passing the word as I went to be ready for a charge. Arriving at a point near the center I gave the command to "charge!" and, mounting the fence, jumped forward on the plowed ground, when a Rebel bullet entered my right hip and I fell to the earth. There was an instant of dizziness, a forgetfulness of everything as I reeled and fell. Quickly regaining consciousness I essayed to gain my feet—only thinking I had stumbled—but again fell. Conscious that I was wounded from the sickening sensation of the warm blood which flowed down my leg and into my boot and warned by the little puffs of dirt around me, as the bullets struck, that the Rebels were disposed to finish the work which they had but partially accomplished, I dragged myself to an old pine stump nearby, where I lay while the regiment swept victoriously past me. The cheers, which rapidly receded in the distance, told that they were driving the foe before them.

I was taken up and carried a short distance in the rear and laid in the shade of the wood, where the horses of the regiment were being held by a portion of the regiment detailed for the purpose. Others from the regiment were brought and laid by my side until a Rebel battery, having got the range of our field hospital, made it so uncomfortable for us that Maj. Gen. D. McM. Gregg, who chanced to pass that way, ordered our removal to a safer distance. I was taken up and carried through the timber and left in the shade of some trees with no one near me but my faithful Negro servant Aaron, who still led my horse about with him. Darkness coming on, he left me and went in search of assistance to take me to some more comfortable place. He returned with two men, bearing a litter, on which I was placed and carried some distance and finally deposited on a straw mattress in an old log house. On the same bed was a young Confederate major, whose name I afterward learned to be Russell. He was mortally wounded and in a voice which clearly indicated his near approach to death, he related to me that in several charges during the day his regiment had nearly all been killed or captured; that he had been home and while there was married; that he received a telegram to rejoin his regiment before the expiration of his leave of absence and had returned to his post the day before, the tenth. He was conscious that his life was of short duration and expressed a desire to see the colonel of his regiment, who was a prisoner in our hands. His request was granted and the colonel, under a guard, was sent to him.

I shall never forget the tall, swarthy, black-haired, and black-eyed individual who came thus to the bedside and received from the handsome young major the dying missives of love to the newly made wife, so soon to become a widow. He had the bearing and look of an Indian. He remained with the major but a moment and was led by the guard away. In the brief interval that I was permitted to know Major Russell he presented the evidences of a noble character. He was youthful, and although his eyes were sunken and his countenance pallid, he was a fine looking fellow.

Late in the evening Dr. R. W. Pease, the medical director of the corps and a warm personal friend, visited me and said he had made out a list of such of the wounded as were to be left, who could not withstand the long march which was before us, and among the number was my own name. Dr. Van Sickler, assistant surgeon of the 10th New York, was to be left in charge of those left behind. The arrangements had been made for the wounded to leave early next morning. There was but six ambulances in the command and between five hundred and six hundred wounded were to be provided for—nearly all of whom would be compelled to ride in the army wagons in which we had transported ammunition and supplies. Dr. Pease was a kind-hearted man, who I knew would advise only what to him seemed best. "A week's journey was before us; the roads were very rough and the weather extremely hot and," said the doctor, "you cannot stand five hours' ride." "But I can die in the attempt, Doctor," I said. "And if there is no transportation for me I have a horse that I will ride; Aaron will hold me on as long as I have life." "If you are determined to go," said the sympathetic doctor, "I will provide a way; rest easy about it," and he took his departure.

It was near midnight when the spirit of Major Russell took its flight, and with the lifeless form by my side, I was left to contemplate the horrors of war and to conjecture what might be my own fate. The surgeons who visited me during the afternoon, as I lay under the elm tree, considered my case so hopeless that they would not even waste the time to dress my wound. As I lay on the litter of straw with the dead Confederate major, a flickering light from a burning faggot in the fireplace cast a sickening light over the wretched room, in which scattered around on the floor lay about a dozen wounded and dead soldiers, the blue and gray lying side by side. The long, weary night of suffering and gloom wore past, and the light of day began to dawn on the twelfth when I was startled to hear just outside, the hurried words, "Hurry up! Get these wounded out!" And the next instant I was seized by two men, thrust into an ambulance and the horses were whipped into a run. Away we sped over cornfields, rocks and corduroys, at a fearful pace! I believed the team to have become unmanageable and running away, but I set my teeth and holding firmly to each side of the ambulance, prepared for the worst. My wound started bleeding afresh and caused a feeling of faintness to come over me. Suddenly we came to a halt and busy preparations of getting the long train of wagons in position and moving off was gone through with. Groans and screams of the unfortunate wounded, who were being jolted about in the heavy army wagons, were heard on every hand.

[Capt. Theophilus F.] Rodenbaugh was assigned to the ambulance with me. [Captain] R. had suffered the loss of an arm the day before. He was in remarkable good spirits for one who had endured so much pain and loss of blood. I think [Captain] R. was taken from the ambulance during the first day and Lieutenant Mason, of the 1st United States Artillery, was substituted. Lieutenant Mason was of a nervous temperament, a splendid young fellow, who loved his profession and was an honor to it. Standing by his own battery, while in action, with his hands by his side, a solid shot from the enemy's battery deprived him of his right hand and tore the flesh from his right thigh. During the eight days' march which we made he suffered much and I afterwards learned he died in Washington a day or two after his arrival. My own sufferings on that long, tedious march were intense, but were somewhat mitigated by the knowledge that there were many whose sufferings were as great or greater than my own in that long train. In many instances the sufferers were compelled to ride in the hot June weather by the side of a comrade who, unable to withstand the hardships of the march and the oppressive heat, had yielded up his life.

Over five hundred wounded were successfully brought off by General [Philip H.] Sheridan under the most discouraging circumstances. A large number of Negroes followed us on the return march to White House. The march being made through a country which had for a long time been occupied by the Rebel army, it was barren of food for either man or beast. Large numbers of horses were broken down, and we were compelled to kill them to prevent their falling into the enemy's hands. A few hours rest would have rendered the poor animals as good as ever, but we were in no position to give them the desired rest, and the result was the faithful creatures who had borne their masters until unable to do so longer were deliberately shot.

During the return march General Sheridan, learning that a Rebel hospital, containing many of our own wounded, was located not far from our line of march, sent a detachment out and brought away such as could be moved. Among others was a Major Wilson, from General [James H.] Wilson's cavalry division, who had been wounded in an engagement and left on the field for dead. He was taken by the Rebels and General Wade Hampton's medical director severed his wounded leg at a point near the body. Word was sent to his wife that he was dead, and he was dropped from the rolls of his regiment as having been killed in action. When we reached Washington he learned from friends that his funeral had been held in his native town in Chenango County, New York, and he was mourned as dead by his wife. On our arrival in Washington he telegraphed his wife that he was on his way home!

The object of the Trevilian raid is given in the following extract from General Sheridan's report of the operations of the cavalry corps: "On June 6 I received instructions from General Meade and the Lieutenant General to proceed with two divisions of my corps to Charlottesville for the purpose of cutting the Virginia Central Railroad, to unite, if possible, with Major General D. Hunter, whom I expected to meet at or near Charlottesville and bring his command over to the Army of the Potomac."

There also appeared to be another object, viz.: to remove the enemy's cavalry from the south side of the Chickahominy, as in case we attempted to cross the James River this large cavalry force could make such resistance at the difficult crossings as to give the enemy time to transfer his forces to oppose the movement. The latter object was fully carried out, but the "uniting with General D. Hunter and bringing his command over to the Army of the Potomac" as will be seen by a further extract from the same report, failed through no fault of General Sheridan's:

> At night (of the eleventh) my command encamped at Trevilian Station and from prisoners, of whom we had captured about five hundred, I learned that Hunter, instead of coming towards Charlottesville, as I had reason to suppose, was at or near Lexington,

> moving apparently, on Lynchburg, on the south side of the James River, and that Breckenridge was at Gordonsville or Charlottesville, having passed up the railroad. I therefore made up my mind that it was best to give up the attempt to join Hunter, as he was going from me instead of coming towards me, and concluded to return.
>
> Directions were at once given to collect our own wounded and that of the enemy. I was still further influenced in my decision to return by the burden which these wounded threw upon me, there being over five hundred cases of our own, and the additional burden of about five hundred prisoners, all of whom must have been abandoned by me in case I proceeded further; besides, one more engagement would have reduced the supply of ammunition to a very small compass.
>
> On the morning of June 12 we commenced destroying the railroad to Louisa Court House, and in the afternoon I directed Torbert to make a reconnaissance up the Gordonsville road to secure a by-road leading over Mallory's ford on the North Anna to the Catharpin road, as I proposed taking this route in returning, and proceeding to Spotsylvania Court House, thence via Bowling Green and Dunkirk to the White House. In the reconnaissance Torbert became heavily engaged, first one brigade, then another, then the last, the battle continuing until after dark. Gregg, during this time, was breaking up the railroad to Louisa Court House.
>
> The result of Torbert's fighting made it impossible to cross at Mallory's ford without enduring a battle next day, in which case the remainder of our ammunition would have been consumed, leaving none to get back with; therefore, during the night of the twelfth we moved back on our track and recrossed the North Anna at Carpenter's Ford.

General Sheridan concluded to return on the night of June 11 and arrangements were accordingly perfected looking to that end. The day's fighting had demonstrated our superiority over the enemy. Every charge and movement made against them on that day had resulted in their discomfiture, and it was on the evening of this successful day's work that General Sheridan concluded to return. The object of the expedition had been accomplished so far as it was possible. The drawing off of the enemy's cavalry from the James River and the destruction of the Virginia Central Railroad were parts of the program fully carried out by General Sheridan. During the night of the twelfth the rumbling of the cars and the whistle of locomotives indicated great activity on the enemy's part in hastening forward reinforcements of infantry of whom they could, in a few moment's time, place in our front a large force, without serious jeopardy to their capital, as the distance was short and facilities for quickly transferring them by railroad excellent.

General Wade Hampton announced the battle officially as a victory. It was just such "victories" as this that wound up the Southern Confederacy. He can only have placed his claim to victory on the second day's (June 12) doings at best, and on that day we have seen that we were carrying out the program made the day before of returning to White House. What of actual fighting took place at Trevilian Station was decidedly a victory for General Sheridan. But two divisions of the Cavalry Corps—the 1st under Torbert and the 2nd under D. McM. Gregg—numbering, all told, about six thousand effective men, were present.

Scouts with Wade Hampton

JOHN S. ELLIOTT,
SCOUT, STUART'S (AFTERWARD HAMPTON'S) CAVALRY

Philadelphia *Weekly Times* 8, No. 11, May, 1884

Soon after the investment of Petersburg, Virginia, by the Federal army under [Lt. Gen. Ulysses S.] Grant in the summer of 1864, I was recalled from my field of operations in Northern Virginia and assigned to duty in the rear of the enemy's lines at Petersburg. I had before me quite an extensive territory, extending from the Petersburg and Weldon Railroad to the James River. It required some time to gain a knowledge of the country, its topography and people, before we could make our plans to the best advantages. Within a month the enemy had established his fortifications and had begun to scour the country outside his lines for the purpose of driving out all citizens who were unfriendly to the Union cause and to capture and disperse scouts and other soldiers who might venture outside the Confederate lines.

There were several scouting parties, whose leaders were George D. Shadburn, Richard Hogan, Isaac Curtis, Ashby, Sanderson, myself and some others. We soon made it a hazardous business for the enemy to scout outside his lines with anything less than a hundred men well mounted and armed. Fight after fight took place between us and these small parties for more than a month. We often made an ambuscade, drawing the Federals into it and making a clean capture. Disputanta Station, on the Petersburg and Norfolk Railroad, was the scene and battle ground of some of the most persistent of these hand-to-hand fights. The enemy soon became more cautious and we became bolder and more daring, frequently going into the Federal lines and capturing the pickets as we came out.

We had a telegraph operator who would cut the enemy's line and attach his wire so as to let the messages pass through his key, and in that way we got a number of important facts. These messages were being sent from the War Department in Washington City to General Grant and from Grant and other generals to the department. One day while we were lying in the bushes listening to the clicking of our little key a battle was going on south of Richmond along the Nine Mile or Charles City road. Some general in command telegraphed to President [Abraham] Lincoln that he had stormed the enemy and captured two lines of breastworks, but the Confederates, reinforced, drove them back with heavy loss in killed and captured. The Federals soon found out that we were intercepting their messages, and they made it too warm for us to continue operations in that line.

We went to work to break up scouting in neutral territory. There was an extensive district of country, interspersed with creeks, swamps, and woods. The population was devoted to the cause of the South, and that gave us great advantages. On one occasion I applied to [Maj. Gen. Wade] Hampton for forty well mounted and armed men to attach and defeat one of these persistent and adventurous patrol parties that had given us a good deal of trouble. They came up with us at times, and greatly outnumbering us we had to resort to flight to avoid being killed or captured. They boasted to the citizens that they intended to have us dead or alive, if we stayed in that country, and the sooner we left the better. The men asked for were furnished.

We hauled down about a half mile of telegraph wire along the Petersburg and Weldon Railroad late in the evening, rolled it into small bundles, and carried it six or eight miles and during the night formed an ambush. We stretched the wire across the road just high enough to catch a man above the saddle and wound it around trees to secure it. This was done at the head of a long cut in the road, and extending it more than a hundred yards back on each side and securing it by wrapping it around the trees we made the wire very much like a partridge net. If we could get the enemy's cavalry into it we intended to charge down on the troopers and the wire in front would sweep the rider off and let the horse go, which would so excite and confuse them that we could capture them without much fighting.

During the night some of my men while scouting along the enemy's picket line met with Ashby and told him where I was and what I intended to do the next day. He gathered several of his party and just before day he joined us. I was very glad to see him and to have his aid. I had been with him in fights and adventures that tried men's courage and knew that there was not a braver or more gallant soldier in General Lee's army. I requested him to take charge of the head of our ambuscade and I would take the rear end, where the fight would begin. Our plan was that every man was to remain hidden until I opened the fight and then all the men were to rush to the front and capture those nearest to them and in that way we would secure all who got into our net. The next day was Sunday, a bright and beautiful morning. We were on the lookout at an early hour with videttes posted some distance out with signals of the enemy's approach. Hour after hour wore away without any sign of their coming. Toward noon two or three scouts from Shadburn's party, who had heard of our intended attack, joined us. They had come from the direction we expected the enemy and saw nothing that indicated a Yankee scout that day. We had begun to despair of any chance that day when one of the videttes came running in and reported the enemy coming in our direction in strong force.

I immediately went to an elevated point nearby, and with my spy-glass could see quite a column of cavalry riding towards us at a leisure gait. I returned and told the boys to get into their blinds and lay low until I opened the fight, and then come out and show their hands. On the enemy came as unconscious as if there was no war. The advance guard of about six men passed into our net laughing and talking, and of course never had the least idea that a deadly snare was set for them in that thick woods on both sides of the road. In a few moments the head of the column came into the snare also. As soon as we got as many as I thought we could manage I sprang from my hiding place to within ten feet of the column, fired a pistol over their heads and hallooed "Charge!" The Federal column broke in an instant, the rear half flying for dear life. We closed in upon the others, and such a scramble was rarely seen during the entire war.

The men came out of their blinds promptly and in fine order, shouting at the top of their powerful voices, "Surrender! Surrender!" and at the same time firing their guns over the heads of the already terrified enemy. The enemy made a grand rush and discovered—as some of the prisoners afterwards said—that they were in a wire net and thought that we intended to murder them. They went with such force against the wire that it broke and the most of them escaped. The first man who struck it was killed and a number of others were badly hurt, all of whom fell into our hands. In their extreme fright quite a number jumped off of their horses and ran through the woods toward their lines. Many of the horses became riderless, and in the excitement ran after their dismounted owners.

The various scouts were exceedingly active and vigilant. The enemy's plans would frequently be discovered in a remarkably short time by them and communicated to General Hampton, whose headquarters were connected with those of General Lee by telegraph. General Lee would know them also in less than an hour after the scouts would report. One night, some time early in the fall, while Shadburn and I were inside the enemy's lines, not far from the James River, our attention was attracted to the lowing of cattle. Shadburn said, "Elliott, what do you reckon that means?" I replied that I did not understand it unless it was a herd of beef cattle. The animals continued to low as if they were separated and excited, and we soon discovered that there were a great many. At least we thought so. He said, "Suppose we look into that matter, and if there is a chance to capture them I think General Hampton will do it." "All right," I said, "I think so, too." We went to work to find them, but before we had time to discover much the approach of day forced us to retire and get out of the lines.

We passed the pickets just as day began to break, about a half mile east of Merchant Hope Church, and went about a mile, got our horses and rode several miles back, where we got breakfast and had our horses fed. During the day we planned the manner of reconnoitering the herd the following night. Shadburn and Merchant were to go to the left and Sneak (whose real name I have forgotten) and I were to go to the right. As soon as darkness came we four rode together until we got a secure place to hide our horses near the enemy's lines. We unsaddled them, arranged a password, or rather a low whistle imitating the tomtit, by which we would recognize each other if we should accidentally meet in the enemy's lines. We soon parted, each party taking the route agreed upon.

Sneak and I crawled up to the enemy's picket line more than a mile east of where Shadburn and Merchant were to go through. After everything got quiet we slipped through two mounted pickets standing about two hundred yards apart and proceeded to look up the cattle. We tried our utmost to find them, but failed until late in the night. They had been driven the day before about two miles west toward Petersburg. The reader may think it strange how we discovered which way they had gone. As soon as we failed to find them at the place where Shadburn and I had seem them the night before we went to work to feel for their tracks, which were so many that it was difficult at times to tell whether they were traveling or merely grazing. But after a long and tedious search we found out that most of the tracks pointed westward. This we told by resorting to low or soft earth, where the animals' weight would make an indenture in the earth one or more inches deep, the point of the hoof of course indicating the direction traveled.

After locating the herd it was difficult to inspect them closely on account of the guards or herdsmen who were constantly prowling around.

On more than one occasion we came very near meeting up with them. If we had it would have necessitated taking them prisoners, which would have forced us to carry them out into our lines. But as luck would have it we did not let them meet up with us. We went up so close to some of the cattle that they would get up and walk off. We could distinctly see that they were large, the cattle, and in pretty fair order. The best judgment we could make from inspecting them was that there were eight hundred or a thousand head. After we had seen all we thought was necessary we retraced our steps to the picket lines, which were fully two and one-half miles from the point where we came in.

Just before day we passed within thirty yards of a citizen's house with bright lights burning in the east-end rooms. My comrade said: "Here is our chance to take a Yankee officer or two with us. Let's slip in and capture them." I objected, for the reason that if we should make such a haul the enemy would become alarmed and increase their vigilance to such a degree that it would be very difficult to get inside of their lines. He agreed with me, and we went quietly away, and were soon near the outside picket. We were crawling on our faces like alligators, trying to avoid discovery as we passed out. Before sunrise we were at our horses. Shadburn and Merchant had not come, so we went to work and saddled all the horses so as to hasten on several miles to the place where it had been agreed we would breakfast. About sunrise, while I was fixing my saddle my horse turned his head suddenly to look at something he had just discovered. I turned, of course, and looked, too, and there were Shadburn and Merchant coming up laughing.

We all had a hurried talk together about where we had been and what we had seen. Shadburn and Merchant had discovered another herd. To sum up our trip it was a success, and we then and there pledged ourselves to do all in our power to keep a watch on the herds and to induce General Hampton to capture them, which we knew he could do. It was agreed that Shadburn should that day see the general and lay before him our discovery and plan. We all mounted and were soon at the appointed place where the kind ladies were waiting for us to partake of our breakfast. It was agreed that not one of us was to say a word, or even hint to anyone, where we had been or what we had seen. After breakfast Shadburn left for our camp, and the rest of us got some feed for our horses and rode far back into a thick woods to take some sleep, which we needed very much. We soon found the place, fed our horses, lay down and slept. Late in the evening we awoke and began talking over what we should do to the best advantage until Shadburn returned.

I suggested that we spend the night in trying to find the enemy's submarine cable, which we had every reason to believe was in the James River. We saddled our horses and rode several miles down the river, which was only about two miles to our left. We secured the animals in the woods not far south of Warwick Swamp and went on foot. It was very difficult to get to the river in places. We cut long poles, tied pieces of iron on the ends to sink them, and swept them along as far out as possible from point to point. We worked industriously, following along the river nearly a mile, until we became very tired and sleepy and gave it up for the time. Next day Shadburn returned and told us General Hampton was very much pleased at our discovery of the cattle, and wished us to keep our watch on the cattle and he would see General [Robert E.] Lee about it.

We continued to go into the enemy's lines by detail for fully two weeks, frequently reporting to the general what we knew to be facts. At length General Lee consented for General Hampton to make the effort. Gen. [William] Mahone was sent to take charge of our position in front of the enemy during our absence. General Hampton, with about two divisions of cavalry and a number of guns from our artillery, started late in the evening, taking a circuitous route to conceal his real purpose. The scouts, about twenty in number, patrolled the country between the enemy's line and the moving columns, and were exceedingly vigilant and active to prevent the enemy from finding out anything going on. We were about two days and nights before we came to within striking distance. The attack was to be made just at daylight. It was understood that we were to join the general soon after midnight of the morning of attack at a certain citizen's residence, where General Hampton told us we would find him at the head of his column.

I arrived at about 1:00 A.M. and found that most of the scouts had arrived with favorable reports. The general expressed himself well pleased with our service. The column moved at about 2:00 A.M., at which time all the scouts had reported. Our column was to open the attack at Merchant Hope Church, near where we had reported the cattle were. As we had worked up the raid and had been the cause of the raid, we asked General Hampton, as a special pleasure as well as honor, to let us lead the charge. He readily assented, and told Col. [Elijah] White, commanding the Maryland cavalry, to support us. Shadburn was to lead us, as he was one of the oldest commanders of scouts in the army. I took position by his side, and when we were ready Colonel White came to the front and asked us some questions respecting the topography of the country, especially concerning the road, church and so on about the enemy's picket posts. When the colonel turned to ride back I said to him: "Colonel, stick to us, and we will give it to them." He replied, laughing: "All right, boys, I'll do it."

As soon as an order came from General Hampton to go ahead, we started. We were just about a half mile from the enemy's pickets, who were standing just in front of the church. We moved on quietly until we came up within two hundred yards of the church. Day was breaking, and we could see the dark outlines of the church as General Hampton came up and said: "Shadburn, you may charge as soon as you can; Colonel White's men are at your backs to sustain you." As the general halted to give us a showing Shadburn gave the order to charge. We went at them in fine order, and when we were within fifty yards of the picket he fired on us and fell back. We charged up and some of us got across the public road when such a volley as alarmed us came from the church and around about it. We drew our pistols and began firing, but to no purpose. The enemy was reinforced in a few moments, when the firing became intense.

We fell back on Colonel White's command, the worst whipped set of fellows we had been for a long time. One of our party was killed and several men and horses were wounded. The colonel came to our relief as he said. He cleared away the rubbish and fallen timber from the road in a few minutes, threw out a line of sharpshooters and moved forward with a grand charge. The enemy fell back in confusion. General Hampton came up and joined in the charge, and in a few minutes more we were in possession of their position, and those who were not prisoners were getting away as fast as feet and horseflesh would carry them. As our men came galloping up they were formed in regimental fronts. By this time it was open daylight. We could see the enemy's cavalry, about a battalion strong, drawn up in line under the hill, about one hundred and fifty yards off. General Hampton sent Tom Scott, one of our scouts, to demand of the Yankee officer his unconditional surrender. Scott bore the message and returned in five minutes with the Yankee colonel's reply, which was:

"Give my compliments to General Hampton and tell him that his demand is not the kind of tactics I learned at school."

General Hampton turned to Colonel White who was with him, and said: "Colonel, capture the Yankees, and also that herd of cattle."

The colonel ordered his command to charge and away we went, the enemy flying for life. Some of the men hallooed: "We are charging into a world of infantry." The cattle were not far off and there were so many of them at first view they did look like so many white tents. We overtook a large number of the fleeing cavalry and captured them. Colonel White dashed on and coming up with the cattle ordered his men to surround and stop them. The enemy, seeing our purpose, did their best to stampede the herd by hooting and shooting among them. We captured the entire herd, said to be about twenty-two hundred.

When I saw Colonel White had the cattle surrounded I charged up to a lot of tents, located in a citizen's garden, or rather where the garden had been, and captured several prisoners and a fine cloak, which I got in an officer's tent. I also untied a fine bay horse and carried him along. The horse, as I understood, belonged to an officer named Gregg, a brother of General [David McM.] Gregg. The horse proved to be a noble animal. I rode him throughout the remainder of the war, and after the surrender I rode him to my home in Alabama, where I kept him for some time and sold him for $200. General Gregg came out and tried to intercept us and recapture the cattle that evening, but we were prepared for him, met him on the half-way ground, and soon convinced him it would not pay. Our herd was safely driven into the Confederate lines and supplied General Lee's army with beef rations for three weeks. Competent judges estimated the entire herd as worth more than $200,000 in greenbacks, or $1,500,000 in Confederate money.

In Petersburg During the Siege

John D. Young,
Captain, Sharpshooter Company, III Corps,
Army of Northern Virginia, C.S.A.

Philadelphia *Weekly Times* 2, no. 17, June 22, 1878

The bloody experiment of Cold Harbor demonstrated to the Federal commander the fact that a direct advance on Richmond from that point, by assault, was as unsuccessful and futile as similar movement had been on the lines of Spotsylvania and the North Anna. Unwilling to waste the time necessary for the slow approaches of siege, [Lt. Gen. Ulysses S.] Grant conceived the bold idea of transferring the base of his operations to the west side of the James River. This change of base was not to be effected, as heretofore, by simply extending his left and marching by flank in front of [Gen. Robert E.] Lee; but emboldened by the success of their last movement he determined to cut loose entirely from their line upon which he had asserted "that he proposed to fight it out if it took all summer," and at the expense of uncovering Washington, and with the Confederate capital still as his objective, to inaugurate the movement by seizing Petersburg. It may be added that in the disastrous repulse at Cold Harbor, in addition to the loss sustained in actual numbers, the morale of his army had been greatly shaken. The need of rest, recuperation, and, above all, new scenes, sustained by the blood of their comrades or associates with the memories of useless slaughter, encouraged the adoption of this plan of operations.

Situated at the head of navigation on the Appomattox River and about ten miles from its confluence with the James, Petersburg, as a covering point of the railway lines, the main feeders of Richmond, was regarded as of great strategic importance, and, as we shall hereafter see, was strongly fortified. The feeler to this transfer was begun on June 8, 1864. When

[Maj. Gen. Benjamin F.] Butler, under the direction of the Federal commander, advanced two columns under [Maj. Gen. Quincy A.] Gillmore and [Brig. Gen. August V.] Kautz against the city, to be supported by an attack from gunboats up the river, Gillmore, moving up from Bermuda Hundred, penetrated to within three miles of the city, seizing in his advance portions of the turnpike and the Richmond and Petersburg Railroad. Being sharply met by [Lt. Gen. Pierre G. T.] Beauregard he halted, and under a stiff pressure from the Confederate forces, retired to the entrenchments at Bermuda Hundred. On the same day the gunboats, moving into action opposite Fort Clifton, on the river, met with such stout resistance as to totally disable one ship, which was abandoned by the enemy, and to compel the others to retire. The advance of Kautz was made from the Prince George side, his force consisting principally of cavalry, with a few light batteries. His movement was so sudden, so spirited and well chosen as to time (Beauregard being then engaged with Gillmore), that he must have been successful but for the heroic defense of the home guards under Col. [Fletcher H.] Archer.

Kautz, timid and uncertain, allowed the appearance of what he conceived to be a heavy field work, but in reality the city reservoir, and a few shots from a battery of horse artillery that happed fortunately to be at hand, to determine his retreat. Thus it appears that the first attempt to capture Petersburg, though well conceived, failed from the incapacity and temporizing conduct of the enemy's commander.

This failure, like many others, acted upon that singular military mind of General Grant like the application of a spur to a restive horse. With a stubbornness of purpose, he determined to renew the attempt, and this time to fall on Petersburg with the entire force at his command. Taught by lessons purchased at the expense of many lives, he laid aside the open and aboveboard movement that had hitherto characterized his strategy. The transfer of the Army of the Potomac to the south of James River was begun on the night of June 12, and was so well carried out that by noon of the sixteenth the whole of the Army of the Potomac was across and before the line of Petersburg.

These lines, now celebrated as the scenes of so many historic combats, were constructed under the personal supervision of Capt. [Charles H.] Dimmock, of the Confederate engineer corps, as early as 1862. The works were located about three miles from the city limits and consisted of forty-five heavy forts, or, more properly speaking, redoubts, so placed as to command the adjacent country, connected partially by strongly entrenched curtains on each particular front. In geometric shape the fortifications

Driving the Confederates out of the Dimmock works (BEYER, *DEEDS OF VALOR*)

formed a huge semi-circle, extending south from the Appomattox River and crossing the Jerusalem plank road well to the right of Blandford Cemetery, bent to the west and enveloping the city in that direction. Although scientifically constructed, and of formidable appearance, this line was not, in the opinion of the best Confederate engineers, well adapted for the defense of Petersburg; besides, what is more to the point at this juncture, the system of these works was of such magnitude and extent that it would have taken two such armies as that of General Lee's to fill them, while Beauregard's forces were barely sufficient to man the batteries in front of the Norfolk road. On the sixteenth [Maj. Gen. Ambrose E.] Burnside and [Maj. Gen. Gouverneur K.] Warren came up in support of the Federal force in front of these works, and all hesitation on the part of the commander or misconception of Grant's intentions was solved by direct orders to assault the lines at once. But already divining Grant's intentions, and no longer threatened by a hostile movement against Richmond from the north side, General Lee had commenced his movement to Petersburg, and, pushing forward the leading divisions of the army, a portion of these veterans were already established in the lines with Beauregard's command. Still, however, this force was so small that under repeated and desperate assaults the enemy were partially successful—driving the Confederates out of the Dimmock works in front of the Norfolk Railroad, and compelling that body to take up a temporary position along the line of the Prince George road. The pressure of Beauregard and the paucity of his forces determined their commander to retire still closer to the city. Such preparations were made as the nature of the circumstances and the projection of this delicate movement would admit, and on the night of the eighteenth the temporary line was abandoned.

I assume that the new line was more the result of an accident than of actual or even casual survey, for General Beauregard, the commander of the Confederate forces, was and is now justly regarded as an officer of great merit and distinction. Skillful as he has over and again proved himself in handling armies, he was particularly successful in that phase of war known as military engineering. Nevertheless, the new line, if tried by the simplest rules of engineering, must be found radically defective and in many instances devoid of the points that combine to make up a strong defensive position. Located on ground commanded at all points by positions already occupied by the enemy, the "new line" ran almost perpendicularly from the river in a southern direction. Striking the Dimmock line at a point where in bearing around the city, these lines (the Dimmock) crossed the Jerusalem plank road, the two lines in conjunction formed what was known as the Rives salient. This new position was almost a straight line without curtains of bastions, or, in fact, formation by which a converging fire could be brought to bear on an advance of the enemy in the front from the river to the Rives salient, and in addition to this defect it was, as before stated, commanded by the range of high ground in possession of the Federals and upon which the enemy had begun to place heavy batteries. With these guns the enemy were enabled to enfilade the Confederate lines right and left; and as they extended further to our right, to obtain a reverse fire on the "new line." But this was not all. It was soon found that the nature of the ground in this particular front was such that the enemy could, free from our observation, easily mass his troops, ready for a rush on our lines, as was the case in the affair of the "Crater." Such were the leading defective features of the new line which, as will be seen, was destined to be held until the evacuation, but only by the enormous cost of building traverses, covered approaches, and all other conceivable works that engineering skill could suggest, to say nothing of the annoyance and sacrifice of life. Why General Beauregard did not retire closer to the city and take up his new position along the Blandford Heights and the ridge of the Jerusalem plank road can only be explained by attributing the new line to accident and to other causes coincident with a reverse movement in the face of the enemy. It was in this new position that Lee, hurrying forward with the main body of his army, found Beauregard; nor was his presence ever more sorely needed. A day later and the defense of Petersburg would never have existed—a monument of the heroic devotion of its defenders worthy to rank in history with Antwerp and Londonderry.

It is said that General Lee's first expression on his arrival at the front was that of dissatisfaction touching the general features of the new line, and, with the view of rectifying this important element of his defense, he called to his assistance Maj. Gen. William Mahone, an officer in whom he reposed great confidence, and who, besides being an engineer by profession, was familiar with the topography of the country around Petersburg. Mahone, surveying the "new line," pronounced it untenable from the river to the Rives salient and advised that a line be constructed still further to the rear and closer to the city, a line formed of regular bastions and curtains running from the river along the high ground of Blandford Heights and covering the Jerusalem plank road, to rest on second swamp, an impassable morass at the head of the Blackwater, some five miles from Petersburg—a position that he then thought could be manned and held by two or three divisions of the army. This position would have commanded the ground occupied by the enemy and given a fair, open, rolling country in their front. Had this line been taken the army would have secured an admirable position, almost impregnable in front, with the left resting on the river, the right on second swamp, that extended for miles in the direction of Norfolk. Such a line, firmly held, would have stopped most effectually the turning movements for which the Federal commander was now so famous. Lee could have given to his army the rest, drill, and discipline of which they stood so much in need, advancing with his reserve to meet the enemy on the chord of the circle that he must describe to further envelop the town. This advice, admirable as it was in all respects, was not adopted, General Lee intimating that his intention then was rather to force a fight than to settle down behind defensive works. When afterward he was forced to adopt this "new line," that position between the river and the Rives salient was strengthened by a rear line of entrenchments.

For a long time the weary but necessary work of building traverses, erecting bomb-proofs and constructing covered approaches to the lines employed the time of the men in the trenches. This occupation, while steady in its way, was now and then varied by repelling sallies or taking quiet shots at the enemy's pickets. The troops on the extreme left, while constantly exposed to danger of a continued fire from the enemy of both cannon and musketry, yet considered these dangers more than balanced by the freedom from drill, so distasteful was this necessary exercise to the average Confederate soldier. Then, too, there were regular reliefs, and either permits were granted to visit the city or they would run the "blockade," as it was called, and in defiance of commands and guards, spend their spare time in its limits.

The condition of the citizens of Petersburg, now for the first time rudely awakened from the contemplation of war far away from their borders to the bloody features of battle at their very portals, was worthy of the high renown that in former days had gained for these people the proud sobriquet of the "Cockade City." Environed with a cruel and relentless foe, who stormed at their doors with shot and shell—their ears stunned with the roar of combats that unceasingly raged around their city—their very eyes saluted with horrid sights of the wounded that streamed from the front and filled the hospitals—they bore themselves in the main with a lofty courage amid scenes of death and danger well calculated to shake the fortitude of the bravest sons of Adam. Such of the men as by reason of age or acquired disability were exempt from service pursued the peaceful avocations of trade or passed their time in discussing news from the front. Others, not satisfied with the numerous exemptions with which they were hedged in and dreading another and more sweeping conscription, amid all the horrid fears of battle, murder and sudden death, devoted their time and energies to putting up political jobs by which they could realize the crowning object of life, a seat in the common council—a body at all times safe, at least from the clutches of the conscript officer. Strange to say, we held an election during the siege and party spirit ran as high as in these times of piping peace. Parties still living recollect the famous "Ashcake ticket" that swept the city and landed in the common council a number of choice spirits that would have in a pinch done better service on the lines than in the common hall. It is a singular fact that the city of Petersburg was never under martial law, and what is more extraordinary, the city government was during the entire siege enabled to maintain order—rarely, if ever, calling upon the provost guard stationed there to assist.

The common council met regularly for the transaction of business. As the shelling increased, however, their meetings were of a proportionately short duration, and it is said that on one occasion, at least, our city fathers made an adjournment so hasty as to omit the usual motion necessary on such occasion. In justice to that honorable body it should be stated that the records of that particular meeting were taken under the shelter of a friendly hill and carefully completed. Members of the council assert that on that day the city, and especially the council chamber, was shelled in a most frightful manner.

The women of the town, unappalled by stories of sack and rapine, bent all their energies to sustain the siege and comfort their defenders. In a more womanly manner they did greatly contribute to alleviate the sufferings and trials of our soldiers, the matrons giving freely from their scant supply of linen, lint, and bandages for the wounded, and carefully nursing the sick and helpless in their various hospitals—in short, doing many necessary things that come most gracefully from women, and all in such a manner as reflected the highest credit on them. The maidens, in another and more pleasing manner to the soldiers contributed their help to carry on the siege and help the veterans to pass away the hours that intervened between duty and pleasure. When the lines were quiet troops of both officers and men, clad in their bravest attire, would hasten to town to devote the spare moments "off duty" to love and beauty. The streets heretofore silent, or mayhap patrolled by a solitary guard on shirking citizens—a silence only interrupted by the shrill scream of a shell or the louder report of its explosion—would be filled with a gay and lively throng. Glittering uniforms commingled with the dull Confederate gray, all on pleasure bent and resolved to make a day of it. It may be said that these visits were of two-fold object, to escape the harassing life of the trenches and to indulge in the fascination of flirting, to which all soldiers are so prone, and last, but by no means least, to secure a really good dinner. Of engagements there were many, and of marriages not a few. Oft and again was the tender tale of love breathed over a homely dish of bacon and greens with its accompanying ashcake, while moment of unalloyed bliss were interrupted by limited supplies of "sorghum and wheat coffee." Balls and parties were of frequent occurrence but owing to the limited state of the commissariat the social gatherings were strictly of a conversational or emotional character. These were aptly styled "starvation parties," and were greatly enjoyed by the soldiers, who, though half-starved themselves, seemed in pleasurable contact with such ample compensation for the customary repast. These parties were often rudely interrupted, and in the midst of mirth and pleasure dread summons to arms would be sounded; there would be a mounting in hot haste, and a rushing of men to the front.

The combats around and near the city were numerous; the affairs numberless. Of the combats, that best known was fought on the eastern front of the city, at the point of the lines known as the "Crater." This action has been most ably and minutely treated by Capt. W. Gordon McCabe, in an oration delivered before the Virginia Division of the Society of the Army of Northern Virginia; a paper (it has since been published) that by all military critics is highly esteemed as a most important contribution to the history of the war. If, however, we except Five Forks, the action of the greatest strategic importance was that of August 18, which resulted in the seizure and holding of the Weldon Railroad, one of the main feeders to the beleaguered city.

When Grant, by executing a series of maneuvers known as the "Deep Bottom movement," which ended in a loss to the Confederates of Battery Harrison, he so seriously menaced Richmond from the north side of James River as not only to draw heavily on Lee's forces at Petersburg for the defense of the Confederate capital, but to demand the presence of Lee himself to take personal direction of affairs on their front. The Federal commander, finding himself checkmated, as it were, on his right and opposed in heavy force, rightly conceived that these very troops must form a large portion of the forces in and around the Petersburg lines. He, therefore, decided that now was the time to seize the Weldon road. Acting at once he turned Warren—then halting on the southern banks of the James, ready to move to the north side—back southward, and pressing these troops swiftly to his left, with but little difficulty placed them on the much-coveted line of communications. Warren arriving on the road at a point about four miles from the city limits, formed a line of battle perpendicular to and across the railroad, then cautiously moved forward in the direction of Petersburg. Up to this time he had met with no hostile force save the few cavalry and possibly a battery of horse artillery. These he brushed out of his way with but slight effort. Now, however, he had scarcely proceeded more than a mile in the direction of Petersburg before he was confronted by a Confederate line. This force proved to be not more than two brigades, with the usual number of guns attached, commanded by [Maj. Gen. Henry] Heth. As the Confederates appeared to be but a small body and, besides, isolated from their lines, Warren determined to deliver battle, and at once made his disposition for attack, when suddenly he found his own position imperiled in a manner as serious as unexpected. Heth, ever on the alert and at all times ready and anxious for a fight, in this respect as well as many others greatly resembled the famous General Pictou. Fiery in nature and of a most chivalric disposition, if he made an error in his combination on the field it was usually found that his intense desire to get at and into the enemy had biased and over-ruled his cooler judgment. Heth had, with a promptness and activity for which he was well noted, already discovered the enemy's position. Leaving a small force in front he passed the greater

Scenes among the rifle pits before Petersburg (ST. NICHOLAS MAGAZINE)

part of his command by the Vaughn road well to Warren's right and falling furiously upon the unprotected flank of [Brig. Gen. Romeyn B.] Ayres' (Federal) division, threw that command back in confusion on their center, capturing a large number of prisoners, colors, and guns. It was soon apparent that Heth's force was too small to follow up his advantage, besides, the closing shades of night quickly put an end to the conflict, leaving Warren still in possession of the Weldon road.

The next day General Mahone, carefully examining from his picket line the position of the Federal forces on the Weldon Railroad, conceived a plan of attack, which he presently suggested to Lt. Gen. [Ambrose P.] Hill, his corps commander. From the appearance of the lines in his front, near Fort Mahone, General Mahone divined that Warren, in his extension to the Confederate right, had failed to keep up a proper communication with the main Federal lines at the Jerusalem plank road. His plan, therefore, was to move to the front and well to the right of the Federal force, pierce their lines and taking Warren in reverse to cut this detached body of troops off entirely. This movement, it was intended, should be supported by an advance from the Confederate force that still confronted Warren on the railroad. This daring scheme was at once referred by Hill to Beauregard, then in temporary command during the absence of Lee. Beauregard, approving the plan, ordered the brigades of [Brig. Gen. Alfred H.] Colquitt and [Brig. Gen. Thomas L.] Clingman to report to Mahone for duty. These two, with one other (Mahone's old brigade), were unfortunately all of the troops that could be spared for this duty. Availing itself of the friendly cover of a wide-mouthed ravine that, running perpendicular from his works, extended far to the front and finally rose to the surface in the deep recourse of the thick woods, to the right of which the enemy lay, Mahone's column swiftly and silently penetrated to the rear of Warren's position without meeting with even so much as a picket. Here, breaking from column, he formed his troops, with Colquitt and Clingman in line of battle, and held the Virginia brigade massed on his defensive flank to be used as occasion demanded. Moving cautiously forward he fell with terrible force upon the astonished and panic-stricken enemy. Nor did they make a stand until so much of Mahone's forces were used for the necessary guarding of his prisoners as to leave him but a handful of them; and Warren had resorted to the cruel expedient of turning his guns on his own men to stop the Confederate advance. Other forces of the Federal army at this juncture came to Warren's assistance. Mahone, with great address and small loss extracted his command from this perilous position. In this brilliant feat of arms, Mahone absolutely captured and brought off more prisoners than he had men engaged—a fact which reflects the highest credit on the masterly manner in which he handled his command. But Warren still held the Weldon Railroad, and it was considered to be of the last importance that it should be dislodged. This resulted in the last of the series of unsuccessful assaults that was delivered for that purpose, and is known as the combat of August 21.

This action was fought by Mahone with a force of six brigades and twelve guns; his design in this instance was to turn the enemy's flank and operate in their rear. But this time he chose their left flank, making for this purpose a wide detour to the right of the Confederate lines. It should be

A Union powder magazine (ST. NICHOLAS MAGAZINE)

understood that by this time Warren was strongly entrenched in his position in front and on his defensive flank, and had also fully connected with the main line on the Jerusalem plank road. His rear, however, was still open to attack. Misled by his guides as to the real position of the enemy's left, and failing to receive from a body of cavalry that he had sent to threaten Warren's rear the co-operation he had expected, or to produce the results he had anticipated, Mahone's attack was unsuccessful, and is now chiefly remembered as the occasion of an incident that at that time was greatly commented upon in army circles—a most singular adventure and exploit of [Brig. Gen. Johnson] Hagood, commanding a South Carolina brigade. When Mahone moved against Warren's works, to guard against accidents, he held Hagood's Brigade in reserve. Deceived by his guides as to the position of the enemy and the nature of the ground, he changed his formation from column into line too soon, and in advancing in line of battle through the chaparral and thick undergrowth his line fell into what is termed in military parlance a "kink." In the act of rearranging the troops the enemy opened upon him a heavy artillery and infantry fire which not only broke but drove back his line. Being informed by one of the brigade commanders that the enemy were advancing Mahone ordered Hagood forward to form on a line perpendicular to his original advance, in order to assail the flank of the advancing Federals. In securing this position Hagood's movement brought his command into the very jaws of the Federal works and almost surrounded by the enemy. As soon as the position of the South Carolina brigade was discovered, Captain Dailey, provost marshal of the 4th Division of Warren's corps, rode out of his entrenchments and, calling to the colonel commanding the regiment on the right flank, summoned that officer to surrender, and at the same time possessed himself of the regimental colors. The regimental commander, sensitive of the perilous condition of his position, submitted to what seemed to him a misfortune that he could not by resistance overcome.

General Hagood, from the left of his brigade, observed the action of Capt. [Dennis] Dailey with a surprise that was increased by the inaction of the enemy as well as the nature of the demand that passed rapidly from the right to his position on the left. Filled with mortification and dismay by the conduct of his officers that threatened to engulf the entire brigade into ruin, he hurried like a raging lion to his right and, accosting Dailey, fiercely ordered him to give up the colors and surrender himself a prisoner. Captain Dailey's reply was worthy of the man who the instant before had faced death to prevent what he considered a useless sacrifice of lives. With a lofty heroism equal to any occasion, he replied: "This regiment, through its officer, has already surrendered to me. You yourself must see that further resistance on your part must end in the total destruction of your command. In the name of humanity I ask your surrender, and refuse to give up the colors." To him speaking came Hagood's answer, quick and stern: "Unless you give up these colors I will shoot you dead," and he leveled a pistol at his foe. Then on Dailey's raising his arm as if to signal to the Federal lines, Hagood shot him through the body, killing him instantly. At the same time seizing the colors he brought off his brigade, but at heavy loss. General Hagood's action in this affair was freely criticized and by many condemned. It is hard to say, even in the lapse of time, what was the proper course to pursue. I know of no case that presents a parallel to this unless it be the shooting of the Indian princess of Delhi by Hodson, of Hodson's Horse, during the mutiny. It was his life or theirs, and he protected himself. The operations of Mahone's column, as before stated, was a failure. That persistent officer, however, determined to make another trial with a larger force, which he had been promised by General Lee, who had at last arrived from the north side; but the troops, however, failed to come up in time, and at night Mahone returned to his lines, leaving Warren still fixed in possession of the road. Thus one of the main feeders to the city was lost. There remained now, if we except the country roads, but two sources of supply to the beleaguered city—the South Side Railroad and the Upper Appomattox Canal. This last line, though now by a series of misfortunes it had degenerated into a mere mill-race, during the siege freighted stuffs from the adjacent country as far up as Farmville, and was a most important medium of transportation to trade and even munitions of war.

During the entire siege buying and selling of every conceivable commodity were pursued with an avidity and eagerness hardly equaled in the more peaceful and balmy days of Petersburg. In the midst of battles and the storm of shells that hurled past, merchants behind barricades of the very goods which they offered coolly made their bargains and carefully noted that their neighbors did not get the best of them in the trade. A glance at the newspapers published at that time disclosed advertisements of every species of saleable property from provisions to patent medicines, from bales of cotton to bundles of cast-off clothing, and all at prices. It can be with truth affirmed that the business operations were on a grander scale than was ever before known in this market. If prices were exorbitantly high, money was proportionately plentiful, of "both old and new issue." It is an instructive and interesting illustration of the fleeting nature of riches to study the bank accounts of some of these operators, at the same time to know that the man who now gazes lovingly on the face and parts most reluctantly with a ten dollar greenback once had his thousands in bank, and during the siege rarely took the trouble to count his deposits, but left that matter to be managed by his clerks. Confederate money was the one thing which we had enough and to spare. Incredible as it may seem, there were some people who even hoarded Confederate money—a currency which, to use their mournful expression, "died on their hands," never to be resurrected here for legitimate purposes; but it is suggested by Maj. John M. Daniel that it will pass current in realms above. Shopkeeping was usually of an ephemeral nature. The stock required, as a general thing, was a barrel of "new dip." This, however, was disposed of on a profit that would now be considered something enormous.

In the time of war as well as in peace banks are a necessity, and in Petersburg there was no exception to this rule; the officers were exempt from military service, and for that reason alone, if no other, stood manfully to their post, while as regards directors, I have heard that board meetings were never before so well attended, not only on discount days but every day. The vaults of the banks were, in fact, the best bomb-proofs in the city. One great relief to the citizens was found in the cessation of tax collecting. There were plenty of summonses but no man could be found brave enough to chase recalcitrant debtors from place to place and force the payment. The disposition of the dead was for a long time a matter of serious thought. The cemetery in Blandford was so near the lines as to be exposed at all times, and the constant fire thereupon rendered it unsafe for the living to bury their dead. Thus the churchyards in the city were first filled and afterward the dead were buried to the south of the town. In spite, however, of the danger attending an interment in Blandford some were found who buried their dead there. I particularly recall one occasion—the burial of Capt. John C. Pegram. This gallant soldier and accomplished gentleman lost his life under the most mournful circumstances. The very evening before the affair in which he was killed he obtained leave of absence from his command for the purpose of being married, and on the morning of that fateful day, when leaving his quarters equipped for the journey, he heard an unusually sharp fire from the front. Being then informed that the enemy were on the move he rode directly to the lines, reporting for duty, engaged, as was his wont, in the thickest of the fight, and in a short time fell, shot through the head, and his remains were brought to the city. Connected on both sides with families of a high ancestry and untarnished fame, they disdained the idea that danger should deter them from placing their beloved dead near the remains of his fathers.

The next night, at the solemn hour of twelve, the burying ground lit up by the rays of torches that glared in defiance of the ceaseless cannonading, his remains in the presence of a sorrowing throng of friends and relations were consigned to camp. So highly was this noble young man esteemed that even tender women were found brave enough to pay by their presence a last sad tribute to his memory; and it is of record that more than six persons were wounded during the short ceremony at the grave, for his last requiem was sounded by the guns of an enemy that he had fought so long and so well—a fitting salute to a soldier so brave, generous and true. The short days of autumn and the shorter rations of our commissariat were now upon us. Military operations, by reason of the state of the roads, were not to be thought of. Furloughs were granted to some few soldiers and taken bodily in the way of desertion by many. The gradual but sure encroachments of the enemy to our right, the bad conditions of things in the far South and in the Valley of Virginia; all served to depress the army. Men began to look one another solemnly in the face and speculate on the end; but soldiers are not found by nature to be melancholy under any circumstances, and such as could now almost foresee the result kept silent and talked in the same strain as when filled with the high hopes of Fredericksburg and Chancellorsville. Gaiety was the order of the day. The medical staff led off with a grand dinner to the artillery of the Third Corps, and not a bad dinner was it, by any means; for from the hospitals and other sources known to these gentlemen of the mortar and pestle, by buying here and borrowing whenever they would, the medicals managed a very fair spread. If the tables of the old Ballingbrook Hotel did not absolutely groan with all the viands of the season, it was certainly most tempting to a body of men who were ready to face the dangers of a charge for a new overcoat or a few pounds of Goshen butter! "Battlefield supplies"—and, I am sorry to say, of the vilest kind—flowed freely and jollity reigned supreme. Regular toasts were drunk and responded to in fine style. A short time afterward the artillery returned the compliment in the shape of a grand "blow-out." This was the event of the season. All the big guns were present. Good things both in shape of bonne-bouches and bon-mots were as plentiful as Confederate notes. The speakers of the occasion were Captains McCabs and Chamberlayne of the artillery; gallant soldiers both, and of whom it may be said that if there was at these times anything that they could do better than fighting a battery it was in making post-prandial speeches. But in the midst of all, the gaunt specter of a depleted army, confronting an ever watchful and increasing foe, forced itself on the minds of thinking men, and set them seriously to study the problem to be solved in a short time.

The March gales had barely hardened the roads sufficiently for military operations before [Maj. Gen. Philip H.] Sheridan, by a splendid stroke of genius, executed a movement that for skill and promptness stands unrivaled since the first campaign in Italy. Riding swiftly up the Valley of Virginia he carried everything before him, and at Staunton, turning short to the left, never drew rein until he had massed ten thousand sabres in front of Lee's extreme right at Petersburg. With this additional force General Grant prepared for the final and decisive blow that was to result in the discomfiture and probable capture of his adversary. For some time back General Lee had been impressed with the uncertain tenure of his hold on Petersburg. His views of touching this grave question had already been laid before the authorities at Richmond; but at this time it needed not the judgment of a soldier to forecast the result. The gradual but sure approaches of Grant's left had reached a point far beyond the Weldon road and seriously threatened the Cox road and rail communications on the south side. It was, therefore, unnecessary, even before Petersburg could be evacuated, that a diversion should be made to draw the enemy off our southern lines. The question of evacuation was practically settled when Warren seized and held the Weldon road. The problem now presented to the Confederate chieftain was to select some point of the segment of the iron circle that seemed gradually to envelop him, break through and hope either to gain a glorious victory, or

Sheridan in the Shenandoah Valley

(HARPER'S NEW MONTHLY MAGAZINE)

at least to inflict such a blow upon the enemy as would relieve the pressure on his left. With a boldness that savored of the days of Chancellorsville, and trusting once more to the chance bad generalship of the enemy—whatever you may term it—Lee deliberately chose what would seem to all the strongest part of the enemy's lines upon which to deliver his blow.

As everything rested upon the success of his undertaking, General Lee determined to use the elite of his army, the direction of the affair to be made under the personal leadership of one of his most trusted lieutenants. [Maj.] Gen. John B. Gordon was selected to lead this forlorn hope, and as in all such affairs as this the success or failure of the action mainly depends upon the leader, it may not be out of place to notice some of the qualities of that officer. Gordon, like many others, had within him a slumbering genius for war that service quickly developed. From the time that he commanded a brigade his conduct was marked in the army as that of a rising man. As division commander he was justly regarded as second to none in that brilliant array of generals that Lee had drawn around him, and his great services were such as to win for him the high grade of a corps commander. A man of tender emotions and dashing gallantry, he was both loved and respected by his men. Untiring in zeal and energy he was esteemed so highly by the commander-in-chief as in Lee's judgment to stand next in succession of the army. In personal appearance Gordon was that type of man that is best calculated to win the affections of an army; with truth, it may be added, that with a striking presence and great military efficiency, he combined a simplicity and purity rarely associated in the same person. With such a leader and a selected band it was hoped that the contemplated movement would be a great success in spite of the difficulties that filled the way. The point of the attack selected was Fort Steadman, on the eastern front of the Petersburg line and well to the Confederate left. To insure a proper support [Maj. Gen. George E.] Pickett's Division was detached from Longstreet's Corps, in front of Richmond, and ordered to be massed in rear of Gordon's works in time to follow up his advance.

Before dawn on March 25, Gordon's column, under the personal supervision of that officer, who stood in front of the works while the assaulting column defiled past him, moved silently from their works, and, successfully capturing the videttes of the IX Corps, burst like a thunderbolt upon the astonished guardians of Fort Stedman. This great battery was instantly carried and its guns turned on the flying enemy; and, again trimming his lines, General Gordon prepared to assail in reverse the entrenchments to his right; but by this time the vast extent of the Federal commander's line was discovered from points both to the right and left in the rear of Stedman, and was seen in the dusky light of approaching day. Grim batteries, too, commanded that work, which poured upon our devoted band an iron hail, while heavy reserves thronged and crowded forward. After vainly waiting for expected supports General Gordon, warned by the increasing light which rapidly disclosed the scarcity of his band, bent all his energies to a successful movement in reverse to the Confederate entrenchments. That he should have accomplished this with comparatively small loss reflected the highest credit upon his conduct on this occasion, and added renewed brilliancy to his renown as a soldier. The failure of this movement, attributed almost entirely to a lack of support, had a most depressing effect upon the minds of both men and leader of our army. This last move of General Lee seemed to have determined Grant to give the signal for the consummation of the movement already carefully prepared to crush him. But four short days after the attack on Fort Stedman the final movement to the Confederate left was begun.

Then probability, the almost certainty of evacuation, was now freely discussed in the city. Already men were preparing for the end by sending off or secreting their goods and chattels. The shelling of the town that had been heretofore slackened was resumed with unabated furry. Shops were closed and the long and silent streets presented the aspect of a city of the dead. Even the bar-rooms that all during the siege had by various devices managed to deal out at enormous prices the vilest decoction that ever soldier or citizen were served with had closed. A deadly quiet everywhere prevailed, only to be broken by the loud explosion of shell and the rattle of shot that pierced the crumbling houses. The people, resigned to their fate, calmly awaited the inevitable.

The fight for Battery Gregg (LIBRARY OF CONGRESS)

Nor had they long to wait. On March 30 news was received in the city of the disastrous battle of Five Forks, in which Pickett and [Lt. Gen. Richard H.] Anderson were totally defeated by Sheridan and hurled reeling and broken to the South, never more in the history of the war to be rallied. On April 1 the city was bombarded along the entire line day and night, and men who watched through the dreadful darkness of that memorable night say that about daybreak an ominous silence fell along the enemy's lines—a stillness that betokened no good for Petersburg. For about that hour a simultaneous advance was made against the lines, an advance which, in spite of the naked condition of the Confederate works, was only successful far to the south of the town, and there chiefly so from the disaster of Five Forks. To the south of Battery Gregg this success was complete. So silently had their assault been delivered here and so slight was the resistance offered, that the division commanders on that part of the line barely escaped with their lives, while to the general of the army who, in the solitude of his quarters, was doubtless trying to solve the difficult problem of a successful withdrawal from the town, their presence was as surprising as overwhelming. Col. Charles S. Venable, an officer of General Lee's staff, who, by gallant and meritorious conduct, has inseparably connected his name with that of the Confederate commanders, was the first one of General Lee's military family to receive the news of the enemy's advance. Without waiting to ascertain the extent of the disaster, Colonel Venable at once reported to General Lee that the enemy had broken the lines. With that fretful petulance in which even General Lee would sometimes indulge, he exhibited his disbelief in a movement so unexpected, by the question: "Did you see them yourself, colonel?" But by this time their troops, rapidly taking position to the south of the town, were in plain view and moving in such a direction as to take the Confederate line in reverse. This advance was stopped at Battery Gregg.

Located to the south of Battery Forty-five, Battery Gregg was mainly intended to form a strong line of defense for the interior line of Petersburg, and, as it happened, presented the first shock to the advancing columns of the enemy. Its defense was rendered immortal by the heroic conduct of a garrison that by chance was hastily thrown in its works—a body of some three hundred men composed chiefly of odds and ends of artillery and scattered detachments of infantry. This mixed body of troops, commanded in some cases, by officers with whom they were utterly unacquainted, proved themselves heroes. Column after column of stormers of the enemy surged against its works to be hurled back routed and broken. At last, taken in reverse, the work was carried, but at the price, as stated by the Federal

General [John] Gibbon, of over one thousand assailants that fell beneath its walls. This delay and the timely arrival of Longstreet prevented a further advance of the enemy and enabled General Lee to perfect preparations for the evacuation, now an immediate necessity.

The irreparable disaster to the lines and the intention of General Lee to withdraw from the town was soon known. Many-tongued rumors, in the shape of "reliable gentlemen from the front," had not only disseminated this news far and wide, but with characteristic fidelity had greatly exaggerated both the extent of our misfortunes and the success of the enemy. The action of the military authorities in the city soon gave color to the worst phase of these rumors. Government stores were piled in the streets and fired. The tobacco warehouses, with the exception of two which held French orders and which were protected by the tri-color, were in flames. The dense columns of smoke and the near approach of battle but served to increase the consternation and excitement that prevailed on all sides. Citizens who had determined to brave everything and remain in the town were busy secreting such valuables and money as they possessed, or with ready hands prepared the affairs of those who decided to trust their fortunes with the army. Among this last class an earnest desire to quit the town in company with the baggage train, then moving, seemed to prevail. The agonizing parting of husband and wife, the tender farewells exchanged between sweetheart and lover, were neutralized by the ridiculous spectacle of some "last ditch man" who, bundle in hand, bravely trudged along with the camp follower of the army.

All day long the battle rolled around the fated city, and when night closed in, with to us a friendly darkness, unlighted save by the burning fuse of passing shells or the fitful fire that at intervals broke out on the picket lines, skillfully and silently the army was withdrawn from the line that for nine long and eventful months they had held against overwhelming numbers under adverse circumstances and with a gallant bearing that challenges the admiration of the world—a defense that has added renown even to that "incomparable infantry" that composed the Army of Northern Virginia. An army that, though soon to go down in the wreck that this movement inaugurated, will even stand among English-speaking people foremost upon the roll of soldiers famous for pluck, pertinacity, and daring. When on the morning of April 2 the serried columns of the enemy moved cautiously through the deserted streets of the city, the only vestige of an opposing force that met their gaze was a struggling squad of Confederate cavalry, who picketed their horses on the Chesterfield Heights overlooking the town. Lee and his army had vanished in the darkness of the night.

The Ride Around Baltimore

Bradley T. Johnson,
Brigadier General, C.S.A.

Philadelphia *Weekly Times* 3, no. 44, December 27, 1879

After the battle of Trevilian Station, June 12, 1864, at which [Maj. Gen. Wade] Hampton beat [Maj. Gen. Philip H.] Sheridan and drove him back from his attempted raid on Lynchburg, to cooperate with [Maj. Gen. David] Hunter, who was moving down the Valley in the same objective, General Hampton gave me permission to undertake an enterprise which I had often discussed with him during the preceding sixty days. My command, the Maryland Line, had by the movement of Lee's army to the lines around Richmond been distributed to the infantry and cavalry and I retained command of the 1st Maryland Cavalry, about two hundred and fifty effective men, and the Baltimore Light Artillery (2nd Maryland Artillery), with five inefficient guns. The gallant Lt. Col. Ridgely Brown, commanding the cavalry, had been killed in the fight at the South Anna bridge, on June 1, and Captain Griffin, with many of his men and two guns, had been captured at the affair at Yellow Tavern, May 11, when [Lt. Gen. James Ewell Brown] Jeb Stuart lost his life charging with the 2nd Virginia Cavalry. At the battle of Trevilian Station I had during the second day been made to do the duty pretty much of a brigade, for which my force was utterly inadequate, and the day after that engagement Hampton gave his consent that I should start on my long projected expedition. This was to pass along the base of the Blue Ridge, through Rappahannock, Culpeper, Madison, and Loudon Counties, cross the Potomac at Muddy Branch at a ford well known to many of the command, who were constantly passing and re-passing it on their way to and from Maryland, surprise the 2nd

Massachusetts Cavalry, generally known with us as the California battalion, and then ride at speed to the Soldiers' Home, where Mr. [Abraham] Lincoln had his quarters, capture him and send him off with a trusty party back over the river to Richmond. I was at the same time to divide the command into two parties—one to cut the railroad and telegraph between Baltimore and Washington and then push across the river at White's Ford, in Montgomery, and the other to move rapidly through Frederick, along the Upper Potomac and cross at the Point of Rocks, or Shepherdstown, or wherever else opportunity was afforded. In case of necessity both parties were to push north into Pennsylvania and escape through West Virginia and even try to get to Canada by way of Niagara.

The total sacrifice of the command would have been well paid for by the capture of Mr. Lincoln, but I did not consider escape utterly hopeless for the main body who were to go through northwestern Maryland. Their object was to create such confusion among the telegraph and railroad and commanding officers that the small detachment having Mr. Lincoln in charge would escape without attracting attention, while pursuit would be directed solely to us. This was my plan, however, and I set out to execute it. I was shoeing my horses and getting up my dismounted men and putting everything in order for sharp and active work when [Lt. Gen. Jubal A.] Early came along a few days after at the head of his column, marching to head off Hunter, then pushing up the Valley on Lynchburg. I knew General Early well and was attached to him by the comradeship of arms, by my respect for his intellect and by my warm love for his genuine, manly, true character and I explained to him my projected movement. He said it would not do. "I'm going to Lynchburg," said he, "and as soon as I mash up Mr. Hunter's little tea party I'm going to Washington myself. You'll put all that out, so you mustn't try it until I come back." He then directed me to move to Staunton and watch the Valley until he got there. By the last of June he came back. I was assigned to the command of the cavalry brigade of William E. Jones, killed at Mount Hope Church on Hunter's advance. We began our movement from Staunton down the Valley—[Maj. Gen. Robert] Ransom's cavalry division on the roads right and left of the Valley Pike and the infantry and artillery on the macadamized road in the middle.

Between Winchester and Martinsburg Early divided his forces, directing Johnson's cavalry brigade and [Maj. Gen. Robert E.] Rodes' Corps of [Maj. Gen. Stephen D.] Ramseur's Division, under Early himself, to the right to cut the Baltimore and Ohio Railroad at Kearneysville and unite with [Brig. Gen. John] McCausland's cavalry and [Maj. Gen. John C.] Breckenridge's Corps at Martinsburg; Johnson and McCausland to make the junction at Hainesville, behind Martinsburg, and thus cut off the retreat of [Maj. Gen. Franz] Sigel, who was at that place. I struck Leetown just after daylight and found it held by General [James A.] Mulligan with two thousand or three thousand infantry, five hundred cavalry, and four guns, and just as the sun rose on July 3, I fired the first gun. Mulligan had a good position on a range of hills. The infantry of Breckenridge was a half day's march behind and I had about eight hundred half armed and badly disciplined mountaineers from southwest Virginia, who would fight like veterans when they pleased, but had no idea of permitting their own sweet wills to be controlled by any orders, no matter from whom emanating. They were as brave and as fearless and as undisciplined as the Highlanders who followed Charles Edward to Culloden. However, after several hours, Mulligan withdrew, and the junction at Martinsburg being then unnecessary by reason of the escape of Sigel, we moved towards Shepherdstown.

Early on July 5 I crossed the Potomac with my command and that night camped two and a half miles from Boonsboro. On the sixth I moved to Middletown, and on the seventh drove a small force that showed itself on the mountain between Middletown and Frederick back to Frederick and pressing after it, arrived in front of the town about midday.

I knew every foot of the country—having been born and bred there—and I had the advantage also of an accurate knowledge of the condition of affairs in the town. I proposed to send one regiment down the Georgetown Pike into the south end of the town, another by the Reservoir road into the north end, and press on in front from the Hagerstown road and on the west side. This would have given me about one thousand prisoners and much baggage, wagons, and artillery. But my commanding officer, General Ransom, thought I was over sanguine because it was my own place and refused to allow the movement to be executed. He directed me to withdraw, under cover of night, to the top of the mountain until the infantry got up. Accordingly, we lay all day the eighth in a drizzling rain on the mountain. At night I was directed to report in person to General Early. I found him on the roadside just south of Middletown, and he then informed me that he had received an order from General Lee by a special officer dispatched to him for the purpose. I was directed to march at daylight of the ninth to get a position to the north of Frederick and watch Early's left until I was satisfied that he was getting on all right in the battle about to take place that day below Frederick and then strike off across the country, cut the railroads and telegraphs north of Baltimore, sweep rapidly round the city, cut the Baltimore and Ohio Railroad between Washington and Baltimore and push on rapidly so as to strike Point Lookout on the night of the twelfth. Captain John Taylor Wood was to be there in an armed steamer which he was to run out of Wilmington. We were to capture the place. I was to take command of the prisoners there—some ten or twelve thousand—and march them up through lower Maryland to Washington, where General Early was to wait for me. The prisoners were to be armed and equipped from the arsenals and magazines of Washington, and thus reinforced, Early's campaign might be still further aggressive.

I told General Early that the march laid out for me was utterly impossible for man or horse to accomplish. It gave me four days to compass near three hundred miles, not counting for time lost in destroying bridges and railroads, but that I would do what was possible for men to do. Accordingly I started from Hagan's, on the Catoctin Mountains, about daylight on the morning of July 9, 1864, moved across to Worman's Mill on the Old Liberty road, two miles north of Frederick and waited until I was satisfied that Early's left flank was free. I was so careful as to communicate my orders only to my assistant adjutant general, Captain George W. Berth; Assistant Inspector General Captain Wilson G. Nicholas, of my staff; [and] Colonel [William E.] Peters, commanding the 21st Virginia, the ranking officer of the brigade. But this caution probably cost me time, as I made an unnecessary detour in arriving at my objective. I moved through Liberty, New Windsor, Westminster, and Reistertown, reaching the latter place about daylight of the tenth. While passing through the latter place a citizen in dishabille was very urgent to be satisfied that the troops were Confederates. At last conviction came upon his doubting mind to his great delight, which he gave expression to as follows, "Well, I told Jake so; ain't I got it on him? He thought they would never come, but I always said they would!" He was much gratified at his superior sagacity. Some hours after, he came to me on the march, begging me to order a horse given back to him, which had been captured by some predatory Confederate, "not that he cared for the horse," he said, "but that Jake would have such a rig on him. That his dear Confederates, so long expected and come at last, should take his horse!" He got it back. We reached Cockeysville, on the Northern Central Railroad, about nine o'clock Sunday, July 10, and burned the bridges there. Here I detached Col. Harry Gilmore, under General Early's instructions, with part of the 1st and 2nd Maryland battalions, to strike the railroad bridge at Gunpowder River on the Philadelphia, Wilmington and Baltimore Railroad, and destroy communication between Baltimore and the North. This Gilmore accomplished the next morning, Monday, July 11, and capturing several trains going north from Baltimore, took prisoner Maj. Gen. [William B.] Franklin, of the United States Army. That night General Franklin escaped from the guard who had him in charge and who were utterly broken down by sixty hours' continuous ride.

I was occupied several hours at Cockeysville and while there dispatched a faithful friend into Baltimore to ascertain the condition of the troops and forces available for the defense of Washington. Early had defeated Wallace at Monocacy the day before and I knew he was going to push into the capital if practicable. After getting an agreeable lunch at Hayfield, the seat of John Merryman, Esq., I left two young gentlemen there to get the report from my Baltimore scout and bring it to me as soon as possible. The charming society, the lovely girls, the balmy July air, and the luxuriant verdure of Hayfield, all combined to make the scene enchanting to soldiers who had been for months campaigning in the battle-scarred plains and valleys of Virginia. From there I moved across the Green Spring Valley, in Baltimore County, and passing near the country residence of the then governor of Maryland—Augustus W. Bradford, Esq.—I detailed Lieutenant Blackstone, of the Maryland cavalry, to burn it, in retaliation for the burning of the home of Governor [John] Letcher, of Virginia, which had been destroyed by General Hunter, at Lexington, under circumstances of peculiar brutality. I bivouacked that night at the Caves, the place of John Carroll, Esq. About midnight I received a message by the two couriers left at Hayfield from the gentleman whom I had sent into Baltimore. He informed me that all the available transportation of the Baltimore and Ohio Railroad was concentrated at Locust Point; that the XIX Corps of Grant's army, under Maj. Gen. [William H.] Emory, and part of the VI Corps were in transports in the stream waiting for the arrival of General Emory to disembark and move to Washington. I at once sent this information to General Early by an officer and escort and moved on. Passing Owens' Mill early in the morning we came across Painter's ice cream establishment, which had a large supply of that luxury for the Baltimore market. As rations were scarce and issued with great irregularity, the ice cream was confiscated and issued to the troops—many of whom had never seen anything like it. The mountaineers thought the "beer" was nice but too cold, so they put it in their canteens to melt.

Pushing on we crossed the Baltimore and Ohio Railroad above Woodstock and passed by Doughegan Manor, the seat of John Lee Carroll, Esq., now governor of Maryland, with whom I had the pleasure of lunching. During the afternoon of that day (Monday, July 11) I dispatched another courier to General Early by a trusty soldier, guided by the son of a friend, who undertook to show him the way across the country. After the battle of Monocacy, fought between Early and [Brig. Gen.] Lew Wallace on Saturday, the ninth, the former had marched direct on Washington. His advance arrived before the fortifications of that place on the morning of the eleventh, but owing to the heat of the weather and the broken down condition of the troops, the column was not closed up and in position before late in the evening of that day. It was then impossible to put the men into a fight, and the attack was postponed until the next morning (the twelfth) at daylight. Troops of the enemy were plainly in sight filing into the works on the Seventh Street road to the right and left, and skirmishers were thrown out in front while an artillery fire was opened on the Confederates from a number of batteries. "Under these circumstances," says General Early, "to have rushed my men blindly against the fortifications, without understanding the state of things, would have been more than folly." After consultation with Major Generals Breckenridge, Rodes, [Maj. Gen. John B.] Gordon, and Ramseur, he determined to make an assault on the enemy's works at daylight next morning unless some information should be received before then showing its impracticability, and he so informed these officers. "During the night a dispatch was received from General Bradley Johnson, from near Baltimore, informing me that he had received information from a reliable source that two corps had arrived from General Grant's army, and that his whole army was probably in motion. This caused me to delay the attack until I could examine the works again, and as soon as it was light enough to see, I rode to the front and found the parapets lined with troops. I had, therefore, reluctantly to give up all hopes of capturing Washington, after I had arrived in sight of the dome of the Capitol and given the Federal authorities a terrible fright."

The preservation of Washington from capture was owing more to the energy and decision of John Garrett, Esq., president of the Baltimore and Ohio Railroad Company, than any merit of the military authorities. Mr. Garrett's railroad telegraph had kept him thoroughly informed as to the movements in western Maryland. He had perceived as early as the Thursday and Friday before that Early had crossed the Potomac in force and that his real object was Washington. He had impressed his views personally upon President Lincoln and the secretary of war, Mr. [Edwin M.] Stanton, and insisted on the necessity of fighting a battle at Frederick, in order either to gain time for troops to be got up for the defense of that city, or, failing that, that preparations could be made for its evacuation. Accordingly, when the battle of Monocacy was fought on Saturday, and he found Early in full march, southward, he immediately prepared the transportation on his road to receive the reinforcements which he was informed would arrive the next day at Locust Point. During Sunday the fleet of transports from Fortress Monroe, with the XIX and VI Corps, began to arrive, but the officer in command refused to land any troops until General Emory should arrive. After striving in vain to start the disembarkation, Mr. Garrett proceeded to Washington on a special engine and so impressed his views on the president and secretary of war that he brought back with him an order to the senior officer of the troops on the transports to report to him until General Emory should arrive. During Sunday night and Monday Garrett, thus actually in command of two army corps, pressed the reinforcements on his cars and hurried them to Washington. Early saw their advance filing into the works on Monday afternoon and the rest of them lining the parapets on Tuesday at daylight.

While these events were taking place I was pressing in hot haste through Howard and Montgomery counties. I reached Tridelphia after 9:00 P.M. that night and unsaddled and fed my horses and let the men get a little sleep. By 12:00 A.M. I received information that a large force of Federal cavalry had gone into camp since my arrival, at Brookville, only a few miles off. I at once got ready and started to attack them, but on reaching that point found they, too, had information of their unwelcome neighbors and had left. Thence I moved to Beltsville, on the railroad between Baltimore and Washington. There I found about one thousand cavalry of [Brig. Gen. James H.] Wilson's Division, which had been dismounted in a recent raid in Lower Virginia and sent north to recuperate. They were mounted on green horses and we drove them after a short affair, down the road toward Bladensburg. It was now the morning of Tuesday the twelfth. I was due that night at Point Lookout, the extreme southeast point of Maryland, in St. Mary's County. It was physically impossible for men to make the ride in the time designated. I determined, however, to come as near it as possible. I sent an officer with a detachment to ride at speed through the country, impressing fresh horses all the way and inform the people along the route that I was coming. They were unanimously my friends and I requested them to have their horses on the roadside so that I could exchange my broken-down animals for their fresh ones and thus borrow them for the occasion. During the preceding day I had been taking horses by flankers on each side of my column and kept a supply of fresh ones at the rear of each regiment. As soon as a man's horse broke down he fell out of the ranks, walked until the rear of his regiment came up, got a fresh horse, left his old one, and resumed his place. By this means I was enabled to march at a trot which, with a cavalry column, is impossible for any length of time without breaking down horses—and broken down horses speedily break down men. With fresh horses, however, I hoped to make a rapid march and get to Point Lookout early on the morning of the thirteenth.

After returning from the pursuit of Wilson's cavalry I turned the head of the column toward Upper Marlboro and proceeded only a short way when I was overtaken by a courier from General Early. He brought me orders to report at once to headquarters at Silver Spring, on the Seventh Street road. I moved down the Washington road to the Agricultural College and thence along the line of the Federal pickets, marching all night, occasionally driving in a picket and expecting at any moment to be fired upon from the works, within range of which I was moving. I reported to General Early after midnight and found the whole army in retreat. I was directed to close up the rear, with Jackson's cavalry brigade behind me. We reached Rockville during the day, where Jackson was pushed by the 2nd Massachusetts Cavalry, who hung on his rear and rendered things very uncomfortable generally. Finding matters getting disagreeable, I put in a squadron of the 1st Maryland, under Capt. Wilson G. Nicholas and Lt. Thomas Grew and charged into the town, scattering our pursuers, who got out of the way with expedition. Their dismounted men, however, stuck to the houses and fences and poured in a galling fire. The dust was so thick that in the charge the men could not see the house in front of them. The horses of Nicholas and Grew were killed, and their riders wounded and taken prisoners. As soon as this loss was discovered I put in another charge and recaptured Grew, but was unable to retake Nicholas, who they had mounted on a spare horse and run off the field.

During the rest of the thirteenth our pursuers treated us with more respect. All night long we marched and stopped, and stopped and marched, with that terrible tedious delay and iteration so wearing to men and horses and it was not until Thursday, the fourteenth, we reached Poolesville. Here we were obliged to stand and keep back the pursuit, while the infantry and artillery were passing over the Potomac. I got my artillery in position and deployed a strong skirmish line in front of Poolesville and checked the enemy for several hours. At last, in the afternoon, a wide line of skirmishers could be seen stretching far beyond each end of those we had been engaged with and which moved steadily forward with a steady alignment, very unusual for dismounted cavalry. I sent for General Ramseur to come up to my position, that the infantry had arrived, and that it was about time for cavalry to leave. He soon joined me and while we were looking at the advancing line through our glasses, which showed their cartridge boxes and canteens plainly—puff! puff! puff! went their fire all along the line. There was no mistaking the sound. The swish of the Minie ball was so clear and so evident that it could not possibly come from carbines. We held on, nevertheless, making a great show with our artillery and repeated attempts to charge them with cavalry, so that we delayed them until their supports could deploy. By this time, however, the enemy had become far advanced and having been notified that everything, including my own baggage and ordnance train had crossed, I withdrew comfortably and got into Virginia about sundown. We had been marching, working, and fighting from daylight July 9 until sundown July 14, four days and a half, or about 108 hours. We had unsaddled only twice during that time, with a halt of from four to five hours each time, making nearly one hundred hours of marching. We had isolated Baltimore from the North and cut off Washington from the United States, having made a circuit from Frederick to Cockeysville to the east, to Beltsville on the south and through Rockville and Poolesville toward the west. We had failed in the main object of the expedition, which was to release the prisoners at Point Lookout, convert them into a new army, capture Washington, establish our communications across the Potomac by Manassas Junction, with Gordonsville and Richmond, and by making this a new base of operations force Grant to let go his hold and come to the rescue of Pennsylvania.

The cooperative movement on Point Lookout failed, I have since understood, because the secret expedition of John Taylor Wood, by sea from Wilmington, was spoken of on the streets in Richmond the day before he was to have started from Wilmington. It was, therefore, countermanded, because the Confederate authorities well knew that the Federal general was so well served that he was accurately and promptly informed of everything as soon as it transpired in Richmond. General Early's attack failed, as I have shown, because of the impossibility of getting to Washington before Monday afternoon. But before then the energy and sagacity of John Garrett had hurried reinforcements from Locust Point, many of which had arrived before Early. His trains were running from Locust Point on Sunday night, all day Monday and on Tuesday night and the last of them had passed over the road not many hours before I reached it at Beltsville on Tuesday morning. The movement on Washington was a feint to draw Grant from Richmond, to be converted into an attack if opportunity offered. I believed that General Grant began to move from Richmond. I knew that two of his corps were on the Patapsco at Baltimore and had information that others had moved up the Potomac. A young man, represented to me as reliable, well-known to some of my people, had left Washington and Georgetown on Monday, and he reported to me that he had seen General Grant in Washington on Sunday. I was therefore forced to believe that Grant was in motion and I so reported to General Early, first from near Baltimore and afterward when I rejoined him on the morning of the thirteenth. I do not know to this day the origin of the story of General Grant's presence in Washington on Sunday. He may have been there, or it may have been another general officer of the same name. I have understood that there was another General Grant in Washington. Be that as it may, it is clear that at no time after Monday morning, July 11, could General Early have been justified in attacking the strong fortifications of Washington. His command consisted of the depleted divisions of Gordon, Rodes, Breckenridge and Ramseur, of about 8,500 muskets, the cavalry division of Maj. Gen. Robert Ransom, consisting of [Brig. Gen. William L.] Jackson, Johnson and McCausland's and [Brig. Gen. John D.] Imboden's brigades of about 2,000 badly armed, worse equipped, and undisciplined mounted men, and three battalions of artillery of forty guns and about one thousand men; making a total effective force of about 11,500 men of all arms. He could only have taken Washington by surprise, and it was impossible to surprise it when General Grant, at City Point, was nearer to it than General Early at Sharpsburg.

Sharpsburg is four marches from Washington. It might be made in three forced marches. The sagacity of Mr. Garrett's recommendation that a battle should be fought at Frederick, even if it were lost, will be appreciated. It would be equivalent to nearly one whole day's march and [would have] extended Early's time from three or four to four or five days. On the other hand, transports from City Point could reach Baltimore on the Patapsco or Washington on the Potomac in twelve hours. They could have transported General Grant's whole army from the James to the Federal Capital before General Early could possibly have marched them from where he was forced to cross the Potomac. In this possibility lay the strength and the weakness of the strategy. If Grant were so inclined, he could have withdrawn his whole force, or such part of it as to have paralyzed his movements on the James, and the threat to Washington would of necessity make him contemplate the necessity of such a move. If Early's movement had induced him so to act, Lee would have been relieved and the South allowed another year for a breathing spell. If it did not so influence him, then we were no worse off than we were before the attempt was made.

I have always considered the movement one the audacity of which was its safety and that no higher military skill was displayed on either side than that shown by General Early in this daring attempt to surprise the capital of his enemy with so small a force.

The Battle of Honey Hill

CHARLES C. SOULE,
CAPTAIN, 55TH MASSACHUSETTS VOLUNTEER INFANTRY (COLORED)

Philadelphia *Weekly Times* 3, no. 12, May 10, 1884, and no. 13, May 17, 1884

The battle fought at Honey Hill, South Carolina, November 30, 1864, is not even mentioned in most histories of the war. It was a disastrous episode in a comparatively unimportant expedition on the coast, occurring at a time when public attention was absorbed in the great movements of the armies under [Maj. Gen. George H.] Thomas, [Maj. Gen. William T.] Sherman, and [Lt. Gen. Ulysses S.] Grant. It deserves, however, some sort of record in our military annals, on account of the stubborn gallantry of most of the troops engaged, and because a successful issue would have given the Charleston and Savannah Railroad into our hands and compelled the immediate evacuation of Savannah or the ultimate capture of its garrison. So important did the action appear to the enemy that the Legislature of Georgia passed a resolution March 9, 1865, thanking General Smith and his command "for their unselfish patriotism in leaving their state and meeting the enemy in the memorable and well-fought battlefield at Honey Hill, in South Carolina."

To the 55th Massachusetts this engagement gave the opportunity which the 54th Massachusetts had at Fort Wagner, of proving that a black regiment, well disciplined and well officered, could behave as gallantly under fire as the best troops in the service.

Sherman's army had started from Atlanta on its "March to the Sea" November 15, 1864. On the thirtieth it had crossed the Ogeechee River and was halted near Louisville, Georgia, two-thirds of the way across the state, the cavalry under [Brig. Gen. Hugh J.] Kilpatrick raiding towards

Augusta and Waynesboro. It was evident by this time that Sherman was aiming, not for Macon and the Gulf, but for the Atlantic coast, and the Confederate troops which had fallen back on Macon were hurried around the flank of our army towards Savannah, where all available troops from North and South Carolina were also ordered to report to Lt. Gen. [William J.] Hardee.

In order to cooperate with the movements of Sherman's forces and for the double purpose of offering to them a safe foothold on the coast and of cutting the only avenue by which reinforcements could reach Savannah, [Maj. Gen.] John G. Foster, commanding the Department of the South, organized an expedition to proceed up Broad River, land at Boyd's Neck, march to Grahamville, and take possession of the Charleston and Savannah Railroad at that point. For this attempt there seemed to be every chance of success. Nearly all the Confederate troops in the district had been sent into the interior to oppose General Sherman's advance. The only force on duty at Grahamville was part of a squadron of the 3rd South Carolina Cavalry.

The distance from the Broad River to the railroad at this point was only seven miles. The gunboats could cover the landing of our troops and offer a secure base of operations. Hilton Head and Broad River had been in our possession for two years—a sufficient time, it would seem, for the officers of the navy to familiarize themselves with the channels and shoals of the coast already thoroughly mapped out by the Coast Survey. Two regiments of Negro troops, recruited from the islands and shores around Hilton Head, ought naturally to have furnished guides familiar with every plantation road, every by-path, and every landmark. While they were slaves they were used to going fifteen or twenty miles from their homes, day and night, or courting, frolicking or religious meetings. There would appear to be no reason—with ample water transportation at hand—why a force could not be collected, ferried quickly and surely up Broad River, and pushed forward promptly to the railroad.

The results would be to sever the communication between Savannah and Charleston, to completely isolate the former city and to enable Sherman at pleasure and without hazard to cross the Savannah River at almost any point below Augusta and establish communications with Port Royal, then the principal Federal depot on the South Atlantic coast.

In order to accomplish these results General Foster assembled at Hilton Head, November 28, all the troops which could be spared from the fortifications along the coast, from Charleston Harbor to Florida. So many regiments had been sent to Virginia that the force thus collected numbered only 5,500 men of all arms. As General Foster was incapacitated by an old wound received in Mexico from active service in the field the command of the expedition devolved on Brig. Gen. John P. Hatch. The expeditionary force was divided into two brigades: the 1st, composed of the 56th New York, Lt. Col. [Rockwell] Tyler; 127th New York, Col. [William] Gurney; 144th New York, Col. [James] Lewis; 157th New York, Lt. Col. [James C.] Carmichael; 25th Ohio, Lt. Col. [N.] Houghton; 32nd United States Colored Troops, Colonel [George W.] Baird; 35th United States Colored Troops, Col. [James C.] Beecher, being commanded by Brig. Gen. [Edward Elmer] Potter; the 2nd, comprising eight companies of the 54th Massachusetts, Colored, Lt. Col. [Henry N.] Hooper; eight companies of the 55th Massachusetts, Colored, Lt. Col. [Charles B.] Fox; 26th United States Colored Troops, Col. [William] Silliman; 102nd United States Colored Troops, Col. [Henry L.] Chipman, being under command of Col. [Alfred S.] Hartwell, of the 55th Massachusetts. The artillery included one section (three-inch Parrots) of Company A, Captain Harmer; 3rd Rhode Island Artillery (which did not go into the action); two sections (four guns) light twelve-pound Napoleons of Captain Mercerean's Battery (B), of the 3rd New York Artillery, and two sections (four guns) light twelve-pound Napoleons of Battery F of the same regiment, commanded by Lieutenant Titus, the whole under command of Lt. Col. [William] Ames, of the 3rd Rhode Island Artillery. Two squadrons of the 5th Massachusetts Cavalry accompanied the expedition.

Rear Admiral [John A.] Dahlgren, having been asked to assist in the land operations, gathered from his fleet and from blockading vessels two navy field batteries of four howitzers each, organized expressly for the occasion and supported by four half-companies of sailor-skirmishers and four depleted companies of marines. This "Naval Brigade," as it was designated in General Hatch's report, was commanded by Commander George H. Preble, and did not exceed 500 men, all told. General Hatch's orders from General Foster were to land at Boyd's Neck, push inland and destroy the railroad near Grahamville, to destroy the bridge to the southward, then march with his whole force and attack the work guarding the Coosawhatchie bridge.

To carry and convey the expedition a fleet of boats and transports had been collected. Admiral Dahlgren, from his flagship, the *Philadelphia*, commanded a flotilla composed of the *Pawnee, Pontiac, Mingoe, Wissahickon, Sonoma, Winona* and the tugs *Daffodil* and *Petite*. These vessels, with the transports, were arranged in single file with orders that each steamer should show no lights except in the stern, and should follow the light of the steamer ahead. Singularly enough there was only one pilot with the fleet, and none of the naval officers had ever ascended Broad River before. The captains of the transports were equally ignorant of the channel, were many of them nervous and incompetent, and at least one of them was so overcome by liquor that the army officers had to navigate his boat as best they could.

At 2:30 A.M. of the twenty-ninth the signal for sailing was given, a red and white light, whose brilliant rays shot across the harbor. A few moments later and it could not have been seen from the vessels, for while they were weighing anchor a heavy fog settled over the harbor, rendering any concerted movement impossible. After two hours of anxious waiting the fog became somewhat lighter. "Feeling about" in his flagship, as he expresses it, Admiral Dahlgren collected his vessels and commenced slowly to grope up the channel with the light-draft tugs in advance. After getting over the shoals at the mouth of Broad River (where the *Wissahickon* grounded and could not be got off in time to take part in the landing), the pilot was sent ahead in the *Pontiac* and the squadron moved slowly up the river in a fog still so thick that the shore was only visible when the vessels were close upon it, and most of the time the gunboats ahead and astern were indistinctly visible. The two tugs continued to feel their way on either side of the flagship. The transports followed, but all of them lost their way in the fog. Some grounded on the shoals and could not be floated off until noon of the thirtieth; others went astray up the Chechesser River (among them the *Canonicus*, carrying the engineers and the material for building landings); others again came to anchor and waited for clearer weather and another tide.

While the transports were thus scattered and delayed the navy vessels kept well together and came to anchor in the creek off Boyd's Landing at about 8:00 A.M. on the morning of the twenty-ninth. As the *Pontiac* in advance approached the landing, a loud whoop was heard through the fog, and a moment later a fresh fire beside a hut on shore showed that the Rebel pickets had been surprised and had barely time to escape. "Not a sign of our troops was anywhere visible," says Admiral Dahlgren in his report, "and I began to fear that some mistake had been made, when a transport appeared flying General Hatch's flag." This was about 11:00 A.M. In half an hour the sailors, marines, and howitzers were landed and advanced about a mile in skirmishing order. The other transports began to arrive and to land troops, who shouted enthusiastically as the fog lifted and showed a picturesque plantation with large pines and oaks, draped with luxuriant Southern moss. The narrow creek was blocked with vessels. The engineers had not arrived with materials to make proper landings.

The debarkation was necessarily slow. Troops were taken ashore in small boats to scramble up the muddy banks on the marsh. Horses were thrown overboard and swam ashore. A dilapidated plantation wharf was utilized as far as possible by the vessels which could reach it. Instead of getting ashore early in the morning, as had been planned, the troops were thus landing all day and through the evening. General Foster, whose boat had been misled in the fog, arrived at 9:00 P.M., but returned to Hilton Head at 4:00 P.M. General Potter arrived with part of his brigade about noon, and Colonel Hartwell, with four companies of the 54th Massachusetts shortly after. The artillery did not leave Hilton Head until nine in the morning and were landed about dark.

The Naval Brigade were ordered forward in the afternoon to occupy the fork where the Coosawhatchie road diverged from the road to Grahamville. They had no guide and their map perplexed them by showing roads where there were none and by magnifying byways and cart paths into roads. Instead of stopping at the crossroads they pushed on to the right, away from Grahamville and toward Ree's Creek and Coosawhatchie. They met, engaged, and drove the Confederate pickets. The 32nd U.S. Colored Troops, one of the first regiments ashore, was sent on to support the Naval Brigade.

About 4:00 P.M., the cavalry and a large portion of the 1st Brigade having landed, General Hatch determined to push forward without waiting for the artillery and the remainder of the infantry and attempt to seize the railroad. General Potter, in advance, turned to the right after the Naval Brigade and came up with them just as they were halting for supper. Here it was discovered that they were on the wrong road and the column retraced its steps to the first crossroad, where the Naval Brigade, thoroughly worn out with the labor of dragging their eight howitzers by hand over the sandy roads, were left for the night, while Generals Hatch and Potter, with the other troops, took the road to the left, on which the advance should have been made at the outset. But bad luck persistently followed the enterprise, for on reaching Bolan's Church, where the Grahamville road turns to the right, and encountering there the enemy's pickets, the guide persisted in following the direct road toward Tenvey's Landing and Savannah. After proceeding on this road four miles without opposition, the guide and the generals became convinced that they had gone astray and countermarched to the church, which they reached at 2:00 A.M., so weary with the night march of fifteen miles that the troops gladly went into bivouac.

Meanwhile Colonel Hartwell had been left in charge at the landing, assigning regiments as they landed to position for the night and making arrangements for a move early the next morning. Boyd's Landing and the plantation settlement near it will be remembered by those who camped there as one of the characteristic scenes of the war. The roomy piazzas of the dwelling house, the dingy picturesqueness of the outbuildings, the background of moss-hung live oaks, the gunboats and transports in the creek, the constant landing of artillery and stores at the wharf, all strongly illuminated by the glow of the campfires, formed a picture to fasten upon the memory of the men, who sank to sleep between the ridges of the old cotton fields that night.

Meanwhile the Confederates had not been idle. Two companies of cavalry which were picketing the coast were called together at Grahamville. Colonel [Charles J.] Colcock, commander of the military district, was summoned in hot haste from the Savannah River, where he was superintending the erection of works to protect the crossings. [Lt. Gen. William J.] Hardee, at Savannah, was promptly advised of the landing of Hatch's expedition. He was in great straits for troops to meet this attack, but by singular good fortune reinforcements arrived just in the nick of time. On the withdrawal of the Federal forces which had been threatening Macon (November 25), [Maj. Gen.] Gustavus W. Smith, who commanded the Georgia troops concentrated there, was ordered to move south by railroad to Albany, Georgia, thence to march across the country to Thomasville and there to take cars for Savannah.

This detour of 150 miles south and then 200 miles northeast was made with great promptness and celerity. The march of fifty-five miles from Albany to Thomasville was made in fifty-four hours. At Thomasville, where five trains had been exported, "the energetic [Brig. Gen. Robert A.] Toombs" had only been able "to frighten the railway officials" into furnishing two trains. In these the 1st Brigade was started after dark, November 29, and reached the outskirts of Savannah at 2:00 A.M. on the thirtieth.

As Savannah General Smith received peremptory orders from General Hardee to proceed at once to Grahamville and repel Hatch's advance. "The officer in command at Pocotaligo," says Gen. Dick [Lt. Gen. Richard] Taylor, meaning probably Grahamville or Coosawhatchie, "had reported that he must abandon his post the following morning unless reinforced. It was absolutely necessary that this communication (the Charleston and Savannah Railroad) should be preserved. Upon it depended the further occupation of Savannah. Over this road must the garrison retreat in the event that it become expedient to evacuate the city. By this route also were reinforcements expected. General Hardee had no troops which he could detail for this important service, except two regular cavalry regiments from

Charleston, and it was feared that they would arrive too late. Not a moment must be lost and it was urged upon General Smith that if he would move at once and hold the enemy in check until 2:00 P.M., several thousand troops en route from North and South Carolina for the reinforcement of the garrison of Savannah would arrive and insure the effectual repulse of the Federals."

Although the statute organizing the state forces (of which General Smith's command was composed) "confined their services and operations to the limits of Georgia; although strictly speaking there rested upon these troops no legal obligation to move beyond the confines of their own State, whose territory they were instructed to defend, although General Smith a qualified authority from Governor Brown to withdraw the Georgia troops under his command from the Confederate service in case they were ordered beyond the limits of the State, and although the commander and command were almost broken down by fatigue and want of rest, realizing that the battle for the salvation of the metropolis of Georgia was on the instant to be fought on South Carolina soil; and after a full conference, with the lieutenant general becoming perfectly satisfied that it was right and proper the movement should be made, General Smith issued the requisite order." The trains were switched across to the Charleston and Savannah Railroad and carried the sleeping Georgians across to South Carolina soil; thus, as General Toombs expressed it, "making them unconscious patriots."

General Smith, with his leading brigade, reached Grahamville at 8:00 A.M. on the thirtieth, the day of the battle. While Smith remained at the railroad until 10:00 A.M., when his second train arrived and also the 47th Georgia, from Charleston, Colonel Colcock, who had been anxiously awaiting with a mere handful of troops the arrival of reinforcements, at once led forward the 1st Brigade toward Bolan's Church. As the Federal advance had occupied before his arrival the position which he had selected for defense, he countermarched the brigade and posted them at works constructed two years before at Honey Hill, equidistant (two miles and a half) from Grahamville and Bolan's Church. In order to delay Hatch's advance until the Confederate troops could be placed in position, Colonel Colcock pushed forward one 12-pounder Napoleon of Kanapaux's Battery, under command of Lieutenant Zealy, together with Company K, Captain Peeples, of the 3rd South Carolina Cavalry. While they held in check the whole Federal column General Smith hastened forward the rest of his brigade and made his dispositions for the defense of Honey Hill.

The situation was an excellent one to repel an attack in front, though weak on the flanks. A substantial open earthwork, pierced for four guns, extended two hundred feet on each side of the road, on the crest of an abrupt slope of about twenty feet. The ground immediately in front of the entrenchments was comparatively open, but at the distance of about 150 yards a shallow and sluggish stream, expanding into a swamp, with a heavy growth of trees and dense underbrush, ran along the whole Confederate front. General Hatch says of this swamp that "it was not impassable, but presented a serious obstacle to our advance." The only practicable approach was by the narrow road, which made so sharp a turn as it passed through the swamp that the earthwork was invisible to a force approaching by the road until they were close upon it.

The force under the command of General Smith was as follows: Infantry—the 1st Brigade of Georgia Militia, Colonel Willis; State Line Brigade of Georgia, Col. [James] Wilson; 17th Georgia (Confederate Regiment), Lt. Col. [Aaron C.] Edwards; 32nd Georgia (Confederate Regiment), Lt. Col. [E. H.] Bacon; Athens Battalion, Maj. [F. W. C.] Cook; Augusta Battalion, Major Jackson. Cavalry—Companies B, E, and C and the "Rebel Troop" of the 3rd South Carolina Cavalry under Maj. [John] Jenkins. Artillery—a section of the Beaufort Artillery, Captain Stuarts; a section of De Pass' Light Battery; a section of the Lafayette Artillery; one gun from Kanapaux's Light Battery; seven pieces. General Smith says that he brought five pieces of artillery into action and that his infantry force, "which was all engaged," numbered 1,400 "effective muskets." This seems rather a low estimate, for on December 5, 906 rations were issued to the 1st Brigade and 469 to the State Line Brigade, 1,375 to the two organizations, and no mention is made in this schedule of the 47th Georgia, which General Smith says arrived from Charleston at ten in the morning. But counting in officers, artillery and cavalry, the Confederate force, before the arrival of reinforcements in the late afternoon, could not have amounted to 2,000 men.

General Hatch's expeditionary force was about 5,500. Deducting two regiments not arrived and one regiment and detachments from others left at the landing as guards, he brought into action on the morning of the thirtieth about 4,000 men, certainly more than two to one though the Confederates had the advantage of position and of knowledge of the country. Captain De Saussure, who served as General Smith's staff for the day, was thoroughly familiar with the ground, as were also Colonel Colcock and Major Jenkins.

The Confederate forces were arranged in a convex semi-circle, the right resting along a fence above the swamp, the center, with the artillery, occupying the earthwork and the left retired toward the Coosawhatchie road, through "an open pine barren." The earthwork seems to have been defective in construction. One account says that it was too high for use by infantry, another that the artillery could not use the embrasures and had to take position in front of the entrenchments. An inspection of the works, as they still stand, contradicts both these statements, and the small loss of the Confederate troops shows that they found satisfactory protection.

Although General Smith was on the field during the action the immediate command of the main line was given to Colonel Colcock, in deference to his position as military commander of the district in which the battle was fought. Col. [Ambrosio J.] Gonzales, of General Hardee's staff, had charge of the artillery and Major Jenkins of the cavalry.

At about 3:00 A.M. of the thirtieth, an attack was made on the Federal pickets beyond the church, but it was repulsed without loss. Desultory picket firing was kept up until morning.

The troops at the landing were astir early. Colonel Hartwell sent forward before daybreak the 56th New York, 35th U S. Colored Troops, and part of the 32nd U.S. Colored Troops to join the 1st Brigade. Leaving the 34th U.S. Colored Troops at the Neck he marched at daylight with eight companies of the 54th Massachusetts, eight companies of the 55th and two batteries of artillery (eight guns), under Lieutenant Colonel Ames. The 26th and 102nd U.S. Colored Troops, comprising the rest of the 2nd Brigade, had not yet arrived. It was a lovely morning, sunny and mild, as these troops marched between the hedges of the plantation roads and along the abandoned cotton fields. They left at the landing a secure base of operations. The double-enders of the fleet, with the *Pontiac*, lay in line, stern to stern, close up to the bank of the creek, presenting a broadside of nineteen heavy cannon and sixteen howitzers.

At the Coosawhatchie crossroads the Naval Brigade, which had camped there for the night, fell into the line of march, and four companies of the 54th Massachusetts, under Capt. [George] Pope, were left to replace them. Shortly after the column had gone on a force of Confederate cavalry came down the Coosawhatchie road and attacked Pope's detachment. Two rifled howitzers of the Naval Brigade, which had been sent back from the church to his support, arrived just in time, and coming up noiselessly (being drawn by hand) behind the hedge-rows opened on the enemy with such effect that they retired in haste. These companies of the 54th were relieved at 11:30 A.M. by the 34th U.S. Colored Troops and marched to the battlefield, arriving between twelve and one. In the afternoon Major Anderson, of Foster's staff, with two companies of the 34th and part of the navy detachment, advanced some distance up the Coosawhatchie road, until fired on at close quarters by the Ree's Creek Battery, when he retired to the cross roads. The enemy made no other demonstration in this part of the field.

At Bolan's Church (which was about three miles from the landing) Potter's Brigade was under orders to march before daylight. If these orders had been executed and a bold push had been made there was no reason why our advance—ever after the loss of twenty-four hours, which had been wasted in missing the way—might not have reached Grahamville without substantial opposition before General Smith's leading brigade arrived by railroad. But for some reason—perhaps because the men were worn out with their night march, perhaps because General Hatch was waiting for the artillery and the 2nd Brigade—the start was not actually made until nearly 9:00 A.M., when the 127th New York was sent forward to skirmish. The cavalry had previously reported that the enemy had appeared up the road with artillery and infantry (these were the guns of Kanapaux's Battery and the company of cavalry, now dismounted and serving as skirmishers, which Colonel Colcock had pushed forward to delay our advance).

At 9:15 A.M. the first skirmish was opened half a mile from the church by a solid shot from Kanapaux's gun, which struck with fatal effect in one of the leading regiments advancing by flank in the narrow road. On our right was a large open field; on our left, for a quarter of a mile from the church, woods with that dense jungle of vines and undergrowth which covered most of the battlefield of Honey Hill. Beyond this was a cotton field and then a wooded swamp, crossing the road and impeding our progress on each flank. The Confederate cannon was placed on a rising ground some distance beyond, commanding the narrow causeway which was the only avenue of approach, and the dismounted cavalry were posted as skirmishers on the further side of the swamp.

A vigorous charge of our skirmish line would have brushed away the meager force—only one company—which thus disputed our passage; but much time seems to have been lost in maneuvering. The 25th Ohio, 144th and 157th New York were advanced and deployed in line to support the skirmish line of the 127th New York. A section of Battery B, 3rd New York Artillery, under Lt. [Edward A.] Wildt, advanced to the edge of the swamp and opened on the enemy, firing seventy-five rounds at six hundred yards. The cavalry sent around the right of the swamp to take the enemy in flank and our excellent force of infantry appears to have been held in check until the artillery and cavalry could produce an effect. Finally an advance was ordered and the Confederates fell back.

Beyond the swamp, up to the entrenchments at Honey Hill, extended on the left heavy woods, with tangled undergrowth. On the right was a large field, in which the Confederates, retiring, had set fire to the tall grass, sedge and broomcorn. A strong wind blew this fire down upon our skirmishers and threw them into temporary disorder, by which the enemy gained further time. Beyond this field were heavy woods on the right. For a mile the road corduroyed part of the way through a swamp, ran between woods so thick that our skirmishers were withdrawn and the leading brigade marched in column on the road. At the end of this straight stretch of road the Confederates made a short stand with their piece of artillery. The advance section of Battery B was again brought into action and fired twenty rounds at eight hundred yards. The Confederates having sufficiently delayed our advance soon retreated, but one of their last shots struck in the groin Lieutenant Wildt, commanding the section, and so nearly carried away his leg that the surgeon who accompanied the advanced amputated it with his pocket knife on the field. Our loss in these skirmishes did not exceed twenty men killed and wounded. Among the latter were Lieutenant Colonel Geary, of the 32nd U.S. Colored Troops, and Captain Penet, of the 144th New York.

These operations consumed nearly the whole morning. Meanwhile General Smith had brought up from Grahamville his whole force and placed them in position along the line already described. The preparations were hardly completed when the advanced gun, having made its last stand at the bend of the road, came back into the entrenchments. Our advance, having withdrawn its skirmishers on account of the density of the thickets on each flank, was marching in column on the road with a few flankers straggling through a vine undergrowth, when, on turning an abrupt bend, it came "unexpectedly" (as General Hatch states in his report) upon the enemy in position. Although the works were said to have been built two years before, their existence was until now unknown and unsuspected by our commanders.

[Charles C.] Jones, in *The Siege of Savannah*, gives the following account of the commencement of the action:

> Upon its appearance about one hundred and twenty yards in front of the works, in a curve of the road, the infantry and artillery opened a murderous fire on the head of the Federal column, before which it melted away. They were advancing in apparent ignorance of the line of field works, and of the serious opposition they were to encounter. Staggered by this fire the enemy recoiled and some time elapsed before they deployed in line of battle. The low ground was wooded to an extent sufficient to conceal the

movements of the enemy, but not to protect them from the heavy fire of infantry and artillery which crushed through their ranks.

What regiment constituted the advance at this time the accounts do not state, and indeed it is somewhat difficult to ascertain the movements or position of each regiment during the rest of the action. The left of Potter's Brigade was at once thrown into line to the left of the road, facing the enemy, along the edge of the swamp. The 127th was next [to] the road, then the 157th New York and the 156th New York, which held our extreme left. The attempt of the right of the brigade to deploy was apparently hindered by the thick undergrowth and the regimental commanders' ignorance of the situation both of our forces and of the enemy. The 32nd U.S. Colored Troops seem to have formed in line and to have met an advanced force of the Confederates posted along an old dam, at right angles with the main road, which formed our line of defense later in the afternoon. The 32nd wavered and the 25th Ohio, which was advancing behind them by the right of companies through the thicket, came into line and charging through the 32nd and a portion of the 144th New York, drove the enemy from their position, inflicting little loss, however, as they were afraid to fire here for fear that some of our own troops were in front of them.

A line was formed on the road which branched off from the main road, parallel with the dam; the 32nd U.S. Colored Troops on the right, the 25th Ohio next, and part of the 144th on the left towards the Grahamville road. There was no firing in front and no enemy visible. After sending forward a party to reconnoiter, Colonel Houghton, of the 25th Ohio, led his regiment forward into the woods, changed front partially towards the left and advanced to the edge of the swamp, where he says "a strong force of the Confederates was met and a severe fight took place." The Savannah *Republican*, in an account of the action, says of this episode: "Our (Confederate) left was very much exposed and an attempt was once or twice made by the enemy to turn it by advancing through the swamp and up the hill, but they were driven back without a prolonged struggle."

The 144th New York does not seem to have advanced at the same time. They were lying down in line shortly after this time, considerably in rear of the 25th Ohio and no further mention is made of them in the report and accounts of the fight until the retreat in the evening. The 32nd U.S. Colored Troops are said by Colonel Hampton to have come up "somewhat tardily" on his right. The further action of the right wing will be shown later on. It may be said here, however, that no general officers or aides appeared, and no orders were received by the right wing while they were in this advanced position. General Hatch says that he "ordered the right to press forward, swing around to the left and flank the enemy, but the dense undergrowth and deep swamp prevented"; but he is mistaken. The undergrowth and swamp were entirely passable, as reconnaissances showed. What was lacking was orders and a commander.

Meanwhile the section of Battery B, already twice engaged (commanded, after Lieutenant Wildt received his wound, by Lieutenant Crocker), was moved to the intersection of the main and branch roads, the only place where artillery could be put. It was a very unfavorable position for the use of artillery. The forest was so thick that the enemy was invisible and the guns could only be sighted at the puffs of smoke which arose over the intervening branches. Shortly afterwards Captain Mercercan brought up the other section of Battery B and the four guns were rapidly worked, although only one section could be placed even in sight of the smoke of the enemy's guns, the left section being masked by woods so dense that there was great difficulty in bringing the two sections into battery. "They were in a very dangerous position," says the author of *Cayuga in the War* [Henry Hall, *Cayuga in the Field: A Record of the 19th New York Volunteers and the 3rd New York Artillery*, Auburn, NY: Truair, Smith and Co., 1873], "being under an unremitting fire of cannon and sharpshooters. Obscured by smoke and shrubbery, however, their exact position was as difficult to make out as that of the rebel battery on the hill. Here seven men of the two sections were wounded. Lieutenant Crocker's eye was shot out, but he wrapped a handkerchief around his head and fought his guns for an hour after the hurt. Captain Mercercan said of him in his report: "I never saw any one display more cool judgment and bravery than he during the whole engagement."

The 35th U.S. Colored Troops, coming up in the rear of the 1st Brigade, was ordered to charge up the road. Forming in line obliquely, with their right resting across the road and their left overlapping in front of the 127th New York, they opened fire and attempted to advance; but the fire they encountered was so hot that they fell back to the rear of the artillery, where they lay down in line and remained during the rest of the afternoon. In the advance Colonel Beecher was twice wounded, but refused to go to the rear. It was now somewhat past noon.

The whole of the 1st Brigade, except the Naval Brigade (held in reserve on the main road), had already become engaged. It was probably of this time in the action that General Smith writes in his report as follows: "In an hour the enemy had so extended and developed their attack that it became absolutely necessary for me to place in my front line my last troops, the 47th Georgia. From time to time alterations had to be made in our lines by changing the positions of regiments and companies, extending intervals, etc., to prevent being flanked." "The gallant 32nd Georgia," says Jones' *Siege of Savannah*, [Charles C. Jones, *The Siege of Savannah in December, 1864*; Albany: Joel Munsell, 1874] "acting as a moveable reserve, always appeared at the most opportune time." The noise of the battle at this time was terrific—the artillery crashing away in the center, while volley after volley of musketry ran down both lines and were reverberated from the surrounding forests.

At the time the first skirmish occurred the 2nd Brigade was halted near Bolan's Church. As the 1st Brigade advanced the 2nd followed, marching by the flank in the road and leaving at the church, as a guard, two companies of the 54th Massachusetts with his slender brigade, of which only eight companies of the 55th Massachusetts and two companies of the 54th Massachusetts were now left, Colonel Hartwell deployed in line in the first cottonfield on the left of the road, then passed the swamp by the flank and crossed the second field (in which the grass was still burning fiercely) in column by company. Halting on the edge of the woods at the further end of the field the brigade rested for half an hour. There was nothing in sight except a battery of artillery in the road at the left. The sound of skirmishing had ceased and the fields and woods wore a Sabbath quiet, when suddenly and violently firing by volley began at the front and the artillery opened again.

The brigade was put in motion and was struggling in column by company through the dense woods, when orders came to Colonel Hartwell to double-quick to the front. Moving by flank to the road, which was so narrow and so thronged with cannon and caissons that the brigade had to thread its way along the roadside and was strung out almost in single file, the brigade passed General Potter, who ordered Colonel Hartwell to support the 127th New York—and afterwards General Hatch, who directed him to support the 35th U.S. Colored Troops, but not to go into action, if possible to avoid it, without further orders, which would be sent to him by an aide.

When the head of the column reached the crossroads, Lieutenant Crocker's section of the artillery was firing rapidly in the road, and the 35th U.S. Colored Troops was in line obliquely across the road beyond, firing at will, and wavering excitedly forward and back. The fire at this point was very hot. It was within close range of the enemy's guns, and as the trees near the road were somewhat thinned out it was more exposed than other points in the line to their infantry fire. Colonel Hartwell directed the leading companies to file to the right down the crossroad, from which the 25th Ohio had just advanced, further to the right. His intention was to form the brigade in line to support the 35th U.S. Colored Troops. Before the 55th Massachusetts could be closed up and formed the 35th had fallen to the rear, and there was nothing to support. Colonel Gurney, of the 127th New York, informed Colonel Hartwell that the left was hard pressed (which appears, by the way, to have been a mistake). The two companies of the 54th Massachusetts were sent to the left and front of the 127th. By the time the 55th Massachusetts was in line, under a hot fire, it became a grave question what should be done.

Colonel Gurney, in his report, says that "Lieutenant Colonel Woodford had reported to General Potter that he would charge the front of the work if a simultaneous charge could be made on the road to his right. The 55th Massachusetts immediately came up and charged. Colonel Gouraud, of Hatch's staff, brought the order for the charge." Colonel Hartwell gave the order to advance in line of battle, but the difficulties of the ground, the swamp and thickets, which had already broken the ranks of the 32nd U.S. Colored Troops and the 35th U.S. Colored Troops allowed the regiment to go forward only two or three rods. The three right companies in this advance got astray in the woods. Forming the other five companies, as well as possible, in column by company on the road, Colonel Hartwell again led them to the front, until the enemy's guns met them at the turn of the road with such a fire of canister that they again fell back.

With the assistance of Col. [George E.] Gouraud, their gallant commander [Hartwell] rallied his men, formed them again in column and led them in a third attempt to charge. This time they fairly turned the corner in the road and crossed the brook, where a rude bridge had been torn up by the Confederates and its planks staked down as an abatis. The shallow stream here spread up and down the road thirty or forty feet, and as the little band, of less than three hundred men, stumbled through sand and water, the five guns of the fort were trained on them with spherical case and canister at 120 yards range and all the infantry of the center and flanks poured in a destructive fire, across the comparatively open ground in front of the works, upon the narrow gorge in the woods through which the road emerged.

Colonel Hartwell had been wounded in the hand in the first advance. As he turned the corner his horse was killed and fell on him in the road. Captain Crane, acting as aide, while shouting, "Come on boys, they are only Georgia militia!" was killed, with his horse, by a charge of canister. Lieutenant Hill, of Hartwell's staff, was knocked from his horse by the explosion of a shell. Lieutenant Boynton, commanding the leading company, was shot in the leg, fell in the water, gained his feet and pressed forward, only to be killed by a canister as he reached the bridge. Color

Sergeant King was killed by the explosion of a shell. Sergeant Mitchell and Sergeant Shorter (the latter had been commissioned, but not yet mustered in as a lieutenant) were severely and Sergeant Major Trotter was slightly wounded.

In an account of a visit to the field next day, the Savannah *Republican* thus describes the carnage at this point: "We found the road literally strewn with their dead. Some eight or ten bodies were floating in the water, where the road crosses, and in a ditch at the roadside, just beyond, we saw six Negroes piled up, one on top of the other. The artillery was served with great accuracy, and we doubt if any battlefield of the war presents such havoc among the trees and shrubbery." "The road," says Colonel Hartwell in his report, "seemed to be swept of everything." No troops in the world could have stood such a fire under such circumstances.

The repulse was instant and final. The five companies had lost over a hundred men killed and wounded in less than five minutes. The survivors fell back, but rallied in the rear of the artillery. Colonel Hartwell would have been left to fall into the hands of the enemy but for the bravery of Lieutenant Ellsworth, who turned back, under that terrific fire, and while one of the men, who was killed the next moment, partly lifted the horse and thus released him, the lieutenant dragged Colonel Hartwell across the ditch into the woods and then to the rear. In thus going from the field Hartwell was hit three times by spent balls, but Ellsworth escaped unharmed. When the 55th were repulsed the Confederates flocked out of their works with loud yells of triumph and trooped down toward the brook, but were quickly driven back by the fire of the regiments on our left.

While the 55th was thus engaged Lieutenant Colonel Woodford led the New York on the left of the road, in line across the swamp, nearly at right angles with the advance of the 55th. They advanced to within a hundred yards of the Confederate works and remained ten minutes firing in a boggy marsh, with water ten or fifteen inches deep, when they were withdrawn to the front and flank of the artillery and there lay down and remained during the rest of the afternoon. There is no record of any movements by the 56th and 157th New York on our left flank, but, as their loss was light, it is probable that they simply held their ground during the afternoon, without attempting to advance and without receiving any attacks from the enemy.

Lieutenant Colonel Hooper, with the two companies of the 54th Massachusetts which had come to the front with Colonel Hartwell, lay all the afternoon to the left and front of the 127th New York, his men lying down and reserving their fire. It was his belief from what he saw in his advanced position that the Confederate right could be easily flanked and he sent a written message to that effect to General Hatch, which, however, had no effect. He writes that General Sherman, riding over the field afterwards with General Hatch, said in his blunt way, "Hatch, why in hell didn't you flank them on their right?"

Captain Pope, who had come up from the crossroads with his four companies of the 54th, hearing no further firing at the front, had halted at the church for dinner, when (just after noon) the sudden burst of firing occurred which indicated that our advance had struck the Confederate works. He double-quicked his command at once to the front and on passing General Hatch was joined by Colonel Bennett, of Hatch's staff, who led the way to the cross roads, where he ordered Captain Pope to charge. This was after the repulse of the 35th and 55th and was an insane order. Captain Pope's men had been separated in coming up by the artillery which still filled the narrow road, and when he received the order to charge he had only one officer and eight men with him. Taking the only view of the situation possible for a sensible man, he led his men back of the artillery and formed them, as they came up, into line. These companies, with the two others which had been first left at the church and had advanced to the front before Pope came up, formed to the right of the 35th, behind the guns, and there lay until dusk.

The three right companies of the 55th Massachusetts, advancing with the regiment in line from the branch road, did not hear the order to form column by company and continued on through the woods and swamp, continually diverging from the rest of the regiment, which had turned to the left of the main road. No enemy was in sight, but the air was full of bullets and of the noise of firing to the right and left. Without orders the men opened fire and as their formation was much broken by the underbrush, the fire of those in the rear was so dangerous to their comrades in front that Colonel Fox ordered the bugler to cease firing.

The right company passed over the 144th New York, which was lying down in line of battle and on reaching the stream, at a considerable distance from the main road, the 25th Ohio was found standing in line and firing excitedly at an unseen enemy—unseen, but not unfelt, however, as a storm of bullets from our left swept away the tops of the grasses and shrubs. Here the companies of the 55th lay down without firing. It was an anxious and perplexing time, for they had entirely lost their bearings and in the thick woods could not tell if the firing on their left came from friend or foe.

A reconnaissance of the front developed no enemy, but there was no general officer nor aide present to give orders for an advance and after remaining by the stream for nearly an hour the whole line—now including the battalion of marines and the 32nd U.S. Colored Troops, to the right of the 25th Ohio—fell back to the branch road and took position behind the old dam, where the Confederates had made a stand earlier in the day. Here they lay all [the] rest of the afternoon. Occasionally the enemy would creep down through the woods and open fire, to which our forces would vigorously respond. But our ammunition was so nearly exhausted and the supplies which were sent up from the rear were so scant that our men were directed to reserve their fire except when thus attacked. The left of this flank, near the corner where the artillery was posted, was much exposed, being in the line of fire down the road from the Confederate works. Here the 54th and 55th Massachusetts lay, losing many men and officers during the afternoon.

By 2:00 P.M. Battery B of the 3rd New York Artillery, having been in action since 9:00 A.M., was completely exhausted. One of the guns had recoiled into the ditch and the gunners had not energy enough to extricate it. The other three guns were overheated and the ammunition was nearly exhausted. Only one of the guns was firing at intervals. Battery F was therefore ordered to replace Battery B. Coming up over the rough corduroy road at a reckless pace, the infantry and stragglers springing aside to right and left to let it pass, it went into battery at the crossroad. Just as they arrived a shell from the enemy exploded the two ammunition chests of a limber of Battery B, severely scorching Lieutenant [George C.] Breck. Lieutenant [Edgar H.] Titus had the guns of this battery taken to the rear by their prolonges, the soldiers lending a hand at the ropes. Two of Titus' pieces were then run up and opened fire, receiving a furious reply. The first gun discharged drew such a fire that nearly every man serving it was wounded. At 4 P.M. this section, its ammunition being exhausted, was withdrawn and its place taken by two howitzers of the Naval Brigade under Lieutenant Commander [Edmond O.] Matthews.

The 102nd U.S. Colored Troops, being landed at 11:00 A.M., hurried at once to the front, arriving at 1 P.M. As General Hatch had been informed by deserters that the enemy were being reinforced from the railroad, the 102nd was held in reserve—two of its companies as well as two companies of the 127th New York being formed across the road to check straggling. At about 4:00 P.M. two companies of the 102nd were engaged in a gallant attempt to draw off the guns of Battery B from their exposed position. As the first company detailed for this work approached the guns they were met by such a fire that Capt. [Arod E.] Lindsay was killed and Lt. [Henry H.] Alvord severely wounded. Sgt. [Jesse W.] Madry, who was left in command, had not been informed of the object of the movement, and filing his men into the woods faced them toward the enemy. "Lieutenant [Orson W.] Bennet, with a detail of thirty men, then brought off the guns in the coolest and most gallant manner."

The Naval Brigade had little chance to distinguish itself, being held in reserve on the main road. The marines, under Lt. [George G.] Stoddard, were sent through the woods to the right flank, where they formed on the right of the 25th Ohio. They also, as well as the 55th Massachusetts, sent forward a reconnoitering party, without finding any enemy in their front, but were obliged to fall back to the cross road with the rest of the line at 3:30 P.M. and lay there until they were withdrawn at dusk. When the guns of Lieutenant Titus' Battery were withdrawn at 4:00 P.M. two of the navy howitzers were sent forward to take their place and were worked with great dexterity by the sailors, who lay down in the road under and around the guns while loading them, retreated to the ditch at the roadside when they fired and after the volley of cannon and musketry which each discharge drew from the enemy sprang again to their guns, thus escaping in a great measure the losses to which the artillerymen of the 3rd New York had been subjected in the same position. An eyewitness says that it was laughable, even under that heavy fire, to see the zeal with which the sailors served their guns and especially to see the tracks they made with their knees in the sand as they crowded about the howitzers.

On the Confederate side, although they had been very fortunate during the day, General Smith confesses that he awaited with some anxiety in the early afternoon the arrival of expected reinforcements. At 11:00 P.M. Brigadier General Robertson came up with artillery, cavalry, and infantry. At midnight Brig. Gen. [James] Chesnut appeared with 350 South Carolina reserves and at daylight, or soon after, of December 1, General Baker brought up his brigade of nearly two thousand men, and Lieutenant General Hardee arrived at Grahamville. Had the Confederates advanced late in the afternoon or evening on the 30th they would have taken our forces at great disadvantage. But most of their men were worn out by continuous marching and riding upon the cars, and General Smith deemed it unwise to attempt any interference with the withdrawal of our troops.

The charge of the 55th was really the culmination of our attack, and when the right wing fell back to the crossroads at 3:30 P.M., it became evident that our enterprise had been foiled and that the best thing to do was to get back to the gunboats. General Potter's arrangements for retreat were excellent. One section of Titus' Battery, supported by two regiments of infantry, took post half a mile back, two regiments of infantry were then withdrawn from the flanks of the front line and posted a mile further to the rear. At dusk the retreat commenced. The Naval Brigade was ordered to occupy the crossroads. The 127th New York and 102nd U.S. Colored Troops, with one section of the Naval Battery, remained at the front, keeping up a slow artillery fire until 7:30 P.M. Meanwhile the wounded were all taken to the rear. The ambulances, which had just come up at dark from the landing, were entirely insufficient for this purpose, so that the 54th and 55th Massachusetts were broken up into squads to carry the wounded back on stretchers extemporized from muskets and blankets.

At 7:30 P.M., the main body being well on the march, the 127th New York and the 102nd U.S. Colored Troops, with the navy howitzers, were withdrawn and covered by the 56th and 144th New York, which in turn were covered by the 25th Ohio and 157th New York. The movement was thus effected without confusion, alarm, pursuit, or loss. Not a wounded man was left on the field except those who fell directly under the fire of the enemy's works, and no stores or equipments fell into the enemy's hands except the blankets and knapsacks which had been thrown aside by our men in their advance through the tangled woods.

The last glimpse our forces had of the scene of the battle was at Bolan's Church, on the way to the rendezvous at Boyd's Landing. On our advance in the morning the little white church, nestled among the moss-hung oaks, presented a beautiful and characteristic Southern picture. As we returned in the evening it wore a very different aspect. Huge fires of rails and brushwood threw a lurid light over the church and the forest behind it. The pews which had been torn out to transform it into a hospital and the stores which had been piled here as a depot were strewn around in wild disorder. Beside the church the surgeons had established their operating tables, and the unconcealed traces of amputations were shocking to behold.

Our loss was reported as being:

Killed	88
Wounded (140 so slightly as not to be in hospital)	623
Missing (of whom 13 wounded and 5 unwounded are known to have fallen into the enemy's hands)	43
Total	754

The Confederate loss was reported at 4 killed and 40 wounded. This disparity is due to the fact that the Confederate forces fought on the defensive, behind breastworks and concealed from us in an unknown position in the woods, while we advanced across their front, over ground which they knew thoroughly. The number of the "slightly wounded" is due to the thick woods, which deflected and partially checked the force of the enemy's fire and increased proportionately the casualties from "spent balls."

The loss by regiments was as follows:

		Killed	**W'nd.d**	**Missing**	**Total**
1st Brigade	25th Ohio	20	118	—	138
	56th N.Y.	6	14	—	20
	127th, N.Y.	5	41	—	46
	144th, N.Y.	17	50	—	67
	157th, N.Y.	—	30	—	30
	32nd, U.S.C.T.	8	56	—	64
	35th, U.S.C.T.	7	107	—	114
2nd Brigade	54th Mass.	2	37	4	43
	55th Mass.	29	108	—	137
	102nd U.S.C.T.	3	20	—	23
Artillery		2	12	—	14
	Cavalry	—	1	—	1
	Naval Brigade (at crossroads)	1	11	—	12
34th U.S.C.T.		5	—	—	5
Totals		**100**	**610**	**4**	**714**

To criticize any operation of the war is an ungracious task, but this paper will not be complete without some comment on the conduct of the expedition. To the behavior of the troops engaged only praise can be accorded. Even the few regiments which appear to have shown momentary disorder remained in line on the field and under fire until ordered to retreat. "The list of killed and wounded," says Hatch in his report, "none of whom fell in retreat, attests good conduct. The affair was a repulse, owing entirely to the strong position held by the enemy and our want of ammunition." "I can not close this report," writes General Potter, "without making honorable mention of the good conduct and steadiness displayed by the officers and men under the most trying of circumstances. Exposed to a heavy fire from a concealed enemy, who was strongly entrenched, and laboring under every disadvantage of ground, they maintained their position with the greatest tenacity and endurances. Nothing but the formidable character of the obstacles they encountered prevented them from achieving success." The Savannah *Republican* concedes that the troops in the center of our line "fought with a desperate earnestness."

But the generalship displayed in the fight was not equal to the soldierly qualities of the troops engaged. There appears to have been a lack of foresight in the preparations. It is strange that only one pilot could be provided for an expedition upon a navigable river, of which our forces had been in full possession for two years. A few reconnoitering expeditions up the river might have familiarized the navy with the soundings and averted the dangers and delays of a fog. And it is more than strange that no better guides could be found in the South Carolina Negro regiments, or among the freedmen who had flocked from the mainland to Hilton Head, than those which misled our advance for a whole day and gave the enemy the time they so much needed to assemble their forces. Again, a little reconnoitering up various roads by the first troops landed on the morning of November 29 would have corrected the errors of guides and maps.

During the action there seems to have been very bad management—the delay in starting on the morning of the thirtieth; the irresolution which allowed one piece of artillery and one company of cavalry to hold in check a whole brigade for three hours; the inaction which left a line of battle without orders and made no systematic attempt at reconnoitering and turning the enemy's flanks, which rested without support or defense in open pine woods; the bad judgment which ordered single regiments to charge successively by a narrow road upon a strongly fortified position, defended by artillery and infantry—these faults cannot be overlooked nor passed by without serious censure. General Potter showed on other occasions such excellent judgment and good generalship that the blame must rest upon his superior officer, General Hatch, who was present at the front and directed operations during the day. To quote [Maj.] Gen. Jacob D. Cox's criticism of the Honey Hill fight from his *March to the Sea:* "It was a fresh instance of the manner in which irresolute leadership in war wastes the lives of men by alternating between an ill-timed caution and an equally ill-timed rashness."

It is only fair to say that the Confederate management seems to have been excellent from first to last. The energy which brought a force from Western Georgia to the coast of South Carolina so opportunely that it got into position only ten minutes before the action opened; the audacity and adroitness which checked the advance of a brigade for several hours with one gun and a few dismounted cavalry and the soldierly ability with which artillery and infantry were so handled as to inflict a loss of 750 men while losing only 50 all deserve the highest praise. On their side it was all good generalship and good luck; on ours it was the reverse.

Hood's Nashville Campaign

J. W. A. Wright,
Major, 36th Alabama Infantry, C.S.A.

Philadelphia *Weekly Times* 8, no. 89, November 15, 1884

Among the many stirring and bloody campaigns of the great war was those begun in November 1864, by [Maj. Gen. William T.] Sherman on the one side and [Lt. Gen. John B.] Hood on the other. On the sixteenth of that month General Sherman marched southward from Atlanta towards Savannah with some 32,000 infantry and artillery and 4,000 cavalry, while on the twenty-first, or only five days later, General Hood moved northward from Florence, Alabama, towards Nashville, with 24,000 infantry, 3,000 artillerymen and 3,500 cavalry. Such, at that date, was the status of these two armies which a few months previously had confronted each other in many a deadly conflict from Dalton to Atlanta—May 6 to September 1—Sherman's effective strength during that momentous struggle being reduced by the casualties of war from 112,000 to 81,000 men, and the army of [Gen. Joseph E.] Johnston and Hood from 70,000 to 40,000, in round numbers.

On December 17, after a month's campaigning, Sherman, having marched 250 miles with no serious resistance, was before the defenses of Savannah and demanded the surrender of that city, while on the same day Hood commenced his retreat from Nashville, with 20,000 men of all arms remaining, after marching some 130 miles to reach the capital of Tennessee and after fighting three pitched battles against [Maj. Gen. John M.] Schofield and [Maj. Gen. George H.] Thomas at Franklin and Nashville.

The purpose of this sketch is to give some of the details of Hood's Tennessee campaign, especially the incidents of the second day's battle at

Nashville, on December 16, 1864, the final results of which made Hood's retreat to the south side of the Tennessee River a necessity.

Hood's Army of Tennessee, 30,500 men of all arms, having spent three weeks at Florence—unexpectedly detained there by vexatious delays in receiving his supplies via Corinth—moved forward, with [Maj. Gen. Nathan B.] Forrest's cavalry in the lead, on November 21 and camped that night twelve miles north of Florence, at Rawhide. Advancing every day with opposition, except slight skirmishes between the Union cavalry and Forrest's vanguard, we passed through the Mount Pleasant country—the garden spot of that part of Tennessee—and on the morning of the twenty-seventh we formed line of battle a few miles south of Columbia. General Schofield's forces—apart of Sherman's army—had arrived the night before by forced marches from Pulaski and had taken position around Columbia for its defense. That night General Schofield withdrew his army—two corps, more than 30,000 strong—across Duck River and outreached about a mile from its north bank.

The Confederates occupied Columbia on the morning of the twenty-eighth and skirmishing, with considerable artillery firing across the river, continued that day and the twenty-ninth. Early on the morning of the twenty-ninth, Hood crossed the river quietly a few miles east of Columbia, with [Maj. Gen. Benjamin F.] Cheatham's and [Maj. Gen. Alexander P.] Stewart's Corps and Johnson's Division of [Maj. Gen.] Stephen D. Lee's Corps, Forrest having crossed with his cavalry at the same point late the previous evening and by a long detour to the right, aimed to seize and hold the Franklin Pike near Spring Hill, twelve miles north of Columbia. This was Hood's noted flank movement, by which he sought to get in Schofield's rear and cut him off from Nashville. At the time this plan was, in the opinion of many of our most experienced and judicious officers, quite equal in its conception to some of Stonewall [Lt. Gen. Thomas J.] Jackson's brilliant flank movements, or those of Sherman against Joe Johnston. It was not successful only because of General Cheatham's extraordinary failure to obey orders and to seize the pike to Franklin, although his command—late in the day, it is true—arrived at its destination in time to execute Hood's plan.

General Lee, with his two remaining divisions, [Maj. Gen. Carter L.] Stevenson's and [Maj. Gen. Henry D.] Clayton's—your correspondent belonging to the latter—had a pontoon bridge constructed on the river at Columbia, under considerable fire of artillery and musketry, late on the evening of November 29 and driving the Federal pickets from some of their advanced pits near the river crossed and confronted Schofield's works, with the intention of attacking them next morning. Before daybreak we were in line of battle and had eaten our cold and frugal breakfast by the light of the stars, not a campfire having been lit during the night. Soon after dawn a dispatch from General Hood to our General Lee was read to every regiment in these words: "I am between the enemy and Nashville. If you will drive them I will catch them."

Our men were informed that they were to charge Schofield's breastworks and take them as soon as the word "Forward!" should be given.

Our line advanced with alacrity and enthusiasm. Indeed, it is worthy of record that during this advance of Hood from Palmetto, near Atlanta, to Franklin the enthusiasm and esprit de corps had materially improved the farther north we marched. It was a matter of interest to observe the difference in the spirits of an advancing and a retreating army. For it is not to be denied that the morale of our Army of Tennessee had become rather shaky under the depressing influence of constant retreats and inevitable earthworks, while they were falling back before Sherman's masterly flank movements, week after week, from Rocky Face Ridge to Atlanta, when many a time the question was asked, "Will we keep falling back to the sea?"

As we moved against Schofield's works in the dim morning twilight on that memorable November 30 not a gun was fired from his trenches, greatly to our surprise. Soon we were in the enemy's trenches, and not a soul was there. Some time after midnight they had "folded their tents like the Arabs and silently stolen away." General Lee pressed forward with his columns at once and we made that morning from 6:00 to 9:00 A.M. in quick time, one of the heaviest of our many marches—nine miles in three hours without a halt. Yet we had scarcely a straggler. All hoped for a decided success, and every moment as we hastened towards Spring Hill we expected to hear the boom of Hood's cannon in his proposed "catching" of Schofield's army. But not a gun was heard, and when our division reached Spring Hill we found to our great disappointment that the bird had flown and that one of the golden opportunities of the war for a Southern army had been lost by the strange failure of one of our best subordinate generals to obey Hood's order to occupy Franklin Pike and to check Schofield's retreat.

After a short halt and rest we marched on towards Franklin at a more moderate pace, the larger part of the army having preceded us. The head of our column of two divisions reached the hills four miles south of Franklin, at 4:00 P.M., just as Hood's line advanced and first took the outer line of breastworks and were then repulsed at the stronger works, near the old Carter gin house and the impenetrable hedge of Osage orange at Carter's

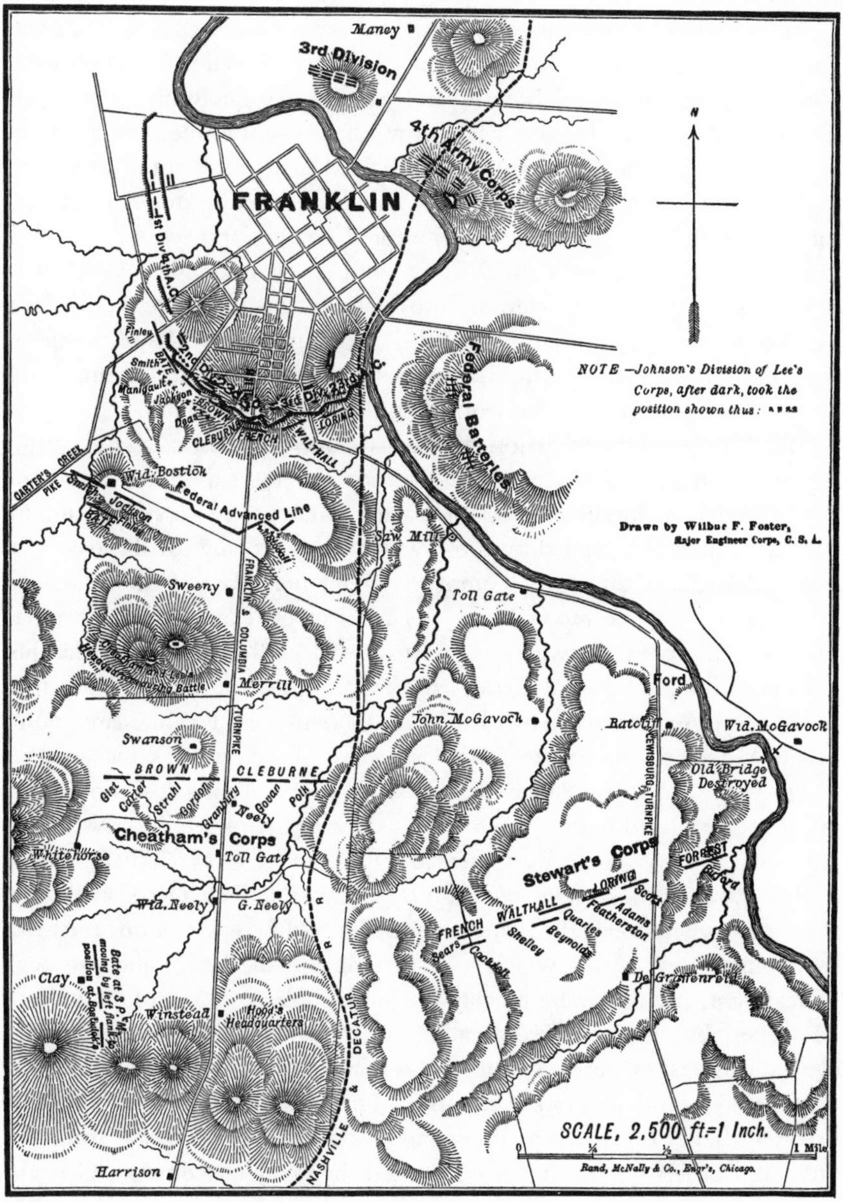

Battlefield of Franklin

(CENTURY MAGAZINE)

farmhouse. [Maj. Gen. Edward] Johnson's Division, which preceded us, as above mentioned, was the only part of Lee's Corps that was actually engaged in the desperate and sanguinary battle of Franklin, they supporting Cheatham on his left. Clayton's and Stevenson's Divisions, which had marched from Columbia that day—upwards of twenty miles—were placed in position on Hood's extreme left, reaching that point some time after nightfall and waited in line till near midnight, expecting orders to charge, for the fighting was continued by repeated charges and repulses of all of Hood's men except our two divisions until about midnight. We were so posted as to have a full view of most of the line of battle, which was marked by the incessant flashes of rifles, sparkling like myriads of fireflies in the darkness of the night. But little artillery was used, Hood not employing his at all out of regard for the women and children in Franklin.

Soon after midnight Schofield left his works for Nashville, and during an hour or more before daylight we witnessed one of the most weird and dismal of sights. Hundreds of bright-blazing torches were moving to and fro over the battlefield, carried by those who were searching for the wounded and the dead. As our corps entered Franklin next day, on the march to Nashville, one of the most ghastly spectacles greeted our eyes that we had witnessed in more than two years of active service. Our dead lay thicker just in front of the gin house at Carter's and on both sides of the pike there than we have ever seen them on any battlefield. It reminded us of the large numbers of Federal dead found by us on some parts of the field of Chickamauga. There were said to be 800 bodies in sight, Hood having lost 4,500 men killed and wounded out of 25,000 engaged, or nearly one-fifth of his attacking force. Some of them were pierced by a number of Minie balls, having evidently been struck again and again by the terrific discharge of small arms as they lay where they fell. I remember being told by some of our men that they found a few bodies which had fallen against the hedge and had been upheld by it, and they were literally riddled by bullets.

When our men entered Franklin in full view of these hundreds of bloody victims of ruthless war, the exclamation was frequently heard: "Here are your temporary breastworks!" This alluded to a promise made by President [Jefferson] Davis and General Hood in addresses to the troops by them and others when the former visited the army at Palmetto, Georgia, September 25, just prior to Hood's advance. This promise was that if, in their future campaigns, they met an entrenched enemy their lives should not be uselessly sacrificed and that they would be ordered to charge only "temporary breastworks."

Our men felt—and with some reason—that here the promise had been disregarded. They held General Hood responsible; from that day their confidence in him diminished and there is no underestimating the effect this fact had in lessening the order of an army that had been growing in enthusiastic valor as they advanced into Tennessee. They brooded over it as the violation of a solemn pledge to them and the influence of this conviction undoubtedly had much to do with the disastrous results of Hood's two battles at Nashville.

It tended to demoralize an army not yet fully recovered from the disheartening effects of constant retreats. Hood says truly in his official report: "Never did troops fight more gallantly." But this was the last of such gallant fighting under Hood of a large part of the army. Even many of his most conservative officers and men wondered why he had not posted himself better on the character of his entrenchments, against which he so persistently hurled his men to a terrific slaughter, for the inner works were certainly too strong to be called "temporary breastworks," and the main attack was on their strongest part.

The general belief was that our gallant commander, as he had proved himself to be, became incensed at the thwarting of his excellent plan at Spring Hill and grew reckless. This idea was strengthened by his saying to some of Cheatham's men as they filed by him that morning, "You would not catch the Yankees when I wanted you to. Now you shall fight them wherever you find then."

Schofield abandoned Franklin so hastily that he left his dead and wounded on the field, and in places his dead were so thickly strewn that his loss seemed almost to equal Hood's. We secured about one thousand prisoners and several battle flags.

Hood followed Schofield's retreating columns early on December 1, and we camped that night near Nashville. Next day our line of battle was formed some two miles south of the city limits or four miles south of the state capital, whose white outlines were in full view from parts of our position. Here substantial earthworks were begun at once, extending in a semicircle from northeast to southwest, parallel to the line of defensive works around Nashville and from three-quarters of a mile to two miles distant from them at different points, their closest parts being about midway between the Granny White pike and the Hillsboro pike.

Along our line the distance between these pikes, as well as from Granny White eastward to Franklin pike, was half a mile each, while northeast from the latter to the Nolensville pike was a mile and three-quarters. The length of Hood's main line of investment was a little more than four miles. Its right was occupied by Cheatham's Corps and extended to the Murfreesboro Railroad; Lee's Corps occupied the center on both sides of Franklin pike and A. P. Stewart's Corps was on his left, extending to and along the Hillsboro pike. Our cavalry held the space from each flank of this main line to the Cumberland River extending on the left about four miles, so that Hood's entire line of investment was at least ten miles long.

On this line, in the opening of an inclement winter, twenty thousand of Hood's men bivouacked, with little or no change of position for two weeks, both armies meanwhile strengthening their entrenchments, while the rest of our army—Forrest's cavalry and [Maj. Gen. William B.] Bate's Division of infantry—sought to dislodge six thousand Federals from Murfreesboro, for the purpose, as General Hood afterwards stated, of opening the routes to Georgia and Virginia.

Hood anticipated that he could defeat Thomas should the latter attack him and hoped in that event to take Nashville, and as enough rolling stock had been captured to operate the railroad running south through Pulaski and Decatur, our Confederate leader began to indulge a fatal sense of security, not seeming once to realize as an element of danger the large reinforcements constantly received by General Thomas during this interval of comparative inactivity. In this two weeks nothing of note occurred outside of the monotonous army work of picket duty and occasional skirmishes between pickets, except some very cold weather and a severe storm on the sixth and seventh.

The ground was frozen hard and snow fell to the depth of several inches. Had not Hood's veterans become by this time well inured to all kinds of hardships by constant exposure to the elements and by scant supplies we would have suffered greatly from this cold snap, in a colder climate than most of us had been accustomed to, for many were thinly clad and poorly shod. But, though we had to rake aside the snow to spread our blankets on the cold ground at night and though we lived in the snow for several days, little or no sickness was caused by this exposure. In fact, nearly three years of service and the roughest of camp life in the open air had made those who survived it decidedly tough. Our part of Hood's men had never had even regular tents to cover us for the last eighteen months prior to that date.

We bade a long farewell to our last tented camp on June 24, 1863, near Wartrace when [Maj. Gen. William S.] Rosecrans began his memorable advance on [Gen. Braxton] Bragg and our army burned most of its tents that we might thenceforth travel lightly. For a year and a half then, during our varied and trying campaigns of Chickamauga, Chattanooga, Dalton to

Atlanta and Jonesboro and lately on Hood's advance of several hundred miles, we had slept most of the time under small tents—so-called—of rubber or woolen blankets, stretched on stakes cut from the woods, with our scant bedding spread on the ground upon leaves, or straw, or rails, or springy saplings, the latter sometimes in their more luxurious form of a spring mattress when time permitted, raised a foot or two from the ground upon forked sticks and cross-poles.

The previous winter our primitive huts built for winter quarters, those near Chattanooga, occupied for only a few days in November 1863, and those at Rocky Face Ridge, near Dalton, did not afford much better accommodations, but were somewhat more roomy than our low-set blanket tents.

During our two weeks of rest near Nashville no movements of our troops occurred, except the withdrawal of Bate's Division of infantry—mostly Tennesseans—from Murfreesboro to our main line and the substitution of [Joseph B.] Palmer's and [Hugh W.] Mercer's infantry brigade for it; also, the recalling of [Brig. Gen. Abraham] Buford's Cavalry Division from Murfreesboro to protect our extreme right on [the] Cumberland River, above Nashville. General Hood was aroused from his fancied security December 15 by the sudden and vigorous attack made by General Thomas, simultaneously on our right and left flanks.

Profiting by this delay of two weeks Thomas had, under General Grant's supervision, doubled the strength of his army by large reinforcements and Hood's 20,000 men investing Nashville were now confronted by an available force of 82,000 men. Many of these were the most experienced veterans of the Federal army—mainly Western men, whose excellent fighting qualities came to be highly respected and somewhat dreaded by Southern soldiers.

Hood had been led to hope for reinforcements, but had received none. Well do the survivors of Hood's army remember how the stillness of that bright winter morning was all at once broken, both on our right and left, by the sullen booming of cannon, soon followed by the sharp rattle of 50-caliber rifles, the latter always sounding in the heaviest firing of any battle like a canebrake on fire. The assault on Hood's right, near the Murfreesboro Railroad, was effectually repulsed by Cheatham's Corps, most of the attacking force being colored troops, who lost heavily, while the Confederate loss was light. On the left of our main line Stewart's Corps was less fortunate. Some of his men, after several attacks had been checked, were overwhelmed and captured with several pieces of artillery in some unfinished redoubts, which Hood was having constructed for the better protection of his left flank.

During this contest our corps—Stephen D. Lee's—had been gradually moved to the left to support Stewart, until most of our brigades were stretched out in single rank along our earthworks. But it was evident that only a light skirmish line was in our front, as the Union forces had been massed in their heavy attack upon Hood's left flank. This was Thomas' true attack, the assault on our right being mainly a feint. The turning of Stewart's left flank made necessary a change in Hood's position. Hence, early that night the Confederate leader withdrew his entire army to a new line from one to two miles farther south, nearly parallel with his former line, but his left flank, thrown considerably back and resting on the Brentwood Hills, immediately west of the Granny White Pike. At the same time Cheatham's Corps was moved from its position on the right to Hood's extreme left and formed that flank as above located. This change placed Lee's Corps on Hood's right and Stewart's in the center, our right flank extending near a deep cut on the railroad to Franklin and bending southward along the eastern slope of Overton Hill, a gently sloping knoll, raising about fifty feet above the surrounding flats.

In its new position Hood's line was considerably contracted. While its full length, following its curves, was some three and a half miles, the distance in a straight line from its right to its left flank was only about two miles and a half. This new alignment being completed by midnight the details for the necessary reliefs of working parties were made and Hood's army went to work, "might and main," with but little rest to refresh them to construct the best defensive works they could for the morrow's deadly strife. Little did any of us dream of the disaster in store for us ere the setting of tomorrow's sun.

In preparing the best defensive works for the conflict of December 16, which was the most general action and by far the bloodiest battle at Nashville, our men along the slope at Overton Hill—who had been made experts in ditching by the Atlanta campaign—found it impossible in the short interval from midnight till the morning's attack was to be expected to construct earthworks of any value. A foot or two below the surface they struck the lime rock and they found it impossible to displace enough soil for their purpose, so our brigade was compelled that night to make the safest breastworks we could of trees we cut near the lines. As it was our men made very good wood-works with head logs, but these were a poor protection, except against Minie balls.

On the day of that bloody and memorable battle our division—Clayton's—formed the right of Hood's line, Stevenson's Division connected with our left and next to the left was Johnson's Division. The respective brigades

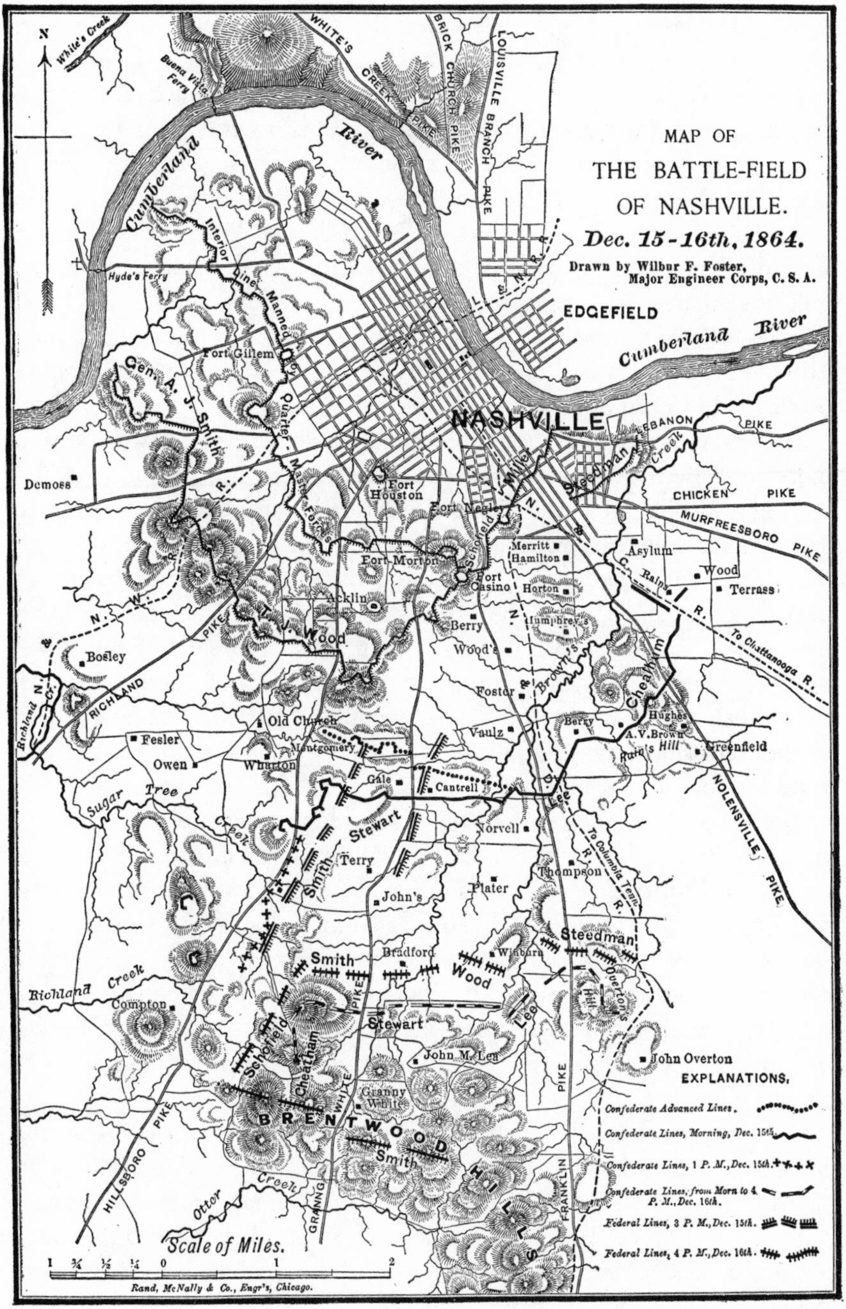

Battlefield of Nashville

(*CENTURY MAGAZINE*)

of our division were posted as follows: [Brig. Gen. Marcellus A.] Stovall's from Georgia on the right, extending east and southward—in a curve to protect our flank—towards the railroad cut already mentioned. Next to the left and westward came [Brig. Gen. James] Holtzclaw's Alabama Brigade, to which my regiment belonged, its left resting on Franklin pike. Immediately to our left was [Brig. Gen. Randall L.] Gibson's Brigade from Louisiana, with its right on Franklin Pike. [Brig. Gen. Edmund W.] Pettus' Brigade of Alabamians supported Gibson's left. Gibson's men were behind a light stone wall, strengthened by such material as they could secure. Stovall's and Pettus' Brigades, [Capt. Charles E.] Fenner's Battery and the rest of Hood's forces had such breastworks as they could hurriedly make with a limited supply of tools in eight or ten hours.

After day dawned we could see our entrenched line of battle with an unobstructed view, unusual in our experience, stretching in nearly a straight line slightly south of west from our position for nearly two miles to the Granny White Pike. This line was almost at right angles to the Franklin Pike, which runs there slightly west of north. The brigades and batteries of our division defended Overton Hill, which is just to the right of Franklin pike as you approach Nashville and which was considered the key to Hood's position. Our hastily constructed line of works extended across the northern slope of Overton Hill. The left of Stovall's Brigade was along the northeastern slope and the right of Holtzclaw's along the north and northwestern slopes of that hill.

In a slight interval between these brigades was Fenner's Battery, with four guns on the line of battle, Captain Fenner himself being in command that day of Eldridge's Battalion of artillery, which was supported by Clayton's infantry. The Eufaula Light Artillery—four pieces—was just in rear of the apex of the hill. These two batteries, or eight guns in all, were the only artillery immediately employed in the bloody work of defending Overton Hill. They rendered signal service—the Eufaula Battery, as General Clayton informed me, being moved by hand, to right and left, as required in the hottest of the fight.

The regiment to which I belonged, the 36th Alabama Infantry, formed the left of Holtzclaw's Brigade, its left resting on Franklin Pike. Capt. Nathan B. Carpenter, of Company B, was in command of our regiment at that time and had charge of its right wing, while the writer, as second in command, had charge of its left, our three field officers being then wounded or in prison. Our post was very favorable for observation in line of battle on the commanding slope near Franklin Pike.

Our regiment had not quite finished its abatis of brush—thrown together hastily and roughly from the limbs and tree tops cut from our logs at night—when between 8:00 and 9:00 A.M. the Federal batteries began a terrific shelling of our works. This was continued till nearly noon. Then came several charges en masse, the chief object of which seemed to be to gain positions near our line, preparatory to the final assault which followed. For when within two or three hundred yards of us they lay down, holding and waving aloft their regimental colors for some time in the midst of irregular musketry and some artillery firing on both sides.

Soon after midday the Federal brigades assigned to this work had taken their positions. They then made their next advance, being met by some desultory firing, such as that mentioned above. Again they paused and lay down for a time. Then suddenly, with a shout along their line, came their heavy charge—the heaviest charge of infantry concentrated on any one point that I witnessed during the war—with the results told very candidly in the Federal official reports.

Our men were lining their works in closer ranks than I ever saw them in any previous or later battle. They had their usual forty rounds of ammunition, and their Enfield rifles were in fine condition. Most of them, in obedience to orders, had remained quiet and were watching anxiously over and under the head-logs for the beginning of the heavy charge which they knew was imminent. At last, soon after 3:00 P.M., the cry arose along our line, "Here they come!" Sure enough they were coming in splendid style in heavy and successive lines, with colored troops in front—one brigade—followed by several brigades of white troops.

We ordered our men to reserve their fire till the assaulting lines were near enough for their aim to do good execution. They obeyed, and when the front line was within some sixty yards of our works the order was given on our part of the line: "Now, boys, give it to them! Aim low! Fire!" And they did fire. They loaded and fired just as fast as they could, and in about half an hour their cartridge-boxes were emptied, though soon replenished from our ordnance stores in the rear. The Federal lines were driven back with fearful slaughter, nor did they charge our division front again, merely advancing to occupy the works we had left when we had fallen back under orders.

After their disastrous repulse we had no opportunity to fully investigate the effects of our fire, as strict orders were passed along the line not to cross our works in pursuit of flying foe, and afterwards between 4:00 and 5:00 P.M., we received orders to fall back on account of the breaking of Hood's

The Federal assault on Overton Hill (MINNESOTA HISTORICAL SOCIETY)

line, more than a mile to our left. Most reluctantly did we withdraw from a position where Hood's right wing had with signal success repelled every attack throughout the day, and for the next twenty-four hours Holtzclaw's Brigade, with other parts of Clayton's Division, became the rear guard of Hood's shattered army.

Allusion has already been made to the unusual distinctness with which from our hillside we could see more than a mile of Hood's line to our left. Beyond that the view was cut off by a thick skirt of woods through which his line of battle passed. No member of our victorious brigades who witnessed that terrible rout can ever forget the surprise and chagrin with which we saw men and riderless horses rushing in wild confusion from that woods towards the Franklin Pike in our rear, closely pursued by the "boys in blue," amid the smoke and carnage of battle, and then regiment after regiment falling back in succession from their works to avoid being flanked, until it became necessary to withdraw the whole of Hood's right wing in haste to prevent our retreat from being cut off by a movement from our left and rear. Soon, over the plains in full view, there was a scene of confusion that baffles description.

The horses of battery after battery—where the horses had not been killed or disabled—were rushed to the front at full speed and hitched to their guns to hurry them off and avoid capture. Towards our left many were too late to save their batteries. In a short time the rout and disorganization were complete. One of those strange fancies to which armies are sometimes subject had seized the most of Hood's men—veterans as most of them were. General Holtzclaw had reason to be proud of his brigade and General Clayton, of his division, for their defense of Overton Hill and their conduct as Hood's rear guard in that most trying emergency. Clayton's command performed here a service for Hood's army such as Thomas had for [Maj. Gen. William S.] Rosecrans at Chickamauga—saved it from total destruction.

How so fatal a breach was made in any part of Hood's line, after every other assault that day had been so completely repulsed, was a mystery and a stunning surprise to the rest of his army who had held their portion of the works. All we could then learn was that part of the division of General Bate (now Governor Bate of Tennessee) had been driven from their entrenchments, and it was asserted that they had not made proper efforts to hold them. As these same troops were charged with failure in duty not long before at Murfreesboro, to the great surprise of their comrades in arms, deep and loud were the curses upon them for bringing this greatest of disasters upon our Southern arms and that in sight of their homes.

It was conceded even then that General Bate was an able and gallant commander, but a deep regret was expressed that part of his command had not acted with a valor worthy of him. It has since been explained that by some error in alignment one of his brigades had a difficult point to hold. In the darkness of the previous night they had occupied a mound, at the base of which it was easy for the Union forces to mass themselves near our works for attack under cover of a heavy artillery fire.

General Thomas took advantage of this and between 3:00 and 4:00 P.M., under a concentrated fire of many field pieces, he pushed forward a division of infantry to the base of this mound, where they were well protected. By a sudden and gallant charge these men scaled the mound and carried the entrenchments that crowned it, Bate's men not venturing to show their heads above their works on account of the storm of shot and shell that swept them incessantly until the assault was consummated. This one breach was so promptly followed up by Thomas' overwhelming numbers that Hood's army was crushed and all chances of his success in Tennessee finally destroyed.

The Confederates lost comparatively few in killed and wounded, but many prisoners, including Gen. Edward Johnson—Sherman says over four thousand—and fifty cannon, in addition to those lost in the unfinished redoubts on the previous day.

In connection with these statements from a Confederate standpoint much interest attaches to reports of the same events by Federal officers and we shall here compare some of them with what we saw and felt. [Maj. Gen. Thomas J.] Wood, whose corps was opposed to General Lee's corps, says in his official report:

"The right of the enemy's line rested on Overton Hill. A close examination of the position satisfied me that if Overton Hill could be carried the enemy's right would be turned, his line from the Franklin pike westward would be taken in reverse and his line of retreat along the Franklin pike and the valley leading to Brentwood (nine miles from Nashville and four miles south of Hood's last line) would be commanded effectually. The capture of half the Confederate army would almost certainly have been the guerdon of success. It was evident that the assault would be very difficult, and even if successful would probably be attended with heavy loss, but the prize at stake was worth the hazard."

This general tells us that Col. [P. Sidney] Post reconnoitered the position and pronounced it "truly formidable," but thought his brigade could take it. We are informed also that, as a first step, Maj. [Wilbur F.] Goodspeed, chief of artillery of Wood's corps, was ordered "to open a concentrated fire on the hill," and that "the order was effectually obeyed." Every man in our position will readily indorse the accuracy of these statements.

The column that assaulted our works on Overton Hill consisted of a colored brigade in the lead, under command of Col. Charles K. Thompson—the 12th and 13th and two other regiments of "United States Colored Infantry." These were followed by Post's and [Col. Abel D.] Streight's brigades, sustained by [Col. Charles H.] Grosvenor's brigade of [Maj. Gen. James B.] Steedman's division. General Wood goes on to say the assault was "welcomed with a most terrific fire of grape and canister and musketry," and mentioned that as the columns got nearer, "his reserves on the slope of the hill rose and poured in a fire before which no troops could live."

Now we must state by way of correction here that we really had no reserves. But these deadly volleys were merely the reserved fire of Holtzclaw's Brigade and especially just at that time, the 36th Alabama. It should be explained in this connection that Gibson's Brigade in our immediate left, as well as Pettus' and Stovall's Brigades, rendered most valuable service at this crisis by a heavy cross fire, the chief assault being concentrated on the front of our brigade, immediately along Franklin Pike and to the right of it as you go toward Nashville.

General Wood adds: "When he had arrived almost at the abatis, while gallantly leading his brigade, the chivalric Post was struck down by a grapeshot and his horse killed under him." Again: "But for the unfortunate fall of Colonel Post, the commander of the assaulting brigade, I think the assault would have succeeded." Those who were in Hood's line beg leave to differ with the general on the latter point. Had he come near enough to see the determined men behind our works thoroughly infuriated because they were then first attacked by Negro troops, he might have changed his mind.

Gen. George H. Thomas' report says of this attack: "The assault was made and received by the enemy with a tremendous fire of grape, canister and musketry, our men moving steadily up the hill until near the crest, when the reserves of the enemy rose and poured into the assaulting column a most destructive fire, causing the men first to waver, then to fall back, leaving their dead and wounded, black and white indiscriminately mingled, lying amid the abatis, the gallant Post among the wounded."

This Colonel Post, of whom such honorable mention is made, was no doubt the officer who was seen by us to ride up to the abatis and actually caught hold of some of the brush and tried to pull it away to make an opening for his men. We saw him and his horse fall there, and my men frequently spoke to me afterwards of his brave act. When the assault was completely repulsed and our firing ceased, Lieutenant Knox of our regiment sallied out with a squad of men across the works and captured the colors of the "13th United Stated Colored Infantry," a trophy retained by our regiment till after the surrender.

They at the same time found the mounted officer that we saw fall and his horse lying near our abatis and if my memory serves me right, took the pistols from his holsters. They reported the dead and wounded, black and white, as strewing the ground very thickly in our immediate front. Colonel Thompson says of the losses of his colored troops: "The loss of the brigade was over twenty-five per cent of the number engaged and the loss was sustained in less than thirty minutes." By the way, that was about the time it took our men to empty their cartridge boxes, as described above.

In numbers he gives 160 killed outright and 766 wounded. I must mention that Colonel Thompson makes two serious mistakes in his official report, which otherwise appears very accurate so far as I can judge. He asserts that some of the colored troops mounted our works. This is certainly not correct. The nearest they came was to our hurriedly constructed abatis, some twenty paces in front of our works. He also says we were reinforced. Our part of the line received no reinforcements, and we had no reserves that came to our support in the fight.

The reserving of the fire of our brigade and the shifting of one of our batteries to the right and left were probably the causes of this wrong impression. It is true that [Brig. Gen. James A.] Smith's Division of Cheatham's Corps was sent to our extreme right, arriving about 2:00 P.M., but this force was merely placed on our right flank to guard against having it turned and it took no active part in the fight.

General Wood gives the loss of his corps during the day's engagement—not including Thompson's Brigade—as follows: killed, officers, 19; enlisted men, 114; wounded, officers, 55; enlisted men, 759; or a total of 947. This makes an entire loss of 1,833 men which occurred in the assault on Overton Hill.

Our loss in killed and wounded was very small, not exceeding twenty in the entire brigade, if I remember correctly, and about 100 out of between 2,000 and 3,000 men of Clayton's entire division in line that day, including his batteries. General Hood gave no statement of the total killed and wounded along his line that day, and it will perhaps never be known exactly, but the number scarcely exceeded 500 men.

General Thomas, while claiming correctly to have routed Hood's army, capturing 53 cannon and he claimed 4,462 prisoners, says of our retreat: "The rear guard, however, was undaunted and firm and did its work bravely to the last." A handsome compliment this from an able commander and a generous foe, and well do the survivors of Holtzclaw's Brigade and Clayton's Division—which did most of the work in covering the retreat from Nashville to Spring Hill—remember the severe fighting of Hood's rear guard, as it withdrew along the route, closely pressed by Federal cavalry on that dismal December 17, before Forrest's cavalry had time to arrive from Murfreesboro to relieve the infantry from that unusual duty.

A heroic act of a Tennessee girl, in the beginning of Hood's retreat, deserves special mention. When Miss Mary Bradford—an accomplished young lady whose acquaintance some of us had formed at the handsome Overton residence, near our lines—saw one of our brigades falling back in disorder, immediately after Hood's line was broken, she risked all the dangers of battle, rushed out among the men and seizing the colors of a regiment most earnestly implored them to rally and stand firm, declaring that she did not fear death and they should not. But by the inexorable fate of battles the retreat had begun and nothing could stem its tide.

As an offset to Miss Bradford's disappointment at the failure of some of Hood's men near Nashville to rally at her appeal it may be pardonable to recall the hearty welcome which some of the ladies of Florence gave to others of Hood's veterans when they first crossed the Tennessee and entered that town, on October 31. This was when Clayton's and Johnson's Divisions of Lee's Corps, protected by a heavy artillery fire, crossed the Tennessee—there one thousand yards wide—on pontoon boats, in the face of one thousand Union cavalry and drove the latter out of Florence, killing, wounding and capturing about forty of them. As is usual this occurred in the principal streets. As Clayton's rough and begrimed skirmishers advanced through the town, driving the Federals before them, some enthusiastic Southern ladies were so overcome with joy that they rushed into the street, threw their arms around their deliverers, as they deemed them, and thanked them for bringing their homes once more within the Confederate lines.

Though more or less skirmishing occurred throughout December 17 along the entire route to Spring Hill there were three special encounters between our rear guard and the pursuing cavalry. The first of these was soon after sunrise at Hollow Tree Gap, near Brentwood, the second about noon, some two miles south of Franklin and the third in a large beech grove, four miles north of Spring Hill, just at dusk.

Wearied by the day's battle and march our division, with its men more scattered than usual, had not gone into camp till 10:00 P.M., and after no refreshing sleep on the wet ground and drenched by one of those heavy rains which so often followed our battles, we were aroused at daybreak to prepare in time for the expected pursuit. It came before we had finished our scanty breakfast of corn bread and bacon. Bledsoe's Battery had been strongly posted, so as to command Hollow Tree Gap and was supported by Pettus' and Stovall's Brigades of infantry, one on each side of the pike, upon a ridge and under the immediate command of General Clayton.

The sun's rays had not yet peeped over the hills upon our bivouac when here came our cavalry from the front at full speed and the Federal cavalry in hot pursuit. Waiting till the last of our cavalry had passed down the pike through our line we opened a heavy fire from battery and rifles upon the head of the pursuing column. Down went many a rider and horse, but those in front had gained such an impetus that some rushed through our lines and fifty or more men and horses were captured, together with several guidons. This checked the pursuit materially at a point between seven and eight miles north of Franklin.

Two miles north of Franklin, however, and near Harpeth River, flanking parties of cavalry appeared. These were readily checked by Gibson's Brigade and Buford's cavalry, so that Harpeth River was crossed with but little interference, its bridge being destroyed by our pioneers under Captain Coleman's direction in spite of a severe fire from Federal sharpshooters. Afterwards about two miles south of Franklin, between noon and 1:00 P.M., the Federal cavalry appeared in such force in our front that a determined stand was made to repel them. Holtzclaw's Brigade was drawn up in line of battle to the right of the pike as the rear guard, our cavalry having passed on towards Spring Hill.

But the heavy and last fighting of the day was just at dusk. A considerable cavalry force, by making a detour, had flanked the Confederate division in front (Stevenson's) and made a sudden and determined attack on Clayton's Division. The latter at once formed a hollow square in the open woods and repulsed the unexpected assault with heavier loss to their assailants than to themselves. From the impetus of the attack some of the Federals dashed down the pike beyond the infantry square in pursuit of our retreating cavalry, even rode side by side unconsciously in the dark with some of the latter and were finally captured a mile or more in the rear of the position where our division made its stand.

Such are some of the details of the fighting of the first day on that memorable retreat which led General Thomas to speak in his complimentary terms (that every Southern soldier must appreciate) of the conduct of Hood's rear guard. For eight days longer this dreary, disheartening retreat was continued, each corps, aided by Forrest's cavalry, acting in turn as rear guard, before Hood's scattered army reached the Tennessee River near Bainbridge, ten miles above Florence. This was on a cold Christmas morning, five weeks after we began the movement on Nashville, which proved so disastrous to Southern arms and to the Confederate cause.

During this dismal retreat through Columbia and Pulaski, in severe winter weather, over hard-frozen roads, Hood's men endured hardships and sufferings not unlike those of [George] Washington's army, when he fell back, after his repulse at Germantown, to his winter quarters at Valley Forge. Weak, badly shod, or even bare-footed, some of our veterans literally left blood-marks in their tracks from lacerated feet. It was estimated then and we believed it was true, that at least one thousand of our men would have been unable to recross the Tennessee but for the aid given them by our mounted officers with their horses.

Among details of the straits to which we were reduced by this unlooked-for defeat may be recorded the fact that the best breakfast some of our regimental headquarters, with good foragers, could "scare up" on that cold Christmas morning was a thin corn "hoe-cake," mixed without salt, baked in a frying pan and washed down with that noted Southern service drink, "corn-meal coffee." Our Christmas dinner was a limited amount of parched corn and salt and our supper that night was only a few slices of fresh fat jowl—and we never asked where the hog came from.

Such was our fare on a hard day's march, during which our corps and perhaps more of Hood's army forded the broad, rocky channel of Shoal Creek, waist deep in places to our wet and shivering [men]. We were obliged to take this "ducking" before our engineers completed a long foot-bridge of rails, because the boom of heavy guns, supposed to be from enterprising Federal gunboats on the Tennessee, was heard, and it was necessary to secure a crossing for our pontoon bridge to save Hood's army from ruin.

Protecting batteries and sharpshooters were soon posted on the river bank and early on the morning of the twenty-sixth the bridge was completed and Hood's main army at once recrossed the Tennessee, some of his stragglers having crossed at Decatur. We at once marched westward along the Memphis and Charleston Railroad, going into camp first at Rienzi and then at Tupelo, Mississippi, January 10, 1865, after a total loss, in this ill-fated campaign, of at least ten thousand men, or one-third of Hood's invading force.

Far be it from me to recall these incidents of our deplorable Civil War for the purpose of renewing its enmities and bitterness, now that the great mass of our people, and especially the surviving soldiers on both sides, sincerely wish to have the wounds of the past healed and should cordially act in concert for the common good of our whole country, striving united to preserve its peace. The truths here recorded recall sad memories of a sad period of our history, but as authentic facts and reminiscences they may form a slight tribute to the brave troops of both armies who confronted each other on some of our bloodiest battlefields.

They show what efforts were made by Thomas on that memorable December 16, 1864, at Nashville, to turn Hood's right; they prove that a prize was at stake and they explain why the important position on Overton Hill was not taken and why, for that reason, Hood was able to withdraw two-thirds of his men from Tennessee.

In the record of such bloody events we see how, in those days of severe trial, the soldiers on both side strove to do their duty and as we, the constantly diminishing survivors of the "boys in blue" and the "boys in gray," seek to recall to mind the stirring scenes of that great and lamentable struggle, how vividly do they dwell upon our memories.

PART FIVE

The War in 1865

The Peace Commission of 1865

ROBERT M. T. HUNTER,
SECRETARY OF STATE, AND SENATOR FROM VIRGINIA, C.S.A.

Philadelphia *Weekly Times* 1, no. 4, March 24, 1877

At the beginning of the year 1865, the country had become much exhausted by the exertions and ravages of the war. Scarce a household but had lost some member of its family in the bloody conflicts of the war, to whose chances parents had hitherto consigned the lives of their children without doubt or hesitation. In General [Robert E.] Lee's skill and patriotism universal confidence was reposed, and among many disposed by nature to be sanguine, hopes of final success were still entertained. But among the considerate and those who had staked and lost both family and fortune in the war, feelings of despondency were beginning to prevail. Particularly was this the case among the older class of legislators. The vacant ranks in our armies were no longer promptly filled, as at the commencement of the war, and an exhibit of our resources, made by Judge [John Archibald] Campbell, our assistant secretary of war, to General Lee, exhibited only a beggarly account of empty taxes.

Propositions to call out boys of not more than sixteen years of age and to place Negroes in the army were already being discussed. The prospects of success from such expedients were regarded as poor, indeed. The chances for the fall of Fort Fisher seemed imminent, as well as that of the complete closure of the ports through which we had been bringing into the Confederacy food, clothing, and munitions of war. These dangers, beginning to be visible, were producing a most depressing effect on our Confederate Congress. When these sources of supply should be cut off, where then would be our resources to prolong the contest? The talk, too, for peace began to be more earnest and open than it had been hitherto. Influential politicians on the other side, formerly of great weight in the party contests of the country and still bound to leading men in the Confederacy by old associations, were openly exerting themselves for peace and appealing to men who used to act with and confide in them to unite with and work with them to procure a peace. [Francis P.] Blair, an old Democratic leader during the time of General [Andrew] Jackson's election to the presidency and his administration and indeed, through the whole period succeeding it up to the election of President Lincoln, adhered to the government party, and labored earnestly for its success. Finding that things were going much further than he had anticipated and becoming alarmed for the consequences, he interposed earnestly in the cause of peace and procured the opportunity to visit Richmond, where he saw many old friends and party associates.

Here his representations were not without effect upon his old confederates who for so long had been in the habit of taking counsel with him on public affairs. He said what seemed to many of us to have much truth, that the disparity of resources was so great in favor of the Federals as would make a much further resistance on the part of the Confederacy impracticable. The United States, he said, if necessary for their purpose, could empty the population of Europe upon the Southern coasts by the offer of the lands of the dispossessed Southern landholders, and they would come in such numbers that any attempt at resistance would be hopeless. If the resistance, too, were protracted much further, such a temper would be exerted among the adherents of the government that they would not object to the exchange, but be quite willing for it. Believing this to be the disposition of our opponents and that a real danger was to be apprehended from the continuance of the war, my own attention was now more seriously directed to peace than heretofore. It turned the thoughts of many Confederates toward peace more seriously than ever before since the commencement of the war. But the very fact of the existence of such disposition on the part of the United States Government showed how small were the chances for a peaceful and friendly settlement of existing differences between the parties.

The talk about peace became so earnest and frequent in the capital of the Confederacy and the indications of a desire for it among many members of the Confederacy became so plain and obvious that President [Jefferson] Davis and his friends began to feel that it was expedient that the Confederate government should show some desire for peace on fair terms. To show no sense of responsibility for the terrible conflict then waging, and no desire for peace on any terms, would injure the Confederate government in the eyes of its own people. The intrinsic difficulties in the way of a fair accommodation were scarcely appreciated, and the desire for change so universal in the human heart was manifest. Many were alarmed at the talk of conscripting Negroes, and mothers, who had shrunk from nothing heretofore, were beginning to flinch at the prospect of seeing their boys of sixteen years of age, or under, exposed to the horrors and hardships such as would then be incurred in military service.

Accordingly, the president, in January 1865, determined to appoint three commissioners and propose a conference between them and others to be appointed by the United States government, on the subject of peace, at some place to be agreed upon between the governments. The persons appointed were [Alexander H.] Stephens, vice president of the Confederate States, Judge John A. Campbell, assistant secretary of war, and R. M. T. Hunter, Confederate senator from the State of Virginia. These were expected to meet President [Abraham] Lincoln and Secretary [William H.] Seward at Old Point and prepared for the conference. General Lee was directed to pass the commissioners through his lines to City Point, from which place it was supposed that [Lt. Gen. Ulysses S.] Grant would transfer them to the place of meeting at Old Point.

Instructions were delivered to them directing, among other things, that they were to treat on the basis of "two countries," thus precluding any idea of reunion, a provision which subsequently gave rise to difficulties in arranging the meeting, and it was rumored that Mr. [Judah P.] Benjamin, secretary of state, foreseeing this, had endeavored in vain to have it stricken out. We were dispatched at once to Petersburg, and it having gotten out that a commission of peace was on its way to Norfolk, we were received everywhere along the line with marks of great interest and curiosity. Of course we did nothing voluntarily to create expectations; and seeing no prospect of negotiating for a settlement of the difficulties between the parties, under our instructions, we did nothing so well calculated to exasperate the difference, as would have been the case had false hopes of peace, wantonly created, been unexpectedly disappointed. But we were not insensible to the manifestations of interest in the question in Petersburg, or that Judge Joynes, on taking leave of us said, as he shook hands, that if we returned with any fair hope of peace, we would be thanked by every man, woman, and child in the city.

When we reached Petersburg an intense state of excitement was soon raised in regard to the commission. This excitement was increased by unexpected delays in passing the commissioners over the enemy's line. The delay was the cause of some wonder to ourselves, until, in subsequently passing over, we observed the lean state of General Lee's defenses and how poorly our lines were lined with defenders. The ground between the two armies was covered with spent minie balls, and it was obvious that if no more carnage had ensued it was not for the want of mutual ill-will and attempts between the combatants. A short time brought us to the river, over which we were conducted to the boat which received us and subsequently conducted us to the place of meeting. Here we were courteously received by General Grant and his officers, and we had abundant means to compare the resources of the respective and opposing lines. Many of the officers in General Grant's lines loudly expressed their desire for peace, wishes which we did not hesitate to reciprocate. Among them was [Maj. Gen. George G.] Meade, who told us he was near being arrested in Chicago at the commencement of the war for expressing such desires and the opinion that the contest would result like the Kilkenny cat fight; and who now, said he, will say that such an opinion was absurd? Some of us said that he had heard the conjecture that General Lee had already fought as many pitched battles as Napoleon in his Italian campaigns. General Meade said that he did not doubt but he had, for many of his skirmishes, as they were called, would have ranked as battles in Napoleon's campaigns.

The officers were courteous in their comments on their enemies, and many of them seemed mindful of old acquaintanceship and old ties. But soon General Grant began to receive returns to his telegrams from President Lincoln and Mr. Seward. A copy of our instructions was transmitted to President Lincoln, and now commenced our troubles. The president and his secretary answered promptly that they could not negotiate on the basis of two countries. President Lincoln said he could negotiate on no hypothesis but one of reunion. We were bound by positive instructions on our side and could make no relaxation of those instructions on that hand. As these difficulties seemed to increase by the persistency on both sides, all partied were annoyed by the hitch. Not only General Grant's officers, but we ourselves, were anxious to know if there was any chance of a settlement and on what terms. It was interesting to us to know whether the other party was aware of our real situation, but nothing occurred to satisfy us on that point; and yet with the system of spies and deserters on both parts and the notoriety of our state of destitution at home, it seemed impossible to suppose that the enemy were not sufficiently aware of our condition to make their knowledge in that particular an important element in the negotiation.

As the difficulties of meeting seemed to increase, the impatience of the bystanders to bring the parties together grew very rapidly. One of General Grant's officers assured us that Mrs. [Julia Dent] Grant had expressed her opinion openly that her husband ought to send us on and permit no vital difficulties to break up the interview. She said we were known to be good men, she believed that our intentions were praiseworthy, and she doubted not but that something good would result if we and Mr. Lincoln could be brought together; but that if Mr. Seward were allowed to intervene between us he would break up all prospect of a settlement of the difficulties by his wily tactics. She seemed to have a poor opinion of his purposes or management. She impressed us very favorably by her frankness and good feeling, but somehow the difficulties were removed, and after a delay of about twenty-four hours steam was gotten up and we were on our way to the place of meeting.

We all moved under some excitement; we were all desirous of a fair settlement and neither expected nor wished unequal advantages or an unfair adjustment. We were no diplomatists, unused in the practices of negotiation; immense events might be in store for us; great possibilities of change ahead of us, and possibly through us seeds might be sown from which new destinies might spring or changes effected which might alter the course of empire itself. We would probably never know what would be the effect of our own actions or how it would result for our country. These were dreary thoughts to any men, but particularly to those who felt the load of a peculiar responsibility for the turn which events might take.

We had formed no particular scheme of negotiation, no definite line of policy by which exciting dispositions on both sides might be molded to satisfactory results. Mr. Stephens seemed possessed with the opinion that secession might be recognized as a conservative remedy by the Northern population, as subsequent conversations proved. He made it evident, too, that he believed the Monroe Doctrine might be made the cement of union among our populations. He acted upon the principle that by a union to drive the French out of Mexico, our people could be reunited at home. The extent to which he carried these opinions was strange indeed. Judge Campbell seemed to repose his hopes on an armistice to be formed by General Grant and General Lee and certain conditions to be declared between them on which this armistice should exist. The intercourse which would subsist during the armistice, it was thought, would hurry about peace and good feeling and the old habits of trade and bring on old feelings generated by the intercourse dictated by self-interest and old association. It was believed, too, that arrangements brought on by General Grant and General Lee to restore old intercourse would be tolerated, which would be rejected if proposed by anyone else.

We met Mr. Lincoln and Mr. Seward aboard the steamer, and soon the conference was commenced by Mr. Stephens, who seemed impressed with the idea that secession was the true conservative remedy for sectional difference and appeared to be animated by the hope that he could convince the president and secretary of the truth of this view. Never was hope more mistaken. Although polite, neither countenanced the idea for a moment. He next proposed another subject upon which he seemed to rely with even more confidence. He revived the old Monroe Doctrine and suggested that a reunion might be formed on the basis of uniting to drive the French out of America, and uniting to organize this continent for Americans. This was received with even less favor than I expected. Both expressed their aversion to any occupancy of Mexico by the French, but if they felt any doubt, expressed none as to the capacity of the United States government to drive the French away. Mr. Blair, while in Richmond, talked of this as a probable basis of reunion.

Mr. Lincoln was evidently afraid that he had uttered sentiments for which he could not be responsible and earnestly disclaimed having authorized this mission—whether this was true I had my doubts then and now. It is impossible but that Mr. Lincoln must have felt anxiety on the subject of peace. If he knew of our destitution he gave no sign of it, but he did not press the peace as I had supposed he would. He distinctly affirmed that he would not treat except on the basis of reunion and the abolition of slavery. Neither Lincoln nor Seward showed any wise or considerate regard for the whole country, or any desire to make the war as little disastrous to the whole country as possible. If they entertained any such desires they made no exhibition. Their whole object seemed to be to force a reunion and an abolition of slavery. If this could be done, they seemed to feel little care for the distress and suffering of the beaten party.

Mr. Lincoln, it is true, said that a politician on his side had declared that $400,000,000 ought to be given by way of compensation to the slaveholders, and in this opinion he expressed his concurrence. Upon this Mr. Seward exhibited some impatience and got up to pace across the floor, exclaiming, as he moved, that in his opinion the United States had done enough in expending so much money on the war for the abolition of slavery and had suffered enough in enduring the losses necessary to carry on the war. "Ah, Mr. Seward," said Mr. Lincoln, "you may talk so about slavery if you will; but if it was wrong in the South to hold slaves, it was wrong in the North to carry on the slave trade and sell them to the South (as it is notorious that they did, he might have added), and to have held on to the money thus procured without compensation, if the slaves were to be taken by them again." Mr. Lincoln said, however, that he was not authorized to make such a proposition, nor did he make it.

It was evident that both the president and secretary were afraid of the extreme men of their party. Certain objects were to be assured, and when once obtained it was no consideration with their party whether the sufferings of the conquered party were to be mitigated or any relief was to be afforded. And yet no statesman and benevolent man, it was obvious that both parties were to be benefited by affording the conquered party some relief for their prostration. The reaction of the sufferings of the South upon the North has been obvious enough for many years. The English government in its scheme of West Indian emancipation saw the necessity of some relief to all parts of the country. It ought to have been obvious enough to wise and considerate statesmen that some relief was the policy here, too. But the North, when placed in power, seemed to be insensible to these views and desired to punish those who had been defeated in the contest. To do this they seemed willing to make their losses irretrievable.

The armistice was promptly opposed by the president and secretary of state. If the only objects were to reestablish the Union and abolish slavery, they were right. If, however, they had any desire for the general good, and to procure relief for parties suffering, as ought to have been felt by men fit to govern such a country and to understand its wants, their views would have been different. We had tried to intimate to General Grant before we reached Old Point that a settlement generally satisfactory to both sides could be more easily effected through him and General Lee by an armistice than in any other way. The attempt was in vain. Lee had too much principle probably to have yielded to such a suggestion, and if Grant would have suffered no principle to restrain him if he had seen his way clear, he had not the ability to weigh truly his responsibility or to understand his opportunities. Generals who are so often accused and blamed for usurping power, often see the best way out of difficulties. Had Caesar or Napoleon been in command of the Union forces there is little doubt but that some settlement would have been made to have relieved us of much of our difficulty.

When a general knows what to do he is often more reliable than the politicians in civil war. England, probably, was better managed by Cromwell than would have been done by the general voice of her civilians. Politicians often make more fatal inroads on the bulwarks of national liberty than military commanders. It is doubtful whether a government formed by the Roman Senate would have been better than Scylla's, and Napoleon's constitutions were probably preferable to what the civilians would have given them. Civil wars often produce emergencies which create new and unexpected wants, and in these I have no doubt but that Napoleon was a more reliable counselor than Lieges. Communications are sometimes produced by the sword that can only be cut by the sword. In this very case some compensation for the Negroes taken away would have been both just and polite. Through a truce or armistice it might have been effected, but otherwise it seems not.

With regard to the Monroe Doctrine, out of which I feared some complications might arise, as Blair had seemed to favor it very much, I took occasion to say to Mr. Lincoln that I differed much from Mr. Stephens and so in my opinion did many of our people, who would be found unwilling to kindle a new war with the French on any such pretense. That for one I laid no such claims to the right of exclusive possession of the American continent for the American people, as had been done by others. That many of us would be found unwilling to have a war upon a mere question of policy rather than of honor or right. That although we would hear and comment as to whatever was said to us on this question, we were not instructed to treat upon it. Nor for one was I prepared to do so. I asked him, however, to communicate the terms, if any, upon which he would negotiate with us. He said he could not treat with us with arms in our hands; in rebellion, as it were, against the government.

I did not advert to the fact that we were with arms in our hands upon this occasion when we came to treat with him, but I replied this had been often done, especially by Charles I, when at civil war with the British Parliament. He laughed and said that "Seward could talk with me about Charles I; he only knew that Charles I had lost his head." I said not for that, but because he made no satisfactory settlement at all. But it was of no use to talk with him upon this subject. It was evident that both he and Seward were terribly afraid of their constituents. They would hint at nothing but unconditional submission, although professing to disclaim any such demand. Reunion and submission seemed their sole conditions. Upon the subject of a forfeiture of lands, Mr. Lincoln said it was well known that he was humane and not disposed to exact severe terms. It was then that I expressed myself more freely on the subject of the negotiation and the condition of affairs. It seemed, I said, that nothing was left us but absolute submission both as to rights and property, a wish to impose no unnecessary sacrifice on us as to landed property on the part of one branch of our government, but no absolute assurance as to this. I might have said it was the expression of an absolute determination not to treat at all, but to demand a submission as absolute as if we were passing through the Candine Forks.

Such a rebuke to negotiation after a civil war of half this magnitude in any European nation probably would have called down the intervention of its neighbors; nor is it probable that the parties to a civil war in any civilized European nation could have met for purposes of adjustment without some plan of relief or amelioration on the part of the stronger in favor of the weaker. Mr. Seward, it is true, disclaimed all demand for unconditional submission. But what else was the demand for reunion and abolition of slavery, without any compensation for Negroes or even absolute safety for property proclaimed to have been forfeited?

The Fall of Fort Fisher

BRAXTON BRAGG,
GENERAL, C.S.A.

Philadelphia *Weekly Times* 4, no. 5, March 27, 1880

In the spring of 1865 the only important seaport remaining open to the Confederates was that of Wilmington, N.C., which, from the peculiarities of the harbor, could only be closed by the capture of its strong defensive earthwork, Fort Fisher, situated upon the peninsula between Cape Fear River and the Atlantic Ocean. An unsuccessful attempt to capture this fort was made by an expedition under General Butler in December 1864. In January the attempt was renewed under Maj. Gen. [Alfred H.] Terry, and resulted in a Union victory. General Terry took 2,083 prisoners, 109 pieces of artillery, and many small arms. The Union loss was in killed 110, in wounded 536. The subjoined letter from General Braxton Bragg to his brother gives a Confederate version of the operations resulting in the fall of the fort:

Wilmington, January 20, 1865

My Dear Thomas: Your very kind note of the thirteenth only reached me this morning, but we are none the less grateful. The unexpected blow which has fallen upon us is almost stunning, but it shall not impair my efforts. Two hours before hearing of the certain fall of the fort I felt as confident as ever man did of successfully defending it. The responsibility is all mine, of course, and I shall bear it as resolutely as possible; but time will make known some matters which may as well be told you now in confidence to be used discreetly. No human power could have prevented the

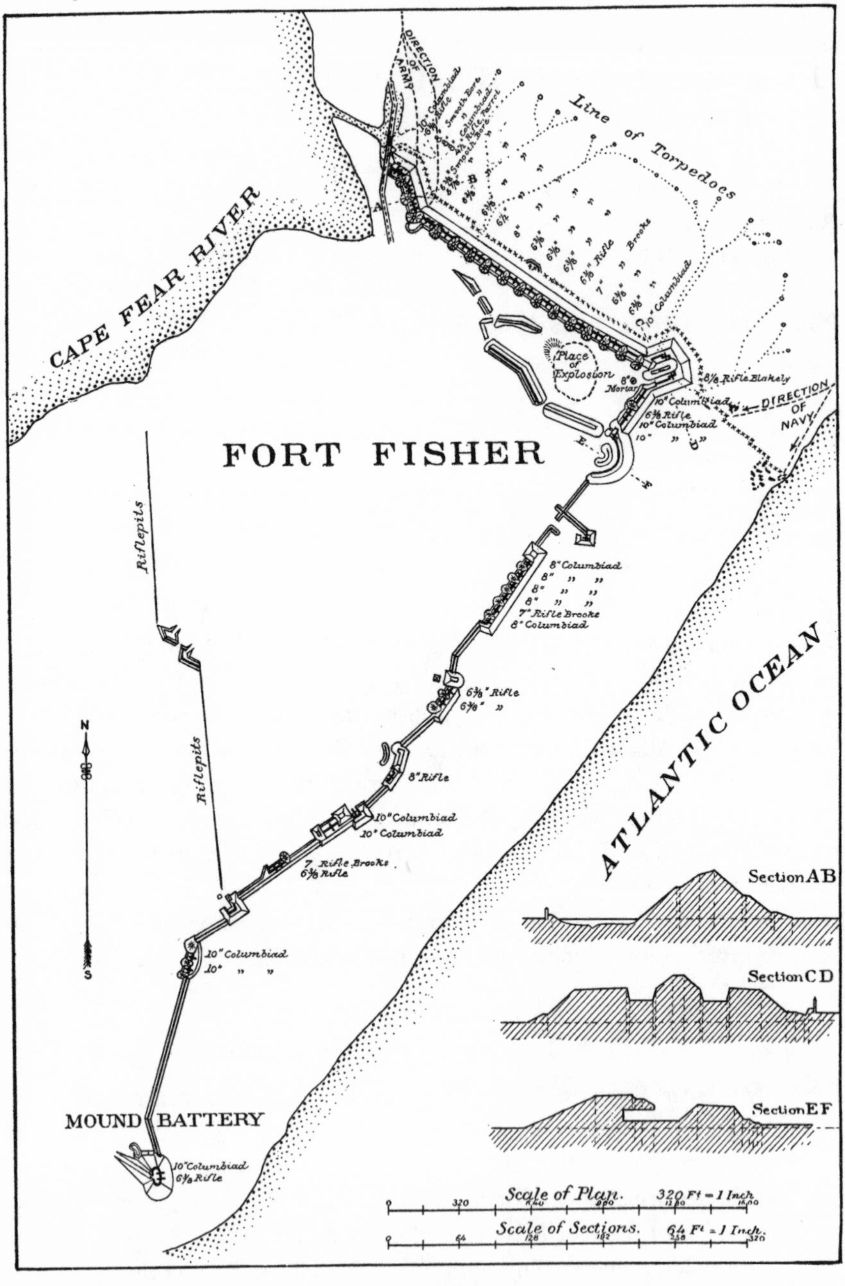

Fort Fisher

(CENTURY MAGAZINE)

enemy from landing, covered as he was by a fleet of ships carrying six hundred heavy guns; anywhere beyond the range of our heavy guns on the fort, our land force could not approach him. Once landed our only chance was to keep him if possible from the fort, with less than half his number; had we extended far enough toward the fort to prevent his movement that way he could have crossed the narrow peninsula north of us and cut us off entirely, when the fort and all must have gone. The land is heavily timbered and very swampy. We then confronted him as closely as possible, to watch his movements and endeavor to strike if he moved from under his shipping. A dense swamp lay between us, and extended three miles toward Fort Fisher. In this position I found the two forces when I reached General [Robert F.] Hoke and took the command just at night on Friday. Cavalry was on our extreme right toward Fort Fisher, and occupying ground entirely to the sea, placing us between the enemy and the fort for observation. These were to report any movement, and the troops lay upon their arms all night, ready to move to the attack toward the fort if the enemy did so. My knowledge of the ground was as good as I knew General Hoke's to be, both of us having been over it. I fully approved his dispositions. We stayed in our camp under the heavy shelling of the enemy's fleet for the night.

No report of any movement having been made we moved out early to reconnoiter, Hoke toward the fort and I to our left. I found the enemy in strong force in front of our left, as well as could be seen across the swamp. But to our great surprise Hoke found him extended beyond our right and entirely across the peninsula between us and Fort Fisher, and strongly entrenched, having, no doubt, been there most of the night. Not a word had been heard from our cavalry and they had evidently withdrawn from their position in the night, and did not themselves know what had occurred, for they fired on Hoke and his staff, who got in front of them in reconnoitering. On hearing this I put the command in motion, and ordered the enemy dislodged, if it was at all practicable. General Hoke and his brigadiers made a close reconnaissance, and expressed to me the opinion that their troops were unequal to the task. I moved forward with them and made a close examination, and after a conference confirmed the opinion and decided not to attack; an attack and failure would have ensured the fall of the fort, and would also have opened the whole state. We could not have succeeded without defeating double our numbers behind entrenchments, while at the same time exposed to a raking fire from their fleet, plainly in sight and within good range, the sea as smooth as glass; but I did not feel the slightest apprehension for the fort. The enemy had landed without artillery and not even a general officer brought a horse. Prisoners captured and deserters coming in concurred in one report that if repulsed once they would immediately retreat and re-embark—the work being considered too strong for them. Believing myself that [Lt. Gen. Ulysses S.] Grant's army could not storm and carry the fort if it was defended, I felt perfect confidence that we were not only safe, but that the enemy had assumed a most precarious position, from which he would escape with great difficulty.

I accordingly ordered Hoke to entrench immediately in his front and push his lines close on him so as to keep him engaged and closely observed. While this was going on I started one thousand of our best men, who had defended forts at Charleston, to reinforce Fisher, and, as I considered the garrison there already as sufficient, being two thousand strong, I ordered about six hundred less reliable troops to come out, considering it an unnecessary exposure of life to keep them there. This order, however, was rescinded on General [William H. C.] Whiting's appeal, and he was allowed to keep the whole. With this garrison I considered the fort perfectly safe and capable of standing any length of siege. We had steamboat communication with it which we could keep open at all times during the night.

Had the cavalry done its duty and promptly reported the enemy's movements, I do not think the result would have been different, such was the configuration of the country and the obstacles that he would have accomplished his object with the force he had. Our only safe reliance was in his repulse, we being the weak and assailed party. The reports from the fort were of the most favorable character up to Sunday evening. Not a gun was reported injured, the fort not damaged and our loss three killed and thirty-two wounded in nearly three days. With these statements I feel confident that when the assault was made it would be easily repulsed, and so telegraphed General Whiting.

During Saturday I was greatly disturbed by the tone and phraseology of General Whiting's dispatches and by reports of others received from him in town. Knowing his great infirmity, which detracted much from his gallantry and efficiency, I concluded to take him out of the fort. As a good officer had been sent in command of the reinforcements, I ordered General Whiting, on Saturday evening, to report to me in person. This order he declined to obey, as he had done once before, about moving troops. My mind was now made up as to his condition, and I felt that the safety of the fort required his prompt relief. Brig. Gen. [Alfred H.] Colquitt was accordingly sent to relieve him. About 3:00 P.M., Sunday, General Whiting informed me the enemy was moving apparently to assault the fort. Hoke immediately moved to attack them under my direction. A feeble musketry fire was heard at the fort, when it closed, not lasting over ten minutes. Hoke found them in very strong position and heavy force ready to receive him. He moved in person close up to their lines with his skirmishers, receiving two balls in his clothes between left arm and breast. Their line was impracticable for his small command, and I did not hesitate to recall him. He could not have succeeded. When the assault commenced on the fort the fleet ceased to fire and in less than half an hour it recommenced with great fury. My inference was that they were repulsed. A report soon reached me, however, from a party across the river, that "the enemy have the fort." As the firing from the fleet on the fort continued, I disregarded the report. At 7:00 P.M. a dispatch from General Whiting reported: "We still hold the fort, but are hard pressed." Soon after another from his adjutant said: "We are still in possession of the fort," etc. My mind was easy. General Colquitt and his reinforcements were hurried forward. The bombardment continued heavily until about 10 P.M., when all became quiet. Unpleasant reports continued to reach me, but nothing worthy of credit until an escaped officer reported from across the river by telegraph that the fort was captured. General Colquitt soon returned and reported he landed at the point about a mile behind the fort at 10:30 P.M., found everything in confusion, hundreds of men without arms, many of them drunk, and no one apparently in command. Colonel [William] Lamb was there, wounded. General Whiting was also pointed out lying on the beach, severely wounded, but fast asleep! The enemy soon approached and Colquitt barely had time to escape in his small boat. Now for statements made by the enemy when meeting us under flag of truce. They assert that they walked into the fort without resistance, not a shot being fired at them, our men all being in the bomb-proofs; that after they got in a small force was rallied and fought them very gallantly, inflicting a heavy loss; but they soon overcame them and captured most of our officers and men without arms under cover of the bomb-proofs, and with the exception of Colonel Lamb, all the officers of any rank and many men were too drunk for duty.

It is known that General Whiting left here for the fort, Friday, in a steamer, with a large party of these money kings, called blockade runners, and a very large supply of the material necessary to produce this result. The fighting done was, no doubt, by the veterans who had reached the fort from Hoke's command. To my mind this is a clear solution of the whole thing. It explains the otherwise inexplicable dispatches I received. It explains how the enemy got into the fort, declared by them as impregnable, and when it had nearly a double garrison.

Blockade-running has cured itself. I knew its demoralizing influence, and even before I came here had urged on the president to remove these officers and troops, replacing them by veterans. All, even to the privates, were more or less interested in the business. Under an arrangement with General Whiting, I learn salvage was regularly allowed on all property saved from wrecks, which was not stolen, and every vessel arriving made certain contributions of luxuries, whisky being the principal. I was at work on these evils, gradually correcting them; but, meeting with the usual denunciation, time was not allowed.

This defense of the fort ought to have been successful against this attack, but it had to fall eventually. The expedition brought against it was able to reduce it in spite of all I could do. The fleet, after dismounting our guns, could have arranged itself above their land forces and no spot for six miles above Fort Fisher could have been held by our land forces. Owing to the depth of water they could get nearer us than they would to Fort Fisher, and could sweep everything to the middle of the river. The same operation on a much smaller scale was entirely successful against the forts at the mouth of Charleston Harbor, except that they were defended by sober, resolute men, until it was necessary to evacuate and the harbor was closed by the fall of Fort Wagner. No one abused General [Pierre G. T.] Beauregard for that, yet he had three times as many troops as I had here. This place is not now what it was.

The people here are not our people, and having lost their occupation preying on the vitals of the country, are clamorous for the Yankees to come in. You hear but that one sentiment, and regret any intention to defend further. But enough for the present. I am both tired and sad.

I knew that my wife would be welcome with you, but I feared it would look badly for me to send her off in the panic, and knowing there was no danger in town, I concluded for her to remain. It has had a great effect on the weak and nervous. We are boarding with a very good family of people where we have privacy and a home, at least for the present. Elise has been quite sick from the cold and sore throat contracted on her last trip. She is now much better, but sadly disheartened.

Will you please send me by express the barrel of flour you have for me? Our only trouble is to get enough to eat, as we pay our board in kind. No one will take a boarder here or anywhere now for money. Our love to all.

Your brother, Braxton Bragg

The Fall of Richmond

GODFREY WEITZEL,
MAJOR, CORPS OF ENGINEERS, AND BREVET MAJOR GENERAL,
UNITED STATES ARMY

Philadelphia *Weekly Times* 4, no. 27, August 27, 1881

[Lt. Gen. Ulysses S.] Grant's instructions for the general movement of the armies operating against Richmond, which resulted in the fall of this city and Petersburg and eventually in the surrender of the Rebel Army of Northern Virginia, were dated City Point, Virginia, March 24, 1865. These instructions have been so often printed and so extensively and widely published that I do not consider it necessary to insert them in this narrative. At the time they were issued I was in command of the XXV Army Corps, with my headquarters east of the Varina road, about one-half mile due north of the H. Cox House. [Maj. Gen. Charles J.] Paine's division of my corps was in North Carolina. My command formed a part of the Army of the James, commanded by Maj. Gen. [Edward. O. C.] Ord. The left of the lines of this army rested upon the Appomattox River, about a mile west of the Point of Rocks, extended thence almost due north to within about three-eighths of a mile of the Varina road; thence northeasterly to a point about a quarter of a mile beyond the New Market road, thence easterly to cover this road. Their total length, not counting the cavalry lines, was about eleven miles.

The force on these lines, commanded by General Ord, consisted of a mixed command under Maj. Gen. George L. Hartsuff; the XXIV Army Corps, commanded by Maj. Gen. John Gibbon; a small division of cavalry, commanded by Brig. Gen. [Ranald S.] Mackenzie; and two divisions of the XXV Army Corps, commanded by me. The divisions of the XXIV Corps

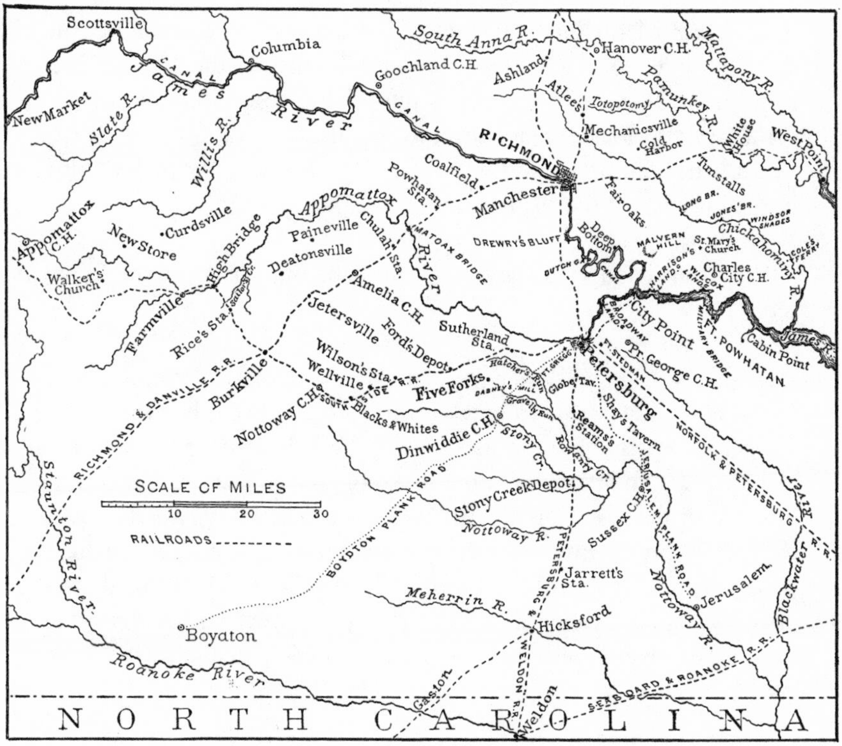

The Petersburg and Appomattox campaigns (CENTURY MAGAZINE)

were commanded respectively by Brigadier Generals Charles Devens, Robert S. Foster, and John W. Turner. Those of the XXV Corps were commanded by Brigadier Generals William Birney and August V. Kautz. Hartsuff's command formed a garrison of that portion of the lines included between the Appomattox and James Rivers; the left of my corps rested on the north side of the James at Fort Brady and the left of the XXIV Corps joined my right near the Varina road and formed the right of the main line. The cavalry was thrown out to the front and right to observe the roads leading into Richmond from that direction.

The part assigned to the Army of the James in the final movement will appear from the following extract from General Grant's instructions:

> General Ord will detach three divisions, two white and one colored, or so much of them as he can and hold the present lines and march for the present left of the Army of the Potomac. During the

movement, Major General Weitzel will be left in command of all the forces remaining behind from the Army of the James. The movement of troops from the Army of the James will commence on the night of the twenty-seventh instant. General Ord will leave behind the minimum number of cavalry necessary for picket duty in the absence of the main army.

The part assigned to me and my command appears from the following extract:

General Weitzel will keep vigilant watch upon his front, and if found at all practicable to break through at any point he will do so. A success north of the James should be followed up with great promptness. An attack will not be feasible unless it is found that the enemy has detached largely. In that case it may be regarded as evident that the enemy are relying upon their local reserves principally for the defense of Richmond. Preparations may be made for abandoning all the line north of the James except enclosed works, only to be abandoned, however, after a break is made in the lines of the enemy.

The final paragraph of these instructions contained general directions applicable to all officers in command of troops left in the trenches. In accordance with the instructions General Ord moved during the night of March 27 with Foster's and Turner's divisions of the XXIV Corps under the immediate command of General Gibbon, Birney's division of the XXV Corps and about 1,500 cavalry commanded by General Mackenzie. He left his department headquarters open for the recording of papers with two staff officers in charge, but I was left in command of the forces which remained behind. His instructions to me were written by himself on two telegraph blanks. This is an exact copy:

Headquarters Department of Virginia, Army of the James,
In the field, March 27, 1865

General Weitzel, commanding Twenty-fifth Corps.

General: If an evacuation occurs during my absence look out for torpedoes and mines. It is now reported that large numbers of the former are put down on Chaffin's farm and Bermuda front. Don't let your columns take the roads. Keep them in the woods

The Army of the James on the march (FORBES, *LIFE OF SHERMAN*)

and by-paths. Send cattle and old horses up the roads first. Tonight and to-morrow keep camp fires going as usual in empty camps and the usual picket on. Make as little change as possible at conspicuous points. If you can do so cover the prominent part of the vacated camps with shelter tents for a day or two or old newspapers. Go on with drills and parades in sight as usual. Adams' 5th Massachusetts (Colored) Cavalry is on its way to Deep Bottom; may arrive to-morrow or day after. Better camp them near where Mackenzie's outside camps were. It is very full. Besides this I leave about five hundred cavalry of Mackenzie's division—commanding officer to report to you. Birney's division will move very quietly soon as 'tis dark, cross at Aiken's, thence cross at Broadway, behind Turner. Both put wagons in front.

Yours, etc., E. O. C. Ord

On the morning of March 28, 1865, I therefore had, under my command the garrison of the Bermuda Hundred front, under General Hartsuff, Kautz's division of the XXV Corps, Devens' division of the XXIV Corps and absent 500 remnants of Mackenzie's Cavalry. The 5th Massachusetts (Colored) Cavalry, a very fine regiment, about 900 strong, commanded by Col. Charles F. Adams, Jr., joined me during the week. Attached to my headquarters I had Barker's very fine company of the 1st New York Volunteer Engineers and a detachment of two companies from the 4th Massachusetts Cavalry. Hartsuff ranked me, but waived his rank on account of my more intimate knowledge of the locality, plans, and troops. Maj. Gen. Alfred H. Terry did this once before to me while we served together in the Army of the James. Those who have had the honor of an acquaintance with these two gentlemen will not be surprised at this. Yet I mention this since I believe such examples of generous unselfishness are as rare as they were seventeen years ago and are therefore brilliant.

The works on the north side of the James, which were open in the rear, were enclosed and all were supplied with ammunition, provisions, and water sufficient for a siege of ten days. They were all armed with artillery, properly manned and had for infantry garrisons mainly those men who could not march well. The remainder of Kautz's and Deven's divisions, numbering about five thousand men each, were disposed of on the lines between these works, so that they could be rapidly concentrated either for attack or defense. During the six days and nights which succeeded the morning of March 28 every man in my command seemed to be fully impressed with the gravity of the situation. There were three high signal towers on my lines—one on Cobb's Hill, in front of Point of Rocks, on the Appomattox River; another near the south bank of the James, opposite Fort Brady; and one a few steps north of my headquarters. These towers overlooked a large part of the enemy's lines and the Richmond and Petersburg pike and railroad, and from the one in front of my headquarters the signal officers could see into portions of Richmond with their glasses on a clear day. I offered special rewards to the men on picket for bringing in prisoners and deserters. Extra officers from division and brigade headquarters were placed on duty on the picket lines, and Colonel Adams with his cavalry was constantly feeling for and hunting up the enemy on the right and front and gathering information. Everything known in warfare and all that the ingenuity of my command could devise were employed in obtaining information concerning the enemy in my front.

I was kept advised daily of the progress of events on the left of the Army of the Potomac by dispatches from Generals Grant and [Maj. Gen. Philip H.] Sheridan, as well as from Colonel Bowers at City Point. As a specimen of dispatches which passed I will here give the following:

U.S. Military Telegraphs, March 31, 1865
(By telegraph from Gravelly Run)

To Major General Weitzel:

Prisoners captured near Hatcher's Run this A.M. report that part of their line strongly reinforced from their left. What news do you get from your front?

U. S. Grant, Lieutenant General

About at the same time when this came I received the following from General Hartsuff on the Bermuda Hundred front:

I have just received the following from the field officer of the day:

General, Since writing this morning I have had communication with the enemy and am positive that four brigades, all of Mahone's Division, is still in front of the Tenth New York Artillery. Not the least change is discernable at other points.

Respectfully,
General Gordon, Officer of Day

J. L. Hartsuff, Major General.

A little later I received the following:

U.S. Military telegraph, March 31, 1865
(By telegraph from 24th Army Corps)

To Major General Weitzel:

The scouting party under Lieutenant Robb, 20th New York Cavalry, has returned. He crossed to the Charles City road, striking it at White's Tavern. He found it was impossible to go through White Oak Swamp, as had been his intention, on account of the height of the water. He therefore proceeded up the road and found the rebel picket about a mile above White's, observed the camp, which was apparently as large as it had ever been, and saw soldiers moving about among tents. Lieutenant Robb was about a mile from the camp, which was behind the enemy's breastwork and apparently infantry. The picket was mounted and about half a mile in front of the breastwork. The picket has usually been found at White's Tavern. Mrs. White says it has been drawn in within the last ten days. There were no tracks on the Charles City road since the rain of this morning about White's. On Wednesday a scouting party of the enemy came down near our picket at Fussell's Mills, as reported to Lieutenant Robb.

All quiet along the cavalry picket today. A few shots fired at the colored troops when first posted.

Charles Devens,
Brigadier General Commanding.

And later the following:

March 31, 1865
(by telegraph from Headquarters 24th Army Corps)

To Major General Weitzel:

Captain Elder, aide-de-camp, reports no apparent change in enemy's camp. He has visited all our picket line in front. Colonel Ripley, First Brigade, has lookouts on trees in three places along the line. They report that they can observe no change.

Charles Devens,
Brigadier General

On Saturday, April 1, things opened lively. First I received a dispatch from General Grant at Dabney's Mills that the wonderfully ubiquitous Mahone's Division was reported over there. Then Brig. Gen. G. H. McKibbon reported from the Bermuda front that there were fewer troops in the enemy's lines on that front than the day before. Then came another from General Grant at Dabney's Mills that they had prisoners, he believed, from every brigade of Pickett's Division, and that nothing had been seen of any of Fields', Kershaw's, or Mahone's Divisions. When I received the first two I requested Hartsuff to open with artillery, to be followed by an attack of infantry, and see what it would develop. Before I heard the result of this General Grant's second dispatch arrived. Hartsuff's artillery fire developed nothing, but a prisoner was captured belonging to Finnegan's Brigade. From his statements Hartsuff was positive that the whole of Mahone's Division was in his front and therefore did not attack with infantry. Then Devens reported no change. At 7:00 P.M. General Grant telegraphed that he did not think that Mahone had moved, unless possibly during the evening. In order to settle this question I requested Hartsuff to attack the next morning and ascertain. This was done as vigorously as he was able to make it. He lost seven killed, 39 wounded (several severely) and 35 prisoners and obtained the desired information. The following is what he said about it:

Hatcher's Farm, April 2, 1865

General Weitzel:

My demonstration this morning resulted in developing the enemy in force along his line. They were driven out of their picket line with ease for a distance of more than half a mile and six of their pickets captured. Our advance was then opened upon by artillery throughout the whole of their line which bore upon it. Having ascertained by this and from the prisoners that their line was still held in force and by Mahone's Division, the troops were directed to withdraw. The enemy followed with a strong line of infantry to their picket line, which they reoccupied.

During this morning a large number of the officers of the James River fleet came on shore and to my headquarters to learn the news. While they were thus assembled I received a dispatch requesting me to inform the senior officer that all the vessels which could be spared were wanted at City Point without delay. This produced quite an excitement and the hasty departure of our web-footed comrades. None of us knew the meaning of it then, but I soon received a dispatch from Colonel Bowers, at City Point, that Parke had captured two forts and two redoubts in his front, and later that the marines and sailors of the fleet were wanted at City Point to guard the great number of rebel prisoners which were continually coming in. Later in the day a nervousness became manifest on some portions of the enemy's lines in my front. In order to assist this I ordered the artillery to open, but no changes of any importance were observed. Then I received a dispatch in the afternoon from the operator at City Point that General Wright had carried the works in his front and that General Parke had carried the works in front of Fort Sedgwick.

About 5:00 P.M. my chief signal officer, Partridge, came down from the tower near my headquarters and reported to me that he had observed evidences of great excitement in Richmond and that people were rushing to and fro in the streets. I immediately gave orders for the concentration of some of my brigades to make an assault and informed General Grant. In the meantime Hartsuff received an order from Grant looking towards an attack at a different point than the one selected by me, and afterwards I received one from him that the success of the day had been so great that he could spare me R. H. Jackson's (formerly W. Birney's) division of my corps, and that he would send it to me and that then I could make sure thing of the attack. Further than this I heard nothing from the other side of the Appomattox during April 2.

Extra vigilance was enjoined on all during the night. I lay down at midnight for a rest, leaving my chief of staff, Brig. Gen. [George F.] Shepley, and my ordnance officer, Capt. George F. Howard, 40th Massachusetts, on guard at my headquarters. A little before 2:00 A.M. I was awakened by General Shepley and informed that bright fires were seen in the direct of Richmond. Shortly after, while we were looking at these fires we heard explosions, and soon a prisoner was sent in from Kautz's front. This prisoner was a colored teamster. He informed me that immediately after dark the Rebels began making preparations to leave and that they had all gone. A forward movement of the entire picket line corroborated this. I, therefore, directed all of my troops to be awakened and furnished with breakfast and to be held in readiness to move as soon as it was light enough to see to pass through the lines of rebel torpedoes without injury.

At the same time I directed my senior aide-de-camp, Maj. Emmons E. Graves, and my provost marshal, Maj. Atherton H. Stevens, Jr., to take a detachment of about forty men from the two companies of the 4th Massachusetts Cavalry attached to my headquarters, and as soon as they could possibly get through the rebel lines to advance towards Richmond on a reconnaissance. I then telegraphed the state of affairs north of the James to Generals Grant and Hartsuff. As soon as I could see I passed through Kautz's lines and the rebel lines in his front with my staff and orderlies. No difficulty was experienced in doing this in single file since the rebels had left passages through the lines of torpedoes for the use of their pickets and these passages were plainly visible at dawn. Soon after passing through the lines we observed a party of mounted men on a slight elevation and but a short distance from us. They wore the overcoats of United States soldiers and were standing still and observing us. At first it seemed as if they were a part of the cavalry detachment which I had sent ahead under Major Graves. But suddenly they wheeled and went off at a gallop. I immediately directed Lieutenant Phillips, 4th Massachusetts Cavalry, of my staff, with an orderly to ride ahead and ascertain, if he could, what they were. He dashed off on a run, followed by the orderly, and ascertained what they were, but could not report the result of his investigation to me until five days thereafter. He then did it by telegraph from Burke's Station.

The mounted party that we saw were Rebel scouts observing our movements. When they saw Phillips and the orderly alone pursuing them they formed an ambuscade and took them in. They in turn escaped at Sailor's Creek, having been in charge of the retreating garrison of Richmond in the meantime.

My staff and I then rode along the Osborne Pike, and when we arrived at its junction with the New Market road we saw Devens' division coming up, the latter marching rapidly. Upon looking to the rear we saw Kautz's division coming up the pike at a similar gait. Only one man was killed in passing through the Rebel torpedo lines. I afterwards understood that the two columns met here and that Devens claimed the pike by virtue of seniority in rank and that Kautz yielded it on this account, but struck out straight across the fields. When we arrived at Battery 2, below Rocketts, we found a solitary sentinel on post in a bright and gorgeous militia uniform. He said he had been posted the night before and not relieved. He had served in the old country and seemed to me to be an Alsatian, for he spoke poor French and worse German. I sent him home to his family. From the time I was first awakened in the light the fires seemed to increase in number and size, and at intervals loud explosions were heard, and now when we entered Richmond we found ourselves in a perfect pandemonium. Fires and explosions in all directions; whites and blacks either drunk or in the highest state of excitement running to and fro on the streets apparently engaged in pillage or in saving some of their scanty effects from the fire; it was a yelling, howling mob.

Major Graves had reconnoitered up to the Capitol Square in the city. Below the latter he had been met by Major Mayo and others of Richmond and received its surrender. They informed him that all the liquor in the city had been ordered destroyed, but it seems that many of the poor wretches had scooped it up from the gutters and drank it. To add to the horror of the scene the convicts broke out of the penitentiary and began an indiscriminate pillage and cut the hose of some of the fire engines. When the mob saw my staff and me they rushed around us, hugged and kissed our legs and horses, shouting hallelujah and glory. This continued until we arrived at Capitol Square. I escaped considerable of this disagreeable infliction by an amusing circumstance. Maj. William V. Hutchings, of Roxbury, Massachusetts rode by my side. He was dressed in full uniform except epaulettes and had the regulation equipments, etc., on his horse. He had quite a venerable and very handsome appearance. I was in undress uniform. The mob naturally supposed Hutchings to be the general, and he received the bulk of the caresses and attentions.

A sad sight met us on reaching Capitol Square. It was covered with women and children who had fled here to escape the fire. Some of them had saved a few articles of furniture, but most had only a few articles of bedding, such as a quilt, blanket and pillow, and were lying upon them. Their poor faces were perfect pictures of utter despair. It was a sight that would have melted a heart of stone. I first ordered my aide, Capt. Horace B. Fitch, of Auburn, New York, to write a dispatch to General Grant, announcing my entrance into Richmond. This was the dispatch which was taken off the wires at City Point and sent to the country via Washington. Then I sent an order to Devens to march his division into the city and endeavor to extinguish the flames and ordered Parsons' engineer company to assist. I directed Kautz to occupy the detached forts nearest the city and Manchester and Adams to picket the roads. Colonel Adams asked as a special favor to be allowed to march his regiment through the city and I granted it. I was told that this fine regiment of colored men made a very great impression on those citizens who saw it. I directed my staff and headquarter orderlies to scour the city and press into service every able-bodied man, white or black, and make them assist in extinguishing the flames. Devens' command anticipated my orders. They marched into the city, stacked arms and went to work. In this manner the fire was extinguished and perfect order restored. Col. Fred L. Manning, provost marshal at department headquarters, reported to me and was placed on duty in the city. General Shepley, my chief of staff, was placed on duty as military governor. He had occupied a similar position in New Orleans after its capture in 1862 and was eminently fit for it by education and experience.

I understood from leading citizens of Richmond that the fires had been started in the large tobacco warehouses, which had been fired by order of [Lt. Gen. Richard S.] Ewell in order that their contents might not fall into our hands. Thus the Rebel capital, fired by men placed in it to defend it, was saved from total destruction by soldiers of the United States, who had taken possession. The bloody victories which opened the gates of Richmond to my command were won at Five Forks and on the left of the Army of the Potomac, but my men won equally as great a one in the city, although it was bloodless. The telegraph corps did not have wire enough to carry the lines into Richmond on the first day and hence the nearest station was about three miles distant. My dispatch announcing my entrance into

Richmond was sent down by cavalry courier, and on his return he brought the following:

April 3, 1865, from Grant's Headquarters

To Major General Weitzel:

I do not doubt that you will march into Richmond unopposed. Take possession of the city and establish guards and preserve order until I get there. Permit no one to leave town after you get possession. The army here will endeavor to cut off the retreat of the enemy.

U. S. Grant, Lieutenant General

In the afternoon I was astonished to receive the following:

April 3, 1865
(by telegraph from Petersburg, Virginia)

To Major General Weitzel:

How are you progressing? Will the enemy try to hold Richmond? I have detained the division belonging to your corps and will send it back if you think it will be needed. I am waiting here to hear from you. The troops moved up the Appomattox this morning.

U. S. Grant, Lieutenant General

I was still more astonished to hear a few days ago that [Adam] Badeau, in his book [*Military History of U. S. Grant*], stated that General Grant did not receive my 8:15 A.M. dispatch until nearly 2:00 P.M. I immediately sent to the office of the Detroit *Free Press* and found that they printed the extra announcing my occupation at 10:00 A.M. The delay was therefore between City Point and General Grant's headquarters.

With this I might consider the narrative of my entry into Richmond as ended, but the history of the letter from Mr. Lincoln directing me to permit the assembling of the Virginia legislature and its subsequent revocation is as intimately bound up with the history of my brief occupation of the city that I will, in order to comply with the request which has been made of me, continue the narrative in regular order of date. I had my headquarters during the day in the Senate chamber of the capitol. After the fires had been extinguished and order restored in Richmond I was desirous to obtain lodging and food. Upon inquiry I found that Major Graves, in the course of his reconnaissance, had found the Davis mansion and that the housekeeper, under instructions from Mr. Jefferson Davis, had surrendered it for the occupancy of the commanding officer of the Federal troops which might occupy the city. In addition to the housekeeper a few servants remained. The supplies in the larder were very scant, but everything else in the house was in good order and furnished elegant quarters for my staff and me. On April 4 received a dispatch, of which the following is a copy:

By telegraph from Headquarters Department Virginia
Army of the James, April 4, 1865

General Weitzel, commanding:

You will seize what tobacco may be within reach to sell for the purpose of feeding the poor of the city. You are appointed governor of Richmond, and in my absence will act as commander of the department in all matters which require prompt action. Let food and necessaries come to the city. Register the white men. Appoint a military commission for the punishment of offenses against law or order. Organize a police force. Start gas and water companies and protect all inhabitants in their property who come forward and take the oath of allegiance on due notice. By property persons are not meant. You will not allow any taxes to be imposed or rents paid other than necessary to recognize ownership of loyal landlords. Be your own treasury agent, allow loyal men to open hotels, but not grog shops.

E. O. C. Ord,
Major General Commanding,

Approved by General Grant

On this day I was delighted also to see Admiral [David G.] Farragut, with whom I became acquainted on the New Orleans expedition of 1862. As soon as he heard that Richmond had fallen he came up the river, regardless of torpedoes, landed at Varina, and rode into the city. He was accompanied by [Brig.] Gen. George M. Gordon, commanding officer at Norfolk. He looked even happier and younger than he did after New Orleans fell. On the next day, April 5, I received a dispatch from City Point that Mr. Lincoln had started for Richmond on the *Malvern*, Admiral Porter's flagship, and the time of probable arrival at the "Rocketts" was given. I ordered my ambulance to be at my office in abundant time for me to reach the "Rocketts" at the appointed time to meet the president. I was therefore very much surprised to hear just about the time I intended to get into my ambulance that the president was already at my quarters. I drove over as hastily as possible and found the report correct. It seems that the *Malvern* came up quicker than was expected, and not finding anyone at the landing to meet him the president started on foot. Porter ordered a guard of marines for an escort, but I am told that Mr. Lincoln saw nothing of his escort on his way. It differed from John Phoenix's cavalry escort to the surveying party in California in this respect, too, that it followed instead of preceding the president. He arrived at the Davis house closely followed by a rabble, mostly composed of Negroes. Some of the rabble had been told that he was Jefferson Davis, and consequently there were some cries of "Hang him! Hang him!"

Soon after my arrival Judge Campbell, General Anderson, and others called and asked for an interview with the president. It was granted and took place in the parlor with closed doors. At the special request of Mr. Lincoln, I was present at this and the subsequent one on the *Malvern*, as his witness. The pith of these interviews was briefly that Mr. Lincoln insisted that he could not treat with any Rebels until they had laid down their arms and surrendered, and that if this were first done he would go as far as he possibly could to prevent the shedding of another drop of blood, and that he and the good people of the North were surfeited with this thing and wanted it to end as soon as possible. Mr. Campbell and the other gentlemen assured Mr. Lincoln that if he would allow the Virginia legislature to meet it would at once repeal the ordinance of secession and that then Gen. Robert E. Lee and every other Virginian would submit; that this would amount to the virtual destruction of the Army of Northern Virginia and eventually to the surrender of all the other Rebel armies, and would ensure perfect peace in the shortest possible time. After the second interview Mr. Lincoln told me that he would think over the whole matter carefully and would probably send me some instructions from City Point on the next day. Immediately after, the *Malvern* steamed down the river. On the next day I received a letter by the hands of Senator Wilkinson, of Minnesota (I think), marked "confidential." The letter was written throughout in Mr. Lincoln's handwriting and was as follows:

Headquarters Armies of the United States,
City Point, April 6, 1865

Major General Weitzel, Richmond, Virginia.

It has been intimated to me that the gentlemen who have acted as the Legislature of Virginia in support of the rebellion may now desire to assemble at Richmond and take measures to withdraw the Virginia troops and other support from resistance to the general government. If they attempt it, give them permission and protection, until, if at all, they attempt some action hostile to the United States, in which case you will notify them and give them reasonable time to leave, and at the end of which time arrest any who remain. Allow Judge Campbell to see this, but do not make it public.

Yours, etc.
A. Lincoln

During the interval between these two interviews I took the president to Libby Prison and Castle Thunder. Both were very crowded with Rebel prisoners. I had considerable conversation with him in regard to the treatment of the conquered people. The pith of his answers was that he did not wish to give me any orders on that subject, but, as he expressed it, "If I were in your place I'd let 'em up easy—let 'em easy."

As soon as I received Mr. Lincoln's letter I directed my chief of staff, [Brig.] Gen. George F. Shepley, to publish a call in accordance with its terms in the Richmond papers. The general looked at me with surprise and asked me whether I was doing this on my own responsibility. I informed him that I was not, but that I had an order to do so. He then asked me to permit him to read the order. I did so. After he had read it carefully he said to me, smilingly: "General, this is a political mistake. Don't you lose that letter, for if you do your major general's commission may not be worth a straw." He afterwards said that he felt confident that the letter would be recalled as soon as the president reached Washington.

General Shepley had a fine legal and judicial mind and had had considerable experience as a politician. General Grant when he was president appointed him judge of the First Circuit—a position which he held until his death in 1878. I turned over to him everything relating to civil administration in Richmond just as General Butler had done in New Orleans. He published the call in the papers of the next day! One of these papers came into the possession of General Sherman and led him into some difficulty in his negotiations with General Johnston in North Carolina.

On the next day, April 6, Mr. Charles A. Dana, assistant secretary of war (now publisher of the New York *Sun*), who had come to Richmond, handed me the following dispatch:

April 6, 1865
(by telegraph from Washington, D.C.)

To Hon. C. A. Dana:

Please ascertain from General Weitzel under what authority he is distributing rations to the people of Richmond, as I suppose he would not do it without authority, and direct him to report daily the amount of rations distributed by his orders to persons not belonging to the military service and not authorized by law to receive rations, designating the color of the persons, their occupation, and sex.

Edwin M. Stanton,
Secretary of War

The poor had been fed from the evening of the day I entered Richmond with the captured Rebel rations and supplies generously furnished by the agents of the Sanitary and Christian Commissions, which accompanied my command. I was fully protected also by the order from General Ord, approved by General Grant, which I have already given. On the afternoon of Saturday, April 8, Dr. Meninger and several other ministers of Richmond called upon me in reference to services on the next day. I, of course, authorized them to hold services, and although I do not remember now the whole of the conversation, I suppose I left it pretty much to themselves who they should pray for. But the dispatch below will show. I believe Mr. Dana was in the room during the interview. On Monday, the tenth, I received a telegram from Mr. Stanton in reference to this subject to which I sent the following reply:

April 10, 1865

Hon. E. M. Stanton, Secretary of War:

The order in relation to religious services in Richmond were verbal and applicable alike to all religious denominations without distinction of sect. They were in substance that no expression would be allowed in any part of any church service in the form of prayer, preaching, or singing which in any way implied a recognition of any other authority than that of the United States or gave any countenance to the rebellion. The clergymen were notified that any prayers for the Rebel government or officials, or for the success of the rebellion, would be considered as treason and punished as such. As in the ritual in use in the Episcopal churches here there was a form of prayer for the Rebel authorities, they were ordered to omit that. No orders were given as to what should be preached or prayed for, but only as to what would not be permitted.

Neither in New Orleans, Norfolk, Charleston, Savannah, or any other captured city, as I have been informed, have the Episcopal churches been ordered at first to adopt the form of prayer for the president of the United States. Do you desire that I should order this form of prayer to be used in the Episcopal, Roman Catholic, Hebrew, and other churches where they have a prescribed liturgy and form of prayer? I have had personally but three interviews with Judge Campbell, two of them in the presence of and the other by a written command of the president of the United States. In neither of these interviews was there a discussion in relation to churches and prayers. These interviews were all held with a view to attain a certain result, and to attain this result I was advised by the president to make concessions in small matters. The above was done in accordance with this advice. The autograph order from the president, which I now have, compels me to hold conference with Judge Campbell on a certain subject. The surrender of Lee's army removes the necessity for further conference. Shall I stop it? The Hon. Green Clay Smith has just called on me and says that in the Episcopal church which he attended prayers were offered for those in authority. Similar prayers, I am told, were offered in other Episcopal churches, and all present understood them to refer to our government. In the course I have pursued, by following the advice of the president, I have intended to show him the greatest respect instead of any disrespect. One of my staff conferred with Mr. Dana, the assistant secretary, and distinctly understood him to authorize and sanction my course upon the subject.

Godfrey Weitzel, Major General

To this I received the following:

(by telegraph from Washington)
April 11, 1865

To Major General Weitzel:

The secretary of war directs me to say that your explanation in regard to the omission of prayers for the president in the city of Richmond is not satisfactory, and that there is a conflict of statements between yourself and Mr. Dana, who asserts that he gave no direction or authority upon the subject to General Shepley or to any other officer. The secretary also directs me to instruct you that officers commanding in Richmond are expected to require from all religious denominations in that city to regard those rituals in no less respect for the president of the United States than they practiced towards the Rebel chief, Jefferson Davis, before he was driven from the capitol.

J. A. Hardie, Inspector General

To this I replied as follows:

April 11, 1865

Lieutenant, Colonel J. A. Hardie, Washington City:

I have the honor to request authority, through the War Department, of his excellency, the president of the United States, to state to the honorable, the secretary of war, conversations, suggestions, and orders which took place and were given me confidentially, in order that I may enable the honorable secretary of war to judge correctly of my action in regard to churches and prayers in this place. Not having had authority to divulge these things I am convinced my action has been judged incorrectly. With regard to Mr. Dana's statement it is a matter between him and my chief of staff (General Shepley).

G. Weitzel, Major General

In reply to this I received the following:

April 12, 1865

(In cipher. By telegraph from Washington)

To Major General Weitzel:

I have seen your dispatch to Colonel Hardie about the matter of prayers. I do not remember hearing prayer spoken of while I was in Richmond, but I have no doubt that you have acted in what appeared to you to be the spirit and temper manifested by me while there. Is there any sign of the Rebel legislature coming together on the understanding of my letter to you?

If there is any such sign inform me what it is. If there is no such sign you may withdraw the offer.

A. Lincoln

On the next day I received another telegram from Mr. Lincoln, in which he directed me to revoke the authority for the assembling of the legislature. I turned this over to General Ord, who had arrived at Richmond and assumed command and started the next day at daybreak, with all the troops of my corps, in the direction of Petersburg. I have been requested to state why this authority for the meeting of the legislature was revoked by the president. I do not know. It seems natural, however, that since Lee had surrendered on April 9 and the original permission was granted simply to disband that army there was no longer any use for the legislature. It seems to me that if General Grant and his subordinate commanders had not pushed matters so much the legislature would have been allowed to meet, and Mr. Lincoln's permission would have been held as another proof of his great wisdom.

I desire to say here in regard to Mr. [Charles A.] Dana's visit to Richmond that he stated to me that he had no intention nor wish to give me any instructions and that he was there only to look on and report. If my memory serves me correctly he sent daily bulletins to the New York *Tribune* from Richmond. He wrote a single note to me while I was in command at Richmond. It was in reference to some Rebel records which he had heard of. I had made the collection of all these documents a special duty for one of my staff officers. While on this subject I desire to touch upon a letter, the existence or non-existence of which has caused considerable correspondence lately in the newspapers of the country. Among the documents found in the drawer of Mr. Davis' desk was a confidential letter written by General Lee and laid before the Confederate Senate in secret session. This letter was written in the previous October, if I recollect correctly, and in it Lee frankly and clearly showed that their cause was lost and I think advised them to make the best terms they could. This letter was considered by me so important that I sent it to the secretary of war by Brig. Gen. H. W. Benham, who was on that day on a visit to Richmond. It certainly ought, therefore, to be among the archives of the War Department.

The object of my departure from Richmond in a southerly direction was to bring together all of my corps stationed in Virginia at some point south or southwest of Petersburg. Here I was to hold myself in readiness to move in the direction of North Carolina, with the VI Corps and the cavalry, all under the command of General Sheridan. The object of this was to be on hand to help General [William T.] Sherman in case General [Joseph E.] Johnston had not surrendered. As I left Richmond on the same day on which the revocation of the call for the Virginia legislature appeared in the papers of that city the rumor was spread and I am told generally believed

Richmond after the war (MCCLURE'S MAGAZINE)

that I had been removed for issuing that call. Advantage of this was taken to fan the east and south winds which had been blowing for me during some time and against which I had been cautioned by warm friends, who were more solicitous about my welfare than I was myself. It fanned these breezes so strongly that even the fair and just mind of General Grant nearly became tainted and a false reputation for myself and corps was nearly started. A few moments' statement of facts to General Grant in person made everything all right, and as the officers of my corps got a fair share of honor in the reorganization of the Regular army I did not consider it necessary to say anything more, either officially or publicly. I can confidently refer to the muster rolls of officers of the XXV Army Corps to prove that as a body they were at that time the peers of any body of officers in any corps in the United States service in every quality that goes to make a good soldier and perfect gentleman. In this narrative I was compelled to name a few, and I would not dare to trust my memory to mention more without doing injustice to others.

I can assure my readers that I was delighted to get out of Richmond and get back to real military duties. I was as happy only once afterwards, and that was when I was relieved on the Rio Grande, in February of the next year. It will be clear to my military readers at least how much trouble it is to satisfy four different commanding officers, two soldiers and two civilians. Richmond was too near Washington and in telegraphic communication with it. There was no trouble in regulating affairs in New Orleans and elsewhere outside of telegraphic communication. I do not believe that the unfortunate people of Richmond ever were aware how near they came to being governed to death after they were rescued from destruction by fire. In saying this I do not wish to reflect in the least on my commanders. They were all kind to me. The disagreeable state of affairs I refer to was the natural result of the great excitement of that period.

Among other minor experiences I had during my ten days' occupation of Richmond were the receipt of abusive letters for extinguishing the fire. Then again I was paraded in some papers, and in one even published in my own home, as a flunky. It was stated that I had placed a guard of colored troops over Mrs. Lee's house and upon her protest had substituted white troops. The truth of this incident is as follows: My brother, Capt. Lewis Weitzel, aide-de-camp on my staff, was riding through the city in obedience to my orders, engaged in gathering all the able-bodied men to assist in extinguishing the fire, when he was hailed by a servant in front of a house towards which the fire seemed to be moving. The servant told him that his mistress wished to speak to him. He dismounted and entered the house and was met by a lady, who stated that her mother was an invalid, confined to her bed, and as the fire seemed to be approaching she asked his assistance. The subsequent conversation developed the fact that my brother was addressing Miss Lee, and that the invalid was no other than Mrs. R. E. Lee. My brother knew that when I was a cadet at West Point, General Lee was superintendent of the academy, and had often heard me speak in high terms of him and his family. He at once, therefore, went to the nearest commander, Colonel Ripley, who furnished him with a corporal, two men, and an ambulance from his own regiment, the 9th Vermont. Captain Weitzel ordered the corporal to remain near the house, and if there were serious danger to remove Mrs. Lee. These men remained on duty until all danger was over. These are the facts upon which the lie was based. As I have herein before stated no colored troops were place[d] on duty in the city. Devens' division of white troops having had more experience in extinguishing fires was alone on duty, with Parson's Company of the 1st New York Volunteer Engineers.

Again, the charge of flunkyism was made against me because I held a review in Richmond of Devens' division and not of Kautz's. The review was ordered for both. In order not to strip the lines completely I ordered Devens' review one day and Kautz's another. The former came off, but before the latter could take place we were under orders to move south. Hence it did not take place. There was some dispute as to which troops first entered Richmond, white or colored. As there was no fighting in going in I did not consider it of much consequence. This narrative gives the facts. Maj. Emmons E. Graves, senior aide-de-camp on my staff, in command, with Maj. Atherton H. Stevens, Jr., and about forty men of the 4th Massachusetts Cavalry were the first to enter.

Then there was some dispute as to the first flag hoisted over Richmond after its capture. This detachment of Massachusetts cavalry had two guidons with it. These guidons were raised first, one at each end of the roof of the capitol building and were therefore the first United States colors raised. When our troops took possession of New Orleans in May 1862, General Shepley was colonel of the 12th Maine Volunteers, and his regiment was detailed to take possession of the new Custom House. As soon as this was done Shepley raised a United States flag, which was his private property, over the building, and many believe today that this was the first United States flag raised in New Orleans after its capture. But this is not true. The first flag was raised over the mint by the navy and was torn down by a mob, headed by W. B. Mumford. The latter was subsequently arrested, tried by a military commission and hung for it. General Shepley had this New Orleans

Custom House flag with him and an aide-de-camp on his staff carried it into Richmond with him and hoisted it over the Capitol. This was therefore the first real American flag which was displayed. The aide-de-camp was Lieutenant de Peyster, son of General J. Watts de Peyster, of New York City, and nephew of Gen. Philip Kearny.

In looking over my notes and copies of telegrams while writing this, I came across some which exhibit the humors of a campaign, and although not properly belonging to the subject matter of my narrative I will here give two as samples. The first is from that great admirer and warm eulogist of the distinguished soldier General Milroy, namely [Brig.] Gen. George H. Gordon, who was in command at Norfolk, Virginia, in April, 1865. It reads as follows:

> April 13, 1865 (by telegraph from Norfolk)
>
> To Major General Weitzel:
>
> General: By your order Colonel Sumner with his command reported to me on the eleventh instant. I ordered him to Suffolk. I learn from General Graham that on the twelfth Colonel Sumner and his command disappeared from my district. I cannot think he has deserted, but I apprise you of the fact of his disappearance that proper steps may be taken to discover his whereabouts.
>
> General Gordon

Colonel [Edwin V.] Sumner [Jr.] is now major of the 5th United States Cavalry. It is probably superfluous to state that he moved away from Gordon in accordance with orders from General Ord's headquarters.

The other is from Hartsuff, who was placed in command of Petersburg and City Point in addition to Bermuda Hundred, with headquarters at Petersburg, on the day I entered Richmond. It had been determined that it would be unnecessary to send any assistance to General Sherman, and, therefore, General Sheridan was moving eastward to get his command more easily supplied. I was moving northward to get a good healthy camp near the Southside Railroad, and thus we were apparently concentrating on Petersburg. I heard that Sheridan had a fine camp and would leave it the next day, and therefore telegraphed to Hartsuff about it, as I had no telegraphic communication with Sheridan.

This is Hartsuff's reply:

April 18, 1865 (by telegraph from Petersburg)

To Major General Weitzel:

Sheridan intends to remain where he is. I fear I shall be unable to defend the city against both, and as I hold the balance of power between you would be glad to know the terms on which you will combine with me against him. I shall make the same proposition to him.

Geo. L. Hartsuff

In conclusion I desire to say that I have written this narrative in the intervals of my duties in the busy season of the year. There may be some slight errors of date, but I believe that I have the facts arranged in order, so that they may easily be comprehended. Such has been my main aim.

The battle at Sailor's Creek proved that my officers were right throughout in their estimate and description of the forces in my front from March 28 to the night of April 2. Besides [Maj. Gen. William] Mahone's Division there was a dispute between us and our forces on the extreme left as to the whereabouts of Corse's and Barton's Brigades. We were right. They were in our front.

The Fighting About Petersburg and the Evacuation of the City

THEODORE S. GARNETT, JR.
CAPTAIN, 9TH VIRGINIA CAVALRY, C.S.A.
(AND STAFF OFFICER TO MAJ. GEN. H. FITZHUGH LEE)

Philadelphia *Weekly Times* 8, no. 20, July 5, 1884

The Army of Northern Virginia after taking position around Petersburg was stripped of all its cavalry except the division commanded by [Maj. Gen. William H. F.] Lee. [Maj. Gen. Wade] Hampton, with [Maj. Gen. Matthew C.] Butler and [Brig. Gen. Pierce M. B.] Young, was sent south in December 1864, [Maj. Gen. Fitzhugh] Lee, with [Maj. Gen. Thomas L.] Rosser, [Brig. Gen. Williams C.] Wickham, [Brig. Gen. Lunsford L.] Lomax, and others having been sent to the Valley in the previous fall. The operations about to be described are such only as came under the limited observation of a staff officer of Maj. Gen. W. H. F. Lee's Division and relate chiefly to the part taken by [Col. William P.] Roberts' Brigade of that division.

The 4th North Carolina Cavalry, the 16th Battalion North Carolina Cavalry, and a small detachment of Georgians formed the command of [Brig. Gen.] James Dearing, who had been promoted from the artillery service, where he had won an enviable reputation. The brigade's first service was rendered during the spring of 1864, when Petersburg was threatened by Butler's troops, though the 4th Regiment had served through the previous year in nearly all the encounters of [Lt. Gen. James Ewell Brown] Stuart with the enemy in Northern Virginia, Maryland, and Pennsylvania. This regiment came to Virginia under the command of Col. [Dennis D.] Ferebee. The 16th Battalion was commanded by Lt. Col. Boyd Edelin.

During the long siege of Petersburg and until February 1865, General Dearing commanded the brigade, but in that month he was ordered to the command of Rosser's Brigade in the Valley, and William P. Roberts, colonel of the 2nd North Carolina Cavalry, was promoted to the rank of brigadier general and assigned to the command which Dearing had just vacated. Upon assuming this command General Roberts had some difficulty in reorganizing the staff and he found the troops in want of nearly everything. But by diligent work and his active energy he soon placed his brigade in excellent condition.

It was on the march from Bellfield, Va., to Stony Creek that he took charge of the brigade, and in less than a week a sudden summons carried W. H. F. Lee's Division by a rapid march to Dinwiddie Court House, to meet a threatened advance of the enemy's cavalry. The alarm proving false the other two brigades of the division were marched back to Stony Creek, leaving Roberts' Brigade to picket the right flank of the army from the vicinity of Burgess' Mill to the Vaughan road.

Brigade headquarters were established on the White Oak road at its intersection with a new military road which ran to Dinwiddie Court House, distant about five miles. Here the brigade remained in comparative quiet and comfort during the month of March 1865, save an occasional alarm on the picket line, when we would hurry down to the support of the squadron reserve, exchange a few shots with the enemy, who would politely retire and leave us to return quietly to our camps. On one of these occasions, shortly after nightfall, [Brig. Gen. Henry A.] Wise's Brigade of infantry on our left ran out of their breastworks and fell back to the heavy works at Burgess' Mill. The flurry was soon over on our end of the line and General Roberts, with the writer, while seeking to re-establish communication with the infantry, was suddenly fired upon by the 34th Virginia Infantry and narrowly escaped death at the hands of our troops.

About March 23, 1865, an order was received from army headquarters directing General Roberts to send one hundred picked men to report for duty to [Maj. Gen.] John B. Gordon at Petersburg. The men were selected and placed under the command of Lt. Col. Edelin, who marched to Petersburg and participated in the attack on the enemy's fortifications on March 25, known as the Hare's Hill fight and which resulted in the repulse of Gordon's magnificent advance, at first successful, but finally overwhelmed for want of proper support. Colonel Edelin returned with his detachment to our camp on the White Oak road just in time to take part in the operations about to be mentioned, but he was captured by the enemy on the second day after his return.

On the morning of March 29, 1865, the enemy commenced that series of movements which resulted in the fall of Petersburg. At dawn Roberts'

Brigade was drawn up in support of our advanced pickets. As the movement developed it became apparent that the advance of the enemy was in such force as to render vain all hope of disputing his progress with our two little regiments. Yet we tried it. Slowly but surely and steadily the heavy columns of infantry formed in our front, deployed and advanced, brushing us away as they enveloped our flanks and without haste or dash closed up on the ground we had stubbornly contested. Twice we checked them, so that they had to reinforce their line, and after losing many of our best men and most gallant officers we saw coming up to our aid the two brigades of Wise and [Brig. Gen. William] Wallace—a mere handful to throw away on the hosts we had encountered. General Wise rode up and requested General Roberts to retire his cavalry as he was about to order his infantry to charge.

It would have been useless to attempt to deter the old man from this rash endeavor by telling him that the enemy were about ten to his one in front. He thought it a mere feint and would not believe our report that a heavy line of battle had been steadily advancing on us for two hours. General Roberts, therefore, mounted his skirmishers and passed with his cavalry to the right while General Wise formed his lines for the charge. We had scarcely reached our position near the Wilson House on the Boydton plank road when we heard the yell of Wise's men as they burst upon the enemy and hurled back his skirmishers upon his main line. We listened for the reply. It came in one tremendous burst of smoke and flame and the rattling thunder of close-ordered volleys told of the fearful check which met Wise's exultant advance. In another moment we saw his broken lines sweeping back, leaving many of their dead and wounded on the bloody field.

General Roberts had formed his brigade along the Boydton plank road, at Wilson's house, in easy range of the field over which Wise had advanced and retreated. Here in the open field, adjoining Wilson's, occurred as brilliant an episode of petit guerre as came under observation in the whole war. From the east side of the Boydton plank road sloped an open field down to a ditch running parallel with that road and distant from it about two hundred or three hundred yards. On the further side of this ditch was rolling ground, quite steep and beyond that rose a hillside of brown straw crowned by a skirt of stunted pines.

Looking from our position on the plank road we observed a strong skirmish line advance from the pines, come down the slope and deploy at the ditch in the open field. Lying there in close range they made everybody keep under cover on our side field. Their fire became galling, their position was menacing and it soon became necessary either to retire or to drive them back. General Roberts determined to attempt the latter by a mounted

The final fighting around Petersburg (FORBES, *LIFE OF SHERMAN*)

charge. One squadron of the 4th North Carolina Cavalry was selected for the work and instructed not to draw rein until they had swept the enemy away. General Roberts led the charge in person. In an instant we were upon them and, strange to relate, the volley with which they received us as we dashed at them killed only two men in our squadron. Before they had time to realize the audacity of the thing they commenced throwing down their arms and surrendering.

But off to our right their line remained intact, and an officer, not so demoralized as those in our immediate front, yelled out: "Don't surrender! Shoot 'em!" And one after another took up the cry, until in another instant they were all firing upon us at close quarters with the very arms they had just thrown down. It was our turn to be surprised now. This complete reversal of our former relations brought about a hasty retreat and we reached the cover of our lines swearing vengeance against those skirmishers and determined to try it once more.

Again the attempt was renewed. Another squadron of the 4th was sent in and the same thing was repeated. Many of the skirmishers surrendered only to be recaptured by those who stood their ground and drove us back by a galling fire. A third time we charged them and being supported by a detachment of the 34th Virginia Infantry, of Wise's Brigade, we dislodged the enemy and they broke and fled. As we pursued them towards the pine thicket their main line of battle, which had been quietly lying down, concealed from us by the tall brown straw, watching our little fight, suddenly rose to their feet and advanced upon us at double-quick, firing as they came. Their volleys, however, flew harmless over our heads. We retreated to the plank road and soon thereafter abandoned its defense. The loss of the 4th North Carolina in this affair was surprisingly small, though it had suffered terribly in the engagement of the morning.

While we were thus occupied reinforcements of infantry were rapidly assembling at Burgess' Mill. Wise's Brigade retired to the fortifications and General Roberts marched towards the White Oak road and camped on the right of [Maj. Gen. Bushrod R.] Johnson's Division. The brigade was ordered to picket the front and right of the army, and it was near midnight before the videttes were fully posted.

Early on the morning of March 30, General Roberts received orders from army headquarters to make a reconnaissance towards the Boydton plank road in the direction of Dinwiddie Court House. General Robert E. Lee desired that a Federal cavalry officer be captured and sent to him as speedily as possible, that he might ascertain the position of [Maj. Gen. Philip H.] Sheridan's Corps, which had not yet made its appearance in the general movement. This request was immediately obeyed, and in less than a half hour, as General Roberts and two of his staff were passing through our outer picket, they stumbled on a detachment of the 2nd Massachusetts Cavalry (eight men and a captain), and after a brief encounter Captain Culp, of the California Battalion, 2nd Massachusetts Cavalry, 2nd Brigade, 2nd Division, Sheridan's Corps, was a prisoner in our hands and was immediately sent on to General Lee at Burgess' Mill.

In a few minutes after this capture the enemy's cavalry advanced upon Roberts' Brigade at Boisseau's house. A sharp contest ensued, in the midst of which General Roberts' horse was shot under him, and the enemy charging at the same moment, he barely escaped capture by leaping on the horse of one of his couriers. The retreat to the White Oak road was conducted in good order, and in view of the fact that only two small regiments of Confederates, say 350 men in all, opposed the advance of this division of Federal cavalry, we felt some satisfaction in preventing the enemy from seizing the White Oak road, the only route by which troops could be hurried to Five Forks.

As we lay there awaiting further attack the infantry of [Maj. Gen. George E.] Pickett's Division commenced passing behind us on their march for Five Forks, distant about two and a half or three miles. [Brig.] Gen. Matt Ransom kindly permitted one of his regiments to remain and assist us in repelling the attack. This regiment of North Carolinians (the number of which is not now remembered) was concealed behind rail-piles along the road in our rear, and General Roberts was to maneuver as if about to retreat and so decoy the enemy to make a charge. The plan worked like a charm. The infantry had scarcely gotten into position before the movement of our brigade had the desired effect.

We rapidly uncovered the front and the enemy dashed gallantly forward in column of fours at a gallop. But the eagerness of the infantry to fire upon them caused the miscarriage of the whole plot, for just as the head of their column appeared over the crest of the hill in front the whole regiment blazed away and the volley passed high over the heads of the charging enemy. Only one man was seen to fall. This checked the advance and the enemy retreated to the Boisseau House, where they established their pickets. It was in following up their retreat that Colonel Edelin, of the 16th Battalion, dashed upon their rear guard and was unhorsed and captured.

On the morning of March 31 General Roberts led his brigade up to Boisseau's house and drove in the enemy's videttes, holding the command in readiness to co-operate with the attack which was about to be made by Generals Pickett, Fitz Lee and W. H. F. Lee upon Sheridan's corps. As soon as the firing began we moved forward, driving in the enemy's pickets, but were halted and forced to await the development of the battle on our right. Towards evening the sound of the guns receding in the direction of Dinwiddie Court House gave us the pleasing assurance that Sheridan was being driven back. Upon our pressing forward the enemy rapidly vacated our front, leaving behind some of their skirmishers, who surrendered to us at long range as soon as they could understand our signals. Pushing on with the brigade, all mounted, General Roberts united his command with the victorious troopers of Fitz Lee and Rosser, then fighting forward toward Dinwiddie Court House and we were about to join in their fight when a remarkable change of front occurred.

We had scarcely reached the left flank of Rosser's line when the rear of Roberts' Brigade was suddenly attacked by what seemed to be an infantry skirmish line, and we had sharp work to hold the ground. It appears that an infantry brigade of the enemy had followed us across the country from the direction of Burgess' Mill and caught up with us just at dusk. Their attack was vigorous, but darkness rapidly descended and put an end to the fight. Under its cover we extricated the brigade from its awkward position and during the night marched over the worst road in the world to the intersection of the Court House road with the White Oak road, the point which on the next day was destined to become famous as the scene of the battle of Five Forks.

On April 1, 1865, General Roberts was on his old line at dawn, about half-way between Five Forks and Burgess' Mill, on the White Oak road. As the sun rose, long columns of the enemy—[Maj. Gen. Gouverneur K.] Warren's Corps—were passing in front of our videttes, pushing on to the relief of Sheridan to turn his recent defeat into a complete victory. Roberts' Brigade continued to guard the White Oak road, and during the forenoon we had a visit from General R. E. Lee. He rode up with only one or two of his staff, and after noting the condition of things in our front, the prospect for a cavalry flight at that moment being unusually good, we were rather pleased to see him bid us "good morning" and ride slowly away in the direction of Burgess' Mill.

In less than ten minutes after General Lee's departure we were charged by [Brig. Gen. August V.] Kautz's division of cavalry. The 11th Pennsylvania led the advance and their first and second squadrons were successively repulsed as they charged up to the road on which we were lying. A handful of men of Roberts' Brigade, not more than fifty or sixty, were dismounted and posted behind rails (the same from which Ransom's men had fired two days before) and these behaved with conspicuous gallantry. Among them Lieutenant Holden, of the 4th North Carolina Cavalry, deserves especial mention.

Being the tallest man in his regiment, like Saul—head and shoulders above his fellows—his commanding presence and encouraging voice as he directed the fire of his skirmishers were particularly prominent. But it is only just to say that every officer and man of that little group did his duty faithfully and well, and it was not until the enemy in overwhelming numbers leaped their horses actually over the rail-piles and got behind our line that we gave up the ground. The woods in our rear afforded excellent shelter to the men and they escaped through them to their led horses with comparatively small loss.

The enemy did not pursue, but turned southward and made their way towards Five Forks, in which direction the sound of battle had at that moment reached our ears. It lasted only a short while, becoming very heavy at times, but soon died away westward, indicating to us the defeat and retreat of Pickett's Division and the abandonment of the line of the White

Oak road. This was, indeed, the sad reality and the beginning of the end. General Roberts retired slowly from the White Oak road, but kept his pickets well out and bivouacked about two miles from the scene of our last encounter. During the night the earth fairly trembled with the roar of the guns, on the lines around Petersburg.

On Sunday morning, April 2, the startling intelligence reached us that Petersburg was evacuated, accompanied by orders from army headquarters directing the line of our retreat. We retired to Sutherland's Station, on the South Side Railroad, where we found a committee of the Richmond Ambulance corps, who were on their way to reach the wounded of the Five Forks fight, but found it impossible to proceed farther. These gentlemen very kindly offered us some supplies, and about 1:00 P.M., after loading a detachment of twenty men with sacks of corn and some provisions, we took up the line of march westward and the retreat began.

The enemy did not pursue on our road and we marched at leisure. But just at nightfall we joined a column of Fitz Lee and Rosser and W. H. F. Lee, then skirmishing with the enemy near Namozene Church. Some of our infantry—a part of Bushrod Johnson's Division—were also in line of battle at this point. We dismounted and took position on the left of [Col. Thomas] Munford's Brigade. One of General Roberts' couriers was killed as we were getting into position. The night was spent on the battlefield, and early next morning we crossed Namozene Creek.

Soon after crossing the creek we were halted, and nearly all of General Fitz Lee's old division passed by us on the march, leaving in our rear only one regiment, the 9th Virginia Cavalry of our division, to guard the ford. We had just taken the road when a great stampede occurred among the led horses of the 9th Regiment. The enemy had forced or flanked their way across the creek, and a few of the 9th, escaping at a run, communicated the demoralization to the ranks of the cavalry who had preceded us and also to a part of our brigade, and soon a panic seized the whole command, except a small part of Roberts' Brigade, which remained steady with General Roberts and did not share in the general consternation and flight.

Men who have witnessed such a scene as this, fortunately of rare occurrence on either side during our war, are puzzled to explain how even the bravest lose their heads and are borne away on the sweeping tide of panic-stricken fugitives long after the cause had ceased and all danger had been removed. To retain self-possession and yield to discipline in the midst of a panic is the truest test of a good soldier, and this was handsomely illustrated by the good men who rode in solid ranks under the immediate eye and command of General Roberts that morning. It is proper also to except from the mass of our cavalry who disappeared so hastily from our sight a small body of men under Colonel Morgan, of Munford's and [Brig. Gen. William H.] Payne's Brigades, who formed squadron on the opposite side of the road from us and awaited the onset of the victorious enemy.

With this little force General Roberts met their advance. It was at first a very feeble attack. They seemed to think we had prepared a trap for them and were not disposed to press their advantage. The country was very open and the movements of both parties could be plainly seen by each. The enemy was slow in finding out the real condition on our side. But they advanced after about an hour's delay and charged us gallantly. They were held in check long enough, however, to enable the command to rally and form at Deep Creek, where late in the evening we joined the remnant of W. H. F. Lee's Division.

It may be proper to state here that near Namozene Church, on a road south of our position at the time the stampede occurred, the enemy attacked and dispersed [Brig. Gen. Rufus] Barringer's Brigade of W. H. F. Lee's Division, and only a small part of that brigade was afterwards with us on the retreat. At Deep Creek we went into camp and spent a quiet night, the enemy occupying the range of hills east of the creek. The next morning we moved towards Amelia Court House. The enemy pushed after us rapidly and by another road than that on which we traveled actually passed beyond us.

On nearing Amelia Court House we were surprised to find a skirmish going on near the town and in our rear. They had cut off a small detachment of [Col. Richard L. T.] Beale's Brigade and were on the point of driving it back into the courthouse. General Roberts hastened forward alone and at the most critical moment put himself at the head of a company of the 14th Virginia Cavalry and gallantly met a charging squadron of the enemy, putting them to flight and saving the village from capture.

It is not saying too much to assert that but for his timely arrival at that particular spot the enemy's cavalry would have charged into Amelia Court House and either taken the commanding general himself prisoner or forced him and his staff to leave the place, for at that moment General Lee had his headquarters in the village, within a quarter or half mile of the scene of this skirmish and had no reason to apprehend the approach of the enemy. Within a very few minutes after this occurrence [Lt. Gen. James P.] Longstreet came to us in person and soon a regiment of his corps was sent to our aid. The evening was spent in desultory firing and at dark we passed through Amelia Court House and bivouacked a few miles southwest of that place.

On the morning of April 5 General Lee ordered General Roberts to make a reconnaissance towards Jetersville. Before reaching that point we encountered another force of Sheridan's corps, who seemed to be picketing the road in our front. We drove them in on their reserve. They received reinforcements and advanced upon us. Here a remnant of Captain Martin's squadron of the 16th North Carolina Battalion made a very gallant fight and repeatedly repulsed and returned the enemy's charges.

In this affair General Roberts, who was constantly present encouraging his troops and charging with Martin's squadron, received a severe blow from a spent ball, which struck him fairly over the heart and rendered him insensible, causing him to reel and fall from his saddle. Fortunately it did not penetrate his body. He revived and resumed the command as soon as he could remount his horse. A large part of the infantry of the Army of Northern Virginia was then assembling in some open country immediately in our rear, and while we were occupied with the enemy they must have been amused spectators of a little incident which occurred here.

The 4th North Carolina was ordered to support Captain Martin in one of his gallant charges. Martin was driven back and the enemy's squadron rushed after him. The 4th North Carolina started in, but failed to get under way in time to resist the headway of the advancing enemy, and the front rank, failing to respond promptly to the "charge," hesitated, broke, and incontinently fled. The enemy pursued only a short distance, but one adventurous and gallant Yankee dashed past his fellows and made for the color-bearer of the 4th North Carolina. He seized the colors and wrested them from him in a hand-to-hand tussle, neither of them attempting to use their pistols or sabers, and so the flag of the 4th Regiment was seen making off at a run as fast as the Federal cavalryman could carry it, who seemed as much astonished at the result of his bold dash as the bewildered color-bearer who had lost it.

A few minutes later a horse and rider at full speed was seen coming out of the woods, and the disordered remnant of the 4th North Carolina mistaking him for another impudent Yankee commenced a fusillade upon him with pistols and carbines. In the midst of it the rider, who proved to be Capt. Thomas W. Pierce, ordnance officer of W. H. F. Lee's Division, was recognized by one of General Roberts' staff and the firing was checked before any damage was done. Captain Pierce had been in the enemy's hands only a few minutes before, but escaped from them by a dash and came near being shot by his own people, his horse having become unmanageable.

It was in the engagement that Captain Coughenour, inspector of Roberts' Brigade, while delivering a message to the general, was severely shot. The bullet entered one side of the throat under the chin and passed out on the other side of and across the throat. It was, of course, deemed a mortal wound, but the gentleman is still alive and well.

The next morning, April 6, after marching and countermarching and repeated skirmishes with the enemy, losing another one of our couriers and several men, we were ordered to pass rapidly to the right flank of a part of General Gordon's Corps, then making preparations to defend the crossing of Sailor's Creek. At a rapid gallop we passed around under the fire of the Federal artillery, who had mysteriously appeared on our flank, and as we neared the ford at Sailor's Creek we found it blocked up by a vast assemblage of wagons, ambulances, and artillery trains. It was seen at a glance that the command could not possibly cross at this ford, so we were marched down the stream and found a rough crossing near an old mill, where we scrambled up the steep banks of the opposite side and placed ourselves on the west bank of Sailor's Creek, just as the final assault was made on the gallant little band of Walker and others, who held the ground until they were actually merged in the swarming masses of the enemy, who enveloped them on both flanks.

From our lofty position on the hill above the ford we saw the final charge and the wild burst of Walker's men as they broke through the enemy in their rear and cut their way out to the ford. We covered the retreat of the few who escaped by a strong line of mounted skirmishers posted well down on the creek, and another night soon closed in around our weary troops. Late that night we reached the High Bridge and crossing the river, rested until daybreak near the foot of the bridge.

The next morning, April 7, found us still acting as the rear guard, and from the High Bridge on to Farmville there was a constant skirmish with the enemy's advance. They moved slowly, and we were kept in observation. Meanwhile a part of [Maj. Gen. William] Mahone's Division had prepared for their reception at a little church near Farmville, and we retired behind our infantry line there. The enemy soon advanced in compact column and formed double lines of battle, attacking Mahone's front with great vigor and determination. They were repulsed in every charge with heavy loss and before dark abandoned the effort to break our line. During the fight General Roberts was ordered to take his command over to the left of Mahone's line and protect that flank. He marched by way of the Ca-Ira road. Just at the point where this road crossed the Farmville road there was a blockade; nearly all the wagons and trains were hopelessly stuck in the mud.

General R. E. Lee was resting quietly at this place looking over a map, with many officers of high rank grouped around him or dismounted near at hand. As we approached the spot a heavy column of Federal cavalry was seen coming at a charge, evidently bent on capturing the trains. Before they could reach the position, however, a regiment of Rosser's old brigade and a part of Munford's command charged the flank of the Federal column, dispersing the whole force and capturing Col. Irvin Gregg and bringing him a prisoner before General Lee. Our brigade went on over to the left and picketed that flank all the night. The end was now near. During the night the blockade was relieved and the trains of the army placed on a parallel road.

Nothing has been said during all this time of the severe toils and privations to which the men had now been exposed for ten days and nights. From April 1 to 9 not a single ration was drawn by our command, and the men had to eke out a scanty substance by sharing with their horses the little corn that could be begged or taken through the country. Night brought no relief from the fatigues of the day, and the result was the sure wasting away of all the energies of man and horse. Captain Martin that night announced to the adjutant general of the brigade with great sorrow the solemn fact that of his old company he had only two men fit for duty, and this not because of desertion or failure of duty, since he could account for every man that had left Petersburg with him—killed, wounded, or captured.

The eighth was marked as the only quiet day of the retreat. An ominous silence reigned all around us. The whole day we moved on the flank of the army, on the right in retreat and parallel to its line of march, and were untroubled by any sign or sound of battle. The distance marched this day was greater than that of any preceding one, and as night came on we passed through the camps of a body of infantry who seemed to be making merry over their misfortunes. Their bands were playing "Dixie" and "The Girl I Left Behind Me," vying with each other in a sort of musical contest, encouraged by the vociferous "Rebel yell," demanding an encore or a "change of air." Throwing ourselves down among the rustling leaves of a fine forest we slept until midnight, at which hour we received orders to report as speedily as possible at Appomattox Court House. Arriving there about dawn we observed the preparations then being made for a general engagement, and shortly after sunrise took position mounted on the right of General Gordon's Corps.

The advance was sounded, and never did the army at any period of its existence respond with more cheerful alacrity or gallantry. With steady step and unwavering front these starved survivors of Stonewall's Corps moved irresistibly upon the solid lines of the Federal infantry and swept them from the field. The VI Corps and one division of the XXIV Corps were in their front and both gave way—the VI giving ground to the left and the XXIV to the right. A battery of United States artillery, four Napoleon guns, in the interval fell into our hands, and panic seemed to have seized the men of the XXIV Corps. Many of that division on our right surrendered without resistance, and to every officer at the front it appeared that the road to Lynchburg had been opened. A single regiment could have cleared the woods on our right, and not much more would have been required to effect the capture of that division of the enemy.

But there was not a man to be spared from Gordon's line, by this time hotly engaged with the VI Corps, who had rallied, and soon, to our utter astonishment, an order came for us to retire from the field and fall back to Appomattox Court House. In another moment the rumor of our surrender was circulated, and in obedience to orders we prepared for that last and bitterest trial which can ever befall the soldier. The scenes at the surrender need no recital.

In conclusion it is proper to add that General Roberts, now the honored auditor of the State of North Carolina, enjoyed the confidence and esteem of all his men. Coming among them from a different command, he soon won their regard by his superior skill and great personal gallantry. He was a soldier of a high order, possessing in a marked degree that aptitude for command which none but men of genius can ever attain. And it is safe to say that if the war had been prolonged even another year he would have added fresh laurels to his enviable reputation and attained high rank among those who achieved honorable fame under the battle flag of the Army of Northern Virginia.

The Death of General A. P. Hill

GEORGE W. TUCKER,
SERGEANT OF COURIERS, HILL'S CORPS, ARMY OF NORTHERN VIRGINIA, C.S.A.

Philadelphia *Weekly Times* 8, no. 40, November 24, 1883

The tragic death of [Lt. Gen.] Ambrose Powell Hill ended preeminent services to the cause he had espoused with singleness of heart and maintained with unexcelled constancy of purpose and courage. He needs no eulogy from any. Those attached to his person, or often in contact, have simply to say, "We loved him." It is for his surviving comrades of the 3rd Corps, and especially those of the old A. P. Hill's Light Division, that the details of their general's last ride of duty are more particularly given.

During the entire winter of 1864-65 General Hill was an invalid and was absent in Richmond on a sick leave from about March 20, returning to his command upon being advised of the operations on the right beyond Hatcher's Run. April 1, accompanied by his staff and couriers, he spent in the saddle from early morning until about 9:00 P.M., returning at night along the works held by his corps as far as those in front of Fort Gregg, where the general halted a considerable time. He passed only a few words with his staff party or those very, very few in the trenches there. He seemed lost in contemplation of the immediate position, at which the Confederate line had become so terribly stretched that it broke that very night, letting in a deluge of the enemy, who, only partly checked by the wonderful defense of Fort Gregg, next morning flooded the country. We then returned to corps headquarters, which were at Indiana, on an extension of Washington Street, Petersburg, and immediately adjoining the Model Farm on the east. General Hill retired to Venable's cottage, just across the road and within

Daybreak in the woods at Hatcher's Run (ST. NICHOLAS MAGAZINE)

fifty yards of his camp, having had there during the winter his wife and two young children.

About midnight the cannonading in front of Petersburg, which had begun at nightfall, became very heavy, increasing as the hours went by. Colonel [William H.] Palmer, chief of staff, woke Major [William N.] Starke, assistant adjutant general, and requested him to find out the cause and effect of the prolonged firing. This was between two and three o'clock on the morning of April 2. Major Starke returned before daylight and reported "that the enemy had part of our line near the Rives salient and that matters looked critical on the lines in front of the city." This he communicated to General Hill at Venable's.

Before sunrise General Hill came over and asked Colonel Palmer if he had any report from Generals [Cadmus M.] Wilcox and [Henry] Heth, whose divisions on the right extended from the front of Fort Gregg to and beyond Burgess' Mill, on Hatcher's Run. The colonel told him that he had heard nothing further to report beyond Major Starke's statement.

The general then passed on to his tent, and a few minutes later the colonel, noticing his colored servant, Charles, leading the general's saddled horse to his tent, ran to him just as he was mounting and asked permission to accompany him. He told the colonel no and desired him to wake up the staff, get everything in readiness, and have the headquarters wagons hitched up. He added that he was going to General [Robert E.] Lee's and would take Sergeant Tucker and two couriers and that as soon as he could have an interview with General Lee he would return.

General Hill then rode to the couriers' quarters and found me in the act of grooming my horse. I did not then have the slightest intimation of what had taken place since our return from the lines the night before. He directed me to follow him with two couriers immediately to General Lee's headquarters. He then rode off rapidly. It was our custom in critical times to have during the night two of the couriers' horses always saddled. I called to [Private] Kirkpatrick and [William H.] Jenkins, the couriers next in turn, to follow the generals as quickly as possible. I saddled up at once and followed them. Kirkpatrick and Jenkins arrived at General Lee's together, only a few minutes after General Hill, who at once directed Kirkpatrick to ride rapidly back to our quarters (I met him on the road going at full speed) and tell Colonel Palmer to follow him to the right and the others of the staff and couriers must rally the men on the right. This was the first information received at corps headquarters that our right had given way. General Hill then rode, attended only by Jenkins, to the front gate of General Lee's headquarters (Turnbull House, on the Cox road, nearly one and a half miles westerly from General Hill's), where I met them.

We went directly across the road into the opposite field and riding due south a short distance the general drew rein and for a few moments used his field glass, which, in my still profound ignorance of what had happened, struck me as exceedingly queer. We then rode on in the same direction down a declivity toward a small branch running eastward to Old Town Creek and a quarter of a mile from General Lee's. We had gone a little more than half this distance when we suddenly came upon two of the enemy's armed infantrymen. Jenkins and myself, who up to this time rode immediately behind the general, were instantly upon them, when at the demand "surrender," they laid down their guns. Turning to the general I asked what should be done with the prisoners. He said, "Jenkins, take them to General Lee." Jenkins started back with his men and we rode on.

Though not invited I was at the general's side, and my attention having now been aroused and looking carefully ahead and around, I saw a lot of people in and about the old log hut winter quarters of General [William] Mahone's Division, situated to the right of Whitworth House and on top of the hill beyond the branch we were approaching. Now as I knew that these quarters had been vacant since about March 15 by the transfer of Mahone to north of the Appomattox and feeling that it was the enemy's troops in possession, with nothing looking like a Confederate anywhere, I remarked, pointing to the old camp, "General, what troops are those?" He quickly replied, "The enemy's." Proceeding still further and General Hill making no further remark, I became so impressed with the great risk he was running that I made bold to say, "Please excuse me, General, but where are you going?" He answered, "Sergeant, I must go to the right as quickly as possible." Then, pointing northwest, he said, "We will go up this side of the branch to the woods, which will cover us until reaching the field in rear of General Heth's quarters. I hope to find the road clear at General Heth's."

From that time on I kept slightly ahead of the general. I had kept a Colt's army pistol drawn since the affair of the Federal stragglers. We then made the branch becoming obscured from the enemy and crossing the Bowdtoin (not "Boydton," as some writers have called it) plank road, soon made the woods, which were kept for about a mile, in which distance we did not see a single person, and emerged into the field opposite General Heth's at a point two miles due southwest from General Lee's headquarters at the Turnbull House and at right angles with the Bowdtoin plank road at the "Harman" House, which was distant half a mile. When going through the woods the only words between General Hill and myself, except a few relating to the route, were by himself. He called my attention and said, "Sergeant, should anything happen to me you must go back to General Lee and report it."

We came into the field near its corner, at the foot of a small declivity, rising which I could plainly see that the road was full of troops of some kind. The general, raising his field-glass, said, "They are there." I understood perfectly that he meant the enemy and asked, "Which way now, General?" He pointed to that side of the woods parallel to the Bowdtoin plank road, about two hundred yards downhill from where our horses stood, saying, "We must keep on to the right." I spurred ahead and we had made two-thirds of the distance and, coming to a walk, looked intently into the woods, at the immediate edge of which were several large trees. I saw what appeared to be six or eight Federals, two of whom, being some distance in advance of the rest, who halted some forty or fifty yards from the field, ran quickly forward to the cover of one of the large trees and, one above the other on the same side, leveled their guns.

I looked around to General Hill. He said, "We must take them," and at the same time drawing, for the first time that day, his Colt's navy pistol. I said, "Stay there, I'll take them." By this time we were within twenty yards of the two behind the tree and getting closer every moment. I shouted, "If you fire, you'll be swept to hell! Our men are here—surrender!" When General Hill was at my side calling "surrender," now within ten yards of the men covering us with their muskets (the upper one the general, the lower one myself), the lower soldier let the stock of his gun down from his shoulder, but recovered quickly as his comrade spoke to him (I only saw his lips move) and both fired. Throwing out my right hand (he was on that side) toward the general, I caught the bridle of his horse and wheeling to the left, turned in the saddle and saw my general on the ground, with his limbs extended, motionless.

Instantly retracing the ground, leading his horse, which gave me no trouble, I entered the woods again where we had left them and realizing the importance, and of all things most desirous of obeying my general's last order "to report to General Lee," I changed to his horse, a very superior one and quite fresh, and letting mine free kept on as fast as the nature of the ground would permit. But after sighting and avoiding several parties of Federal stragglers and skirmishers, I felt that it would be best to take to the open country and run for it. After some distance of this I made for the Mahone Division log-hut winter quarters, which were still full of the enemy, upon the principle of greater safety in running through its narrow streets than taking their leisurely fire in the open. Emerging thence downhill to the branch, along the north side of which General Hill had so shortly ridden in his most earnest endeavor to reach our separated and shattered right and in a straight line for General Lee's headquarters, I came in sight of a mounted party of our own people, who, when the branch was crossed and the hill risen, proved to be Lieutenant General [James P.] Longstreet and staff, just arrived from north of the Appomattox. Meanwhile, meeting Colonels Palmer and Wingate and others of General Hill's staff and couriers and halting a moment to answer the kindly expressed inquiries of General Longstreet, we rode on and found General Lee mounted at the Cox road in front of army headquarters. I reported to him General Hill's last order to me. General Lee then asked for details, receiving which and expressing his sorrow he directed me to accompany Colonel Palmer to Mrs. Hill. General Lee said, "Colonel, break the news to her as gently as possible."

The 5th Alabama Battalion, provost guard to General Hill's Corps, skirmishing, found the general's body, which was still slightly warm, with nothing about it disturbed. The Federal party were doubtless alarmed at what had been done and must have instantly fled. The writer did not again see General Hill's body, which was brought to Venable's by a route still further to our rear, having, with the staff and couriers of the 3rd Corps, been ordered to General Longstreet, who soon became very actively engaged. I learned that the ball struck the general's pistol hand and then penetrated his body, just over the heart. Captain Frank Hill, aide-de-camp (and nephew) to the general, in charge, and Courier Jenkins were of the party detailed to escort the body, with Mrs. Hill and her children, to "a Mr. Hill's," near the banks of James River, in Chesterfield County, where the general's body was temporarily buried and afterward removed to Hollywood Cemetery, Richmond, Virginia.

The Fall of Charleston

C. F. HOLLINGSWORTH,
U.S. NAVY

Philadelphia *Weekly Times* 3, no. 29, September 13, 1879

Charleston—the hotbed of secession, the birthplace of nullification, and looked up to during the whole progress of the rebellion as the embodiment of the "last ditch"—was our destination as we sailed from Baltimore in January 1865, in the steamer *Winona*, one of the original screw gunboats. We did a little cruising along the Atlantic coast and captured a steamer up one of the North Carolina rivers with a boat expedition, and lost it as soon as captured through overweening confidence. It was about the beginning of March when we first crossed the bar of Charleston Harbor and steamed up to where the *Harvest Moon*, or, as the sailors had dubbed her, the *Horn Spoon*, an old river boat converted into a temporary flag-ship by Admiral [John A. B.] Dahlgren, was anchored.

About three years had passed since that eventful day when the heart of the great North was thrilled by the news of the bombardment of Fort Sumter and its surrender after a magnificent resistance, and yet the end seemed as far off as ever. One year before the daring and determined attack on Sumter had resulted in the riddling of that structure with the fifteen-inch shells and rifled bolts from the monitors, and the incessant bombardment from Morris Island had reduced the massive walls of the fort to a stubborn earthwork that only grew stronger as the shot and shell were poured into it. The highest part lay toward Morris Island, and near the center were the flagstaff with the cross-barred flag of the Confederacy flying at the head. Ever and anon a single sharpshooter would let fly with his long-range telescopic sighted rifle at some person or object in the naval battery at the end of Cumming's Point, on the upper end of Morris Island. So accurate were these rifles that they could, even at that distance of 1,160 yards, hit any object the size of a man.

To the left lay Morris Island, with its entrenchments, while beyond Sumter could be seen Charleston in the distance, the three steeples of the churches—St. Michael's, St. Phillip's, and St. Paul's—looming up grandly. From the clock in the steeple of the latter we could see the time of day, when the weather was clear, with the aid of telescopes. Between us and the city, however, and beyond Sumter, could be seen the formidable looking pile barrier erected to keep out our vessels, in case they succeeded in dashing past the batteries. Near these was the deep channel, named, years before the days of accession, as if in a spirit of prophesy, "Rebellion road."

When the weather was clear we could see, up the Cooper River, the Confederate ironclads, made after the model of the *Merrimac.* But they never came in long range even of our heavy guns. On the right of the harbor entrance, at the head of Sullivan's Island, was the picturesque little village of Moultrieville, above it being Battery Beauregard and just below the large Fort Moultrie, with its outworks and a number of smaller batteries. Away down at the lower end of Sullivan's Island was the massive work Fort Marshall, guarding Beach Inlet and the inner channel along the island, the beautifully wooded Mount Pleasant being almost in range of the upper bastion. Inside the bar the most conspicuous vessel was the huge ironclad *New Ironsides*, and then the half dozen ironclad turret boats, gunboats, and supply vessels. Outside of the bar were anchored the powder ships. The investment of the harbor and Confederate works by our fleet seemed to be an unending job. Month after month elapsed and with the exception of the fierce attack on the forts in the fall there was hardly an incident to break the monotony of the blockade. Day by day the telescopes were leveled anxiously in the direction of the city to see if there were any change.

In the opening of 1865 the end seemed to be apparently as far off as ever. In her accustomed place the *New Ironsides* lay at anchor day after day, an object of terror to and closely watched by the enemy, who seemed to have the most unbounded respect for her prowess. Let her up anchor and move but a hundred yards or so, and battery after battery would open on her with shot and shell from their heaviest guns. Near the *Ironsides* were the half dozen turreted boats with their battered sides. Every night a couple of the ironclads went up to within rifle shot of the beach under Fort Moultrie, and, of course, in close range of their heavy guns. But close as it was they were seldom disturbed, as the turrets were hard to hit in the first place, and still harder to hurt at close range. At a long range of a mile or a mile and a quarter the heavy shot from the ten-inch Columbiads would plunge on the deck, driving great holes through the inch plates, and in one or two cases shot went clear through the deck and the bottom. Up in close to the channel that swept past Moultrie, the ironclads kept under way all night in support of the numerous small boats and stream launches that rowed noiselessly up and down the channel on the lookout for the blockade runners that wanted to get in and out. When the nights were dark, the moon not shining and clouds sweeping across the sky, the picket boats were the most watchful, for then the steamers tried their best to run in and out, and often succeeded even though carrying a few shot and shell with them. The history of the unsuccessful attempts were written on the low, sandy shores of Sullivan's Island, all the way from Fort Moultrie down to Fort Marshall, a score or so of them being there wrecked. As we lay on picket so close in were we that through the long hours of the night we could hear the challenges of the pickets on shore as they tramped on their beats on the ramparts of their batteries.

As day would begin to dawn the boats were called in and the ironclads retired from their advanced position, and the daily routine of watchfulness and of incessant artillery practice was kept up. Years of practice had given the gunners on either side a surprising accuracy in their firing, and the soldiers on both sides generally kept close to shelter. Having a perfect range of the several batteries the gunners on either side would frequently exchange their fiery compliments. At the upper end of Morris Island or Cumming's Point our men had built a naval battery, armed with nine-inch Dahlgren shell guns, distant about 1,165 yards from the nearest side of Sumter. Sharpshooters on the latter, armed with their heavy Spencer rifles with telescopic sights, could strike an object the size of a man in the naval battery at that immense distance, and on a clear day one could see the puff of smoke, followed by the sharp report, recurring at intervals all day.

This was the condition of affairs until towards the close of January 1865, when there began to be rumors of the close approach of [Maj. Gen. William T.] Sherman's "bummers," as his army of veterans were nicknamed. The effect of these rumors were shown in the apparent uneasiness of the Confederates and in the frequent spasmodic shelling of our line, and more especially in their placing a large number of prisoners at a point near their batteries of Moultrie, where shells from our vessels from Morris Island would be apt to cause damage to our own men. Fort Marshall at this time was strengthened and more extended outworks thrown up, and a crisis was evidently at hand. One day as we were lying at anchor out of range, as we thought, we were all startled by a shell bursting high over our heads. It came like a clap of thunder from a clear sky. Before we had recovered from our surprise, a second, and in a few minutes a third shell burst, and then they went even farther and burst over some vessels still further from the Confederates, and finally the shells began to burst in uncomfortable proximity to the powder ships at the outer bar, a distance of over five miles. Things were getting to be decidedly interesting when the visitors ceased coming. We afterwards found out the cause of the eccentric firing. The Confederates had mounted a long iron 32-pound gun as a mortar to experiment with long-range firing as a last resort to shell us out, but their gun was burst after a couple hours' firing, and that was the end of that experiment.

Thus matters were on the evening of February 17, 1865, when our boats, the *Nantucket* and the *Nahant*, got ready to go on picket for the last time, although we had no idea that such was to be the case at the time. The defenses appeared to be as impregnable and the capture as far off as at any time during the past three or four years. All night, as we were on picket, we could hear more than the usual number of noises in the several batteries. The lights appeared to be moving around more than had been noticed, and the tramp of armed men was heard. The noise of steam whistles could be heard in the city, and over the latter could be seen a sultry glare, as if some great fire was raging. But leaving these noises and strange sights aside, there was not much to excite unusual suspicions, the sentries going their regular rounds and the sounds of their challenges being heard all through the night. Shortly after midnight a picket launch stopped at our vessel and informed us that there was a suspicious movement going on up the Ashley River, and that there was signaling from Fort Sumter and a small steamer going backwards and forwards between city and fort. But nothing else appearing out of the way, our boats continued to maintain their position, still keeping an anxious outlook.

Just before starting to leave our position, as the gray streaks of early dawn appeared in the eastern sky on the morning of the eighteenth, seeing an unusual number of men at Moultrie, we brought the 15-inch gun to bear on them, and sent a shell that exploded right in the center of the work. No answering shot was returned. It was the last shot fired at the Confederate works around Charleston. Soon the batteries began to stand out in the clear light of the early morning and stand out sharp against the sky, and then it was that they presented an unwonted appearance of solitude. All along the long line of ramparts not a sentinel paced his beat, and both army and navy started to investigate. The enemy had taken French leave and escaped from almost certain capture by the columns of Sherman that were folding in around them like a constrictor around its prey. Lt. Col.

[Augustus G.] Bennett, commanding the 21st Regiment of United States Colored Troops, and holding the advanced post of our army, sent Maj. [John A.] Hennessey, of the 52nd Pennsylvania Volunteers, to Fort Sumter, and finding it to be deserted raised the Stars and Stripes on the flagstaff in the fort, being the first time it had flown on the works since Major [Robert] Anderson was compelled to lower it in April, 1861.

Almost immediately a boat started from one of our vessels and from Colonel Bennett's post, and the crews of both strained every nerve to get first to Fort Moultrie. By this time every officer and man in the fleet and on Morris Island was intensely gazing in the direction of Sullivan's Island. Lustily the two crews bent to their oars, but the army men had the start, and their comrades gave a hoarse cheer as their boat struck the beach first, and almost instantly, with a responsive "hurrah!" rushed up the beach, into and across the ditch and over the ramparts of the fort, and in a moment or two we heard the hoarse cheering of the soldiers and sailors, the latter being only a few seconds behind, and the Confederate flag came down, whirling around and around like a huge snake as it was lowered and trampled in the dust. And as the Stars and Stripes went whirling up to the place so long held by the Stars and Bars, the soldiers on shore and the officers and crews of the fleet greeted it with cheer on cheer, and the men and officers danced around as if almost insane with joy. Before the sun had fairly arisen the flag of the Union saluted its first rays from Fort Marshall to Sumter, and the long, long, weary vigil was at an end and Charleston was ours.

Our forces were quick to follow up the retreating Confederates, who, the people on shore on Sullivan's Island told us, had not entirely left the vicinity. Colonel Bennett, with a squad of men, arrived at the point gardens shortly after seven o'clock. As he passed the Ashley River on his way up he saw the three ironclads up the river on fire, and also saw a large fire burning in the city. Almost as soon as he landed the ironclad *Palmetto State* burst up with a heavy rumbling sound, and huge volumes of smoke and flame were issuing from the ports of the *Chicora* and the *Charleston*—the latter blowing up at eleven o'clock and the other at nine o'clock. Without pausing to investigate the ironclads, Colonel Bennett pushed on with his men until informed that the Confederate rear guard were still in considerable force in the city. An officer who was with Bennett, going on by himself on horseback, came across a Confederate body of about fifty men, who halted him and demanded his horse. But before securing the latter the men got frightened and made off.

In a few hours the city was entirely clear of the Confederates and the mayor made a formal surrender and under control of our forces. In the meantime the soldiers and sailors had gone to investigate the batteries on Sullivan's Island and Fort Sumter. They found confusion worse confounded. Before they reached Battery Beauregard the latter blew up with a tremendous report, the entire interior being scooped out to the depth of nearly thirty feet, and guns, carriages, and timbers, etc., hurled into the air, falling in many cases at the distance of hundreds of yards. Fortunately no one was hurt. Anticipating that our men would visit the works, the Confederates had placed about two hundred barrels of powder in the center of the work and left a slow match burning as a fuse in the midst. It burned a little too fast, exploding before our men reached it.

Our men rapidly ran down the line of batteries, and in several cases were just in time to snatch up and extinguish burning slow matches that had been inserted in huge piles of cannon powder piled up outside of the inner entrances of the casemates of the batteries, in some cases higher than a man's head. They had apparently emptied barrel after barrel on those piles, then scattered a number of boxes of percussion caps and primers over the mass, so as to make it easy to send whoever stepped on them incautiously into eternity. But either owing to good luck or by the bad quality of the caps and primers, nothing of the kind occurred.

The casemates themselves were composed of a large room with a winding entrance, the roof composed of heavy timbers with earth packed on top of them to the depth of ten to fifteen feet. They were dark, damp, and smelled musty, but were very effective as far as protection was concerned. In one of them we found several Bunsen's batteries connecting with an ordinary telegraphic apparatus, the insulated wires extending down the beach and into the water. At one time a large iron cylindrical torpedo, charged with several hundred pounds of powder, with which the wires were connected, was directly under the *New Ironsides*, and the officer in charge of the battery tried again and again to fire the torpedo, and wondered why it failed at the very last moment. We found out the secret—a Confederate conscript, who was at heart a Union man, having cut the wire just as it entered the water.

In the city prompt measures had been taken by the commanding general to establish order, and there was very little external evidence of a change in the army of occupation. Placing the inhabitants under martial law, a stringent order was issued that no liquor should be sold by anyone, unless on the prescription of a physician. This was deemed necessary to prevent too exuberant a manifestation on the part of all over the end of the long blockade. That it was not more honored in the breach than in the observance we saw for ourselves. Stepping into a drug store on King Street the following morning, the proprietor immediately brought out his jar of fine brandy and asked us to take something. There were three of us, and none refused, and we drank to the old flag. We offered him payment, and he refused to take any; couldn't think of such a thing, etc., etc. We found out the cause of his goodness later. Another circumstance that we noticed was that many of the Negroes, instead of passing us on the pavement, would pass out into the street, and the women would curtsy and the men uncover their heads. It was a relic of their past usage, and spoke eloquently of the social customs of the old regime.

As we passed through the city the ravages of the bombardment became clearer to the least observant. Many of the houses were riddled with shot and shell and a broad swath of buildings had been burned out by the great fires. The handsome residences down on White Point fronting the beautiful gardens of the Battery had already been taken possession by families and communities of Negroes, who flocked in from the country as the Confederates left the city. In the upper part of the town many buildings were deserted and in most cases the furniture taken away. The shells here appeared to have played fearful havoc, and plunging through roof and wall entered and tore up the streets into great holes, into which a horse and cart could be thrown. Some of the larger and better class of houses, however, had been left with everything standing, and the camp followers commenced to plunder them. Thus the residence of Judge Duncan was left with its fine furniture and valuable library, and the latter was recklessly torn down and trampled on the floor and portable articles of value removed by the plunderers, who seemed to think that war gave a license for pilfering.

A short time after we had taken possession of the city the enthusiasm of the colored element held a jubilee celebration that culminated in a street parade of thousands of the colored population, the biggest proportion of which consisted of colored picaninnies from six to twelve years of age, of all shades of color from cream to charcoal, and all conditions from the ragged yet happy little wretch, clad in a piece of coffee bag, to the comparatively well dressed. As they marched through the streets to the sounds of vocal and instrumental music, they displayed primitive yet expressive sketches on banners and transparencies and devices. One of the latter was a huge coffin, containing the remains of the Confederacy. At one time the whole line struck up the melody "John Brown's body lies moldering in the grave," and it was wonderful to hear the rich melody coming from such untutored throats, some of the children especially having rich tenor and alto voices.

As time wore on and the Union successes continued it became evident that a grand celebration of the capture of Fort Sumter was necessary to crown them all, and we soon heard of great preparations making at the North. At noon of Saturday, April 8, 1865, the *Arago*, with Captain Gadsden, set sail from New York with a large company of distinguished guests on board. Shortly after it reached Charleston, however, we got the first news of the surrender of General [Robert E.] Lee and his army on the evening of April 13, by the steamer *Oceanus*. The news was announced at the theatre and then at the Charleston Hotel, producing the wildest enthusiasm. Speeches were made by Senator Wilson and General Washburne and others at the hotel and the bands of the 127th New York and 14th Maine Regiments played the national airs.

On the *Oceanus* was a large number of visitors from Brooklyn, New York. The following day the *Arago* came down with Reverend Henry Ward Beecher and a large number of guests aboard. Other steamers came from Savannah and Beaufort and Port Royal with army and navy officers aboard to be present at the celebration. In the meantime the old Fort Sumter had been prepared for the thousand of guests who were to be present at the raising of the old flag. A number of Charleston ladies had had the rubbish cleared from the ruins as much as possible. Inside the crumbled walls a large oblong platform had been erected with an arched canopy overhead draped with the American flag and brightened with festoons and wreaths of evergreens and flowers. On this stand would be the speakers and General Anderson and the representatives of the navy, army, and the civil authorities. On the stage, by the speaker, was a large golden eagle, holding in his beak a wreath of evergreens and roses. In the center was a great flagstaff nearly one hundred and fifty feet in height, the halyards of which had been adjusted by three volunteers from the crew of the United States steamer *Juniata*, men who had taken part in the assault upon Sumter by Admiral Dahlgren's fleet, September 9, 1863.

At six o'clock in the morning the steamer *Diamond*, Maj. Gen. [Quincy A.] Gillmore's boat, with self, staff, and visitors aboard, left the wharf for Sumter, the wharves and streets in the vicinity being crowded with people. At eight o'clock the entire fleet of Admiral Dahlgren hoisted their flags, and almost in an instant every ship in the harbor was strung from deck to trucks with colored bunting, the news of Lee's surrender causing the display at an earlier hour than was intended. The *Pawnee*, to which I had then been transferred, *Senora, Philadelphia, Santiago de Cuba, New Ironsides*, the turret ironclads and gunboats, then each fired a salute of twenty-one guns in front of the city. This was the first time the citizens of Charleston had a chance to get a near view of the terrible ironclads. At the same time the national ensign was thrown to the breeze from all the forts and batteries around except from Sumter, where the ceremonies were to culminate with the re-raising of Anderson's old battle-scarred flag.

The steamers *Canonieus, Blackstone, Oceanus, Delaware, W. W. Colt, Nellie Baker, Golden Gate, Anna Maria,* and even the funny-looking *Planter*—the latter Captain Small's steamer—were conveying people from the city to the fort. On their arrival the guests passed from the wharf newly erected at the west angle to the parade ground. Detachments of marines and sailors, under Lieutenant Commander Williams—the survivors of the assault on Sumter—and detachments from the 127th New York and 35th Massachusetts formed in line as a guard of honor. At 11:00 A.M. Admiral Dahlgren made his appearance on the fort, accompanied by Captain [Gustavus W.] Fox, assistant secretary of the United States Navy, and Mr. [John] Nicolay, private secretary to the president, and followed by Fleet Captain Bradford and over two hundred officers, mostly in full dress uniform. In front of the platform the seats, accommodating three thousand or four thousand, were rapidly filled—a large number of ladies from the North and a goodly number of Charleston being present. Shortly after twelve o'clock, noon, General Gillmore arrived, attended by General Anderson and daughter and a large number of officers, and at half-past twelve o'clock Reverend Henry Ward Beecher, the orator of the occasion, appeared and was accorded an enthusiastic welcome—the whole assemblage arising to their feet.

The speakers' stand and the platform now showed a very distinguished array. On it could be seen Maj. Gen. Q. A. Gillmore and staff, in full uniform; Admiral Dahlgren, Fleet Captain Bradford, Commodore Stephen C. Rowan, Fleet Engineer R. Danby, Paymaster Watmough, Judge Advocate Cowley, Colonel Charles Anderson (brother of the general), with one or two hundred other army and navy officers; Theodore Tilton, of the New York *Independent;* Justice Swayne, of the United States Supreme Court; Judge Story and Thompson and Hon. W. D. Kelley, of Pennsylvania; W. Lloyd Garrison, George Thompson, Professor Davids, of West Point Military Academy; General [Abner] Doubleday, General E. D. Townsend, adjutant general, United States Army; General John A. Dix, Provost Marshals Generals Fry and Thompson, Colonel S. L. Woodford and wife, Judge Holt, General Saxton and staff, Medical Director Clymer, Colonel Bogert, Major Burger, Captains Bragg and Merrill, Reverend M. Harris and Reverend R. S. Steers, Jr., D.D., and others. Joseph Hoxie and Sergeant Hart, with the old flag and the Fort Sumter mail-bag, the latter dated April 14, 1861, were also on the stand.

The exercises were commenced by singing a song written for the occasion, entitled "Victory at Last," joined in by all present. After prayer by

Reverend M. Harris, chaplain of United States Army, who had offered prayer at the raising of the old flag when the fort was occupied by Anderson, December 27, 1860, selections of psalms were read by Reverend Dr. Storrs, the people responding. Maj. Gen. E. D. Townsend then read the dispatch sent to the secretary of war by Major Anderson from the steamship *Baltic*, off Sandy Hook, April 17, 1861, announcing the surrender of Fort Sumter to General Beauregard. General Anderson then stepped forward and said:

> My friends and fellow citizens and brother soldiers: By the considerate appointment of the honorable secretary of war I am here to fulfill the cherished wish of my heart through four long years of bloody war—to restore to its proper place this dear flag, which floated here during the peace before the first act of this cruel rebellion. I thank God that I have lived to see this day, and to be here to perform this duty to my country. My heart is filled with gratitude to that God who has so signally blessed us—who has given to us blessings beyond measure. May all the world proclaim, Glory to God in the highest and on earth peace and good will toward men.

Hearty cries of "Amen, amen!" sounded from the vast assemblage as he closed, and he stepped forward, and taking hold of the halyards commenced to raise the old flag, which had been done up in a bunt or knot, hand over hand until it was half-way up. There he became almost paralyzed with emotion, the tears rolling down his weather-beaten cheeks in streams, and Sergeant Hart sprang forward to assist him. Overcoming his emotion, the general and sergeant rapidly ran the flag to the truck and with a sudden jerk loosed the old flag which, caught by the breeze, streamed out beautifully. As it flaunted, the whole assemblage rose to their feet, threw hats in the air and cheered again and again, until many were so hoarse they could not speak, and it was full fifteen minutes before order was secured; in the meantime the battery on the fort, the vessels in the fleet, Fort Moultrie, Battery Bee, Fort Putnam on Morris Island, [and] Fort Johnson on James Island [were] firing their salutes of one hundred guns.

After order had been established Reverend Henry Ward Beecher stepped from the stand and with a few preliminary remarks, delivered a stirring and eloquent address. The effect was marred, however, by his reading his address from slips of manuscript. The exercises of the day closed with the singing of the doxology, "Old Hundred," and a prayer and benediction by Reverend Dr. Storrs. In a few hours the fort was comparatively deserted, but in the evening the celebration was continued by a grand ball at Hibernia Hall, given by General [John P.] Hatch's staff, and the whole city presented an aspect of a grand victory being celebrated, as it was. It took many days for the place to tone down to the dull routine of everyday life.

The Beginning of the End

Alexander R. Boteler,
Colonel, C.S.A.

Philadelphia *Weekly Times* 2, no. 25, August 17, 1878

It is well known that the evacuation of Petersburg by the Confederate forces on the evening [of] April 2, 1865, precipitated the fall of Richmond on the same eventful night and that the surrender of the latter long-beleaguered city was marked by the horrors of a fearful conflagration, which was made more terrible by the excesses of a drunken mob of plunderers, who were as fierce, as pitiless, and as unrestrained as the destroying flames around them. There were few, if any, scenes of the Civil War that came under my personal observation, from the John Brown raid to Gen. [Robert E.] Lee's surrender, which made so deep an impression on me at the time of their occurrence and which my memory retains with more distinctness at the present day.

It had been an extremely hard winter on our troops around Richmond and Petersburg, especially on those entrenched in front of the latter place, which was the key to the Confederate capital. For, apart from the hazards and hardships consequent upon the operations of hostile lines in close proximity and always on the alert for strategic advantages, they suffered exceedingly from short rations, insufficient clothing, and constant exposure to the inclemency of the weather; the effect of which was to reduce their numbers to less than thirty thousand men, many of whom were unfit for duty from physical exhaustion and some few undeniably demoralized by their sad surroundings.

In looking back now, through the medium of more than a dozen years, to those "distressful times of internecine strife," I can hardly realize the facts of my own experience in the privations to which we were subjected; and it is no exaggeration to say that the Army of Northern Virginia, while at Petersburg during the last winter of the war, was frequently in a condition bordering on actual starvation, which was mainly, if not altogether, owing to the mismanagement of the commissariat at Richmond.

To give an idea of the meagerness and uncertainty of our supplies, I need only to cite our own mess as an illustration. There were but three of us in it—Col. William B. Rodman, of North Carolina; Col. John M. Patton, of Virginia; and myself—and we probably fared as well as most of the other officers, having certainly as many facilities for supplying our wants; yet, for days and even weeks together, it seemed impossible for us to get a particle of fresh meat, or, indeed, meat of any kind, except an occasional ration of rusty bacon, half-cured and wholly spoiled, which was not fit for a dog to eat.

Sometimes the only food we could obtain would be a few handfuls of moldy hardtack made of bran flour, which was so tough as to defy the teeth and when crushed, was found to be vermin filled. At other times we had to content ourselves with a tack or two of musty cornmeal which puzzled the ingenuity and exhausted the patience of our experienced and painstaking cook in vainly attempting to make it palatable. We tried it as "pone," as "hoe-cake," as "dodger," and in divers other forms familiar to the cuisine of the South, including children's mush and sick men's gruel, but it was "no go"—certainly no gout that was at all agreeable—for, in whatever fashion it was served, baked or boiled, it was simply abominable and seldom tempted as to a second taste.

Tea and coffee being unattainable I ventured once—and only once—to substitute for the latter luxury a carefully prepared decoction of roasted peanuts; but the process of boiling those popular American esculents developed their latent peculiarities to such a degree that the beverage made from them was too vulgarly vile for civilized humanity.

Taught by experience that the country darkies who infested the camps could not be relied on to cater for our mess table, we one day detailed on that important duty a trusty old soldier. Mounting him at sunrise on a serviceable horse, with an ample supply of "blue backs" in his pocket, we told him to scour the entire county of Dinwiddie rather than fail to find something fresh for our dinners. He was gone all day, while we in the meantime tempered our fast with anticipations of the savory feast of fat things he would be sure, we thought, to secure for us. But alas! For the vanity of earthly hopes and the emptiness of human expectations. When our purveyor returned, which was long after nightfall, instead of bringing us the pack-horse load of provisions that we looked for—the roasting pigs, poultry, hams, fruits, vegetables, et cetera—all that he had to show for his whole day's foraging was a poor, miserable, insignificant head of cabbage, not a bit bigger than his two fists, wilted without and worm-eaten within, for which he had to pay nine dollars and fifty cents. When I say that we were ruefully and wrathfully disappointed I but fully express what we felt at such a sequel to our sanguine expectations. Our sudden transition from the pleasures of hope to the pangs of despair was severe.

Yet the price paid for the specimen of spoiled cabbage by our improvised commissary of subsistence was not out of proportion with the current rates then ruling in that region for other commodities, as those were the days of a redundant and inconvertible currency, when money was the only thing that was cheap and when it was said of our people at the South that in going to market they toted their small change in bushel baskets and took home their purchase in *portemonnales*. This inflation of prices, however, had one good effect. It tended to preserve the morale of the army by making it almost impossible for either officers or men to indulge in strong potations—as the few who were festively inclined and could command the means for an occasional "frolic" were obliged to pay not less than a hundred dollars for a bottle of bad whisky and three dollars apiece for candies—"tallow dips," at that! So that the Southern soldiers, apart from those considerations of propriety which governed the conduct of most of them, had to confine themselves strictly to cold water as their beverage.

But it is useless to multiply illustrations to show what was the condition of the Confederates at the siege of Petersburg. Let it suffice to say that their sufferings during that dreary winter did more to diminish their numbers and to destroy their efficiency than had been done by force of arms in any of the previous campaigns. The soldierly bearing, however—the "manhood," as [Lt. Gen. Ulysses S.] Grant termed it—of most of those who were left of the Army of Northern Virginia remained unbroken, and they continued to display the same resistless dash and indomitable daring that had enabled them during the four preceding years to cover their banners all over with trophies and inscriptions of victories won from their gallant adversaries under adverse circumstances and at the greatest odds. For no matter how poorly armed they were, no matter how scantily clad, how pinched by cold, how weakened by hunger, wearied by watches or worn down by work, whenever the "long roll"—the battle-beat to arms!—resounded through their ranks they never faltered, never failed to follow their leaders to the front and with self-sacrificing alacrity to fling themselves, if need be, into the very jaws of death, utterly forgetful of everything but the fact that they were soldiers—soldiers of the South—fighting in obedience to their own conscientious convictions of duty and in filial defense to the mandate of their mother state for what they honestly believed to be the heritage of their rights, the tenure of their property, the safety of their families, and the sanctity of their homes!

But what could their valor avail under the circumstances that then surrounded them? How could it be expected that they would succeed when they had to contend against gaunt famine in their midst as well as the multitudinous and magnificently equipped "Grand Army of the Potomac" in their front, which outnumbered them four to one! Consequently, by midwinter, it became apparent to every one of us not willfully blind or woefully obtuse, that when the spring campaign should open, Grant's first movement would be, by an extension of his lines, to flank Lee's little army of half-starved Confederates out of their entrenchments.

Toward the last of March I got a few days' leave of absence to go to Richmond on business requiring my personal attention there, which I was anxious to arrange before the anticipated movement of the Federal army should inaugurate action operations in the open field. My leave expired on Sunday, April 2, when it was necessary of me, of course, to report my return to camp. Soon after breakfast, therefore, that day, I left the hospitable home of the Richmond friend with whom I had been adjourning and made my way leisurely to the depot to take the train back to the battle-scarred city of Petersburg. It was a lovely morning—such as makes one glad to be alive. A few floating vapors, interfused with light, softened the rays of the sun and the atmosphere, refreshed by recent rains, was filled with the fragrance of the early flowers of spring. The streets were unusually silent, and the city, in its "Sunday solitude," seemed to be reposing in the holy calm of peaceful security. "There was a Sabbath stillness in the air," and nothing to indicate that the dreaded day had come at last, which was to witness the destruction of the doomed capital of the Confederates States.

But on reaching the depot it presented quite an animated spectacle. The regular passenger cars were crowded with soldiers. There were extra troop trains on the sidings also filled to their utmost capacity and a considerable body of men beside were waiting for means of transportation. So that I was not surprised to learn when I had squeezed myself into one of the cars, that they were then "fighting hard in Petersburg," and had sent to Richmond for reinforcements. Soon after crossing the James River we met a train of cars containing several hundred Federal prisoners, some of whom had been taken by [Maj. Gen. Fitzhugh] Lee on the Friday before, at Five

Forks, and others a few days previous by the gallant [Maj. Gen. John B.] Gordon in his capture of Fort Steadman on Hare's Hill. The two trains stopping for a few moments side by side, "the boys" in each began to chaff those in the other, good-humoredly as usual, and to their mutual amusement.

"Oh, Johnny Reb, I'm sorry for you. Oh, so sorry!" said a boy in blue, shaking his head with mock solemnity.

"It's a good sign, Yank, when you are sorry," replied the boy in gray, with a merry laugh.

"For," continued the blue, "you'll get special thunder at Petersburg this evening."

"And you 'Castle Thunder,' at Richmond, this morning," was the gray's rejoinder.

"Say, Yank," asked another, "how did you find it at Five Forks, day before yesterday?"

"Hot as ——, Johnny!"

"Then, Yank, you got a foretaste of your future state."

"I don't thing my state will be hotter than Virginny is just now, Johnny!"

"Bye, bye!, Yank. Tell 'em to take care of you at the Hotel Libby,"

"Ta, ta! Johnny—same to you at the hot h—ll Petersburg."

And so the two trains, separating, moved off toward their respective destinations—one taking its passengers to prison and the other bearing those on board of it to battle. When we got near Petersburg we saw dense columns of smoke rising from different parts of the city, which indicated that our people were burning the cotton and tobacco stored in the town and caused us to fear that the Confederates had had reverses which would compel an evacuation of the place.

But we were not prepared for the startling intelligence we received upon our arrival, the details of which may be briefly summed up as follows: On March 25 [Maj. Gen. Philip H.] Sheridan had reached Petersburg, bringing with him the largest and most thoroughly equipped, if not the best, body of cavalry that had ever been seen on this continent. General Grant, on thus being reinforced, determined, if possible, to turn Lee's extreme right resting on the Southside Railroad, at a point some fifteen miles west of Petersburg and also to destroy the road itself.

Accordingly orders were given to Sheridan on March 29 to get on the right rear of General Lee's line the next morning; and to enable him to execute the order, two corps of infantry were detached to cooperate with his cavalry—making the force under Sheridan about 25,000 men. From the night of the twenty-ninth to the morning of the thirty-first it had rained so constantly that the roads were rendered almost impassable for wagons and artillery. This delayed but did not prevent the projected movement, as, on the 30th, Sheridan advanced from Dinwiddie Court-House toward Five Forks, where he was confronted by Fitz Lee's cavalry and [Maj. Gen. George E.] Pickett's Division of infantry.

On the following day, Friday, March 31, the Federals attempted to turn the Confederate right and were handsomely repulsed, being driven back to Dinwiddie Court House; but, on being heavily reinforced the next day, Saturday, April 1, they had compelled the Confederates, in their turn, to retreat, and flanking them at Five Forks, had captured some five thousand prisoners. Thus they were on the right rear of General Lee's lines.

To meet these movements General Lee had been obliged to detach seventeen thousand men, viz. the two corps commanded by Pickett and [Maj. Gen. Bushrod R.] Johnson, the brigades of [Brig. Gen. Henry A.] Wise and [Brig. Gen. Matt W.] Ransom, Hager's Battalion of artillery and Fitz Lee's Division of cavalry. Consequently, his lines in front of Petersburg were so weakened that there was left but one Confederate to every fifty yards.

General Lee, as soon as he saw the necessity for sending off so large a detachment to protect the point menaced by Sheridan, had taken the precaution to telegraph for reinforcements from Longstreet, who was in command of the defenses around Richmond. But, before they arrived at Petersburg, Grant had that morning—Sunday, April 2—finally assaulted Lee's attenuated line and had pierced it in three different places. The VI Corps had broken through at a point near the western extremity of the city; the XXIV Corps further west and the IX Corps eastwardly, near the Jerusalem plank road, so that the shattered remnants of the Confederate army, driven back to their inner line of defense, were then resolutely resisting the concentrated attacks of an overwhelming force of the enemy in their front and on both flanks, with the Appomattox River in their rear. Such was the situation that morning when we arrived at Petersburg, and, as may be imagined, it was anything but pleasant to contemplate from a Southern point of view, it being evident that the city had to be abandoned without further delay and that it was an extremely difficult undertaking for General Lee to extricate his little army from its dangerous position.

On my way out to where had been our winter quarters in the southwestern suburbs, I saw that the evacuation of the city had been already ordered, as long lines of army wagons were hurrying out of town loaded with ammunition, provisions, and such other stores as it was necessary to save, followed by vehicles of almost every description belonging to citizens and accompanied by a heterogeneous cavalcade of non-combatants. At the same time details of men were busy burning the cotton and tobacco, many hundred hogsheads of the latter staple having been piled up, weeks before, on vacant lots and in the least frequented streets, to be destroyed in anticipation of the disaster that was then impending. I was, therefore, in some measure prepared for the disappointment that awaited me at our quondam quarters in finding them vacated: that my two messmates, in obedience to orders, had packed up and packed off everything belonging to us three and that they themselves had left the city some hours before.

Abandoned to my own resources, I was both unmounted and unarmed, my weapons, horse, and harness being, at that time, miles away from me. And, as every available animal thereabout was then in active use—those not in the military service being employed in taking persons and property out of town—it was clearly impossible for me that morning to get another horse in Petersburg.

Nothing, therefore, remained for me to do but to make a virtue of necessity and, by the patient exercise of a little peripatetic philosophy in accommodating myself to circumstances, to take the chances. Wishing to see what I could of the position of affairs on the field, I walked out to the vicinity of our lines, which were not far off, as the tide of battle had surged up to the very suburbs of the city, and I there learned fuller particulars of the fight that morning and also got some official information of the movements in contemplation. Some of the incidents of the morning were very exciting, and none more so than those connected with the defense of Fort Gregg, which was one of a series of detached earthworks thrown up at intervals behind the whole length of the outer line of the Confederate defenses. It was manned by [Brig. Gen. Nathaniel H.] Harris' Mississippi Brigade, numbering 250 men. When the Federals had carried the outer line of the Confederates opposite to Fort Gregg—which they did without much difficulty and at little loss—flushed with their success they sprang forward to the assault of the fort. But the brave little garrison drove them back. Five times did the Federal forces attack the fort, and in each instance were they repulsed by the undaunted Mississippians.

It was, indeed, as President [Rutherford B.] Hayes says, "Greek meeting Greek," and as there were, as usual, many more Northern Greeks than Southern engaged in this affair, Confederate valor had to succumb to Northern numbers, and the fort finally fell into the hands of its enemies—but not until its entire garrison of 250, with the exception of thirty men, had been shot down at their post of duty, and between five and six hundred of their Federal assailants had shared the same fate. There were other instances of self-sacrificing gallantry during the day which are worthy of record and remembrance, but which the prescribed limits of this article do not allow me to particularize.

After seeing and hearing all that I could I returned to town toward sunset. In the meantime the firing on both sides had slackened. Indeed, since morning there had been no heavy engagement. The Federals seemed to be satisfied with what they had accomplished, and the Confederates were maintaining their position mainly to give time for the wagon trains (which were altogether not less than twenty miles long) to get well on their way from Petersburg and to be enabled themselves to make an orderly retreat under cover of the ensuing night—a movement which I thought it high time for me also to consider and provide for properly, if possible.

Accordingly, before dark, I went out to Dunlap Station, some two miles from town, on the Richmond Railroad, where a kinsman of mine (Dr. Clagett) was surgeon in charge of a field hospital and where I thought I might be able to get a horse. But failing to find one there I finally concluded to return by rail to Richmond, where I took it for granted I should have no difficulty in equipping myself in time to overtake our army next day on its retreat from Petersburg. They were then getting a train ready at Dunlap's, but it was delayed until after 9:00 P.M. in order to place on board of it as many of our wounded as could be safely transferred to Richmond—none of us dreaming of the condition in which we should find that city on reaching it. There were several hundred of the wounded to be sent off by the train, and a sad sight it was to see the poor fellows as we put them in the cars, but sadder still to witness their patient sufferings while trying to make them comfortable on our melancholy journey—the sickening horrors of which I have not the heart to attempt to describe.

It was nearly midnight when we arrived at Richmond, and as I left the cars at the depot, the first person I met was my genial old friend, Dr. Charges Magill, formerly of Hagerstown, Maryland, but then, as now, a resident of Richmond, who greeted me with the exclamation:

"Good heaven, Boteler, what in the name of wonder has brought you here tonight?"

"Why do you ask, doctor?" I inquired, in some surprise at the tone and manner of his salutation.

"Don't you know," said he, "that Richmond's evacuated, and that the Yankees will be here by daylight, if not before?"

"Impossible!" I exclaimed, utterly amazed at the information.

"It is so, I assure you," he continued. "The president, cabinet, governor, and all the rest of the officials went off this evening—most of them by the Danville train. Everybody's gone who could go—soldiers and all—and the city is completely abandoned to the enemy!"

It is told of [Lt.] Gen. Jubal A. Early that when he heard of Lee's surrender he stood for some seconds in silent amazement and then, suddenly looking up to the sky, exclaimed with characteristic emphasis: "Gabriel! Blow your horn!" But the astonishment of the gallant old general at that announcement could not have been greater than mine was at Doctor Magill. I could hardly realize the fact that Richmond, which I had left this morning so calm, so peaceful and apparently so serene, was actually surrendered—that the long struggle for the Confederate capital was over and that the next day's sun would see it in full possession of its persistent and now victorious enemies! When it is remembered how the news of that important and indeed decisive event thrilled the hearts of the whole country, North and South, it will be readily understood that the time, place, and circumstances of its announcement to me gave startling significance to the portentous fact. Although I had all along supposed that the fall of Petersburg would probably be followed by the evacuation of Richmond, I had no idea that the two catastrophes would occur so suddenly, in the same night and that I would be so unpleasantly involved in both of them.

As a matter of course, my predicament had now become more embarrassing than ever. While there was a greater necessity for me to be mounted to make my escape, the chance of getting a horse at that late hour in Richmond was proportionately less than it had been in Petersburg. How I did wish, then, for my own bonny bay mare! But there was no time for sentimental regrets or vain desires. Remembering a certain black mare belonging to a German friend of mine on Grace Street, which was one of the best and most beautiful animals in the city, it occurred to me that if I could only get hold of her the difficulties of my position would at once be obviated. So I started forthwith for the residence of my friend, feeling assured that, if at home, he would be happy to verify to me the truth of the proverb that "a friend in need is a friend indeed." On my way up the street I called at the headquarters of General Ewell, who had command within the city, and was agreeably surprised to find him yet in town, though just about to take his departure—his horse and those of his staff being then at the door in charge of the couriers.

The general confirmed the information given me by Doctor Magill, told me that the pickets had been withdrawn from around the city, and advised me to get out of it with the least possible delay. After receiving from him some suggestions as to the best route for me on the other side of the river, in order to rejoin Lee's army, which he informed me was then in full retreat, I resumed my walk up Grace Street and soon arriving at my friend's door had no difficulty in arousing him from bed, as, like almost every one else in Richmond then, he was passing a night of sleepless anxiety. Welcoming me with his accustomed cordiality, he expressed no less surprise than pleasure in seeing me, as he knew I had gone that morning to Petersburg.

"Of course," said he, "you'll stay here, now, and surrender yourself tomorrow morning, as there is no longer any hope for the Confederacy."

"Why that would be downright desertion, for which I would deserve to be shot," said I, amused at the artless sincerity of his well-meant suggestion. "No, indeed! So far from it. My sole business in Richmond is to obtain the necessary equipment to enable me to follow General Lee, and I want your black mare."

"What!" he exclaimed, "My mare! My pet! Why, don't you know that I never lend her to anybody!"

"Yes," I replied, "I know that perfectly well—that you never lend her, that no reasonable amount of money can buy her and that you keep her so securely stabled that thieves cannot break through and steal her—nevertheless I must have her."

"So! That is cool!" said he. "You tell me, and you say truly, that my mare cannot be borrowed, bought, nor stolen, and yet that you must have her! Well, how do you expect to get her? Tell me that."

"Oh!" I answered, "that is a problem for you yourself to solve. Only let me remind you that when the Federal army of occupation comes in tomorrow morning some of those cute fellows will soon find your pet, and, of course, confiscate her to their own use, as contraband of war!"

"Ah! That is so!" said he, reflectingly. "That is so, indeed. Some of them are good judges of horseflesh, and they'll take her from me, certain! So I'll tell you what I'll do. I'll just make you a present of her. How will that answer?"

"Admirably well!" I exclaimed. "You are the same old, big-hearted trump I always took you for." And, as in duty bound, I made my most profound acknowledgements for the timely favor he had done me.

But in presenting me with the mare my friend's munificence was by no means exhausted, for, after calling up a servant to saddle her for me, he asked if I'd been to supper, and on my saying that since breakfast I had not so much even as thought of a meal, he seemed to be really distressed at my protracted fast and at the poor prospect of my finding anything fit to eat on the route of a retreating army. So he began to bustle about his sideboard and pantry, "on hospitable thought intent," until he had collected and placed before me an appetizing, cold collation. Nor was this all, for while I was doing justice to my improvised repast, he laid a package by the side of my plate, saying:

"Take that, too."

"What's all this?" I asked.

"All that," said he, "was called money here yesterday, but it will hardly go by that name tomorrow; so you just take it with you and make the most of it."

"No, no!" said I, "this won't do at all! I'm a thousand times obliged; but I've money enough in my pocket, and can't take any of yours."

"Excuse the question, but I am curious to know how much you happen to have about you now."

"Oh, some several hundred dollars," I answered, carelessly.

"Yes? Confederate, of course, and your some several hundred dollars," said he, "won't buy a pair of boots. Pshaw! Now, come, don't be proud and foolish! Take this package of Confederate notes, and mind what I tell you. When you catch up with the treasury department you just make 'em change these notes into gold, or silver, or coffee, or something or other that you can use by and by as money. Now be sure and change it, my friend, every bit of it, and as soon as you can—if you have to pay five hundred for one. Because, I tell you, the bottom has fallen out of the Confederacy and it's all gone to the bow-wows! You understand?"

"All right, old fellow," said I, finally. "I'll take the notes and change them if I have a chance. But it must be for you not for myself."

The package contained upward of twenty thousand dollars of Confederate issues, which I hardly need say never were exchanged on any terms—not even for the intrinsic value of the paper on which they were printed.

"And now," said he, as I arose from the table, feeling wonderfully refreshed in mind, body, and estates, "tell me if I can do anything more for you tonight?"

"Nothing in the world, I thank you, unless," said I, "you have a spare pistol to lend me, as I am totally unarmed."

"Pistol? Be sure I have, and a sword, too, at your service, which I'll be glad if you'll take out of the house before the Yankees come and find 'em all."

And he forthwith brought down to me a light cavalry saber with its belt, to which was attached a holster containing a new English revolver, already charged, with a case of ammunition—all which he supplemented with a luncheon for next day and a handful of cigars. I could hardly have had my wishes more pleasantly complied with and my wants more completely supplied than they were that night by my good, genial friend from Frankfort-on-the-Main, Gustav Lersner, who certainly did his best to give me a good sendoff. It was now about 2:00 A.M. So bidding my kind and considerate host good-bye, I mounted his mare—for I could not conscientiously consider her mine—and made my way toward the lower or business part of the city, my purpose begin to cross the river at Mayo's Bridge.

As I rode down Grace Street, which was dark, silent, and deserted, I noticed a red reflection in the sky to the right indicating an extensive conflagration near the river, in the neighborhood of the depot; and presently perceiving the baleful glare of another farther down, in the direction of Rockett's, it became apparent to me that the city had been fired at different points and that the danger of a disastrous and widespread calamity was more imminent from the ominous fact that no alarm was sounded, that no fire engines appeared upon the streets, and that no efforts seemed to be made by citizens to arrest the progress of the flames.

When near the Capitol Square I met a few persons who were walking rapidly, but not in the direction of the fires. In passing the Mechanic's Institute, which had been used for the War Department, several men in the middle of the street there were burning piles of papers which they were replenishing with bundles of what I took to be official documents of the department that were being brought out to them in baskets from the building. At a short distance from the Spottswood Hotel I turned into Main Street, and after passing two or three groups of disorderly persons, who seemed to be intoxicated, some of whom were making the night hideous with their wild yells and horrible profanity, I had gotten down at far as Mitchell & Tyler's jewelry store, when, suddenly, without any premonition, I found myself in the midst of a promiscuous crowd of both sexes and of all colors, who, coming swiftly and silently up the street, had surrounded me before I was aware of it. It was a reckless mob of pillagers—a marauding rabble of the most disreputable classes, who, under cover of the darkness and confusion that prevailed, had emerged from their haunts in the slums of the city and were prowling through the streets like a pack of hungry wolves in pursuit of prey, committing all kinds of depredations with impunity. They had been plundering the stores further down town and were just about to ransack the jewelry establishment when I met them. At first supposing they would pass on quietly, I reined up to allow them to do so, but when I perceived that they had stopped to break into the store—the door of which they were battering with axes—I attempted to push my way through the crowd, when a huge bareheaded ruffian seized my bridle and, forcing the mare back almost on her haunches, demanded in a rough tone, with an oath, what I was riding over him for.

"Take care, man!" said I, quickly, "my mare will hurt you—she bites!" and the fellow stepped back immediately, letting go the rein. At the same instant a crash and the jingle of shattered glass apprised the crowd that the store door was broken down and there was a general rush in that direction, which enabled me to extricate myself from the throng without further difficulty. The city council having, at a late hour that night, directed that all the spirituous liquors in town should be destroyed, hundreds of barrels of it had been rolled out of the warehouses, their heads stove in and their contents emptied into the gutters. This was especially the case in Cary Street, so that when I entered that approach to the bridge the whisky was fetlock deep in some parts of it. Its fumes so filled the atmosphere that they affected my head and I had to hurry beyond their influence to prevent being overcome by them. After considerable trouble in getting around and over the barrels, boxes, and bales that obstructed the roadway, as well as the sidewalks of that vicinity, I finally reached Mayo's Bridge, getting there just in time to be the very last horseman to cross over it, as they were then setting it on fire in several places.

Arriving at an elevated open space on the Manchester side of the river, I stopped and turned to take my last look at Richmond. The spectacle it then presented was a fearful one, though nothing, I presume, to what it was a few hours after. The three bridges spanning James River—that of the Petersburg Railroad, of the Danville Railroad, and Mayo's—were all on fire, the two former being wrapped in flames from end to end and the latter beginning to blaze. Extensive fires were also raging in the western, central, and eastern sections of the city, near the river, which seemed from the reflection to run red with blood. Vast volumes of lurid smoke rolled in billowy clouds across the crimson sky, "blotting out the stars," while innumerable sparks whirling in eddying coruscations, with flakes of fire falling on houses far and near, were rapidly extending the conflagration. Above the sullen roar of the flames, which sounded like the monotone of the surf upon a rocky shore, were heard at frequent intervals the crash of falling timbers accompanied with such yells and shrieks as made a very midnight pandemonium.

While I was gazing with unutterable sadness on this exciting scene of destruction, there was suddenly in the direction of the river, just below me, a blinding flash and a terrific explosion, louder that the loudest thunder, which seemed to shake the very foundations of the hill itself. My mare,

General Lee at Appomattox

(*HARPER'S NEW MONTHLY MAGAZINE*)

frantic with fright, sprang so suddenly across the road as nearly to unseat me, and before I had fairly readjusted myself in the saddle there was another dazzling flash and tremendous report followed in a few seconds by a third, both of which were no less startling than the first. They were caused, as I subsequently learned, by the blowing up of the ironclads *Virginia, Richmond* and another vessel of war whose name I do not now remember.

After watching the progress of the fires for more than half an hour, I left the environs of Manchester and made my way across the country in the direction of General Lee's lines of march, and that evening overtook his retreating army. From that time forth, throughout the following week, that never-to-be-forgotten week that preceded the surrender, the nature, number, and variety of our personal experiences were sufficient to fill a folio volume and would require a far abler pen than mine to describe them.

In closing this imperfect sketch I take occasion to say that within a week after our surrender at Appomattox I returned to Richmond and had the pleasure of restoring to my German friend his beautiful black mare, which, though reduced in flesh, was perfectly sound in wind and limb and almost as full of life as when I first mounted her at her master's door in the memorable night of the fall of Richmond and of Lee's retreat from Petersburg.

Jefferson Davis' Week at Danville

William D. Coleman,
18th Virginia Infantry, C.S.A.

Philadelphia *Weekly Times* 5, no. 14, May 28, 1881

When the chief officials of the Confederate States fled from Richmond on the memorable night of April 2, 1865—taking with them the hurriedly gathered archives of the Confederacy—they proceeded as rapidly as the worn-out rails and burned-out locomotives of the Richmond and Danville Railroad would permit to the then small town of Danville, on the south side of Dan River, within three miles of the state line dividing Virginia from North Carolina, by the ancient survey of Col. William Byrd, of Westover. Here they halted with the purpose of establishing anew the capital of the Confederacy, hoping for General [Robert E.] Lee to realign his army along the Staunton River, and resolved (as their president, Jefferson Davis, proclaimed) to "meet the foe with fresh defiance, with unconquered and unconquerable hearts."

About 3:00 P.M. on Monday, April 3, five trains of cars reached Danville, bringing President Davis, several members of his cabinet and other government officials, some members of the Virginia legislature and a few private citizens of distinction. In the forenoon of the same day, some hours before the arrival of these trains, but when it was known that they were en route, the citizens of the town in general had assembled at the call of James M. Walker, then mayor, and appointed a committee to make all necessary arrangements for throwing open the houses in the town for the hospitable reception and entertainment of President Davis and the other government officials and the private citizens accompanying him. The committee was composed of the following citizens: Captain W. T. Clark, the Rev. C. H. Hall (Methodist), the Rev. J. M. Kirkpatrick (Presbyterian), the Rev. C. C. Chaplin (Baptist), William Ayres, Dr. J. M. Smith, Dr. J. M. Waddill, and Messrs. C. W. Watkins, P. W. Ferrell, and E. N. Sorey. At the same meeting of citizens the mayor and the president and members of the town council were appointed a committee to meet the distinguished refugees on their arrival at the depot and tender them the hospitalities of the town.

Both of these committees zealously discharged the duties assigned them. On the arrival of the trains President Davis and several members of his staff, after their formal reception by the mayor and the town council, were invited by Mr. [William T.] Sutherlin, then the post quartermaster at Danville, into his private carriage and conveyed to his elegant residence near the head of Main Street, where they became his guests. All the other refugee Confederates were also received with cordial hospitality, and that night there were but few families in the town which had not some of them as guests.

It is quite foreign to my purpose in preparing this paper to attempt any description of the scenes and incidents of the week succeeding the arrival of the Confederate officials at Danville—"the last capital of the Confederacy." The excitement and apprehension among the resident population, the anxiety and solicitude among the recently arrived were, in truth, almost indescribable. All the telegraph lines had been cut down or otherwise rendered unavailable for the transmission of information, and there was no mode of communication between the town and the armed forces of the Confederacy in any direction. The railroad bridges between it and Richmond had nearly all been destroyed, and no trains were running or could run any considerable distance in that direction. Southward there was limited communication with Goldsboro, fifty miles distant, by the Piedmont Railroad and thence toward Charlotte, North Carolina; but this limited means of communication was entirely monopolized by the Confederate officials, and was, moreover, hourly threatened with immediate destruction by a cavalry raid which [Maj. Gen. George] Stoneman was then making from the direction of Southwest Virginia through Northwest North Carolina, which [Maj. Gen. William T.] Sherman's army, having accomplished its famous "March to the Sea," was known to be approaching from southeastern North Carolina. No communication could be had with General Lee's army and even its exact location was unknown, while the whereabouts of Gen. Joseph E. Johnston and his army were altogether conjectural among the people in Danville at that time. But right nobly did they stand the test of such a situation. Old and young, men, women and children, their hearts were in the cause and they deemed no sacrifice too great, even then in the waning fortunes of that cause, for them to make in its behalf. But my purpose is simply to embody herein a narrative of facts touching the last days of the Confederacy which may interest those who wish to know what was the conduct and bearing of the chief actors in those historical events.

On the morning of April 4, being the next day after his arrival in Danville, President Davis prepared an "Address to the People of the Confederate States of America." This address was published in but one newspaper of the period because there was no way by which it could be sent to any other. From a copy of the Danville *Register*, dated April 5, 1865, now before me—a little 12x18 sheet, printed on the dingy substance known as "Confederate printing paper," and now still dingier from age—I transcribe as follows:

> To the People of the Confederate States of America:
>
> The general-in-chief of our army has found it necessary to make such movements of the troops as to uncover the capital, and thus involve the withdrawal of the government from the city of Richmond. It would be unwise, even if it were possible, to conceal the great moral, as well as material, injury to our cause that must result from the occupation of Richmond by the enemy. It is equally unwise and unworthy of us, as patriots engaged in a most sacred cause, to allow our energies to falter, our spirits to grow faint, or our efforts to become relaxed under reverses, however calamitous. While it has been to us a source of national pride that, for four years of unequaled warfare, we have been able in close proximity to the center of the enemy's power to maintain the seat of our chosen government free from the pollution of his presence; while the memories of the heroic dead, who have freely given their lives to its defense must ever remain enshrined in our hearts; while the preservation of the capital, which is usually regarded as the evidence to mankind of separate existence, was an object very dear to us, it is also true and should not be forgotten, that the loss we have suffered is not without compensation. For many months the largest and finest army of the Confederacy, under the command of a leader whose presence inspires equal confidence in the troops and the people, has been greatly trammeled by the necessity of keeping constant watch over the approaches to the capital, and

has thus been forced to forego more than one opportunity for promising enterprise. The hopes and confidence of the enemy have been constantly excited by the belief that their possession of Richmond would be the signal for our submission to their rule, and relieve them from the burden of a war which, as their failing resources admonish them, must be abandoned if not speedily brought to a successful close. It is for us, my countrymen, to show by our bearing under reverses how wretched has been the self-deception of those who have believed us less able to endure misfortune with fortitude than to encounter danger with courage.

We have now entered upon a new phase of a struggle, the memory of which is to endure for all ages, and to shed ever increasing luster upon our country. Relieved from the necessity of guarding cities and particular points, important but not vital to our defense, with our army free to move from point to point, and strike in detail the detachments and garrisons of the enemy, operating in the interior of our own country, where supplies are more impossible, and where the foe will be far removed from his own base and cut off from succor in case of reverse, nothing is now needed to render our triumph certain but the exhibition of our own unconquerable resolve. Let us but will it and we are free, and who, in the light of the past, dare doubt your purpose in the future?

Animated by that confidence in your spirit and fortitude, which never yet has failed me, I announce to you, fellow countrymen, that it is my purpose to maintain your cause with my whole heart and soul; that I will never consent to abandon to the enemy one foot of the soil of any one of the states of the Confederacy; that Virginia—noble state, whose ancient renown has been eclipsed by her still more glorious recent history; whose bosom has been bared to receive the main shock of this war; whose sons and daughters have exhibited heroism so sublime as to render her illustrious in all time to come; that Virginia, with the help of the people and by the blessing of Providence, shall be held and defended, and no peace ever made with the infamous invaders of her homes by the sacrifice of any of her rights or territory. If by stress of numbers we should ever be compelled to a temporary withdrawal from her limits or those of any other border state, again and again will we return, until the baffled and exhausted enemy shall abandon in despair his endless and impossible task of making slaves of a people resolved to be free. Let us, then, not despond, my countrymen, but relying on the never-failing and protecting care of our God, let us meet the foe with fresh defiance, with unconquered and unconquerable hearts.

Jefferson Davis.
Danville, April 4, 1865

This address appeared on Wednesday morning April 5, 1865. Its effect upon the public mind as far as it could be disseminated among the people was exciting, reassuring, and encouraging. The impression prevailed universally, or at least as far as I could observe, that President Davis intended to maintain the Confederate government to the bitter end, and that under no circumstances would he consent to the removal of the capital of the Confederacy and the archives of the government beyond the Virginia state line. That this impression was erroneous the swiftly coming subsequent events too plainly showed for comment now. But the prevalence of this impression created great popularity for President Davis, and praises of his presumed determined purpose were to be heard on every hand. Still there was great anxiety among the people, which became greater and greater as day after day passed and nothing could be heard from Lee's army. Wednesday and Thursday passed in this terrible uncertainly and anxiety, and day after day in like manner, until at last on the Monday evening following, as will be shown in the sequel, came at last, not "news of battle," but of overthrow. More than one party of volunteer scouts went forth from the town, going in the supposed direction of Lee's army, hoping to bring back intelligence there from, but none of these parties had succeeded up to Friday morning. That morning Capt. [William P.] Graves, formerly commanding Company A (Danville Blues) 18th Regiment Virginia Infantry, was sent for by Col. [Robert E.] Withers, then commanding the post at Danville, and by him requested to report to [Brig. Gen. Henry H.] Walker for a special service. Captain Graves had just returned from a voluntary scouting expedition into North Carolina, west of the Piedmont Railroad, which he had made at the request of Colonel Withers, in order to ascertain the facts in relation to the reported raid of Stoneman in that section of the country.

At this point I might describe the situation of affairs in Danville at the time under consideration; how President Davis with his cabinet ministers was in almost continual consultation; how the heads of departments were busily at work reorganizing their clerical corps and getting the government "in working order" at this newly chosen capital of the Confederacy; and how, above all, not a whisper of a suspicion even that Lee would ever surrender, or that his army could ever be vanquished, was heard from any quarter. But I shall refrain from any extended digression and conclude this paper with a simple narrative of how the news of Lee's surrender was obtained and brought to President Davis, and how it was received by him. And this I will do as nearly as I can in the words of Captain Graves, who obtained and delivered this crushing intelligence to Mr. Davis in person, and who has related the story to me.

Captain Graves is herewith quoted:

> I reported to General Walker, as requested by Colonel Withers, and he asked me if I would undertake an important service which it was necessary should be promptly performed. I readily consented, of course. General Walker then told me that President Davis desired that the present location of the Army of Northern Virginia should be ascertained at once and a line of couriers established between General Lee's headquarters and the nearest point from which telegraphic communication could be had with Danville. The telegraph wires along the line of the Richmond and Danville Railroad had been repaired as far, I believe, as Roanoke Station, on Staunton River, and it was proposed to continue the repairs on to Drake's Branch in Charlotte County, some fifteen miles further on, and establish telegraphic communication from that point to Danville. General Walker then directed me to proceed at once to Drake's Branch and take command of a company of cavalry which he was informed had been raised in the neighborhood and which he said I would find there.
>
> With this company of cavalry he directed me to go and find General Lee's headquarters and establish the line of couriers from there to Drake's Branch. He gave me authority to take a special train—consisting of a locomotive and a single car—from the Richmond and Danville Railroad to carry me over the line of that road to Drake's Branch.
>
> Accordingly, on the afternoon of the same day (Friday, April 7), I left Danville on my "special train," no one attending me except the engineer and fireman. We made the run from Danville to Clover Depot, a distance of some forty-six miles, in pretty good time, and on arriving there I reliably ascertained that there was no such company of cavalry at Drake's Branch as General Walker had told me I would find there, and in consequence I saw I would have

to change the plan of operations I had in mind on starting from Danville.

At Clover Depot I was joined by Captain R. L. Henley, the enrolling officer (generally called "conscript officer") for that district, and he accompanied me on to Drake's Branch at once. Here we met Maj. Richard V. Gaines, who lived near by and had enlisted a small party of volunteers, consisting in part of citizens of the neighborhood and in part of soldiers belonging to the army who happened to be at home (on sick leave, I believe), with purpose to go through the country in search of information touching the whereabouts and movements of General Lee's army. Some of these volunteers were pretty well mounted and others but poorly so. Major Gaines agreed to turn this party over to me for the expedition I had been sent upon by General Walker, but they could not be gotten together and made ready to set out until next morning, as it was then already night.

Upon this understanding I concluded to return to Clover Depot with Captain Henley and spend the night there, as I could find no place at Drake's Branch to stay at. I accordingly returned to Clover Depot and remained there quiet until next morning.

On Saturday morning, April 8, I took my special train at Clover Depot again and, accompanied by Captain Henley, proceeded to Drake's Branch and there took charge of the party of volunteers which Major Gaines had gotten together. The party consisted of about fifteen men, but I can now recollect the names of but a few of them. Those whose names I recollect were John H. Redd, Isaac Overbrey, Ben Franklin Jenkins (a Northern man, who was on a visit South when the war commenced and volunteered as a Confederate soldier), and Luther Jeffress, a lad only seventeen or eighteen years old. The names of the others, all of whom were entire strangers to me, I cannot now recall.

With this party, some of whom were but poorly mounted, I left Drake's Branch on Saturday morning (April 8), intending to proceed by the most direct route practicable to reach some point on the South Side Railroad, above Farmville, hoping by so doing to obtain the intelligence I was seeking in the speediest manner. We proceeded by way of Charlotte Court House, which is a little village called Marysville, five miles from Drake's Branch, and here we were detained several hours in getting together some better horses, which were needed for those of the party who were poorly mounted; but we got our needed horses and got away from Marysville about noon, intending to go by way of Chickentown and make directly for Pamplin's Depot on the South Side Railroad, about twenty miles west of Farmville. On reaching Concord on Sunday I found I could not there obtain any reliable information as to the whereabouts of General Lee or the situation of his army. Strange that there, within less than twenty miles of the spot on which at that very hour the supreme transaction of the whole four years' war was being enacted, the people whom we encountered could tell us nothing of what was going on. But most of the few people whom we saw seemed to be dazed and bewildered and hardly able to give intelligent answers to simple questions.

Getting no satisfactory information at Newlin's Store we proceeded along the line of the South Side Railroad in an easterly direction, intending to keep on to Farmville, if necessary, but determined not to turn back until I had gotten the information I had been sent to obtain or was captured by the enemy in trying to do it. But we had proceeded but a few miles along the line of the railroad when we encountered [Brig. Gen.] Thomas L. Rosser, who was attended by and in command of a remnant of his Confederate Cavalry Brigade. I was personally acquainted with General Rosser, having formed his acquaintance at the first battle of Manassas, when he was in command of one of the batteries of the Washington Artillery from New Orleans, and I had also met him several times subsequently after he had gone into the cavalry arm of the service. After our mutual recognition and the exchange of salutations, I informed General Rosser of the mission on which I had been sent, of my anxiety to accomplish it and of the importance of my being able to return to Danville with the required intelligence for President Davis as speedily as possible. Thereupon he took me aside, with Captain Henley, who was accompanying me, and in a sort of confidential manner imparted to us the most disastrous intelligence I could possibly bear to President Davis. He told us of the overthrow of the Army of Northern Virginia. He also related an astounding story to the effect that General Lee had disappeared the previous night and that [Lt. Gen. James P.] Longstreet was at that hour, while we were speaking, at [Lt. Gen. Ulysses S.] Grant's headquarters making a total surrender of the Confederate army.

He went on to say further that, with the remnant of his command of cavalry accompanying him, he intended to go on to Lynchburg and there join in with [Maj. Gen. Lunsford L.] Lomax and whatever cavalry General Lomax might have, and having united their forces, he and General Lomax would push on and make their way into North Carolina, there join Gen. Joseph E. Johnston's army and continue the fight. With great animation, General Rosser exclaimed at this point: "By God, sir, the cavalry ain't whipped!"

After some little further conversation General Rosser counseled us that it would be futile to attempt to proceed onwards, for that if we did we would most certainly be captured by the enemy. He urged this dissuasion upon me with great earnestness. Upon this advice I returned to my party, whom I had left at some paces distant, and informed them that I had learned that if we proceeded any further we should probably all be captured by the enemy. I told them that as to myself, I intended to go on and take the risk of capture, for I was unwilling to turn back, without fuller information than I had as yet obtained, but I did not wish any man of the party to go on with me unless by his own free will and accord he, knowing the risk, was willing to take it with me. I then directed that all who wished to turn back and go home should fall out of ranks and go at once. The whole party thereupon fell out of ranks and turned back except Captain R. L. Henley and Mr. John H. Redd. Captain Henley had been with me when General Rosser was telling me what he did, as I have related, and knew it all as well as I did, but it was different with Mr. Redd, so I took him aside and told him exactly and in detail just what information General Rosser had imparted to me, and added that I was unwilling to take him along with me under any possible misapprehension of the situation; but that if, with full knowledge of the risk to be run, he was still willing to go with me I would be glad to have him do so. He said he would go.

All my party except Captain Henley and Mr. Redd having thus turned back and left me, I bid General Rosser farewell, and he went on his way toward Lynchburg. With Captain Henley and Mr. Redd, I proceeded further along the line of the railroad for a mile or so and then we met [Brig. Gen. Thomas T.] Munford, who was coming along alone, though at that time I believe in command of [Brig. Gen. Williams C.] Wickham's old brigade of cavalry. With him, also, I was personally acquainted and on meeting we exchanged salutations. After a few moments' conversation in the nature of inquiries and answers, I informed him also of the mission on which I had been sent, as I had previously informed General Rosser. General Munford then told me that General Lee (and not General Longstreet, as General Rosser had said) was at that hour at General Grant's headquarters surrendering the Army of Northern Virginia. He advised me to go on and try to get full information to take back to President Davis, and said that two miles further down the railroad I would come to our picket, in sight of whom was also the Yankee picket. He further advised me, if possible, to get under convoy of one of the flags of truce he said I would find frequently passing between General Grant's headquarters and our own lines, and by that means I might get access to General Lee. On getting access to General Lee I could inform him of the president's presence in Danville and of the mission on which I had been sent.

I at once determined to take this advice, and parting with General Munford I pressed on with Captain Henley and Mr. Redd until we came to the picket station which General Munford had mentioned. We found it a short distance off the line of the railroad track and upon a country road running parallel thereto. On reaching the camp of this picket station I asked for the officer in command. He appeared and we introduced each other. His name I cannot now remember, but I do remember that he had the rank of colonel, I informed him of the mission on which I had been sent from Danville, mentioned my meeting with General Rosser and General Munford, and the advice which the latter had given me, and then requested him to allow me as quickly as possible to accompany a flag of truce to General Grant's headquarters, so that I might obtain an interview with General Lee. But he positively refused to allow me to do so. I then remained at this picket camp several hours entirely inactive, a mere looker-on, because I could do nothing further. During this time I saw several flags of truce passing and repassing between our lines and the Yankee lines, but could get no information as to the particulars of what was going on.

About 4:00 P.M., I had utterly despaired of being able to communicate with General Lee at all and was pondering in my mind as to what I had best do under the circumstances. But I concluded to demand a further conference with the colonel who was in command of the picket post. He readily accorded it. At this conference the colonel urged it upon me that it was entirely impracticable for me to see General Lee; that I had obtained full and perfectly reliable information of the fact that the surrender of the army was taking place and in a few hours would be completed, and that if I remained longer I would also be embraced in the surrender and detained as a prisoner. He suggested that it was best for me to set out at once on my return to Danville and report to President Davis the information I had obtained. After considering the matter I concluded to adopt the colonel's suggestions, and accordingly at four that Sunday afternoon I, together with Captain Henley and Mr. Redd, set out to return to Danville, bearing the tidings I had obtained.

We retraced our way back along the line of the railroad a short distance, and then leaving the railroad to the right, made directly by way of the country roads for Campbell Court House, which we reached about sunset. On arriving at Campbell Court House we heard a rumor that a considerable body of Yankee raiders were advancing upon the village. Surmising that this party of raiders was the same which had made a foray upon the village of Chickentown the previous day, and which we had made a detour to avoid, I considered it best to get away from Campbell Court House as quickly as possible so as to avoid them again.

At Campbell Court House we were joined by Colonel R. W. Withers; we left that village very speedily and went on, making our way by the most direct route, over the country roads to Danville. From Campbell Court House we went directly to the residence of Mr. Payne, who was the father-in-law of Colonel Withers, our guide. This house was about four miles from Pannill's Bridge, across Staunton River, and we reached it about an hour before daybreak. Here we were hospitably entertained, Captain Henley, Mr. Redd, and myself, provided with a good supper, comfortable beds in which we slept for an hour or two, and then after breakfast, about sunrise, proceeded on our way to Danville, leaving Colonel Withers at the house of his father-in-law.

We proceeded rather leisurely until we got to Pannill's Bridge and Pannill's Store, which are in sight of each other, but here we learned that no one had crossed Pannill's Bridge with news of Lee's surrender, and I therefore decided that it was highly important for us to hurry on and bear the news to Danville as quickly as possible. Previously, we had presumed that intelligence of the surrender would have reached Danville long before we could get there, and, therefore, had made no great haste. But now I came to a contrary conclusion and consequently we spurred up and hastened on. At Pannill's Store I procured a fresh horse, that [which] I had ridden from Drake's Branch being pretty well exhausted.

Shortly after passing Pannill's Bridge Captain Henley parted from us and turned to make his way by a different route to Clover Depot; the point at which he first joined me. Accompanied now by Mr. Redd alone I hastened on to Danville. Our route lay along the country roads from Pannill's Bridge by way of the residence of the Rev. Joel Hubbard, a famous Baptist preacher in Pittsylvania County, and through Riceville, thence on by Spring Garden and Beavers' to Danville—the distance from Pannill's Bridge to Danville being about fifty miles, which we accomplished in a little less than nine hours. After we had gotten a short distance beyond Riceville we overtook a party of horsemen, comprising Dr. E. D. Withers, Captain W. Hayes Otey, and Mr. F. G. Claiborne, who had been sent out from Danville on a mission somewhat similar to my own. They were returning to Danville, and upon inquiry I found that they had not heard of General Lee's surrender. I gave them that information and then pushed us ahead of them with Mr. Redd, making still more urgent haste to reach Danville as soon as possible.

Mr. Redd and I arrived at Danville at 3:00 P.M., and immediately reported to General H. H. Walker at his headquarters. We found him in an upstairs room of a house known as the old Price building, at the corner of Main and Union Streets (since burned down), where he had established his headquarters. I gave him the information I had obtained, and this was the first time the dreadful tidings was told in Danville, then the capital of the Confederacy. Mr. Redd parted with me here, and General Walker requested me to go with him at once to see President Davis.

The executive offices for the president, the secretary of state and, I believe, some other departments of the government had by this time been established in a large brick building on Wilson Street. Here General Walker and I went to find President Davis and to communicate to him the news of the surrender. On arriving at the house we were informed that the president was at dinner. General Walker directed the messenger in attendance to tell him that we desired and respectfully requested an immediate audience. The messenger returned presently and reported that the president said he was at dinner and suggested that if the general's business was not very pressing he might wait until the dinner was over. General Walker sent word back that his business was very urgent and that he must see the president at once. Thereupon President Davis came out of the dining room into the reception room to meet General Walker and myself. He had the appearance of having just arisen from the dinner table. He spoke to General Walker and the ordinary salutations were interchanged between them.

General Walker then presented me to the president and informed him that I was the officer who by his direction had been sent to establish a line of couriers for communication with General Lee and that I had important information to communicate. The president merely bowed or nodded his head and invited us to be seated. I took a seat on a sofa and the president came and took a seat beside me, General Walker taking a chair near by us. As soon as we were thus seated President Davis again bowed his head to me as a signal for me to proceed. I then, in as few words as possible, gave him a full statement of the information I had obtained of General Lee's surrender. During my recital of this information President Davis rested his elbow on the side of the sofa and kept his hand on the side of his brow, listening with the profoundest attention but uttering not a word, either of comment or inquiry. After I had finished the telling of my terrible news he still sat for a few moments resting his brow upon his hand, as if in profound meditation.

Presently, still without one word of comment upon the news I had brought him or of inquiry as to further particulars, he turned to General Walker and myself in a most courteous manner and inquired whether we had dined. The general replied that he had, but I had not. In fact I had not tasted food since leaving Mr. Payne's that morning at sunrise and had ridden over fifty miles since. "Then," said President Davis to me, "walk in, Captain, and take some bread and meat with me." As he said this he arose from his seat on the sofa. I did likewise, thanked him for his invitation and followed him as he led the way to the dinner table.

On entering the dining room I found seated at table a number of gentlemen who were members of the president's official family, including several of his cabinet ministers, but there were no ladies present. He invited me to a seat at the table, took a seat himself and recommenced eating his dinner. As this was to me a memorable "state dinner" I have well remembered the "bill of fare" and can give it now. It consisted of a boiled ham of bacon, some Irish potatoes and some fried eggs; no pastry, no dessert and no wines or liquors of any kind, but bread and water in plenty. While we remained at the dinner table President Davis uttered not a word in relation to the news I had brought him and made no allusion to the subject whatever. He seemed to be profoundly meditating all the time, and when addressed by any of the gentlemen around him always made very courteous replies, but in the fewest words possible, and took no other part in the conversation. On rising from the table, however, he accompanied me back to the reception room, where we rejoined General Walker, who had been waiting for me.

We resumed our seats in the reception room as before, and then President Davis turned to me and made the most careful and special inquiries touching the news I had brought him and all that I had seen and heard during my expedition to the lines of the army. All these inquiries I answered fully and explicitly. When he had gotten through questioning me and seemed ready to close the interview I arose to leave, as did General Walker also. As I was taking leave of him I said: "Mr. President, if there is anything further I can do to serve you, please command me." As I said this he seemed for the first time to exhibit any emotion, but he answered me with considerable feeling, saying; "Ah, Captain, I fear there will be but few now who would make such an offer." With this we shook hands and General Walker and I left the president and I saw him no more.

That night at 10:30 P.M. all the Confederate officials left Danville, taking the archives of the government with them and went southward by way of Greensboro, North Carolina.

The Defense of Spanish Fort

PHILIP D. STEPHENSON,
PRIVATE, 5TH COMPANY, WASHINGTON ARTILLERY OF NEW ORLEANS, C.S.A.

Philadelphia *Weekly Times* 8, no. 23, July 26, 1884

Who knows of Spanish Fort? Not many readers of the "Annals of the War," I suspect, yet it was the scene of one of the most thrilling and romantic episodes of the war. It was one of the very last incidents, too, for we evacuated the place on the night of April 9, 1865, the day of [Gen. Robert E.] Lee's surrender. Spanish Fort was one of the outer defenses of Mobile. It was situated about twelve miles below the city and across the bay, on the eastern shore. Look on the map of Alabama and turn to Mobile Bay. At the mouth you notice two islands almost closing the bay, having but a narrow passage. Guarding the passage and facing each other are Forts Gaines and Morgan. Further up the bay, on the eastern side, on a tongue of land not represented on the map, was Spanish Fort, and still further up, nearer the city, was Blakely, another fortified place.

The sole approach to the city through the bay was a tortuous and narrow channel, marked out by stakes, which ran zigzag across to Blakely, then down to Spanish Fort and then on out to the Gulf; all the rest of the bay was filled with torpedoes and a variety of other obstructions. Early in March 1865, the 5th Company of Washington Artillery was having a "good time" in the city of Mobile. The place was a sort of Paradise to them. They had been detached from the veteran Army of Tennessee, and with it had just passed through the almost unparalleled hardships of [Lt. Gen. John B.] Hood's disastrous Nashville campaign. Mobile was one of the protected cities of the South, one of the last places, if not the very last, to feel the direct clutch of the hand of war. Consequently a semblance of the ways of peace still existed there. Coffee houses were in full blast where "coffee" could be bought for a dollar a cup, with an "ironclad" pie thrown in. The theatre was in vogue ($5 admittance), where the hero was a second rate but able-bodied "artist," whom the soldiers hissed for not being in the ranks, and the "villain" was a poor lame fellow with a squeaky voice, who could not disguise his hobble as he strode furiously across the stage. Some of us had been paid and we indulged with reckless joy in boots at a cost of $100 or so, or in linen shirts at a like fabulous sum. The band played in the city park and strenuous was the effort to get off from duty for a promenade there, or on "Government Street," and truly inventive was the genius developed in the way of arranging or "getting up" toilets for the occasion.

One day orders came to be ready to move at a moment's notice, and not long after we found ourselves on the bay, threading the channel for the eastern shore. The enemy were approaching Mobile by land and water—that was the occasion of our move. I remember we had a grand review in the streets of Mobile. Every one who could carry a gun was in the ranks. The artillerists were armed as infantry. I suppose there were ten thousand men under arms. The great majority of these were fragments of other commands, boy militia, etc.; a few were veteran troops. Our commander was [Maj. Gen.] Dabney H. Maury, "every inch a soldier," but then there were not many inches of him. The soldiers called him "puss in boots," because half of his diminutive person seemed lost in a pair of the immense cavalry boots of the day. He was a wise and gallant officer.

Other reinforcements accompanied us to Spanish Fort. I suppose the garrison, when attacked a few days after, amounted to 1,800 men of all arms. Brig. Gen. Randall Gibson, now United States Senator from Louisiana, was in command.

We found ourselves in a curious little tongue of high land jutting out into the bay in a southwesterly direction. This high land broke off abruptly in bluffs on the western or water side, leaving but a narrow margin of beach, while, on the eastern or inland side, it sloped off into a marsh, which ran around us and above us into the bay between us and Blakely. Our works were arranged to resist an attack from the interior, and, beginning at the southern and lip end of the "tongue," ran in a semi-circle around the inside rim of the high land, resting at each end on the bay. Or rather, they would have done so on the north as well as south, only the march interfered, and we had no time to complete them. This was our weak point, and yet in a sense our strong point. We had no defenses in that marsh, yet a dense jungle supplied the defense, so dense that our leaders confided in it greatly and placed only a picket line there. These works of ours consisted of three "forts" (of earth), one at each end and one in the center, connected by rifle pits. The one in the center was assigned to our battery. The whole extent of our line from end to end was but little over a mile and a half.

We felt ourselves to be in a trap as soon as we took in the situation. If [Adm. David G.] Farragut's fleet should pass Forts Gaines and Morgan at the mouth of the bay, all he would have to do would be to sail serenely up in our rear and shell us at his leisure and cut us off from Mobile, while a land force could invest us and starve us into surrender. So prominent was the thought in our minds that I remember my messmate [Cordelius Johnson] "Tony" B[arrow] and I ("Tony" is now a staid merchant and man of family in Louisiana) sat on the parapets one afternoon soon after getting there and planned a way of escape for ourselves. Casting our eye towards the bay we noticed a chain of little, low marshy islands, hardly above the water, which fringed our shore at a distance of six to eight hundred yards from the land and stretched northward up towards Blakely. "If the place were taken by assault," we thought, "we might make for one of these and by swimming from one to the other, finally get to Blakely." Little did we dream that the whole command was eventually to escape from under the very clutches of the enemy by means of one of those very islands.

Several days elapsed before the enemy made his appearance. The time was spent in "planting" torpedoes all through the woody marsh in front of us, in strengthening our works and in making great bomb proofs right behind our works for our wounded, our ammunition and so on. These bomb proofs were made, some of them, on a vast scale. One I worked upon was about 16×20 feet in dimensions and 10 to 12 feet deep. We cut down great trees, rolled the trunks over the mouth, then put a layer of heavy logs crosswise, then a layer of brush and dirt, until the roof was six to eight feet thick.

At last the enemy were in sight. Farragut's fleet appeared first. How gallantly ship after ship came up the bay and how we watched them! Then suddenly the foremost was hid in a dense cloud of smoke and water. When she came in view again her bow was up in the air and she was evidently sinking. From where we were we could hear no report, but we knew that she had struck one of our torpedoes. The channel was full of them. This was why our leaders left us so exposed, apparently, in our rear. This stopped the advance for the time on the water side. But soon the pop, pop, pop of our pickets' guns drew our attention to our immediate front; the firing grew into volleys, our men came into view through the woods, slowly falling back and finally retiring to the line already marked for them as their permanent posts, the blue waves of the Federal forces circled around us and by nightfall we were invested.

I think it was about March 22 or 23, 1865. I know we were invested seventeen days and made our escape about April 9. Those seventeen days were sufficiently thrilling and eventful. Imagine our position and you can readily believe me. A force reported to be thirty thousand strong, under [Maj. Gen. Frederick] Steele in front, massed and crowded around our little semi-circle line, their artillery packed thick along the works they were already throwing up and the ships now drawn within easy range in our rear. The shells from one end of their line could reach the other end of ours, and raked us, while the guns of the fleet could send their shells plump into our backs. Every day was full of incident, and it soon got so that we had no rest day or night. Each side had little detached pits, facing each other, with squads of four or five men in each, and constant was the effort of the one side to surprise and capture the other. We had two little coehorn mortars in our battery (about fifteen inches long), and Corporal Charlie Fox, especially, became so expert with them that he emptied the pits of the enemy repeatedly with his shell.

The boy militia referred to, mere lads many of them, from thirteen to seventeen or eighteen years of age, excited the mingled grief and admiration of us veterans. In vain did we tell them when going to the skirmish line to shelter themselves as much as possible. They thought it was "not soldierly," and they stood up and were shot down like sheep. A spring just inside of our works became a point of thrilling interest. It soon became so that we could not leave our works and run back to the rear to the usual place for water, and it was either use that spring or famish. Yet it was in full sight of the enemy. It occupied a depression in the hillside and was commanded by their sharpshooters. There was but one recourse—we must go there by night. Men, strung around with the canteens of their comrades, would steal down to the ravine in the darkness. Sometimes numbers would be gathered there waiting hours for their turn to fill and leave. Alas, that spring became baptized in blood. The enemy had the range and kept up a fire, though they could not see, and many a poor fellow fell around that spring.

Artillery duels became of daily occurrence, our head logs were constantly knocked down upon us, bruising and crippling us, squads of sharpshooters devoted their especial attention to our port holes or embrasures and poured a steady stream of bullets through them from early morn till dewy eve; mining and counter-mining began, and I remember one gallant fellow along the line to the right of us crept one night with a detail of men down the ravine where the spring was, out beyond our skirmish pits, into the lines of the enemy's pickets and finding the mouth of their mine, which occupied a rather advanced position, he captured the whole batch of miners and got back to our works without firing a shot or losing a man.

But the end came at last. We knew it was coming. We could feel it in the air. And then, too, certain ominous indications came from the enemy. For several days we could see that they were preparing for something unusual. Suddenly one afternoon a most extraordinary fire opened upon us from three points, from the two ends of their line and from their center. It seemed to concentrate upon our one battery. No doubt we had done them mischief, and perhaps more mischief than the other forts, for our gunners had gained experience in a score of battles; but we were not prepared for such an especial compliment as this. They were shelling us with mortar shells, huge fifteen-inch bombs, so large that we could see them with the naked eye shortly after leaving the mortar's mouth; see them as they arose up into the air, describing a graceful curve and then begin hurrying with vicious impetus down full upon our helpless heads.

They had six of those mortars, two at each point, moved, I suppose, from their ships, and from that time on, both day and night, those fearful things came down upon our heads. There was no shelter from those bombs—no defense from that fire. We had to stand and take it. Their force was terrible. They would go six feet in the solid earth and exploding tear up a space fifteen or twenty feet square. They went through that tremendous bombproof roof, of which I have spoken, as though it was paper, and we were in constant expectation of losing all of our ammunition and provisions. Those abominable mortars were the last item in their preparations. They practiced on us to get the range, and then we got it.

The last day, the day of assault, came. What a day that was! And yet the enemy's tactics were they rained upon us from front and flank and rear and top, from field guns, siege guns, ship guns and mortars, such a tempest of shot and shell as defies description. Think of seventy-five or a hundred guns massed in a semicircle around us; think of those huge mortars belching forth their monstrous contents upon us; think of the fleet in our rear pouring its fire into our backs! Suddenly that storm burst forth, but it ceased not for a moment through all that interminable day. The very air was hot. The din was so great it distracted our senses. We could hardly hear each other speak and could hardly tell what we were doing. The crackling of musketry, the unbroken roaring of artillery, the yelling and shrieking of the shells, the bellowing boom of the mortars, the dense shroud of sulphurous smoke thickening around us—it was [as] though the mouth of the pit had yawned and the uproar of hell was about us. And it was not taking

The capture of Spanish Fort (BEYER, *DEEDS OF VALOR*)

away from this infernal picture to see men, as I did, hopping about, the blood bursting from eyes and ears and mouth, driven stark crazy by concussion or some other cause.

It was utterly idle to try to return that fire. After a few rounds we did not even attempt to do so. We stood around sheltering ourselves as best we could. Our works were no longer a protection to us, except against the fire in front. But that we did not mind. Our thoughts were of the fire from the rear, and above all, of those huge descending bombs. And now occurred a strange scene. We deserted the cover of our works and went out in the space behind them. And there, exposed to the full range of all the rest of that fearful fire, we devoted ourselves entirely to the work of dodging those mortar shells. And they were dodgable.

There was a certain man in the battery gifted with a peculiarly accurate and rapid power of measuring distances with the naked eye. He had found out that by watching the bomb as it left the mortar and after describing the curve began to descend he could tell pretty near where and when it would strike. His comrades found out this talent, and rallying around him would run at his signal out of harm's way. And it was funny to see our officers (and a braver act never lived) edging near and in a nonchalant manner say: "Sing out, Shoot, and tell us which way to run!" One of those bombs towards the close entered the big bomb proof of which I have spoken and exploded. The place was crowded with men who, in spite of warning, sought shelter there. The havoc made I know not, for it was just awhile before we left, but I shudder to think of it.

Night came at last. Oh, how delicious, how inexpressibly comforting is the coming of night oftentimes to the soldier in war. But it gave respite only by a change of incident and not by bestowing the sweet gift of balmy sleep. The most striking and romantic of all the acts of this drama was now upon us, viz: our escape. The assault, as I have said, came about 3:00 P.M. But it was a very feeble affair where we were, and was evidently a feint. The main attack was on our left. They penetrated through that dense marshy jungle, which we looked upon as almost impenetrable, and, pushing back the feeble picket line we had there got to the bay between us and Blakely, thus cutting us off. There, as we afterwards found out, they planted a battery. From that point they came on down our line driving our slender force before them until they got to the fort on our left, which they captured. It was only a few hundred yards from us and we could see them there moving about in the moonlight. Why they did not come right on and take us, too, we could never understand. It was one of those curious blunders which happened so often on both sides during the war.

It was with their dusky outlines in full view, on the fort above us, that we made our preparations to leave, and did leave. And now, as to that leaving. Not one of the readers of this article has less notion of what we were going to do, or where we were going, than did we, the rank and file, as we received the whispered orders to prepare silently for departure. We were completely bewildered. "Escape? How escape?" We were completely cut off, surrounded, nay, the enemy were in our works, in sight of us. Yet we did escape, and that, too, with scarcely the loss of a man. It was a brilliant moonlight night. About ten o'clock, after spiking our guns, we left our works and made directly for the beach. Did the enemy see us? They ought to have seen us. Why they did not I cannot tell. We got to the bluffs overlooking the bay.

What next? Behold, the head of the column seemed to melt gradually into the earth, and as we moved up to supply their place we understood their disappearance. The face of the bluff was creased with great fissures or ravines opening out upon the water. The head of our column had disappeared down one of these! Down we followed pell-mell, right down the almost perpendicular sides of the gorge, clinging to vines, saplings, the sides of the rocks, any way to keep our hold, until we reached the bottom fifty feet or so below. And there, to our amazement, we found the beginning of a tread-way one or two planks wide. At the word all shoes and boots were off and we stood in our stocking feet in single line upon that narrow tread-way. And then, after orders to keep our guns on the off side from the enemy to prevent their glistening being noticed (for artillerists though we were, we still had our infantry accoutrements) and after orders not to whisper a word on pain of being court-martialed we went forth, literally not knowing whither we were going.

The tread-way first debouched upon the beach, then turning to the right it went up the shore for quite a distance. Just how far I cannot say, but I know we passed so close to the enemy's pickets stationed in the marsh that we could hear them talking, and went right under the nose of their battery. Finally the tread-way turned and struck out into the bay. The water was shallow and we walked just above the water's surface. Suddenly a shot came; it was from that battery. Imagine our consternation. But it was not repeated for some time. It was evident they did not see us, but were merely firing periodically across what they supposed to be the channel, in order to prevent any succor reaching us. The very last thing they were thinking of was our attempting to escape.

We came to the end of that tread-way at last. It ended on one of those very marshes by which my comrade Tony [Barrow] and I had planned to escape. A chain of them, as I have said, ran up the bay, some six or eight hundred yards from the shore. The channel was outside of them, and when we jumped off the tread-way on to the island where it terminated there, out in the water, were the dusky forms of several gunboats waiting to carry us away. But will I ever forget those few minutes on that island? When I jumped from the tread-way I sank to my waist in mud. It was a bog. Every one sank more or less deep. There we were, right under the guns of that battery, helplessly floundering up to our middle in mud. Suppose they discovered us! And there. Forth from the shore came a confused uproar of noises—the shouts of baffled men, volleys of musketry, the deep boom of cannon. They have discovered our flight back in our works; they have found us out. But not that battery. Periodically its shot goes down the bay, but not towards us. It is still in blissful ignorance and we are still safe!

But we must be quick. Our first aim is to struggle up the island, as much out of the range of those guns as possible. All order vanishes; it is no wonder, situated as we were. Tony B[arrow] and I had stuck together throughout. Looking out on the water we saw a yawl pulled cautiously to the shore. We looked around—no one was nigh, as we thought, no fear of swamping her. In we plunged, rushing up to our necks in water, and throwing our guns in first, pitched into the boat, head over heels, laughing, spluttering, struggling. When we had got upright the boat was full to sinking and we though we were the only ones near it. We were soon on board of one of the gunboats, and in an incredibly short time that whole command was off that island and sailing jubilantly up the bay. Then that battery found us out, and before we left sent some right well aimed shots through our rigging. I remember I had curled down on deck near the boiler, for I was wringing wet, and as those shots came viciously near the thought came, "What a shame to be sunk in this boat after what we have gone through this day." But we were not sunk. We steamed up the bay, touched at Blakely for a while (it was stormed an hour or so after we left), went across to Mobile and in a few days evacuated the place with the rest of the troops there and surrendered shortly after at Meridian, Mississippi.

MAP AND ILLUSTRATION CREDITS

Maps and illustrations are from the following sources:

Beyer, W. F., and O. F. Keydel. *Deeds of Valor*. Detroit: Perrien-Keydel Co., 1907. (Cited in captions as Beyer, *Deeds of Valor*.)

Forbes, Ida B. *General Wm. T. Sherman, His Life and Battles; or, From Boyhood to His "March to the Sea."* Illustrated by Edwin Forbes. New York, 1886. (Cited in captions as *Life of Sherman*.)

Frank Leslie's Illustrated Newspaper.

Harper's New Monthly Magazine.

Hearst's Magazine.

Johnson, Rossiter. *Campfire and Battlefield*. New York, 1894. (Cited in captions as Johnson, *Campfire and Battlefield*.)

Knox College, Galesburg, Illinois. Ray D. Smith Civil War Collection.

Library of Congress Photographic Collections.

Magazine of American History.

McClure's Magazine.

Minnesota Historical Society, St. Paul, Minnesota.

Scribner's Magazine.

St. Nicholas Magazine.

INDEX